Library of
VOID
Davidson College

THE GREAT
DR. BURNEY

THE GREAT
Dr. BURNEY

HIS LIFE ~ HIS TRAVELS
HIS WORKS ~ HIS FAMILY
AND HIS FRIENDS

By PERCY A. SCHOLES
M.A., D.Mus., Dr. ès Lettres, F.S.A.

VOLUME II

GREENWOOD PRESS, PUBLISHERS
WESTPORT, CONNECTICUT

927.8
B965s
v.2

Originally published in 1948 in two volumes
by Oxford University Press, London, New York, Toronto

Reprinted with the permission
of Oxford University Press, Inc., New York

First Greenwood Reprinting 1971

Library of Congress Catalogue Card Number 74-104254

SBN 8371-4017-X (Set)
SBN 8371-6242-4 (Vol. II)

Printed in the United States of America

76 - 6621

TABLE OF CONTENTS

VOLUME II

LIST OF PLATES

VOLUME II

XXXVIII. THE STREATHAM COTERIE BREAKS UP

(1782; Burney aged 56, Fanny 30, Mrs. Thrale 41, and Johnson 73)

IN June 1779 Burney had a trying experience at Streatham. His chaise was at the door, waiting to take him home, when another vehicle drove up bringing his friend Thrale in a condition of semi-consciousness. Says Mrs. Thrale,[1] 'I called Dr. Burney, begged him to fly in the post-chaise, which was then waiting for him, and send me some physician—Sir R. Jebb or Pepys, or if none else could be found, my old accoucheur, Doctor Bromfield of Gerrard Street'. Evidently either there was then no doctor at Streatham or nearer than London itself, or else Mrs. Thrale felt little confidence in local or ordinary general practitioners, these three hastily suggested to Burney being not only friends of the family but men high in their profession—respectively Physician in Ordinary to the King, Physician Extraordinary to him, and Surgeon to the Queen.

It was Dr. Bromfield who came, and he diagnosed the trouble as an apoplectic seizure.

Thrale, it seems, had been at the house of a sister in town, to attend the opening of the will of her husband who had recently died; the will had been read and he had sat down to dinner when he suddenly dropped unconscious. Then the foolish sister and her daughter, instead of calling a doctor, had thrust him into the carriage and driven him down to Streatham.

As a result of this trouble, and of a trouble also amongst the clerks at Thrale's brewery who quarrelled, and one of whom just now ran away with eighteen hundred pounds, Mrs. Thrale suffered a miscarriage; and since the brewery business required constant attention and Thrale was no longer the man he had been the family moved to their Southwark house and Mrs. Thrale looked in at the office every day and did what she could to get its tangled affairs straightened.

For nearly two years (June 1779 to April 1781) Thrale lingered. His own imprudence was a constant anxiety to his wife and friends. The doctors warned him gravely against his long-rooted habit of grossly over-eating but he could not be brought to deny himself: 'He must eat prudently in future', said Sir Richard Jebb, but there was no enforcing this command.

Mrs. Thrale wrote to Johnson:

> 'Burney [she means Fanny] and I and Queeny [her daughter] tease him every meal he eats, and Mrs. Montagu is quite serious with him; but what can one do? He will eat, I think, and if he does eat I know he will not live. It makes me very unhappy, but I must bear it.'[2]

[1] Hayward, *Autobiography . . . of Mrs. Piozzi* (1861).

[2] Letter inserted in Croker's edition of Boswell's *Johnson*.

Then Thrale (never a highly prudent business man and now disturbed in his wits) began to lavish money unwisely on a new building at his brewery and this soon became another source of worry. And then the musician Piozzi broke it to her that her husband was organizing a grand domestic entertainment to be given at the Southwark house and had entrusted him, Piozzi, with the preparation of its musical part, authorizing him to engage 'the Parsees—a set of Orientals, who were shown at all the gay houses—the lions of the day'. The sopranist Roncaglia and the great opera composer Sacchini were also engaged—Roncaglia probably to sing arias of Sacchini accompanied by the composer.[1]

When Mrs. Thrale told her husband's doctors of this intended excitement they were alarmed and 'tried to counteract [countermand] the frolic but in vain'. The most they could achieve was the obtaining of a promise that immediately the entertainment was over he would go back to the quieter life of Streatham, but even this concession he was reluctant to make ('Leave London! lose my Ranelagh season!').

What happened on the day set for the entertainment is told by Hannah More in her letters:

> 'Mrs. Garrick and I were invited to a fine assembly at Mrs. Thrale's. There was to be a fine concert and all the fine people were to be there; but the *chief attraction* was to meet the Bramin and the two Parsees . . . but just as my hair was dressed, came a servant to forbid our coming, for that Mr. Thrale was dead.'

There was found in Fanny's papers, after her death, a hurried note to her from Mrs. Thrale ('Write to me—pray for me!') endorsed by Fanny, 'Written a few hours after the death of Mr. Thrale, which happened by a sudden stroke of apoplexy, on the morning of a day on which half the fashion of London had been invited to an assembly in his house'.[2]

After Thrale's death the Burneys can for a time have seen but little of Mrs. Thrale and of their old Streatham circle, since, taking up residence at Southwark, Mrs. Thrale says, she 'kept the counting house from nine o'clock every morning till five o'clock every evening till June, when God Almighty sent us a parcel of rich Quakers who bought the whole, and saved me and my coadjutors from brewing ourselves into another bankruptcy'.[3]

[1] Hayward-Lobban, 191. Roncaglia, like Sacchini, was a friend of Burney (see Burney's letter to Martini of 22 June 1778, preserved in the archives of the Liceo of Bologna).

[2] *Diary and Letters*, i. 468 n.

[3] Hayward. The allusion to a previous bankruptcy is something of an exaggeration; it refers to a crisis that occurred shortly before Burney came into association with the Thrales, when the brewer had been taken in by a visionary whose grand commercial schemes included one for making beer without malt or hops. The 'parcel of rich Quakers' were the Barclays, whose name together with that of Thrale's foreman, Perkins (see I. 375 n.), is still associated with the brewery.

And now Mrs. Thrale was free to wander at will, without the cares of husband or business. And it so happened that Piozzi fell much into her company.

After the lamentable party at St. Martin's Street of which we have read (the one in 1777 at which Mrs. Thrale apparently first met this musician and at which her shocked host had to check her exuberant love of fun) she seems not to have met the man she had then mimicked until about three years later—in the summer of 1780, when, being in residence at Brighton, she caught sight of him at the door of a lending library and accosted him in Italian, asking him if he would give her daughter some holiday lessons in Italian. 'He replied, coldly, that he was come thither himself merely to recover his voice, which he feared was wholly lost; that he was composing some music, and lived in great retirement.' He had apparently failed to recognize her but must have been enlightened by the tradesman who kept the library, for as Mrs. Thrale and her daughter repassed it a little later he 'started out of the shop and begged my pardon for not knowing me before, and protested his readiness to do anything to oblige me'. The next morning arrived a letter from Fanny to Mrs. Thrale, telling her that 'her father's friend, Mr. Piozzi, was gone to Brighthelmstone [Brighton], where she hoped we would meet, for though he had lost his voice, his musical powers were enchanting, and that I should find him a companion likely to lighten the burden of life to me, as he was just a man to my natural taste'. Piozzi's 'musical powers' could hardly be expected to be 'enchanting' to the unmusical Mrs. Thrale, but perhaps this was a tactful suggestion on Fanny's part, designed to lead to the provision of some congenial distraction for her friend's husband, who had suffered his first stroke and gone to Brighton to recuperate. And indeed 'Mr. Thrale found his performance on the piano-forte so superior to anything then heard in England, and in short, took such a fancy to his society, that we were seldom apart, except while Mr. Piozzi was studying to compose the six fine sonatas that he dedicated to his favourite pupil, Miss Child, afterwards Lady Westmoreland'.

We have evidence of the intimacy that now grew up between Piozzi and the Thrales in a letter of Mrs. Thrale of December of that year (1780):[1]

'My Master keeps upon his Legs very prettily, & we have had a merry Xmas: Mr. & Mrs. Davenant—kind Creatures—are with me still, & I kept Mr. Harry Cotton with me as long as he would stay: two or three young Men & Maidens of an agreeable sort filled our Society—& that delightful Mortal Piozzi, the famous Italian singer spent a day or two in entertaining us with *his* astonishing Powers. What most amazed the People of the *Ton*, was *his* condescending to play Country Dances (for the 1st Time of his Life) while we pretty Masters & Misses set to Dancing. I coax him to teach

[1] Quoted in James L. Clifford, *Hester Lynch Piozzi* (1941), 193.

Hester the Vocal part of Musick, while Doctor Burney works her at the Harpsichord.'

The next year was that of Thrale's death; and then, with indecent eagerness, society began to discuss a second marriage—'Every man that comes to the house is put in the papers for me to marry. . . . I wrote to-day to beg the "Morning Herald" would say no more about me, good or bad.'

The family friendship with Piozzi that had grown up suggested him to the gossipers as one of the possible candidates for her hand. So indeed he in time became. The incidents connected with the growing affection between the brewer's widow and the musician, and that led up to their marriage in July 1784, after rather over three years of the former's widowhood, have been told time after time in the numerous books devoted to Mrs. Thrale, in which, rather than in this one on the Burneys, they have their place.[1] What does claim mention here is the estrangement that now occurred.

Johnson objected to the marriage, and so did all Mrs. Thrale's friends—amongst them the Burneys. Fanny's comments nearly half a century later are still hysterical, though as far as she feels able she now defends her old friend. She recalls that at the period of the growing infatuation (as she would describe it) she was for some months domiciled with Mrs. Thrale, at Streatham, and goes on:

'And here let a tribute of friendship be offered up to the shrine of remembrance, due from a thousand ineffaceably tender recollections. Not wildly, and with male and headstrong passions, as has currently been asserted, was this connexion brought to bear on the part of Mrs. Thrale. It was struggled against at times with even agonizing energy; and with efforts so vehement, as nearly to destroy the poor machine they were exerted to save. But the subtle poison had glided into her veins so unsuspectedly, and, at first, so unopposedly, that the whole fabric was infected with its venom; which seemed to become a part, never to be dislodged, of its system.'[2]

About the Piozzi connexion Fanny apparently told her father nothing at the time, but he began to realize what was happening and—

'In taking her home with him one morning, to pass a day in St. Martin's Street, he almost involuntarily, in driving from the paddock, turned back his head towards the house, and, in a tone the most impressive, sighed out: "Adieu, Streatham!—Adieu!"

'His daughter perceived his eyes were glistening; though he presently dropt them, and bowed down his head, as if not to distress her by any look of examination; and said no more.

'Her tears, which had long been with difficulty restrained from overflowing in his presence, through grief at the unhappiness, and even more at

[1] They are very intelligently and interestingly narrated in C. E. Vulliamy, *Mrs. Thrale of Streatham*. There have been as many pages written about this marriage (and by as many people) as, perhaps, about any marriage in history.

[2] *Mem.* ii. 246.

what she thought the infatuation of her friend, now burst forth, from emotions that surprised away forbearance.

'Dr. Burney sat silent and quiet, to give her time for recollection; though fully expecting a trusting communication.

'She gave, however, none: his commands alone could have forced a disclosure; but he soon felt convinced, by her taciturnity, that she must have been bound to concealment. He pitied, therefore, but respected her secrecy; and, clearing his brow, finished the little journey in conversing upon their own affairs.'[1]

There was much to be said in favour of Mrs. Thrale's remarrying, for her first marriage had been one rather of duty than of inclination, and having at last met a man whom she could and did love, why should she not reconstruct her domestic life on a more genuine foundation? There was much, too, to be said in favour of Piozzi. The poet Rogers, in his *Table Talk*, describes him as 'a very handsome, gentlemanly and amiable person', and Mrs. Thrale herself, in a letter to Johnson (1784), says that he was 'a religious man, a sober man and a thinking man'. And he was no fool and had always been able to maintain a high position in the profession he was now in effect abandoning. Like all of us he had his little faults. For instance, he was jealous of Pacchierotti; Susan Burney says, 'He walked off from me at a concert on seeing him approaching'.[2]

The actual advances towards an engagement were not made by the gentleman but left to the lady: the decision lingered and there was a good deal of backwards-and-forwards work between the two—much more than there need have been if he had cared to exert pressure.

What was the basis of the very decided objection on the part of Mrs. Thrale's many friends to her remarriage? Apparently the facts that Piozzi was a foreigner; that he was a Roman Catholic; that, though not poor, he was yet very greatly inferior to her in wealth; and also that he was a professional musician.

Mrs. Thrale was herself no snob, but in that she was superior to the generality of her countrymen and countrywomen of the eighteenth century—and even, alas! to many of those of the twentieth. There had been an after-dinner discussion on unequal marriages, at Streatham, about the time that Burney started to frequent the house.[3] It arose out of a recent case of 'a young lady who had married a man much her inferior in rank'. Boswell contended that the young lady's relations should treat her with 'an inflexible steadiness of displeasure', Mrs. Thrale was 'all for mildness and forgiveness', and Johnson held forth in characteristic style:

'Madam, we must distinguish. Were I a man of rank, I would not let a daughter starve who had made a mean marriage; but having voluntarily

[1] Ibid. 248.
[2] *Early Diary*, i., p. lxxxviii.
[3] See Boswell, under 1775.

degraded herself from the station she was entitled to hold, I would support her only in that she herself had chosen; and would not put her on a level with my other daughters. You are to consider, Madam, that it is our duty to maintain the subordination of civilized society; and when there is a gross and shameful deviation from rank, it should be punished so as to deter others from the same perversion.'

Boswell's after-ruminations on this discussion only confirmed the severity of his view:

'If indulgence be shewn to such conduct, and the offenders know that in a longer or shorter time they shall be received as well as if they had not contaminated their blood by a base alliance, the great check upon that inordinate caprice which generally occasions low marriages will be removed, and the fair and comfortable order of improved life will be miserably disturbed.'

The worst features of the match were the trouble it created between mother and children and the throwing off of Dr. Johnson. But Johnson, now nearing his end, was becoming exceedingly 'difficult', and this letter to her at Bath is pardonable only when we recall his state of health—

'Madam.—If I interpret your letter right, you are ignominiously married: if it is yet undone, let us once talk together. If you have abandoned your children and your religion, God forgive your wickedness; if you have forfeited your fame and your country, may your folly do no further mischief. If the last act is yet to do, I who have loved you, esteemed you, reverenced you, and served you, I who long thought you the first of woman kind entreat that, before your fate is irrevocable, I may once more see you. I was, I once was,

Madam, most truly yours,
Sam: Johnson.

I will come down, if you permit it.'[1]

It is comforting to find that a few days later, in reply to a spirited rejoinder from his old friend, he could write in a kinder vein:

'I wish that God may grant you every blessing, that you may be happy in this world for its short continuance, and eternally happy in a better state; and whatever I can contribute to your happiness I am very ready to repay, for that kindness which soothed twenty years of a life radically wretched.'

Well, the Burneys' Streatham joys were over and the Streatham hostess vanishes from the pages of the Burney records, to reappear in them only once or twice, and at long intervals.

And unfortunately, though Mrs. Piozzi might profess to despise the attacks upon her, they bit deep—and all the deeper because she believed her old friends the Burneys to be implicated. In *Thraliana*, under date 1 August 1788, is found:

[1] *The R. B. Adam Library relating to Dr. Samuel Johnson and his Era.*

'Baretti has been grossly abusive in the European Magazine to me; that hurts me but little: what shocks me is that those treacherous Burneys should abett and puff him. He is a most ungrateful, because unprincipled wretch, but I am sorry that anything belonging to Dr. Burney shd. be so monstrously wicked.'

The words 'grossly abusive' are, indeed, not too strong. Baretti calls her:

'The frontless female, who goes now by the mean appellation of Piozzi; La Piozzi, as my fiddling countrymen term her; who has dwindled down into the contemptible wife of her daughter's singing-master.'[1]

We see from a passage in Mrs. Piozzi's *Autobiographical Notes* where that injudicious lady got her ideas that the Burneys were abetting Baretti. Speaking of the period in question she says:

'Libels and odd ill-natured speeches appeared sometimes in the public prints, and one day of the ensuing winter, when I was airing my lap-dogs in a retired part of Hyde Park, Lord Fife came up to me, and after a moment's chat, said, "Would you like to know your friends from your enemies?" in a Scotch accent. "Yes, very much, my lord," was the reply. "Ay, but have you strength of mind enough to bear my intelligence?" "Make haste and tell me, dear my lord," said I. "Why then the Burneys are your enemies, that you so fostered and fondled; more than that, Baretti has been making up a libel . . . and every magazine has refused it entrance except a new work carried on by the female Burney."'

All this, of course, was mere mischief-making gossip. *The European Magazine* was not 'carried on by the female Burney', who heard with 'great concern' of Baretti's treatment in it of her old friend.[2]

Fanny came across Mrs. Thrale after six years (in 1790) at an assembly at her friend Mrs. Locke's (when, says Fanny, both parties 'offered indication of subsisting happiness', and, says Mrs. Piozzi, 'all ended, as it should do, with perfect indifference'), and again, later, at Windsor, 'on the way to St. George's chapel'. One of Burney's now very rare meetings with his old hostess and friend is recorded by Fanny as follows:

'It was at one of the charming concerts of the charming musician, Salomon, that this occurred. Dr. Burney knew not that she was returned from Italy, whither she had gone speedily after her marriage; till here, with much surprise, he perceived among the audience, il Signor Piozzi.

'Approaching him, with an aspect of cordiality, which was met with one of welcoming pleasure, they entered into talk upon the performers and instruments, and the enchanting compositions of Haydn. Dr. Burney then

[1] The attacks appeared in *The European Magazine* for 1788 (xiii. 313, 393; xiv. 89). See George Birkbeck Hill's edition of Boswell's *Johnson*, iii. 49 n.

[2] *Diary and Letters*, iv. 20. Mrs. Piozzi was wrong as to the responsibility for the article in *The European Magazine*, but one wonders whether she ever knew that Burney himself was the author of the article on her 'Anecdotes of Johnson' in *The Monthly Review* (lxxiv, 1786, p. 374). It is discriminating, but frank blame predominates.

inquired, with all the interest that he most sincerely felt, after *la sua consorte*. Piozzi, turning round, pointed to a sofa, on which, to his infinite joy, Dr. Burney beheld Mrs. Thrale Piozzi, seated in the midst of her daughters, the four Miss Thrales.

'His pleasure seemed reciprocated by Mrs. Piozzi, who, sportively ejaculating, "Here's Dr. Burney, as young as ever!" held out to him her hand with lively amity.

'His satisfaction now expanded into a conversational gaiety, that opened from them both those fertile sources of entertainment, that originally had rendered them most agreeable to each other; the younger branches, with amiable good-humour, contributing to the spirit of this unexpected junction.'[1]

Apparently, after this, occasional meetings or correspondence took place, for a letter of Burney to Mrs. Piozzi, in 1807, says:

'We are not come to a right understanding yet. I plainly perceive that I labour under some suspicion of neglect wh. disturbs me. It is totally unfounded.—This being "the truth, and nothing but the truth" . . . let not dear Madam, cold Etiquette, after we have fortunately met, keep us asunder. —Your old, your very old and obliged servant.'[2]

What was probably the last meeting of all occurred at Bath in the following year (1808), when Burney was eighty-two and Mrs. Piozzi sixty-seven, and when nearly a quarter of a century had gone by since the parting. Burney was at Bath for his health and was pleased and surprised when Mrs. Piozzi's name was brought up to him:

'I was much surprised but desired that she might be admitted; and I received her as an old friend with whom I had spent much time very happily, and never wished to quarrel. . . . We shook hands very cordially and avoided any allusion to our long separation and its cause.'

And then, apparently, Burney called on her husband, who like himself was in Bath for his health.[3]

It is pleasant to know that Mr. and Mrs. Piozzi lived in perfect happiness together for a quarter of a century (he died in 1809): this, then, was the upshot of what Macaulay, long after the parties were in their graves, still stigmatized as 'a degrading passion'. From 1813 onwards Fanny and the widowed Mrs. Piozzi were meeting and corresponding again, and we possess letters that passed between them and letters from Fanny to her family in which the renewed friendship

[1] *Mem.* iii. 198.

[2] This letter, dated 21 Jan., is quoted in the R. B. Adam Catalogue, vol. iii.

[3] To the end Mrs. Piozzi had moods in which bitterness towards the Burneys came over her again (Lord Fife having done his work only too well). So, on Burney's death she remarked in her commonplace book, with a heedless mixture of metaphors: 'Burney—dead at last I am told at 89 Years old; and in the full possession of his Faculties:—they were extremely fine ones. He *thought* himself my Friend once I believe, whilst he *thought* the World was so:—when the Stream turned against the *poor* Straw, he helped retard its Progress with his *Stick*: & made his Daughter do it with her *Fingers*—The Stream however grew too strong, and forced the little Straw forward in *Spite of them*—Oh then they cowr'd, & sneaked again, and would again have plaid the *Parasite*' (Jas. L. Clifford, *Hester Lynch Piozzi*, 414 n.).

is mentioned. We have in one of Fanny's letters an agreeable picture of Mrs. Piozzi celebrating what she considered to be her eightieth birthday (really the seventy-ninth anniversary of her birth) at Bath, in 1820, by giving a ball to seven or eight hundred people, and leading off the dances with her adopted son, nephew of her late husband.[1] This adopted son (adding to his original name her maiden name) became Sir John Piozzi Salusbury, Sheriff of Flintshire. There are still 'Piozzi Salusburys' to be met (see *Who's Who*), perpetuating the memory of this eighteenth-century romance that so needlessly disturbed our Burneys.

Let us close this account of the ending of a happy association with Fanny's parting tribute to her old friend when, during the year following the Bath festivities just mentioned, she heard of her death:

> 'I have lost now, just lost, my once most dear, intimate, and admired friend, Mrs. Thrale Piozzi, who preserved her fine faculties, her imagination, her intelligence, her powers of allusion and citation, her extraordinary memory, and her almost unexampled vivacity, to the last of her existence. She was in her eighty-second year, and yet owed not her death to age nor to natural decay, but to the effects of a fall in a journey from Penzance to Clifton. . . . She was, in truth, a most wonderful character for talents and eccentricity, for wit, genius, generosity, spirit, and powers of entertainment.'[2]

The Streatham circle, as we have seen, broke up about 1782. That is the year in which, as is stated, Burney was a competitor for the position of organist at the church of St. Martin in the Fields, close to his dwelling. This, we are told, he lost to Benjamin Cooke, who for thirty years had been connected with Westminster Abbey, having been appointed deputy organist in 1746, at the age of twelve, and organist sixteen years later, at the age of twenty-eight. Cooke continued his occupancy of the position at the Abbey until his death in 1793, so in accepting that of St. Martin's he became a pluralist.[3]

In 1783 Burney made the acquaintance of 'the famous Linguet, during the residence in England of that eloquent, powerful, unfortunate victim, of parts too strong for his judgement, and of impulses too imperious for his safety'.[4] It was no doubt chiefly as a distinguished writer that Linguet interested Burney—as author of the *Histoire du siècle d'Alexandre le Grand*, of the *Fanatisme des philosophes*, the *Histoire des révolutions de l'Empire Romain*, and perhaps (though this might not interest Burney so much) the *Théorie des lois civiles*. We know that Burney possessed some of this author's works, for we hear of Mrs. Montagu losing one of them.[5]

[1] *Diary and Letters*, vi. 399. [2] Ibid.

[3] The statement as to Burney's competing for this post at St. Martin's I take from C. F. Abdy Williams, *Degrees in Music*, 1894. I do not remember meeting with it elsewhere, but Abdy Williams (a careful writer) must have done so and, on the face of it, it seems very likely that Burney, on a vacancy occurring at his own parish church, would apply for it.

[4] *Mem.* ii. 334. [5] *Diary and Letters*, i. 121.

Said she to Fanny, 'I am afraid he thinks me a thief with his *Linguet*, but I assure you I am a very honest woman, and I spent a full three hours in looking for it.'

Linguet, after his first prudent removal to London, had foolishly gone back to France and spent two years in prison. Now, released, he had returned to the land of liberty. We are not told much of the commerce between Burney and Linguet, but are told more of another famous French writer and politician whom Burney met in Linguet's London apartment—Brissot de Warville, Carlyle's 'restless, scheming, scribbling Brissot . . . a man of the windmill species, that grinds always turning towards all winds; not in the steadiest manner'. To judge by what follows, Brissot evidently had a high opinion of *Evelina* and of the recently published *Cecilia*:

'At this time, 1783, Brissot de Warville announced himself as a member of a French committee employed to select subjects in foreign countries, for adding to the national stock of worthies of his own soil, who were destined to immortality, by having their portraits, busts, or statues, elevated in the Paris Pantheon. And, as such, he addressed a letter to Dr. Burney. He had been directed, he said, to choose, in England, a female for this high honour; and he wrote to Dr. Burney to say, that the gentlewoman upon whom it had pleased him to fix—was no other than a daughter of the Doctor's!

'At that astonished daughter's earnest supplication, the Doctor, with proper acknowledgements, declined accepting this towering compliment.

'M. Brissot employed his highest pains of flattery to conquer this repugnance; but head, heart, and taste were in opposition to his pleadings, and he had no chance of success.'[1]

Then Brissot 'earnestly besought permission' to introduce to what he called 'l'Hôtel du Grand Newton' the young wife he had just married, and the Burneys found her to be 'pretty, gentle, and with a striking air of youthful innocence'. The pair seemed to be 'perfectly satisfied in following literary pursuits', but, as Fanny says, they came later to realize that his being in London was, in reality, connected with 'some deep political projects of which he afterwards extended the practice to America'.

It is generally understood that Brissot's visit to America was in connexion with the movement for the abolition of slavery (as representative of the 'Société des Amis des Noirs'), but the Burneys apparently did not believe his mission was so innocent as this. Did that fashionable harpsichord and piano teacher, Dr. Burney, one wonders, ever come across a copy of Brissot's account of his experiences there—*New Travels in the United States of America*? And if so what had he to say to the following passage?

'Music . . . begins to make a part of their education. In some houses you hear the forte-piano. This art, it is true, is still in its infancy. . . . God grant

[1] *Mem.* ii. 334.

that the Bostonian women may never, like those of France, acquire the malady of perfection in this art! It is never attained but at the expense of the domestic virtues.'[1]

Anyhow the Burneys did not take to Brissot. He had 'a certain low-bred fullness and forwardness of look, even in the midst of professions of humility and respect that were by no means attractive to Dr. Burney'. So this 'latent demagogue' was cold-shouldered ('completely shirked' is Fanny's term) and 'nothing more was there seen or known of him till his jacobinical harangues and proceedings, five years later, were blazoned to the world by the republican gazettes'.

Fanny really becomes very hot about poor Brissot, who, forty years before she wrote, had perished under the guillotine—as had Linguet, to whom was owing the Burneys' acquaintance with him. And though he had been 'deluded into showing hospitality':

'Great was his thankfulness, that the delusion had not been of such strength, as to induce him to enrol a representation of his daughter in a selection made by a man of principles and conduct so opposite to his own; however, individually, the collection might have been as flattering to his parental pride, as her undue entrance into such a circle would have been painfully ostentatious to the insufficient and unambitious object of M. Brissot's choice.'

Another prominent Frenchman who sought out Burney and struck up an acquaintance with him was the Duc de Chaulnes—the eminent physicist and chemist who had published twenty years earlier an ingenious method of minute graduation 'by replacing the points of a pair of beam compasses by two micrometer microscopes',[2] and who was also the discoverer of the alkaline carbonates. In a memorandum left by Burney he says:

'In 1783, I dined at the Adelphi with Dr. Johnson and the Duc de Chaulnes. This extraordinary personage, a great traveller, and curious inquirer into the productions of art and of nature, had recently been to China; and, amongst many other discoveries that he had made in that immense and remote region, of which he had brought specimens to Europe, being a great chemist, he had particularly applied himself to the disclosure of the means by which the Chinese obtain that extraordinary brilliancy and permanence in the prismatic colours, which is so much admired and envied by other nations.

'I knew nothing of his being in England till, late one night, I heard a bustle and different voices in the passage, or little hall, in my house in St. Martin's-street, commonly, from its former great owner, called Newton House; when, on inquiry, I was informed that there was a foreign gentleman, with a guide and an interpreter, who was come to beg permission to see the observatory of the *grand* Newton.

[1] Translation of part of the work in No. 126 of the *Old South Leaflets*, published 'by direction of the Old South Work, Old South Meeting House, Boston' (1905).

[2] *Encyclopaedia Britannica*, s.v. 'Graduation'. A full description of this new method is therein given.

'I went out of the parlour to speak to this stranger, and to invite him in. He accepted the offer with readiness, and I promised to shew him the observatory the next morning; and we soon became so well acquainted, that, two or three days afterwards, he honoured me with the following note in English: which I shall copy literally, for its foreign originality.

'The Duke of Chaulnes' best compliments to Doctor Burney: he desires the favour of his company to dinner with Doctor Johnson on Sunday next, between about three and four o'clock, which is the hour convenient to the excellent old Doctor, the best piece of man, indeed, that the Duke ever saw.'[1]

This dinner, it appears, turned out rather sadly. Johnson was within a year or so of his death, and was 'in a state of bodily uneasiness and pain that unfitted him for exertion'. He did his best, but 'his physical force refused consent to his efforts'.

However, soon afterwards the Duke came to tea in St. Martin's Street, entering the house 'with reverence, from a knowledge that he was treading boards that had been trodden by the great Newton'. He explained his Chinese researches, 'examined the Doctor's library', and demanded to be introduced to novelist Fanny. Poor Fanny! The ceremony was, on the Duke's part, so pompous and eulogistic that she was embarrassed to the point of utter silence, and the Duke—

'finding, when it was over, she simply bowed, and turned about to make the tea, without attempting any conversational reply, he conceived that his eloquent *éloge* had not been understood; and after a little general talk with Mr. Hoole and his son, who were of the evening party, he approached her again, with a grave desire to the Doctor of a second presentation.

'This, though unavoidably granted, produced nothing more brilliant to satisfy his expectations; which then, in all probability, were changed into pity, if not contempt, at so egregious a mark of that uncouth malady of which her country stands arraigned, bashful shyness.'

'This *maladie du pays*', confesses Fanny, 'has pursued and annoyed her through life, except when incidentally surprised away by peculiar persons or circumstances.'

Then there was the celebrated writer who, without intending it, was the means of enriching the French dictionary with a new word. A Berquinade is defined as an 'Ouvrage écrit pour la jeunesse, à la manière de Berquin. Œuvre fade, sans intérêt'. Berquin came to London about 1783 or a little later, and, according to his own statement, the first inquiry he made was for the 'Hôtel du Grand Newton'. Here

'he offered up incense to the owner, and to his second daughter, of so overpowering a perfume, that it would have derogated completely from the character of verity and simplicity that makes the charm of his tales for juvenile pupils, had it not appeared, from passages published in his works after his return to France, that he had really wrought himself into feeling the enthusiasm that here had appeared overstrained, unnatural, and almost, at least to the daughter, burlesque.'

[1] *Mem.* ii. 337.

The joke was that whilst Monsieur Berquin was delivering his soul of such fine sentiments, and begging Mrs. Burney to present to his fellow author, Fanny, on his behalf, a set of his famous *Ami des Enfants* (twenty-four volumes; no less!), Fanny was sitting in that very room, as she wrote to Susan, 'quietly scollopping a muslin boarder and making entreating signs to my mother not to betray me'.

It was only when Berquin came again that he found out how he had been fooled, and then he took it gracefully.

> 'But his rapture every time I speak is too great to be excited often! therefore, I am chary of my words. You would laugh irresistibly to see how *enchanté* he deems it fit to appear every time I open my mouth! holding up one hand aloft, as if in sign to all others present to keep the peace!'

This Berquin, who was to French children much what Burney's friend, Mrs. Barbauld, was to British ones, was some years later appointed tutor to the Dauphin, but did not enjoy the honour long, for the Revolution came to rob him of it.

XXXIX. BURNEY AMONGST THE WATER NYMPHS

(1783; aged 57)

A VERY public, but rather ludicrous, honour came Burney's way in the late 1770's. In one of a series of paintings which half London flocked to see he was exhibited rising from the water in the company of a bevy of Nereids. This series happily exists to the present day, and the passenger along the Strand or the Embankment may, if he cares to turn aside for a moment and ask permission of the Royal Society of Arts, in John Street, enjoy the sight of Burney in the strange company not only of the ladies just mentioned but also in that of Drake, Raleigh, and Cabot, and, more reasonably, his actual acquaintance, 'the late Captain Cook, of amiable memory'. These four nautical worthies are propelling a triumphal car in which sits 'The Thames, steering himself with one hand and holding in the other a mariner's compass'. And in front of the car are four figures representing Europe, Asia, Africa, and America. Mercury, as 'the emblem of Commerce', is represented at the top of the picture as summoning the nations, and the Nereids following the car carry several articles of the principal manufactures of Great Britain. 'The sportive appearance of some of these Nereids gives a variety to the picture and is intended to show that an extensive commerce is sometimes found subversive of the foundation of virtue'[1]: thus is a delicate touch of moral warning brought into the composition. (See opposite.)

But what on earth, the reader may breathlessly inquire, is Burney doing in this doubtful company? Or, rather, What in the water is he doing? Fanny herself was, to the end, puzzled. In old age she says:

'Amongst the many contemporary tributes paid to the merits of Dr. Burney, there was one from a celebrated and estimable artist, that caused no small diversion to the friends of the Doctor; and, perhaps, to the public at large; from the Hibernian tale which it seemed instinctively to unfold of the birthplace of its designer.

'The famous painter, Mr. Barry, after a formal declaration that his picture of *The Triumph of the Thames*, which was painted for the Society of Arts, should be devoted exclusively to immortalizing the eminent dead, placed, in the watery groupes of the renowned departed, Dr. Burney, then full of life and vigour.'[2]

It will be fairest to let the painter give his own explanation and to accord him the space and time he feels himself to require. He had, partly, sound patriotic purpose:

'As music is naturally connected with matters of joy and triumph, and

[1] A *Note on the Pictures by James Barry in the Great Room of the Society of Arts*, by Sir Trueman Wood (who has incorporated therein, as the reader may have surmised, some of the choicest phrases of the contemporary description).

[2] *Mem.* ii. 340.

PLATE 23. *BURNEY IN STRANGE COMPANY*

THE GREAT ROOM OF THE ROYAL SOCIETY OF ARTS
With the paintings by Burney's eccentric friend, Barry (*see* ii. 14 et seq.).

'COMMERCE, OR THE TRIUMPH OF THE THAMES'
Burney was a member of the Society. If he sometimes attended the meetings it must have interested him to see the prominence given to his own face and figure (behind the Nereid's outstretched left arm), and those of his late acquaintance, Captain Cook (in front of Neptune's car). Did he recall the exclamation of 'a dowager of fashion'—*It irks me to see my good friend Dr. Burney paddling in a horse-pond with a bevy of naked wenches?*

that according to all necessary propriety, the retinue of the Thames could not appear without an artist in this way, I was happy to find that there was no necessity for my co-operating with those who seem inclined to disgrace our country by recurring to foreigners, whilst we can boast a native, so eminently distinguished for his musical abilities as doctor Burney, whom I have introduced here, behind Drake, and Rawleigh. . . . When we reflect upon the expence and attention which our people so eagerly bestow upon Italian operas, and other foreign musical entertainments, in a language unintelligible to the many, and even but ill understood by the few, one is almost tempted to think that our musical feelings are very superior to those of the Italians, since we appear to the full, in as much extacy from the mere sensation of hearing only, as the people of Italy are from the joint operation of their ears and their understandings. 'Tis odd enough, that on the banks of the Tyber and the Arno, music should necessarily require words for an exponent, and to be enforced by the language that was intelligible and familiar to all; whilst we on the banks of the Thames, from our superior sensibility and greater quickness of apprehension, should stand in no need of any such requisition. But the philosophical critics will not allow us to reason after this manner; they will say, that this very extraordinary relish is, for the most part, affectation; and it is possible they may call it by its right name. But if ever the musical genius of our islands should be suffered to emerge, and that it may be rationally hoped that we too should, in our turn, have our ears and our hearts equally affected by the sterling vigour and persuasive sentiments of our own poetry, cloathed in all the harmony, majesty, and eloquent melting sensibility of those co-operating tones, which form the proper colouring, and give the last finish, perfection, and energy to that vehicle of our sentiments language; if ever these things are likely to come to pass, it must be under the auspices of such a leader as Doctor Burney, whose plan for establishing a national school of music not long since, at the Foundling Hospital,[1] which, to all rational people, seemed so useful and practicable; and after being unanimously voted by the governors, was set aside by the cabal of a few fanatics only. We might expect every thing under such a director, whose admirable history of music shews a mind capacious and excursive, that has left nothing unexplored from which his art might derive perfection, and appears no less fraught with elegant observation, and a vigorous display of the spirit, and beauties of our poetry, which his animated translations manifest, than for every kind of agreeable and useful information respecting his own very pleasing art.'[2]

Barry was a personal friend of the Burneys and an habitué of their house. Fanny calls him 'the most striking, though by no means the most reasonable converser amongst those who generally volunteered their colloquial services in St. Martin's Street', and she deplores his enmity to that other painter friend of theirs, Reynolds—who, as she reminds us, was not likely to be the blameworthy party in the dissension,

[1] See I. 261–3.

[2] *An Account of a Series of Pictures in the Great Room of the Society of Arts, Manufactures and Commerce, at the Adelphi, by James Barry, R.A.* (*1783*). Barry got Burney's brother-in-law, Arthur Young, to correct this pamphlet for him and begged him 'in charity spare not the rod, as it may save the child' (*Autobiography of Arthur Young*, 116).

for, says she, adopting Johnson's dictum, 'Sir Joshua Reynolds possesses the largest share of inoffensiveness of any man I know':[1] Barry 'had many admirable and uncommon properties', and cherished 'moral sentiments' that were 'liberal, nay noble', but he was also full of eccentricities and extremely quarrelsome.

In 1842 Haydon (a painter who in general conception of the purpose of his art much resembled Barry) went to look at these paintings at the Society of Arts. He found there somebody who could give him an interesting account of their execution sixty years before:

'Went to the Adelphi, and looked at Barry's pictures. Miss Corkings, the housekeeper, was a girl of twelve years old when Barry painted the work. She told me many anecdotes. She said his violence was dreadful, his oaths horrid, and his temper like insanity. She said he carried virtue to a vice. His hatred of obligation was such that he would accept nothing. Wherever he dined he left 1*s.* 2*d.* in the plate, and gentlemen indulged him. The servants were afraid to go near him; in summer he came to work at five, and worked till dark, when a lamp was lighted, and he went on etching till eleven at night.

'She said, when coaxed to talk, his conversation was sublime. She thought the want of early discipline was the cause of his defects. He began his work in 1780 [should be 1777], and was seven years [should be six years] before he concluded it. She remembered Burke and Johnson calling once, but no artist. She really believed he would have shot anyone who had dared. He had tea boiled in a quart pot, and a penny roll for breakfast, dined in Porridge island [the cheap cook-shop quarter of the Strand neighbourhood], and had milk for supper, which was prepared in the house.

'There is a grasp of mind there nowhere else to be found, as Johnson said, but no colour, no surface, beauty, or correct drawing. Still, as the only work of the kind, it is an honour to the country.'[2]

Burney may have smiled, with others, at the oddity of his own translation to a liquid element, but he must have been gratified also. He had many personal reasons for being interested in the matter. He himself had been elected to the Society of Arts long before (in 1764, when he was still in Poland Street), and his brother-in-law, Arthur Young, who appeared in another of Barry's pictures in the same room, was also a member, had been Chairman of its Committee on Agriculture, and had been awarded gold medals by the Society for his system of fattening hogs and for an account of the 'Clustered Potato'. Amongst other friends of his who were members were his early patron the Earl of Holdernesse, his late friend the Earl of Sandwich, his old master Arne, and his friends Sir Joseph Banks, Boswell, Sir Robert Chambers,

[1] Barry despised mere portrait-painters. To him painting was a medium for the expression of *noble ideas*—in fact a branch of literature.

[2] *Autobiography and Memoirs of B. R. Haydon,* under date of 4 Jan. 1842. Barry was at work on this big series of paintings until 1783. From the above it appears that when daylight went he stayed on the premises etching.

Garrick, Hawkesworth, Soame Jenyns, Johnson, Sir William Pepys, Reynolds, Sir Robert Strange, Thrale, and Horace Walpole.

Then the artist was the particular protégé of his friend Burke, who had first brought this brother Irishman of his to London and introduced him into artistic society, and had given him an allowance to help to maintain him during a four years' period of study in Rome.

And no doubt, too, Burney was amused by all the quips that his quaint picturing produced. Fanny gives us one *jeu d'esprit* by the Burneys' friend, Owen Cambridge. It alludes to 'an accident that had just occurred to the celebrated Gibbon; who, in stepping too lightly from or to a boat of Mr. Cambridge's, had slipped into the Thames':

'This morning a letter was brought into my room, and the maid said it came from Mr. Cambridge, but that the messenger was gone. I opened, and will copy it. The lines were suggested by my father's portrait in Barry's great painting.

When Chloe's picture was to Venus shown,
Surprised, the goddess took it for her own.—Prior.

When Burney's picture was to Gibbon shown,
The pleased historian took it for his own;
"For who, with shoulders dry, and powdered locks,
E'er bathed, but I?" he said, and rapp'd his box.

Barry replied, My lasting colours show
What gifts the painter's pencil can bestow.
With nymphs of Thames, those amiable creatures,
I placed the charming minstrel's smiling features:
And let not, then, his *bonne fortune* concern ye,
For there are nymphs enough for you and Burney.'[1]

[1] *Diary and Letters*, ii. 224; *Mem.* ii. 342.

XL. THE BURNEYS COME TO KNOW OLD MRS. DELANY AND FANNY TO LEARN COURT ETIQUETTE

(1783; Fanny aged 31, her father 57, and Mrs. Delany 83)

WHILST the Burneys were in St. Martin's Street there was living ten minutes' walk away, in St. James's Place, a wonderful old lady, whom in 1783 they came to know and whose friendship, during the five years she had still to live, was to mean a good deal to Burney himself and to introduce Fanny to new scenes and, indeed, to transform her whole manner of life.

This was Mrs. Delany (see pl. 34, II. 104), 'the fairest model of female excellence of the days that were passed', as their friend Burke described her to them[1]—high-bred, accomplished, and sensible, amiable benevolent, and devoutly Christian in the composed eighteenth-century style. In her twenties she had been the 'Aspasia' of the romantic correspondence circle of which a young Fellow of Lincoln College, John Wesley, was the 'Cyrus' and his brother, Charles, the 'Araspes'; later she had been the friend and correspondent of Swift. She had intimate memories of Handel, dating back to the earlier part of his English career; this great figure of the past had frequented her house, had talked over with her particular passages in his music, and, 'in the best humour in the world', had 'played lessons and accompanied all the ladies that sung from seven o'clock to eleven'.[2] She had once made 'a drama for an oratorio, out of Milton's *Paradise Lost*, to give Mr. Handel to compose to' (it cost her 'a great deal of thought and contrivance', but he does not seem to have made use of it). 'Just as I came to this place', she ends a letter in 1747, 'in came Mr. Handel, and he has prevented my adding any more.'

Swift was long ago dead and so was Handel, and so were most of her earlier circle, but, whilst she lamented the loss of old friends she was always making new ones, and now, having read *Evelina* (or rather, it must be, having had it read to her, for she was nearly blind), she wanted to know Fanny Burney. And Fanny, who must have heard a great deal about her from Horace Walpole and the Dowager Duchess of Portland and from innumerable other friends of her own and her father, wanted to know her, too.

It was by the intervention of one of the Bluestockings, 'the respectable Mrs. Chapone', that Fanny 'was first conveyed to the dwelling of Mrs. Delany in St. James's Place', where she was at once captivated by a charming exhibition of the high-toned courtesy of a period even more

[1] *Mem.* ii. 300.

[2] Letter to her sister of 12 Apr. 1734, in R. Brimley Johnson, *Mrs. Delany*. (For the various facts and expressions here quoted see pp. 98, 130, 136, and 160 of that work.)

formally polite than her own, and was delighted to examine her hostess's own paintings, and 'ornaments of her own execution, of striking elegance . . . partly copied from antique studies, partly of fanciful invention, but all equally in the chaste style of true and refined good taste', and above all a very famous piece of work now to be admired by us, too (in the Print Room of the British Museum), for:

'At the request of Mrs. Chapone, she instantly and unaffectedly brought forth a volume of her newly-invented Mosaic flower-work; an art of her own creation; consisting of staining paper of all possible colours, and then cutting it into strips, so finely and delicately, that when pasted on a dark ground, in accordance to the flower it was to produce, it had the appearance of a beautiful painting; except that it rose to the sight with a still richer effect: and this art Mrs. Delany had invented at seventy-five years of age!'[1]

And then, after there had been eaten a 'plain, well-cooked and elegantly served' little dinner, there came in Mrs. Delany's regular evening visitor, the Dowager Duchess above mentioned, a friend of the earlier days of Daddy Crisp, whom the Duchess described as 'one of the most ingenious and agreeable men she had ever known', regretting 'his having sequestered himself so much from the society of his former friends'. Fanny was glad to find the Duchess 'not merely free from pride, but free from affability—its most mortifying deputy' (an acute touch, Novelist Fanny being always a discerning observer of human nature in its many delicate shades and colours). And there was much very gratifying talk about *Evelina*. And, in fact, this first meeting of Fanny and the old lady passed off famously and was worth the long account of it recorded in the diary on the return to St. Martin's Street—from which account (also later largely transcribed into Fanny's *Memoirs* of her father) the present one is taken.[2]

This was but the beginning of a close friendship between the older lady and the younger one. Indeed Fanny was soon an habituée of the

[1] 'Sir Joshua Reynolds admired the floral mosaics, looking on them as works of a beautiful applied art; while Banks and Solander admired them equally as the most accurate of all botanical reproductions. "They are the only imitations of nature I have ever seen," declared Banks, "from which I would venture to describe botanically any plant without the least fear of committing an error." . . . The "paper mosaick" is not an overpowering manifestation of genius. On the other hand, it is far more than a mere marvel of elegance. It is an original accomplishment, unique of its kind, ingenious, exquisite, one of the loveliest minor works of the century. In turning over the pages of the volumes one is literally astounded by the delicacy and the firm daintiness of the work, by the extraordinary skill with which the most minute snippets or shreds of paper, sometimes thin as hair, are fixed in position, and by the admirable sense of effect and arrangement in placing flowers on the background. Every one who loves the eighteenth century and its typical graces ought to visit the Print Room and ask to see the *Flora Delanica*: there is nothing else comparable to the peculiar and intensely personal charm of this work.' C. E. Vulliamy, *Aspasia: the Life and Letters of Mary Granville, Mrs. Delany* (1935), 256. The many large albums containing these mosaics were bequeathed to the British Museum by Lady Llanover in 1897. The present writer strongly endorses the above eulogy of them.

[2] *Diary and Letters*, ii. 193 et seq.; *Mem.* ii. 300 et seq.

house in St. James's Place. And this naturally led to Burney's going there, too, and drawing upon Mrs. Delany's store of reminiscences for his own writings. At the special request of the King, Mrs. Delany's warm admirer, she searched her memory for Handelian recollections; and in the last volume of the *History of Music* Burney gives us not only an account of the vocal career of 'the celebrated Mrs. Anastasia Robinson', but also (and this was surely hardly essential in such a work) a longer one of her romantic affair with, and ultimate marriage to, the Earl of Peterborough—all this 'communicated to me by the late venerable Mrs. Delany, her contemporary and intimate acquaintance'.

And now approached a pleasantly anticipated day when Fanny was to have a carriage sent for her from the Duchess of Portland's country-house at Bulstrode Park, beyond Watford, so that she might pass some time there with the Duchess and Mrs. Delany. But then came the shock of a heart-broken letter from Mrs. Delany, already at Bulstrode, to say that the Duchess had suddenly passed away.

So Fanny went for a time to live with her bereaved friend in St. James's Place. But the upkeep of the house there was soon found to be too expensive for Mrs. Delany to maintain, since her old friend, the Duchess, whilst always leaving her her cherished independence, had been in the habit of tactfully supplying 'unnumbered little auxiliaries to domestic economy', and these were received no more. So the King stepped in—and in royal fashion. Mrs. Delany, he said, must come and live at Windsor, where he would 'fit up' for her a house near the Castle, and where she should enjoy a pension of three hundred pounds a year. And there the old lady settled, her pension handed to her half-yearly in a pocket-book by the Queen in person, so as to avoid taxation (how sluggish is the fiscal conscience, even in palaces!), and the last years of a fading life were made comfortable.

Soon the Queen, an admirer of *Evelina*, began to ask Mrs. Delany why she had not brought Fanny to her new home at Windsor, and Fanny was invited and duly came down. At first she contrived to slip out of the way when the Queen was announced or the King strolled over the Park and knocked at the door. There exists, in a letter from Fanny to her people at home,[1] a long and amusing account of how she was at length taken unawares by the King's arrival and how he questioned her, in the minute way he had of questioning people, as to how she came to write *Evelina*, and how she managed to arrange for its secret publication, and what her father (that 'very agreeable and entertaining man', as the Queen called him) was at the moment engaged in doing:

'"Is your father about anything at present?"

'"Yes, sir, he goes on, when he has time, with his history."

'"Does he write quick?"

'"Yes, sir, when he writes from himself; but in his history, he has so many

[1] *Diary and Letters*, ii. 314 et seq.

books to consult, that sometimes he spends three days in finding authorities for a single passage."

'"Very true; that must be unavoidable."'[1]

And then the Queen arrived, and the King went on catechizing Fanny and repeating all her answers to the Queen, and Fanny got into a panic, fancying, by the drift of the talk, that they were going to make her play the harpsichord. And, sure enough, at last:

'The King came to me again, and said, "Are you musical?"

'"Not a performer, sir."

'Then going from me to the Queen, he cried, "She does not play."

'I did not hear what the Queen answered; she spoke in a low voice, and seemed much out of spirits. . . .

'"Are you sure you never play?—never touch the keys at all?"

'"Never to acknowledge it, sir."

'"Oh! that's it!" cried he; and flying to the Queen, cried, "She does play—but not to acknowledge it!"

'I was now in a most horrible panic once more; pushed so very home, I could answer no other than I did, for these categorical questions almost constrain categorical answers; and here, at Windsor, it seems an absolute point that whatever they ask must be told, and whatever they desire must be done. Think, but, then, of my consternation, in expecting their commands to perform! My dear father, pity me!

'The eager air with which he returned to me fully explained what was to follow. I hastily, therefore, spoke first, in order to stop him, crying—"I never, sir, played to anybody but myself!—never!"

'"No?" cried he, looking incredulous; "what, not to ——."

'"Not even to me, sir!" cried my kind Mrs. Delany, who saw what was threatening me.

'"No?—are you sure?" cried he, disappointed; "but—but you'll——"

'"I have never, sir," cried I, very earnestly, "played in my life, but when I could hear nobody else—quite alone, and from a mere love of any musical sounds."

'He repeated all this to the Queen, whose answers I never heard; but when he once more came back, with a face that looked unwilling to give it up, in my fright I had recourse to dumb show, and raised my hands in a supplicating fold, with a most begging countenance to be excused. This, luckily, succeeded; he understood me very readily, and laughed a little, but made a sort of desisting, or rather complying, little bow, and said no more about it.'

And then there followed an anecdote about poor 'Mr. Webb'. This was evidently William Webb, Organist of St. George's Chapel, Windsor, who (as Brown and Stratton's *British Musical Biography* tells us) 'died in 1788 from loss of blood, after undergoing an operation for removal of a wen in the nostril', an operation we can well believe he desired since we hear from Fanny that he had 'a nose of so enormous a size that it covered all the middle of his face'. The little Princess

[1] Ibid. 323.

Sophia, it appears, was to have music lessons from Webb, and the Queen warned her 'to remember that this was a misfortune—for which he ought to be pitied, and that she must be sure not to laugh at it, nor stare at it'; and Sophia, on Mr. Webb being announced, ran up to a lady present and said, 'Lady Cremorne, Mr. Webb has got a very great nose, but that is only to be pitied—so mind you don't laugh!' And the King added, 'Poor Mr. Webb was very much discountenanced when he first saw me, and tried to hide his face, by a great nosegay, or I believe, only a branch, which he held before it; but really that had so odd a look, that it was worse and more ridiculous than the nose; however I hope he does not mind me now.'

And so the talk went on, and there were other similar talks on other evenings, and Fanny, despite her invincible shyness, clearly became a great favourite. Once there was talk of Rousseau, to whom, when he was in England, the King had made an allowance, and there were anecdotes told 'all charging him with savage pride and insolent ingratitude'. Here Fanny 'thought it but common justice to the memory of poor Rousseau' (he had died seven or eight years before) to put in a word:

'"Some gratitude, sir," said I, "he was not without. When my father was in Paris, which was after Rousseau had been in England, he visited him, in his garret, and the first thing he showed him was your Majesty's portrait over his chimney."[1]

Then there was the evening when the King opened his heart to Fanny about Shakespeare in phrases to-day still well remembered and phrases punctuated with plenty of his favourite 'What?' ('Was there ever such stuff as great part of Shakespeare? only one must not say so. But what think you? What? Is there not sad stuff? What, What?')

And so Fanny gradually became habituated to royalty and the manner in which it should be treated and was able to send to her sister Hetty in London a long memorandum—'Directions for Coughing, Sneezing, or Moving, before the King and Queen'. This document, from its mere practical utility, deserves a larger publicity than it has yet obtained, but shall here be given more in the light of an entertaining digression from the serious historical matter that has so far occupied this chapter:

'*Directions for Coughing, Sneezing, or Moving, before the King and Queen.*

'In the first place, you must not cough. If you find a cough tickling in your throat, you must arrest it from making any sound; if you find yourself choking with the forbearance, you must choke—but not cough.

'In the second place, you must not sneeze. If you have a vehement cold, you must take no notice of it; if your nose-membranes feel a great irritation, you must hold your breath; if a sneeze still insists on making its way, you must oppose it, by keeping your teeth grinding together; if the violence of

[1] *Diary and Letters,* ii. 342. See I. 182–3 of the present work.

the repulse breaks some blood-vessel, you must break the blood-vessel—but not sneeze.

'In the third place, you must not, upon any account, stir either hand or foot. If, by chance, a black pin runs into your head, you must not take it out. If the pain is very great, you must be sure to bear it without wincing; if it brings the tears into your eyes, you must not wipe them off; if they give you a tingling by running down your cheeks, you must look as if nothing was the matter. If the blood should gush from your head by means of the black pin, you must let it gush; if you are uneasy to think of making such a blurred appearance, you must be uneasy, but you must say nothing about it. If, however, the agony is very great, you may, privately, bite the inside of your cheek, or of your lips, for a little relief; taking care, meanwhile, to do it so cautiously as to make no apparent dent outwardly. And, with that precaution, if you even gnaw a piece out, it will not be minded, only be sure either to swallow it, or commit it to a corner of the inside of your mouth till they are gone—for you must not spit.'[1]

Fanny was clearly becoming an authority on Court procedure, and now there came a time when her father thought that she might be useful to *him*. Back in London, she was, one Sunday morning in 1786, just setting out to church when her father unexpectedly appeared. He had heard late on Saturday night of the death of blind Stanley, the fine old musician who for some years had held the position of Master of the King's Band of Music, and he had, apparently, first thing next morning rushed out to see his friend Mr. Smelt, one of the Court officials. Smelt had advised him how to go about obtaining the position which he had been promised when Stanley's predecessor, Boyce, died, and had not then been given (see Appendix, II. 323). He was to go to Windsor at once. 'Take your daughter in your hand,' said Smelt, 'and walk upon the terrace [the South Terrace where the Royal Family were wont to take their evening promenade; see pl. 24, II. 24]. The King seeing you at this time, he will understand, and he is more likely to be touched by a hint of that delicate sort than by any direct application.' By a coincidence, just as Fanny was changing her dress for this journey a letter was put into her hand saying that the Queen wished her to go to Windsor again to visit Mrs. Delany, so the omens were propitious.

The carriage was called and off they went, father and daughter, and in the evening they duly appeared on the Terrace, finding the Royal Family there before they arrived:

'The King and Queen, and the Prince of Mechlenberg, and Her Majesty's mother, walked together. Next them the Princesses and their ladies, and the young Princes, making a very gay and pleasing procession, of one of the finest families in the world. Every way they moved, the crowd retired to stand up against the wall as they passed, and then closed in to follow.'[2]

First the Queen and then the King spoke to Fanny, who had been taken under the care of one of the ladies; they alluded to the fact that

[1] Ibid. 352.

[2] Ibid. 358.

her father, who stood a little way off, was present but they did not approach him, and this looked like a bad sign:

'We stayed some time longer on the terrace, and my poor father occasionally joined me; but he looked so conscious and depressed, that it pained me to see him. There is nothing that I know so very dejecting as solicitation. I am sure I could never, I believe, go through a task of that sort. My dear father was not spoken to, though he had a bow every time the King passed him, and a curtsey from the Queen. But it hurt him, and he thought it a very bad prognostic; and all there was at all to build upon was the graciousness shown to me, which, indeed, in the manner I was accosted, was very flattering, and except to high rank, I am told, very rare. . . .

'We did not get home till past eleven o'clock. We were then informed that Lord Brudenel had called to say Mr. Parsons had a promise of the place from the Lord Chamberlain.' [The Lord Chamberlain was Lord Salisbury.]

So that was it! Parsons, whom, when he was a youth, Burney had befriended in Rome (see I. 179), was the lucky man. It seemed that 'the place had been given away instantly on the death of Mr. Stanley, without any consultation with his Majesty' (What it is to be a King!), and, it was 'generally surmised, much to his Majesty's displeasure', as it certainly was to Burney's:

'But not, however, against the successful rival, Mr. Parsons, afterwards Sir William, was this displeasure directed: he was wholly blameless, not only in this superseding promotion, but in the tenor of his life at large. He might even be uninformed of Dr. Burney's prior claims. And such, in fact, was Dr. Burney's belief.'[1]

As to 'his Majesty's displeasure' it was openly expressed about three years later when His Majesty, during one of his periods of temporary derangement, being released from the usual restraints of his judgement, expressed his mind freely to Fanny:

'He now spoke of my father, with still more kindness, and told me he ought to have had the post of Master of the Band, and not that little poor musician Parsons, who was not fit for it. "But Lord Salisbury," he cried, "used your father very ill in that business, and so he did me! However, I have dashed out his name, and I shall put your father's in—as soon as I get loose again!"'[2]

[1] *Mem.* iii. 78. In Lady Llanover's *Autobiography and Correspondence of Mrs. Delany* there are two letters from Mrs. Boscawen to Mrs. Delany which refer to this occurrence:

'23 May 1786

'I long to know your opinion of Dr. Burney's success, which I am sure has your good wishes, for the love you bear his amiable daughter. I heard they were both at Windsor last Sunday, and I have great hopes that His Majesty will think him worthy to succeed the late Mr. Stanley.'

'27 May 1786

'I am sure you regret with me that *Lord Salisbury* had a *favourite* amongst the musical people, so as not to prefer the *most worthy*, and Dr. Burney is thus esteemed by so many people. . . .'

[2] *Diary and Letters*, iv. 249. See II. 103 of the present work for another allusion to this meeting of Fanny's with the King.

GEORGE III

Patron of music, Handel enthusiast, and admirer of Burney's literary activities (*see* ii. 20–4, 71–3, 99–101, 179, 295–7).

QUEEN CHARLOTTE

Employer and friend of Fanny Burney, whose skill as a novelist she highly appreciated (*see* ii. 20–4, 95–109).

THE KING AND QUEEN ON THE WINDSOR TERRACE

By 'Hamilton'.

This picture is in the Stuttgart Gallery, there being, apparently, another copy at Düsseldorf. The present writer happened to come upon it and reproduces it here since it chances perfectly to illustrate the incident of Burney's disappointing attempt of 1786 to secure the vacant post of Master of the King's Band of Music, as described at ii. 23—'*Take your daughter in your hand*', said Smelt, '*and walk upon the Terrace. The King seeing you at this time, he will understand and he is more likely to be touched by a hint of that delicate sort than by any direct application.*'

(The painter was probably Hugh Douglas Hamilton, 1734–1806, a popular painter who made portraits of George III and his Queen; certainly not C. W. Hamilton, as suggested in Baedeker's *Germany*, for he died six years before George III came to the throne.)

PLATE 25. *BURNEY'S WONDERFUL 'COURT SUIT'*

There has come down to one of Burney's descendants (Mrs. Ayres, formerly Miss Evelyn d'Arblay Burney) a puzzling relic in the shape of what has been long known in the family as his 'Court Suit'. It consists of a waistcoat (which shows signs of having been worn) and the front parts of a coat (which, strangely, appears never to have been made up). The very delicate embroideries embody floral and musical motives of the highest beauty.

The COAT (upper picture) is of thick stiff brown silk, with a design of white leaves, and wine-red, pink, yellow, green, and pale blue flowers. The WAISTCOAT (lower pictures) is of very thick black taffeta, ornamented with groups of flowers, musical instruments, and music books, in white and pastel shades of pink, blue, yellow, and green. The stitchery is throughout of satin thread.

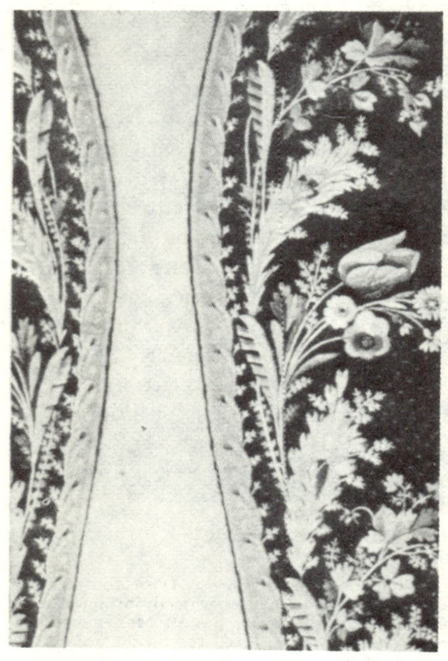

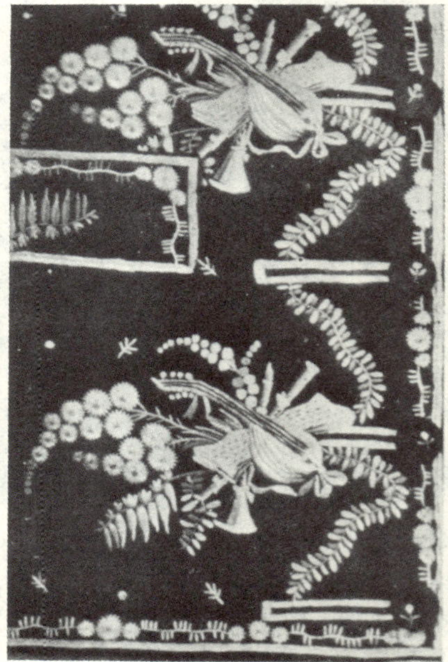

XLI. BURNEY'S CHILDREN AND STEPCHILDREN IN 1783

(Burney aged 57)

AND now let us take a look at the children of Dr. and Mrs. Burney's three families—his, hers, and theirs. We will take the year 1783 as our fixed point.

ESTHER (or 'Hetty'), in 1783, was about thirty-four years old. She was thoroughly happy with her husband and had now at least five or six children, the eldest being about twelve years old. (In the end she was to reach a total of eleven children, but, of course, that ruthless eighteenth-century infant mortality was to rob her of a number of these—how many we do not know, for the records are vague.) It is surely to the 'wifish' Esther's credit ('the wifish Hetty' seems to have been a family expression) that with such abundant family cares she kept her harpsichord playing up to so high a standard as the accounts of it all indicate.

In 1780, as a result of the alarms of the Gordon Riots, Esther had had a serious illness, in which she was nursed by that good creature Betty Hatton,[1] her father's old cook, whose marriage will be chronicled on a later page. Hetty and her husband were apparently living in Charles Street, Long Acre, so were not very far from the family headquarters.

JAMES (or 'Jem' or 'Jemm'), in 1783, was thirty-three. He had been round the world with Captain Cook (1772–4), and then to America, where he had taken part in a few skirmishes with the rebels in Massachusetts Bay (1775), had made the further circumnavigation (the one on which Cook lost his life), commanding one of the ships on the homeward voyage, and had (October 1780, when anchored off Yarmouth) been officially confirmed in the rank of Commander—and on arriving at Deptford had been welcomed home by Johnson, who, it seems, visited him on his ship,[2] and who on return to Streatham 'pronounced an actual eulogium upon Captain Burney to his listeners—how amiable he was, and how gentle in his manners, tho' he had lived so many years with sailors and savages'.[3]

Then he had spent a merry Christmas with Fanny at Chesington, delighting Daddy Crisp with 'Journals, Maps, Plans, Charts, &c. . . . besides a thousand little anecdotes',[4] and just after Christmas had become engaged to Sally Payne, daughter of Tom Payne, the well-known bookseller of Castle Street, St. Martin's-in-the-Fields (publisher

[1] *Early Diary*, i. 50 n.
[2] Manwaring, *My Friend the Admiral*, 155.
[3] From a letter of Mrs. Thrale to Fanny (*Diary and Letters*, i. 454).
[4] Hutton, *Burford Papers*, 60.

of Hawkins's *History of Music*, see I. 302), but had quickly been drawn off to sterner activities.

'A most delightful incident has happened since I came hither. We had just done tea on Friday, and Mrs. Hamilton, Kitty, Jem, and Mr. Crisp, were sitting down to cards, when we were surprised by an express from London, and it brought a "Whereas we think fit" from the Admiralty, to appoint Captain Burney to the command of the *Latona*, during the absence of the Honourable Captain Conway. This is one of the best frigates in the navy, of thirty-eight guns, and immediately, I believe, ready for service. Jem was almost frantic with ecstasy of joy; he sang, laughed, drank to his own success, and danced about the room with Miss Kitty [the quaint, elderly niece of Crisp's hostess-landlady] till he put her quite out of breath. His hope is to get out immediately, and have a brush with some of the Dons, Monsieurs, or Mynheers, while he is in possession of a ship of sufficient force to attack any frigate he may meet.'[1]

It was on hearing the news of this appointment that Dr. Johnson made his further well-remembered pronouncement, quoted in an earlier chapter—'I question if any ship upon the ocean goes out attended with more good wishes than that which carries the fate of Burney'.

After this short voyage as deputy for the Commander of the *Latona* he had been appointed to a definite command of his own, the *Bristol*, of forty guns, and had sailed for the East Indies—after making many protests to the Admiralty about his sailors being largely 'prest men, almost destitute of clothes', and the supply of 'portable broth' for the 'sick and hurt' being only one-fifth the requisite quantity, and the ammunition being 'such as does not fit our guns, and after firing, sticks so fast as to render the gun for some minutes useless'—and so on.[2]

In 1783 James took part in the action at Cuddalore, and at this point we will, for the moment, leave him.

FRANCES ('Fanny'), in 1783, was thirty-one. She had just followed up the success of *Evelina* by the almost equal success of another novel, *Cecilia, or the Memoirs of an Heiress*—in no less than five volumes.

Burney, when he read the manuscript of this second romance of his gifted daughter, thought it even more wonderful than her first.[3] Daddy Crisp, though admiring the book, wanted her to alter one chapter of it, but the authoress, true to some sturdy advice that Crisp himself had given her shortly before, 'never to alter or give up one tittle of anything she wrote merely because of the opinion of her friends, let their talents

[1] *Diary and Letters*, i. 452.

[2] See Manwaring, *My Friend the Admiral*, 168, for a shocking revelation as to the incapacity and inhumanity of our Admiralty at this time. Apparently the treatment of the men had not much improved since the Seven Years' War, during which, for one man killed in battle, nearly a hundred died of disease or were reported 'missing'—which latter term, probably, might usually be interpreted 'deserted in disgust and despair'. (The actual figures, as given in *The Annual Register* for 1763, are 1,512 killed as against 133,708 'missing', or died of disease.)

[3] *Diary and Letters*, ii. 58.

or taste be ever so great', stuck to her own conviction, saying: 'The conflict scene for Cecilia, between the mother and son, to which you so warmly object, is the very scene for which I wrote the whole book, and so entirely does my plan hang upon it, that I must abide by its reception in the world, or put the whole behind the fire.'[1]

And so, in June 1782, *Cecilia* appeared, published jointly by 'honest Tom Payne' (her brother James's father-in-law to be) and Cadell. The publisher of *Evelina*, Lowndes, was much chagrined that he had not been given the opportunity of publishing its successor, and wrote to Dr. Burney a petulant letter ('at a Meeting of Booksellers this Day, I was asked Why I had not *Cecilia?* I answered I did not know, but I would tell them soon—I beg you'll tell me the Reason'), to which Fanny herself replied in very proper terms:

'The author of *Evelina* is much surprised that Mr. Lowndes should trouble himself to enquire any Reason why he did not publish *Cecilia*. She is certainly neither under Engagement or Obligation to *any* Bookseller whatever, and is to no one, therefore, responsible for chusing, and changing as she pleases.

Surrey, Sept. 16, 1782.

'To Mr. Lowndes, Bookseller,
'Fleet Street.'[2]

One reason, no doubt, why Fanny had not given Lowndes the chance of publishing *Cecilia* was the very poor terms (as she must by now have realized) that he had made with her, in her inexperience, for *Evelina*. But another reason may be suggested. Lowndes's grandfather, also a bookseller, is supposed to be the original of one of the characters in *Cecilia*—the miserly *Briggs*.[3] It would hardly have been fitting! And this time Fanny pocketed not the miserable £30 that Lowndes had given her for *Evelina* but a solid £250 (which Crisp advised her to invest in the three-per-cent. annuities),[4] though, wrote Charlotte, 'Most people say she ought to have had a thousand' as, indeed, she ought. But she got additional payment in all sorts of public and private approval—amongst the latter a long and lordly letter from Burke, thanking her 'for the new present bestowed upon the public', and ending:

'In an age distinguished by producing extraordinary women, I hardly dare tell you where my opinion would place you amongst them. I respect your modesty, that will not endure the commendations which your merit forces from everybody.'[5]

Which is certainly first quality butter! (This letter was prefixed to later editions of the work.)

Queen Charlotte, Fanny was told, objected to just one character, the

[1] Ibid. 69, 72.
[2] Ibid. 482.
[3] *D.N.B.* s.v. 'Lowndes, William Thomas'.
[4] *Diary and Letters*, ii. 99.
[5] Ibid. 93.

miserly Mr. Briggs just mentioned,[1] but as he was a favourite with most other readers, Fanny could bear that.

There was a French translation of *Cecilia* promptly published at Neuchâtel (the year after its first appearance, i.e. 1783), but we may take it for granted that the author received no payment for that.

The motif of *Cecilia* is the same as that of *Evelina*. Indeed all of Fanny's novels could have borne much the same sub-title as her first one, 'History of a Young Lady's Entrance into the World'—from which the psycho-analysts can draw what conclusion they like as to Fanny's own mentality, which, despite all the self-esteem which the later pages of her diary and correspondence (and, above all, some parts of her *Memoirs* of her father) sometimes seem to show, was probably deeply tinged to the last with a naïve diffidence.

The plot of *Cecilia* turns largely upon a loss of money, such as her own stepmother had experienced (see I. 131). The book begins rather heavily, but brightens up when the vulgar Briggs makes his appearance. There is a certain extravagance about the whole work, especially as concerns rather too frequent and remarkable meetings that occur purely by chance yet are providential for the plot, pushing it forward just when it needs it. In reading *Cecilia* we often feel the dreamlike strangeness of another world, but then the eighteenth century *is* another world from ours.

Well, as Professor Vaughan says in the *Cambridge History of English Literature*, Fanny does possess 'a talent not easily to be matched amongst English novelists, for telling a story'. And she does deserve Johnson's name for her (after reading *Cecilia*)—'my little character-monger'.[2] And all that makes for entertaining reading.

The first edition of *Cecilia*, consisting of 2,000 copies, was sold out in three months, and there have been very many editions since.[3]

Probably many late-eighteenth-century babies were named after *Cecilia*. Two seem to have been, at any rate—one of Mrs. Thrale's, in 1783, and Esther Burney's, in 1789. And from a phrase emphasized by capitalization on one of the closing pages of *Cecilia* Jane Austen, thirty years later, took the title of one of her own novels (this not being her only honest debt to Fanny):

> 'The whole of this unfortunate business', said Dr. Lyster, 'has been the result of PRIDE and PREJUDICE. . . . Yet this, however, remember; if to PRIDE and PREJUDICE you owe your miseries, so wonderfully is good and evil balanced, that to PRIDE and PREJUDICE you will also owe their termination.'

[1] *Diary and Letters*, ii. 153. There had been similar objections to the vulgar old sea-captain in *Evelina*.

[2] Told in the dedication to Fanny's later novel, *The Wanderer*.

[3] To the shame of present-day publishers there appears to be, at the moment this is written, no edition at all on the market, but Messrs. Dent's edition of 1893 and other editions can easily be procured by any of the more competent second-hand booksellers, to one of whom the present reader, if he has never read the book, is strongly recommended to apply.

It looks as though this expression of Fanny's (an expression that she had so emphasized) 'caught on': two or three times, soon after the book's appearance, we find Mrs. Thrale, in her diary, applying it to the objections of her daughters to her second marriage.[1]

To the student of the eighteenth century's musical manners *Cecilia* is of special interest. It includes vivid descriptions of opera rehearsal and performance, and of Vauxhall, the Pantheon, and other places of musical entertainment. And Fanny has neatly embedded in it some praise of the St. Martin's Street favourite, the *evirato* soprano, Pacchierotti (so balancing what she had done in *Evelina* for one of his rivals, Millico), and also an unobtrusive advertisement of the pianofortes of her father's friend Merlin—of whom more anon. The passage describing the opera rehearsal and Pacchierotti's performance thereat was a favourite with contemporary readers. In 1789 Fanny, being at Lord Mount-Edgcumbe's, near Weymouth, 'saw amongst a small collection of books' *Cecilia*:

'I immediately laid a wager with myself the first volume would open upon Pacchierotti; and I won it very honestly, though I never expected to be paid it. The chapter, An Opera Rehearsal, was so well read, the leaves always flew apart to display it.'[2]

SUSANNA ELIZABETH (or 'Susan'), in 1783, was about twenty-eight. She was a lively person—a pretty good harpsichordist (see I. 335; and for a portrait of Susan, see pl. 44, II. 244), a singer, and a very descriptive correspondent. Her letters (such of them as are now available[3]) much resemble Fanny's, and when Mrs. Burney began at last to have a dim suspicion that *Evelina* might have originated in her own house her idea was that Fanny and Susan might have concocted it in concert.[4]

Of all the sisters Fanny and Susan were the most alike, and so Johnson, when Fanny had become his close intimate and favourite, said to Susan, 'I think one should love you too—if one did but know you'. And one who came to know her came to love her too—her brother James's old comrade of Cook's last voyage, the heroic Molesworth Phillips, Lieutenant of Marines.

As already recounted (cf. I. 287–8) Phillips had been with Cook when he was killed, had himself been stabbed between the shoulders, but had leapt into the sea and swum to one of the ship's boats that was standing off the shore. Then, seeing that one of his company of marines, who was also swimming, was in danger of capture, he leaped into the sea

[1] A. Hayward, *Autobiography, Letters and Literary Remains of Mrs. Piozzi* (1861); J. H. Lobban, *Dr. Johnson's Mrs. Thrale* (1910), 213, 226.

[2] *Diary and Letters*, iv. 321.

[3] As an Appendix at the end of *Early Diary*.

[4] *Early Diary*, ii. 237, 247. Susan tells in one of her letters of 'an extraordinary man of Ayrshire, born and bred a *Ploughman*, who, tout en suivant la chance, has composed some pieces of poetry which, if situation be considered, are wonderful, and even setting that aside seem the production of a real genius'.

again, and though struck on the head with a stone, seized the marine by his pigtail and towed him to safety.[1]

Susanna was married to Phillips (now Captain) in January 1782. And now the Burneys had an accession to their family pretty much after their own heart. Phillips was a man who loved the drama ('when a raw youth' visiting London for the first time, he had 'pawned his shirt to see Garrick'), and he loved music and had some skill in it. So he at once became an accepted member of the Burney inner circle.[2] And there, for the moment, we will leave Susan and her courageous Captain of Marines.

CHARLES, in 1783, was twenty-six. His crime was well behind him and he had settled down to an entirely virtuous life—even, indeed, a life of training others to be virtuous. It was in this very year of 1783 that he married, and this was also the year in which he commenced author, writing articles on classical subjects for *The Monthly Review*, of which his father-in-law and headmaster, Rose, was the editor. At this point of the Burney narrative there need be no more said about Charles.

CHARLOTTE ANN, in 1783, was twenty-four. Her education had been at some school in Norfolk. Fanny described her, in her school days, as 'mighty pretty and a dear good girl', and 'my sweet little Charlotte'. She had 'a cherubical face' and a reputation for liveliness.[3] Garrick called her his 'little Comedy' (from a supposed resemblance to a figure in Reynolds's picture of *Garrick between Tragedy and Comedy*) and his 'little Dumpling Queen'. He threatened to run away with her—but then he was always threatening to run away with one or other of the Burney girls. She was rather slangy and flippant and perhaps a little flirtatious. And, like Fanny and Susan, she had a very descriptive pen.

Charlotte had as yet done nothing special in life (merely amused and pleased all about her), so need not here be written about at length.

And that completes the list of Burney's then living children by his first wife. By his second he had two.

RICHARD THOMAS (or 'Dick') was, in 1783, fifteen years old, and was still at Winchester. As Mrs. Thrale wrote him 'monitory letters', we may suppose he had some schoolboy faults—or was thought to have them. He had a way of 'playing the buffoon', to amuse the company, but (to judge from his after career) had solid parts also. Anyhow, as the youngest boy of the family, he was a general favourite.[4]

SARAH HARRIET ('Sally'), in 1783, was about thirteen. When younger she had been 'one of the most innocent, artless, queer little things you ever saw and altogether a very sweet and very engaging

[1] *Early Diary*, ii. 269 and *D.N.B.* (Supplement), s.v. 'Phillips, Molesworth'.
[2] *Family Memoranda*, 122; *Early Diary*, ii. 270; *D.N.B.* Supplement.
[3] *Early Diary*, i. 61, 102, 206, 221, 225; ii. 31, 272.
[4] *Diary and Letters*, i. 158, 206.

child'.[1] She was later to come into wide public notice, but that lay at this date far in the future.

We now come to the three children whom Burney took over with his second wife—the Allens.

STEPHEN (age unknown) is a shadowy figure. He was to enjoy a comfortable clerical career and by this time must have embarked upon it. As we know so little of him we may as well finish him off now. He is apparently the 'Rev. Stephen, afterwards Dr. Allen, of Shouldham Hall', once curate of Lynn and a musical man, as mentioned by Alvis in his *History of King's Lynn*.

MARIA, in 1783, was thirty-two. Her runaway marriage to the sportsman, Rishton, has been noted. She had now been Mrs. Rishton for eleven years. The records about her and her husband are full of dogs and horseback riding, and driving in a 'whiskey', and shooting and cricket, and quoits, with an occasional lapse into literature, for, says Fanny on one occasion:

'It is not possible for a man to make a better husband than Mr. Rishton does. He spends almost every moment of his time with his wife, and is all attention and kindness to her. He is reading Spencer's "Fairy Queen" to us, in which he is extremely delicate, omitting whatever, to the poet's great disgrace, has crept in that is improper for a woman's ear.'[2]

Maria respected Dr. Burney and once wrote, 'I must be the most ungrateful of human beings coud I for a moment forget the paternal kindness I received from him while I boasted his protection'. She was clearly not continuously perfectly happy in her marriage, or she would not have added (looking back at her own elopement and another just about to be mentioned) 'a sincere wish that none of my family had ever quitted his sheltering roof till placed under the protection of a worthy husband'.[3]

ELIZABETH's ('Bessy's) age, in 1783, we do not know, but by adroitly putting together various odds and ends of information and drawing shrewd inferences it can be fairly safely guessed at about twenty-one.

And now must be mentioned another elopement in the family. In August 1777 Mrs. Burney went to Paris and Burney, his fashionable pupils probably all dispersed for the summer, to stay at Streatham.[4] Bessy Allen, now aged about fifteen, was in Paris, whither she had been sent two years before under the care of Mrs. Strange, 'for the purpose of completing her education and refining her manners'.[5] Burney then returned to St. Martin's Street, where in October he received bad news, which he communicated to the Thrales now gone to Brighthelmston

[1] *Early Diary*, ii. 87.
[2] Ibid. i. 252.
[3] Ibid. 278.
[4] Ibid. 284.
[5] W. Wright Roberts, *Charles and Fanny Burney in the Light of the New Thrale Correspondence n the John Rylands Library*, 9. Also *Early Diary*, ii. 87, 129.

(Brighton). Johnson was not at this moment with them (he was just beginning his *Lives of the Poets* and that kept him in London) and Mrs. Thrale, who apparently had been ill (perhaps after the birth of one of her many babies) wrote to him, passing on the news:

'Well when I was at the worst I would scarcely have changed Places with Mrs. Burney: She is the Doctor's second Wife you know, & had a fine Daughter—a great Fortune—by her former husband; whom she has kept some Years in France and about two or three Months ago she went over to fetch the Girl home, and I have seen some of her Letters to her Husband expressing the happiness she was enjoying at Paris in Company of this fine Daughter; how she delayed her Return because this Daughter so introduced her into high Company &c. but no sooner was Burney gone home to his Family . . . but he writes to me word that Mrs. Burney was coming over from Dieppe to Brighthelmstone *all alone* in great Distress, her fine Daughter having eloped from her at Paris—& so in fact she *did* come yesterday, expecting to find the Dr. with us, but he was gone, & greater & more real Distress have I seldom seen.'[1]

Mrs. Thrale's expressions of sympathy with his wife Burney acknowledged in the wan and cheerless way we should expect from such a man at such a moment:

'You were very good ("but 'tis a way you have") to try to comfort poor Madam after her unfortunate Campaign on the Continent. She changed her Resolution, & came to London the [day?] after her Landing, & the Day following we went together into Surry, for a week. She is now in Town, but invisible; 'tis humiliating to tell melancholy Stories ab^{t} one's Self, & more so to hear People pretend to pity one, when we know they have no more Feeling than *Punch*. I hate to think of the Trick that has been played her, & still more to talk about it.'[2]

And there the episode ends. We know very little more of this second strayed sheep from the second Mrs. Burney's little flock save that she had become Mrs. Meeke and that, according to Crisp, her husband was 'an adventurer' and that if any definite evidence ever existed of her being unhappy as a result of her youthful escapade, as is to be suspected, Fanny has excised it from the family documents, which occasionally, as the years go by, mention her name and rarely anything more.

Apparently her mother and stepfather forgave her, since little more than three years later we actually find them sending their youngest child, Sally (Sarah Harriet), then aged about ten, to stay with her in Geneva.[3] Which does not look so bad after all!

[1] Roberts, op. cit., 9. There is a good deal about this affair in some contemporary letters of Eliza Draper to Miss Strange, printed in *Notes and Queries*, clxxxvii. 27, 48 (15 and 28 July 1944).

[2] Roberts, op. cit. 10.

[3] W. H. Hutton, *Burford Papers*, 60.

XLII. OTHER FAMILY MATTERS

(Up to 1783, when Burney was 57)

It may be as well, at this point, to take a bird's-eye view of the other Burneys and Burney connexions, as they were at about the period we have now reached—of some of whom we have been losing sight. Burney, for all his moving in a wide social field, was a good 'family man'. With some of his relatives left behind in Chester and Shrewsbury we do not hear of his having much further association, though he may have done so. But he seems to have brought to London his mother and sister, and with his brother Richard, in Worcester, he kept up a constant intercourse. And as for Richard's children, those he delighted to have about him.

Burney's Mother and Sisters

In 1775 Burney's mother, Mrs. Ann Burney, died. She had lost her husband a quarter of a century before, and then, after living for some years with daughters and stepdaughters in apartments in Chester Castle, offered her by her husband's patron, Lord Cholmondeley, had come to London where she lived in York Place, Covent Garden. Three female members of the family of Burney's own generation continued to live with her—'Aunt Gregg' (identity doubtful), 'Aunt Becky' (Rebecca, Burney's half-sister, a year older than he), and 'Aunt Ann' (Burney's sister).

We have not enough material to construct any sort of a portrait of Burney's mother, but, from a rhyming letter her granddaughter Fanny, when sixteen, wrote from Lynn, we know one of her traits (not entirely peculiar to her, however):

Why Fanny!—child!
My dear! you're frantic—mad—quite wild!
I'm lost in wonder and amaze;
Ah! Things were different in my days!
When *I* was young, to hem and sow [*sic*]
Was almost all I wish'd to know:
But as to writing *verse* and *rhimes*—
O dear! Oh dear! How chang'd the times![1]

We do not find many other allusions to old Mrs. Burney. We are told that she showed a little proper resentment at some of the vulgar Mrs. O'Connor's gross impertinences to Fanny respecting poor, disappointed Mr. Barlow (see Ch. XXVII), and then find Fanny writing to Crisp:

'My poor grandmother Burney, after a long, painful, lingering illness, in the course of which we all contributed our mites towards assisting as nurses, has breathed her last.'[2]

[1] *Early Diary*, i, p. lxxx.

[2] Ibid. ii. 83–5.

Of 'Aunt Gregg' the present writer knows nothing whatever.

'Aunt Becky', it seems, was very 'good-natured' and 'remarkably good tempered', and in the Burney girls' younger days functioned usefully as a chaperon to dances and parties.[1] It does not seem to have been entirely of her own free will that she remained unmarried, for she was one of those who, when Fanny refused Mr. Barlow, thought that the foolish child might come to repent of her lost chance—'When you are like *us*'.[2]

'Aunt Ann', 'Aunt Anne', or 'Aunt Nanny', held a particular importance in the economy of the Burney family, for in her their good fortune had given them 'the best nurse in England, tender, careful, and affectionate—and but too well experienced in illness'. She was one of those who, in the Poland Street days, helped to save the life of fifteen-year-old Susan when the apothecary had lugubriously announced that 'she had a *very* poor chance of recovery'.[3] We unexpectedly meet her once as a bridesmaid, with two of her young nieces, Hetty and Fanny, as colleagues; this was at the marriage of a 'Mr. John Hatton, glass polisher' to 'Mrs. Betty Langley, our old cook', on which occasion we are told that the senior bridesmaid could 'count years with the bride herself', and the bride was 'a maiden of about fifty'.[4] It was the judicious Aunt Anne whom Fanny used as ambassadress to the officious Mrs. O'Connor in the famous Barlow affair, 'desiring her to forbear these attacks', and letting her know, in as civil words as possible, that Fanny was 'too determined for them to answer any possible purpose'.[5] The nurse and diplomat could also, when called upon, take her part in amateur theatricals—and take a male part, too, and, made up as 'Dr. Prattle', become the cause of much merriment.[6] She was in the *Evelina* secret. Altogether a very dependable and serviceable aunt.

We may not have occasion to meet these aunts again, so will just say that the mysterious 'Aunt Gregg' fades completely out of the chronicles, and that Aunts Rebecca and Anne long waited for a legacy from one of their uncles (the uncle was already gone, and the waiting was due to the fact that duty had obliged him to give a favourite servant the first use of the money; however, the favourite servant providentially acquired 'a habit of taking strong Rum and Brandy and water, to which at last she fell a victim').

Aunt Anne was in 1778 settled at Brompton with a friend from Worcester, Miss Humphries, but in 1791 Fanny speaks of her 'good aunts' as being 'at their Richmond abode',[7] and in Burney's Will, dated 1807, Aunt Rebecca is described as 'of Richmond, Surrey'.

Aunt Rebecca died in 1809, 'at the great age of 85', and 'as she had

[1] *Early Diary*, i. 77 et seq., 124; ii. 61.
[2] Ibid. ii. 84.
[3] Ibid. i. 41.
[4] Ibid. 49.
[5] Ibid. ii. 88.
[6] Ibid. 176.
[7] *Diary and Letters*, i. 24, v. 37.

almost outlived her intellects, her death was considered as a happy release'.[1]

Burney's Brother Richard

It is time to say something more about Burney's brother Richard, the dancing-master and musician who, as we have seen (I. 33), in 1754 settled in Worcester. Yet there seems to be little that can at this period be said about him. He lived for many years in a house he had bought, Barborne Lodge, about a mile from the centre of Worcester. He apparently held a good position in the city and county generally, and, with the help of his sons Richard Gustavus and James Adolphus and that of another assistant who is mentioned, was probably monopolizing all the better-class dancing teaching of the country-side—and doing most of the music teaching too (so far as the cathedral organist, Elias Isaac, did not monopolize that), and also the harpsichord tuning—and the piano tuning, if any.

He had lost his wife in 1771, 'after a painful and lingering disease'.[2] His sons Charles Rousseau, the musician, and Edward, the artist, were in London, but he had with him in Worcester two other sons already mentioned (until in 1778 one of them, James Adolphus, settled in Shrewsbury), and also a son, Thomas Frederick (probably a drawing-master—see II. 42), and three daughters.

A letter in the present writer's possession, addressed by the artist Edward F. Burney to his cousin Charles, exiled at Aberdeen (dated merely '4th of March'), may be quoted both as an example of Edward's epistolary style and as giving a description of the situation of Richard Burney and his family in 1781 or 1782:

'You are so kind in yours as to ask after the present state of the Family which when I left them (about 3 weeks ago) stood thus. My Father having evacuated Barborne lodge has strongly fortified himself with Port Folios at his Lodgings in Worcester, the Garrison consisting of only him and Tom, they are in good health and spirits and have a good stock of ammunition in the print way [Richard Burney was a great collector of books and prints] and as they are not very closely Blockaded, they have supplies coming in every day. Barborne Lodge is occupied by the Hawkins *new raised* Regiment. Mr. Hawkins [cf. II. 42] who is Governor was a Roman Catholic Priest, but having changed his Religion, while I was down at Barborne was married to my sister [Ann, otherwise Hannah, or Nancy]—then, Richard, a kind of Light Horseman, is quartered half the week at Gloucester and half at Barborne. James's Head Quarters are at Shrewsbury, where he has Rebecca to take care of his Baggage Waggons and Stores while he makes excursions and Forageing Parties to Bridgenorth &c. and once a fortnight by forced marches sups with the Governor at Barborne. The Enraged Drawing Mistress is promoted by the late change of affairs from E. W. Burney [Elizabeth

[1] For the last days of these aunts the authority is *Family Memoranda*.
[2] *Family Memoranda*.

Warren Burney] to be Miss Burney, and goes sometimes Recruiting into Worcester.'

And that is about all there is, at this moment, to say about Richard Burney of Worcester. But there will be something more to be added shortly—and alas! something tragic.

Burney's Harpsichordist Nephew, Charles Rousseau

Charles Rousseau Burney (born 1747) seems to have been both a very amiable man and a first-rate musician. Fanny always speaks well of him; 'the good and dear Mr. Burney' had 'an obliging disposition', 'extreme worth' and 'excellent though unpretending understanding', and lived 'a meritorious life'.[1] As for Charles Rousseau Burney's harpsichord performance, when Dr. Burney gave a musical party it was this nephew of his who became 'the King of the evening', and his playing always 'raised a general astonishment'. His execution was virtuosic; we find such reports as 'Mr. Burney went to the harpsichord; he played with his usual successful velocity and his usual applause'.[2] A special feature of his technique was his nimble shake. The fashionable Italian composer-harpist-vocalist, Millico, at one of the St. Martin's Street musical evenings, admired this:

> 'It is impossible to express the delight which his performance gave to Millico. His amazing execution really excited in him the most hearty laughs. The Italians cultivate harpsichord-playing so little, giving all their time to the voice, that execution such as Mr. Burney's appeared miraculous, and when Millico saw him make a fine and long shake with his fourth and little fingers, and then change from finger to finger, while his left hand kept on the subject, he was really almost convulsed . . . and when it was over, rising from his seat, he clapt his hands and cried with emphasis and in a very droll accent, "It is terrible, I really tink."'[3]

And when Fanny wishes to praise the marvellous *prima donna*, Agujari, she does it by this comparison:

> 'Then her *shake*—so plump—so true, so open! It is as strong and distinct as Mr. Burney's upon the harpsichord.'[4]

The duet playing of Charles Rousseau Burney and his cousin-wife, Esther, had great fame, and that they might be heard by distinguished people was a frequent motive in arranging musical parties at St. Martin's Street. So we find record of 'a little concert we had at which assisted a most superb party and company', which was 'occasioned by the desire of Dr. King to have Prince Orloff, of Russia, hear Mr. Burney and my sister in a duet before he left England.'[5]

[1] *Early Diary*, i. 105, 124; *Diary and Letters*, iii. 356; vi. 310.

[2] *Early Diary*, i. 178; ii. 5, 59.

[3] Ibid. i. 219.

[4] Ibid. ii. 79.

[5] Dr. John King, F.R.S. (see I. 131 n.), had been chaplain to the English Factory at St. Petersburg and wrote some books on Russia. This Prince Orloff was 'the identical man

Sometimes the young Burney couple played one of Dr. Burney's own harpsichord duets (see II. 203), but their great *cheval de bataille* was 'Müthel's Duet', which was always 'heard with great applause'. Müthel's works appear to be now entirely unknown, and to the best of the present writer's knowledge not one of them is in print. He was a pupil of J. S. Bach (we may say his last pupil, for when he went to Bach to receive what we may call 'finishing lessons' Bach was within three months of his death). Burney speaks most highly of the quality of his music; it was, for its day, extremely difficult, and little of it was published. What the Burneys called 'Müthel's Duet' was doubtless the *Duetto für 2 Claviere, 2 Flügel oder 2 Fortepiano*, which appeared at Riga in 1771; Forkel mentions it in his Life of Bach, and there is a copy in the British Museum. Burney gave some account of the career of Müthel at the end of the *German Tour* and in the German edition the translator considerably augmented it. Müthel (*né* Moetlin) was born about 1720.

It may be remarked that Charles Rousseau Burney and his wife, in addition to their harpsichord prowess, occasionally performed in the more domestic gatherings, as violinist and vocalist respectively.[1]

In 1767 and 1770 we find Charles Rousseau Burney (a prophet not without honour in his own country) as one of the artists at the Worcester Festival. We also hear of his playing at Covent Garden before the King. But the most attractive account of his playing, apart from that in his own home or his uncle's, comes properly at a rather later period than that we are now treating. It is one of his playing in prison. Dr. Burney's friend, William Beckford, who had been of great service to him in Italy (see I. 174), was in the Fleet (presumably for debt, but possibly for libel—anyhow 'unjustly'). Dr. Burney himself used to visit him there. He says in a letter to Fanny (8 October 1791):

> 'I intend to try to get Sir Joshua [Reynolds] and Sir Joseph Banks, his old acquaintances, to visit him there with me. I was with the dear, worthy and charming man, two hours on Wednesday, and love him and honour him more than ever. What a place—surrounded with fresh horrors!—for the habitation of such a man.
>
> 'My most worthy and good nephew Charles, of Titchfield Street, goes to him generally once a week, and dines, and plays to him on a miserable pianoforte for five or six hours at a time.'[2]

who was the reigning favourite with the Empress of Russia [Catherine the Great] at the time the Czar was murdered'; his diamonds, which enjoyed European fame, quite dazzled the company that gathered in the St. Martin's Street music-room (*Early Diary*, ii. 93). In Chambers's *Encyclopædia* (1925 edition) there is a description of one of Orloff's diamonds (still a famous stone), with a 'life-size' picture which shows it to be an inch across. Orloff carried about with him not only diamonds but gold, and at Covent Garden Theatre was robbed of a jewelled snuff-box worth £30,000. The thief, George Barrington (whom Orloff, for some reason, declined to prosecute), was later, for another crime, transported to Botany Bay, and so became the author of a number of books on Australia, earning a page or two in *D.N.B.* as 'Barrington, George, Pickpocket and Author.'

[1] *Early Diary*, i. 32, 99; ii. 60, 93, 97, 108, &c.

[2] *Diary and Letters*, v. 36. This was not, of course, William Beckford, the author of *Vathek*

Burney's Dancing-Master Nephews, Richard and James

Richard Gustavus Burney, of Worcester, who stands out pretty boldly on Fanny's vivid canvases, is almost as distinct and amusing an individual as anyone whose personality she pictures in her novels.

Her cousin Richard, she says, though amusingly vain and boastful, was 'a young man of uncommon talents and parts, and of the utmost sweetness of disposition'. He was a most entertaining companion, taking off 'with incomparable mimicry, the airs of his neighbours', and poking as much fun at himself as at those around him.[1]

His profession was that of his father; he taught dancing and music in Worcester and in a wide district around it, constantly riding and driving about the country-side to give his lessons. We hear of his teaching singing in a school at Hartlebury. He had a good voice and Fanny commends his catch singing, and in 1770 we find him playing (apparently) both violin and violoncello at the Worcester Festival.[2] According to his own account he was supposed by his family at Worcester to make his frequent journeys on horseback, but preferred to use a chaise and, indeed, to do all his travelling in the greatest style:

'I go from Barborne on my own horse—and so the good folks there think I ride all the way—Ha—Ha—Ha!—but the first inn I come to—I leave the poor jade behind me, order a chaise and four—and stop as I return at the same inn—and go back to Barborne on my horse! . . . Do you know it stands me in a hundred a year for chaises;—the time I spend at inns . . . and there I can only get Port and Madeira—for people, hang 'em wont sell anything better. . . . Then they keep monstrous tables in the country—not that I care for the victuals—not in the least—only the *shew*—nay I dislike their dishes—though I always eat them—but then the beef is always put on the side table!—so I swallow the ragout that is before me—though, faith, I love the beef best of all things!—but it would be impossible to call for it, you know. O, utterly —that would be having such a *vulgar appetite*. Ha—Ha—Ha!—*a vulgar appetite*!'[3]

And (again according to his own account) he was called on to officiate

(1759–1844), but William Beckford, the author of books on Jamaica, &c. (d. 1799). The writer in the *Dictionary of National Biography* does not seem to know of his ever finding his way into prison. In another place Fanny writes 'The unfortunate, but truly amiable and high-minded Mr. Beckford was amongst the greatest favourites and most welcome visitors to Dr. Burney; whose remembrance of the friendly zeal of that gentleman in Italy, was a never failing call for every soothing return that could be offered to him in the calamities which, roughly and ruinously, had now changed his whole situation in life—leaving his virtues alone unalterable' (*Mem.* iii. 133). The King's Bench and Fleet prisons seem to have, at one time or another, harboured a good many of Burney's acquaintances. Burney tells us of the male soprano Tenducci being confined in the former. He 'embellished that residence by his talents and amused its inhabitants', and was allowed to accept concert engagements outside the prison 'attended by a *garde du corps*', a certain 'Jewish lady, his patroness', taking him (and presumably the *garde du corps*) to and from the concerts in her carriage.

[1] *Early Diary*, i. 166 et seq.

[2] Lysons, Amott, Lee Williams, and Chance, *Origin and Progress of the Meeting of the Three Choirs* (1895), 47.

[3] *Early Diary*, i. 167.

as 'Master of the Ceremonies at all the Balls and Conductor at all the Concerts', and was President of all the Musical Clubs in and about Worcester (the weekly meetings for music-making, at this time so common all over England):

'O—ma'am, why I have it all my own way I have all power—I direct and fix everything—nothing can be done without my consent. I have a casting vote—I make all the motions—in short, my power is unlimited.'

'And I don't doubt but that you make a good use of it—and keep them all in order. And what else do you do?'

'Why I put about the wine—take care they all give their toasts—First we go round with sentiments, and then the ladies.'

'And you take care they take but half glasses I am sure?—or at least that they drink half water?'

'O Lord no, ma'am—that is always an affront—no, a full bumper always!'

'And do you all give toasts?'

'O yes, ma'am, everybody.'

'And how many have you? three or four?'

'Three or four! Lord bless me! three or four and twenty!'

And to Fanny's remark, 'I can't imagine how you find time for all this', the reply was:

'O, with great difficulty, but there would be no living in the country without. All day I am fagging at business—then in the evening I begin to live. We never break-up till morning. Sometimes I go to bed at 3 or 4—and am up again at 6, and begin my rides—which keep me in health. But I am convinced that people may live upon a third part of the sleep they give themselves, if it is sound—It is all custom—For my part I can't bear bed—it is such a total loss of time!'

Richard was pretty often in London, with his cousins at St. Martin's Street. In 1778, when he was twenty-seven, he was staying with his Aunt Ann at Brompton and fell ill, amusing himself hugely during his convalescence by having read and re-read to him, and almost getting by heart, *Evelina*, of which all London was then talking—and amusing Fanny and her sisters by his excited admiration of it, and his anxiety to know who was its author. He thought Dr. Burney might have written such a book:

'Such amazing knowledge of characters, such an acquaintance with *high* and *low* life, such universal and extensive knowledge of the world; I declare, I know not a man breathing who is likely to be the author,—unless it is my uncle.'

Much more than that could be told about 'Cousin Dick', and much to his credit, for, with all his volubility and volatility, he had a sound foundation of sense and good feeling. In 1783 we find him staying in London with Burney's friend North, Bishop of Worcester, and Bishops even in those days (and even 'worldly' ones) did not invite the mere

Library of Davidson College

amusing rattles of dancing-masters of their dioceses to stay with them at their town-houses.[1]

Richard's brother, James Adolphus (of nearly his own age, born in 1753), was 'a good-natured, unaffected, good-hearted young man', not possessing 'the power of entertainment of his brother Richard, but so well-disposed, and so sweet tempered that it is hardly fair and possible to find fault with him'.[2] Like young Richard, he followed the parental profession of dancing-master and music teacher. With Richard he went to Paris in 1777, to improve himself professionally, and stayed there some weeks. And in the next year 'business opening in Ludlow and Bridgnorth', he settled in Shrewsbury.

And that is pretty nearly all that the present writer knows about James Adolphus, except that he died in 1798, 'universally and deservedly respected'.[3]

Burney's Artist Nephew, Edward

In 1776[4] a notable nephew of Burney's, Edward Francis (or Francisco), came to London, rather against his father's wishes, to study art. Apparently he was soon recalled, and in April 1777 his walk in life was, apparently, still not settled, for we find Crisp writing to Fanny, 'Has your lordly uncle yet given his consent that his son shall be allow'd

1 The London and Worcester Burney families were always on happy terms with this episcopal friend of theirs. A letter from him in the present writer's possession, dated 1782, when he had become Bishop of Winchester, runs:

Farnham Castle
Decr ye 27th 1782.

Dear Sir,

We have a very agreeable party of Burneys at this place, and are *almost* as happy as good society can make us but (which rarely happens) we are all agreed as to what would make us completely so. It is in your power to give us this Addition. I trust therefore you will not resist the joint solicitation of all this House, that you will spare us a few Days of your recess from business at this season. If I thought it necessary, I would say all the precise things which Formality prescribes by way of regular Invitation, but I will neither disgust you nor so grossly bely myself, Mrs. North and this Party. Formality besides rendering the sincerity of our wishes suspected, is subject to so easy a refusal, that it would in no respect answer our purpose. With frankness therefore we beg you will join us in the ease and cheerfullness of a Winter Party in the Country and you may be assured that none of them will be more happy in the pleasure of seeing you than Mrs. North and Dear Sr

Your very Faithful
Servant
B. Winchester.

It is not perfectly clear to whom this letter was addressed—apparently to Dr. Burney himself.

The Bishop was brother to Lord North, who, when reproached with the early age at which his brother had secured one of the best endowed bishoprics in the country, replied that 'his brother was, no doubt, young to be a bishop, but when he was older he might not have a brother who was Prime Minister'. The Bishop's London house, which the Burneys frequented, is reputed to have been furnished 'in a style of uncommon splendour'.

2 *Early Diary*, ii. 163.

3 The *Birmingham Chronicle*, quoted in *Family Memoranda*.

4 Dates on the authority of Samuel Redgrave, *Dictionary of Artists of the English School*, 1874. For a self-portrait of Edward Burney, see pl. 27, II. 41.

PLATE 26. *SOME OF THE BURNEYS*

BURNEY'S SECOND WIFE. Miniature in the possession of Canon Burney (painter unknown). RICHARD, ESTHER, AND CHARLES R. BURNEY. Burney's brother (*see* i. 33, ii. 35 and 124–6) and eldest daughter with her cousin-husband. By Hudson.

TWO PORTRAITS OF CHARLES ROUSSEAU BURNEY

Burney's nephew and son-in-law (more prominently known as a virtuoso harpsichordist than as a violinist). Portraits (left) by Edward F. Burney (*see* ii. 41) and (right) by Gainsborough.

PLATE 27. *BURNEY'S PAINTER NEPHEW*

EDWARD F. BURNEY'S SELF-PORTRAIT
(For his career *see* ii. 40–2 and 283–5.)

THE WALTZ

A discovery in the Victoria and Albert Museum, in 1931, revealed this artist in a forgotten capacity—that of caricaturist. What some people thought of the dance style recently imported from the continent can be equally well remembered from the above picture or Burney's own remark (in Rees's Cyclopaedia)—*The verb 'walzen', from which is derived the name of this dance, implies to roll, wallow, welter, tumble down, or roll in the dirt or mire.*

to make a figure in the world and do honour to himself, family, and country?'[1]

On this important question of Edward's career it appears that the head of the London Burneys had to fight the head of the Worcester Burneys. Dr. Burney, it appears, consulted his friend Reynolds about Edward, and triumphantly threw at his brother the great man's words, already quoted in Chapter II of the present book: 'His propensity to painting is so strong that I believe we must call it genius.'

Edward was then allowed to study in the Royal Academy School, where in 1780 he won a medal.[2] And, with the high approval of Reynolds, his illustrations to his cousin Fanny's *Evelina* were in the same year submitted for the Academy's exhibition, and they were accepted. Young Charlotte Burney, who admired the designs enormously, joyously wrote to Fanny, then in Bath, that 'Mr. Barry, who is mightily struck with them, has promised of his own accord, to endeavour to procure a good place for them'.[3] The young artist, in one of these designs, paid a pleasant and tactful compliment to an honoured friend of the Burney family, for in the parlour of the good old clergyman, Mr. Villars, we see a portrait of Dr. Johnson hanging on the wall. Fanny would approve of that!

Edward Burney appears to have lived at first with his aunts in York Place, Covent Garden, but he was much with his St. Martin's Street cousins. We find him accompanying some of them to a Masquerade at the Pantheon dressed as a native of Otaheite; 'he went privately to Sir Joshua's and took a sketch of Omiah's dress,[4] which he copied in his own pretty exactly', and as he 'cooked up' his dress out of 'Jemm's Otaehietie Merchandize' and then was admitted to the hall on Dr. Burney's 'Proprietor's Ticket', he enjoyed a cheap evening's entertainment, mystifying fellow masqueraders with 'broken English, except now and then, that he touched 'em up with a speech in the Otaehitie language that he had got by heart', and staying until five o'clock in the morning—'and it answered to him excessively well, as indeed you may suppose, being the first Masquerade that he ever was at'.[5]

Edward became a portraitist (his portraits of his cousin Fanny are favourable specimens of his art, and he painted Daddy Crisp and others of the circle). Then, being an excessively diffident sort of fellow (Fanny several times tells us of this, and Charles Lamb in one of his essays mentioned on II. 284–5 makes it very clear), and not at all a 'pusher', settled down as a favourite book illustrator, designer of symbolic frontis-

[1] *Early Diary*, ii. 161.

[2] Letter of Miss Joan Evans in *The Times*, 16 Jan. 1931, also a letter from Edward himself to his cousin Charles, in the present writer's possession.

[3] *Early Diary*, ii. 290. James Barry was, as we have seen (II. 14–17), at this time engaged on a painting of his own that had a special interest for the Burneys.

[4] See I. 287.

[5] Letter of Charlotte to Fanny (*Early Diary*, ii. 289).

pieces and charming vignettes, and adorner of ladies' 'Keepsakes', annual 'Fashionable Pocket Repositories', and the like—all his work in this kind being extremely graceful and elegantly perfect, but hardly justifying the word 'genius' that had been applied to him in his youth. (More about him will be found on II. 283–5.)

Other Worcester Nephews and Nieces

Thomas Frederick Burney, born 1765, was, like his brother Edward, a capable draughtsman with 'an uncommon genius for pen and ink drawings'.[1] There are some of his drawings of Worcestershire churches (as also of his brother Edward's) to be seen in the Prattinton Collection of the Society of Antiquaries. He was 'droll and good-humoured'.[2]

Ann, or Hannah, known as 'Nancy', must, apparently, have been born in the early 1770's. We know little of her beyond the fact that she was an attractive little maiden who later became Mrs. Hawkins, and that her husband was a Roman Catholic priest turned Anglican clergyman (cf. II. 35), of whom we hear in 1792 that he was 'engaged in writing notes for answers to Paine, Mackintosh, Rouse, Priestley, Price, and a score more of Mr. Burke's incendiary antagonists', so that he was evidently a bold, 'let-'em-all-come' sort of fellow.[3]

Elizabeth Warren Burney, born in 1755, grew up into a paragon. As the Worcester Journal tells the world:

'To give a character of Elizabeth Warren Burney, b. 1755, would only be to enumerate all the virtues belonging to a woman, without one drawback to counterbalance. She was not a shining character, but she had a cheerful mind, well stored, not only with useful knowledge, but with good taste; and her judgment could always be consulted with conviction that she was right. She was pious without gloom, or fanaticism, charitable without ostentation, and made herself useful to her family, without officiousness; she was a general favourite with them all.'[4]

Rebecca was the youngest of the Worcester Burneys. She was 'a sweet open-hearted girl, and totally free from pride', and so that

[1] *Family Memoranda*, in which is to be found a lengthy account of this young man.

[2] Who was 'F. H. Burney' who, in 1848, illustrated a keepsake, *The Musical Bijou*? Him I have not traced. One would guess him to be a member of this artistic family, but he is not mentioned in *Family Memoranda*, which includes mention of sixty members of the family.

[3] We may as well part now with Mrs. Hawkins, so will note that in 1819 she was 'released from pain' (R. Brimley Johnson, 381).

[4] *Family Memoranda*. But alas, even paragons die and in 1832, when she was seventy-seven, dropsy attacked this one's legs. 'Her ingenious nephew' (Rev. Richard Allen Burney, a Somersetshire rector), to satisfy her desire to keep up church attendance, 'constructed a seat with poles, to carry her backwards and forwards', but soon 'her pure spirit departed this life, well prepared for a better', and she 'left an affected family to deplore her loss'. And—'the funeral was a most respectable one'. Some years before this melancholy occurrence she had been much gratified by being introduced to the Bonaparte family, 'Monsieur Lucien and his family being confined at this time as Prisoners of War, at Thorn Grove, 4 miles from Worcester' (R. Brimley Johnson, 398).

'remarkably pleasant man', Mr. Sandford, a Worcester physician, probably got a very good bargain with her.

Arthur Young

There is one other relation of Burney's, a relation by marriage, of whom something should now be said—his brother-in-law (in the sense of two men marrying sisters), Arthur Young. His earlier career has already been briefly sketched (I. 136–7) and we have now to account for a further period of twenty years. It was, like every period in Young's life, both a busy and an uncomfortable one. He had gone on pouring out his agricultural treatises—his four-volume *Six Months' Tour through the North of Ireland*, his *Farmer's Tour through the East of England*, his *Farmer's Guide in Hiring and Stocking Farms*, his *Rural Œconomy*, his two-volume *Course in Experimental Agriculture*, his *Farmer's Calendar*, and his *Observations on the Present State of the Waste Land of Great Britain*. And with these he had also published some political works, such as his *Proposals to the Legislature for Numbering the People* (proposals not adopted by that legislature until thirty years later), his *Political Arithmetic* ('immediately translated into many languages and highly commended in many parts of Europe') and his *Political Essays concerning the Present State of the British Empire*. And of a number of these he had had to prepare second and third editions. Little wonder that he declared, 'No cart-horse laboured as I did at this period'.[1]

It was in the year 1783 that he began his serial publication, *The Annals of Agriculture*, of which the King took in two sets, one for himself and one for his farmer at Windsor, and what is more, to which the King himself twice contributed (but discreetly and under the name of that farmer). When Young was received by the King upon the terrace at Windsor the King said to him, 'Mr. Young, I consider myself as more obliged to you than to any other man in my dominions', and the Queen added that the King and she never travelled without his *Annals* in their carriage.

And with all this literary activity he had combined, at various points in the period, practical farming on his own account, reporting also, for a time, the debates in the House of Commons for *The Morning Post* (at five guineas a week, and he had to walk seventeen miles home to his farm at North Mimms every Saturday and seventeen miles back every Monday). He had, for a part of the period now in question, undertaken the management of Lord Kingsborough's estates in Ireland, living there for about two years, and on return having his luggage stolen *en route* with all the specimens of soils and minerals that he had collected. And he had had the honour of election as F.R.S.—in 1774, the year after his brother-in-law, Burney.

[1] For a portrait of Young (at a somewhat later period) see pl. 44, II. 244.

Two or three times, disappointed with the material fruits of all his activity, he had been on the point of emigrating to America.

Then, in 1769, his son Arthur had been born, and in that very year of 1783 which we have taken as our present term, there had also been born to him the child nicknamed 'Bobbin'—'my lovely Bobbin', the correspondence between whom and her father is a charming feature of the latter's *Autobiography* and whose life was the greatest joy of a life that had not too many joys, as her death, at fourteen, was to be its greatest sorrow (see pl. 44, II. 244).[1]

Young was a frequent visitor to the Burneys at Poland Street and then at St. Martin's Street; there he got the distraction he needed, 'fascinated by Hetty's performance on the harpsichord and singing of Italian airs', and enjoying Dr. Burney's talk ('I never met with any person who had more decided talents for conversation, eminently seasoned with wit and humour, and these talents were so at command that he could exert them at will'). He often amused the girls by his odd ways, as when he appeared 'absurdly dressed for a common visit, being in light blue, embroidered with silver, a bag and a sword, and walking in the rain!' But the story of how he came to be 'walking in the rain', if amusing, was also a little distressing to the good-humoured Burney family, for, on a polite inquiry being made as to his wife, he replied, 'We just now parted in a pet, but, I think, we were to meet here':

> 'Soon after she came in a chair. After common salutations—"Pray how came you to leave me so, Mr. Young?" cried she—"Only think," turning to us—"the fellow of a coachman drove the horses' heads towards a court in Soho Square, and pretended he could not move them; and Mr. Young was fool enough to get out, and let the man have his way,—when he deserved to be horse-whipped." "Instead of which," returned he, "I gave him a shilling! Where's the difference?" "Who but you" cried she "would not have made the man come on with us? or else not have paid him?—and so I was forced to run into a toyshop, where he politely left me to my fate—and where I chanced to meet with a chair."'[2]

Fortunately these matrimonial jars at last ceased. Of Young and Mrs. Young (the latter now grown immoderately fat) Fanny tells us in 1771:

> 'They have however given over those violent disputes and quarrels with which they used to entertain their friends, not that Mrs. Young has any reason to congratulate herself upon it, quite the contrary, for the extreme violence of her overbearing temper has at length so wearied Mr. Young that he disdains any controversy with her, scarce ever contradicting her, and lives a life of calm, easy contempt.'[3]

The Young couple, though they may have ceased open warfare, never again, apparently, got on to even reasonably good terms. Fanny's

[1] All these various particulars from the *Autobiography*, and from Fanny's *Early Diary*.

[2] *Early Diary*, i. 98.

[3] Ibid. 121.

diary has many references to extravagance, debt, distress, and bickerings ('He vehemently added that if he was to begin the world again no earthly thing should ever prevail on him to marry')—and a few to gleams of sunshine, as when he dined with her and Susan and she was able to write, 'Fortune, I hope, smiles on him again, for he again smiles on the world'. Sometimes the Burneys and the Youngs would go together to Marylebone Gardens or the Opera, and these seem to have been bright spots in poor, ingenious, and magnificently useful Arthur Young's tortured life.

That, then, is the chequered account of how Dr. Burney's relative by marriage and always dear friend had been spending his life in the interval since, in the present work, we last met with him.

XLIII. THE BURNEYS LOSE SOME OLD FRIENDS

(*1783–1784; Burney aged 57–58*)

DURING the years 1783 and 1784 the Burneys experienced three sad losses—those of Crisp, Bewley, and Johnson.

Something of the position Crisp held in the affections of the whole Burney family must have become evident to the reader from the allusions to him in previous chapters. Burney's friendship with him had begun nearly forty years before (see Ch. IV), and as each child had been added to the family and came to years of discretion he or she had been admitted to an equal friendship.

Crisp's retreat at Chesington was the continual resort of every member of the family. They went there for holidays, and they went there for convalescence after illness. They shared all their joys and sorrow with Crisp and they went to him for advice in every great emergency. It was Crisp's exhortations that had at length pulled Burney out of exile in Lynn back to the wider opportunities of London. It was to Crisp's house that Burney had repaired after each of his continental tours to recover from their effect on his health and to put in order his journals for publication. 'It was primarily to gratify Mr. Crisp' that Burney had begun 'while yet in Poland Street, those little musical assemblages' that came to take so important a place in the family's social life;[1] it would appear that these gatherings (and perhaps they alone) drew Crisp occasionally from his retirement.

'But how he wished for our dear Mr. Crisp. Do pray, now leave your gout to itself, and come to our next music meeting. Or if it needs must cling to you, and come also, who knows but that music, which has

"Charms to sooth the savage breast,
To soften rocks, and bend a knotted oak—"

may have charms also, To soften Gout, and *Un*bend Knotted Fingers?'[2]

All the Burney news was at once descriptively imparted to Crisp—the meetings with notabilities, such as Reynolds, Burke, Horace Walpole, and Gibbon (with 'cheeks of such prodigious chubbyness that they envelope his nose so completely, as to render it, in profile, absolutely invisible'), and many a celebrity of those days less well known to the general reader of ours, such as Soame Jenyns, and Owen Cambridge, and the various Bluestocking ladies—Mrs. Carter, Mrs. Chapone, Mrs. Montagu, and the rest of them. Never did family enjoy the encouraging and understanding sympathy of a loving grandfather or uncle more than did the Burneys those of their dear 'Daddy Crisp'.

And now, early in 1783, Susan (now Mrs. Phillips), staying at Chesington, wrote to her father that Crisp's gout had reached a point past curing or alleviation, and that his end was near. Fanny rushed down

[1] *Mem.* ii. 9. [2] Ibid. 18.

into the country (Burney, apparently, could not get free from business, or perhaps it was felt that he should not add to the congestion of a smallish house the presence of a useless male), and the two girls had soon to send the sad news of the end. To which Burney replied, 'Not an hour in the day has passed since the fatal catastrophe, in which I have not felt a pang for the irreparable loss I have sustained.' He wrote an *Elegy on the Death of a Friend*:

> The guide and tutor of my early youth,
> Whose word was wisdom, and whose wisdom truth.

And it was he who drafted a paragraph for the newspapers and the epitaph for the monument still to be seen in the village church:

To the Memory

of

SAMUEL CRISP, ESQ.,

who died April 24, 1783, aged 76.

May Heaven—through our merciful REDEEMER—receive his soul!

> Reader! This rude and humble spot contains
> The much lamented, much revered remains
> Of one whose learning, judgment, taste, and sense,
> Good-humour'd wit, and mild benevolence
> Charm'd and enlighten'd all the hamlet round,
> Wherever genius, worth—or want was found.
> To few it is that bounteous heaven imparts
> Such depth of knowledge, and such taste in arts;
> Such penetration, and enchanting powers
> Of brightening social and convivial hours.
> Had he, through life, been blest, by nature kind,
> With health robust of body as of mind,
> With skill to serve and charm mankind, so great
> In arts, in science, letters, church, or state,
> His fame the nation's annals had enroll'd,
> And virtues to remotest ages told.
>
> C. BURNEY.

The above is the epitaph as Fanny gives it in the *Memoirs* of her father. Comparison with the monument itself shows slight discrepancies—as though Fanny had either (*a*) had access to a copy showing the poet's afterthoughts, or (*b*) had, in transcribing his work, added slight improving touches, or (*c*) had written it out from memory.

In September of the same year Burney's dear friend, the village doctor of Massingham, Bewley ('the Broom Gentleman', as Johnson called him; see I. 93, 94), died at Burney's own house in St. Martin's Street.

Bewley 'had never before visited the metropolis, except to pass through it upon business; his narrow income, and confined country practice, having hitherto stood in the way of such an excursion'. Now, wishing to meet his old friend again, and also to consult 'the wisest of his brethren of the Æsculapian tribe, upon the subject of his own health, which was now in a state of alarming deterioration', he resolved to go to London. His wife accompanied him; and they went first to Birmingham, where Bewley, himself no mean scientist, wished to visit the celebrated Priestley, Unitarian minister and discoverer of oxygen. Then they travelled to town, Bewley apparently much better for his journeyings. Burney, as a good host and an affectionate friend, took him about to see pictures and to meet interesting people, and in the evening entertained him with performances from 'favourite old musical composers of Mr. Bewley; or favourite new ones of Dr. Burney, now first brought forward to his friend's enraptured ears'. The greatest thrill of the country doctor's London visit, however, came with his visit to Johnson, to whom Burney presented him as 'the humble but devoted preserver of the bristly tuft of the Bolt Court Hearth-Broom'.[1] Then acute illness seized him, and eminent physicians of the day, Hunter (John or William?), Potts, Warren (Richard), and Jebb, who all, out of respect for his attainments and character, attended him without fee, could arrive at no satisfactory diagnosis—the disease being afterwards discovered to be cancer.

On Bewley's death Burney sent this account to the Norwich newspaper:

'On Friday last died, at the house of his friend, Dr. Burney, in St. Martin's-street, where he had been on a visit, Mr. William Bewley, of Massingham, in Norfolk; whose death will be sincerely lamented by all men of science, to whom his great abilities, particularly in anatomy, electricity and chemistry, had penetrated through the obscurity of his abode, and the natural modesty and diffidence of his disposition. Indeed, the depth and extent of his knowledge on every useful branch of science and literature, could only be equalled by the goodness of his heart, simplicity of his character, and innocency of his life; seasoned with a natural, unsought wit and humour, of a cast the most original, pleasant and inoffensive.

'Hobbes, in the last century, whose chief writings were levelled against the religion of his country, was called, from the place of his residence, the Philosopher of Malmesbury; but with how much more truth and propriety has Mr. Bewley, whose life was spent in the laborious search of the most hidden and useful discoveries in art and nature, in exposing sophistry and displaying talents, been distinguished in Norfolk by the respectable title of the Philosopher of Massingham.'[2]

[1] All these lordly phrases are Fanny's (*Mem.* ii. 347 et seq.), and represent the style of her writing in old age. She is wrong about Bolt Court, for the 'Hearth-Broom' incident (see I. 93) had occurred in one of Johnson's earlier residences.

[2] Ibid. 352.

It was in April 1783 that Crisp died, and on 5 September of the same year that Bewley died. The day after Bewley's death there died also the blind poetess Anna Williams, whom for over thirty years the charitable Johnson had entertained in his house. Johnson pathetically wrote to Burney as follows:

'I came home on the 18th at noon to a very disconsolate house. You and I have lost our friends; but you have more friends at home. My domestick companion is taken from me. She is much missed, for her acquisitions were many, and her curiosity universal; so that she partook of every conversation. I am not well enough to go much out; and to sit, and eat, or fast alone, is very wearisome.'[1]

Johnson himself, it will be noticed, was at this time ill. Fanny's diary records on 19 June 1783 how she and her father at once called at the house in Bolt Court, for Fanny remembered that 'he had earnestly desired me, when we lived so much together at Streatham, to see him frequently if he should be ill'.

Johnson, it appeared, was suffering from a paralytic stroke confined to his tongue. The incident is now well known to us all. The blow had fallen at four o'clock in the morning, and he had risen and 'composed in his own mind a Latin prayer, to the effect that God might "spare his intellects" and let all his sufferings "fall upon his body"'. And when he had composed the prayer he had 'endeavoured to speak it aloud, but found his voice was gone'. However, to Fanny and her father's great relief, when they arrived at the house they learnt that 'the physicians had pronounced him to be in no danger, and expected a speedy recovery'.

And so it was. Next month their friend was able to go to Rochester, whence he passed on to Salisbury. And in December he had so fully resumed his wonted zest for social life as to found a new Club, meeting at the 'Essex Head', an inn in Essex Street, Strand, kept by an old footman of the Thrales, whom he wished to help: 'We meet thrice a week, and he who misses forfeits twopence'. Burney, who became a member of this club, a little later (1784) became also a member of Johnson's 'Literary Club', founded nearly twenty years before (and still in existence to-day), and it is difficult to see how he, an incessantly busy man, could attend not only some of the fortnightly meetings of that club but also any considerable proportion of the 'thrice weekly' of this new 'Essex Head Club' (or 'Sam's Club'—so named after the former ex-footman, not after its founder!), but apparently he did so.[2]

[1] Boswell.

[2] *Mem.* ii. 261, 377; iii. 257, 297. To be elected to the Literary Club was a very substantial mark of respect. A little time before Burney was elected the Bishop of St. Asaph had said that election was an honour 'not inferior to that of being the representative [in Parliament] of Westminster or Surrey'—and on the night the Club elected this Bishop they refused another (Porteus, Bishop of Chester), and also Lord Camden. The original members (1764) were Reynolds, Johnson, Hawkins, Burke, Goldsmith, Topham Beauclerk, Bennett Langton,

He must, however, one guesses, have been called on for a good many twopences.

Despite the apparent new lease of life Johnson's health was progressively declining. At one of the early meetings of the new Club (in January 1784) he was taken ill and had difficulty in reaching home, and in April he wrote that he had been confined to the house for '129 days, more than the third part of a year, and no inconsiderable part of human life'. However, he was able to 'return thanks to God, in St. Clement's church, for his recovery'.[1] He then visited Oxford with Boswell, and seemed to be very much his old self ('How he does talk!' said a lady in the coach; 'Every sentence is an essay'). And he even projected a winter in Italy, for the benefit of his asthma.

In the summer of 1784 he made further travels in England. From Ashbourne in Derbyshire he wrote to Burney (2 August 1784),[2] and alluded to a recent illness of Mrs. Burney and to his own state of health:

'My journey has at least done me no harm, nor can I yet boast of any great good. . . .

'I have lost dear Mr. Allen, and wherever I turn the dead or the dying meet my notice, and force my attention upon misery and mortality. Mrs. Burney's escape from so much danger, and her ease after so much pain, throws however some radiance of hope upon the gloomy prospect. May her recovery be perfect, and her continuance long.

'I struggle hard for life. I take physick, and take air. My friend's chariot is always ready. We have run this morning twenty-four miles, and could run forty-eight more. *But who can run the race with Death?*'

Johnson announced his return to London in the following little note:

Samuel Dyer, Dr. Nugent, and Chamier (Under-Secretary for War)—most of these personal friends of Burney, so that it is a little curious that he did not become a member earlier than he did (see John Timbs, *Clubs and Club Life in London*, 1872). His election took place 17 Feb. 1784 (Boswell, ed. Croker, 1831, i. 529).

There is an amusing instance of the awe with which membership of this Club was regarded in Rev. Richard Eastcote, *Sketch of the Origin, Progress, and Effects of Music*, 1793. The book opens with a note on Burney, the author explaining that he will often have to quote him and hence supplying his 'young readers' with some information. He quotes Johnson on Burney and then dwells on the honour of membership of the Literary Club ('When we know that a single black ball excludes a candidate', &c.), finally supplying a list of 'Original and Present Members'. All this to introduce Burney, with adequate dignity, to 'young readers'!

For the Essex Head Club see *Diary and Letters*, ii. 235, and Boswell's *Johnson*. It was less exclusive than the Literary Club, and Hawkins, in his *Life of Johnson*, speaks disrespectfully of it: 'I was not made privy to this his intention but, all circumstances considered, it was no matter of surprise to me when I heard that the great Dr. Johnson had, in the month of December 1783, formed a sixpenny club at an ale-house in Essex-street, and that though some of the persons thereof were persons of note, strangers, under restrictions, for three pence each night might three nights in a week hear him talk and partake of his conversation.' To which Hawkins's own daughter (L. M. Hawkins, *Memoirs* i. 103) pointedly rejoins: 'Boswell was well justified in his resentment of my father's designation of this club as a sixpenny club, meeting at an ale-house. . . . Honestly speaking, I dare say my father did not like being passed over.'

[1] Mrs. Piozzi, *Letters to and from the late Samuel Johnson, LL.D.* (1788), ii. 365.

[2] Letter in George Birkbeck Hill's *Boswell*, iv. 360. (The original was sold at Sotheby's, 30 July 1930.)

'Mr. Johnson, who came home last night, sends his respects to dear Dr. Burney and all the dear Burneys, little and great.'[1]

Burney now made a duty of paying him frequent visits, but the favourite Fanny was not usually able to accompany her father, and, indeed, Burney was a little afraid of his daughter going to Bolt Court lest the sight of her should set the mind of Johnson again on the subject of the Thrale quarrel, and so throw him into agitation.[2] But one morning, when driving into the City on business, Burney dropped his daughter at Johnson's door, promising to call for her on his return—and, sure enough, the embittering topic *was* broached: 'She cares for no one!' he exclaimed (meaning Mrs. Thrale); 'You only—You she loves still! But no one and nothing else!'

The subject was turned, and then Burney came in and took his daughter away.

At the beginning of September it became clear that the end was near. Johnson made his Will, appointing Burney's rival, Hawkins (a legal man and, whatever his social faults, a sound man of affairs), as one of his executors.

Fanny called at the house and sent up a message. Johnson had with him his old and dear friend George Strahan, Vicar of St. Mary's, Islington, and son of the chief publisher of the famous dictionary, and sent him down to thank Fanny for calling and to say that 'he was so very bad, and very weak, that he hoped she would excuse his seeing her'. A few days after it proved possible for the dying man to receive her father:

'Dr. Burney found him seated on a great chair, propt up by pillows, and perfectly tranquil. He affectionately took the Doctor's hand, and kindly inquired after his health, and that of his family; and then, as evermore Dr. Johnson was wont to do, he separately and very particularly named and dwelt upon the Doctor's second daughter; gently adding, "I hope Fanny did not take it amiss, that I did not see her that morning?—I was very bad indeed!"

'Dr. Burney answered, that the word *amiss* could never be apropos to her; and least of all now, when he was so ill.

'The Doctor ventured to stay about half an hour, which was partly spent in quiet discourse, partly in calm silence; the invalid always perfectly placid in looks and manner.

'When the Doctor was retiring, Dr. Johnson again took his hand and encouraged him to call yet another time; and afterwards, when he was again departing, Dr. Johnson impressively said, though in a low voice, "Tell Fanny—to pray for me!" And then, still holding, or rather grasping, his hand, he made a prayer for himself, the most pious, humble, eloquent, and touching, Dr. Burney said, that mortal man could compose and utter. He concluded it with an amen! in which Dr. Burney fervently joined; and which was spontaneously echoed by all who were present.

'This over, he brightened up, as if with revived spirits, and opened cheerfully

[1] Boswell, under date 1784. [2] *Mem.* ii. 358.

into some general conversation; and when Dr. Burney, yet a third time, was taking his reluctant leave, something of his old arch look played upon his countenance as, smilingly he said "Tell Fanny—I think I shall yet throw the ball at her again!"'[1]

Next morning, Sunday, after church, Fanny called, but Johnson had again to ask to be excused, 'for he feels himself too weak for such an interview'. And the following day Burney was bereft of a friendship that had opened nearly thirty years before and become progressively closer, and Fanny of an affectionate association that, though it had lasted only six years or so, had been very intimate.

According to William Seward, close friend of both the Burneys and Johnson:

'Johnson the day before he died was visited by Dr. Burney. After having taken an affectionate leave of his old friend he said, taking his hands between his, "My good friend, *Do all the good you can*".'[2]

As will be remembered by readers of Boswell, Johnson, a few days before his death, 'asked Sir John Hawkins, as one of his executors, where he should be buried, and on being answered, "Doubtless in Westminster Abbey", seemed to feel a satisfaction very natural to a Poet; and indeed very natural to any man of any imagination who has no family sepulchre in which he can be laid with his fathers'. Burney, with his fellow members of the Literary Club, attended the funeral, as did his son Charles.[3]

Windham in his diary has this entry under date 20 December 1784:

'20th.—A memorable day—the day which saw deposited in Westminster Abbey the remains of Johnson. After our return from the Abbey I spent some time with Burke on the subject of his negotiation with the Chancellor. We dined at Sir Joshua Reynolds, viz. Burke and R. Burke, Metcalf, Colman, Hoole, Scott, Burney and Brocklesby.'[4]

There was a good deal of dissatisfaction over the way the ceremony was conducted. Charles Burney, junior, wrote the next day:

'The executor, Sir John Hawkins, did not manage things well, for there was no anthem or choir service performed—no lesson—but merely what is read over every old woman that is buried by the parish.'[5]

And Burney himself, in a letter to Twining on Christmas Day, wrote:

'The Dean and Chapter of Westminster Abbey lay all the blame on Sir

[1] *Mem.* iii. 11; there is much the same account in *Diary and Letters*, ii. 279 et seq.

[2] *European Magazine* (1798), 92. The same anecdote occurs, in slightly different wording, in Seward's *Biographiana* (1799).

[3] *Mem.* iii. 16.

[4] *Diary of the Right Hon. William Windham* (1866), i.

[5] Quoted in John Johnstone, *Memoirs of Dr. Samuel Parr*, in the first volume of Parr's *Collected Works*.

John Hawkins for suffering Johnson to be so unworthily interred. The Knight's first inquiry at the Abbey in giving orders, as the most acting executor, was—"What would be the difference in the expense between a public and a private funeral?" and was told only a few pounds to the prebendaries, and about ninety pairs of gloves to the choir and attendants; and he then determined that, "as Dr. Johnson had no music in him, he should choose the cheapest manner of interment." And for this reason there was no organ heard, or burial service sung; for which he suffers the Dean and Chapter to be abused in all the newspapers, and joins in their abuse when the subject is mentioned in conversation.'[1]

Burney, in the same letter, deals severely with certain statements about Johnson's morals in earlier life, which he alleges emanated from Hawkins. And he exclaims, in a tone of disgust:

'The knight, Sir John, and I met two or three times during his sickness, and at his funeral. He steps forth as one of poor Johnson's six or eight biographers, with as little taste or powers of writing worthy of such an occupation as for musical history.'

In the long run Burney's condemnation has been pretty well confirmed. Posterity thinks better of Hawkins's *History of Music* than did Burney, but it says few good words for his *Life of Johnson*.[2]

In closing the account of this special period of the Burneys' bereavement it seems proper here to add an extract from a letter from Burney to his daughter Fanny, written just after the death of Crisp, which lays down a wisely reasoned principle upon which (as there is other evidence) he steadily tried to act throughout his life:

'However as something is due to the living, there is, perhaps, a boundary at which it is right to endeavour to stop lamenting the dead. It is very hard, as I have found it all my life, to exceed these bounds in our duty or attention, without its being at the expense of others. I have lost in my time persons so dear to me, as to throw me into the utmost affliction and despondence which can be suffered without insanity; but I had claims on my life, my reason, and my activity, which drew me from the pit of despair, and forced me, though with great difficulty, to rouse and exert every nerve and faculty in answering them. It has been very well said of mental wounds, that they must digest, like those of the body, before they can be healed. Necessity can alone, perhaps, in some cases, bring on this digestion; but we should not prevent it

[1] Twining, *Country Clergyman*, 129.

[2] For some contemporary views on Hawkins see Boswell in Hill's edition, i. 28. Malone, referring to Hawkins's *Life of Johnson*, used the word 'malignancy'. Boswell thought this a little too strong and preferred the word 'malevolence'. Bishop Percy thought Hawkins was 'a most detestable fellow'. Dyer said he was 'a man of the most mischievous, uncharitable and malignant disposition'. The usually mild Sir Joshua Reynolds said that Hawkins, 'though he assumed great outward sanctity was not only mean and grovelling in disposition but absolutely dishonest'. Most of these expressions are as reported by Malone (see Prior's *Malone*, pp. 425–7); they may not be verbally accurate but seem to represent a general consensus of opinion against Hawkins, and, of course, they all come from people who were closely associated with him in the Literary Club or otherwise.

by caustics or corrosion; let the wound be open a due time, but not treated with violence. To quit all metaphor, we must, alas! try to diminish our sorrow for our calamity, to enable us to support one another; as a national peace is but time to refit, a mental is no more. So far, however, am I blaming your indulgence of sorrow on the present occasion, that I both love and honour you for it; and therefore shall add no more on that melancholy subject.'[1]

[1] *Diary and Letters*, ii. 212.

XLIV. BURNEY BECOMES ORGANIST OF CHELSEA HOSPITAL

(1783; aged 57)

IN 1784 Burney, after nine years of tenancy of the house in St. Martin's Street, during which period his hospitality had made it a centre of attraction for the musical and literary minds of London, began to think of leaving it. Fanny tells us the story of this impending change of residence. On one and the same day in December 1783 she had the sadness of visiting the failing Johnson ('who is indeed very ill, and whom I could hardly bear to leave') and the happiness of receiving a visit from Burke:

'The year 1783 was now on its wane; so was the administration in which Mr. Burke was a minister;[1] when one day, after dinner at Sir Joshua Reynolds', Mr. Burke drew Dr. Burney aside, and, with great delicacy, and feeling his way, by the most investigating looks, as he proceeded, said that the organist's place at Chelsea College [i.e. Chelsea Hospital;[2] see pl. 28, II. 58] was then vacant: that it was but twenty pounds a year, but that, to a man of Dr. Burney's eminence, if it should be worth acceptance, it might be raised to fifty.[3] He then lamented that, during the short time in which he had been Paymaster General, nothing better, and indeed, nothing else had occurred more worthy of offering.

'Trifling as this was in a pecuniary light, and certainly far beneath the age or the rank in his profession of Dr. Burney, to possess any thing through the influence, or rather the friendship of Mr. Burke, had a charm irresistible. The Doctor wished, also, for some retreat from, yet near London; and he had reason to hope for apartments, ere long, in the capacious Chelsea College. He therefore warmly returned his acknowledgements for the proposal, to which he frankly acceded.

'And two days after, just as the news was published of a total change of administration, Dr. Burney received from Mr. Burke the following notice of his vigilant kindness:

"I had yesterday the pleasure of voting you, my dear Sir, a salary of fifty pounds a year, as organist to Chelsea Hospital. But as every increase of salary made at our Board is subject to the approbation of the Lords of the Treasury, what effect the change now made may have I know not;—but I do not think any Treasury will rescind it.

"This was *pour faire la bonne bouche* at parting with office; and I am only

[1] The short-lived Portland ministry, Apr.–Dec. 1783.

[2] Chelsea Hospital took the place of the buildings originally intended as a divinity school, 'King James' Colledge at Chelsey' (begun 1609). Some old inhabitants of Chelsea even to-day speak of the Hospital as 'the College'.

[3] There was, in addition, a customary annual fee of two pounds for 'locking up the organ', whatever that might be!

sorry that it did not fall in my way to shew you a more substantial mark of my high respect for you and Miss Burney.

I have the honour to be, &c.

EDM. BURKE.

Horse Guards, Dec. 9, 1783.

"I really could not do this business at a more early period, else it would have been done infallibly. . . ."

'A short time afterwards, Mr. Burke called himself in St. Martin's-street, and—for the Doctor, as usual, was not at home—Mr. Burke, as usual, had the condescension to inquire for this Memorialist; whom he found alone.

'He entered the room with that penetrating look, yet open air, that marked his demeanour where his object in giving was, also, to receive pleasure; and in uttering apologies of as much elegance for breaking into her time, as if he could possibly be ignorant of the honour he did her; or blind to the delight with which it was felt.

'He was anxious, he said, to make known in person that the business of the Chelsea Organ was finally settled at the Treasury.

'Difficult would it be, from the charm of his manner as well as of his words, to decide whether he conveyed this communication with most friendliness or most politeness: but, having delivered for Dr. Burney all that officially belonged to the business, he thoughtfully, a moment, paused; and then impressively said: "This is my last act of office!".'[1]

There is perhaps a slight suggestion of a desire for a quieter life, and perhaps for some financial retrenchment, in Burney's accepting this new office. He had been making a good income, but at the cost of incessant activity and great outlay. Having a most fashionable clientele he was able to charge a guinea a lesson, and there is a letter of Johnson to Mrs. Thrale mentioning that Burney had given fifty-seven lessons during the preceding week, so that if, considering that exceptional, we put the average weekly earnings at forty-five guineas, we shall be moderate. Then there was the 'Entrance Money' for new pupils, which was one guinea.[2] As for the proceeds from his books we will write those off, since the expenses of the tours abroad, which constituted a part of their preparation, must, one guesses, have much more than counterbalanced any profits; however, the harpsichord compositions, which no doubt Burney used with all his pupils, were certainly a source of revenue. Allowing for a considerable drop in earnings during the summer months we may suppose that Burney had for some years

[1] *Mem.* ii. 373.

[2] Cf., in *D.N.B.*, one of Burney's rivals, a fashionable London harpsichord teacher, Joseph Kelway, who charged two guineas 'entrance money'. Burney's friend, Samuel Wesley, writing in 1830, looked back to the period now in question as the Golden Age for Music Masters—'Instruction in music was much better in those days than it is at present. The inferior masters were used to receive two guineas for eight lessons, and two guineas entrance also. Three guineas for eight lessons was a very usual price with masters of the higher order, and four for those of the highest. At different periods I myself have received a guinea a lesson, and from some pupils as much as twenty-five shillings.' (J. T. Lightwood, *Samuel Wesley, Musician,* 114.)

been making at least £1,500 a year, and quite possibly £2,000, apart from his wife's income.

But then his expenses had been proportionately great. They had to be if he was to maintain his position with the 'society' people from whom he drew his income. As his brother-in-law, Arthur Young, says of him,[1] he was 'sought after' by 'the first nobility', 'dressed expensively', and 'always kept his carriage'.[2] He had probably given dowries with his girls. It is quite likely, then, that up to this date Burney had not a great sum of money put away, and one means of economy would be a reduction in the rent and upkeep of his house—at that time a fairly large one.

His children Esther, James, Susanna, and Charles were now off his hands, and so were all his three stepchildren. The three girls Fanny, Charlotte, and Sarah Harriet were at home and Dick would come home from Winchester for the holidays. But the household was much diminished and could be accommodated in a smaller place and with a reduced domestic staff. The reduction in expenses would permit of a reduction in work, and though fifty-seven years is but a moderate age, still it is an age at which that same number of lessons per week is likely to be felt as, to say the least, a considerable bore and also something of a physical strain.

It will be seen by a remark in the quotation from Fanny's *Memoirs* of her father, above, that Burney 'had reason to hope for apartments, ere long, in the capacious Chelsea College'. He had, then, no such apartments assigned him, as a part of the emoluments of office,[3] and it seems to have been three or four years before any rooms fell vacant. Then (mid 1787) he rented, for £12 a year, the five-room apartment next to the chapel officially assigned to the First Chaplain, who was non-resident. In those days a large proportion of the beneficed clergy of England took stipends and then underpaid some poor devil to do their duty, pocketing the difference.[4] And it was the same in government

[1] *Autobiography*, 101.

[2] Our historically minded Burney has recorded for after ages the name of 'the first English music-master who kept his carriage'—William Savage, 'master of the boys in St. Paul's cathedral' and a well-known bass singer and fashionable teacher of singing. Burney, during his first period in London, was in touch with him (see I. 55). Looking back to the conditions of those times he says: 'No master had then more than two guineas a month; but servants' wages, house-keeping, and house-rent, were in proportion.' Poor Savage, who died in 1789, 'out-lived fashion so much as to walk on foot during the last years of his life'.

[3] Indeed he never had, but always rented, according to the present occupant of the very apartments now to be in question, Captain C. G. T. Dean, who is engaged in compiling a history of the hospital, and has studied the official records, generously supplying the present writer with a good deal of material for this chapter. A paper by Captain Dean on 'Dr. Burney's Connexion with the Royal Hospital, Chelsea', will be found in *Transactions of the London and Middlesex Archaeological Society*, New Series, viii, pt. 3 (1944).

[4] This kind of thing, of course, went on much longer than the period at which we have now arrived. There is, for instance, in the nineteenth century, the case of the Precentor of St. Paul's Cathedral, whose face was so entirely unknown to the vergers that when, in 1852, on the occasion of the Duke of Wellington's funeral, he presented himself there, he was refused admission. This Christian minister, threatened by the redoubtable reformer, Miss Hackett,

service; at this period practically everybody on the staff of Chelsea Hospital paid deputies to do their work, as did this chaplain. Burney himself, to some extent, fell in with the custom. In 1798 there is record of his employing a deputy at £12 a year;[1] he may have done this from the beginning of his tenure of the office, or may have done so only when he became older, and began to spend a good deal of time travelling about the country to stay with some of his grand friends at their country seats. There were services twice daily in the chapel, but one may guess that these would be read and that the organ would be called into use only on Sundays; if it was used daily, then, of course, the need for a deputy is fully explained and the £12 may have been very fully earned. In any case, as Burney was concurrently Organist of Oxford Chapel he may have needed a deputy to take one of the Sunday services.

Burney's predecessors in this post were not men of any particular distinction, but it may be worth while to set forth their names and dates, from the building of the organ by the famous Renatus Harris ninety years before:

1693. PETER DUMAS, a recently naturalized Huguenot refugee.
1719. THEOPHILUS COLE.
1730. BARNABY (or BARNABAS) GUNN. (His Christian name appears in both forms in the Hospital's records: the contemporary Barnabas Gunn, Organist of Gloucester Cathedral, may have been his father.)
1753. THOMAS RAWLINS, a pupil of Pepusch and a member of Handel's orchestra in his opera and oratorio performances.
1767. THOMAS WOOD. Mentioned in Burney's *History* as leader of the band at Covent Garden Theatre and Organist of St. Giles's Church, as well as Chelsea Hospital.

It is worth mention that Burney's successor, when the time came thirty years later, was to be the able Charles Wesley, junior.

The date when Burney settled in Chelsea Hospital is very variously stated. Grove's *Dictionary* says 1783, which, in view of the date of the above letter, would mean quick work! All sorts of odd dates are given in continental books of reference—Fétis, 1790; Mendel, 1789; Abert, Riemann, and Schmidl, all the impossible 1782. These discrepancies are not important, as it cannot matter much to foreign readers at what date Charles Burney left one abode for another; but one wonders at their variety and speculates as to their origin. A careful comparison of entries in Fanny's diary, and also of letters of Susanna now in the Public Library of Armagh, shows that Burney was in possession of his Chelsea apartments well before the end of the summer of 1787 and Boswell says he breakfasted with him there on 3 November 1787, yet other entries

with prosecution for neglect of his duties, boldly asserted that his position had been given him as 'a perfect sinecure'.

[1] Burney's employment of this deputy at this salary is mentioned in the 34th Report (1798) of the Select Committee on Finance (i.e. a Report on the whole question of government finance). The Report is in the State Papers at the British Museum.

PLATE 28. *BURNEY'S LAST DWELLING*

THE RIVER FRONT OF CHELSEA HOSPITAL
As Burney knew it (*see* ii. 55 et seq.).

THE HOSPITAL CHAPEL
Showing Burney's organ.

BURNEY'S FIRST APARTMENT
The porch by Adam.

show that he was also in possession of the St. Martin's Street house up to at least June 1788 and the Rate Book shows him as responsible until 1789, after which the house had no tenant for a year. For a period there are mentioned meetings in both places with members of the family and with friends.

It would seem that when the suite of apartments in the hospital fell vacant Burney promptly took it, but that, his lease of the St. Martin's Street house being as yet unexpired, he kept that on also. There would be no great difficulty in this, as the hospital itself supplied and maintained the furniture in the apartments it allotted to the chaplain and other officials. Indeed, one object in keeping the St. Martin's Street house for a time may have been that of accommodation of furniture not required in the new abode. Burney's library was evidently not at once transferred, for Susanna, in a letter of 6 August 1787, talks of going with her father to 'rummage in St. Martin's Street' and of helping him 'in his search of music'.

This temporary occupation of two dwellings is doubtless the basis of a clause in the final passage of the article on Burney, a few years later, in Gerber's *Historisch-Biographisches Lexicon der Tonkünstler* (Leipzig, 1790). It mentions admiringly not only the eminence to which Burney's children were already climbing, but also his own lordly possession of 'a competency, two houses in London, and his own carriage'.

Burney's new dwelling was, and is, a pleasant little place, with a porch by Adam which had been added to it a few years before he came into residence and which remains one of its principal features (see pl. 28, II. 58). He occupied it until 1798, when a new Chaplain was appointed, one who wished to reside. He then moved to the Second Chaplain's flat, on the second floor of the main building, and there remained to the end. This flat in the early years of the present century again became the organist's apartment. It appears to be now much in the condition in which it was in Burney's day. It is very odd that for this smaller flat he paid £30 a year (then quite a high rent), as against the £12 for the larger apartment he had just quitted.[1]

1 Captain Dean gives me this figure from the 1812 Report of the Commissioners for Military Enquiry. He adds:

'It was certainly a high rent, especially for the Second Chaplain's flat on the 2nd Floor, which was considerably smaller than the First Chaplain's on the ground floor. The Quarters were furnished at public expense until 1793. Furniture then in the various apartments was left for the occupants' use. Both Chaplains also received an allowance of £25 p.a. in lieu of furniture after 1793, so they certainly did not suffer by the changes!

'Various apartments in the Hospital were let at this period. In 1793 the Chelsea Board ordered that deputies were to be appointed only with their permission, which was then formally granted to the absentee First Chaplain, Comyn. In 1796 the Board authorized Dr. Burney to continue renting the First Chaplain's Quarters, and in 1798 they approved his renting the Second Chaplain's Quarters (vide *Chelsea Journal*, i.e. contemporary extracts from the Board Minutes preserved among the Hospital Records).'

An allusion to Burney's ejection from his first apartment at Chelsea, and 'fears of removal on account of the twenty thousand volumes', will be found in *Diary and Letters*, v. 403.

Burney's organ (see pl. 28, II. 58), built by Renatus Harris the Third in 1693, was in the west gallery of the chapel and had a beautiful oak case, which fortunately was retained when the instrument was rebuilt in 1817 and again in 1936. No particulars of its specification have apparently been preserved. Burney had no choir, and there was, indeed, none until 1834, but the girls of the Royal Hospital School sat in the gallery and probably led the singing. Four years after Burney was appointed there was held a special service to celebrate the recovery of George III from one of his bouts of illness and mental derangement, and on this occasion, the records tell us, the children of local charity schools and Sunday schools marched to the chapel in procession, with all the local big-wigs, and the organ was 'animated by Dr. Burney'; the ceremonies ended, the children were given a good dinner whilst the In-pensioners of the hospital rapidly liquidated the sum of £81 that had been distributed amongst them.[1]

There is just one little matter to clear up before we leave Burney in possession of this new post. It does not seem to have been a very valuable gift on Burke's part; indeed, after considering all the circumstances above detailed, most readers will probably remain more than a little surprised that it should have been worth Burney's acceptance. Anyhow, such as it was he owed the appointment to the respect felt for him by his fellow club member and friend, Edmund Burke, and there seems little warrant for Morley, in his Life of Burke, representing it as solely of the nature of a tribute to Burney's daughter Fanny. Admittedly Burke admired both *Evelina* and *Cecilia*, but that is no reason for saying:

'He showed his regard for the authoress in a more substantial way than by compliments and criticism. His last act, before going out of office, in 1783, was to procure for Dr. Burney the appointment of organist at the chapel of Chelsea.'[2]

Burke had constantly dropped in 'uninvited and unexpectedly to the little tea-table in St. Martin's Street, and the Doctor and his wife visited Burke and his wife in their apartments at the Treasury'.[3] When Burke asked for Burney's vote for a friend in a Westminster election and Burney's principles made it necessary for him to refuse it Burney evidently sent Burke a letter alluding to the Chelsea appointment and regretting that he had to refuse anything to the friend to whom he owed it. To this Burke replied:

'You have little or no obligations to me; but if you had as many as I really wish it were in my power—as it is certainly in my desire—to lay upon you,

[1] Thomas Faulkener, *Historical and Topographical Description of Chelsea*, 1810 edition, p. 440 (not in the 1829 edition). Faulkener is quoting the *London Evening Post* of 14 Mar. 1789. He mentions in his book that Burney was a Governor of the Chelsea Sunday Schools.

[2] John Morley, *Burke* (1888).

[3] *Mem.* ii. 371.

I hope you do not think me capable of conferring them, in order to subject your mind, or your affairs, to a painful and mischievous servitude.'

And this generosity of mind Burney acknowledged as follows:

'Your delicacy, dear Sir, in refraining from the least hint of allusion that could be construed into a wish that I should go with you in the late struggle, though you had a fair claim upon me, redoubles my desire to give you some voluntary testimony of the great respect and regard with which I have the honour to be, &c.'[1]

This is a correspondence which is creditable to both men!

[1] Ibid. iii. 123.

XLV. THE HANDEL COMMEMORATION[1]

(*1784; Burney aged 58; Handel 25 years dead*)

THE indications of the approaching marriage of Mrs. Thrale (about which her friends excited themselves so unnecessarily, as it now looks to us), and the still sadder indications of the approaching death of Dr. Johnson, made the early part of 1784 a trying time for Burney. However, he had a new and congenial activity to occupy his mind. As Fanny puts it, in phrases which are best quoted intact, since the present writer could not even distantly approach their charm and dignity:

'A new and brilliant professional occupation fell, fortunately, to the task of Dr. Burney, drawing him from his cares, and beguiling him from his sorrows, by notes of sweetest melody, and combinations of the most intricate, yet sound harmony; for this year, which completed a century from the birth of Handel, was alloted for a public Commemoration of that great musician and his works.

'Dr. Burney, justly proud of the honour paid to the chief of that art of which he was a professor, was soon, and instinctively wound up to his native spirits, by the exertions which were called forth in aid of this noble enterprize. He suggested fresh ideas to the Conductors; he was consulted by all the Directors; and his advice and experience enlightened every member of the business in whatever walk he moved.'[2]

The Directors mentioned were the Earls of Exeter, Sandwich, and Uxbridge, Sir Watkin Williams Wynn, Bt., and Sir Richard Jebb, Bt., with Joah Bates as conductor. Some of these (perhaps all) were personal friends of Burney. Of his relations with Lord Sandwich we already know a good deal (see I. 193–4, 195 n., 285); and 'the admirable prescriptions and skill of the eminent physician, Sir Richard Jebb' (see reference at II. 1) had often been employed to the advantage of Burney's family and had once saved Burney himself when 'dangerously attacked by an acute fever'.[3]

Joah Bates was a Yorkshireman married to a Lancashire woman—a former Eton and Cambridge scholar married to a former factory girl, but one who had won fame as a vocalist. His brilliant classical career at Cambridge had terminated in a tutorship at King's, and he had had the son of Lord Sandwich as a pupil: this led to Lord Sandwich's taking him into the Admiralty as his private secretary, and to his subsequent promotion to the Commissionership of the Victualling Office. At this

[1] For various pictures illustrating this Commemoration, see pls. 29–32, II. 64, 65.

[2] *Mem.* ii. 379. They were, of course, wrong about the birth of Handel, who was born not in 1684 but in 1685. Handel's obituary notice in *The Gentleman's Magazine* in 1759 had the correct birth date of 1685 but Mainwaring's Life of Handel (1760—the earliest life published) had for some reason 1684; for a long time every English writer followed Mainwaring and the wrong date was engraved on the monument in Westminster Abbey.

[3] *Mem.* ii. 133.

office, on Tower Hill, he had his private residence and here, with his friends, he concocted his bold plan for the Commemoration of Handel.

Bates was a very expert musician (a fine performer on the harpsichord, says Burney) and at Cambridge the acknowledged leader in all musical activities. When the parish church of his native Halifax acquired an organ, 'determining that it should be opened with éclat, he, for the first time that any oratorio had been performed north of the Trent attempted the *Messiah* . . . and it was universally acknowledged by the best judges that the Messiah had never been so well performed'.[1] It was he who was responsible for the bringing into existence of the 'Concert of Antient Music', otherwise known as 'The King's Concerts', which ran from 1776 to 1848, and he was long the regular conductor of this enterprise. All his co-directors in this Handel Commemoration were Directors of the 'Antient Concert', of which the Commemoration was, indeed, an offshoot.

Besides the Directors there were eight Assistant Directors, all professional musicians (Drs. Benjamin Cooke, Samuel Arnold, and Edmund Ayrton, and Messrs. Redmond Simpson, T. S. Dupuis, H. T. Aylward, and William Parsons).[2] And there was an Assistant Conductor, John Ashley, the eminent bassoonist.

The charitable object of the Commemoration (for, of course, it *had* to have a charitable object) was to assist the funds of the 'Musical Fund', or 'Society for Decayed Musicians' (to use Burney's cheerless title for the charity)—a most appropriate destination of any profits, since Handel had been one of the original promoters of this fund (in 1738), had composed concertos and given concerts for it, and when he died had left it a thousand pounds.[3]

[1] Burney, in Rees's *Cyclopaedia*, s.v. 'Bates, Joah'. Herschel, the musician-astronomer (see II. 153), wrote in his diary in 1766: 'Mar. 7. Halifax. The Messiah. This Oratorio was performed at a private club of chorus singers held at the Rev. Mr. Bates, the Clerk [? vicar] of the Parish Church and father of the well-known musical Mr. Joe Bates, where it was agreed to rehearse the same Oratorio every other Friday, in order to perform it in the church at the opening of a new organ erecting there. I was the leader of the orchestra and Mr. Joe Bates, who played a chamber organ, directed the performance; his brother played the violincello.' (*The Herschel Chronicle*, ed. Constance A. Lubbock, 1933; 35.) (What is this reference to a chamber organ? Possibly it was in the house of Bates's father, and used for the rehearsals.)

[2] Burney quaintly says, on the closing page of his book on the Commemoration: 'The worthy noblemen and baronets, who honoured the undertaking with their countenance and direction, wisely and generously hung out honourable lures of wands, good cheer, medals, and importance, to those who, without performing, were willing to take an active part in the business; yet it is but justice to say, that the honour of HANDEL and benefit of their favourite Society, stimulated their zeal more powerfully than any other considerations.'

It appears that rings exist which were made for some of the officials—'of plain gold with a framed portrait of Handel, printed in black on white satin', the frame being 'of an oval shape . . . about an inch and a half long by three quarters of an inch broad' (see *Notes and Queries*, IV. viii. 39 and V. vi. 207, 315).

[3] To finish with the charitable side of the Commemoration, it may be mentioned that the fund received £6,000 and a few years later (1789) was granted a charter by George III, under the new name of 'Royal Society of Musicians', under which name it to-day still carries

Burney's part in this great enterprise was not confined to the suggestive and consultative activities above mentioned; he proposed to the Directors that he should 'become the Historian of the transaction', producing a book to be sold for the further benefit of the fund. This offer was 'accepted with pleasure and gratitude' and, putting aside, for the time, his work on the third volume of his *History*, he 'now delegated all his powers to the furtherance of this grand scheme; and drew up a narrative of the festival, with so much delight in recording the disinterestedness of its voluntary performers; its services to the superannuated or helpless old labourers of his caste; and the splendid success of the undertaking; that his history of the performances in Commemoration of Handel, presents a picture so vivid of that superb entertainment, that those who still live to remember it, must seem to witness its stupendous effects anew: and those of later days, who can know of it but by tradition, must bewail their little chance of ever personally hearing such magnificent harmony; or beholding a scene so glorious of royal magnificence and national enthusiasm'.[1]

He desired to prefix to his volume an accurate account of Handel's life. He had, as we have seen, known Handel, and had personally watched his later career, but he required details of the great man's life during the period previous to his coming to England, and for these he wrote to some of his many German friends—being helped, also, as already mentioned by old Mrs. Delany, who cherished memories of Handel in his first years of life in England.

All the musical writers of that period tell us something about that wonderful Commemoration, but it is from Burney's official account that we get the best idea of it, and from that is derived most of the information that is now to follow.

The originally announced three performances took place during the last week of May—on Wednesday at noon in Westminster Abbey, on Thursday evening in the Pantheon in Oxford Street, and on Saturday, at noon, in the Abbey again. They were, however, so successful that, 'By Command of His Majesty', two performances were added on the Thursday and Saturday noons of the following week, both of these in the Abbey.

The 'reserved seat' system does not seem to have existed in those days (at the theatre people used to have to send their servants hours before the time of opening, to sit in their places until they came), and so for those twelve o'clock Abbey performances the doors were announced to be open at nine—at which hour there was such a throng of rank and fashion

on its good work. Burney had joined this body in 1749, when he was twenty-three years old. He was one of the four eminent musicians who signed the petition for the charter, the others being Dr. Benjamin Cooke, Organist of Westminster Abbey, Dr. Samuel Arnold, Organist of the Chapel Royal, and Dr. Edmund Ayrton, Master of the Children of His Majesty's Chapels. For the charter, with the names of these four, see *Mus. Times*, Oct. 1905.

[1] *Mem.* ii. 380.

DESIGNS FOR TICKETS

The first one is by Cipriani. Both are engraved by Bartolozzi.

JOAH BATES

[illegible] conducted seated at the organ (*see* ii. 62 and 65).

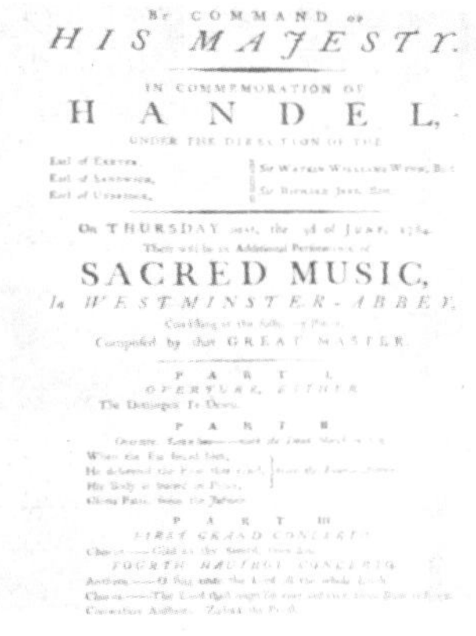

BY COMMAND OF

HIS MAJESTY.

IN COMMEMORATION OF

HANDEL,

UNDER THE DIRECTION OF THE

[illegible]

On THURSDAY next, the [illegible] of JUNE, [illegible]

[illegible]

SACRED MUSIC,

In WESTMINSTER-ABBEY,

[illegible]

Composed by that GREAT MASTER.

PART I.

OVERTURE, ESTHER.

The Dettingen Te Deum.

PART II.

[illegible]

PART III.

FIRST GRAND CONCERTO.

[illegible]

FOURTH HAUTBOY CONCERTO.

[illegible]

A PROGRAMME

For one of the 'Additional Performances' (*see* ii. 64).

THE PANTHEON IN OXFORD STREET

Where the secular programme was performed (*see* ii. 64 and 171–7).

PLATE 30. *THE GREAT HANDEL COMMEMORATION*, II

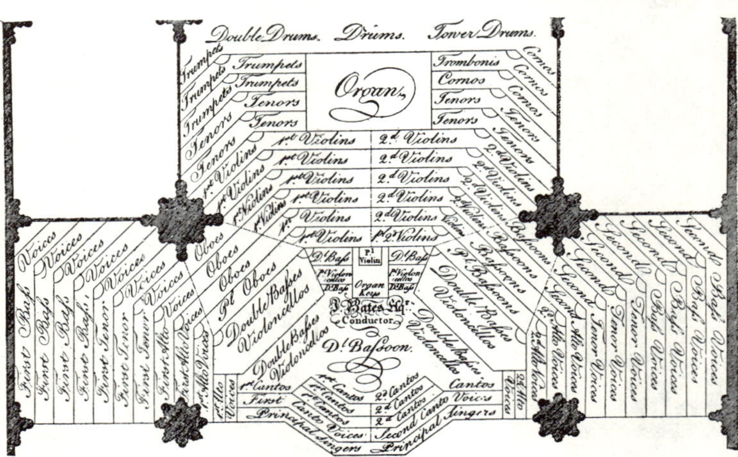

THE CHORAL AND INSTRUMENTAL FORCES

(West end of the nave) By Burney's nephew, E. F. Burney.

The Conductor, Joah Bates, sits at a detached Organ Console. The Orchestra, of 250 performers, is placed between him and the Organ and to his right and left. The Choir is in front and in side galleries, as shown in the diagram but not in sight in the picture. 'Cantos' are soprano singers. There were no Chorus Contraltos in those days—only Male Altos. The 'Tenors' indicated (as distinct from the 'Tenor Voices') are Violas. For further information of the disposition and control of these large forces *see* ii. 67–70.

assembled with their guinea tickets in their hands that there resulted a good deal of 'dishevelled hair' and a good many 'torn garments'. (Even at this long distance of time one feels sorry about that 'dishevelled hair', for, as one of the singers, the well-known Michael Kelly, tells us, 'such was the rage to procure seats that ladies had their hair dressed the night previous to get to the Abbey in good time'[1]—and, with the loftily-built-up and highly elaborate hair-dressings of that day, this meant sitting up all night, so as not to derange the edifice:[2]

'In less than an hour after the doors were opened, the whole area and galleries of the Abbey seemed too full for the admission of more company; and a considerable time before the performance began, the doors were all shut to every one but their Majesties, and their suite, who arrived soon after Twelve; and on entering the box, prepared for their reception, pleasure and astonishment, at the sight of the company and disposition of the Orchestra and Performers, were painted so strongly on their countenances, as to be visible to all their delighted subjects present. Eagerness and expectation for the *premier coup d'archet* were now wound up to the highest pitch of impatience; when a silence, the most profound and solemn, was gently interrupted by the processional symphony of the Coronation Anthem, composed in 1727.

'And from the time that the first sound of this celebrated, and well-known composition, was heard, to the final close, every hearer seemed afraid of breathing, lest it should obstruct the stream of harmony in its passage to the ear.'[3]

Burney here alludes to 'the disposition of the Orchestra and Performers'. What that disposition was can be gathered by the reader who will take the trouble to study the picture by Burney's nephew Edward and the explanatory chart that goes with it, which are here reproduced from Burney's book (see pl. 30, II. 65). The accommodation for the musicians, it will be understood, had all been built up at the west end of the nave, and a special organ there installed by 'the ingenious Mr. Samuel Green, of Islington', who, as the accounts show (Burney supplies a detailed statement of receipts and expenditure), got a hundred pounds for his services.

'It was fabricated for the cathedral of Canterbury, but before its departure for the place of its destination, it was permitted to be opened in the capital on this memorable occasion. The keys of communication with the harpsichord, at which Mr. Bates, the conductor, was seated, extended nineteen feet from the body of the organ, and twenty feet seven inches below the perpendicular of the set of keys by which it is usually played. Similar keys were first contrived in this country for Handel himself, at his Oratorios; but to convey them to so great a distance from the instrument, without render-

[1] *Reminiscences of Michael Kelly*, 1826.

[2] Fanny (*Early Diary*, ii. 146) speaks of a lady with 'hair higher than twelve wigs stuck one on the other'.

[3] Burney, *Handel Commemoration*, 26. But if the reader wishes to turn to the original of any passage quoted he should note that the book has a double pagination—one series of numbers for the Life of Handel and another for the description of the Festival.

ing the touch impracticably heavy, required uncommon ingenuity and mechanical resources.'[1]

At the east end of the nave, in front of the normal organ screen, and hiding it, was (Wyatt was the architect employed and he was allowed to spend nearly £2,000) 'a throne in a beautiful Gothic style corresponding with that of the Abbey and a center box, richly decorated with crimson satin, fringed with gold, for the reception of their Majesties and the Royal Family'. On the right of this was 'a box for the Bishops', and on the left one for the Dean and Chapter.

'Immediately below these two boxes were two others, one on the right, for the families and friends of the Directors, and the other for those of the prebendaries of Westminster. Immediately below the King's-box was placed one for the Directors themselves; who were all distinguished by white wands tipped with gold, and gold medals, struck on the occasion, appending from white ribbands. These their Majesties likewise condescended to wear, at each performance. Behind, and on each side of the throne, there were seats for their Majesty's suite, maids of honour, grooms of the bedchamber, pages, &c.'[2]

The body of the nave was 'filled up with level benches, and appropriated to the early subscribers', and the aisles were 'formed into long galleries, ranging with the orchestra, and ascending, so as to contain twelve rows on each side'.

We may now consider the musical forces engaged. The original motive of the promoters, Burney says, was to provide an occasion for bringing together 'the number of eminent musical performers of all kinds, both vocal and instrumental, with which London abounded', which 'was far greater than in any other city of Europe'. They had lamented that there had hitherto been 'no public periodical occasion for collecting and consolidating them into one band', so that 'a performance might be exhibited on so grand and magnificent a scale as no other part of the world could equal'. They now certainly achieved their ambition of removing this cause for distress, for they 'collected and consolidated' no fewer than 513 musicians (including a certain number of provincials), which, as Burney is at pains to show by the exhibition of such statistics as he could collect, far exceeded any previous 'collection and consolidation' in the whole history of musical effort.

'Pope more than forty years ago, imagining that his [Handel's] band was more numerous than modern times had ever seen or heard before, contented himself with calling him *Centimanus*, where he says:

"Strong in new arms, lo! Giant HANDEL stands,
Like bold Briareus with his *hundred hands*."

But if our great bard had survived the late Commemoration, when the

[1] Burney, *Handel Commemoration* (second part), 8.

[2] Ibid. (second part), 10. See the plate opposite. again drawn by Edward Burney for his uncle's book.

'VIEW OF THE GALLERY'

(EAST END OF THE NAVE)

is is one of Edward F. Burney's illustrations in his Uncle's *Account of the Musical Performances in stminster Abbey and the Pantheon in Commemoration of Handel* (*see* ii. 71 et seq.). It is described as 'VIEW OF E GALLERY PREPARED FOR THE RECEPTION OF THEIR MAJESTIES, THE ROYAL FAMILY, DIRECTORS, AND NCIPAL PERSONAGES IN THE KINGDOM'. (For a brief description of the splendours of this Gallery *see* ii. 66.)

THE MONUMENT AND MEMORIAL IN WESTMINSTER ABBEY

E. F. Burney's picture, for his Uncle's book, of the famous statue of 1761, in the Poet's Corner—'perhaps Roubiliac's most popular effort', as the *Dictionary of National Biography* suggests. (*See* ii. 74 for a discussion of the lettering.)

Above is seen the tablet recording the Commemoration.

productions of Handel employed more than five hundred voices and instruments, he would, perhaps, have lost a pun, a simile, and a *bon mot*, for want of a classical allusion to lean on.'

Here is a summary statement of the instrumental forces engaged:

STRINGS

1st Violins, 48; 2nd Violins, 47; Violas (called 'Tenors' in the chart), 26; Violoncellos, 21; Double Basses, 15.

Burney greatly enjoyed hearing these 157 instruments tune. He says: 'The most sudden and surprising effect of this stupendous band, was, perhaps, produced by simultaneous tuning: as all the stringed-instruments performed this task, *à double corde*, and these strings being all *open*, their force was more than equal to that of two stopt-strings, upon two different instruments.'

WOOD WIND

1st Hautboys, 13; 2nd Hautboys, 13; Flutes, 6; Bassoons, 26; Double Bassoon, 1.

BRASS

Trumpets, 12; Trombones, 6; Horns, 12.

PERCUSSION

Kettledrums, 3; Double Kettledrum, 1.[1]

ORGAN

The modern eye is a little startled at the sight of the large contingent of Hautboys and Bassoons; certain solo passages were played by twelve Hautboys, 'which united in such a manner', says Burney, 'as to have the effect of a single instrument'. Clarinets there were none, for those had only gradually been coming into use during Handel's lifetime and were not provided for in his scores, and some good orchestras, even in 1784, did not have them. The Trombones (which Burney also calls 'Sacbuts' or 'Double Trumpets'), the Double Bassoon, and the Double Kettledrum require a special word or two, which Burney himself shall be allowed to supply:

'In order to render the band as powerful and complete as possible, it was determined to employ every species of instrument that was capable of producing grand effects in a great orchestra, and spacious building. Among these, the SACBUT, or DOUBLE TRUMPET, was sought; but so many years had elapsed since it had been used in this kingdom, that, neither the instrument, nor a performer upon it, could easily be found. It was, however, discovered, after much useless enquiry, not only here, but by letter, on the continent, that in his Majesty's military band there were six musicians who played the three several species of sacbut; tenor, base, and double base.

[1] This is as given in the 'List of Instrumental Performers'. As will be seen from Burney's remarks below, the four drummers had at their disposition a varied collection of instruments, though just what these were seems to be a little difficult to grasp.

'The Double Bassoon, which was so conspicuous in the Orchestra and powerful in its effect, is likewise a tube of sixteen feet. It was made with the approbation of Mr. Handel, by Stainsby, the Flute-maker, for the coronation of his late majesty, George the Second. The late ingenious Mr. Lampe, author of the justly admired Music of *The Dragon of Wantley*, was the person intended to perform on it; but, for want of a proper reed, or for some other cause, at present unknown, no use was made of it, at that time; nor, indeed, though it has been often attempted, was it ever introduced into any band in England, till now, by the ingenuity and perseverance of Mr. Ashly, of the Guards.

The Double-Base Kettle Drums were made from models of Mr. Asbridge, of Drury-lane orchestra, in copper, it being impossible to procure plates of brass, large enough. The Tower-drums, which by permission of his grace the duke of Richmond, were brought to the Abbey on this occasion, are those which belong to the Ordnance stores, and were taken by the duke of Marlborough at the battle of Malplaquet, in 1709. These are hemispherical, or a circle divided; but those of Mr. Asbridge are more cylindrical, being much longer, as well as more capacious, than the common kettle-drum; by which he accounts for the superiority of their tone to that of all other drums. These three species of kettle-drums, which may be called tenor, base, and double-base, were an octave below each other.'[1]

Now for the Vocal Performers. They were as follows:

Trebles

6 Principals, headed by Burney's old friend Madame Mara (see I. 230), and 55 others (of these only 6 were women, the rest being all choirboys of the Abbey, St. Paul's, the Chapel Royal, &c.).

Counter Tenors

3 Principals and 45 others. (Note that there were no contraltos—and a

[1] As to the Double Bassoon, compare the *Musical Memoirs* of the eminent oboist, W. T. Parke (1830), vol. i, p. 42. 'At these musical performances Mr. Ashley, a sub-director, and first bassoon at Covent Garden Theatre, played for the first time on a newly-invented instrument called a double bassoon, an appropriate appellation, it being double the size of the common ones. This instrument, which rested on a stand, had a sort of flue affixed to the top of it, similar (with the exception of smoke) to that of a Richmond steam-boat. I am ignorant, however, whether it produced any tone, or whether it was placed in the orchestra to terminate the prospect.'

The Double Bassoon occurs in the score of Handel's *L'Allegro* (1740).

What were Burney's real feelings about those newfangled noise makers? In writing the official book of the Commemoration he had to restrain himself; he could not offend his friend Lord Sandwich and the other directors. Twenty years later, when writing in Rees's *Cyclopaedia* (s.v. 'Solo') he could let himself go, and did:

> 'At the Commemoration of Handel, the double drums, double curtals [i.e. double bassoons], tromboni, &c. augmented his lordship's pleasure, in proportion to the din and stentorophonic screams of these truly savage instruments.'

He admits that 'in so wide a building as Westminster Abbey and softened by so powerful a chorus of voices and instruments as were assembled for the Commemoration' these instruments 'had occasionally a fine effect', and that is as far as he will go.

The Earl of Sandwich was probably the instigator of the use of the 'double drums'. He was himself an ardent percussionist (see II. 178 n.).

century later at the Leeds Festival of 1883 there were only 17 contraltos against 42 male altos or counter tenors.)[1]

TENORS

3 Principals and 77 others.

BASSES

5 Principals and 83 others.

It is startling to us to hear that this large force was brought into action almost unrehearsed. A week before the festival began there had, apparently, been no rehearsal at all, and the one then held was merely for the purpose of testing (presumably separately) 120 singers whose names and abilities did not happen to be known to the conductor; of these he discarded merely two as inefficient. There was, after that, one general rehearsal for each performance (probably on the day preceding it). And that was that!

Then remember that Joah Bates's conducting was done entirely from the organ, and that though he could see most of the performers, and occasionally (if they happened to be looking) help them with a nod or a frown as he played, others had their backs to him. Burney was very proud of the results obtained without a time-beater (It is to be doubted if he had any conception of a 'conductor' in the modern sense, though, as it will be seen shortly, he used the word):

'Foreigners, particularly the French, must be much astonished at so numerous a band moving in such exact measure, without the assistance of a *Coryphaeus* to beat the time, either with a roll of paper, or a noisy *baton*, or truncheon. . . .

'As this Commemoration is not only the first instance of a band of such magnitude being assembled together, but of *any* band, at all numerous, performing in a similar situation, without the assistance of a *Manu-ductor*, to regulate the measure, the performances in Westminster-Abbey may be safely pronounced, no less remarkable for the multiplicity of voices and instruments employed, than for accuracy and precision. When all the wheels of that huge machine, the Orchestra, were in motion, the effect resembled clock-work in every thing, but want of feeling and expression.'

And his reflections that follow this bold statement are expressed with a dignity of phrase and an apt choice of epithet that came, perhaps, from his long association with one to whom the conversational grand style was habitual:

'And as the power of gravity and attraction in bodies is proportioned to their mass and density, so it seems as if the magnitude of this band had commanded and impelled adhesion and obedience, beyond that of any other of inferior force. The pulsations in every limb, and ramifications of veins and arteries in an animal, could not be more reciprocal, isochronous, and under the regulation of the heart, than the members of this body of

[1] For the tardy introduction of the contralto voice see the article 'Alto' in *The Oxford Companion to Music.*

Musicians under that of the Conductor and Leader. The totality of sound seemed to proceed from one voice, and one instrument; and its powers produced, not only new and exquisite sensations in judges and lovers of the art, but were felt by those who never received pleasure from Music before.

'These effects, which will be long remembered by the present public, perhaps to the disadvantage of all other choral performances, run the risk of being doubted by all but those who heard them, and the present description of being pronounced fabulous, if it should survive the present generation.'[1]

It is fair to admit that the audience's appreciation was expressed in the very best way. The behaviour of audiences in those days was in general what we should now call scandalous. Fanny's Evelina, when she made her first visit to the opera, wrote home: 'I could have thought myself in Paradise, but for the continual talking of the company around me', and when she went to the Pantheon, was 'quite astonished to find how little music is listened to in silence, for though everybody seems to admire, hardly anybody listens'. And Fanny's Cecilia, when she, in her turn, went to the opera, 'discovered that she had no chance of hearing', because 'the place she had happened to find vacant was next to a party of young ladies, who were so earnestly engaged in their own discourse, that they listened not to a note of the Opera', and so infinitely diverted with their own witticisms, that their tittering and loquacity allowed no one in their vicinity to hear better than themselves'; and when she went to a Pantheon concert found that 'no one of the party

[1] Burney, *Handel Commemoration* (second part), 14. Here, from Rees's *Cyclopaedia*, is the article on 'Battre la Mesure, *Fr. to beat time, in Music*'. It is by Burney himself, for he wrote the musical articles in this work (see Ch. LVIII):

'There are various ways of marking the measure and accents in music: by dividing each bar into 2, 3, or 4 equal parts with the motion of the hand, the foot, a *baton*, or a roll of paper. In common time of 2 minims or 2 crotchets in a bar, called *binary* measure, the hand is merely moved down and up. In time of 4 crotchets in a bar, the French frequently mark each portion of it, by *beating* the hand down to the first crotchet, moving it to the left for the 2d, to the right for the 3d, and lifting it up for the last. In triple time, or *ternary* measure of 3 minims, 3 crotchets, or 3 quavers, it is usually beaten, 2 down and one up, or the 1st down, the 2d to the left, and the 3d up.

'The beating time is of great antiquity. The ancient Greeks had various ways of regulating the accents of song, and steps of the dance.

'The Italians often beat the two first portions of a bar, and lift the hand up for the rest, both in common and triple time.

'At the Opera, concert-spiritual, and even at private concerts (formerly) there was a person at Paris, armed with a truncheon (*baton de Mesure*) like a general, whom Rousseau, in his Dictionary, ridicules, and says that he had been very aptly called the *Bucheron*, or wood-cutter; though when he wrote his musical articles for the *Encyclopédie*, the Italians and other nations, still had a *Corista* to regulate the measure in the numerous bands employed in their churches when there was a *gran Funzione*, in celebration of some saint or holy time. But it was in England, at the Commemoration of Handel in Westminster-abbey, that, in the most numerous band that ever was assembled in modern times, a Coryphaeus was first dispensed with.'

The 'first dispensing' with the 'Coryphaeus' seems to refer to occasions of great performances *in churches* (the sentence is badly worded and a little ambiguous). It will be seen from I. 123–4 of the present work that in Burney's day orchestral conducting at concerts in Britain was done from a keyboard instrument. (For a brief general discussion of the history of conducting see *The Oxford Companion to Music*, 6th and later editions.)

but herself had any desire to listen, no sort of attention was paid, the ladies entertaining themselves as if no Orchestra was in the room and the gentlemen, with an equal disregard of it, struggling for a place by the fire'.

That, then, was the general standard of behaviour that the Burneys found in places of music-making in their time. But here, at last, was an exception! Says Burney:

'In justice to the audience, it may be said, that though the frequency of hearing good Music in this capital, of late years, has so far blunted the edge of curiosity and appetite, that the best Operas and Concerts are accompanied with a buz and murmur of conversation, equal to that of a tumultuous croud, or the din of high 'Change; yet now, such a stillness reigned, as, perhaps, never happened before in so large an assembly. The midnight hour was never sounded in more perfect tranquillity, than every note of these compositions. I have long been watching the operations of good Music on the sensibility of mankind; but never remember, in any part of Europe, where I attended Musical exhibitions, in the Church, Theatre, or Chamber, to have observed so much curiosity excited, attention bestowed, or satisfaction glow in the countenances of those present, as on this occasion.'[1]

In every way, then, Burney had a congenial task in the compilation of his *Account of the Musical Performances in Westminster Abbey and the Pantheon in Commemoration of Handel.* Just one detail, apparently, irked him. He quickly finished the text of his book and then found publication delayed by 'the business of the plates'. Why they should have taken so long to engrave is difficult to guess, but so it was, and this 'laxity of progress by no means kept pace with the eagerness of the Directors, or the expectations of the public', the Directors often 'making known their disappointment through the channel of the Earl of Sandwich'.

However, there was one little advantage gained by the delay. The King became a contributor to the publication; Fanny tells us:

'The King himself deigned to make frequent inquiry into the state of the business; and when his Majesty knew that the publication was retarded only by the engravers, he desired to see the loose and unbound sheets of the work, which he perused with so strong an interest in their contents, that he drew up two critical notes upon them, with so much perspicuity and justness, that Dr. Burney, unwilling to lose their purport, yet not daring to presume to insert them with the King's name in any appendix, cancelled the two sheets to which they had reference, and embodied their meaning in his own text.'[2]

[1] Burney, *Handel Commemoration* (second part), 14.

[2] *Mem.* ii. 384. Fanny's attribution of the delay entirely to the engravers seems to be hardly correct. Burney almost rewrote the first (biographical) part of the book after it had been set in type. A study of the peculiar pagination and of the list of cancels in the instructions to the binder on the last page will confirm this assertion; and there exists a letter of Burney to J. C. Walker, the Irish antiquarian and writer on music, stating that he had at first relied on Mainwaring's *Life of Handel*, and later found it 'very deficient and inaccurate' (Quaritch's catalogue No. 471, 1933, p. 100).

Any readers who happen to possess Burney's Handel book may care to see what royal music criticism is like. They will find the King's contributions as follows:

p. 80. Passage on the chorus, 'He trusted in God'.

p. 105. Passage on the hautbois playing of Fischer.

A letter from Burney, in the British Museum (Add. MS. 35532, fol. 364), goes farther than the above; it says that the King read the book 'in MS. sheet by sheet, in fact as it was written', and we can safely accept this rather than Fanny's statement made in her old age.[1]

There were, it appears, ill-natured people who considered that Burney 'swanked' too much about the royal collaboration. Fanny, in 1785, mentions the 'vile Probationary Odes', and in 1788 does so again.[2] She refers to Mr. Michael Angelo Taylor, M.P., as being 'coupled to my dear father most impertinently and unwarrantably'. *The humorous Probationary Odes by the Various Candidates for the Office of Poet Laureat to His Majesty, In the Room of William Whitehead Esq., deceased* (cf. I. 302 n.), are supported by a number of satirical essays and one of these is a mock 'Testimony to the great powers of Mr. Taylor's Ode by Dr. Burney'. It includes a story of Taylor's supposed early life and includes the following passage:

> 'This anecdote was majestically inserted in my manuscript copy of Handel's Commemoration by the Great Personage to whose judgement I submitted it (I take every occasion of shewing the insertion as a good puff—I wish, however the same hand had subscribed for the book).'

Burney dedicated his book to the King in sonorous phrases that Johnson provided for him. (This really masterly little composition must have been one of Johnson's last literary tasks, if not his very last one, before he died.)[3] And when the book appeared 'a splendid copy of the work was prepared for the King'. Lord Sandwich 'offered his services for taking the Doctor under his wing to present the book at the levee', but the King sent a pleasant message to the effect that he would prefer to see Burney in private audience:

[1] In Lady Llanover's *Life and Correspondence of Mrs. Delany* is a letter from the Queen in which she encloses one from the King, both letters referring to Handel information Mrs. Delany had procured from her brother, Bernard Granville (see reference to him later in the present work—II. 75 n.): 'The King is much pleased with the very correct manner in which Mrs. Delany has obligingly executed the commission of obtaining an exact catalogue of Mr. Granville's collection of Mr. Handel's music, and desires she will forward it to Dr. Burney; at the same time, as Mrs. Delany has communicated Mr. Granville's willingness of letting the King see those vols. that are not in the original collection, he is desired at any convenient opportunity to let the following one's, be sent to town, and great care shall be taken, that they shall be without damage returned.' [A list of eight volumes follows.]

[2] *Diary and Letters*, ii. 320 and iii. 492.

[3] A letter from Johnson to Burney, now in the Morgan Library, discusses some suggestions Burney had made as to slight changes and additions and proposes the paragraph beginning 'But that this pleasure' which Burney duly incorporated. The letter is dated 'Ashburn [Ashbourne] Augst. 28, 1784'.

'He found their Majesties together, without any attendants or any state, in the library; where he presented both to the King and to the Queen a copy of his Commemoration.

'They had the appearance of being in a serene *tête à tête*, that bore every mark of frank and cheerful intercourse. His reception was most gracious; and they both seemed eager to look at his offerings, which they instantly opened and examined.

'"You have made, Dr. Burney", said his Majesty, "a much more considerable book of this Commemoration than I had expected; or, perhaps, than you had expected yourself?"

'"Yes, Sire," he answered; "the subject grew upon me as I proceeded, and a continual accumulation of materials rendered it almost daily more interesting."

'His Majesty then detailed his opinion of the various performers; and said that one thing only had discredited the business, and that was the inharmonious manner in which one of the bass singers had sung his part; which had really been more like a man groaning in a fit of the cholic, than singing an air.

'The Doctor laughingly agreed that such sort of execution certainly more resembled a convulsive noise, proceeding from some one in torture, than any species of harmony; and that, therefore, as he could not speak of that singer favourably in his account, he had been wholly silent on his subject; as had been his practice in other similar instances.

'The Queen seemed perfectly to understand, and much to approve, the motive for this mild method of treating want of abilities and powers to please, where the will was good, and where the labour had been gratuitous.

'The King expressed much admiration that the full *fortes* of so vast a band, in accompanying the singers, had never been too loud, even for a single voice; when it might so naturally have been expected that the accompaniments even of the softest pianos, in such plenitude, would have been overpowering to all vocal solos. He had talked, he said, both with musical people and with philosophers upon the subject; but none of them could assign a reason, or account for so astonishing a fact. . . .

'The Doctor then begged permission to return his most humble thanks to his Majesty, for the hints with which the work had been honoured during its compilation. The King bowed; and their Majesties both re-opened their books to look at the engravings; when the King, remarking to several of them the signature of E. F. Burney, said: "All your family are geniuses, Dr. Burney. Your daughter. . . ."'[1]

But what Their Majesties thought about 'Your daughter' must stand over for another page.

As already stated, this new book of Burney's appeared in 1785. Its publisher was Thomas Payne, who was a month or two later to become James Burney's father-in-law (the name Robinson, of Paternoster Row, also appears on the title page). It was a largish quarto. The same year an octavo edition appeared in Dublin, where a good deal of music

[1] *Mem.* iii. 17–19.

publishing went on in those days (aided by the fact that no copyright law existed between the two countries, so that English publications like this could be safely pirated), and where there still remained, no doubt, a rather special interest in the composer, who had spent some time there and there first performed his *Messiah*. Grattan Flood says that the publisher was that strange creature, Luke White, who soon after became a lottery broker and developed into a millionaire, an M.P., and finally into 'the founder of the Annaly peerage'.[1]

There was also a German edition—*Nachricht von Händels Lebensumständen und der zu ihm in London . . . angestellten Gedächtnissfeyer*. The translator was Eschenburg and the book was published in 1785 in Berlin and Stettin.

When Lord Sandwich was pressing Burney to push on the publication of the book he also 'entered into correspondence with the Doctor, relative to future anniversary concerts upon a similar plan, though on a considerably lessened scale'. Such further commemorations of Handel (not always on 'a lessened scale', by any means) took place in the three following years, 1785–6–7, and then in 1791, and at the last of these the performers are actually recorded as numbering 1,068 (though, according to W. H. Husk, in Grove's *Dictionary*, s.v. 'Handel Commemoration', they probably did not all appear together in any one performance). Then, in 1834, there was another such festival[2] and this was made the occasion, twenty years after Burney's death, for a reprint of his work (8vo; copy in the British Museum).

It is said that of the first (1785) edition of Burney's book 'one copy was liberally presented to every musician who had assisted on that splendid occasion'.[3]

There is a curious little point concerning one of the engravings of the book—the one picturing Handel's monument in the Abbey (see pl. 32, II. 67). The actual monument gives the date of Handel's death as 'April XIV, MDCCLIX', but Burney had had this altered in his plate to 'Good Friday, April XIII, MDCCLIX' so giving the impression that the date thus stands on the monument itself.

In his text (p. 31) he refers to this date as having been given him by Dr. Warren, who attended Handel in his last illness (and who was also

[1] But *D.N.B.* says that Judge John Gore was the first Baron Annaly (1766). I leave this unimportant question undetermined. As regards the Irish pirating of English publications, Dr. R. W. Chapman, in the chapter, 'Authors and Publishers', in *Johnson's England* (1933), 313, says: 'Throughout the period any book likely to be saleable was immediately, and as a matter of course, reprinted in Dublin. The practice was sometimes complained of, but was generally regarded as respectable. When Johnson in 1773 published a revised edition of his *Dictionary* a reprint of it was issued in Dublin by subscription, and one of the subscribers was Johnson's friend, Edmond Malone.' Similarly, at this period, a book published in Paris was frequently reprinted immediately in Geneva, Neuchâtel, or Amsterdam, &c.

[2] There was an attempt to continue the festivals after this, but bigotry stopped it. In 1836 the Duke of Newcastle brought up in the House of Lords the question of 'desecration' of the Abbey and the Bishop of London put his foot down (see Schoelcher, *Handel*, 351).

[3] Busby, *Concert Room and Orchestra Anecdotes*, 1825, ii. 55.

a personal friend of his own[1]). He speaks of the 'April XIV' date as 'at first erroneously engraved on his monument'. But the date he treats as erroneous is *still* to be seen there, and, as a matter of fact, has now long been accepted as correct.[2]

The point is unimportant except for the facts, (*a*) that many people, from what we may call a good sentimental reason, like to think that Handel's wish (expressed to Burney's friend, Warren) to die on Good Friday, was duly fulfilled, and are therefore inclined, unless put right, to carry on the tradition; and (*b*) that Burney has been severely blamed for consciously 'circulating a misrepresentation', on the ground that his words '*at first* erroneously engraved' imply that the monument's date was later altered.[3] Rockstro, in his still standard *Life of Handel* (1883; p. 362), fairly meets this last charge against Burney:

> 'Burney was a thorough gentleman, and therefore incapable of falsifying anything. Moreover, the falsification of an existing inscription, openly exposed to the public, would be absurd. Is there, then, any difficulty in accepting the theory that he recommended the Dean and Chapter to correct the date which he supposed to have been "at first erroneously engraved" on the monument; and published his engraving in the expectation that it would be altered accordingly?'[4]

An odd little echo of these Handel Festivals of the 1780's crops up in *The Torrington Diaries*. In 1789 Torrington, on one of his tours, rode into the little Derbyshire market town of Dronfield, where, after having 'procur'd some slices of fried gammon of bacon and eggs and being refresh'd', he 'sought the key of the church', and heard, to his surprise, that Dronfield could rise to oratorio:

> 'The clerk's wife said "There would be a *Rory Tory* in a few days, and the Sheffield men to sing it".—For since the fame of the abbey musick, the country has gone wild in its imitations: which indeed may be of use, as drawing people to see the inside of churches.'[5]

So did the influence of the grand Commemoration that our Burney

[1] See *Early Diary*, ii. 308.

[2] The question of the day of Handel's death was at last settled, in 1861, by the publication of *The Autobiography and Correspondence of Mary Granville, afterwards Mrs. Delany* (edited by Lady Llanover; 6 vols.), which contains a letter written to her brother, Bernard Granville, by a friend of Handel's and his, giving all particulars of the event.

[3] See Grove's *Dictionary*, article 'Handel Commemoration' (the charge is to be found in all the four editions of the *Dictionary* that have appeared to date, i.e. to the one of the year 1940).

[4] It is odd that Victor Schoelcher, *Life of Handel* (1857), p. 348, speaks of the date as having originally appeared on the monument as April XIV and as now appearing as 'Good Friday April XIII'. He says, 'Since they changed the day of his death in order to be correct they ought now to change the year of his birth'. Probably Burney's book led him into thinking that the change had been made, and, though living for twenty years in England and studying Handelian matters all the time, he never looked carefully at the inscription on the monument.

[5] *The Torrington Diaries containing the Tours through England and Wales of the Hon. John Byng (later Viscount Torrington)*, ed. C. Bruyn Andrews, 2 vols. (1930). The passage quoted is at ii. 26.

had helped to promote spread to out-of-the-way, and even tiny, centres of population.

Let us close lyrically these memories of a novel and notable artistic effort. An anonymous bard published in 1786, as a shilling pamphlet, *The Commemoration of Handel—a Poem.* A third of a century later a second edition revealed his identity as that of the sturdy and untiring warrior for the cause of Jenner and Vaccination, John Ring, whom we thus find to have been a musical as well as a medical man. It is but a tiny portion of his eloquent versification for which space can here be found:

In those fam'd walls which Thames is wont to lave
With winding stream and with translucent wave,
Where commerce dwells, and Freedom's bounty springs,
The seat of Empire, the delight of kings;
Behold assembl'd an illustrious band,
The chiefs in harmony from ev'ry land!
Fir'd at the name, they lend no venal aid
To pay due honors to their Handel's shade.

. . . . .

The vocal bands of high-resounding fame
Rank first, and as of right precedence claim.
Their various aid unnumber'd leaders bring,
Skill'd in the tones of ev'ry tuneful string.
These duly rang'd in splendid rows beneath,
Soft flutes above delightful murmurs breathe;
There hautboy sweet and clarion shrill is found,
There solemn base, and warlike trumpets sound.
On either hand the drum salutes our ears,
Like thunder rolling through the distant spheres;
To crown the whole the wondrous organ tow'rs,
Matchless alike in stature as in pow'rs.

. . . . .

What other age, what other happy land
Could boast so num'rous or so choice a band?
Here no mean parts, no common talents meet,
But ev'ry tuneful excellence we greet;
Unbrib'd, unsought from ev'ry shore they came
To raise bright trophies to their Handel's name.

XLVI. BURNEY AND THE BURGLARS

(*1785; Burney aged 59*)

In the year following the great Handel Commemoration the house in St. Martin's Street suffered a burglary by which Burney was a serious loser. Fanny's account of this affair is exciting:

'Early one morning, and before he was risen, Mrs. Burney's maid, rushing vehemently into the bedroom, screamed out: "Oh, Sir! Robbers! Robbers! the house is broke open!"

'A wrapping gown and slippers brought the Doctor down stairs in a moment; when he found that the bureau of Mrs. Burney, in the dining parlour, had been forced open; and saw upon the table three packets of mingled gold and silver, which seemed to have been put into three divisions for a triple booty; but which were left, it was supposed, upon some sudden alarm, while the robbers were in the act of distribution.

'After securing and rejoicing in what so fortunately had been saved from seizure, Dr. Burney repaired to his study; but no abandoned pillage met his gratulations there! his own bureau had been visited with equal rapacity, though left with less precipitancy; and he soon discovered that he had been purloined of upwards of £300.

'He sent instantly for an officer of the Police, who unhesitatingly pronounced that the leader, at least, of the burglary, must have been a former domestic; this was decided, from remarking that he had gone straight forward to the two bureaus, which were the only depositories of money; while sundry cabinets and commodes, to the right and to the left, had been passed unransacked.

'The entrance into the house had been effected through the area; and a kitchen window was still open, at the foot of which, upon the sand on the floor, the print of a man's shoe was so perfect, that the police-officer drew its circumference with great exactitude; picking up, at the same time, a button that had been squeezed off from a coat, by the forced passage.

'Dr. Burney had recently parted with a man servant of whom he had much reason to think ill, though none had occurred to make him believed a house-breaker. This man was immediately inquired for; but he had quitted the lodgings to which he had retired upon losing his place; and had acquainted no one whither he was gone.

'The officers of the police, however, with their usual ferretting routine of dexterity, soon traced the suspected runaway to Hastings; where he had arrived to embark in a fishing vessel for France; but he had found none ready, and was waiting for a fair wind.

'When the police-officer, having intimation that he was gone to an inn for some refreshment, entered the kitchen where he was taking some bread and cheese, he got up so softly, while the officer, not to alarm him, had turned round to give some directions to a waiter, that he slid unheard out of the kitchen by an opposite door: and, quickly as the officer missed him, he was sought for in vain; not a trace of his footsteps was to be seen; though the inward guilt manifested by such an evasion redoubled the vigilance of pursuit.

'The fugitive was soon, however, discerned, on the top of a high brick wall, running along its edge in the midst of the most frightful danger, with a courage that, in any better cause, would have been worthy of admiration.

'The policeman, now, composedly left him to his race and his defeat; satisfied that no asylum awaited him at the end of the wall, and that he must thence drop, without further resistance, into captivity.

'Cruel for Dr. Burney is what remains of this narration: the runaway was seized, and brought to the public office, where a true bill was found for his trial, as he could give no reason for his flight; and as the button picked up in the area exactly suited a wanting one in a coat discovered to be in his possession. His shoe, also, precisely fitted the drawing on the kitchen floor. But though this circumstantial evidence was so strong as to bring all the magistrates a conviction of his guilt that they scrupled not to avow, it was only circumstantial; it was not positive. He had taken nothing but cash; a single bank note might have been brought home to him with proof; but to coin, who could swear? The magistrates, therefore, were compelled to discharge, though they would not utter the word acquit, the prisoner; and the Doctor had the mortification to witness in the court the repayment of upwards of fifty guineas to the felon, that had been found on him at Hastings. The rest of the three hundred pounds must have been secured by the accomplices; or buried in some place of concealment.

'But Dr. Burney, however aggrieved and injured by this affair, was always foremost to subscribe to the liberal maxim of the law, that it is better to acquit ten criminals, than to condemn one innocent man. He resigned himself, therefore, submissively, however little pleased, to the laws of his noble country, ever ready to consider, like Pope,

"All partial evil universal good".'[1]

All the above was written by Fanny in old age, nearly half a century after the event, but we may suppose that she had in her diary a contemporary record of the details upon which she drew.[2]

After this account of the burglary she asks a rhetorical question, as a preliminary to revealing at last a well-kept family secret—'Would it be just, could it be right, to leave unqualified to the grief of his friends, and to the rage of the murmurers against destiny, a blight such as this to the industry and welfare of Dr. Burney; and not seek to soften the concern of the kind, and not aim at mitigating the asperity of the declaimers, by opening a fairer point of view for the termination of this event, if fact and fair reality can supply colours for so revivifying a change of scenery?' And to this rather ponderously expressed question she herself gives the answer (one with which, our curiosity thus aroused, we must all agree): 'Surely such a retention, if not exacted by discretion or delicacy, would be graceless. A secret, therefore, of more than forty-

[1] *Mem.* iii. 28 et seq.

[2] It is not included in the printed version of the diary, in which there are many gaps caused by her ruthless deletions.

seven years' standing, and known at this moment to no living being but this Memorialist, ought now, in honour, in justice, and in gratitude, to be laid open to the surviving friends of Dr. Burney':

'About a month after this treacherous depredation had filled the Doctor and his house with dismay, a lady of high rank, fortune, and independence, well known in the family, mysteriously summoned this Memorialist to a private room, for a *tête à tête*, in St. Martin's-Street.

'As soon as they were alone, she scrutinizingly examined that no one was within hearing on the other side of either of the doors leading into the apartment; and then solemnly said that she came to demand a little secret service.

'The Memorialist protested herself most ready to meet her request; but that was insufficient: the lady insisted upon a formal and positive promise, that what she should ask should be done; yet that her name in the transaction should never be divulged.

'There seemed something so little reasonable in a desire for so unqualified an engagement upon a subject unknown, that the Memorialist, disturbed, hesitated and hung back.

'The lady was palpably hurt; and dropping a low curtsey, with a supercilious half smile, and a brief, but civil, "Good morrow, ma'am," was proudly stalking out of the room; when, shocked to offend her, the Memorialist besought her patience; and then frankly asked, how she could promise what she was in the dark whether she could perform?

'The lady, unbending her furrowed brow, replied, "I'll tell you how, ma'am: you must either say, I believe you to be an honest woman, and I'll trust you; or, I believe you to be no better than you should be, and I'll have nothing to do with you."

'An alternative such as this could hardly be called an alternative: the promise was given.

'The smile now of pleasure, almost of triumph, that succeeded to that of satire, which had almost amounted to scorn, nearly recompenced the hazarded trust; which, soon afterwards, was even more than repaid by the sincerest admiration.

'The lady, taking a thick letter-case from a capacious and well-furnished part of the female habiliment of other days, yclept a pocket, produced a small parcel, and said, "Do me the favour, Ma'am, to slip this trifle into the Doctor's bureau the first time you see him open it; and just say, 'Sir, this is bank notes for three hundred pounds, instead of what that rogue robbed you of. But you must ask no questions; and you must not stare, Sir, for it's from a friend that will never be known. So don't be over curious; for it's a friend who will never take it back, if you fret yourself to the bone. So please, Sir, to do what you please with it. Either use it, or put it behind the fire, whichever you think the most sensible.' And then, if he should say, 'Pray, Miss, who gave you that impertinent message for me?' you will get into no jeopardy, for you can answer that you are bound head and foot to hold your tongue; and then being a man of honour, he will hold his. Don't you think so, Ma'am?"

'The Memorialist, heartily laughing, but in great perturbation lest the

Doctor should be hurt or displeased, would fain have resisted this commission; but the lady, peremptorily saying a promise was a promise, which no person under a vagabond; but more especially a person of honour, writing books, could break, would listen to no appeal.

'She had been, she said, on the point of *non compos* ever since that rogue had played the Doctor such a knavish trick, as picking his bureau to get at his cash; in thinking how much richer she, who had neither child nor chick, nor any particular great talents, was than she ought to be; while a man who was so much greater a scholar, and with such a fry of young ones at his heels, all of them such a set of geniuses, was suddenly made so much poorer, for no offence, only that rogue's knavishness. And she could not get back into her right senses upon the accident, she said, till she had hit upon this scheme: for knowing Dr. Burney to be a very punctilious man, like most of the book-writers, who were always rather odd, she was aware she could not make him accept such a thing in a quiet way, however it might be his due in conscience; only by some cunning device that he could not get the better of.

'Expostulation was vain; and the matter was arranged exactly according to her injunctions.'

Happily the time was to come when 'the Memorialist', as Fanny always calls herself, was able to obtain permission to divulge her secret to her father. The mysterious lady 'without child or chick', who acted under the stress of such generous feelings to the 'scholar with such a fry of young ones at his heels', was Lady Mary Duncan, a lady 'whose solid worth and faithful friendship compensated for manners the most uncouth, and language the most unpolished'; this lady employed an 'uncultivated, ungrammatical, and incoherent dialect', exhibited a 'comic but arbitrary manner', and 'constantly dressed according to the fashion of her early days, in a hoop with a long-pointed stomacher and long-pointed ruffles, and fly cap', but was a paragon of 'generosity, spirit, and good humour', expressing in practical ways the promptings of a mind 'munificent and nobly liberal'. She was a daughter of the Earl of Thanet, the widow of an eminent London physician, Sir William Duncan, Bt., and the aunt of Admiral Duncan (after the famous victory of 1797, Viscount Camperdown). She exceeded even the Burneys in an admiration for Pacchierotti and she remained a warm friend of Fanny and her father to her dying day, her country house being one of the many at which Burney in his later years used happily to pass a little time.[1]

[1] For her Pacchierotti mania see Horace Walpole's letter to Mason of 3 Jan. 1782. He says: 'There is a nightingale-woman, I am told, called the Allegranti, who sings so sweetly that Lady Mary Duncan and Lady Mount-Edgcumbe turn their backs when she warbles, because you know people only hear with their faces, and nothing is fit to be heard but Pacchierotti. As I have no ear but in my eyes I shall go to see this Philomel.' (See also letter of 4–7 July 1791.) There can be no doubt that Pacchierotti was one of the most innately artistic, as well as one of the most accomplished, singers, who has ever appeared. For a good description of him, as musician and man, see Burney's friend, Rev. Thomas Twining (*Recreations and Studies of a Country Clergyman*, 75 et seq.).

XLVII. THE BURNEYS AMONGST THE BLUESTOCKINGS

(*The 1780's and 1790's; Burney in his fifties and sixties and Fanny in her thirties and forties*)

DURING the 1780's and 1790's Burney and his daughter Fanny were much amongst that 'Bluestocking community' that grew into existence as a protest against the current attitude of, and towards, woman—then regarded as a pet, a plaything, or a domestic ornament rather than as a rational creature of intellectual capacity. They are frequently found at 'the blue assemblages in town of Mrs. Montagu and Mrs. Vesey'[1] and at other 'blue assemblages' also. It is probable that the connexion between the Burneys and the Blues began through their meeting Mrs. Montagu at the Thrales, where she was frequently to be found.

The application of the word 'Bluestocking', or 'Bas Bleu', to these parties where leaders in the worlds of fashion and of literature were brought together for serious conversation, to the exclusion of card-playing and frivolity, began, it appears, with MRS. VESEY. Fanny gives an explanation of the name. She connects it (and the connexion is generally accepted) with a detail of the dress of the naturalist and general man of letters, Benjamin Stillingfleet.

Stillingfleet had practised as a medical man in King's Lynn and had been connected by friendship with the Windham family at Felbrig. He was an amateur of the violoncello and wrote an anonymous work on *The Principles and Power of Harmony* (see II. 383), which was later to be highly praised and minutely analysed by Burney in Rees's *Cyclopaedia*. It is, then, quite possible, and indeed almost certain, that the Burneys knew Stillingfleet himself, and although he died rather before they began to be gradually drawn into the London Bluestocking coterie, it is likely enough that they heard from him of the origin of the term 'Bluestocking', as so applied. It must be premised, before giving the relevant quotation from Fanny, that Stillingfleet ('always happy, always cheerful and seems to me a worthy honest man', reports the poet Gray) was poor to the point of lodging in a garret and dressing with great simplicity. Fanny says that the Bluestocking community:

'Owed its name to an apology made by Mr. Stillingfleet, in declining to accept an invitation to a literary meeting at Mrs. Vesey's, from not being, he said, in the habit of displaying a proper equipment for an evening assembly. "Pho, pho," cried she, with her well-known, yet always original simplicity, while she looked inquisitively at him and his accoutrements; "don't mind dress! Come in your blue stockings!" With which words,

[1] *Mem.* ii. 74.

humourously repeating them as he entered the apartment of the chosen coterie, Mr. Stillingfleet claimed permission for appearing, according to order. And those words, ever after, were fixed, in playful stigma, upon Mrs. Vesey's associations.'[1]

Mrs. Vesey, an Irishwoman, 'well-bred and of agreeable manners', but at times amusingly informal and apt, by lapse of memory, when she opened her mouth to put her foot in it, is always reckoned to be not only the originator of the name but also the founder of the English Bluestocking movement. She adroitly managed to create an unofficial connexion between her parties and the Literary Club (see II. 49), of which her husband, Agmondesham Vesey, an Irish M.P., was very proud to be a member. After the Club dinners, every other Tuesday, the members used to stroll round to her house in Bolton Row (later in Clarges Street), to join the 'Blue' party there arranged for the same evening.

One peculiarity of Mrs. Vesey's management of her parties is often referred to by her contemporaries. She believed in 'breaking up' the company:

'Her fears were so great of the horror, as it was styled, of a circle, from the ceremony and awe which it produced, that she pushed all the small sofas, as well as chairs, pell-mell about the apartments, so as not to leave even a zig-zag path of communication free from impediment: and her greatest delight was to place the seats back to back, so that those who occupied them could perceive no more of their nearest neighbour than if the parties had been sent into different rooms: an arrangement that could only be eluded by such a twisting of the neck as to threaten the interlocutors with a spasmodic affection.'[2]

This anti-geometrical insistence of Mrs. Vesey is alluded to in Hannah More's long, smooth-rhymed poem, *The Bas Bleus; or Conversation*:

See Vesey's plastic genius make
A Circle every figure take;
Nay, shapes and forms which would defy
All science of Geometry;
Isosceles and Parallel,
Names hard to speak and hard to spell.

[1] *Mem.* ii. 262. Fanny's account must not be misunderstood. The actual term 'Blue-stocking' is older than the period here in question, and seems somehow to have originated long before in France, or possibly in Italy, in a somewhat similar connotation (see various books of reference and also Timb's *History of Clubs*, 1872, p. 169). But it was the Stillingfleet incident that led to this already existing term being humorously transferred to the Vesey and similar social gatherings and so acquiring the precise sense it bears to-day in English speech.

Boswell pretty well confirms Fanny's account of the matter: 'One of the most eminent members of these societies when they first commenced was Mr. Stillingfleet, whose dress was remarkable, grave and, in particular, it was observed that he wore blue stockings. Such was the excellence of his conversation that his absence was felt as so great a loss that it used to be said, "We can do nothing without the *blue stockings*" and thus by degrees the title was established.'

[2] *Mem.* ii. 264.

Th' enchantress wav'd her wand, and spoke!
Her potent wand the Circle broke;
The social Spirits hover round,
And bless the liberated ground.
Ask you what charms this gift dispense?
'Tis the strong spell of Common Sense.

By the time the Burneys became Bluestockings Mrs. Vesey had become not only very 'wrinkled, sallow and time-beaten' but also very deaf. Fanny describes her as rushing about the room, wherever she saw going on what she thought must be interesting conversation, with 'two, three or more ear-trumpets hanging to her wrist and slung about her neck', trying them in turn upon the various speakers and sometimes in her haste to miss nothing, putting the wrong end of the trumpet to her ear.[1]

At her gatherings, however, though you might be amused at your hostess, you could not but feel admiration for the skill with which she had skimmed the very cream off English intellectual society—leading statesmen, writers, painters, and actors, together with the most widely read and clear-thinking women of the day. She herself might be able to hear little of the conversation but those who did hear it went away inspired and enlightened.

At least equal in importance to the gatherings of Mrs. Vesey were those of MRS. MONTAGU (see pl. 33, II. 86). By the time that the Burneys joined the Blue group she was, apparently, occupying her fine new house in Portman Square—'a superb new house', as Fanny tells us, one 'which was magnificently fitted up and appeared to be rather appropriate for princes, nobles, and courtiers, than for poets, philosophers, and blue-stocking votaries'. In 1791 Mrs. Montagu received George III and his Queen there. One feature of the house was the 'Feather Room' (so large that on one occasion she entertained in it 700 to breakfast); its walls were hung with every species of feather (a most dust-collecting, and hence insanitary, species of decoration, as we should nowadays think). This room is commemorated in the poem of Cowper beginning:

The birds put off their every hue
To dress a room for Montagu.

Mrs. Montagu's arrangement of her guests was as formal and geometrical as Mrs. Vesey's was haphazard or, rather, deliberately asymmetrical:

'At Mrs. Montagu's, the semi-circle that faced the fire retained during the whole evening its unbroken form, with a precision that made it seem described by a Brobdingnagian compass. The lady of the castle commonly placed herself at the upper end of the room, near the commencement of the curve, so as to be courteously visible to all her guests; having the person of highest rank, or consequence, properly on one side, and the person the most

[1] Ibid. 266.

eminent for talents, sagaciously, on the other; or as near to her chair, and her converse, as her favouring eye, and a complacent bow of the head, could invite him to that distinction.'[1]

It will be realized, then, that whilst Mrs. Vesey's gatherings partook of the nature of a club, with separate conversations everywhere in progress simultaneously, those of Mrs. Montagu were more suggestive of a public meeting directed by a capable chairman. And the chairman's own contributions to discussion were important: 'her conversational powers were of a truly superior order; strong, just, clear, and often eloquent.'[2] Johnson said, 'Mrs. Montagu is a very extraordinary person; she has a constant stream of conversation, and it is always impregnated; it has always meaning'.[3] But he did not think highly of her much lauded book in which she refuted Voltaire's contemptuous opinions on Shakespeare: 'Reynolds is fond of her book, and I wonder at it; for neither I, nor Beauclerk, nor Mrs. Thrale could get through it'[4] (But then Johnson rarely did 'get through' a book—see I. 239).

Mrs. Montagu was really a very formidable personage—very rich, very well-connected, very well-informed, very self-assured. But she had a soft side to her nature and it came out at least once a year—on May Day, when she entertained the chimney-sweeper climbing-boys of London to roast beef and plum pudding on her lawn. Fanny in her *Memoirs* of her father becomes very eloquent on this subject, rising to heights where the use of such a commonplace word as 'chimney-sweep' or even 'boy' could not be tolerated. And those words never *are* uttered throughout the whole page given to the subject; instead we read of 'jetty objects' and 'sooty little agents', and 'those hapless artificers, who perform the most abject offices of any authorized calling, in being the active guardians of our blazing hearths'.

'Not all the lyrics of all the rhymsters, nor all the warblings of all the spring-feathered choristers, could hail the opening smiles of May, like the fragrance of that roasted beef, and the pulpy softness of those puddings of plums, with which Mrs. Montagu yearly renovated those sooty little agents to the safety of our most blessing luxury.'[5]

There is a dreadful secret about Mrs. Montagu that has only lately come out, and that, we may suppose, was never revealed to any Burney. She did not like *Evelina*—or so Mrs. Thrale told Johnson:

[1] *Mem.* ii. 270. [2] Ibid. 271.

[3] Boswell, *Johnson*, s.v. 1784.

[4] Boswell, *Tour to the Hebrides*, under 23 Sept. It is fair to say that Mrs. Thrale, by then Mrs. Piozzi, contradicted this assertion as concerned herself. See Postscript to her *Anecdotes of the Late Samuel Johnson, LL.D.* (1786), included in George Birkbeck Hill's *Johnsonian Miscellanies* (1897), i. 351. (See, however, Jas. L. Clifford's *Hester Lynch Piozzi* (1941), p. 260, for doubts cast on the value of her repudiation.)

[5] *Mem.* ii. 272. It is such a passage as this from poor octogenarian Fanny that almost justifies Macaulay in his allusion to Fanny's later style as 'the worst style that has ever been known among men'. In this annual entertainment Mrs. Montagu anticipated Elia's 'pleasant friend, Jem White', of the essay, 'The Praise of Chimney Sweepers'.

'Mrs. Montagu cannot bear *Evelina*—let not that be published—her Silver-Smiths are Pewterers, she says, & her Captains Boatswains.'[1]

Mrs. Montagu was, of course, not the only reader of *Evelina* who objected to the coarse brutality of Captain Mirvan, but as to the Holborn silversmiths, the Branghtons, some people with quite as much real taste as the refined Mrs. Montagu (Johnson certainly) chuckled over their delightfully natural vulgarity and quoted their phrases with relish.

There were other blue-connoisseurs than Mrs. Vesey and Mrs. Montagu. Fanny mentions 'the HONOURABLE MISS MONCKTON . . . one of those who stand foremost in collecting all extraordinary or curious people to her London conversaziones, which, like those of Mrs. Vesey, mix the rank and the literature and exclude all besides'.[2] At her house in Charles Street, Berkeley Square, she used, says Boswell, to exhibit 'the finest bit of blue'. Miss Monckton (later Countess of Cork) was, when the Burneys first knew her in 1782, 'between thirty and forty, very short, very fat, but handsome; splendidly and fantastically dressed, rouged not unbecomingly, yet evidently and palpably desirous of gaining notice and admiration'. Fanny was pleased when she received her first invitation to one of Miss Monckton's assemblies ('a most perfumed note, on French paper, gilt, bordered, glazed, inclosed in a finely decorated cover, and sealed with a miniken figure'), for, 'though in small parties it is necessary to like the mistress of the house, in large assemblies it is but like going to a better-regulated meeting place'.[3]

Miss Monckton, like Mrs. Vesey, believed in a dispersed disposition of her forces:

'Not merely as fearful of form as Mrs. Vesey was Miss Monckton; she went farther; she frequently left her general guests wholly to themselves. There was always, she knew, good fare for intellectual entertainment; and those who had courage to seek might partake of its advantages; while those who had not that quality, might amuse themselves as lookers on. . . .

'Miss Monckton usually sat about the middle of the room, lounging on one chair, while bending over the back of another, in a thin, fine muslin dress, even at Christmas; while all around her were in satins, or tissues; and without advancing to meet any one, or rising, or placing, or troubling herself to see whether there were any seats left for them, she would turn round her head to the announcement of a name, give a nod, a smile, and a short "How do you do?—" and then, chatting on with her own set, leave them to seek their fortune.'[4]

Fanny tells us, on one occasion:

[1] W. Wright Roberts, *Charles and Fanny Burney in the Light of the new Thrale Correspondence in the John Rylands Library*, 12.

[2] *Diary and Letters*, ii. 123.

[3] Ibid. 130.

[4] Ibid. 134.

'Some new people now coming in, and placing themselves in a regular way, Miss Monckton exclaimed—"My whole care is to prevent a circle"; and hastily rising, she pulled about the chairs, and planted the people in groups, with as dexterous a disorder as you would desire to see.'[1]

Then there was MRS. CHAPONE (see pl. 33, opposite), authoress of *Letters on the Improvement of the Mind* (dedicated to Mrs. Montagu, by the way), and consequently an educational authority. There is an allusion to this useful treatise in Sheridan's *The Rivals*, where Lydia hears her aunt and Sir Anthony Absolute coming up to her room and hastily prepares to receive them: 'Fling *Peregrine Pickle* under the toilet; throw *Roderick Random* into the closet . . . now lay Mrs. Chapone in sight and leave Fordyce's Sermons open on the table.'

Mrs. Chapone was accomplished but not rich, and lived in the relatively unfashionable Dean Street, Soho. And, as she suffered from a 'palpable and organic deficiency in health and strength', she could not make her parties gay—they 'always wanted spirit, a want which cast over them a damp that made the same interlocutors who elsewhere grouped audiences around them from their fame as discoursers appear to be assembled here merely for the grand purpose of performing a duty'.

The Burneys, though they attended Mrs. Chapone's Blue parties, preferred her when she was to be found in a more private and intimate character. 'Her sound understanding, her sagacious observation, her turn to humour, and the candour of her affectionate nature, all then came into play without effort. It was thus that she struck Dr. Burney with the sense of her worth.'[2] As for Fanny, she described Mrs. Chapone as 'the most superiorly unaffected creature you can conceive, and full of *agrémens* from good sense, talent, and conversational powers, in defiance of age, infirmities, and uncommon ugliness', and added 'I really love as well as admire and esteem her'.[3]

It wàs Mrs. Chapone who introduced Fanny to Mrs. Delany (see Ch. XL), and so diverted the current of her life into a new channel in which it flowed for several years. It was Mrs. Chapone, also, who brought about a meeting between Fanny and the learned, active, and useful MRS. BARBAULD, poet, prose-writer, editor of the British Novelists and, as Fanny reminds us,[4] 'the authoress of the most useful books next to Mrs. Trimmer's, that have been yet written for dear little children'. In this last department Mrs. Barbauld was, with her brother, Dr. Aikin, a good deal of a pioneer (the present writer, as a 'dear little child', read and re-read the *Evenings at Home*, a full set of which happily came down his family as far as his own generation). Mrs. Barbauld, despite her being the wife of 'a dissenting minister' (and the Burneys were not

[1] *Diary and Letters*, ii. 134. A most vivid description of one of Miss Monckton's parties is there given.

[2] *Mem.* ii. 284.

[3] *Diary and Letters*, ii. 239.

[4] Ibid. v. 419.

MRS. MONTAGU

Vhom Johnson spoke of as 'a very extraordinary person' (*see* ii. 81 and 83–5).

ELIZABETH CARTER

Who, Johnson said, could 'make a pudding as well as translate Epictetus' (*see* ii. 88).

HANNAH MORE

these latter days maliciously described as 'a ;e conger-eel in an ocean of dingy morality' (*see* ii. 88 and 89).

HESTER CHAPONE

Called by Fanny Burney, who had a great respect for her, 'the most superiorly unaffected creature whom you can conceive' (*see* ii. 86).

the people to approve of dissent), was much esteemed by Fanny Burney, though she agreed with Mrs. Chapone, that her 'almost set smile' and air of 'determined complacence and prepared acquiescence' were fatiguing. As Mrs. Chapone put it, 'She is a very good young woman, as well as replete with talents; but why must one always smile so? It makes my poor jaws ache to look at her.'

Mrs. Barbauld was neither rich enough nor fashionable enough to be a Blue hostess, but she lived on the fringe of the blue-tinted country of the social man. Johnson, according to Burney, once made to Burney some sneering remarks about Mrs. Barbauld. She had, he said, been a child prodigy of learning, and in what had it resulted—'In marrying a little presbyterian parson, who keeps an infant boarding school.' But that was petty and unfair, and if the remark was made in the presence of Fanny Burney we may believe that she told him so. In 1788, when the Court was at Cheltenham, Fanny had the pleasure of introducing Mrs. Barbauld to 'the good and dear King'.

Another Bluestocking circle was that of 'MRS.' REYNOLDS (the unmarried sister of Sir Joshua). She had written an *Essay on Taste* which she submitted to the criticism of her friend Johnson, who said that 'her notions, though manifesting a depth of penetration and a nicety of remark such as Locke or Pascal might be proud of, must everywhere be rendered smoother and plainer' (if it was to be published, that is—but it never was). He doubted whether her ideas were 'very clear even to her own mind'.

There was an 'excessive oddness and absurdity' about Mrs. Reynolds; she was always doing something strange and, when she realized it, being overcome with shame.[1]

It was at Mrs. Reynolds's that Fanny first met Dr. Percy, Bishop of Dromore and 'collector and editor of the beautiful reliques of ancient English poetry', and it was she whom Johnson introduced in his disrespectful extempore parody of the ballad style that Percy admired more than he:

> I therefore pray thee, Renny dear,
> That thou wilt give to me,
> With cream and sugar softened well,
> Another dish of tea.

Mrs. Reynolds was a frequent visitor of the Burneys in their St. Martin's Street days, and though she lived 'in an habitual perplexity of mind and irresolution of conduct which to herself was restlessly tormenting and to all around her teazingly wearisome', they esteemed her highly for 'her many excellent qualities'. As already mentioned (I. 2 70–1), Mrs. Reynolds once painted Burney's portrait.

Amongst other notable Bluestocking women with whom Fanny and

[1] Ibid. ii. 164. There are some amusing anecdotes of 'Mrs.' Reynolds there.

her father forgathered were Mrs. Carter, Hannah More, Mrs. Ord, Mrs. Boscawen, and Mrs. Gregory.

ELIZABETH CARTER (see pl. 33, II. 86; her 'Mrs.', too, was but a brevet rank) is the lady of whom Johnson so warmly approved: the highest praise that he could give a certain scholar was that 'he understood Greek better than anyone whom he had ever known except Elizabeth Carter'.[1] But his commendation went farther than that. Upon hearing another lady praised for her learning he said:

'A man is in general better pleased when he has a good dinner upon his table than when his wife talks Greek. My old friend, Mrs. Carter, could make a pudding as well as translate Epictetus.'[2]

At the Essex Head Club once: 'He told us, "I dined yesterday at Mrs. Garrick's with Mrs. Carter, Miss Hannah More and Miss Fanny Burney. Three such women are not to be found".'[3]

Poor Mrs. Carter all her life suffered from frequent and severe headaches as a result of her youthful study of Latin, Greek, and Hebrew, and all her life she was addicted to snuff-taking, from a habit early contracted 'of taking snuff . . . in order to keep herself awake during her studies, which she frequently protracted during great part of the night, and was afterwards unable to give up the custom, though it was very disagreeable to her father'. (Her biographer adds a footnote: 'Besides the taking snuff, she owned that she used to bind a wet towel round her head, put a wet cloth to the pit of her stomach, and chew green tea and coffee. To oblige her father, she endeavoured to conquer the habit of taking snuff, and would not resume it without his consent. This he at length reluctantly gave, finding how much she suffered from the want of it.')

She was a musician and 'played both on the spinnet and German flute, and certainly took some pains to acquire this accomplishment, as there is a great deal of music for both instruments in her own hand writing'.[4]

Mrs. Montagu, in 1775, settled an annuity of £100 upon her friend Mrs. Carter. Fanny could say of her, 'I never saw age so graceful in the female sex yet, her whole face seems to beam with goodness, piety and philanthropy',[5] and as for Fanny's father:

'The Doctor truly revered in Mrs. Carter the rare union of humility with learning, and of piety with cheerfulness. He frequently, and always with pleasure, conveyed her to or from her home, when they visited the same parties; and always enjoyed those opportunities in comparing notes with her on such topics as were not light enough for the large or mixed companies which they were just seeking or had just left: topics, however, which they

[1] Montagu Pennington, *Memoirs of the Life of Mrs. Elizabeth Carter* (1807), 9.

[2] Sir John Hawkins's edition of Johnson's *Works* (1787), xi. 205. The translation of Epictetus was published in 1758.

[3] Boswell, 15 May 1784.

[4] Pennington, op. cit. 7.

[5] *Diary and Letters*, i. 391.

always treated with simplicity; for Mrs. Carter, though natively more serious and habitually more studious than Dr. Burney, was as free from pedantry as himself.'[1]

HANNAH MORE (see pl. 33, II. 86) is, of course, well remembered to-day. The Burneys must have seen a good deal of her at the house of their friends the Garricks, with whom she used to stay for months at a time—though in the later period of her long life she drifted into the very different orbit of the evangelical and philanthropic Wilberforce.

When Fanny was appointed to Court (we shall hear all about this shortly), Hannah More was one of those who welcomed the announcement: 'It was the very joy of my heart, on seeing the other day in the papers that our charming Miss Burney has got an establishment so near the Queen. How I love the queen for having so wisely chosen'.[2] (And the Queen evidently approved of Miss More, also, for she lent Fanny her valuable moral work, which had just appeared, 1788, *Thoughts on the Importance of the Manners of the Great to General Society*.[3]) But when Fanny's health suffered under the confinement at Court Miss More was one of those who 'expressed the most flattering solicitude'.

Fanny's pamphlet on behalf of the French clergy (to be discussed on a later page) seems to have been anticipated by one of Hannah More's, likewise addressed to 'the Ladies of Great Britain'.[4]

Miss More gives a distressing account of her experience at one of the 'Blue' gatherings:

'The other evening they carried me to Mrs. Ord's assembly; I was quite dressed for the purpose. Mrs. Garrick gave me an elegant cap, and put it on herself; so that I was quite sure of being smart: but how short-lived is all human joy! and see what it is to live in the country! When I came into the drawing-rooms, I found them full of company, every human creature in deep mourning, and I, poor I, all gorgeous in scarlet. I never recollected

[1] *Mem.* iii. 341. Mrs. Carter was something of a poet, too, and Richardson, in *Clarissa*, inserted her 'Ode to Wisdom' so that his heroine might 'set part of it to her harpsichord' (whatever that may mean).

[2] William Roberts, *Memoirs of the Life and Correspondence of Mrs. Hannah More* (2nd ed. 1834), ii. 42; also George Birkbeck Hill, *Johnsonian Miscellanies* (1897), ii. 191.

[3] Roberts, op. cit. ii. 359. Let us hope that the volume the Queen lent to Fanny did her good. Here is what Augustine Birrell says in his *Men, Women, and Books*: 'The celebrated Mrs. Hannah More is one of the most detestable writers that ever held a pen. She flounders like a huge conger-eel in an ocean of dingy morality. She may have been a wit in her youth, though I am not aware of any evidence of it—certainly her poem, "Bas Bleu", is none—but for all the rest of her days, and they were many, she was an encyclopaedia of all literary vices. You may search her nineteen volumes through without lighting upon one original thought, one happy phrase. Her religion lacks reality. Not a single expression of genuine piety, of heart-felt emotion, ever escapes her lips. She is never pathetic, never terrible. Her creed is powerless either to attract the well-disposed or make the guilty tremble. No naughty child ever read "The Fairchild Family" or "Stories from the Church Catechism" without quaking and quivering like a short-haired puppy after a ducking; but, then, Mrs. Sherwood was a woman of genius, whilst Mrs. Hannah More was a pompous failure.' One may reasonably ask, perhaps, whether Birrell had himself read those 'nineteen volumes through', and it may be recalled that the lady so roundly condemned enjoyed the respect of many good judges of character, including Garrick.

[4] Roberts, op. cit. ii. 359.

that the mourning for some foreign Wilhelmina Jaquelina was not over. However I got over it as well as I could, made an apology, lamented the *ignorance* in which I had lately lived, and I hope this false step of mine will be buried in oblivion. There was all the old set, the Johnsons, the Burneys, the Chapones, the Thrales, the Smelts, the Pepyses, the Ramsays, and so on ad infinitum. Even Jacobite Johnson was in deep mourning.'[1]

Mrs. Ord was 'a lady of great mental merit, strict principles and dignified manners', who, 'without belonging to what was called the Blues or *Bas Bleu* Society, except as a receiver or visitor',[2] yet 'selected parties from that set to mix with those of other, or of no denomination'. And, according to Burney, the mixing was skilfully done. As he put it (using a metaphor perhaps a little below the dignity of the subject), 'Mrs. Ord is an excellent cook and employs all the refinements of her art in taking care not to put clashing materials into the same mess'. Hers was 'the first coterie into which the Doctor, after his abode in St. Martin's Street, initiated his family; Mrs. Burney as a participator, his daughters as appendages, of what might justly be called a *conversazione*'; and on leaving the house at the end of the first visit he expressed himself to his hostess in the true Blue spirit:

'"I rejoice Madam," he said, "to find that there are still two or three houses, even in these dissipated times, where, through judgment and taste in their selection, people may be called together, not with the aid of cards, to kill time, but with that of conversation, to give it life."'[3]

We have already noted some variety of practice amongst the Blue hostesses in the arrangement of their company. Mrs. Ord adds to this, for she seems to have adopted a ground plan described as 'not in groups, nor yet in a circle, but seated square, i.e. close to the wainscot, leaving a vacancy in the middle of the apartment sufficient for dancing three or four cotillons'—an arrangement that not a little disconcerted our modest Fanny when, after the publication of *Cecilia*, she was invited there as the lioness of the evening and arrived to find the rest of the guests thus formally placed to receive her and all rising ceremoniously to do so.[4]

It was Mrs. Ord who, when Fanny took up her Windsor appointment, drove her and her father down to Windsor (see II. 96–7). And when the years of confinement in that situation were happily ended it was Mrs. Ord, again, who accompanied Fanny to Bath and the West of England on a four months' tour of recovery, and at last 'delivered the invalid to her family nearly re-established'.[5]

And when in the course of nature Mrs. Ord was gathered to that world where card-playing and frivolity are, we suppose, unpractised, and the protest of an organized Blue Brigade is hence unnecessary, Fanny

[1] Roberts, op. cit. i. 170.

[2] She is the only lady mentioned in the present chapter who has not her niche in the *Dictionary of National Biography*.

[3] All the above quotations come from *Mem.* i. 336–8.

[4] *Mem.* ii. 288.

[5] Ibid. iii. 125.

was able to record that so perfect had been her conduct here below that she might be described as 'one of those few beings whom censure passed by as unimpeachable'.

Apparently, in addition to her actual blue, or conversational parties, Mrs. Ord sometimes gave musical parties, for we hear of Esther and her husband, Charles Rousseau Burney, playing to her guests.[1]

The accomplished Mrs. Boscawen was the widow of the great admiral of that name. She was one of the ladies who kept subscription lists for Fanny's *Camilla* (see II. 134), and when, on its publication, the King and Queen had been given the first and second sets of its volumes, she was presented with the third set, which the King thought very right, as 'Mrs. Boscawen, I hear, has been very zealous'. She admired Burney, that is to say she 'spoke of my dearest father with her usual true sense of how to speak of him', and is consequently extolled as 'dear, good Mrs. Boscawen' and as a lady 'all elegance and good breeding'.[2]

Miss Gregory was the daughter of Dr. John Gregory, author of *A Father's Legacy to his Daughters*. After his death, in 1773, she lived with Mrs. Montagu, until in 1784, 'with the world's approbation though against Mrs. Montagu's',[3] she married the Rev. Archibald Alison, later author of the *Essay on the Nature and Principles of Taste*—a book long famous, but one which frightened Fanny when presented to her, 'for I dread attacking metaphysics, but I have thanked her cordially for her *kind remembrance*'.[4]

Miss Gregory was 'a fine young woman, and seems gentle and well bred', said Fanny on the occasion of one of her early meetings with her, and later she found her to be 'frank, open, shrewd and sensible, and speaks her opinion both of matters and things with a plumpness and honesty and readiness that both pleases and diverts me, and though she now makes it a rule to be my neighbour whenever we meet, she has never made me a hint of a compliment, and that is not nothing as things go'.[5]

And all this, though it does not by any means exhaust the tale of the Bluestockings, is surely enough about them for most readers of the present book.

But there is a poem to reproduce—not a great one, but one which in its day made a social stir. In 1782 we find Fanny Burney writing to her sister, Susan:

[1] *Diary and Letters*, i. 391.

[2] Ibid. v. 292, 341, 404. For a full and attractive account of this lady see Brigadier-General Aspinall-Oglander, *Admiral's Widow: the Life and Letters of the Hon. Mrs. Edward Boscawen, from 1761 to 1805* (1942). There exists in the London of to-day an odd unrecognized relic of the Boscawens. Opposite No. 2 St. James's Square is a lamp-post the base of which has only lately been noticed to be a cannon, mouth upwards. This, it appears, was captured by Admiral Boscawen at the victory over the French off Cape Finisterre in 1747, and presented to his brother, Lord Falmouth, who then lived in the house on this site. (H. V. Morton, *Ghosts of London*, 1939.)

[3] *Diary and Letters*, ii. 283.

[4] Ibid. iv. 351.

[5] Ibid. i. 120, 353.

'Do you know they have put me again into the newspapers, in a copy of verses made upon literary ladies—where are introduced Mrs. Carter, Chapone, Cowley, Hannah More, Mrs. Greville, Mrs. Boscawen, Mrs. Thrale, Mrs. Crewe, Sophy Streatfield, and Mrs. Montagu? In such honourable company, to repine at being placed, would, perhaps, be impertinent; so I take it quietly enough; but I would to Heaven I could keep clear of the whole. However, my dear father is so delighted, that, though he was half afraid of speaking to me at all about them at first, he carries them constantly in his pocket, and reads them to everybody! I have a great suspicion they were written by Mr. Pepys, as they are just what I have heard him say of all the people, and as every creature mentioned in them, but Mrs. Cowley, Greville, and Crewe, were invited to be at his house on the very day they were printed.'[1]

Pepys was a regular habitué of the Blue salons and could well have written it, but denied having done so. Whose was it? In 1822 'a manuscript copy was found, among Dr. Burney's papers, with so many erasures, interlineation, and changes, as to give the most direct internal evidence that it was the doctor's own composition'.[2] Sly dog! He did not tell even his daughters, and his secret was never in his lifetime discovered. The poem is typical of the personal and society matter that newspaper editors were then willing to print. It appeared in the *Morning Herald* for 12 March 1782.

ADVICE TO THE *HERALD*

Herald, wherefore thus proclaim
Nought of woman but the *shame*?
Quit, oh, quit, at least awhile,
Perdita's too luscious smile;
Wanton Worsley, stilted Daly,
Heroines of each blackguard alley;
Better sure record in story
Such as shine their sex's glory!
Herald! haste, with me proclaim
Those of literary fame.
Hannah More's pathetic pen,
Painting high th' impassion'd scene;
Carter's piety and learning,
Little Burney's quick discerning;
Cowley's neatly pointed wit,
Healing those her satires hit;
Smiling Streatfield's iv'ry neck,
Nose, and notions—*à la Grecque*!
Let Chapone retain a place,
And the mother of her Grace,
Each art of conversation knowing,
High-bred, elegant Boscawen;

[1] *Diary and Letters*, ii. 76.

[2] Note by Fanny's niece, Mrs. Barrett, in her edition of the *Diary and Letters* (1842–6).

Thrale, in whose expressive eyes
Sits a soul above disguise,
Skill'd with wit and sense t'impart
Feelings of a generous heart.
Lucan, Leveson, Greville, Crewe;
Fertile-minded Montague,
Who makes each rising art her care,
'And brings her knowledge from afar!'
Whilst her tuneful tongue defends
Authors dead, and absent friends;
Bright in genius, pure in fame:—
Herald, haste, and *these* proclaim!

It would take too much space to elucidate all the personal references in this poem, but a word may be said about that celebrated charmer, Sophie Streatfield. She was a Greek scholar as well as a beauty, and in Burney's couplet about her this is alluded to. But Johnson (who admitted that he 'loved her very much' and that she was 'a sweet creature') is said to have asserted that 'taking away her Greek she was as ignorant as a butterfly'.[1]

The celebrated Sophie appears repeatedly in Fanny Burney's diary, and a good many times in Mrs. Thrale's, too. Here is something from the latter, and note that its date is only a month or two before that of Burney's anonymous poem:

'*Streatham, January 1st, 1782.* Sophy Streatfield has begun the new year nicely with a new conquest. Poor dear Dr. Burney! *he* is now the reigning favourite, and she spares neither pains nor caresses to turn that good man's head, much to the vexation of his family; particularly my Fanny, who is naturally provoked to see sport made of her father in his last stage of life [he had a third of a century still before him!] by a young coquet, whose sole employment in this world seems to have been winning men's hearts on purpose to fling them away. How she contrives to keep bishops, and brewers, and doctors, and directors of the East India Company, all in chains so, and almost all at the same time, would amaze a wiser person than me; I can only say let us mark the end!'[2]

It is in keeping with Burney's association with the Bluestockings that at the period when it was at its height he should have been enrolled amongst the writers of *The Monthly Review*—a journal that for nearly a century (1749–1845) maintained a very high position in the literary world, devoting its pages exclusively to the notices (often very extended) of all the important books that appeared. As may be remembered Burney's friend, Twining, did much of its reviewing of scientific books and now the books on musical subjects were entrusted to Burney himself.

[1] *Diary and Letters*, i. 102, 231.

[2] A. Hayward, *Autobiography, Letters and Literary Remains of Mrs. Piozzi* (1861), and J. H. Lobban, *Dr. Johnson's Mrs. Thrale* (1910), 182. After charming such multitudes of men Sophie died unmarried in 1835.

Burney retained his position on the staff of the *Review* from 1785 to 1802, resigning it only because of his having undertaken another engrossing task. His articles, like others in the same pages, are solid in style and ample in quotation from the works under treatment. They are also frank—even outspoken. He naturally drops heavily on an author who expresses the opinion that Bruce's famous Abyssinian Lyre (see I. 267) was imaginary. Of Thomas Robertson's *Inquiry into the Fine Arts* (1786) he says that the title is inaccurate and should be *An Inquiry into all the Books the Author could find on the Fine Arts*, and of an allusion in this work to Lord Kelly (see I. 119) he declares of his lordship, 'After his return to Britain [from musical study abroad] he was more assiduous in the service of Bacchus than Apollo'. But an author who attacks the famous Handel Festivals (see Ch. XLV) in a pamphlet called *Sense against Sound; or a Succedaneum for Abbey Music* (1788) is treated almost impolitely, the notice opening:

'We used to imagine that Dr. Monro, and his assistant keepers and matrons of Bedlam, took better care of their patients, than to suffer those fit only for a strait waistcoat to be indulged with pen and ink. This is letting them loose upon the public with an instrument in their hands as dangerous as that of the Irish Mohawk in Queen Anne's time, who used to run about the streets in the dusk of the evening, armed with a pen-knife with which he slit the nose of every single passenger he met, crying out when the bloody deed was done, "Arrah, my dear, I beg your pardon, but it's a way I have", and then ran away in pursuit of another victim.'

A good deal has been rightly said about Burney's gift for making and keeping friends, but he was not afraid to make enemies also!

XLVIII. FANNY ENTERS THE ROYAL SERVICE

(*1786; Fanny aged 34, her father aged 60*)

IN July 1786 Fanny, being at Mrs. Delany's, was called upon by a gentleman of the Court, who brought her a singular offer. The Queen, having first admired Fanny as a novelist, had then, on coming to know her personally, admired her for herself and now wished to have her near her. She proposed, therefore, says Fanny, 'to settle me with one of the princesses, in preference to the thousands [*sic*] of offered candidates of high birth and rank, but small fortunes, who were waiting and supplicating for places'. Fanny would have apartments in the palace, a good table ('a very magnificent table', indeed, as it turned out to be), a footman, and £200 a year. And, added the messenger, 'In such a situation, so respectfully offered, not solicited, you may have opportunities of serving your particular friends—especially your father—such as scarce any other could afford you'.

This messenger was the same Mr. Smelt[1] who had advised Burney and Fanny in the matter of the Mastership of the King's Musick (see II. 23). His advice on that occasion, we remember, was to the effect that Burney should make use of his daughter's popularity with the Royal Family to bring his own claims tactfully to their notice, and perhaps had the Mastership still been open when the advice was given and so faithfully followed, it would have been given to Burney: we may guess that this incident was in Mr. Smelt's mind when he insinuated the diplomatic advantage of a position about the Court for Fanny, for though the post of Master of the King's Musick was now irrevocably gone other opportunities might occur.

To most women the chance of a place at Court would in those days have appeared delightful, and by most women then it would have been eagerly grasped, but to Fanny the prospect of being immured in a Court was little more attractive than would have been that of being immured in a convent. So to Smelt's surprise Fanny hung back; he returned to the Queen without a positive 'Yes' or 'No', and then again to Fanny with the demand that she should herself attend on the Queen to discuss the matter.

As for Burney, as soon as the proposal was mentioned to him he took it for granted that it must be accepted, and Fanny (who, at thirty-four, looked on it as 'a matter that ought to be settled by himself') wrote: 'I cannot . . . even to my father utter my reluctance; I see him so much delighted at the prospect of an establishment he looks upon as so

[1] For Smelt, a military engineer of distinction, and a man of independent mind though a courtier, see *D.N.B.*, where, however, he is called 'Leonard' whereas Fanny calls him 'Lemuel'.

honourable. But for the Queen's own word *permanent*, but for her declared desire to attach me *entirely* to herself and family, I should share in his pleasure; but what can make *me* amends for all I shall forfeit?'[1]

What *would* she forfeit? Her home, which she loved; the daily society of her father and the frequent meetings with her married sisters, Hetty, Susan, and Charlotte; the brilliant circle of friends amongst whom she was such a favourite; her literary career, already one of public fame; and, above all, her freedom ('I have always and uniformly had a horror of a life of attendance and dependence', she writes to a friend whose counsel she seeks).

It is difficult for us to-day to realize what could be the attractions in Burney's mind of a post of this sort for his daughter. We agree with Macaulay[2] that it was absurd to think 'that she should consent to be almost as completely separated from her family and friends as if she had gone to Calcutta, and almost as close a prisoner as if she had been sent to gaol for a libel', but, in justice to her father, we must remember that to conscientious parents unprovided daughters were in those days (as they often are even to-day) a source of anxiety; that Burney, nearing sixty, and often in bad health, had no certainty of long earning powers before him; that Fanny's authorship was in those days an even less dependable means of support than it would be now; and that not only Burney but all the members of the distinguished circle in which he moved looked upon an offer of a life position about the Court as an enormous honour. When Fanny, as in duty bound, accepted the post (which was raised in importance from that of attendant on one of the princesses to that of one of the 'Keepers of the Robes' to the Queen) Burke 'hastened in person to St. Martin's Street with his warm gratulations'. Hannah More, as we have noted, on seeing the announcement in the newspaper, wrote to a friend, 'It was the very joy of my heart', and other men and women of sense and information wrote and spoke in similar terms. In fact the illusion attributed to Burney by Macaulay was in those days general—the illusion 'that going to court was like going to heaven; that to see princes and princesses was a kind of beatific vision; that the exquisite felicity enjoyed by royal persons was not confined to themselves, but was communicated by some mysterious efflux or reflection to all who were suffered to stand at their toilettes, or to bear their trains'. 'My dear father is in raptures', wrote Fanny to her sister Charlotte (now Mrs. Francis); 'that is my first comfort. Write to wish him joy, my Charlotte, without a hint to him, or any one but Susan, of my confessions of my internal reluctance and fears'.

So on 17 July 1786 there set off from London Fanny and the Doctor

[1] This and most other material of this chapter come from *Diary and Letters*, ii. 360, to the end of iv, and from *Mem.* iii. Some of the incidents are also related by Mrs. Papendick (see Bibliography), but obviously very inaccurately, so that this last source has not been drawn upon here.

[2] Essay, 'The Diary and Letters of Madame d'Arblay'.

with their friend, Mrs. Ord, in Mrs. Ord's carriage, with the Doctor's carriage following 'as a baggage waggon for my clothes'.

And the Queen received Fanny in the dressing-room that she was for some years to know so well as the principal scene of her duties. And she had dinner with the peevish, small-minded Mrs. Schwellenberg, who (perhaps from jealousy at seeing an Englishwoman take over duties that had always hitherto been performed by a German) was to make herself the curse of her life. And at tea afterwards she met a bishop and other company (for when invitations were issued by the King and Queen it was the staff who carried out the duties of hospitality—particularly as concerned male visitors, since no male except the King himself, on any account, sat in the Queen's presence) and an equerry who cheered her by talking of the Worcester Burneys, whom he well knew. And one of the young Princesses came in and greeted her politely. And then, from an adjoining music room floated the strains of the King's evening concert, for, like the German courts, this one had music every evening—'Nothing but Handel' on this occasion, as on most occasions hereafter. And then at night she was summoned to the Queen's dressing-room, at which 'the Queen arrived handed by the King', and the King said a kindly word to her, and the Princesses came to kiss the Queen's hand and say good-night, and on leaving 'curtsied condescendingly' to Fanny, and the Queen did her best to set her at ease, talking to her about her father, and at last had her night-dress put on and wished Fanny good-night.

And at six next morning Fanny rose to be ready to attend the Queen at seven, and the Schwellenberg and she dressed the Queen for prayers in the Castle Chapel.[1] And then at noon Dr. Burney appeared, to say good-bye to his daughter, and the routine of attendance on her mistress,

[1] It is comforting to learn that there was no compulsory chapel for the Queen's attendants. A humorous equerry (and how delightfully Fanny always reproduces his spirited conversation!) warned her at the outset thus:

> ' "One thing, pray let me caution you about—don't go to early prayers in November; if you do, that will completely kill you! Oh Ma'am, you know nothing yet of all these matters!—only pray, joking apart, let me have the honour just to advise you this one thing, or else it's all over with you, I do assure you!"
>
> 'It was in vain I begged him to be more merciful in his prophecies; he failed not, every night, to administer to me the same pleasant anticipations.
>
> ' "When the Princesses," cried he, "used to it as they are, get regularly knocked up before this business is over, off they drop, one by one:—first the Queen deserts us; then Princess Elizabeth is done for; then Princess Royal begins coughing; then Princess Augusta gets the snuffles; and all the poor attendants, my poor sister at their head, drop off, one after another, like so many snuffs of candles; till at last, dwindle, dwindle, dwindle—not a soul goes to chapel but the King, the parson, and myself; and there we three freeze it out together!" '

It must be remembered that the Court did not then occupy Windsor Castle itself, which was at that time in a ruinous condition, but what were called the Upper Lodge (for the King and Queen and two elder Princesses and attendants) and the Lower Lodge (for the younger Princesses and attendants). These lodges were cold and draughty temporary buildings erected by Dr. Burney's friend, the architect Sir William Chambers. They happily disappeared in 1823.

from seven a.m. to midnight, had been established as it was to run on for the coming years—for ever and ever, as was understood; and Fanny is soon found making a pun—she thinks the last four letters of the word 'toilette' superfluous.[1]

On the following Saturday night young Charles Wesley appeared to play the harpsichord at the evening concert: he played 'extremely well and next day after service, by the King's order, he played six or seven pieces all of Handel, so well suited to the organ and so well performed on a remarkably good instrument that it was a great regale to me to hear them' (indeed, absorbed in the music, Fanny was late for her duties in the Queen's dressing-room), and the same evening she heard floating in from the music room 'the sweet-flowing, melting, celestial notes of Fischer's hautbois'. So there were, at any rate, to be musical alleviations of the deadening monotony of the Court life.

So it went on day after day, with confinement to the royal apartments and to menial duties, summoned by a bell when wanted by her mistress, looking after her mistress's 'little dog' and filling her mistress's snuff-box (she soon acquired a reputation as a mixer of snuff). Of course there were a few hours free, but the day was so broken into by duties that Fanny could not get far away and the danger of infringement of Court etiquette made it difficult to receive friends. And, worst of all, Fanny was tied to the vulgar-minded Mrs. Schwellenberg almost as one galley-slave is chained to another.

There were regular days for going to the palace at Kew, and regular days for the 'Drawing Rooms' at St. James's Palace. At all these palaces Fanny had her own apartments and at St. James's Palace she sometimes received her father and her sisters; her father, being *persona grata* with the King and Queen, could appear at the 'Drawing Rooms', and now and again did so. Fanny tells us of one occasion at St. James's Palace[2] when on arrival she found in her room, 'my dearest father waiting for me, quite well, full of spirits, full of Handel, full of manuscripts, and full of proof-sheets'. That was Burney!

There were sometimes expeditions—as one to Oxford. On this occasion the staff were at first very cavalierly treated by the host and hostess of the party, Lord and Lady Harcourt at Nuneham, and when they went on to Oxford no arrangements had been made to feed them, so that they had to stand (always to stand, through the whole day)

[1] Lady Llanover, in her *Autobiography and Correspondence of Mary Granville, Mrs. Delany* (Series II, vol. iii), has some rather spiteful remarks about Fanny in her Court position, many of them clearly ill founded, as anyone who has read Fanny's diary can at once see. The following may be true, and if so is probably explained by Fanny's short-sightedness, which often embarrassed her: 'Queen Charlotte used to complain to Mrs. Delany that Miss Burney could not learn to tie the bow of her necklace on Court days without giving her pain by getting the hair at the back of the neck tied in with it.'

[2] Buckingham Palace, then called 'The Queen's House' (settled on the Queen as a dower house), was not then used for these state occasions, though the royalties sometimes themselves occupied it for a few days.

whilst their Majesties, in Christ Church Hall, partook of a 'cold collation', and they would have starved if some of the 'worthy doctors' had not seen their plight and caused refreshment to be brought up for them, which they consumed surreptitiously, 'standing in a double row, with one to screen one throughout the troop' so that the crime might not be discovered.

There were some humorous incidents, as one when in the Sheldonian the professors and doctors came forward to kiss the King's hand, and the Professor of Music, poor Dr. Hayes (Philip Hayes, for his corpulence called 'Fill-Chaise'; he had 'the reputation of possessing the largest person and most unsociable temper in England'), found himself in difficulties. Fanny, in a letter to her father describing this royal visit to Oxford,[1] told him:

'When poor Dr. Hayes came forward, he was so unconscionably fat and heavy, and had so much difficulty to kneel and so much more still to arise, that it raised a general buzz throughout the theatre. He really looked as if dressed up and stuffed for a Falstaff. I admired much to see the King, the only person who kept his countenance upon the doctor's plumping down before him.'[2]

Fanny herself was occasionally in danger of providing some of the comic relief of the British Court, until 'by constant practice' she acquired, more or less reliably, 'the power and skill of walking backwards, without tripping up my own heels, feeling my head giddy, or treading my train out of the plaits—accidents very frequent among novices in that business'.

And her father innocently provided some amusement. He came down to Windsor for an after-Christmas visit of three days with Mrs. Delany. Fanny told the Queen of this coming visit, of which 'she heard with the most pleased and pleasing expression of approbation', and the Queen told the King, who showed 'real satisfaction'. The Queen told her to ask her father to dine with her and Mrs. Schwellenberg, so with Mrs. Delany and the gentlemanly Mr. Smelt and another congenial spirit or two a very happy dinner-party was made up. After dinner, when all had gone into Fanny's room for coffee, the King came to fetch Mrs. Delany, but 'not for that solely, for his behaviour to my father proved his desire to see and converse with him':

'He began immediately upon musical matters, and entered into a discourse

[1] This letter is given in great part in Constance Hill, *Fanny Burney at the Court of Queen Charlotte*, 66 et seq.

[2] Burney probably chuckled when he read of poor Hayes's discomfiture. Here is what he later wrote of the man in Rees's *Cyclopaedia*: 'With a very limited genius for composition, and unlimited vanity, envy and spleen, he was always on the fret; and, by his situation, had a power, which he never spared, to render all other musicians uncomfortable. No one entered the university occasionally, or from curiosity, that did not alarm him. His extreme corpulency will be longer remembered than his abilities, of which he has left no example that we can recollect worthy to be recorded.' We almost get the impression that Burney, who had got on so well with Dr. William Hayes (see I. 144, 145), did not like his son Philip.

upon them with the most animated wish of both hearing and communicating his sentiments; and my dear father was perfectly ready to meet his advances. No one, at all used to the court etiquettes, could have seen him without smiling; he was so totally unacquainted with the forms usually observed in the royal presence, and so regardless or thoughtless of acquiring them, that he moved, spoke, acted, and debated, precisely with the same ease and freedom that he would have used to any other gentleman whom he had accidentally met.

'A certain flutter of spirits, which always accompanies these interviews, even with those who are least awed by them, put my dear father off the guard which is the customary assistant upon these occasions, of watching what is done by those already initiated in these royal ceremonies: highly gratified by the openness and good-humour of the King, he was all energy and spirit, and pursued every topic that was started, till he had satisfied himself upon it, and started every topic that occurred to him, whether the King was ready for another or not.

'While the rest, retreating towards the wainscot, formed a distant and respectful circle, in which the King alone moves, this dear father came forward into it himself, and, wholly bent upon pursuing whatever theme was begun, followed the King when he moved away, and came forward to meet his steps when he moved back; and while the rest waited his immediate address ere they ventured to speak a word, he began and finished, sustained or dropped, renewed or declined, every theme that he pleased, without consulting anything but his feelings and understanding.'

However, the King, 'whose good sense instantly distinguishes what is unconscious from what is disrespectful', quite understood the ardour of a brother musical enthusiast, and stayed an hour in 'perfect good humour', receiving and returning Burney's 'sprightly and informal sallies', and a week afterwards, 'in consequence of the gracious speeches' Fanny had heard about him, she got him down to Windsor again; and again, by the Queen's invitation, he had dinner with his daughter.

'This evening proved indeed a pleasant one; the honours paid my dear father gladdened my heart. The King came into my room to see Mrs. Delany, and conversed with him so openly, so gaily, and so readily, that it was evident he was pleased with his renewed visit, and pleased with his society. Nor was this all; soon after, the Queen herself came also, purposely to see him. She immediately sat down, that she might seat Mrs. Delany, and then addressed herself to my father, with the most winning complacency. Repeatedly, too, she addressed herself to me, as if to do me honour in my father's eyes, and to show him how graciously she was disposed towards me. I had previously entreated my father to snatch at any possible opportunity of expressing his satisfaction in all that related to me, as I knew it would not only give pleasure to her benevolence, but was a token of gratitude literally expected from him.

'My Susan, however [Fanny is writing to her sister], knows our dear father, and will know him by the following trait: he had planned his speech, and was quite elevated with the prospect of making it, and with the pleasure of my pointing it out, and being so happy! Dearest father! how blessed in that facility of believing all people as good and as happy as he wishes them! Nevertheless, no sooner did the King touch upon that dangerous string, the history of music, than all else was forgotten! Away flew the speech,—the Queen herself was present in vain,—eagerly and warmly he began an account of his progress, and an enumeration of his materials,—and out from his pockets came a couple of dirty books, which he had lately picked up, at an immense price, at a sale, and which, in showing to the King, he said were equally scarce and valuable, and added, with energy, "I would not take fifty pounds for that!" Just as if he had said—little as he meant such meaning—"Don't hope for it to your own collection!"

'Was not this a curious scene?'

And then Burney reached 'the height of his Windsor ambition', for the King took him off to the concert room.[1]

And a few days later, the Queen's birthday occurring, Fanny, at her father's behest, had somewhat embarrassingly to present to her on his behalf a loyal poem he had written for the occasion.

Some of the happier hours of Fanny's life at Court have just been mentioned. There were, it is clear, far more dull and trying ones. And there were some sad ones, as in April 1787 when she fell terribly ill and her sister Susan had to be sent for to nurse her, and the Queen came to visit the sisters and brought some noisy creatures with her ('How silly I was to bring those Dogs'); but at last she was better and 'eat some asparagus with an appearance of appetite', and then Susan was able to depart and Fanny to resume her daily round. And one of the worst

[1] The following description of the sufferings of the King's personal suite during the music-makings comes from one of Fanny's accounts of her conversations with the humorous equerry already mentioned ('Colonel Goldsworthy' is the name she attaches to him). He had been chattering away, and, says Fanny:

'In this manner he ran on, till General Budé reminded him it was time they should appear in the concert-room.

'"Ay," cried he, reluctantly, "now for the fiddlers! There I go, plant myself against the side of the chimney, stand first on one foot, then on the other, hear over and over again all that fine squeaking, and then fall fast asleep, and escape by mere miracle from flouncing down plump in all their faces!"

'"What would the Queen say if you did that?"

'"Oh, ma'am, the Queen would know nothing of the matter; she'd only suppose it some old double bass that tumbled."

'"Why, could not she see what it was?"

'"Oh no! ma'am, we are never in the room with the Queen! that's the drawing-room, beyond, where the Queen sits; we go no farther than the fiddling-room. As to the Queen, we don't see her week after week sometimes. The King, indeed, comes there to us, between whiles, though that's all as it happens, now Price is gone. He used to play at backgammon with Price."

'"Then what do you do there?"

'"Just what I tell you—nothing at all, but stand as furniture! But the worst is, sometimes, when my poor eye-peepers are not quite closed, I look to the music-books to see what's coming; and there I read 'Chorus of Virgins': so then, when they begin, I look about me. A chorus of virgins, indeed! why, there's nothing but ten or a dozen fiddlers! not a soul beside! It's as true as I'm alive! So then, when we've stood supporting the chimney-piece about two hours, why then, if I'm not called upon, I shuffle back out of the room, make a profound bow to the harpsichord, and I'm off."'

periods of all was when Mrs. Delany died—showing to the last her old-world courtesy, for before receiving Fanny for a final 'good-bye' she had left with her housekeeper a message to be given her when all was over: 'To say to me, when she was gone, how much comfort I must always feel in reflecting how much her latter days had been soothed by me.' Mrs. Delany's Will included this provision: 'I bequeath to Miss Burney the two medallions of the King and Queen now in my closet at Windsor, also Sacharissa in oils, a portrait of my own painting' (this was a copy of a picture of Vandyke).[1]

Then there was the excitement of attendance in Westminster Hall at many of the sessions of the trial of Warren Hastings, for which the Queen sometimes gave Fanny tickets for herself and her father—but as he could not go she took her brother Charles and on another occasion Jem, whose seamanlike readiness to express his feelings, however, kept her trembling (all the Burneys were very much on the side of Hastings and consequently on this occasion opposed to many old friends—Burke and Windham and others[2]).

There was, too, the Royal Visit to Cheltenham, where, for the King's health, the Court spent two months. As they drove thither 'all the towns were filled with people, as closely fastened to one another as in a playhouse. Every town seemed all face; and all the way upon the road we rarely proceeded five miles without encountering a band of the most horrid fiddlers, scraping "God save the King" with all their might, out of tune, out of time, and all in the rain.'

The Western road had rarely or never been so thronged as it now became and the prices of lodgings in Cheltenham have perhaps not been so high from that day to this. We get a hint of the way London fashion promptly poured westward in this extract from the *Morning Post*, referring to the day of the King's leaving:

> 'It is an absolute fact that no less than *sixty-seven hairdressers* set off for Cheltenham in one *drove* on Saturday morning last.'

At Cheltenham there were rather gay doings; it was possible for Fanny to see something of the Worcester Burneys, and when the royal party attended the Three Choirs Festival, at Worcester, she got permission from the Queen to sit with her cousins at a cathedral performance that proved to be 'very long and tolerably tedious, consisting of Handel's gravest pieces and fullest choruses', and concluding with a sermon concerning the institution of the charity, preached by Dr. Langhorne, which sermon had, perhaps, some effect, since the History of the festival tells us that at a later performance during the week there was 'the

[1] See *Autobiography and Correspondence of Mary Granville, Mrs. Delany*, edited by Lady Llanover, Series II, vol. v.

[2] Burney wrote to Fanny on 7 May 1795, 'And so Dear Mr. Hastings is honourably acquitted; and I visited him next morning, and we cordially shook hands' (*Diary and Letters*, vi. 36).

liberal donation of £200 put in the plate by his Majesty'. An evening concert in the College Hall was not so agreeable, for though Fanny, again with her cousins, had a seat, she had to look on at the sufferings of her colleagues who were on duty—Lord Orford and Lady Harcourt and the equerries who, 'no sort of resting place' having been 'considered' for them, were 'forced to stand perpendicular all the evening'. (Why did kings and queens in those days so neglect their attendant company?)

Then, after return to Windsor, the King's indisposition, to relieve which the Cheltenham expedition had been undertaken, became worse and declared itself openly for what it was. And then, for nearly five months (October 1788 to March 1789), there was the gloom and anxiety of a court with a mad King and an almost despairing Queen. It is to this period that belongs the well-known incident of the King, at a time when he was supposed to be kept in complete seclusion and everybody was ordered to keep out of his sight, meeting Fanny by chance in the gardens of Kew palace (see also II. 24). She ran away as hard as she could, pursued by the King and he pursued by his doctors (the clever and humane Willises, father and son)[1] and by his attendants. Then, as running was bad for the King, the Doctors called to Fanny to stop. '*Why did you run away?*', cried the King, and putting his hands round her shoulders, kissed her on the cheek. 'What a conversation followed', says Fanny. 'He opened his whole heart to me, expounded all his sentiments, and acquainted me with all his intentions.' Then he amazed her by asking after her very trying colleague, the Schwellenberg, and crying, '*Never mind her! don't be oppressed; I am your friend! don't let her cast you down! I know you have a hard time of it—but don't mind her!*'

So Fanny's sufferings had, after all, been observed. She had never known that before![2]

He added, '*Stick to your father—stick to your own family—let them be your object*', and putting his hand on his breast, 'he gravely and slowly said, *I will protect you; I promise you that, and therefore depend on me!*'

'He then talked to me a great deal of my dear father, and made a thousand inquiries concerning his *History of Music*. [The concluding two volumes were about to be published.] This brought him to his favourite theme, Handel; and he told me innumerable anecdotes of him, and particularly that celebrated tale of Handel's saying of himself, when a boy, "While that boy lives, my music will never want a protector." And this, he said, I might relate to my father.

'Then he ran over most of his oratorios, attempting to sing the subjects of several airs and choruses, but so dreadfully hoarse that the sound was terrible.

[1] These Willises seem to have done pretty well out of the business of curing mad monarchs. The *Observer* of 4 Mar. 1792 has the following: 'Dr. Willis, on Friday morning, set off from London for Lisbon, to the Queen of Portugal. He is to have £20,000 down and £1,000 per month. The Queen's malady is mentioned to be of the most violent nature.'

[2] Fanny's tolerance of her colleague was due to her intense loyalty to the Queen. She felt that it would be wrong, she says, 'to shock her with murmurs against one who, however to me noxious and persecuting, is to her a faithful and truly devoted old servant'.

'Dr. Willis, quite alarmed at this exertion, feared he would do himself harm, and again proposed a separation. "No! no! no!" he exclaimed, "not yet; I have something I must just mention first."'

At last, with some final admonitions not to mind the hateful Schwellenberg, for he would protect her, and another kiss, the Monarch and the Keeper of the Robes parted. Next day Fanny was relieved to read the medical bulletin to the effect that 'His Majesty passed yesterday quietly, has had a good night, and is much as usual this morning'. And thence onward (as a result of this encounter, with its reminder of his old life, or in spite of it?), the King improved in health, and about three weeks later Fanny met him again, in the Queen's dressing-room:

'On opening the door, there he stood! He smiled at my start, and saying he had waited on purpose to see me, added, "I am quite well now. I was nearly so when I saw you before—but I could overtake you better now!" And then he left the room.

'I was quite melted with joy and thankfulness at this so entire restoration.

'End of February, 1789. *Dieu merci!*'

Now were official 'Prayers of Thanksgiving' read in all the churches of the kingdom: London was illuminated, and the Queen and the elder princesses went to town to see it all, and be seen, by the populace (see Cowper's poem, *On the Queen's visit to London the Night of 17th March 1789*), whilst the King and the youngest princess, little Amelia, stayed quietly at Kew Palace but saw the special domestic illumination which Mr. Smelt had arranged there, and 'when it was lighted and prepared, the Princess Amelia went to lead her Papa to the front window, but first she dropped on her knees and presented him with a paper—a paper with a poem that Fanny had composed at the Queen's request beginning:

Amidst a rapt'rous nation's praise
That sees Thee to their prayer restor'd

and ending:

The little bearer begs a kiss
From dear Papa for bringing this.

And later the Queen presented Fanny with 'a medal of green and gold and a motto, *Vive le Roi* . . . as well as a fan ornamented with the words —*Health restored to one, and happiness to millions*'.[1]

[1] In the Douce Collection in the Bodleian Library there is a cutting from some unnamed newspaper (fol. 211) which reads as follows:

'King's Recovery. Musicians' Address. "To join the general chorus of congratulation" is the passage in their Address which divided the Society. The word *chorus* was objected to as hacknied by Parke, Dance, etc. Burney and Arnold defended it. But it went to Ballot, 45 for it—39 against it. The address is Burney's. It will be presented in a day or two.'

The 'Society' was obviously the one now known as the 'Royal Society of Musicians'. In the same year as it presented this Address to the King, a petition for a Royal Charter was presented to him, signed by Burney, Arnold, and two other members, and duly granted.

Overture Porus.
Concerto Oboe
Chorus N. 1. Alex. Feast
5. Grand Concerto Hand. 6
Concertante Bass et Horno
Chorus N. 2 Alex. Feast
Overture Parthenope
Concerto Violino
Chorus N. 3. Alex. Feast

HANDEL PROGRAMME BY GEORGE III

who, in his capacity of one of the Directors of the 'Concert of Antient Music' (often known as 'The King's Concert'; *see* ii. 178–80), enjoyed the privilege of taking his turn at selecting the pieces to be performed.

MRS. DELANY

Much-beloved personal friend of the King and Queen and of Fanny Burney and her father (*see* ii. 18–24, 102).

THE PRINCE OF WALES

Friend of Burney and his son Charles—able to discuss music with the one and Greek literature with the other (*see* ii. 306).

DESIGNS ON A COMMEMORATIVE SILK SCARF

(For the King's recovery in 1789 *see* ii. 104–5.)

There followed the famous visit to Weymouth, and, as on the journey to Cheltenham, there were crowds all the way and bands playing *God save the King*. For instance, at Romsey:

'On the steps of the Town-Hall, an orchestra was formed, and a band of musicians, in common brown coarse cloth and red neckcloths, and even in carters' loose gowns, made a chorus of "God save the King", in which the countless multitude joined, in such loud acclamation, that their loyalty and heartiness, and natural joy, almost surprised me into a sob before I knew myself at all affected by them.'

Apparently *God save the King* was at that time, despite its being nothing but an address to the Deity, looked upon as something of a secular song, since Fanny tells us, writing of the five days' stay made at Lyndhurst:

'On the Sunday we all went to the parish church; and after the service, instead of a psalm, imagine our surprise to hear the whole congregation join in "God save the King!" Misplaced as this was in a church, its intent was so kind, loyal, and affectionate, that I believe there was not a dry eye amongst either singers or hearers. The King's late dreadful illness has rendered this song quite melting to me.'

At Weymouth itself it was *God save the King* everywhere:

'Not a child could we meet that had not a bandeau round its head, cap, or hat, of "God save the King"; all the bargemen wore it in cockades; and even the bathing-women had it in large coarse girdles round their waists. It is printed in golden letters upon most of the bathing-machines, and in various scrolls and devices it adorns every shop and almost every house in the two towns. . . . The King bathes, and with great success; a machine follows the Royal one into the sea, filled with fiddlers, who play "God save the King", as His Majesty takes his plunge!'[1]

Back from Weymouth there were various London plays and opera performances to be attended with the royal party.

There could happen little adventures on such occasions, as once (at a rather earlier date) when the Court went to a performance of Holcroft's play, *Seduction*, Fanny being seated in one of the royal boxes directly opposite to that occupied by the King and Queen. At the end she was leaning forward, examining through her opera glass the actress who was declaiming the Epilogue, when, to her confusion, she suddenly heard a flattering allusion to her own *Cecilia*. She shrank back in confusion, her fan in front of her face as she saw the King and Queen, amused, looking at her through their opera glasses. And afterwards she had to endure some chaffing from them. The King's remark was,

[1] His Majesty's sojourn at Weymouth and some of these incidents will be familiar to many readers from their treatment by Thomas Hardy in *The Trumpet Major*. George III's bathing-machine (octagonal, with a pyramidal roof, and with the Royal Arms above the door) was in regular public use at Weymouth down to the summer of 1914, when 'it was removed from its wheels and degraded to some mean use, apparently a tool shed' (letter by L. G. Wickham Legg in *The Times*, 29 June 1933). So the one-time loyal memories of Weymouth have, in these latter days, completely evaporated!

'I took a look at you. I could not help that, I wanted to see how you looked when your father first discovered your writing [i.e. of *Evelina*]—and now I think I know!'

Then there were a further Handel Commemoration or two to attend; and the King put Fanny's name down among the contributors to the 'Tottenham Street Oratorio' (i.e. the Antient Concert, at which he himself used to be present; see II. 179). We have, too, an account of a concert at the Pantheon, to hear the great Pacchierotti and a Madame Benda whom Burney had advised 'to try her powers' there and on whom the Queen was interested to have Fanny's report. Dr. Burney called for Fanny at St. James's Palace and took her to this concert, where she sat with her sister Esther and Esther's eldest child Marianne. 'And, oh, how Pacchierotti sung!' How!—with what exquisite feeling and penetrating pathos!' But 'Poor Madame Benda pleased neither friends nor foes', having 'a prodigious voice, great power of execution, but a manner of singing so vehemently boisterous that a boatswain might entreat her to moderate it'. So Madame Benda, we may guess, was *not*, on Fanny's report, taken into royal favour.

And, talking of boatswains and bluff sea manners, who should now appear in the concert hall but Brother Jem, eagerly asking, 'Will there be war with Spain?' and more eagerly adding, 'If there is, I should be glad of a frigate of thirty-two guns. Now if you ask for it don't say a *frigate* and get me one of twenty-eight.' Brother Jem had had no command at all since he came home nearly five years before, but all Fanny can remark on this request for her intervention in the country's naval management, is, 'Poor innocent James!'

However, James was very much in earnest and actually declared 'he intended coming to court'—to which, 'very much frightened', Fanny begged him first to come and drink tea with her and talk it all over. And so, a day or two later he did, and brought his wife, the quondam Sally Payne, and was joined there by his and Fanny's brother-in-law and his old shipmate, Captain Phillips. And, as a result of the confabulations, Fanny agreed to mention his wishes to the Queen, which she did that evening, but alas, on seeing James again three days later, Fanny found him 'quite amazed' at not having had 'a vessel, just such a one as he wished, instantly given him'.

Jem once tackled the Burneys' friend William Windham (an important man in Parliament and soon to be Secretary for War):

'"How do you do, Captain Burney?"

'"My Lord, I should be glad to be employed."

'"You must be sensible, Captain Burney, we have many claimants just now, and more than it is possible to satisfy immediately."

'"I am very sensible of that, my Lord; but, at the same time, I wish to let your Lordship know what I should like to have—a frigate of thirty-two guns."

'"I am very glad to know what you wish, sir."

'He took out his pocket-book, made a memorandum, and wished James good morning.'

But again nothing happened. Fanny says, 'I perpetually brought in my wishes for poor James'. But, alas, 'poor James', with all his varied experience, his high naval reputation, and the advantage of a sister at Court (remember Mr. Smelt's suggestions as to the value of that!), never, as long as he lived, got another command—presumably because there were others with either prior claims or a more direct influence in actual Admiralty quarters.

In passing we may note the apparent modesty of James's demand—'a frigate of thirty-two guns'. We see the explanation of this in the following passage from Admiral Sir Herbert Richmond's chapter, 'The Navy', in *Johnson's England.*[1]

'Though the pay in the ships of the line was higher than in the smaller classes, captains often—possibly "generally" would be nearer the mark—preferred a frigate command; for it gave opportunities for making a fortune in prize money. Captain Pasley, when commanding a 50-gun ship—a large frigate, in effect—refused an offer to exchange into a higher-paid 74. "A 74-gun ship is not the thing in that country." If, however, he should be offered to exchange into a smart 32-gun frigate, the *Active*, he might accept. "With my connections I think a Fortune in a couple of years would be a certainty."'

In 1791 Fanny's name appeared in the newspapers in connexion with the shocking theft from Buckingham House of 'a pair of silver snuffers and stand, and two candlestick nozzles, the property of his majesty'—the thief being a former footman of hers, a German, who had been recommended to her by his former employer 'a nobleman'.[2]

And so Fanny's Court life went on—not devoid of enlivening incidents but these so placed against a background of dull dressing-room duties and recriminations from an utterly uncongenial colleague as to lower her spirits and her physical health.

For there were no holidays. 'Mais, Monsieur, est-ce possible,' said the Comtesse de Boufflers once to Burney, 'Mademoiselle votre fille, n'a-t-elle point de vacance?' When Burney repeated this to his daughter she was at last emboldened to open her heart:

'I owned the species of life distasteful to me: I was lost to all private comfort, dead to all domestic endearment; I was worn with want of rest, and fatigued with laborious watchfulness and attendance. My time was devoted to official duties; and all that in life was dearest to me—my friends, my chosen society, my best affections—lived now in my mind only by recollection, and rested upon that with nothing but bitter regret. With relations the most deservedly dear, with friends of almost unequalled goodness, I lived like an orphan—like one who had no natural ties, and must make

[1] 1933, i. 61.

[2] *Annual Register*, Feb. 1791. See also *Notes and Queries* for 150 years later, 22 Feb. 1941.

her way as she could by those that were factitious. Melancholy was the existence where happiness was excluded, though not a complaint could be made! where the illustrious personages who were served possessed almost all human excellence,—yet where those who were their servants, though treated with the most benevolent condescension, could never, in any part of the livelong day, command liberty, or social intercourse, or repose!

'The silence of my dearest father now silencing myself, I turned to look at him; but how was I struck to see his honoured head bowed down almost into his bosom with dejection and discomfort!—We were both perfectly still a few moments; but when he raised his head I could hardly keep my seat, to see his eyes filled with tears!—"I have long", he cried, "been uneasy, though I have not spoken; . . . but . . . if you wish to resign—my house, my purse, my arms, shall be open to receive you back!"'

Then came a plain-spoken letter from Horace Walpole, 'Were your talents given to be buried in obscurity?' and the like.

Then Boswell turns up again. At Windsor, one day, he met Fanny, as by chance, at the gate of the choir of St. George's Chapel. He wanted, for his coming *Johnson*, 'some of your choice little notes of the Doctor's; we have seen him long enough upon stilts; I want to show him in a new light. Grave Sam, and great Sam, and solemn Sam, and learned Sam,—all these he has appeared over and over. Now I want to entwine a wreath of the graces across his brow; I want to show him as gay Sam, agreeable Sam, pleasant Sam; so you must help me with some of his beautiful billets to yourself.' But he had another preoccupation, too:

'"You must come forth, Madam!" he vociferated; "this monastic life won't do. You must come forth! We are resolved to a man,—we, The CLUB, Madam! ay, THE CLUB, Madam! are resolved to a man, that Dr. Burney shall have no rest—poor gentleman!—till he scale the walls of your august convent, to burn your veil, and carry you off."

'At the iron gate opening into the lawn, not daring to force his uninvited steps any farther, he seriously and formally again stopped her, and, with a look and voice that indicated "Don't imagine I am trifling!" solemnly confirmed to her a rumour which already had reached her ears, that Mr. Windham, whom she knew to be foremost in this chivalrous cabal against the patience of Dr. Burney, was modelling a plan for inducing the members of the Literary Club to address a round-robin to the Doctor, to recall his daughter to the world.

'"And the whole matter was puissantly discussed", added Mr. Boswell, "at THE CLUB, Madam, at the last meeting—Charles Fox in the chair."'

Fanny later saw Windham and, with difficulty, persuaded him to stop the proposed intervention of the Literary Club in her personal affairs. But at last it became clear that Fanny must insist upon a retirement from her place at Court. Her father and stepmother saw this plainly, but, says she:

'I could not . . . summon courage to present my memorial; my heart always failed me, from seeing the Queen's entire freedom from such an expectation:

for though I was frequently so ill in her presence that I could hardly stand, I saw she concluded me, while life remained, inevitably hers.'

However, terrified as Fanny was at the thought of taking such a step as her health demanded (her brother-in-law, Mr. Francis, the physician, was insistent on this last point), she at last indited a longish and very humble and indeed reverential epistle to her royal mistress, kept it by her for two months, and finally summoned up courage to present it. There were still efforts to retain her services, but the newspapers ('how and by whom instigated' she knew not) took up the subject of her seclusion from the world and 'dealt round comments and lamentations profusely'. And then came 'a terrible illness'—and at last a tender conversation with the Queen, who told her she could go and added, 'You know what you now have from me; the half of that I mean to continue', and the King is reputed to have acquiesced in this provision for Fanny's future, saying, 'It is but her due. She has given up five years of her pen.' There was a final interview, in which the Queen 'had a handkerchief in her hand or at her eyes the whole time', and Fanny, as soon as she got out of the room, 'nearly sobbed', and the King, seeing her so much moved, quietly stepped away.

And then, very gratefully, Fanny, with her promise of a pension of £100 a year, took leave of the Queen and the King and the princesses, in mingled happiness and sorrow, and set forth to claim the welcome her father had promised her.

'We shall expect you here to dinner by four,' wrote her father.

'The great grubbery will be in nice order for you, as well as the little; both have lately had many accessions of new books. The ink is good, good pens in plenty, and the most pleasant and smooth paper in the world!

Come, Rosalind, oh, come and see
What quires are in store for thee!'

'Here, therefore', writes Fanny, 'end my Court Annals; after having lived in the service of Her Majesty five years within ten days—from July 17, 1786 to July 7, 1791.'

And many readers of *Evelina* and *Cecilia*, we may be sure, were glad to read the news of Fanny's release. A publication of 1788 (*Catalogue of Five Hundred Celebrated Authors of Great Britain now living*), after describing her as 'the author of two of the best novels in the English language', had expressed public feeling by the quiet conclusion: 'Since that time the hours of this celebrated genius are said to have been chiefly occupied with the folding of muslins.'

XLIX. BURNEY AND HIS FRIEND HAYDN

(*1791–1795; Burney aged 65–69, Haydn 59–63*)

In Burney's own reminiscences, recorded in those 'sundry manuscript volumes, of various sizes containing the history of his life from his cradle nearly to his grave', which Fanny to our everlasting dismay so ruthlessly destroyed, was to be found, it appears, a passage running as follows:

'1791.—This year was auspiciously begun, in the musical world, by the arrival in London of the illustrious Joseph Haydn. 'Tis to Salomon that the lovers of music are indebted for what the lovers of music will call this blessing. Salomon went over himself to Vienna, upon hearing of the death of the Prince of Esterhazy, the great patron of Haydn, purposely to tempt that celebrated musical genius hither; and on February 25, the first of Haydn's incomparable symphonies which was composed for the concerts of Salomon was performed. Haydn himself presided at the piano-forte: and the sight of that renowned composer so electrified the audience, as to excite an attention and a pleasure superior to any that had ever, to my knowledge, been caused by instrumental music in England. All the slow middle movements were encored; which never before happened, I believe, in any country.'[1]

It was on New Year's Day that Haydn first set foot on British soil. On arrival in London he stayed a night with the music publisher, Bland, in Holborn—whence the *Rasiermesserquartett* ('Razor Quartet').[2] Then he lodged in the same house as his impresario, Salomon, in Great Pulteney Street (having also a room for composing at Shudi and Broadwood's pianoforte shop in the same street); thence moving to Bury Street, St. James, and afterwards to the then rural retreat of Lisson Grove.

Haydn's first visit in London was to Burney. We learn this from his friend Griesinger's biography of him, published the year of the composer's death.[3] Griesinger, who was Secretary of the Saxon Legation at Vienna, also acted as an intermediary between the Leipzig publisher, Breitkopf, and Haydn. His friendship with Haydn dated from 1799, when he first came to Vienna, so that at the time of the English visit he did not know him, but he claimed to have later drawn the material for his book largely from the lips of the great man himself and the book makes it clear that he had access to Haydn's diaries of the English

[1] *Mem.* iii. 132. For Thomas Hardy's portraits of both Haydn and Salomon painted in London about this time, see opposite.

[2] The tale is of the composer, in exasperation when shaving, exclaiming, 'I'd give my best quartet for a new razor', and of his host taking him at his word, and so becoming proprietor of the String Quartet in F minor, sometimes called 'No. 61', and sometimes 'Op. 55, No. 2'. The story is sometimes told as referring to Bland's stay with Haydn at Esterház, but more probably belongs to Haydn's stay with Bland in London.

[3] In the *Allgemeine Muzikzeitung*, July–Sept. 1809. The following year it appeared in book form.

PLATE 35. *HAYDN IN ENGLAND*

HAYDN AND HIS LONDON IMPRESARIO, SALOMON

Both painted by Thomas Hardy. For Haydn's London visits see Chapters XLIX and L (ii. 110 et seq.).

HAYDN COMPOSES FOR A BRITISH CHARITY

A page of his manuscript of the march composed for the 1792 Anniversary Festival of the Royal Society of Musicians—the charity in which his friend Burney was so deeply interested.

visits.[1] We may, therefore, reasonably suppose that Griesinger had warrant for his statement.

Burney had long been in correspondence with Haydn.[2] It was twenty-eight years before that he had first met with his name, in Breitkopf's catalogue, and he had then, no doubt, procured his music, for Burney was always on the look-out for anything new. When in Vienna, nine years later (1772), he had, we may be sure, hoped to meet Haydn, but must have been disappointed, since he does not mention doing so (most likely Haydn was at the time at his patron's country seat of Esterház). Six years after that (1778) he had been alarmed by a rumour of Haydn's death and had applied to the British Ambassador at Vienna, Sir Robert Keith, as to the truth of the rumour; Sir Robert relieved him by the happy news that Haydn was still alive, and, setting his German secretary to work, procured for him those biographical particulars which, prefaced by eulogy, afterwards appeared in the fourth volume of the *History*. Thereafter Burney and Haydn had got into direct touch by correspondence, and now, at last, they met.

'I am now happily arrived at that part of my narrative where it is necessary to speak of HAYDN! the admirable and matchless HAYDN! from whose productions I have received more pleasure late in my life, when tired of most other Music, than I ever received in the most ignorant and rapturous part of my youth, when every thing was new, and the disposition to be pleased undiminished by criticism or satiety.'[3]

The occasion of Haydn's arrival in England was not, in Burney's opinion, any ordinary one. It must be celebrated with all possible éclat; in fact it demanded a poem! So Burney came out with his glowing *Verses on the Arrival in England of the Great Musician Haydn*, published with the imprint of James Burney's father-in-law, Payne, and of three other booksellers in various parts of London.

These verses open with a magnificent metaphor, in which the art of music is boldly lifted to the level of a jorum of punch:

Music! the Calm of life, the cordial bowl,
Which anxious care can banish from the soul.

They soon proceed to an ingenious rhyming catalogue of Italian composers who gallantly did their bit and, for a time, satisfied humanity:

Italia both Scarlattis gave, Corelli,
Geminiani, Somis; and Jomelli,
Durante, Pergolesi, and Tartini,
Vinci, Piccini, Sarti, and Sacchini.

They then continue through an account of the efforts of 'Germania' and England, at length arriving at a description of a stage at which, sated

[1] The diary of the 1791–2 visit has been published in translation (but apparently not quite complete) in Henry E. Krehbiel, *Music and Manners in the Classical Period* (1898).

[2] *Mem.* ii. 327.

[3] *Hist.* iv. 599 (Mercer, ii. 958).

with the old stuff and longing for novelty, tired humanity was obliged to admit of all her composers that:

> . . . dry and stale become, they ceased at last,
> To please and charm us in the ear's repast.

At which point, the verses tell us, there providentially appears 'Great Haydn,' whose

> . . . new and varied strains
> Of habit and indiff'rance broke the chains;
> Rous'd to attention the long torpid sense,
> With all that pleasing wonder could dispense.

And so, after a series of similar metaphors, with a Burneyan touch or two of astronomical allusion to Copernicus and Newton, the muse flaps her wings more vigorously still and at last mounts to this apostrophe (the best part of the poem):

> Welcome, great master! to our favour'd isle,
> Already partial to thy name and style;
> Long may thy fountain of invention run
> In streams as rapid as it first begun;
> While skill for each fantastic whim provides,
> And certain science ev'ry current guides!
> Oh, may thy days, from human suff'rings free,
> Be blest with glory and felicity.
> With full fruition, to a distant hour,
> Of all thy magic and creative pow'r!
> Blest in thyself, with rectitude of mind,
> And blessing, with thy talents, all mankind!

Well, our Burney was not a heaven-inspired poet, but he did what he could, and no doubt Haydn (whom we may suppose to have been no minute and petulant critic of English verse) was gratified.[1]

The reception of Haydn in 'our favour'd isle' was all that his poetical friend could desire. He had been brought over by Salomon to appear at his concerts with six specially composed symphonies, and did so with great éclat. Burney was now writing for *The Monthly Review* (see II. 93–4), and it was quite possibly he who wrote the article which includes these words:

'His compositions, long before his arrival in this country, had been distinguished by an attention, which we do not remember to have been bestowed on any other instrumental music before; but at the concerts in Hanover square, where he has presided, his presence seems to have awakened such a degree of enthusiasm in the audience, as almost amounts to a frenzy.'[2]

But Haydn was also heard at the King's Theatre (in concert per-

[1] The poem is quoted in part at the end of C. F. Pohl's *Mozart und Haydn in London* (Vienna, 1867) and in full at the end of Botstiber's third volume to Pohl's unfinished *Joseph Haydn* (Leipzig, 1927).

[2] *The Monthly Review*, 1791, v. 223. This short article is nominally of the nature of a review of Burney's poem, but as it does not criticize or praise the poem in any way Burney himself may have been the writer.

formances, not opera), and at the Annual Dinner of Burney's pet Royal Society of Musicians, this last with a specially composed march (of which the autograph score is still in the possession of the Society, see pl. 35, II. 110). Then he was present as a member of the audience at the Westminster Abbey Handel Commemoration of that year (where he wept at the Hallelujah Chorus and uttered his often afterwards quoted testimony to Handel—'He is the master of us all'), and as a member of the audience again at the meeting of the Charity Children in St. Paul's Cathedral (where he wept again—at Jones's Chant in D sung by the 4,000 boys and girls). He was within one week a guest at two Guildhall banquets (that of the outgoing Lord Mayor and that of the incoming one), leaving in his diary a curious and unflattering account of the eating, drinking, dancing, and music,[1] and was taken to Oxford to receive an honorary Mus.D., which honour it is traditionally and plausibly stated was paid him at Burney's suggestion.[2]

Probably owing to Fanny's destructive mania in her old age, the actual records of the many meetings that must have taken place between Haydn and Burney are very sparse. We do have clear record of one such meeting in Burney's own rooms at Chelsea. His friend, Twining, wrote to him on 4 May 1791, from Colchester:

'I don't know anything—any musical thing—that would delight me so much as to meet him in a snug quartett party, and hear his manner of playing his own music. If you can bring about such a thing while I am in town, either at Chelsea or at Mr. Burney's [i.e. Charles Rousseau Burney's], or at Mr. Salomon's, or at I care not where, if it were even in the black hole at Calcutta (if it is a good hole for music)—I say, if by hook or by crook you could manage such a thing, you should be my Magnus Apollo for the rest of your life.'[3]

[1] 'Nothing but minuets are danced in this room; but I couldn't stay longer than a quarter of an hour; first because of the heat caused by so many people being crowded into so small a room, second, because of the wretched dance music, two violins and one violoncello composing the whole orchestra. The minuets were more Polish than German or Italian. Thence I went into another room which looked more like a subterranean cave. There the dance was English; the music was a little better because there was a drum which drowned the blunders of the fiddlers. I went on to the great hall where we had dined; the music was more sufferable. The dance was English but only on the elevated platform where the Lord Mayor and the first four members had dined. The other tables were all newly surrounded by men who, as usual, drank right lustily all night long. The most singular thing of all, however, was the fact that a part of the company danced on without hearing a note of the music, for first at one table, then at another, some were howling songs and some drinking toasts amidst the maddest shrieks of "Hurra! Hurra!" and the swinging of glasses.' (From Haydn's 1791 Note Book transcribed in translation in Henry E. Krehbiel, *Music and Manners in the Classical Period*, 60. A good deal of this note-book also appears in *The Harmonicon*, 1827, 5.)

[2] Miss Rosemary S. M. Hughes has thoroughly investigated this tradition and finds no source for it other than G. A. Griesinger's *Biographische Notizen über Joseph Haydn* (Vienna, 1810) and A. C. Dies's *Biographische Nachrichten von Joseph Haydn* (same place and date). Griesinger, however, is a good authority—see *ante*, II. 110. See Rosemary S. M. Hughes, 'Dr. Burney's Championship of Haydn', in *The Musical Quarterly*, Jan. 1941. See also the same author's 'Haydn at Oxford 1773–1791', in *Music and Letters*, July 1939.

[3] Twining, *Country Clergyman*.

We find in Fanny's diary a reference to an evening in her father's rooms at Chelsea in that same month of May 1791, when she, Burney's old friend Twining, and Haydn were all present, and 'there was some sweet music of his performed', but 'Esther, his best exhibitor, was not well' and was 'missed in all ways'.[1] And we know that it was Burney who introduced to Haydn the Moravian minister and composer, Rev. Christian Ignatius Latrobe, for a letter from Latrobe to Vincent Novello says:

'Haydn arrived in England in 1791. I was introduced to him by Dr. Burney, who well knew the value I should set upon the personal acquaintance of a man whose works I so greatly admired, and of which I may say, that they had been a feast to my soul.'[2]

And we know that Haydn then called on Latrobe:

'When he entered the room he found my wife alone, and as she could not speak German, and he had scarcely picked up a few English words, both were at a loss what to say. He bowed with foreign formality, and the following short explanation took place:

'H. "Dis, Mr. La Trobe house?"

'The answer was in the affirmative.

'H. "Be you his Woman?"

'"I am Mrs. La Trobe", was the reply.

'After some pause he looked round the room and saw his picture, to which he immediately pointed and explained: "Dat is me. I am Haydn!" My wife instantly, knowing what a most welcome guest I was honoured with, sent for me to a house not far off and treated him with all possible civility.'

We also know from Latrobe that Haydn gave Burney some of his music (he probably gave him a good deal), since Latrobe tells Novello:

'I have begun to get a 17th Volume of my Selection engraved, and wished much to have consulted you about my introductory piece, which is the Kyrie Eleison in the Mass of Haydn formerly in Dr. Burney's Collection. . . . Haydn himself gave the Doctor that Mass as far as the Creed, and he, out of great goodwill, permitted me to copy it in the year 1805.'

And it seems that Fanny, too, was given some music, as witness this entry in Sotheby's catalogue of a sale on 8–10 June 1931:

'541. HAYDN (J. F.) Auto. Music, 2 pp. oblong folio, clearly written, for two trebles and two basses, endorsed by Fanny Burney "June 5. 1795, Rec'd from Dr. Haydn".'

Or, as the catalogue of the same firm described it when it came up for sale again on 31 July and 1 August 1944:

[1] *Diary and Letters*, iv. 459. Haydn's diary of his second English visit gives us lists of the different categories of London musicians at the time, and it includes amongst *Pianists* 'Burney' and 'Mrs. Burney' (i.e. Esther's husband and herself). Amongst *Compositores* we find 'Dr. Burney', and amongst *Doctors* 'Burney'.

[2] Letter from Latrobe to Vincent Novello, 22 Nov. 1828 (British Museum, Add. MS. 11730, fol. 112). It is reprinted in *Musical Times*, Sept. 1851, which has also a good article on Latrobe by Edward Holmes.

'HAYDN (Joseph) MS. music, 2 pp. oblong folio, pour piano à 4 mains, en mi bémol, 16 bars complete, from his string quartette, endorsed by Fanny Buracy [*sic*] "*June 5th, 1795. Recd. from Dr. Haydn, 1795*".'

It was not until the end of June 1792 that this visit to England, which had by then lasted eighteen months, came to an end, and in February 1794 Haydn was back in London again, for another eighteen months' visit. Altogether, then, between January 1791 and August 1795 Haydn spent three years on British soil, and we may be sure that his friend Burney saw much of him. There was a geniality in the two men that well accorded and when they took a journey to Bath together they must have enjoyed a happy companionship.

If they ever *did* go to Bath together . . . ? Tradition determinedly asserts that they did. Lives of Haydn say that they did. Books of reference say that they did. But Haydn's own diary entry mentions two companions and ignores Burney. The visitors' list in *The Bath Chronicle* of 6 August 1794 gives the names of Haydn and one of these companions—and no Burney. *The Bath Herald and Register* of 8 August gives the name of Haydn and the same two companions he himself mentions—but no Burney![1]

During Haydn's second visit Burney was present at his benefit concert (May or June 1795). This he mentions in a letter to Fanny:

'Three huge assemblies at Spencer House; two dinners at the Duke of Leeds'; two clubs; a *déjeuner* at Mrs. Crewe's villa at Hampstead; a dinner at Lord Macartney's; two ditto at Mr. Crewe's; two philosophical conversaziones at Sir Joseph Banks's; Haydn's benefit; Salomon's ditto, etc. etc. What profligacy! But what *argufies* all this festivity?—'tis all vanity and exhalement of spirit. I am tired to death of it all, while your domestic and maternal joys are as fresh as the roses in your garden.'[2]

It is not at all improbable that Haydn was a guest with Burney at that dinner at Lord Macartney's, for in his diary, at just this time, he records a lot of information that Lord Macartney, whose name he mentions, had apparently given him respecting the Great Wall of China and similar subjects.[3] Burney had helped to fit out Lord Macartney (a fellow member of the Literary Club) for his famous mission to China, with 'whatever belonged to musical matters, whether instruments, compositions, band, or decoration, that might contribute in that line, to its magnificence'. And Macartney had recognized his help by the gift of 'a superb and very costly silver inkstand, of the most beautiful

[1] The diary entry begins 'Den 2ten August 1794 gieng ich frueh um 5 Uhr nach Bath mit Mr. Asher und Mr. Cimandor (ein junger Violin Virtuose und Komponist), langte abends um 8 Uhr dahin', i.e. 'On 2nd August 1794 I set off at five o'clock in the morning to Bath with Mr. Asher and Mr. Cimador [for that is the correct spelling], a young violin virtuoso and composer, and arrived in the evening at eight o'clock.' The diary of the second English visit has been published by J. E. Engl, as *Joseph Haydns handschriftliches Tagebuch aus der Zeit seines zweiten Aufenthaltes in London, 1794 und 1795* (Breitkopf & Härtel, 1909).

[2] *Diary and Letters*, v. 258.

[3] Op. cit. 31.

workmanship, upon which he had engraved a Latin motto, flatteringly expressive of his esteem for Dr. Burney.'[1]

We have a glimpse of Haydn and Burney together in Burney's article 'Mozart', in Rees's *Cyclopaedia*:

'When Haydn was asked in our hearing by Broderip, in his music-shop, whether Mozart had left any MS. compositions behind him that were worth purchasing, as his widow had offered his unedited papers at a high price to the principal publishers of music through-out Europe; Haydn eagerly said; "Purchase them by all means. He was truly a great musician. I have been often flattered by my friends with having some genius; but he was much my superior."

'Though this declaration had more of modesty than truth in it, yet if Mozart's genius had been granted as many years to expand as that of Haydn, the assertion might perhaps have been realised in many particulars.'

This anecdote is confirmed in the manuscript notes of R. J. S. Stevens, the glee composer. He says:

'He called on Broderip in the Haymarket, and urged him to purchase *all Mozart's compositions*. Such a genius he never knew.

'I *saw Haydn* leave Broderip's shop, after he had made this declaration. Mr. Broderip mentioned Haydn's words to me.'[2]

(It is satisfactory to know that Broderip did his best to act upon Haydn's advice.)

Most of the Burney–Haydn correspondence seems to have disappeared, but we have this letter of Burney (apparently written in English, of which language Haydn possessed by now, of course, a degree of knowledge):

Chelsea College, Aug. 19, 1799.

My dear and much-honoured Friend,

The reverence with which I have always been impressed for your great talents, and respectable and amiable character, renders your remembrance of me extremely flattering. And I am the more pleased with the letter with which you have honoured me, of July 15th, as it has pointed out to me the means by which I may manifest my zeal in your service, as far as my small influence can extend. I shall, with great pleasure, mention your intention of publishing your oratorio *Della Creazione del Mondo* ['The Creation'], by subscription, to all my friends; but you alarm me very much by the short time you allow for solicitation. In winter it would be sufficient, but now (in August) there is not a single patron of music in town. I have been in Hampshire myself for three weeks, and am now at home for two or three days only, on my way to Dover, where I shall remain for a month or six weeks, and where I shall see few or none of the persons whom I mean to stimulate to do themselves the honour of subscribing to your work. I wish it

[1] *Mem.* iii. 218. See reference to this inkstand (or 'standish') in Burney's will, II. 269. Lord Macartney procured for Burney's brother-in-law, Arthur Young, much information on Chinese agriculture.

[2] Article by Professor J. B. Trend in *Music and Letters*, Apr. 1933, 130.

were possible to postpone the delivery of the book in England till next winter. The operas, oratorios, and concerts, public and private, seldom begin in London till after Christmas, nor do the nobility and gentry return thither from the country till the meeting of Parliament about that time. Now, three months from the date of your letter, my dear Sir, will only throw your publication to the middle of October, the very time in the whole year when London is the most uninhabited by the lovers of field sports, as well as music.

I had the great pleasure of hearing your new quartetti (Opera 76) well performed before I went out of town, and never received more pleasure from instrumental music: they are full of invention, fire, good taste, and new effects, and seem the productions, not of a sublime genius who has written so much and so well already, but of one of highly-cultivated talents, who had expended none of his fire before. The Divine Hymn, written for your imperial master, in imitation of our loyal song, 'God save great George our King', and set so admirably to music by yourself, I have translated and adapted to your melody, which is simple, grave, supplicating and pleasing. *La cadenza particolarmente mi pare nuova e squisitissima.* I have given our friend, Mr. Barthélemon, a copy of my English translation to transmit to you, with my affection and best respects. It was from seeing in your letter to him, how well you wrote English, that I ventured to address you in my own language, for which my translation of your hymn will perhaps serve as an exercise; in comparing my version with the original, you will perceive that it is rather a paraphrase than a close translation; but the liberties I have taken were in consequence of the supposed treachery of some of his Imperial Majesty's generals and subjects, during the unfortunate campaign of Italy, of 1797, which the English all thought was the consequence, not of Buonaparte's heroism, but of Austrian and Italian treachery.[1]

Let me intreat you, my dear Sir, to favour me with your opinion of my proposition for postponing the publication of your oratorio, at least in England, till March, or April, 1800. But whatever you determine, be assured of my zeal and ardent wishes for your success, being, with the highest respect and regard,—Dear Sir,

Your enthusiastic admirer and affectionate Servant,

CHARLES BURNEY.[2]

Al Celeberrimo Signore Giuseppe Haydn, in Vienna.

In a letter to Fanny a little later in the year Burney is able to tell her: 'I have gotten twenty-nine subscribers for Haydn.'[3]

Haydn did, as Burney suggested, defer the publication of *The Creation* —until early the next year apparently, for the first edition bears the date of 1800, and when it was given in London (by two rival impresarios, Ashley and Salomon, respectively) on 28 March and 21 April of that year, we may suppose that Burney was present. And we know that he was, as he had promised, active in 'solicitation', for in 1810 he

[1] For more on this translation of the Austrian Hymn see II. 298–9.

[2] In *The Harmonicon*, 1827, 63. It has been reprinted in several other publications since it there appeared, e.g. Pohl, *Mozart und Haydn in London* (1867), and *The Choir*, Aug. 1928.

[3] *Mem.* iii. 283.

made a note: 'I procured him more subscribers for that sublime effort of genius, the Creation, than all his other friends, whether at home or abroad, put together.'[1] From the following letter we see that the subscribers' copies did not arrive in London until some time after the performances had taken place.[2]

Chelsea College,
July 25, 1800.

Gentlemen,

I am obliged to you for informing me that Dr. Haydn's books for wch. I have procured subscribers, are at length arrived. I shall want 87 copies, though more than half the subscribers are gone into the country for the summer; and as no money has yet been received, I shall probably, if I send the books after them, wait till they return to town ere the subscription will be paid.

It was unlucky that when I called at your warehouse this morning, the person I spoke to did not inform [me] that the Oratorio of the Creation was arrived, as I cd. have taken the books with me in the carriage. However, as I shall be able to spare my carriage during 2 hours to-morrow morning, if you will deliver the no. of copies above mentioned to the bearer of this letter, I will be accountable for them, and forward them to the subscribers as soon as possible.

May I ask you, Gentlemen, whether no letter, or particular book for my own use was directed to me by Dr. Haydn in the bale of books? I have recd. no answer to either of two letters which I wrote to him since Xmas. In one of his letters to me, on the subject of his Oratorio, Dr. Haydn says: 'non mancherò di mandare a V.S. un Esemplare.'

I have the honour to be
Gentlemen, your obedient
humble servant
CHAS. BURNEY.

[1] *Mem.* iii. 393.

[2] I am indebted to Mr. C. B. Oldman, of the British Museum, for calling my attention to this letter, which is inserted in a grangerized copy of Watt's *Byron* in the Museum (C. 44. e–g), vol. xv.

L. THE 'MUSICAL GRADUATES'

(*From 1790; Burney aged 64*)

THERE is one social event during Haydn's first visit to England that calls for just a little special mention. Haydn, having been elected a member of the Musical Graduates' Meeting (of which Burney was also a member), entertained his fellow members to dinner.

There is in the British Museum an interesting manuscript of Burney's friend, Dr. J. W. Callcott,[1] a pretty full *Account of the Graduates' Meeting, a Society of Musical Professors, established in London Novr. 24, 1790.*

The idea of establishing such an organization seems to have arisen out of the graduation of Parsons (who, as we have seen, secured a royal post that Burney coveted) and of Dupuis (whom Haydn, in his London diary, singles out as 'a great organist'). Here is Callcott's description of the inception of the meeting:

'Wm. Parsons Esqr. Master of the Kings Band and T. S. Dupuis Esqr. Organist and Composer to his Majesty having taken the accumulated degrees of Bachelor and Doctor in Music June 1790, the small number of Musical Graduates was honorably encreased. At that time Drs. Arnold, Ayrton, Burney and Cooke with Messrs. Bellamy, Callcott, Guise and Henderson, were the only Graduates resident near London.

'At an accidental visit paid to J. Beard Esqr.[2] at Hampton, August 1790, by Drs. Arnold and Dupuis, Messrs. Callcott and Hudson the conversation in the journey happened to turn on the late establishment of the Glee Club and the rapid success which an institution of barely three years date had found, the number of candidates exceeding that of the 30 members.

'Dr. Dupuis, who had been a principal in the formation of the Glee Club and who had given to the Society the name it now bears, suggested the idea that the Musical Graduates were sufficiently numerous to constitute a select party and which might be held alternately at the house of each member at equal distances of time throughout the year.

'This proposal was gladly received and in the ensuing Autumn about the beginning of November a previous meeting was held at Dr. Dupuis, at which all the Graduates were present, Dr. Cooke excepted, who having lately lost the situation he had held so many years at the Academy of Antient Music by the appointment of Dr. Arnold, felt himself so much dissatisfied that he declined being considered as a Member. But the high respectability of his character and the great opinion generally entertained of his ability made his absence no small cause of regret to several members who thought it a most desirable object that "Brethren should dwell together in unity" and to the acute observations of Sir W. P.[3] and his extensive knowledge of the world

[1] Add. MS. 27693, fols. 6–36.

[2] The famous tenor vocalist.

[3] Parsons is here spoken of both as 'Esq.' and 'Sir. W.' He was knighted in 1795, when he was on a visit to Dublin, by the Lord Lieutenant of Ireland, being the first British musician to be knighted; i.e. he was 'Esq.' at the time that occurred the events related and 'Sir' at the time when Callcott wrote. He was a worthy man who, curiously, ended up as a London

we owe the subsequent attendance of Dr. Cooke to whom invitations were regularly sent and whose irritated passions were cooled by the respect continually shewn.'

The first gathering was held at the house of Dr. Arnold, in Craven Street, Strand; the second at the house of Richard Guise, Mus. B. (Master of the Choristers of Westminster Abbey), in Dartmouth Street; the third at Dr. Ayrton's, in St. James Street; then came Burney's turn, and on 11 May 1790 he entertained his fellow members in his rooms at Chelsea College. After this Parsons received the society at his house in Shepherd's Bush.

The account goes on:

'A new and illustrious Member was added to the List by the University of Oxford who conferred the Degree of Dr. in music upon the celebrated Haydn, and it was with much concern to Mr. Callcott, who held the sixth meeting at Kensington Gravel Pitts on the third of August, and to Mr. Hudson, whose day was fixed for Sept. 14 at St. Peters Hill, that Dr. Haydn's summer engagements prevented his attendance. At the Eighth Meeting however, given by Dr. Dupuis at Grosvenor Gate, Oct. 26, the presence of the new member was highly gratifying to all.'

'The ensuing term at Oxford added three more names to the list of the Society', and so, at the Ninth Meeting, in December 1790, occurred 'the most numerous meeting that has ever yet been united', the 'Company present' being—Dr. Arnold, Dr. Aylward, Dr. Ayrton, Dr. Burney, Dr. Cooke, Dr. Dupuis, Dr. Haydn, Dr. Parsons, Mr. Bellamy, Mr. Callcott, Mr. Guise, Mr. Hindle, Mr. Hudson, and Mr. Smith.

Haydn had, of course, to take his turn at entertaining his fellow graduates, and, as he had no house of his own, he did it in a coffee-house:

'1792. Dr. Haydn previous to his leaving England gave the Graduates his dinner on the 20th of June at Parsloes in St. James St. to which at his particular request, Mr. Salomon was admitted, partly as the intimate friend of Dr. Haydn partly as an interpreter, Dr. Haydn having not made sufficient progress in the English Tongue.'

There is record of Burney's entertaining the members in 1794, 1795, 1796, and 1799,[1] on which occasions he doubtless provided the statutory (or at any rate, habitual) 'two plain dishes, with soup and fish ad libitum', and the usual toasts were given of:

'The King and Constitution
The Queen and Royal Family

Stipendiary Magistrate. The joke that went about was that he was 'knighted on the score of his merits, not on the merit of his scores'.

[1] In 1797 (and possibly 1798) Burney, having lost his wife, was too discouraged to 'meet his graduated brethren'. Letter to J. W. Callcott, 24 Jan. 1797 (in the possession of the present writer). It is written in the third person. 'The not having been able to meet his graduated brethren at their usual cheerful dinners, during the present winter, has been much lamented by Dr. B. among other privations wch a late melancholy event has occasioned. *Time* only can blunt the edge of regret & sorrow for what we lose;—but quaere—does it not, likewise, diminish our appetite for what remains?'

Viva la Musica
The two Universities
Our Absent brethren.

With such occasional sentiments as the circumstances of the time might excite.'

There is a special mention of Burney in 1793:

'Dr. Burney having in his possession an original drawing of Purcell of which the merit appeared considerably great it was proposed in honour of our Countryman and the Society to publish an engraving of it at the joint expence. The delay of the artist, together with the resignations and death of several members who had pledged themselves to support the undertaking render the future publication extremely hypothetical, as the concern is now entirely limited to the risque of a few.'[1]

Though good feeling seems generally to have prevailed within the ranks of the graduates there were occasional lapses. For instance, we learn that 'the name of Mr. Hudson ceased to appear in the list' (Robert Hudson, Almoner and Master of the Children of St. Paul's Cathedral).

'In a letter of excuse to one of the Members he declined the pleasure of attending the Graduates since he was never accustomed to dine at his own table without the company of his wife and daughter. If this reason had originated in the purity of his wishes to preserve decency and restrain the effects of excess it might have been respected and admissible, but since he often signed himself in joke what he felt himself to be right earnest, Jerry Sneak, that ridicule was justly incurred which never fails to accompany singularity in which Virtue and Principle claim no share.'[2]

The charitable construction to put upon Hudson's defection is, surely, that he had to bow to *force majeure*—was under petticoat government.

Then there followed the resignation of Bellamy (Richard Bellamy, who, in the pluralist fashion of those days, had accumulated membership of the choirs of Westminster Abbey, St. Paul's Cathedral, and the Chapel Royal). Bellamy, it seemed, was peeved at the non-acceptance of a bright idea of his, 'namely that no Person should be elected to any musical place in the Cathedrals of this Kingdom without a previous testimony of their abilities from the Society of Musical Graduates'—which his fellow members sagely judged would be a piece of legislation 'not only ridiculous but impossible to put in execution'. However, these two resignations provoked few tears:

'It must ingenuously be confessed that of all the Members Messrs. Hudson and Bellamy could be best spared although the noise of the former was qualified by the silence of the latter.'

[1] This appears to be a drawing from Kneller's now well-known portrait of Purcell as a young man. It descended for several generations in the Burney family and then passed to the Print Room of the British Museum. It is included in the list of Purcell portraits given in Grove's *Dictionary of Music*, its Burney associations being there mentioned.

[2] 'Jerry Sneak' was a hen-pecked husband in Foote's *Mayor of Garratt* (Haymarket, 1763).

The tone of the gatherings seems for a time to have oscillated between edification and conviviality. There were 'several important discussions of harmonical questions with occasional anecdotes of former musicians', but there were also 'moments when the power of wine conquered that of reason', and at these times, by less serious members, 'all improvement of the mind was stigmatized with the title of parish business'. However, 'it must be also allowed in justice that whenever matters of real and momentous consequence occurred the attention of all was easily obtained'.

The account ends on a note of doubt. At what date it was written cannot be determined but by then, apparently, the social element had overshadowed the element of learned discussion:

'Friendship and Conviviality are now openly stated as the ultimate end of the Society, to know each other, to shew the world that the heads of our profession preserve unanimity in the midst of conflicting interests, and that harmony of sentiments unites those whom particular pursuits keep generally apart.

'How far the exclusion of useful and improving investigations will make the continuance of friendly and convivial parties permanently agreeable is hereafter an object of consideration for those who are sensible of the shortness of life and who are willing to shew posterity their time has not been idly though perhaps unprofitably spent. But at the request of the Society the Author has presumed to draw out these facts and observations and subscribes himself with great respect their most devoted Servt.

J. W. Callcott.'

As already indicated there seems to be no definite information as to when the Graduates' Meeting came to an end. The society called 'Concentores Sodales', which was founded in June 1798, is spoken of in Grove's *Dictionary* (2nd, 3rd, and 4th editions) as 'to some extent the revival of the Graduates' Meeting', but this cannot be correct.[1] The periods of existence of the two bodies considerably overlapped. The present writer possesses a letter from Burney to Callcott inviting the graduates to dinner in Burney's rooms in Chelsea College at four o'clock on 13 November 1799, and the gatherings went on considerably later than that, as will be seen by the following passage in a note from Callcott to Burney.[2]

'Our loss of Dr. Arnold has suspended all our Graduates' Meetings, and as your time is too important to be lost I shall not be the first to propose any meeting which may diminish it.'

Arnold died in October 1802. Whether the meetings were ever resumed after his death is not clear.

[1] Some muddle seems to have occurred in the Grove article through the editor inserting a parenthesis of a speculative nature. The article as it stood in the original edition of Grove did not make the statement just mentioned.

[2] British Museum, Add. MS. 27667, fols. 59b–69b.

LI. DISASTERS AMONGST THE WORCESTER BURNEYS

(1785–1792; Burney himself aged 59–66)

IN 1786 Burney's daughter Esther and her husband Charles Rousseau Burney became troubled about their boy, Charles Crisp, now about eleven years old. He is described as an intelligent little fellow 'having an uncommon share of youthful volatility'[1] but a distaste for application and perseverance.

There had been Burneys of this kind in earlier generations. We have a hint or two that Burney's own father was like that. Burney's Uncle Joseph, to whom the whole of the Macburney possessions had been left, began badly and 'contrived early in life to dissipate his patrimony'. Then there were Burney's brother, Thomas, the dancing-master in London, who made a mess of things, deserted his family, and went off to America; and, also, Thomas's son, who had 'so unimprovable a disposition that he became a clog on the family' (I. 33). It is hardly true to say, as we often do, that 'there is a black sheep in every flock', but a good many flocks do have one, and of this the Burney flock is an instance.

Coming back to young Charles Crisp Burney, it seems to have been thought that a change of scene might do him good. So he was sent down to Worcester, with some idea that his 'youthful vivacity' would cheer his paternal grandfather, 'and as he attended a very good free school, and received instruction from his grandfather in music, it was an advantage to both'.

But before long 'C.C.' (as he is called in the Worcester Journal) disappeared, to the great anxiety of his family. Then somebody told them that he had been seen on the road to London, and there, in due course, he appeared, having walked the whole way.

He was 'for a time kept separate from his brothers and sisters and by remonstrance and admonition made to acknowledge his error', and after a fortnight, at his own request, put on the Worcester coach and returned to his grandfather.

The next time he gave cause of anxiety he did it in a more innocent way. 'His violent spirits' and 'love of boisterous play' occasioned his meeting with an accident'—a broken hip. However that, in time, mended, and when he was thirteen he was launched into a new life.

It seems to us almost incredible, but at that tender age C.C. became a member of the medical profession—a very humble member, of course, a mere apprentice; but at thirteen!

It may be remembered that one of C.C.'s aunts, Rebecca, had

[1] Practically all the particulars of this chapter come from *Family Memoranda*.

married a Mr. Sandford, a physician. He was now living at Wellington, near Shrewsbury. The boy was offered to him as an apprentice, and as he 'thought that C.C. was in most respects well adapted for the profession', he accepted him.

And so for two or three years, from his fourteenth year to his sixteenth, young C.C. lived in Wellington as a medical apprentice.

And then on 15 February 1791 he was missing again. And a 'respectable tradesman call'd to inform Mr. Sandford that an apprentice of his, of the name of Kinder, was missing, too, and that he had left behind him a letter saying that he and C.C. were walking to London'.

Mr. Sandford at once wrote to Charles's parents in London, Esther and Charles Rousseau Burney, and they waited for the boy to turn up again, as he had done on the previous occasion:

> 'Instead of which, to their great surprise, they received on the 20th a short letter to the following effect; that if they wish'd to save their son Charles from ruin, they must send someone who knew him, to London Bridge the next day, where he would endeavour to detain him till one o'clock, after which all further search would be fruitless. Sign'd KINDER.'

Unfortunately this letter, sent by the 'penny post', arrived too late—on the evening of the day mentioned. Members of the family next day stationed themselves on the bridge, but nothing happened.

> 'They then concluded that either the letter had arrived too late, or that he had caught a distant glimpse of some of his family, and had hastened away; and that, as he had always shown a taste for travelling, his intention must certainly have been to go abroad. This idea gave them great uneasiness, as he was very ill-prepared for any arduous enterprise; and they continued in anxious, and daily expectation of either seeing or hearing from him.'

But no member of the Burney family ever did again see Charles Crisp Burney, though, as we shall find, the mystery of his disappearance was, some years after, fully cleared up.

Meantime a further disaster came upon the family. This was, indeed, a period of trial for the Worcester Burneys, and for Esther, who had married one of them. In 1785 Richard Burney's son, Thomas Frederick (see II. 42), the pen-and-ink draughtsman of 'uncommon genius', had died at the age of nineteen or twenty. In 1790 his brother, the gay and popular Richard Gustavus (see II. 38), died at the age of thirty-nine. In 1791 the boy 'C.C.' disappeared. And in 1792 catastrophe overwhelmed the head of the house, Dr. Charles Burney's elder brother Richard himself, now aged sixty-eight.

He had come to London on business, and taken lodgings there. One evening he set out for the theatre, as was thought. He did not return, and next morning the person with whom he lodged came to report the fact to Esther and her husband. All day the members of the family searched London, but without result, so on the following morning

Edward, the artist, set out on a systematic tour of inquiry of all the watch-houses in the theatre district.

There are still a certain number of these watch-houses to be seen in London,[1] of which the best known, perhaps, is one dating from the year before the event now being narrated and attached to a corner of the church of St. Sepulchre, Holborn. Each ward of London then had its watch-house, which served as a headquarters for its watchmen—mostly decrepit and useless old fellows, incompetent and venal. It was at these places that Edward made his inquiries.

'When he arriv'd at one of them, he was inform'd that an elderly gentleman had been brought there the preceding Friday evening, by a Hackney Coachman who said he did not know what to do with him; he therefore left him there for that night; and the next day, they had convey'd him to Covent Garden Workhouse, as he was then incapable of speech, and there were no papers in his pockets by which they could find out his name or place of residence. The account the Coachman gave them was, that the Gentleman had been he supposed at the Play, and having got into his Coach, had order'd him to drive to a part of the town, where he had a house for a short time, when he was first married! On arriving there, his senses were in so confused a state, that after some search for a supposed house, he was obliged to give it up. He then told the man to take him to York Street, Covent Garden, where he said he had sisters living. This not having been the case for a number of years, and no such name, or house to be found, the man began to get angry; and supposing him to be in an intoxicated state, said he would take him to the watch-house, and no further. On his getting out of the Coach, he stagger'd and fell down upon the pavement, and the man carried him into the house.'

So to Covent Garden Workhouse Edward hurried and there he found his father insensible. He was put into the coach and taken back to his lodgings, and 'a celebrated surgeon and anatomist' was sent for, who said that the head was badly injured and that the then terrible operation of trepanning was necessary. Ten days after the injury (surely much too late!) this operation was carried out; the brain was found to have suffered an incurable injury, and Richard Burney quickly died. He is buried in Marylebone Churchyard.

Edward Burney now set to work to investigate the sad occurrence. He closely questioned the people at the watch-house, but they 'either could not or would not give any information of the Coachman who conveyed him to their house' and there the inquiries came to a dead end. There was no money in the unfortunate man's pockets, which suggested either that he had been robbed or that 'the Coachman had taken care to pay himself' (or, surely, that the watch or workhouse people had made a little haul), but his silver buckles were still on his shoes.

And so vanished Dr. Burney's favourite brother—a man of 'a great

[1] See list in Kent, *Encyclopædia of London*, 1937.

taste for literature', a collector of books, prints, and paintings, a successful teacher of dancing and music, and an amateur poet, excelling chiefly in 'humorous compositions'.

And now we return to the missing youth, Charles Crisp Burney.

Years went by, and Mr. Sandford, the physician, left Wellington. In 1799, eight years after the disappearance, he had occasion to write to that town and made inquiries as to whether anything had ever been heard of the apprentice, Kinder, who had been C.C.'s companion in his flight. And the reply was that Kinder was 'return'd from abroad and settled in the grocery business at Nuneaton in Warwickshire'.

So to Kinder Mr. Sandford wrote, and at last the whole story was revealed. Charles Crisp Burney had died in Calcutta. This is what had happened.

The two youths had set out from Wellington meaning to go to France. (Those were still the early days of the Revolution, and many Englishmen had not foreseen to what it was to lead and were filled with ideas of a new extension of human freedom; Wordsworth was in France at that very time.) To carry out this bold enterprise their combined financial resources had amounted to three shillings and sixpence, Kinder having also a watch that could be turned into money and young Burney a 'surgical pocket-book'.

They had walked all the first night and had arrived in the early morning at Wolverhampton. Thence they had trudged on to Birmingham and then had found themselves too footsore to walk farther. They had therefore sold Kinder's watch and had taken the coach. Arrived in London they had got cheap lodgings in a public house. They had now had the sense to realize that a journey to France on such slender capital was out of the question.

Kinder had then, unknown to C.C., sent the letter to C.C.'s parents, and had beguiled him on to the bridge, but as C.C.'s relatives had not appeared he had come to the conclusion 'that his conduct had irritated them and that they were determined to give him up to his fate'. (He later blamed himself for 'not making a personal application', but 'shame, the certain concomitant of rash and ill-concocted projects in youth, prevented his doing so'.)

> 'Charles was extremely solicitous to see his Brother, hoping by his mediation to be restored to the affection of his parents, and for this purpose, we saunter'd one evening about Mr. Burney's house in Titchfield Street more than 2 hours, during which time an Uncle enter'd but no Brother appearing, we return'd to our lodging.'

Their money exhausted, the youths had listened to a rascally recruiting officer of the East India Company, and had signed on for a period of five years' service as soldiers under the Company.

They had embarked and spent four months, 'associated with the lowest order of human beings', on a voyage to Sumatra. There they had landed, and waited for another ship to take them to Calcutta. Charles now, bitten by mosquitoes, had contracted dysentery, and 'malignant ulcers on both legs, which encreased in size and gangrenous appearance during the passage to Calcutta'. The boat that took them there was a small one and the 330 soldiers crammed into her had found both the accommodation and the water very insufficient. On arrival in Calcutta (more than seven months out from London), both boys had had to go into hospital. A humane 'surgeon on the Bengal establishment', out of his own pocket, had paid for 'attentions much beyond the comforts of a military hospital'.

'My friend was possess'd of that Noble and manly spirit which always resisted the least inducement to complain, nor did I ever hear him during his painful illness, repine at the dispensations of Providence. He often exulted in the idea of having changed his name; so delicately sensible was he of avoiding the least imputation of disgrace that might alight on his friends from his imprudent conduct.

'I was at the time of his death, so much emaciated by the dysentry, that it was with great difficulty I quitted my bed, to witness the aweful exit of my dear friend. Aweful, did I say? Judge, Sir, what must have been my feelings,—worn out by a disorder which evidently threatened my own existence, far distant from other dear connexions—deprived at such a time of the cheerful voice of friendship, this was a stroke almost too powerful for the utmost efforts of humanity to sustain! I should then have met death as I would a welcome friend.

'Charles had been for 3 or 4 days, sensible of his approaching dissolution, and often in that time spoke in the most feeling manner of his Parents, and particularly of a Brother, for whom he had unbounded affection. He requested that I would inform them of his death (which happen'd on the 24th of December 1791), with an assurance of his sincere penitence, which I did in a letter address'd to his Father, dated Hospital Calcutta, Jany. 7th 1792.'

Kinder's letters were unfortunate. This one may have been lost at sea. At all events it never reached the anxious parents.

Kinder, at the end of six months' illness, being found to be better educated than the ordinary run of the soldiers, had been given clerical work. He had served out his five years and then got his discharge and returned to England, where a generous uncle had settled him 'in a comfortable business, fully determined to expiate for the gross follies of youth by a rigid attention to the duties of maturer age'.

'This account, however circumstantial, and satisfactorily given, was of a nature so truly melancholy, as to give great affliction, not only to the parents of poor Charles, but his relations in general. Had the letter been received, which Mr. Kinder mentions having written from Calcutta, it would have saved his family much uncertainty, and painful suspense. It was likewise perhaps an unfortunate circumstance for Charles, that he had changed his name; for soon after his departure, Mrs. Burney [Dr. Burney's wife is evidently intended] wrote to her son Richard (who was settled at Calcutta) giving him a particular account of him, and his elopement. Mr. R. Burney, in return, said he had made many fruitless researches for him at that place. Thus at the early age of seventeen did this ill-fated young man fall a victim to rash enterprise, and immature projects.'

LII. FANNY'S ROMANTIC MARRIAGE

(*1793; Fanny aged 41, her Father 67*)

IN or about the year 1783 the Burneys came to see a little of the Locke (or 'Lock') family, of Norbury Park,[1] near Mickleham, Surrey, and in 1785 Susan and her husband, Captain Phillips, settled in a house at Mickleham, and thenceforth there sprang up a great intimacy between the two families, Mrs. Locke on the one hand and Susan and Fanny on the other becoming (and remaining for life) devoted friends.

Space is here lacking to say what might be said of the Lockes. The father of the family, a wealthy and cultured man, was well known in his own day as a lover of the arts. The *St. Ursula* of Claude, now in the National Gallery, was once his, and so was certain statuary now in the British Museum. The *Dictionary of National Biography* notices William Lockes in three generations—the one just mentioned; his son, who was not only, like him, a patron of art but also himself a painter and etcher; and *his* son (almost outside the period of which the present book treats), a captain in the Life Guards who was also an amateur painter.

In 1792, when with the death of Mirabeau all hope of a constitutional monarchy in France vanished and when such of the French nobility and clergy as could escape were flying to England for safety, a number of refugees settled in the Mickleham neighbourhood, and in particular in a large house there, Juniper Hall, which became a centre of interest on account of the important members of French society who were there to be found. Amongst early arrivals there were the Comte de Narbonne, formerly Minister of War; the Duc de Montmorency; Baron de Lameth; the Marquis de Jaucourt; the Marquise de la Châtre and her son; and General Alexandre d'Arblay, formerly Adjutant to Lafayette. A little later Madame de Staël arrived and became the acknowledged 'head of the colony'.[2]

Susan soon made the acquaintance of this distinguished little company and wrote of them to Fanny, and Fanny, when next she went to Mickleham, came to know them too.

Of one of them, General d'Arblay (see pl. 36, II. 130), Fanny had heard at Bradfield Hall, Berkshire, which was now the home of Arthur Young. There she had lately met the Duc de Liancourt, whose action in persuading Louis XVI to appear in the National Assembly had been so important an incident in the earlier phase of the revolutionary

[1] By the spirited action of Mr. W. M. Willcocks, a London solicitor, Norbury Park was bought by the Surrey County Council in 1930 to save it from becoming a 'building estate'. The house itself was bought by Dr. Marie Stopes and part of the woodlands is now National Trust Property.

For the history of the Lockes, with many sidelights on members of the Burney family, see *The Locks of Norbury*, by the Duchess of Sermonetta (1940).

[2] *Diary and Letters*, v. 117, 169.

movement. Liancourt, as an enthusiast for modern methods in farming, had long been in close touch with Young, to whom in happier times he had entrusted the agricultural education of his sons. They and he had also visited Burney at St. Martin's Street, on which occasion he had particularly wished to meet the Doctor's literary daughter, who, however, from shyness, had prevailed on her father to let her be out of the way when the visit took place. Now at last she made acquaintance with the Duke, who, a refugee himself, questioned her about the little refugee colony at Juniper Hall and said that he 'should most like to meet M. d'Arblay, who was a friend and favourite of his eldest son'.[1] This was in October 1792, and in November Susan was writing to her sister about this same d'Arblay:

'He seems to me a true *militaire, franc et loyal*—open as the day—warmly affectionate to his friends—intelligent, ready, and amusing in conversation, with a great share of *gaité de cœur*, and, at the same time, of *naïveté* and *bonne foi. . . .*

'He mentioned his fortune and his income from his appointments as something immense, but I never remember the number of hundred thousand livres, nor can tell what their amount is without some consideration. "Et me voilà, madame, réduit à rien, hormis un peu d'argent comptant, et encore très peu. Je ne sais encore ce que Narbonne pourra retirer des débris de sa fortune; mais, quoique ce soit, nous le partagerons ensemble. Je ne m'en fais pas le moindre scruple, puisque nous n'avons eu qu'un intérêt commun, et nous nous sommes toujours aimés comme frères."

'M. d'Arblay was the officer on guard at the Tuileries the night on which the King, etc., escaped to Varennes, and ran great risk of being denounced, and perhaps massacred, though he had been kept in the most perfect ignorance of the King's intention.'[2]

A little later and Fanny, staying with the Lockes, wrote to her father apropos of the news of the execution of Louis XVI and its effect on the minds of the Juniper Hall residents:

'M. de Narbonne and M. d'Arblay have been almost annihilated: they are for ever repining that they are French, and, though two of the most accomplished and elegant men I ever saw, they break our hearts with the humiliation they feel for their guiltless birth in that guilty country!—"Est-ce vrai," cries M. de Narbonne, "que vous conservez encore quelque amitié, M. Lock, pour ceux qui ont la honte et le malheur d'être nés François?"—Poor man!—he has all the symptoms upon him of the jaundice; and M. d'Arblay, from a very fine figure and good face, was changed, as if by magic, in one night, by the receipt of this inexpiable news, into an appearance as black, as meagre, and as miserable as M. de la Blancherie.'[3]

(M. de la Blancherie was a particularly cheerless and painfully constant visitor of the Burneys at St. Martin's Street.)

[1] *Diary and Letters*, v. 134. In Young's *Travels in France* he gives an interesting description of a visit to Liancourt in 1757.

[2] *Diary and Letters*, v. 139–43.

[3] Ibid. 165.

PLATE 36. *FANNY BURNEY AND HER HUSBAND*

FANNY BURNEY
One of the two extant portraits of her by her cousin, Edward F. Burney.

GENERAL D'ARBLAY
By 'Vernet' (presumably Carle Vernet, 1758–1835). *See* ii. 129 et seq., 224 et seq., and 280.

FANNY BURNEY
Miniature. Artist unknown; his background symbolizes her literary activities.

Burney himself was almost as much overcome as his daughters' friends, Narbonne and d'Arblay. He wrote to his daughters a long and vigorous letter condemning Fox for his *Letter to the Electors of Westminster* (which had urged that Britain should not allow itself to be drawn into war with France), and ended with a description of a meeting of the Literary Club:

'At the club, on Tuesday, the fullest I ever knew, consisting of fifteen members, fourteen seemed all of one mind, and full of reflections on the late transaction in France; but, when about half the company was assembled, who should come in but Charles Fox! There were already three or four bishops arrived, hardly one of whom could look at him, I believe, without horror. After the first bow and cold salutation, the conversation stood still for several minutes. During dinner Mr. Windham, and Burke, jun., came in, who were obliged to sit at a side table. All were *boutonnés* [close, reserved] and not a word of the martyred King or politics of any kind was mentioned; and though the company was chiefly composed of the most eloquent and loquacious men in the kingdom, the conversation was the dullest and most uninteresting I ever remember at this or any such large meeting. Mr. Windham and Fox, civil—young Burke and he never spoke. The Bishop of Peterborough as sulky as the d—l; the Bishop of Salisbury, more a man of the world, very cheerful; the Bishop of Dromore, frightened as much as a barndoor fowl at the sight of a fox; Bishop Marlow [Marlay] preserved his usual pleasant countenance. Steevens in the chair; the Duke of Leeds on his right, and Fox on his left, said not a word. Lords Ossory and Lucan, formerly much attached, seemed silent and sulky.

'I have not time for more description. God bless you both, and all!

C. B.'

To this Fanny replied with a letter beginning, 'How exactly do I sympathise with all you say and feel, my dear sir, upon these truly calamitous times', and ending:

'M. de Narbonne has been quite ill with the grief of this last enormity; and M. d'Arblay is now indisposed. This latter is one of the most delightful characters I have ever met, for openness, probity, intellectual knowledge, and unhackneyed manners. M. de Narbonne is far more a man of the world, and joins the most courtly refinement and elegance to the quickest repartee and readiness of wit. If anything but desolation and misery had brought them hither, we should have thought their addition to the Norbury society all that could be wished. They are bosom friends.[1]

Your F. B.'

And three weeks later, still at Mickleham, she wrote to him:

'M. d'Arblay is one of the most singularly interesting characters that can ever have been formed. He has a sincerity, a frankness, an ingenuous openness of nature, that I had been unjust enough to think could not belong to a Frenchman. With all this, which is his military portion, he is passionately fond of literature, a most delicate critic in his own language, well versed in

[1] Ibid. 171.

both Italian and German, and a very elegant poet. He has just undertaken to become my French master for pronunciation, and he gives me long daily lessons in reading. Pray expect wonderful improvements! In return I hear him in English; and for his theme this evening he has been writing an English address à Mr. Burney (i.e. M. le Docteur).'[1]

This letter she sent by the hand of no less important a messenger than Talleyrand, who had been visiting Juniper Hall (as, apparently, he often did) and was returning to his lodgings in Woodstock Street, Oxford Street, and who, presumably, called on Burney at Chelsea (everybody knew or wished to know Burney), to deliver the letter.

And so the interest of Fanny in d'Arblay (for that is what we are driving at!) grew and, pity proverbially being 'akin to love', about May of this same year (1793) d'Arblay felt that he could write to Fanny a proposal of marriage in due form—accompanied by a candid admission that he saw very little chance of ever regaining the fortune of which the Revolution had robbed him. And Fanny retired to Chesington, which after Crisp's death (still kept up by his old friend Mrs. Hamilton and her niece Kitty Cooke) remained a place of retreat for all Burneys, and thought it over. There d'Arblay one day appeared, and was feasted by Kitty, who had prepared 'half a ham boiled' and chocolate. Mrs. Hamilton questioned him about the Revolution and 'shed tears at the recital', and he went away again—apparently without an answer as yet, but with hopes.

Then he wrote letters to Fanny and she could see that in his loneliness he was 'desparately dejected'. She evidently loved him but was troubled by the problem of an income. He had almost nothing and she had her pension of £100 a year plus, presumably, a small sum from the invested proceeds of *Cecilia*. She consulted Mr. Locke, who 'was of the opinion that the £100 per annum might do, as it does for many a curate'. *But was the pension to be depended upon? Might the Queen withdraw it if she married a Roman Catholic and an alien?* If it were not withdrawn and if Fanny could do some more writing ('with peace of mind I have resources that I could bring forward to amend the little situation') then the partnership might be possible.

The doubtful step was taken. There exists a letter from Fanny to her brother Charles, dated 23 July 1793, announcing her engagement but warning him to keep it entirely dark until the Queen has been informed:

> 'As this affair must be conveyed to the Q—— before it is made public, even among my friends, I entreat you to keep its design to *yourself* till you hear further. It is of the highest importance that no accidental information should anticipate my communication.'

The proper manner of approaching the Queen had been a matter of perplexity. Nearly two months before this d'Arblay himself had

[1] *Diary and Letters*, v. 175.

proposed to write, as Fanny wrote to Susan in a letter from Chesington of 31 May:

'His own idea, to write to the Queen, much as it has startled me, and wild as it seemed to me, is certainly less wild than to take the chance of such a blow in the dark. Yet such a letter could not even reach her. His very name is probably only known to her through myself.'

Most likely, in the end, Fanny commissioned one of her former colleagues to break the news at Court. This seems the most natural thing to do.[1] All might yet be well. Perhaps, even, the General, by marriage to a British subject, could be considered as eligible for some employment. Fanny, despite her grand friends amongst the lords and ladies and her years of life in a palace, had never come to look upon high comfort and style as necessities of life and was able to write to her Susan, 'You must all know that to me a crust of bread, with a little roof for shelter and a fire for warmth, near you, would bring me to peace, to happiness.'[2] Then her father got wind of what was going on in her mind and wrote to warn her. He was very uneasy, and begged her not to 'entangle herself in a wild and romantic attachment'—'M. d'Arblay is certainly a very amiable and accomplished man, and of great military abilities, I take for granted; but what employment has he for them of which the success is not extremely hazardous? His property, whatever it was, has been confiscated . . .' and so on, the sort of letter that any father in such a situation would write, and be justified in writing.

However, Fanny's mind was made up (perhaps a little opposition had helped towards this), and on 31 July 1793, 'in Mickleham Church, in presence of Mr. and Mrs. Lock, Captain and Mrs. Phillips, M. de Narbonne and Captain Burney, who was father to his sister, as Mr. Lock was to M. d'A.', the marriage ceremony took place, being repeated a few days later at the Sardinian Chapel in Lincoln's Inn Fields, so that the union of a Protestant and a Roman Catholic might be firmly established from both points of view (and the Roman Catholic ceremony had, besides, a practical object—'that if, by a counter-revolution in France, M. d'Arblay recovers any of his rights, his wife may not be excluded from their participation').[3]

It will be noticed that Burney himself was not present at the wedding ceremony. 'His apprehensions from the smallness of our income', says Fanny, 'have made him cold and averse; and though he granted his consent, I could not even solicit his presence; I am satisfied, however, that time will convince him I have not been so imprudent as he now thinks me.' And sure enough, the hard-hearted parent did soften, and there is even a hint that he made some sort of a financial contribution. The Queen's pension was not withdrawn; she had never disapproved the marriage, as she told Fanny later. And soon Fanny was busy on a

[1] Constance Hill, *Juniper Hall*, 162–4.

[2] *Diary and Letters*, v. 202.

[3] Ibid. 207.

new novel that might be expected to bring in money. So things did not look too black—for a couple prepared to live in the greatest simplicity, as this one was.

For some months the d'Arblays had rooms in a farm-house near Bookham (about two miles from Susan and the Lockes), and then they rented a cottage in the same neighbourhood, and in this latter, in December 1794, a son was born to them ('Alexander Charles Louis, son of Alexandre Gabriel Pieuchard D'Arblay and Frances his wife', as the baptismal register announces him).

Then, in 1796, a new novel appeared—*Camilla, or a Picture of Youth.* Adopting Burke's suggestion respecting the previous book, Fanny published this one by subscription, and instead of the booksellers keeping the subscription lists these were kept by some of Fanny's lady friends—ladies of high influence in fashionable and in Bluestocking circles.[1] Burke himself took four copies and in payment sent banknotes for £20; Warren Hastings canvassed British India; three Miss Thrales took ten copies amongst them; and other sympathizers did their bit too, so that, it is said, Fanny cleared no less than three thousand guineas. The d'Arblays were now in a position to build, and next year came into existence the dwelling that Burney called 'Camilla Cottage' and to which the name 'Camilla' ever after adhered. It was placed on a site belonging to Mr. Locke and was planned by d'Arblay to be 'as small and cheap as will accord with its being warm and comfortable'.[2]

Sir Frederick Bridge, Organist of Westminster Abbey, gave in 1892 an account of the 'cottage' as it then was:[3]

'Although greatly enlarged, this residence still includes the rooms which formed the modest little home which was named Camilla Lacy, after one of Miss Burney's successful novels. A few days ago, while staying in the neighbourhood, I had the opportunity, by the kind invitation of the present occupants, of visiting and inspecting the various interesting relics of its former owner preserved there. In a small room, designated the "Burney Parlour", are kept the MSS. of her three celebrated novels, enclosed in glass cabinets, which effectively preserve them from the busy fingers of inquisitive visitors. Round the walls hangs a splendid collection of portraits, principally line engravings, of Fanny Burney herself and her intimate friends. Among them is also a copy of the well-known portrait of Dr. Burney, familiar to all readers of his *History*. Dr. Johnson, Garrick, Talleyrand, Mrs. Thrale, and Piozzi are conspicuous, and under each portrait, enclosed in a glass case, are autograph letters addressed to Fanny Burney herself, by the person depicted. This interesting collection has been made by Mr. and Mrs. Wyllie at the cost of much labour and patience, and forms altogether a most interesting memorial of Dr. Burney and his contemporaries.'

[1] The method of publication of *Camilla* was settled on only after long discussion in the Burney family. Fanny's father and her brothers James and Charles all had their own ideas to which they tenaciously held. In the Armagh library there is a long letter from Susan to Fanny (3 July 1795), relating the various views and trying to help towards a decision.

[2] *Mem.* ii. 259.

[3] *Musical News*, 19 Feb.

In recent times this house was in the possession of Mr. F. Leverton Harris, M.P., who inherited it from his uncle, the Mr. Wyllie above-mentioned, and continued to collect in it interesting Burney relics—all destroyed by fire in 1919, after which the house was rebuilt and a new collection undertaken.

By 1931 this house built 'small and cheap' had developed to the point where it could be described in a sale advertisement in *The Times* (19 November) as a 'modern Tudor-style residence with 15 bed and dressing rooms, 5 bath rooms and complete offices', with 'spacious lawns shaded by magnificent forest trees, sports grounds, hard and grass tennis courts, large covered riding school, ranges of garages and stabling, and the wonderful rock garden—one of the finest in the South of England'—its humble origins being kept in mind, however, by 'The Burney Garden where Fanny Burney is reputed to have written her books'.

The garden in question was, in its beginnings, one of utility rather than of ornament, and its making and upkeep were a capital concern of d'Arblay, who, says Fanny, 'dreams now of cabbage-walks, potato-beds, bean-perfumes, and peas-blossom'. Burney had sent his son-in-law a book on garden management (Miller's *Gardener's and Florist's Dictionary*—a very famous book, first published seventy years before this), and Fanny was soon able to calculate that Camilla Cottage grew a third of what it consumed.

This was surely a triumph for a military man turned gardener; we do not hear that the General literally beat his sword into a ploughshare but already at Bookham we have a statement that he made use of it for cutting hedges and pruning fruit-trees. Of course, as a novice, he sometimes made mistakes, as when, they being still in lodgings at Bookham, 'he cleared a considerable compartment of weeds and, when it looked clean and well, he showed his work to the gardener, and the man said he had demolished an asparagus bed;' though in self-defence 'M. d'Arblay protested nothing could look more like *de mauvaises herbes*'. When Fanny's husband was not gardening he was reading or studying English or was writing (perhaps poetry, for he was a bit of a poet; Burney said of his poems, 'I believe I have a few in an old "Almanach des Muses"')—in fact he proved to be a very domesticated man.

Before *Camilla* there was undertaken a literary work of smaller scope. The Archbishop of Canterbury had sent a circular letter to all the parishes in England, 'authorising the ministers of these parishes to raise a subscription for the unfortunate French clergy'.[1] Then the Burneys' lifelong friend, Mrs. Crewe, 'having seen at Eastbourne a great number of venerable and amiable French clergy suffering all the evils of banishment and beggary with silent resignation', got up a

[1] *Diary and Letters*, v. 189. In view of the strongly Protestant feeling of eighteenth-century Anglicanism this is a fact worth noting, as reflecting favourably on its Christian charity.

Ladies' Committee, to supplement the pittance these poor men were already receiving from the general Refugees' Committee, and she roped in as secretary the indefatigable Burney. The number of clergy to be helped was evidently between 4,000 and 5,000, for Burney calculated that to allow them only eight shillings a week apiece would run away with the enormous sum of £7,500 a month.[1] Fanny, indeed, says there were 6,000. Burney's friend, Thomas Twining, the clergyman, got a letter from his brother, Richard, the tea-merchant, who was on a summer tour, saying:

'At Winchester we saw the cathedral and the college—usual sights. We also saw the unusual and melancholy sight of the French priests, who live in the King's House. There are about six hundred of them. I had much satisfaction in bringing forth my little stock of French, to converse with such as came in my way. We saw several of them in the chapels which they have fitted up. We visited one of the apartments in which they sleep. There were two gentlemen in it, praying. I apologised for disturbing them. They were glad to hear their own language, and would fain have introduced us to their Superior. But I understood that he was often much affected at the sight of strangers. We met several parties of priests as we walked about the city, and they always pulled off their hats to us. Some were in the cathedral, during the time of service.'[2]

The secretary kept his family busy: 'Your mother', he says in a letter to Fanny, 'works hard in packing and distributing papers among her friends in town and country, and Sally in copying letters.'[3] He pressed Fanny's pen and literary fame into his service and she wrote for him a little eighteenpenny booklet of about thirty pages designed to stimulate the flow of subscriptions and also, by its own profits, to contribute to the fund. It was called *Brief Reflections Relative to the Emigrant French Clergy earnestly submitted to the Humane Consideration of the Ladies of Great Britain, by the Author of Evelina and Cecilia.*

This is a book of noble Johnsonian diction, full of sonorous and rhythmic phrases. It opens:

'However wide from the allotted boundaries and appointed province of Females may be all interference in public matters, even in the agitating season of general calamity; it does not thence follow that they are exempt from all public claims, or mere passive spectatresses of the moral as well as of the political œconomy of human life.'

And the ending is even grander than the beginning:

[1] *Diary and Letters*, v. 227. [2] *Selections from Papers of the Twining Family*, 200.

[3] Burney had to get his friend Windham to help him in certain approaches to people, and apparently there were delays. On 7 Nov. 1793 Windham writes to Mrs. Crewe telling her that to his former subscription of £25 he would add another sum, admitting that he had been a bit negligent in working for the fund and adding: 'I meant by this very post to have written to Dr. Burney. I am glad that the pen of Madame Abry, or whatever the name is, is going to be exerted in the cause' (*Windham Papers* i. 172). Burney's friend, Rev. Thomas Twining, preached a sermon in aid of the fund, 'and got them about 20 guineas—more than I expected in so small a parish, and the best collection in Colchester' (Twining, *Country Clergyman*, 179).

'Come forth, then, O ye Females, blest with affluence! spare from your luxuries, diminish from your pleasures, solicit with your best powers; and hold in heart and mind that, when the awful hour of your own dissolution arrives, the wide-opening portals of heaven may present to your view these venerable sires, as the precursors of your admission.'

And, after the word 'Finis' comes an intimation, 'N.B. a Translation of this Tract is preparing for the press by M. d'Arblay' (though what good a French translation would do is difficult to see, and it is doubtful if it ever appeared), and an instruction as to where to apply for 'Plans and Advertisements' of the scheme for which help was so much desired.

There is no hint throughout Fanny's 'tract' (which, if its pompous style be accepted as suitable to the purpose at that period, is really extremely well written) of any responsibility on the part of the French clergy themselves for the bringing upon their country and themselves of such disasters. When the charitable Burneys were hobnobbing with and helping the French emigrant nobility and clergy it does not seem to have been remembered by them that for centuries the French nobility and clergy had been almost monopolizing the revenues of their country, leaving to the poorer classes almost a monopoly in the payment of taxes. Surely Fanny and her father had read the latest work of Burney's brother-in-law, the Burney family's favourite Arthur Young, issued the very year previous to Fanny's tract. This book was the *Travels in France during the years 1787, 1788, 1789*. In the appendix to this book, entitled 'On the Revolution in France', are many such eloquent and judicious passages as the following:

'It is impossible to justify the excesses of the people in taking up arms; they were certainly guilty of cruelties; it is idle to deny the facts, for they have been proved too clearly to admit of a doubt. But is it really the people to whom we are to impute the whole? Or to their oppressors who had kept them so long in a state of bondage? He who chooses to be served by slaves, and by ill-treated slaves, must know that he holds both his property and life by a tenure far different from those who prefer the service of well-treated freemen; and he who dines to the music of groaning sufferers, must not, in the moment of insurrection, complain that his daughters are ravished, and then destroyed; and that his sons' throats are cut. When such evils happen, they are surely more imputable to the tyranny of the master, than to the cruelty of the servant. The analogy holds with the French peasants—the murder of a seigneur, or a chateau in flames, is recorded in every newspaper; the rank of the person who suffers attracts notice; but where do we find the register of that seigneur's oppressions of his peasantry, and his exactions of feudal services, from those whose children were dying around them for want of bread? Where do we find the minutes that assigned these starving wretches to some vile pettifogger, to be fleeced by impositions, and a mockery of justice, in the seigneural courts? Who gives us the awards of the intendant and his *sub-delegués*, which took off the taxes of a man of fashion, and laid them with accumulated weight, on the poor, who were so unfortunate as to be his neighbours? Who has dwelt sufficiently upon explaining all the ramifications of despotism, regal, aristocratical, and ecclesiastical, pervading the whole mass of the people; reaching, like a circulating fluid, the most distant capillary tubes of poverty and wretchedness? In these cases, the sufferers are too ignoble to be known; and the mass too indiscriminate to be pitied.'

And that clerical fanaticism had itself, not so long before, approved the death of thousands of innocent persons and the driving out of the country of nearly half-a-million of the most sober and industrious part of the population was completely out of Fanny's mind.

She writes a paragraph like this:

'All ages have furnished examples of individuals who have been distinguished from their contemporaries by actions of Heroism: but to find a similar instance of a whole body of men, thus repelling every allurement of protection and preferment, of home, country, friends, fortune, possessions, for the still calls of piety, and private dictates of conscience, precedent may be defied, and the annals of virtue explored in vain.'

And so doing she, amazingly, forgets utterly the Revocation of the Edict of Nantes, only a century before.

Let us hope the readers forgot it too, for when charity is to be invoked a little forgetfulness is often desirable and if we wait until entirely worthy beneficiaries of our generosity are available our generous instincts will wither away in perpetual inactivity.

And now for *Camilla*—what sort of a book was that? Well, it must be admitted that, as Fanny's first novel, *Evelina*, was her best, and her second, *Cecilia*, her second best, so her third, *Camilla*, was her second worst, there following it a fourth and absolute 'rock bottom' production, of which more anon!

Burney did not expect an altogether happy reception for *Camilla*. The trouble was that Fanny had refused the offer for it of the publisher Robinson, and Robinson, unfortunately, owned *The Critical Review*, the rival to *The Monthly Review*, to which both Burney and his son Charles were contributors. In a letter to Charles junior Burney said:

'It was always my opinion, that if Robinson had no share in Camilla, he wd. be a formidable enemy to her and her mother. He said "Mm. d'Arblay was determined to fill 5 volumes—and had done it in such a manner as wd. do her no credit. He had seen the critical reviewers that morning, and they did not like it—they had said that the book wd. be praised in the M. Review by Dr. Charles B.—and that's all the praise it would get". . . . It wd. be cruel if a work of such intrinsic merit were to be stigmatized and blasted merely because Mr. R. is not proprietor of the copyright. He has now the Crit. R. so entirely under his own management and direction, that every work is abased or exalted according to his fiat. . . . The work if it has fair play must do credit, not only to Fanny, but to us all.'[1]

[1] Letter quoted in Messrs. Myers's Catalogue No. 331, 1940—to which Dr. L. F. Powell has kindly called my attention. As will be seen in a footnote below, the allegation that Burney himself would become responsible for the discussion of *Camilla* in *The Monthly Review* was a bad guess.

Once again we have the narration of a young lady's difficult course through life. The plot is involved. There are happy passages of humour in which simple people talk in simple language, and passages in which the reader is hopefully expected to wade through dialectical glue like this:

'Where opinion may humour systematic prepossession, who shall build upon his virtue or wisdom to guard the transparency of his impartiality?'[1]

There were people who loved *Camilla.* Burney himself did. Writing to his son Charles he said:

'What think you all of your little niece and kinswoman Camilla? She soon fastened upon me, and with the partial fondness of an old Grandfather I doat on her so much that I think of nothing else night or day. Besides the story entertainment there is here and there better writing and deeper thinking than in either of her former novels—less oppressive distress than in the last volume of Cecilia, and a wider and deeper reach in the knowledge of the world and of the human heart—the moral tendencies are so numerous, delicate and free from severity and cant, that the work seems to me the best and most impressive system of female education that I have ever seen.'

And then he went on to analyse all the characters in detail. This approval from Fanny's father went round the family. Charles let Fanny see it, and she copied it into a letter to Susan.[2]

Jane Austen was a subscriber to *Camilla*, and, in *Northanger Abbey*, coupling it with Fanny's own *Cecilia* and Miss Edgeworth's *Belinda*, speaks of it as a 'work in which the greatest powers of the mind are displayed, in which the most thorough knowledge of human nature, the happiest delineation of its varieties, the liveliest effusions of wit, and humour, are conveyed to the world in the best chosen language'.

In a later chapter of *Northanger Abbey*, Fanny's *Camilla* reappears, too candidly described by one of the characters:

'"I was thinking of that . . . stupid book, written by that woman they make such a fuss about; she who married the French emigrant."

'"I suppose you mean *Camilla*!"

'"Yes, that's the book; such unnatural stuff! An old man playing at see-saw; I took up the first volume once, and looked it over, but I soon found it would not do; indeed, I guessed what sort of stuff it must be before I saw it: as soon as I heard she had married an emigrant, I was sure I should never be able to get through it."'[3]

Charles Lamb, in a sonnet of 1820[4] (prompted by the publication of a

[1] A passage candidly described by *The Monthly Review* as 'singularly obscure', though, as Austin Dobson has suggested, it is more obscure than singular, since 'there are other passages to pattern'. Dr. Burney was very indignant at the strictures of *The Monthly Review*, and so was his son, James, but Fanny proposed to bear up under them (*Diary and Letters*, v. 297).

[2] Given in Brimley Johnson's *Fanny Burney and the Burneys*, 223.

[3] In *Northanger Abbey* the references are in chs. v and vii.

[4] *Morning Chronicle*, 13 July of that year; reprint in E. V. Lucas's edition of Lamb's works, v. 82. Reference in Austin Dobson's *Fanny Burney*, 189.

book by Fanny Burney's half-sister, Sarah Harriet), shows admiration for *Camilla*.

The verdict of the present-day reader (if the book has one) will probably be somewhere between that of Miss Austen and that of her 'Mr. Thorpe'. But 'Mr. Thorpe', if he only knew of it, could claim some authoritative contemporary support, for Horace Walpole, in a letter to Miss Mary Berry (16 August 1796) detailing the many callers of a busy day, says:

> 'Next arrived Dr. Burney, on his way to Mrs. Boscawen. He asked me about deplorable *Camilla*—alas! I had not recovered of it enough to be loud in its praise. I am glad, however, to hear that she has realized about two thousand pounds—and the worth (no doubt) of as much in honours at Windsor, where she was detained three days, and where even Monr. Darbelay was allowed to dine.'

Walpole's reference to the visit to Windsor can be filled out from a long letter from Fanny to her father.[1] She had dedicated her book to the Queen (presumably by permission), and she and her husband drove down to Windsor to present to the dedicatee the first copy to be put into circulation, 'M. d'Arblay helped to carry the books as far as to the gates' (there were two sets, for King and Queen, ten volumes in all), and there an old colleague of Fanny met them and insisted on taking them, 'terrified I imagine, lest French feet should contaminate the gravel within'. The Queen was in her dressing-room, and Fanny presented the volumes 'on one knee'. Then the King came from his concert to receive his set, and, as usual (he was always terribly curious about the business of authorship), questioned Fanny minutely as to how, when, and where she had carried out her task. Next day d'Arblay had a happy time in consulting the royal gardener 'about our cabbages, so if they have not now a high flavour we are hopeless', and then Fanny went again to the palace and chatted with the Queen and the Princesses and she and her husband, by royal invitation, dined with the royal staff of which she had formerly been a member. Her successor, Mademoiselle Jacobi, now drew her aside and put into her hands 'a little folded packet' which was found to contain fifty guineas from the King and fifty guineas from the Queen, as a mark of appreciation of the gifts she had made—the said mark being accompanied by a message that robbed it of any taint of payment and gave it, instead, the dignity of a gracious acknowledgement.

There was another friendly reception of Fanny by the Princesses and on the next evening, as the weather, which had been bad, had cleared, the Royal Family made their usual parade of the Terrace, where the King singled out General d'Arblay and engaged him in one of his pleasant catechisms.

And then Fanny was received again by the Queen and Princesses and

[1] *Diary and Letters*, v. 270.

found that the Queen had already got through fifty pages of her book: 'But I am in great uneasiness for that poor little girl, that I am afraid will get the small-pox! and I am sadly afraid that sweet little other girl will not keep her fortune! but I won't peep; I read quite fair.'

So the d'Arblays climbed again into their hired chaise very happy and 'at a little before eleven we arrived at our dear cottage, and to our sleeping Bambino'.

A quite successful little jaunt!

LIII. THE TRAGEDY OF SUSAN BURNEY

(*1786–1800; Susan aged about 32–46 and Burney himself 60–74*)

SUSAN's marriage to her heroic Captain of Marines, Molesworth Phillips, had seemed to be a very happy one. The family and friends approved the bridegroom—'a noble, brave, open, agreeable fellow', as Crisp called him, expressing also the reassuring opinion that 'now he is married and settled (apparently in a high degree to his own liking) he will prove Œconomical, for which he naturally has a turn, when not led away by high Spirits or Company'.[1] The captain seemed 'perfectly to adore' his wife, 'which she returns very properly', and, says Crisp, 'I think she has great luck'.

And besides other good personal qualities Phillips had that of possessing a hobby, which is said to be always satisfactory in a husband, as keeping him occupied and happy:

> 'He is a most ingenious Creature; and such a Gentleman mechanic I believe is not in the kingdom; he has presented the Museum with Models of a vast Variety of Vessels, Utensils, Arms, &c., &c., &c., executed with his own hand alone with a degree of neatness and accuracy that cannot be surpass'd; for which he has rec$^{d.}$ a letter of thanks and acknowledgement in form from the Governors of the Museum; and a Ticket of Admission for ever for himself, and Company with him to visit every part of it whenever he pleases. These Models are of the many uncommon things he met with in going round the World.'[2]

The happy couple stayed for a short time at Chesington and then went to Ipswich, where the Captain was on recruiting service and where Fanny visited them, writing to her father:

> 'I would that you could but look on at the unaffected happiness, gaiety, and lightness of heart of this dear creature, and the worthiness, good-humour, sense, drollery, and kind-heartedness of her excellent help-mate. I could have no greater happiness myself . . . than I receive from witnessing their mutual comfort.'[3]

For a time they were living in Boulogne, apparently for Susan's health, and then they settled in Mickleham, and, as we have seen, were much in touch with the Juniper Hall refugees.

At last, Phillips having inherited from an uncle in 1787 an estate in Ireland, at Belcotton, near Drogheda, he went there, to Susan's great

[1] Hutton, *Burford Papers*, 75.

[2] Ibid. 76. The Museum seems to be the British Museum, for Mrs. Lefroy, daughter of John Rickman, the friend of both James Burney and Phillips, says that Phillips was often to be seen there 'lounging and offering advice, or a hand, when any novelty arrived'. See G. E. Manwaring, *My Friend the Admiral*, 165 n. A letter of Manwaring's in *The Times Literary Supplement* of 24 Oct. 1930 asked for information as to the present whereabouts of Phillips's models—but in vain.

[3] Constance Hill, *The House in St. Martin's Street*, 324.

grief ('My dear Phillips left me; I passed an hour in affliction, and the whole day in great sadness').[1]

After two months, at the beginning of November, Phillips was back again:

'Fanny [her little daughter] was sitting quietly at her lesson as usual when behold—the door opened, and an exclamation and shriek declared *Papa*. He looks quite well, and is so thank Heaven and sends my Fanny [her sister] his very kind love. I despatched news of his arrival to my ever kind and sympathising friend who has just been here from church with her sweet girls and Mr. William [Locke], all congratulating me with eyes and with voice in the sweetest and most expressive manner. My Fanny is quite happy in Papa's return, who has loaded her with little presents; but Norbury's remembrance of him and fondness is quite surprising. He would not come from his Papa yesterday even to *me* who was never refused before, and who now joyed in *being* refused. "No *tanky* Mama" he said "Papa caddy Norbudy". He brought him all his little playthings, and told him the history that belonged to them all—who gave, and who broke, and who should mend them—but here is a Papa who will not let me write a word more, so Heaven bless my dearest Fanny.'[2]

A pleasant domestic picture! But something was soon to go wrong. What? There is a gap of over six years in the letters preserved, so evidently the discreet Fanny destroyed all the correspondence of that period. When in 1795 letters are again available for our scrutiny we find that Phillips, now promoted brevet-major, has again been for some time in Ireland and that he has with him Norbury (aged perhaps twelve or thirteen—the date of his birth does not seem to have been preserved). During a good part of 1795–6 Susan and her two remaining children seem to be staying at Chelsea with her father, or sometimes with her brother James.[3]

In October 1796 Phillips was in England, and he and Susan now set out together for Ireland, taking with them little Fanny and William. They travelled very slowly—'scarcely more than two stages a day' (perhaps 20 miles), which suggests that Susan was not in a very robust state, and they had a dreadful crossing from Parkgate to Dublin, lasting from nine o'clock on Saturday evening to two o'clock on Monday afternoon, none of the party able to eat anything the whole time (quite the other way, in fact!), 'tho' the Major had laid in a sufficient sea store and the passengers were good natured and liberal in offers of supply'.

And thus arrived in Dublin, Susan found her Norbury, and the family was once again complete.

Susan's parting with her father had been a particularly sad one, for

[1] Letter to her sister Fanny in the Armagh Library, reproduced in Brimley Johnson, 161.

[2] Letter to her sister Fanny in the Armagh Library, reproduced in ibid. 179.

[3] Burney's old friend of the Lynn days, John Hayes, of the Exchequer Office, had lately died, and had left James his house in James Street (now Buckingham Gate), leaving to Dr. Burney himself his 'finely chosen and beautifully bound collection of books'.

his wife was obviously dying. Burney himself was much touched, and wrote a poem:

'ON THE DEPARTURE OF MY DAUGHTER SUSAN TO IRELAND.

My gentle Susan! who, in early state,
Each pain or care could soothe or mitigate;
And who in adolescence could impart
Delight to every eye and feeling heart;
Whose mind, expanding with increase of years,
Precluded all anxiety and fears
Which parents feel for inexperienced youth
Unguided in the ways of moral truth.

. . . .

On her kind Nature, genially her friend,
A heart bestowed instruction could not mend;
Intuitive, each virtue she possessed,
And learned their foes to shun and to detest.
  Nor did her intellectual powers require
The usual aid of labour to inspire
Her soul with prudence, wisdom, and a taste,
Unerring in refinement; sound and chaste.
  Yet of her merits this the smallest part—
Far more endeared by virtues of the heart,
Which constantly excite her to embrace
Each duty of her state with active grace.'[1]

Arriving at her husband's estate at Belcotton, Susan found a ramshackle, unfinished house: 'It is not comfortable and, *entre nous*, can never be elegant, but it is the passion of its Master, and I wd. not for the world he shd. suppose that I shd. publish my objections to it; the country around is flat and, I think, very dreary.'[2] And soon Susan realized that Belcotton was subject to 'malignant damps, ungenial and inclement weather', which, as we realize later, made it a very unsuitable place of residence for her. Probably, too, she had financial worries. Her father's Will, made many years later, alludes to this son-in-law's affairs at about the period in question as being 'in a deplorable state', and in a letter of 1806, looking back on his own various financial losses, he mentions as one of them a mortgage 'in Ireland of £2,000', on which he had for many years received no interest, and now, 'I fear, gone beyond recovery'—which suggests that he had been lending his son-in-law money.[3]

[1] *Early Diary*, ii. 270.

[2] Letter in Armagh Library, quoted in Brimley Johnson, 244–5.

[3] 'Beyond recovery.' It was never recovered in his lifetime, but a letter written the year after his death by his son Charles to his daughter Fanny (in the present writer's possession) has as its purpose the announcement of the receipt from Ireland of the sum of £1,823. 4*s*. 3½*d*., which, when taxes and legal expenses had been paid, would leave in the Executors' hands £1,754. 5*s*. 1½*d*. (the precision of those halfpennies!). This must refer to a repayment of the mortgage.

Then there were alarms. French invasion was threatened. The major joined a local Yeomanry Corps. Fortunately, owing to terrific gales, the attempted landing of De Galles and Hoche at Bantry Bay, in January 1797, ended in a fiasco. This event stirred brother James, in London, to literary activity, and he published a *Plan of Defence against Invasion*, of which, in a few months, a second edition was demanded. (His scheme was one of a register of all able-bodied males between the ages of eighteen and fifty-five, in London and the south and eastern coasts, with weekly drills.)[1] Possibly Phillips's activities in the organization of the Yeomanry had something to do with his promotion as brevet-colonel in January 1798.

Susan's state of health was soon a cause of anxiety to her friends at home. She was much touched when Fanny wrote saying that d'Arblay had promised, in case she ever became really ill, at once to rush over, bringing Fanny to nurse her.[2]

But the big trouble was Phillips's infatuation with a female neighbour. Susan had had a hint of this before leaving London. Whilst she was staying with her brother James he and his wife had received a call from a young sailor, named Brabazon, who came with an introduction from Phillips. And this young man 'gave James the idea that his sister Jane was too much noticed by the Major, and that her family thought it foolish and were embarrassed by it'.

The morning after Susan arrived at Belcotton the first thing Phillips did was to tell his little daughter Fanny 'to get ready for a ride in the gig and (privately) to dress herself as well as she cd.' And when the child was brought back she said that, instead of being taken 'to the seaside, just for an airing', as promised, she had been taken to the Brabazons and that 'she thought Papa would never come away'.

And next day, Sunday, when the Phillips family went to church, where as Fanny knew they possessed a pew of their own, Phillips led the way up the aisle to a pew occupied by a lady and gentleman, whom Susan found to be Miss Brabazon and a brother. This led to an after-service conversation in which Susan found herself much attracted to the lady.

'The next day she called on me with her Brother, and pressed a thousand offers of assistance wth great sweetness—seemed shocked and uneasy at the unfinished state of the house, and surprised me by breaking out into exclamations upon the thoughtlessness of the M[ajor]. "I assure you", s^{d} she, "*the whole country is in arms* against him for bringing you at such a season of the year to such an unfinished place as this—and now I have seen it I shall not be able to say a word in his defence". Presently, after she supposed he w^{d} not be in a hurry to shew himself at Drogheda adding that he was not at all *popular* just then, she spoke of Norbury with the tenderest affection and

[1] There is a good account of this pamphlet in G. E. Manwaring, *My Friend the Admiral*, 210.
[2] Letter in Armagh Library, quoted in Brimley Johnson, 264.

interest: s^{d} he had been *her child* whilst at Rath, in consideration of wch she hoped I w^{d} not consider her as a new acquaintance, for she had been so much in the habit of conversing with him about his absent Mama, that she felt as if she had intimately known me for near two years.'[1]

Quickly this sympathetic lady, whom Phillips was so publicly pursuing, became his wife's most intimate friend, and her most helpful one at a period when she badly needed moral support.

For Jane Brabazon was in no way responsible for the difficult position in which Susan found herself:

'Her modest firmness I am convinced has awed M[olesworth] from anything like open declarations, or rather from *any* declarations save of friendly regard—but this can certainly be known only by themselves, and in the meanwhile his pursuit of her is flagrant and his assiduity unceasing. I am but too well persuaded these have been very generally remarked, and you will not require now to conceive the *drawbacks* at which I hinted. I am far enough removed from a jealous wife by my nature, and circumstances have rendered any tendencies of that kind for many years impossible—yet it w^{d} be as repugnant to my feelings as to every idea I have of rectitude to submit to being considered as *la complaisante de mon Mari* in such a situation. I sh^{d} be in the present case doubly wounded by such a suggestion, because it w^{d} be as injurious to an amiable and innocent girl as it w^{d} be offensive to myself. . . .

'My drawbacks however end not here—for I am become an object of jealousy; and the acquaintance between us wch at first was desired, is become a cause of suspicion, and every means employed to interrupt it.'[2]

Soon the fears of a French invasion of Ireland, of dangers from the Irish rebels, and of a further deterioration of Susan's health, and the knowledge of her troubles with her husband, were causing her brothers and sisters to urge her to come back to England. Phillips being in financial difficulties, James offered to pay any expenses, and the d'Arblays, too, out of their little stock, offered a hundred pounds. Jane Brabazon wished herself to take Susan to England, and 'having just received a sum of money' proposed to pay the expenses out of that. Everybody agreed that Susan and her children should come home—except her husband, and he kept changing his mind and, indeed, behaving very foolishly and tyrannically.

It now became necessary, for safety, to fly to Dublin, which, however, was itself soon almost surrounded by the rebels. Susan's friends protested to Phillips, but their alarms were treated as a 'subject of derision' and produced 'fits of outrage and phrenzy the mere apprehension of which', writes Susan to her sister, 'is an evil amongst the most difficult to support'.

Dr. Burney begged Susan to come over and live with him. He had now lost his wife and was lonely, and he 'sighed for an answer from

[1] Letter in Armagh Library, quoted in Brimley Johnson, 268.

[2] Letter in Armagh Library, quoted in ibid. 270–1.

Ireland' that would promise him the opportunity to 'comfortably form his new establishment'.[1]

Jane Brabazon now became engaged to a clergyman. Soon she was married, and perhaps this had something to do with inducing Phillips to give way. Anyhow, in December 1799, Dr. Charles Burney junior set out in his carriage from London to meet Susan and her family (less the beloved Norbury whom his father still insisted on keeping in Ireland) and to bring them to Chelsea. Susan landed at Parkgate, but never travelled farther. There on 6 January 1800 she died, and near there she is buried.

Burney wrote the epitaph which was long to be seen over her grave in Neston churchyard, but which I cannot now find there—possibly owing to the church having been rebuilt.

In Memory of

MRS. SUSANNA ELIZABETH PHILLIPS,

Third daughter of Doctor Burney, and wife of Major Phillips, of Belcotton, in Ireland; who, on her way to visit her father at Chelsea College, died at Park Gate, 6th of January, 1800.

Learn, pensive reader, who may pass this way,
That underneath this stone remains the clay
That held a soul as pure, inform'd, refin'd,
As e'er to erring mortal was assign'd.
Closed are those eyes whose radiance, mild, yet bright,
Beam'd all that gives to feeling soul's delight!
Quench'd are those rays of spirit, taste, and sense,
Pure emanations of benevolence,
That could alike instruct, appease, control,
And speak the genuine dictates of the soul.

C. B.

And then—Phillips, once so much in love with Susan Burney and then with Jane Brabazon, married a Miss Maturin, sister of his son Norbury's excellent tutor. And somehow he must in the course of a few years have been considered to have expiated his faults, and been forgiven even by sturdy brother James. For we find Charles Lamb, six years later (1806), writing to his friend John Rickman, 'The Capt. and Mrs. Burney and Phillips take their chance at cribbage here on Wednesday. Will you and Mrs. R. join the party?'[2] And a little later (1809) we find Mary Lamb alluding to a Lamblike jollification in which James's son, Martin, and Phillips are to take part together.[3]

[1] Letter in Armagh Library, reproduced in ibid. 287. The Duchess of Sermonetta (op. cit.) says that Burney 'lived in London in straitened circumstances and would certainly not be able to provide her with any comforts'. There must be some mistake here. Burney's circumstances were certainly quite reasonably easy and he was moving in the highest social circles, to which Susan, too, would have had access.

[2] E. V. Lucas, *The Letters of Charles Lamb*, i. 429.

[3] Op. cit. ii. 72.

Phillips appears in one of Lamb's essays as 'the high-minded associate of Cook, the veteran Colonel, with his lusty heart still sending cartels of defiance to old Time'.

And John Thomas Smith, Keeper of the Prints and Drawings in the British Museum, in his *Nollekens and His Times* (1829, when Phillips was seventy-three), alluding to the once so tyrannous husband as 'Lieut.-colonel Phillips, whose venerable age is not beyond his politeness', acknowledges to him various anecdotes of Queen Charlotte catching Mrs. Garrick in the act of peeling onions, and sitting down to peel onions with her (which anecdote Phillips possibly got from Fanny); of the Burneys' friend, Sir Joshua Reynolds, spilling snuff on the Duchess of Marlborough's carpet at Blenheim; of the celebrated Dr. Monsey (an acquaintance of Burney, since he was resident physician of Chelsea Hospital) attending in a 'filthy dirty shirt' one of those evening parties of Mrs. Montagu's at which Fanny and her father were so often present; of Hogarth promising to give a 'breakfast lecture' on some of his pictures to Dr. Burney's acquaintances, Horace Walpole and Topham Beauclerk; and of Dr. Burney, when Nollekens the sculptor rashly essayed music criticism, firmly putting him in his right place.

Burney himself does not seem easily to have regained a good opinion of Phillips. In a letter to Malone, in 1808, he denounces Phillips as a 'worthless father':

'I have a long and melancholy story to tell of the hardship of poor Norbury Phillips's case with respect to a Fellowship for wch. he had been working so hard; and I find it was one of the new *Royal Fellowships* wch. he hoped to obtain; but I am grieved to tell you, in confidence, that from his worthless Father not having made any provision for his college expenses, he has been induced to accept for the present summer of a proposal made for his instructing, out of College, Ld. Miltown, during the vacation, by wch. appointment he has a retreat, and *perhaps* will return to College with sufficient savings to pay for his Rooms etc.'[1]

Phillips died of cholera in 1832, and was buried in the graveyard of St. Margaret's Westminster, the gravestones of which have now been sunk beneath the sward. On his death-bed he had begged to be buried in the grave of his 'earliest and most deservedly respected friend', James Burney.[2]

Of the defection of Phillips and of his rehabilitation in the good opinion of decent people, including, apparently, some of the Burneys, no explanation can be offered here. Perhaps some reader who has sounded the mysteries of the human heart more deeply than has the present author can divine one.

[1] Bodleian, MS. Malone 38, fol. 146.

[2] G. W. Manwaring, *My Friend the Admiral*, 282.

LIV. BURNEY AGAIN A WIDOWER

(1796; Burney aged 70)

THE year 1796 was an eventful one for Burney. He published his big book on Metastasio; his much loved daughter, Susan, as we have just seen, left for Ireland, never to see him again; and his wife died.

Of Burney's visit to Metastasio, in Vienna a quarter of a century earlier, something has been said in a previous chapter, where also Metastasio's work as the universal opera librettist of the period has been discussed. Burney's admiration for him was enormous and he wished to make his book a worthy tribute. He corresponded with the poet's niece, long his companion ('the accomplished Madlle. Martinetz', he calls her), and went to a great deal of trouble to procure Metastasio's posthumous works, which had, he heard, been recently published in Vienna. A letter to a friend, the poet Mason,[1] explains his intentions. During the preceding winter he had been for three months confined to the house by illness, and had used the opportunity to push on with this work.

The *Life and Letters of Metastasio* occupy three volumes and, alas! these have become virtually unreadable. Few people to-day are possessed of an interest in the once so famous poet so strong as to constitute a motive power adequate to the task of pushing through the book. It is a dull thing and has never been reprinted.

When Susan was leaving for Ireland Fanny advised her to avoid seeing her stepmother, who was in a very weak state, and by whom violent emotions were better avoided.[2]

This was in early October 1796, and on the 20th of that month Mrs. Burney died. She had for many years been a valetudinarian, but, having great force of mind, was able repeatedly to surmount danger that seemed to threaten her, and so until near the end it had been supposed by those around her that she could again pull through.

When the event occurred Burney hurried off a message to Fanny at Bookham and she and her husband hastened to Chelsea:

> 'There she found the Doctor encircled by most of his family, but in the lowest spirits, and in a weak and shattered state of nerves; and there she spent with him, and his youngest daughter, Sarah Harriet, the whole of the first melancholy period of this great change.'[3]

On 26 October Mrs. Burney was interred in the little burying ground of Chelsea Hospital, and, as Burney says, he returned to his 'melancholy home, desolate and stupified':

> 'Though long expected this calamity was very severely felt. I missed her

[1] In the present writer's possession. It is dated 10 May 1795.

[2] *Diary and Letters*, v. 292.

[3] *Mem.* iii. 223.

counsel, converse, and family regulations; and a companion of thirty years, whose mind was cultivated, whose intellects were above the general level of her sex, and whose curiosity after knowledge was insatiable to the last. These were losses that caused a vacuum in my habitation and in my mind, that has never been filled up.

'My four eldest daughters, all dutiful, intelligent, and affectionate, were married, and had families of their own to superintend, or they might have administered comfort. My youngest daughter, Sarah Harriet, by my second marriage, had quick intellects, and distinguished talents; but she had no experience in household affairs. However, though she had native spirits of the highest gaiety, she became a steady and prudent character, and a kind and good girl.'[1]

It is difficult for us to-day to arrive at an estimate of the second Mrs. Burney's character. In reading Fanny's diary and her letters one is struck by the comparative absence of mention of her; either Mrs. Burney's stepdaughters did not often allude to her or (more likely) the allusions were later struck out by the family archivist, the prudent Fanny. When they do allude to her it is sometimes under the title of 'the Lady', and one fancies that the word is to be pronounced with a slight flavour of superciliousness or of disapproval.

It is odd that two of the second Mrs. Burney's own children by her first marriage should have run away with their lovers and contracted clandestine marriages. One guesses that she was not a quite sympathetic personage.[2] However, Burney during the twenty-nine years of their life together found her a good companion:

'She was the admirer and sincere friend of that first wife, whose virtues and intellectual powers were perhaps her model in early life. Without neglecting domestic and maternal duties, she cultivated her mind in such a manner by extensive reading, and the assistance of a tenacious and happy memory, as to enable her to converse with persons of learning and talents on all subjects to which female studies are commonly allowed to extend; and through a coincidence of taste and principles in all matters of which the discussion is apt to ruffle the temper, and alienate affection, our conversation and intercourse was sincere, cordial, and cheering.'

[1] *Mem.* iii. 225.

[2] Since this book was in proof I have been favoured by Mr. William Woods, of North Sutton, New Hampshire, with a copy of a long letter in his possession from Fanny to her stepbrother, the Rev. Dr. Stephen Allen. Its date is evidently 1832 or early 1833. Fanny's three-volume *Memoirs* of her father had just appeared and Stephen felt that they did not do justice to his mother—Fanny's stepmother. Fanny defends herself by a tactful recital of the circumstances which justified her statements in the *Memoirs*, says that if Stephen's sister Maria (Mrs. Rishton) had been alive she would have had her support, and concludes:

'I have always done justice to the real virtues of my Father's 2d. choice; & always admired and esteemed her good qualities, which were manifold and charming. Her Temper alone was in fault, not her heart or intentions. But for that impracticable Temper, I should always have loved her as I did at the first. But, alas, I, & all my Brethren suffered more than you,—so rarely in the scene of action—can well conceive from her unhappily ever varying disposition. But of this no more. Peace to her Manes, & rest to her Soul! Such is my truly sincere prayer—& such I uttered it—Sarah can tell you—over her Coffin.'

Mrs. Burney was certainly considerate of her husband's comfort. Fanny writing to Susan in Ireland, a few days after the funeral, records a touching last example of this:

'Let me not forget to record one thing that was truly generous in my poor mother's last voluntary exertions. She charged Sally and her maid, both, not to call my father when she appeared to be dying; and not to disturb him if her death should happen in the night, nor to let him hear it till he arose at his usual time. I feel sensibly the kindness of this sparing consideration and true feeling.'[1]

'Yet', adds Fanny, 'not thus would I be served. O never should I forgive the misjudged prudence that should rob me of one little instant of remaining life in one who was truly dear to me!'

Overwhelmed by his loss Burney shut himself up for some weeks. He tried to write, but what he wrote, as he told Fanny, were 'melancholy, heart-rending letters which have oppressed me greatly'. He tried to read, but, said he, 'I "pronounce the words without understanding one of them", as Dr. Johnson said, in reading my Dissertation on the Music of the Ancients'.[2] He started 'sorting and examining papers', 'ransacking, depositing or demolishing regretful records'.[3] Fanny thought this revival of memories of the past bad for him. She wished him to engage in some task that would direct his thought forward rather than backward. Their friend Mrs. Crewe had the bright idea of employing his mind by setting him to work as a regular contributor to a new journal to be called *The Breakfast Table*, which Fanny was to edit, but Fanny herself at once refused the position, pointing out, quite reasonably, that 'the editor of such a censorial and didactic work' as was proposed should be a watchful frequenter of public places and live in the midst of public people'—which she no longer did.[4] She put forward another idea. He had sometimes talked of compiling a *Musical Dictionary*. Could he not get to work on that?[5] Then, helping him to grapple with his mass of accumulated documents, she happily came upon:

'the fragment of a poem on Astronomy, begun at the period of the first ascent from balloons, and formed on the idea that, by their help, if, in process of

[1] *Diary and Letters*, v. 300.

[2] *Mem.* iii. 227. The dissertation mentioned is that at the opening of the *History of Music*.

[3] *Mem.* iii. 226; *Diary and Letters*, v. 300.

[4] *Mem.* iii. 235. Two or three years later, apparently, Mrs. Crewe had not abandoned her idea of Fanny editing a journal. See the letter from Burney to Fanny on II. 299 of the present work.

[5] As we shall find, Burney did later engage in a task of this sort—but as contributor of the musical articles to a general work of reference. See Ch. LVIII. Before Johnson's death Burney had expected to be called on by him for a smaller task of the same nature. The following note from Burney occurs in Malone's edition of Boswell's *Johnson*: 'He owns in his preface the deficiency of the technical part of his work; and he said, he should be much obliged to me for definitions of musical terms for his next edition, which he did not live to superintend' (1799; i. 261).

time, a steerage was obtained, and the art of keeping them afloat, and ascending to what height the steersman pleased, was also discovered, parties might easily and pleasantly undertake voyages to the moon; and, perhaps, to the planets nearest to the earth, such as Mars and Venus: without considering that each planet and satellite must have its vortex and atmosphere filled with different beings and productions, none of which can subsist in another region.'[1]

And this 'wild fancy' put it into Fanny's head to incite him 'to attempt a serious historical and didactic poem on the subject of astronomy', and, says Burney, 'having been a dabbler all my life in astronomy I was not averse to the proposition':

'Very early in life I collected all the books I could attain upon this subject. I was already, therefore, in possession of a good number; to which I now added whatever I could procure from France, as well as in England. And with these, having the free run of Sir Joseph Banks' scientific library, with that of the Royal Society, and of the Museum, I obtained such ample materials, that I took my daughter d'Arblay's advice, and, in little more than a year from the time that I began the work, I had made a rough sketch of an historical and didactic Poem on Astronomy.'[2]

Fanny had found for her father the best distraction from his sorrow, the best occupation for his loneliness. Soon we find him writing:

'Every spare minute I now devote to astronomy and its history, which I incessantly try to versify, but find very difficult to render poetical. This probably, however, may be the case with most didactic poems.'

He began, too, to mingle again in society, and wrote to Fanny describing 'his various whirls of business and engagements'. As ever, he was now burning the candle at both ends (was there ever such an unsleeping worker?). The day's social and business duties over he says, 'after fulfilling them all, instead of going to sleep like a mere dull mortal, I take a flight upon Pegasus to the moon or to some planet or fixed star'. We must remember that Burney was a man with a fixed opinion as to the sinfulness of giving way to sorrow (see II. 53). Once the first shock was past he believed in occupying the mind and not brooding.

[1] *Mem.* iii. 226. [2] Ibid. 249.

LV. BURNEY AND HERSCHEL—ASTRONOMERS

(1797–1799; Burney aged 71–73, Herschel 59–61)

BURNEY and Herschel, as Fellows of the Royal Society (elected at the same meeting; see I. 43), and indeed for a time colleagues on its Council, had long been in touch. They had plenty of common ground, being both musicians as well as, in their very different degrees, astronomers. This is not the place to go into the details of Herschel's musical career, but the reader may be reminded that his father was an oboist in the Hanoverian army band; that he himself became one; that settling in England he was appointed bandmaster of a Militia band quartered at Richmond, Yorkshire (if two hautboys and two horns can be called a band and their chief player a bandmaster); that he lived in Sunderland, riding about much as Burney did at Lynn, playing and giving lessons on the violin and other instruments, and composing symphonies (seven of them in the seven months, June 1760 to January 1761); that he directed weekly orchestral concerts in 'a garden after the style of Vauxhall' at Newcastle, and then concerts at Leeds, where he lived for four years; that as violinist he led the orchestra at Joah Bates's great *Messiah* performance in Halifax parish church (see II. 63 n.) and was elected organist of this church; and that finally (for this was the last move in his musical career) he moved to Bath, as a member of the Pump Room orchestra and as Organist of the fashionable Octagon Chapel there, meantime training his sister Caroline as a public singer, organizing oratorio performances, and composing glees, catches, and other music.[1]

All this time Herschel, aided by his devoted sister, Caroline, was studying astronomy, polishing lenses, making ever bigger and better telescopes, and publishing astronomical papers in the transactions of scientific societies. In 1780 he discovered the planet Uranus and in 1782 he was summoned to Windsor by the King to exhibit his latest and greatest telescope to the royal family; then, on the recommendation

[1] Here, as a matter of interest to musicians, is the specification of Herschel's organ at Bath (as given by J. T. Lightwood, in *The Choir* some years ago; Mr. Lightwood was able to inspect the instrument, stored in an organ factory but no longer in good order):

GREAT ORGAN

	Feet		Feet
Open Diapason . . .	8	Twelfth	$2\frac{1}{2}$
Stopped Diapason . .	8	Sesquialtera	various
Flute	4	Clarinet	8
Principal	4		

SWELL ORGAN

Bourdon	16	Principal	4
Open Diapason . . .	8	Piccolo	2
Stopped Diapason . .	8	Oboe	8

This organ was built by Snetzler, who also built Burney's organ at Lynn.

of Burney's friend, Sir Joseph Banks, appointed Court Astronomer, he removed to the Windsor neighbourhood, his final residence, at Slough, a mile or two away, becoming a place of pilgrimage for scientific men (as well as mere curious people and celebrity hunters) from all parts of Europe.[1]

The first meeting between Herschel and Burney may have occurred on the occasion of one of Burney's several visits to Bath in search of health, for Burney was not the man to visit any city without taking the opportunity of making acquaintance with any musical or astronomical notabilities that happened to be resident there. (We have seen how, in his continental tours, he sought out not only the musicians but the astronomers, and a combination musician-astronomer would exercise a compelling attraction.)

When Fanny took up her position at Windsor she, too, naturally saw something of Herschel, who was much about the Court. In August 1786 she records that one evening he came to take tea with her and her colleagues:

> 'The King has not a happier subject than this man, who owes wholly to His Majesty that he is not wretched: for such was his eagerness to quit all other pursuits to follow astronomy solely, that he was in danger of ruin, when his talents, and great and uncommon genius, attracted the King's patronage. He has now not only his pension, which gives him the felicity of devoting all his time to his darling study, but he is indulged in licence from the King to make a telescope according to his new ideas and discoveries, that is to have no cost spared in its construction, and is wholly to be paid for by His Majesty.
>
> 'This seems to have made him happier even than the pension, as it enables him to put in execution all his wonderful projects, from which his expectations of future discoveries are so sanguine as to make his present existence a state of almost perfect enjoyment. . . . He seems a man without a wish that has its object in the terrestrial globe.'[2]

Herschel's attendance on the occasion just mentioned was for the purpose of exhibiting to the King and his family 'the new comet lately discovered by his sister, Miss Herschel . . . the first lady's comet', and, says Fanny, 'I was very desirous to see it'. At Princess Augusta's invitation she went into the garden, where Herschel 'with all the good humour with which he would have taken the same trouble for a brother or sister astronomer', showed her that comet and 'some of his new-discovered universes'.

[1] For both the musical career and the scientific career of Herschel, see *D.N.B.* (not entirely correct about the former) and *Encyclopædia Britannica*, and authorities mentioned in these. Also, and especially, *The Herschel Chronicle; the Life-story of William Herschel and his sister Caroline Herschel*, edited by his granddaughter, Constance A. Lubbock (1933). There is a paper (in English), 'The Musician Astronomer', in the *Monthly Journal* of the Internationale Musikgesellschaft, 22 Oct. 1907, and there are, too, some allusions to Herschel's musical career in Southey's *The Doctor*.

[2] *Diary and Letters*, iii. 17.

THE GIANT TELESCOPE AND ITS MAKER
(*See* ii. 153–8.)
The portrait of Herschel is by J. Russell, R.A.

LADY CREWE
(*See* i. 42, ii. 160 et seq., 254–6.)

WILLIAM WINDHAM
(*See* i. 344, ii. 254–5.)

ABRAHAM REES, D.D.
(*See* ii. 184–201.)

J. W. CALLCOTT, D.Mus.
(*See* ii. 187.)

The portrait on the left (from the *European Magazine*, 1785) may be a reproduction of the missing one by Miss Reynolds (*see* i. 271). The portrait on the right is by Dance (1794).

Burney's Coat of Arms was granted in 1807. It is described as—

Azure, two bars erminois counter-embattled, on a canton argent a cross pattée-fitchée of sable. Cross a dexter manche, counter-embowed, gules, charged with a lyre or, the hand grasping a cross pattée-fitchée sable.

The Bust is that by Nollekens, exhibited at the Royal Academy in 1802 (*see* i. 144 n.), of which copies are to be seen in the British Museum and in the Oxford Music School.

THEATRE ROYAL, DRURY-LANE.
1795/6

Free Admiſſion Card.
Dr Charles Burney
By Order of the Proprietors.
W. Westley
Treaſurer.

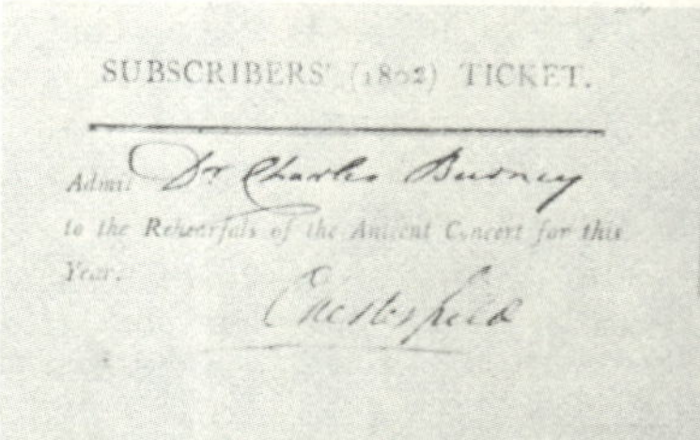

SUBSCRIBERS' (1802) TICKET.

Admit Dr Charles Burney
to the Rehearsals of the Antient Concert for this Year.
Chesterfield

Tickets now in the Print Room of the British Museum.

Later in the same year Burney, being in Windsor, called for his daughter and took her to Herschel's house, where they inspected his wonderful instruments and walked through his immense telescope.[1] A few months later Mrs. Delany took her there again, and this time she had the pleasure of meeting Herschel's famous sister and invaluable assistant (who on the occasion of the first visit had been sleeping after an astronomical vigil):

'She is very little, very gentle, very modest, and very ingenuous; and her manners are those of a person unhackneyed and unawed by the world, yet desirous to meet and to return its smiles. . . . I inquired of Miss Herschel if she was still comet-hunting, or content now with the moon? The brother answered that he had the charge of the moon, but he left to his sister to sweep the heavens for comets.'[2]

On another occasion Fanny met Herschel at the house of a colleague in Windsor, and heard him play the violin.

And now Burney, a year after his wife's death, distracting his mind with his great astronomical poem and making steady progress in its composition, wished to discuss this with his friend, Herschel, and, in reply to a letter to that effect, received another stating that 'he will be happy to talk over with me any subject of astronomy that I may be pleased to lead him to'.[3]

And so he set off for Windsor and spent a night with the astronomer and his family:

'I had a string of questions ready to ask, and astronomical difficulties to solve, which, with looking at curious books and instruments, filled up the time charmingly till tea, which being drank with the ladies, we two retired again to the *starry*.

'Now, having paved the way, we began to talk of my poetical plan, and he pressed me to read what I had done. Heaven help his head! my eight books, of from 400 to 820 lines, would require two or three days to read. He made me unpack my trunk for my MS., from which I read him the titles of the chapters, and begged he would choose any book or character of a great astronomer he pleased. "Oh, let us have the beginning."

'I read him the first eighteen or twenty lines of the exordium, and then said I rather wished to come to modern times; I was more certain of my ground in high antiquity than after the time of Copernicus, and began my eighth chapter, entirely on Newton and his system.

'He gave me the greatest encouragement; and said repeatedly that I perfectly understood what I was writing about; and only stopped me at two places: one was at a word too strong for what I had to describe, and the other at one too weak.

[1] In 1791 Haydn, too, went to see this giant telescope, which he reports in his diary as being '40 feet long and 5 feet wide'. He then gives a concise biography of Herschel, with particulars of his salary, his wife's age and dowry, and so forth (Pohl, *Mozart und Haydn in London*, ii. 207; Krehbiel, *Music and Manners*, 64). For a picture of the telescope and a portrait of its famous designer, see pl. 37, II. 154.

[2] *Diary and Letters*, iii. 322.

[3] Ibid. v. 342.

'The doctrine he allowed to be quite orthodox, concerning gravitation, refraction, reflection, optics, comets, magnitudes, distances, revolutions, etc. etc., but made a discovery to me which, had I known sooner, would have overset me, and prevented my reading any part of my work: he said he had almost always had an aversion to poetry, which he regarded as the arrangement of fine words, without any useful meaning or adherence to truth; but that, when truth and science were united to these fine words, he liked poetry very well; and next morning, after breakfast, he made me read as much of another chapter on Des Cartes, etc., as the time would allow, as I had ordered my carriage at twelve.

'I read, talked, asked questions, and looked at books and instruments till near one, when I set off for Chelsea.'[1]

And a month or two later Herschel, in his turn, stayed with Burney at Chelsea, and listened to the first five books of the ambitious poem—'without one objection except a little hesitation at my saying, upon Bailly's authority, that if the sun was to move round the earth, according to Ptolemy, instead of the earth round the sun, as in the Copernican system, the nearest fixed star, in every second, must constantly run at the rate of near a hundred thousand miles'.

' "Stop a little," said he; "I fancy you have greatly underrated the velocity required, but I will calculate it at home." And at his second visit he brought me a slip of paper, written by his sister, as I suppose he had dictated—"Hence we see that Sirius, if it revolved round the earth, would move at the rate of 1426 millions of miles per second. Hence the required velocity of Sirius in its orbit would be above 7305 times greater than that of light."

'This was all that I had to correct of doctrine in the first five books, and he was so humble as to confess that I knew more of the history of astronomy than he did, and had surprised him with the mass of information I had got together.

'He thanked me for the entertainment and instruction I had given him. "Can anything be grander?"—and all this before he knows a word of what I have said of himself, all his discoveries, as you may remember, being kept back for the twelfth and last book. Adad! I begin to be a little conceited.'[2]

Six months later Burney had to go down to Slough again, to read more of his poem to the great astronomer. And this time the Herschel family and Burney placed themselves on the Windsor Terrace to see the Royal Family at their evening promenade. (For Burney's spirited account of his reception there, see his letter to Fanny reproduced on II. 295–7.)

Then Herschel proposed to take Burney to the King's evening concert, 'he having permission to go when he chooses, his five nephews (Griesbachs) making a principal part of the band'.[3] And, said he, 'I

[1] *Diary and Letters*, v. 346.

[2] Ibid. v. 430.

[3] Some of these Griesbachs are mentioned incidentally in Grove, in connexion with 'Griesbach, John Henry', son of one of them. This John Henry was not only a composer of operas, oratorios, symphonies, &c., but also a violoncellist, a solo pianist, a writer of books on acoustics, and other musical subjects, a painter, an entomologist, a mathematician, and, like

know you will be welcome'. And so he was, the King discussing with him both his astronomical poem and the music of the evening.

'And now', the reader may ask, '*Where is this wonderful poem to be seen?*'

Alas, nowhere! It served its purpose of distracting Burney's mind in the period when his bereavement was fresh upon him and then—was destroyed unfinished! Fanny was never told why and did not dare to ask.[1] Just one stanza survives. For the present writer takes the following to be a relic of the poem. He finds it in an old exercise book of Burney's that has come into his possession, an exercise book that has been turned from its first purpose, pages being removed and the one containing this stanza left because it happened to have a blank space that could be filled with the new matter for which the book was now being used:

> Great Newton's comprehensive soul
> Saw system after system rowl.
> Could read the rules, explain the Cause
> Which kept them firm to given Laws.

From this sample it would appear that though we may have lost a clear and succinct exposition of the history of Astronomy we have not lost great poetry.

There are several portraits of Herschel extant and they confirm all the accounts of his genial kindness (especially that by William Artaud, showing him in old age). Perhaps his granddaughter[2] may be right when she remarks that Herschel was 'no doubt aware' of Fanny's object in inciting her father to this tremendous astronomical-poetical project and that 'it was a feeling of true friendship which enabled him to listen patiently for hours to the reading of Dr. Burney's verses'. Was it a desire for help or a desire to be helpful that led to the visit alluded to in the following? Probably both!

> 'Herschel came hither today to ask me if I could furnish him a Latin or Greek name for the small stars that have lately been found, and called by some Planets, and by others Comets; yet so small that they cannot be found by a Telescope. . . .'[3]

This absorption in a new pursuit was clearly having the effect for which Fanny in proposing it had hoped. We see a happy spirit returned in a letter she received from her father at this period:

> 'My cough is better; and so am I; and, as Horace Walpole used to say, "I am now at my best—for I shall never be better!" I work at my astronomy, polish, make notes, &c., and often see Herschel, with whom I dearly love

his great-uncle, an astronomer. A versatile family, the Herschels and those deriving from them! (See the entries under 'Herschel' and 'Griesbach', in the various biographical and musical works of reference in English and German.)

[1] *Mem.* iii. 416.

[2] Constance A. Lubbock, *The Herschel Chronicle.*

[3] Letter quoted in Messrs. Myers's Catalogue No. 331, 1940—to which Dr. L. F. Powell had kindly called my attention.

to conjure—as Daddy Crisp called all commerce upon the sciences. I review an article now and then for Griffith; I have had a most comic letter from dear Twi.; I have gotten twenty-nine subscribers for Haydn; and to-morrow I shall have the musical graduates to dine with me.—And now I must run and dress.

'So here's my history;—and so good night, and God bless you and your Alexanders, the Great and the Little. . . .

'A Burney party dined with me yesterday; and we were as merry, and laughed as bonnily as the Burneys always do when they get together, and open their hearts, and tell old stories, and have no fear of being quizzed by interlopers.'[1]

[1] *Mem.* iii. 283. 'Griffith' was the proprietor-editor of *The Monthly Review*; 'dear Twi.' was 'Twining'; the 'subscribers' were those for Haydn's *The Creation* (see II. 116–18); the 'two Alexanders' were Fanny's husband and son.

LVI. THE DEATH OF BURKE AND A VISIT TO THE SCENES OF BURNEY'S YOUTH

(1797; Burney aged 71 and Burke 68)

For twenty years or more Burney had been on terms of intimacy and even affection with Burke. They were fellow members of the Literary Club. They had innumerable friends and acquaintances in common —members of the literary and artistic circles, such as Baretti and Barry the painter, and many of the most important figures, male and female, in the social and political world. On a good many questions they differed, as, for instance, the Hastings trial; on others they warmly agreed, as, for instance, the French Revolution. But they always respected one another's sincerity, and it will be remembered that when Burney, indebted as he was to Burke for the Chelsea appointment, was yet unable to give him political support, his honesty of purpose was at once appreciated (see II. 60).

Burney, as he exclaimed in a letter to Fanny (of whose ability as a novelist, it will be remembered, Burke was one of the warmest admirers), looked on his friend as 'certainly one of the greatest men of the century' and 'the best orator and statesman of modern times'. Despite some 'passions and prejudices', to which, says Burney, 'I did not subscribe', he ardently admired his 'great abilities, his warmth of friendship, and his constitutional urbanity'. And Fanny was able to reply:

'I feel it, with my whole heart, and participate in every word you say of that truly great man. That he was not, as his enemies exclaim, perfect, is nothing in the scale of his stupendous superiority over almost all those who are merely exempt from his defects. That he was upright in heart and intention, even where he acted erroneously, I firmly believe: and that he asserted nothing that he had not persuaded himself to be true, even from Mr. Hastings being the most rapacious of villains, to the King's being incurably insane. He was as liberal in sentiment as he was luminous in intellect, and extraordinary in eloquence; and for amiability, he was surely, when in spirits and good-humour—*all but* the most delightful of men.'

And then, to account for the occasions on which Burke had, in her view and that of her family, been guilty of bad judgement (and probably especially that of the Hastings trial, on which she felt deeply), she added, rather acutely, this very tactfully worded reservation:

'Though superior to envy, and glowing with the noblest zeal to exalt talents and merits in others, he had, I believe, an unavoidable, though not a vain consciousness of his own greatness, that shut out from his consideration those occasional and useful self-doubts that keep the judgment in order, by making us, from time to time, call our motives and our passions to account.'

These reflections of Fanny and her father were prompted by the sad news of their friend's death, which had come to Burney in the following form:

Dear Sir,

I am grieved to tell you that your late friend, Mr. Burke, is no more. He expired last night, at half-past twelve o'clock.

The long, steady, and unshaken friendship which had subsisted between you and him, renders this a painful communication; but it is a duty I owe to such friendship.

I am, Dear Sir, etc.
EDW. NAGLE.

Beaconsfield, 9th July 1797.

Of Burney's presence at the final scene he wrote thus to his daughter:

'Malone and I went to Bulstrode together, in my carriage, with two added horses. We found there the Dukes of Portland and Devonshire. Windham arrived to dinner. The Lord Chancellor and the Speaker could not leave London till four o'clock, but were at Bulstrode by seven. All set off together for Beaconsfield, where we found the rest of the pall-bearers, Lords Fitzwilliam and Inchiquin, Sir Gilbert Elliot, Frederick North, Drs. King and Lawrence, Dudley North, and very many of the great orator's personal friends; though, by his repeated injunctions, the funeral was ordered to be very private. He left a list to whom rings of remembrance were to be sent, in which my name honourably occurs; and a jeweller has been with me for my measure.

'After these mournful rites, the Duke of Portland included me in his invite back to Bulstrode, with the Duke of Devonshire, the Chancellor, the Speaker, Windham, Malone, and Secretary King: and there I continued the next day.

'The Duke pressed me to stay on, and accompany him and his party to a visit, the following morning, in honour of Mr. Burke, that was to be made to the school, founded by that enlarged philanthropist, for the male children of the ruined emigrant nobility, now seeking refuge in this country. But it was not in my power to prolong my absence from town.'[1]

And now Mrs. Crewe, who had for several years been pressing Burney to go down to her husband's Cheshire seat, prevailed on him to leave London, where he had lately suffered such losses:

'The die is thrown; and I have agreed, at last, to go down with Mrs. Crewe to the family mansion in Cheshire, which Mr. Crewe, as well as herself, has so long pressed me to visit. M. le Président de Fronteville, a very agreeable French gentleman, is to be of the party. But dear Mr. Crewe, with his daughter, sets off first, to pass a condoling day or two with poor Mrs. Burke at Beaconsfield. We are then to join at Wycomb and thence to Oxford, &c.'

Burney has left a particularly clear and interesting account of this visit in another letter to Fanny, with which this chapter may fittingly conclude:

[1] These letters are included by Fanny in her *Memoirs* of her father, iii. 239–41.

Crewe Hall, 2d. August.

I could not get a moment to write on the road, as we travelled at a great rate, with Mrs. Crewe's four horses, followed by four post. I have now only time to name what places we passed ere we got to old Shrewsbury, which lies forty miles out of the right road of dear Mrs. Crewe; who so kindly made a point of carrying me thither. Blenheim—Shakespeare's Stratford-upon-Avon,—where I visited the mansion, or rather *cabane* of our immortal bard, now a butcher's shop! I sate on his easy chair, still remaining in his chimney corner; and wondered more than ever how a man living in such a miserable house and town, should have attained such sublime ideas of grandeur in the most exalted situations. Birmingham—Wolverhampton—Shifnal by the Rekin–Watling, thought a Roman road—Lord Berwick's—and, at five o'clock in the afternoon, on Monday, old Shrewsbury.

I ran away from Mrs. Crewe, who was too tired to walk about, and played the Cicerone myself to Miss Crewe, who has both understanding and curiosity for gaining knowledge, and to M. de Fronteville, to whom I undertook to shew off old Shrewsbury; of which I knew all the streets, lanes and parishes, as well as I did sixty years ago. . . .

I found my way, without a single question, to the old Town Hall, the New Town House, High Street, and Raven Street, where I was born. And then to the Free School, founded by Henry VIII, and endowed by his daughter Bess.

We went up to the top of the highest tower in the Castle, which Sir William Pulteney now inhabits. He has repaired every one of the lofty and venerable towers in their true ancient and Gothic style. After dinner, I laid out *a shilling or two* with an old bookseller, whom I catechised about old people and old things,—but alas! of the first, not one creature is now alive whom I remember, or who can remember me! . . .

The next morning, Tuesday, I set off alone, at seven o'clock, to visit the new church, St. Chad's; which is a very fine one but so irreverently secular, that it would make a very handsome theatre. I then walked in that most beautiful of all public parks, as I still believe, in the world, called the Quarry; formed in verdant and flower-enamelled fields, by the Severn side, with the boldest and most lovely opposite shore imaginable.

I found my way, also, from this walk to a new bridge, called the Welsh Bridge; which leads to Montgomeryshire. On the former old one there was a statue, which was supposed to be of Llewellen, Prince of Wales; but is now discovered to be of the Black Prince. It is well preserved, and is not of bad sculpture. I was driven back to the inn by the rain.

We all adjourned to breakfast with Dr. Darwin, who is newly married to a daughter of Mr. Wedgewood's. They are very intelligent, agreeable, and shrewd folks.

In a most violent rain, nearly a storm, we left my dear old Shrewsbury; and without being able, in such weather, to get to my dearer old Condover.

Yet I could have found nothing there but melancholy remembrances; all gone for whom I had cared,—or who had cared for me!

Crewe Hall was built in the reign of James the First, of half Gothic, half Grecian architecture. It is the completest mansion I ever saw of that period. It is a noble house; well fitted, and well applied to hospitality. Mr. Crewe is one of the politest men in his own house, and one of the best landlords that I know.

The park, in the midst of which the mansion stands, is well wooded and planted. There is a noble piece of water in sight of my window, nearly of the same effect as that of Blenheim, allowing for the different magnitude of the mansion and grounds. Mrs. Crewe has a little *ferme ornée*, to which she sometimes retires when the house is crowded with mixed company. 'Tis fitted up with infinite fancy and good taste. She has established there a school of forty girls, who are taught needle-work and reading. The outside is built in imitation of a convent, and the matron is called the Abbess.

When I had passed, most agreeably, about a fortnight at Crewe Hall, Mrs. Crewe fulfilled her kind promise of making an excursion to Chester, knowing how much I yearned to see again that city of my youth. Miss Crewe, and M. le President alone made the party; which turned out most pleasantly. I ran about Chester, the rows, walls, cathedral, and castle, as familiarly as I could have done fifty years ago; visited the Free School, where I Hic, haec, hoc'd it three or four years; and the cathedral where I saw and heard the first organ I ever touched.

From Chester we went to Liverpool by water, on a new canal that communicated with the river Mersey. The passage-boat was very convenient, and the voyage very pleasant. The sight of the shipping from the Mersey is very striking. We put up at the Hotel; passed all the morning in visiting Liverpool, the docks, warehouses, &c., which we were shewn by Mr. Walker, a rich and great ship-broker, and an acquaintance of Mr. and Mrs. Crewe's. Mrs. Walker is a really elegant and an agreeable woman.

Eight Jamaica ships had come in for Mr. Walker a few days before our arrival, by which he cleared £10,000. We dined at his villa, two or three miles from the town, on turtle; and afterwards went to the play, at a pretty theatre, where the performance was good.

We then took a little dip into a charming part of Wales, about Wrexham, and visited Lady Cunliffe, wife of Sir Foster, *capo di casa* of a very old and worthy family of my acquaintance of very many years. She is an elegant and most pleasing woman; the house is just finished by Wyatt, in exquisite taste; as is the furniture.

At the end of a month, the President and I took leave, reluctantly, of Crewe Hall, and set off together for London. Mrs. Crewe made a party with us, the first day, to Trentham Hall, the very fine place of the Marquis of Stafford. We were very hospitably as well as elegantly received by the Marchioness. The park, through which the river Trent runs; the woods; the valley of Temps; the iron bridge over a large and clear piece of water; the pictures, all fine in their way; and the house, lately altered and enlarged by Wyatt: all this we saw to great advantage, for almost all, in compliment to Mrs. and Miss Crewe, was shewn us by the Marchioness herself.

We thence went to Wedgewood's famous pottery, called Etruria, and witnessed the whole process of that ingenious and beautiful manufactory, of which the produce is now dispersed all over the world. Mrs. Crewe wanted to send you a mighty pretty hand churn for your breakfast table; but I was sure it would be broken to pieces in the journey, and did not dare take it in charge. Here I parted with that dear Mrs. Crewe.

The President and I got to Litchfield about ten o'clock that night; and the next morning, before my companion was up, I strolled about the city with one of the waiters, in search of Dr. Johnson's good negro, Frank Barber, who, I had been told, lived there; but upon enquiry, I found that his residence was in a village four or five miles off: I saw, however, the house where Dr. Johnson was born; and where his father, 'an old bookseller', died. The house is stuccoed; has five sash windows in front; and pillars before it. It is in a broad street, and is the best house thereabouts, though it is now a grocer's shop.

I next went to the Garrick mansion; which has been repaired, stuccoed, enlarged and sashed. Peter Garrick, David's elder brother, died nearly two years ago, leaving all his property to the apothecary who had attended him: but the will was disputed and set aside not long since; it having been proved at a trial, that the testator was insane at the time the will was made; so that Mrs. Doxie, Garrick's sister, a widow with a numerous family, recovered the house and £30,000. She now lives in it with her children, and has been able to set up her carriage. The inhabitants of Litchfield were so pleased with the decision of the Court, that they illuminated the streets, and had public rejoicings on the occasion.

I next tried to find the abode of Dr. James, the inventor of the admirable fever powder, which has so often saved the life of our dear Susan, and of others without number; but the ungrateful Litchfieldites knew nothing about him! I could find only one old man who remembered or knew even that he was a native of the town! 'The man who has lengthened life' to be forgotten at his natal place! and already!

The Cathedral here is the most complete and beautiful Gothic building I ever saw. The outside was very ill-used by the fanatics of the last century; but there are three perfect spires still standing, and more than fifty whole-length figures of saints in their original niches. The choir is exquisitely beautiful. A fine new organ is erected, and was well played. I never heard the cathedral service so well performed, to that instrument only, before. The services and anthems were of middle-aged music, neither too old and dry, nor too modern and light; the voices subdued, and exquisitely softened and sweetened to the building.

I found here a monument to Garrick; and another just by it to Johnson. The former put up by Garrick's widow; the latter by Johnson's friends. Both are beautiful, and alike in every particular of workmanship.[1]

[1] *Mem.* iii. 243. Cf. I. 370 of the present work, where the last passage appears in a slightly different form, from Fanny Burney's *Diary and Letters*. Similarly the passage about Dr. James will be found in a variant on I. 370: these variants are an example of Fanny's not quite faithful treatment of her father's writings.

LVII. LONDON MUSIC-MAKING TOWARDS THE END OF THE EIGHTEENTH CENTURY

In an earlier chapter we have seen something of the musical activities of London at the time Burney first lived there, i.e. in the 1740's and early 1750's. Let us now look at them at a period roughly half a century later.[1]

The activities discussed in connexion with the earlier period were as follows:

1. *Opera.* Handel's Operas; Ballad Opera.
2. *The Gardens*, especially Vauxhall, Ranelagh, and Marylebone.
3. *Concert Organizations.* The Castle Concerts; the Swan Concerts; the concerts at Hickford's Rooms.
4. *Choral Music.* Oratorio; the Academy of Antient Music; the Madrigal Society.

Let us now see how these various classes of entertainment, and some others, were carried out in the latter part of the century.

Opera

The course of opera in England up to the year 1788 is very fully set out (far too fully for most readers!) in the final volume of Burney's *History*. Here are mentioned about fifty composers, of not one of whom has the ordinary opera-goer of to-day heard any work, with the single exception of Gluck, and of him he has heard only one opera of the three Burney mentions—*Orfeo ed Euridice.*

There does not seem to be evidence that Burney ever heard any of the operas of Mozart, though some of these attained London performances during the last decade of his life (*La Clemenza di Tito* and *Don Giovanni* in 1806, the latter in a mere amateur performance; *Così fan Tutte* and *Die Zauberflöte*, in 1811; *Figaro* in 1812).

The King's Theatre, in the Haymarket, was the great operatic centre of England throughout Burney's lifetime.[2] In reading Burney's enormous chapter on Italian Opera in England one is apt to become confused owing to his various synonyms for King's Theatre. For variety he sometimes calls it 'the great opera-house', the 'great theatre', or the 'Great Theatre in the Haymarket' (to distinguish it from the 'little theatre in the Haymarket', in which, very occasionally, he records opera performances as taking place). At times he calls it merely 'the opera', or 'the Opera-house'. Whenever no other theatre is expressly

[1] For a few examples of the elaborate and often beautiful tickets for musical entertainments common at this period, see pl. 40, II. 168.

[2] It was opened in 1705 and called 'Queen's Theatre' until the accession of George I, then 'King's Theatre'. It is now 'His Majesty's Theatre'. It was burned down in 1789 (see II. 165) and reopened in 1790: in its new form it possessed a large separate concert room. The present theatre dates from another conflagration in 1867.

mentioned, in all the latter part of the chapter above mentioned, Burney is to be taken as writing of the King's Theatre, the one steady home of Italian Opera in England during the latter part of the eighteenth century.

In 1771 the entertainments of Mrs. Cornelys (see II. 168) threatened to infringe the virtual monopoly of the King's Theatre, and she had to be put down (see II. 170). In 1789, when the King's Theatre was out of use through fire, the Pantheon (to be alluded to shortly) was fitted up as an opera house, but in 1792 this, too, was destroyed by fire, and when it was reconstructed its theatrical character was abandoned. There were one or two other attempts to use the Pantheon as an operatic rival to the King's Theatre but they were shortlived.

In addition to the fashionable Italian opera there was the more 'popular' English opera, by English composers and with English singers, which did not interest Burney so much. The old ballad opera, which began with *The Beggar's Opera* just after Burney was born, was already moribund when in 1744 he came to London (see I. 21–2). From the 1760's onwards a more elaborate type of English opera took its place —one less purely native in its musical style. As Burney says:

'Indeed in 1763 [should be 1762] the English pasticcio burletta of *Love in a Village* [compiled by Arne], and in 1765 *The Summer's Tale* [pasticcio from about twenty composers, with some original music by Arne] and *The Maid of the Mill* [Dr. Samuel Arnold] betrayed us into a taste for Italian melody which has been the model of most of our vocal composers, in and out of the theatre, ever since.'

He then goes on to mention, as composers of such pieces, Dr. Samuel Arnold, Dibdin, Shield, Linley, and Jackson of Exeter, all of whom very judiciously complied with the reigning taste, and imitated or adopted the opera style in all its vicissitudes.

The pieces he mentions were given at Covent Garden, which was the regular home of English Opera as well as being one of the chief theatres for the spoken play. At Covent Garden you got almost every kind of stage entertainment except Italian opera—Shakespeare, Goldsmith, Sheridan, English Opera, and Pantomime. Covent Garden also had an annual season of oratorio (see below, II. 177, 180).

The Gardens

Vauxhall and Ranelagh continued active, but Marylebone Gardens were closed in 1778. Ranelagh expired long before Burney's lifetime ended (in 1803); Vauxhall lasted long after his death (to 1859). From 1774, for forty-six years, James Hook was the organist and composer at Vauxhall: his enormous production of operas, songs, catches, &c. (over 2,000 in all), has to-day dwindled down to one or two favourite airs, such as *The Lass of Richmond Hill* (1789) and *Within a Mile of Edinboro' Town*.

Concert Organizations

The Castle Concerts and Swan Concerts (see I. 22–3) had ceased (the present writer knows not when, but Burney in the last volume of his *History* speaks of them as a thing of the past). Apparently, however, there were other concerts at City taverns, for Henry Angelo, born in 1760, writing of a period when he had arrived at a concert-going age, says:

'About this period there were several musical societies and concerts, held at certain taverns on the east of Temple-bar. I remember one, at the Old Queen's-Arms tavern, situated on the north side of Newgate-street, to which, on Thursday nights, admission was obtained by tickets at two shillings each. The performers at this time were in part professional and others were amateurs. Here Shore, the renowned trumpet, used to perform, and Fischer occasionally gave them a solo on his oboe—two such players as may not be heard again for a hundred years. Here, as I have been informed, at one period, Corelli's quartets were played in genuine style; latterly, the society sunk into second and third-rate performers, and I believe the concerts ceased about thirty years ago' [i.e. about the end of the century].[1]

The Subscription Concert series at Hickford's Room declined, says Burney, after the death of the violinist Festing, who led them (as he did the Castle and Swan Concerts), and:

'Another was established by Mrs. Cornely, in Soho-square, where the best performers and the best company were assembled, till Bach and Abel uniting interests, opened a subscription, about 1763, for a weekly concert, and as their own compositions were new and excellent, and the best performers of all kinds which our capital could supply enlisted under their banners, this concert was better patronised and longer supported than perhaps any one had ever been in this country; having continued for full twenty years with uninterrupted prosperity.

'The same concert now subsists in a still more flourishing way than ever, under the denomination of the Professional Concert, with the advantage of a greater variety of composition than during the regency of Bach and Abel, to whose sole productions the whole performance of each winter was chiefly confined. Fischer, indeed, composed for himself, and in a style so new and fanciful, that in point of execution, his piece was always regarded as one of the highest treats of the night, and heard with proportionate rapture. Here Cramer, Crosdil, Cervetto, and other eminent professors, established their reputation, and by every new performance, mounted still higher in the favour of the public.'[2]

Of 'Mrs. Cornely' (or 'Cornelys') more will be said below. Bach was, of course, John Christian Bach; Abel, Karl Friedrich Abel, a pupil of J. C. Bach's father, the great Bach, and a renowned player of the viola da gamba. These two men kept house together and were very leading

[1] *Reminiscences of Henry Angelo* (1828–30), i. 277.

[2] *Hist.* iv. (Mercer, ii. 1017). Fischer was the great hautboy player (cf. II. 195); the Cramer mentioned is Wilhelm Cramer, the violinist; Crosdill and Cervetto (see I. 138) were eminent 'cellists.

figures in London music until Bach died in 1782 (Abel died five years later). Their concerts were latterly given in a building they had in 1775 erected for the purpose (in partnership with the Swiss dancing master and opera manager, 'Sir' John Gallini)—the long-famous Hanover Square Rooms.[1]

As Burney indicates, after the Bach–Abel partnership was ended by Bach's death (1782) the PROFESSIONAL CONCERT (with Abel as a participant) carried on the scheme—but at first under the title 'Hanover Square Great Concert', the term 'Professional Concert' being adopted two years later. The subscription was six guineas and there were twelve meetings in the season; the number of subscribers was limited to 500.

In its first programme, in 1783, this series included a Haydn symphony, and Haydn's name remained prominent throughout. Royalty and nobility flocked to the Professional Concert, which from 1786 took place every Monday. A committee of subscribers managed the affair. This committee tried to get Haydn to London but failed. Salomon succeeded (see II. 110), and to meet the dangerous competition thus established the committee engaged Pleyel. He conducted his first concert in February 1792; the programme contained symphonies by Mozart, by Haydn, and by Pleyel himself, and Haydn attended. In 1793 these concerts ceased and a feeble attempt to revive them in 1799 did not succeed.

THE ANACREONTIC SOCIETY was founded in 1766 and held fortnightly concerts in the ballroom of the Crown and Anchor tavern, in the Strand. It had a male membership of merchants, bankers, and the like, with professional musicians (as honorary members) to supply the performances. Orchestral and chamber music, choral music, and solo vocal music made up the programmes. After each concert there was a supper and then some vocalist of standing sang John Stafford Smith's *To Anacreon in Heaven*,[2] and catches and glees followed—sometimes continuing until 3 a.m.

Ladies were (sometimes, at any rate) present in the gallery, as the following account of a visit of Haydn to the Society in 1791 shows:

'Before the grand finale the celebrated Haydn entered the room, and was welcomed by the Sons of Harmony with every mark of respect and attention.

'A small party of ladies occupied the gallery that overlooks the Concert-Room, seemingly so well pleased with the instrumental performance that they returned after supper, joining chorus with "Anacreon in Heaven" and his convivial votaries, till "Sigh no more, Ladies" gently whispered the restraint which modesty ever imposes on the midnight crew.'[3]

[1] For portraits of Bach and Abel see pl. 39, II. 168.

[2] The melody was in 1814 attached to Francis Scott Key's poem, 'The Star-Spangled Banner' which was adopted in 1931 as the official national anthem of the United States. For its history see O. G. Sonneck, *Report on 'The Star-Spangled Banner'* (Library of Congress, 1914).

[3] Report in *The Gazetteer*, 14 Jan. 1791 (quoted in *The Musical Times*, Oct. 1902, 642).

It was a row amongst the members owing to the singing of some comic songs that were considered to be unfit for the ears of the ladies' gallery that broke up the Society, three years after this (1794).

It may be of interest to give an account of this Society by one who was often present at its gatherings. Michael Kelly, in his *Reminiscences* (ii. 101), speaking of his friend Dodd, the actor, says:

'He was a constant attendant of the Anacreontic Society, held at the Crown and Anchor in the Strand, which was admirably conducted by a set of bankers and merchants. They had a good concert in the early part of the evening, by a most excellent band led by Cramer; after which, the company retired to the large room, where supper was provided. The principal vocal performers of the day were to be found there. Old Charles Bannister, after supper, uniformly sang, with powerful effect, "Anacreon in Heaven", which was there originally sung by Webster. There were the best catches and glees, sung by Webbe, Danby, Dignum, Hobbs, Sedgwick, Suett, &c. relieved by some famous songs of Dodd's. I passed many delightful evenings in this society, and was extremely sorry when it was discontinued.'

A more free and easy organization somewhat on the same lines as the last was the MULBERRY TREE CLUB, held at a coffee house in Bow Street. The members and any of the public who cared to buy tickets (for there was nothing exclusive about this 'club') dined together at three o'clock on Saturdays. Vocalists from the theatres largely made up the membership and they provided the entertainment (the proprietor of the coffee house, Matt Williams, was himself an actor and a favourite with his colleagues, who, apparently, rallied round him).[1] There were probably many more of these informal dining and music clubs scattered about the central parts of London at that time.

MRS. CORNELYS'S ENTERTAINMENTS

We must now discuss two organizations that, possessing extensive and grandiose premises, used them not merely for concert-giving but also for the carrying out of masquerades and similar fashionable entertainments of a lighter and more social kind.

'On Wednesday evening', writes Fanny in her diary during April 1770, 'we went to Mrs. Cornely's with papa. . . . The magnificence of the rooms, splendour of the illuminations and embellishments, and the brilliant appearance of the company exceeded anything I ever before saw. The apartments were so crowded we had scarce room to move, which was quite disagreeable, nevertheless the flight of apartments both upstairs and on the ground floor seemed endless.'[2] And, in *Humphry Clinker*, Smollett's heroine is equally enthusiastic—'Between Ranelagh and Vauxhall I have been at Mrs. Cornely's assembly, which, for the rooms, the dresses, and decorations, surpasses all description'.

[1] *Reminiscences of Henry Angelo* (1828–30), ii. 163.

[2] *Early Diary*, i. 89. For a portrait of Mrs. Cornelys see opposite; for one of her tickets see pl. 40, II. 169.

JOHN CHRISTIAN BACH AND KARL FRIEDRICH ABEL
Oil painting by their friend Gainsborough and etching by W. N. Gardiner.
(For Burney's description of the Bach–Abel activities *see* ii. 166–7.)

MRS. CORNELYS
or her adventurous career, her fashionable cial and musical activities in London, and her ultimate disaster, *see* ii. 168–71.

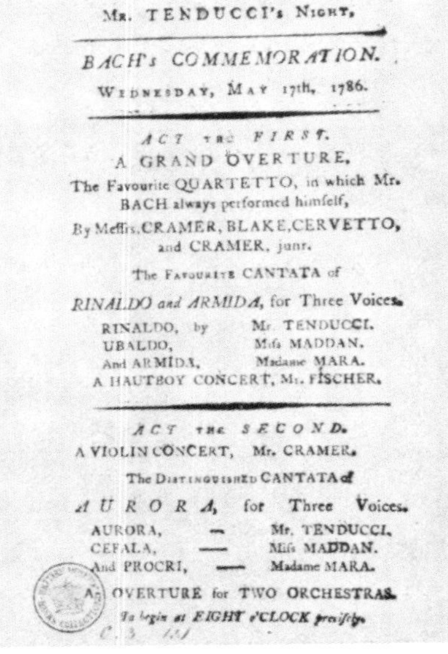

MR. TENDUCCI's NIGHT,

BACH's COMMEMORATION.

WEDNESDAY, MAY 17th, 1786.

ACT THE FIRST.

A GRAND OVERTURE,

The Favourite QUARTETTO, in which Mr. BACH always performed himself,

By Meffrs. CRAMER, BLAKE, CERVETTO, and CRAMER, junr.

The FAVOURITE CANTATA of

RINALDO and ARMIDA, for Three Voices.

RINALDO, by	Mr. TENDUCCI.
UBALDO,	Mifs MADDAN.
And ARMIDA,	Madame MARA.

A HAUTBOY CONCERT, Mr. FISCHER.

ACT THE SECOND.

A VIOLIN CONCERT, Mr. CRAMER.

The DISTINGUISHED CANTATA of

AURORA, for Three Voices.

AURORA,	—	Mr. TENDUCCI.
CEFALA,	—	Mifs MADDAN.
And PROCRI,	—	Madame MARA.

AN OVERTURE for TWO ORCHESTRAS.

To begin at EIGHT o'CLOCK precifely.

A MEMORIAL CONCERT
The celebrated sopranist, Tenducci, four years after J. C. Bach's death announced this commemorative programme of his compositions.

PLATE 40. *WHEN CONCERT TICKETS WERE WORKS OF ART*

By CIPRIANI; engraved by BARTOLOZZI

Designed and engraved by WM. SHARP

By CIPRIANI; engraved by BARTOLOZZI

Designed and engraved by BARTOLOZZI

By WM. LAWRENSON; engraved by BARTOLOZZI

A Charity Concert Ticket

By ROBERT SMIRKE; engrave
by JAS. HEATH

At the period of Fanny's diary entry, just quoted, the fame of Mrs. Cornelys's entertainment was at its height, but the very next year she was indicted for keeping 'a common disorderly house', and the year following she was bankrupt.

This Mrs. Cornelys (*née* Imer), at the date of this visit of Burney and some of his daughters to her entertainment, was a woman of forty-eight. She had been born in Venice in 1723; had at seventeen become the mistress of a senator named Malipiero; had passed into Bavaria and at thirty become mistress of the reigning Margrave of Bayreuth; had married a dancer named Pompeati, who went mad (and no wonder!) and then committed suicide; had won the admiration of Prince Charles of Lorraine, who entrusted to her 'the direction of all the theatres in the Austrian Netherlands' (a strange circumstance, but all the accounts of her give it, or something like it); and had lived in Amsterdam under the name of Madame Trente but there married a certain Cornelis de Rigerboos, and hereafter called herself 'Cornelys'.[1]

She was apparently a vocalist of some quality, for when Gluck made his early visit to England she is said to have taken part in the performance of his opera. This statement, often made, is presumably based upon the following passage in Burney's *History*:

> '1746. There was no opera attempted at the great theatre in the Haymarket, till January 7th, when LA CADUTA DE' GIGANTI, set by Gluck, was performed before the Duke of Cumberland, in compliment to whom the whole was written and composed. The singers were Monticelli, Jozzi, and Ciacchi; with Signora Imer, Pompeati, afterwards better known by the name of Madame *Cornelie*, and Frasi. The first woman, Imer, never surpassed mediocrity in voice, taste, or action; and the Pompeati, though nominally second woman, had such a masculine and violent manner of singing, that few female symptoms were perceptible.'[2]

After this early visit to England the adventurous Mrs. Cornelys may have returned to the Continent, but in 1760 she was back in London, for in that year she bought Carlisle House, Soho Square (built by an Earl of Carlisle seventy or eighty years earlier), and fitted it up in the style described above by Fanny Burney. Casanova, who claimed to be the father of Mrs. Cornelys's son and daughter, appeared in London about this time, and he records her as saying, 'You must know that I give twelve balls a year for the nobility and the same number for the middle-class people. I have sometimes as many as six hundred people

[1] See *D.N.B.*; Edward Walford, *Old and New London* (1872–8); *Notes and Queries*, 8th Series, ix. 282; &c. But it is impossible to reconcile with exactitude all the accounts of this adventurous life.

[2] *Hist.* iv. 452 (Mercer, ii. 844). There are two oddities about this passage. Firstly the first and second women bear respectively the maiden name and first married name of Mrs. Cornelys. What does this mean? Secondly Burney uses the spelling 'Cornelie', whereas elsewhere he calls her 'Cornely' and his daughter and other people all use 'Cornelys': this latter small point, however, has obviously little significance.

in my rooms—at two guineas a head.' Casanova says that Mrs. Cornelys was then living in a big way—'three secretaries, thirty-two domestics, six horses, a pack of hounds and a lady companion' (Casanova's own order of going in; the present writer would not treat a 'dame de compagnie' thus cavalierly).

Mrs. Cornelys had the adroitness to associate with her some of the leaders of fashion as a 'Society', and Casanova records the circumstance of Lady Harrington persuading him to buy a ticket from her and giving him a receipt for his two guineas.

In 1764 Mrs. Cornelys extended the scope of her activities. She began to give occasional musical performances. Next year these became the regular series already mentioned as directed by John Christian Bach and the great gamba player, K. F. Abel. The Balls and Assemblies also continued, and were attended by notable people, such as, in 1768, the King of Denmark. Members of the British royal family are found amongst the company, as also Burney's friends, Mrs. Crewe and Lord Sandwich.

Then came the sudden collapse above mentioned. The concert scheme seems to have been taken as dangerous rivalry by the managers at the Italian Opera at the King's Theatre, and they found one or two different ways of setting the law in motion.[1] And just at this time the Pantheon opened, which probably gave the finishing blow. And so in 1772 Carlisle House and all its contents were advertised for sale by auction. Whether it was sold and, if so, who bought it, is not clear, but it was, apparently, still available for entertainments and we find Mrs. Cornelys herself making an occasional attempt to get the public into it again—as in 1774 when Fanny had a ticket for one of her Assemblies offered by a young gentleman:

'"What Assemblies do you frequent, Ma'am?" "Me, Sir? Indeed I never dance; I go to none!" "To none? bless me! but—pray, Ma'am—will you do me the honour to accept any tickets for Mrs. Cornely's?" "Sir, I am obliged to you; but I never—" "No, Sir;" said my father [gravely]; "she does nothing of that sort."'[2]

And so in 1775 when there was announced a 'Rural Masquerade', and 1776 when there was announced a Masked Ball with a number of 'bands of music' in the various rooms, we hear that:

'It is to be much wished the company may convene early, as, about half-past eleven, a numerous and select party of Gentlemen (who have formed the plan) mean to enter the Great Gallery as cavalry, and parade through every room till past twelve, when the supper will be announced by the sounding of trumpets and beating of kettle drums, who will march playing,

[1] Horace Walpole gives a spicy account of the attacks on Mrs. Cornelys and her attempts to parry them (letter to Horace Mann, 22 Feb. 1771; in Toynbee's edition, viii. 12). He speaks as though the Carlisle House 'Harmonic Meetings' were really opera performances.

[2] *Early Diary*, i. 298.

and the company walking in regular procession back again, through the large suite of apartments already described, to the bottom of the Great Stairs (the illuminations of which will be new and striking) which leads the company up to the front Drawing-room; which, with the middle Drawing-room, will be laid out in a manner, it is presumed, will give an agreeable surprize to the spectators, as they are to be displayed as sideboards, or beaufets, exactly in the same manner as was performed by the city of Paris in honour of the marriage of the Dauphin of France to the Infanta of Spain. From these rooms they will proceed to the Star-room, which will also be rendered worthy of the reception of the company by illuminations, music, &c.; and from there will be a most delightful perspective view of the great Ball-room, where the supper is to be served, and in such a taste, as to admit of many hundred people being all seated at one time, at different tables, and yet have a distinct and pleasant view of one another, at the same time a grand band, superb decorations, and the illuminations perfectly after a new taste.'[1]

However, nothing now succeeded; the gorgeous Carlisle House was doomed. Various people tried to make it 'go' again, but without much success. Horace Walpole alludes to what may have been a last despairing effort on the part of Mrs. Cornelys herself in 1781. In 1785 the property was in Chancery, and in 1788 and 1792 its two detached portions (joined by a 'Chinese bridge') were pulled down, a Roman Catholic chapel (predecessor of the one that now stands there) then being built on one part of the site.

As for Mrs. Cornelys she tried keeping an hotel at Southampton; transformed herself somehow into 'Mrs. Smith'; sold asses' milk in Knightsbridge; got into the Fleet Prison and got out again during the Gordon Riots; got in again and, aged seventy-four, there died in 1797. What a life!

The Pantheon

Now for the other great musical, dancing, and assembly enterprise.

'What do you think of a winter Ranelagh erecting in Oxford Road at the expense of sixty thousand pounds?' writes Horace Walpole from Strawberry Hill to his friend Sir Horace Mann in Florence. That was in May 1770, and twelve months later he refers to it again. He has been mentioning an occurrence in France that amuses him, and goes on:

'If we laugh at the French they stare at us. Our enormous luxury and expense astonishes them. I carried their Ambassador, and a Comte de Levi, the other morning to see the new winter Ranelagh in Oxford Road, which is

[1] Quoted in E. F. Rimbault (Ed. George Clinch), *Soho and its Associations* (1895), 60. Much of the information here given as to Mrs. Cornelys's life and activities comes either from this book or from the *Mémoires de Casanova*, especially vol. v, ch. xvii (The edition consulted is that of Flammarion of Paris, but from the list of references given at the end of the article 'Cornelys' in *D.N.B.* to the Brussels edition of 1881 it is clear that the arrangement of volumes, chapters, and pages in these two editions tallies). There are also a number of useful references to Mrs. Cornelys in Horace Walpole's letters (see index to Toynbee's edition) —the last being dated 1781.

almost finished. It amazed me myself. Imagine Balbec in all its glory! The pillars are of artificial *giallo antico*. The ceilings, even of the passages, are of the most beautiful stuccos in the best taste of grotesque. The ceilings of the ball-rooms and the panels painted like Raphael's *loggias* in the Vatican. A dome like the Pantheon [i.e. the original one in Rome], glazed.... Monsieur de Guisnes said to me, "Ce n'est qu'à Londres qu'on peut faire tout cela."'

Later Walpole calls the London Pantheon 'the most beautiful edifice in England' (Burney goes farther and in Rees's *Cyclopaedia* roundly calls it 'the most elegant structure in Europe, if not on the globe'; for pictures of both exterior and interior see pl. 29, II. 64). And when Walpole goes to an entertainment there he enthuses:

'There has been a masquerade at the Pantheon, which was so glorious a vision that I thought I was in the old Pantheon, or in the Temples of Delphi or Ephesus, amidst a crowd of various nations, and that formerly

Panthoides Euphorbus eram,

and did but recollect what I had seen. All the friezes and niches were edged with alternate lamps of green and purple glass, that shed a most heathen light, and the dome was illuminated by a heaven of oiled paper well painted with gods and goddesses. Mr. Wyat, the architect, has so much taste that I think he must be descended from Sir Thomas.'[1]

Johnson and Boswell went to see the new wonder of the world (31 March 1772):

'We then walked to the Pantheon. The first view of it did not strike us so much as Ranelagh, of which he said, the *coup d'œil* was the finest thing he had ever seen. The truth is, Ranelagh is of a more beautiful form; more of it, or rather indeed the whole *rotunda*, appears at once, and it is better lighted. However, as Johnson observed, we saw the Pantheon in time of mourning [the King's mother was just dead] when there was a dull uniformity; whereas we had seen Ranelagh when the view was enlivened with a gay profusion of colours. . . .

'I said there was not half a guinea's worth of pleasure in seeing this place.

'JOHNSON. "But, Sir, there is half a guinea's worth of inferiority to other people in not having seen it."

'BOSWELL. "I doubt, Sir, whether there are many happy people here."

'JOHNSON. "Yes, Sir, there are many happy people here. There are many people here who are watching hundreds, and who think hundreds are watching them."

'Happening to meet Sir Adam Fergusson, I presented him to Dr. Johnson. Sir Adam expressed some apprehension that the Pantheon would encourage luxury. "Sir, (said Johnson,) I am a great friend to publick amusements; for they keep people from vice."'

Gibbon, about the same time, paid the place a visit and called it 'the wonder of the eighteenth century and of the British empire'.[2]

[1] *Letters of Horace Walpole* (Toynbee), vii. 379; viii. 28, 162, 313. The last reference is, of course, to the early-sixteenth-century poet, Sir Thomas Wyatt.

[2] Gibbon, *Misc. Works*, ii. 74.

Six years after the Pantheon had been opened Fanny sent her Evelina there, and made her write home:

'I was extremely struck with the beauty of the building, which greatly surpassed whatever I could have expected or imagined. Yet it has more the appearance of a chapel than of a place of diversion; and though I was quite charmed with the magnificence of the room, I felt that I could not be as gay and thoughtless there as at Ranelagh; for there is something in it which rather inspires awe and solemnity, than mirth and pleasure. However, perhaps it may only have this effect upon such a novice as myself.'

And when *Cecilia* appeared the Pantheon figured in that also. In fact, as Fanny's two heroines were in London they *had* to go to the Pantheon. Everybody did, though as Fanny makes clear to us a great many people who went to the concerts there did so with the object Johnson mentions (that of seeing and being seen), and were very supercilious about the music.

'"I believe that solo will never be over; I hate a solo; it sinks, it depresses me intolerably."

'"You will presently, Sir," said Cecilia, looking at the bill of the concert, "have a full piece; and that, I hope, will revive you."

'"A full piece! Oh insupportable! no taste in it, no delicacy, no room for the smallest feeling."

'"Perhaps, then, you are only fond of singing?"

'"I should be, if I could hear it; but we are now so miserably off in voices, that I hardly ever attempt to listen to a song, without fancying myself deaf from the feebleness of the performers. I hate every thing that requires attention. Nothing gives pleasure that does not force its own way."

'"You only, then, like loud voices, and great powers?"

'"O worse and worse!—no, nothing is so disgusting to me. All my amazement is that these people think it worth while to give Concerts at all; one is sick to death of music."

'"Nay," cried Cecilia, "if it gives no pleasure, at least it takes none away for, far from being any impediment to conversation, I think every body talks more during the performance than between the acts."'

It will be gathered that the entertainments at the Pantheon were largely social. There was even card-playing there (on occasion at any rate), for Charlotte Burney records, 'I went with my Father to the Pantheon . . . and there we saw Dr. Warren's two sons,[1] who were playing cards in the gallery, and we stopt and spoke to them and staid till Mr. Charles Warren call'd out—"Dr. Burney, you've made me lose deal."'[2]

Burney says, 'During the first winter there were assemblies only, without dancing or music, three times a week. On other days each person paid five shillings for seeing the building only.' And these gatherings were enormously successful: 'The great room, though spacious,

[1] The Dr. Warren who attended Handel in his last illness (see II. 74), and also Johnson.

[2] *Early Diary*, ii. 307.

was so crowded on all these occasions that in July a general meeting of the proprietors was advertised in order to take into consideration the enlarging of the building.'[1]

Mr. Talbot Hughes, in *Johnson's England* (i. 403), says:

> 'A famous masquerade given by the Savoir Vivre Club at the Pantheon in 1775 was attended by fourteen thousand masks, and in the following year sixteen thousand masks attended the fête given jointly by the Savoir Vivre, Almack's, Boodle's, Sanderson's, and the Thatched House Clubs.'

It is difficult to realize that such numbers could be accommodated—and have room to promenade. Our present Royal Albert Hall, with its balconies, accommodates a *seated* audience of only 10,000.

Perhaps it was the enlarging of the building that led to the enlarging of the scheme of entertainment. At all events concerts soon began, and in 1776, Burney tells us in his *History*, the managers did a bold thing. They engaged the celebrated prima donna, Agujari 'at the enormous salary of £100 a night for singing two songs only!' And, says he, it paid them, and when later they went 'a more œconomical way to work' they were involved in disgrace and ruin.[2] The Burneys were impassioned admirers of Agujari, who was frequently at their house in St. Martin's Street, and they rejoiced to see her flourish at the Pantheon:

> 'It was here that the Agujari and Pacchierotti exercised their talents; it was here that the king, queen, and royal family, with all the first nobility in the kingdom, assembled, at the commemoration of Handel in 1784; and it was here that one of the first bands in Europe graced the orchestra, alternately headed by Giardini, La Motte, Cramer, or Giornovichi, who, with Fischer, Crosdil, Cervetto, etc., produced effects in symphonies, concertos, solos, and vocal accompaniments, which had never before been heard in this country.'[1]

The attempt to find a worthy successor for Agujari met with an unexpected obstacle. The directors of the enterprise tried to secure Madame Mara (Burney does not give a date, but it must have been in the late 70s), and were foiled by no less a person than Frederick the Great:

> 'There had been a correspondence opened between this admirable singer and the proprietors of the Pantheon, who wished much to engage her as a successor to Agujari; but the king of Prussia would not let her quit his capital; and after she had executed an article which engaged her in the service of the Pantheon, and money had been remitted to her to defray the expences of her journey, on his Prussian majesty discovering that she intended to quit his service *à la sourdine*, he had her arrested and thrown into prison; and it was with extreme difficulty that she contrived, by means of our ambassador, Sir James Harris, to let the proprietors of the Pantheon know that she could not fulfil her engagement, and entreated them, for God's sake, not to write to her any more. She, however, very honestly

[1] Rees's *Cyclopaedia*, s.v. 'Pantheon'.

[2] *Hist.* iv. 504 (Mercer, ii. 882).

returned the money that had been advanced to her by the proprietors of the Pantheon.'[1]

It was this disappointment, apparently, that caused the proprietors to engage Banti. They gave her £800 a year (a very different figure from Agujari's £100 a night!) 'upon condition that £100 should be deducted each season out of her salary for payment of an able master to cultivate her voice'—a surprising clause in the agreement of a *prima donna*, but Banti's great gifts were apparently all bestowed by nature; they had stood her in good stead as a street and café singer in her native Venice but now needed the embellishments of art. The proprietors engaged Sacchini as her teacher, but 'he quitted her as an incurable patient' and they then engaged Piozzi, 'whose patience was likewise exhausted before she became a perfect singer'.

In 1779 Banti 'returned to Italy as ignorant of music as when she left that country'.[2]

In 1780 Frederick the Great at last released Madame Mara and she travelled about the Continent for a time, arriving in London in the spring of 1784, and duly appearing at the Pantheon—at first with small success, owing to the excitement of a general election, but then, after her appearances at the Westminster Abbey Handel Festival had made her merits known, with high éclat.

Burney's article 'Pantheon', in Rees's *Cyclopaedia*, which must have been written during the first years of the nineteenth century, ends sadly:

'No person of taste in architecture, or music, who remembers the Pantheon, its numerous, splendid, and elegant assemblies, can hear it mentioned without a sigh!'

What is this about a sigh? Well, from 1789 the character of the Pantheon changed and shortly afterwards destruction had come upon it. Burney says:

'After the opera-house in the Haymarket was burnt down in 1790 [really 1789], this master-piece of architecture was transformed into a theatre for the performance of operas; when, though many of its internal beauties were hidden and annihilated, it still was a perfect model of a complete theatre in its new form. But unhappily, before it had been used as a lyric theatre two seasons, it was burnt down by some fatal accident or design, which has never yet been divulged to the satisfaction of the public.'[3]

[1] Rees's *Cyclopaedia*, s.v. 'Mara'.

[2] These particulars from Burney's article 'Banti', in Rees, and his treatment of the subject in his *History*.

[3] For the Pantheon in its temporary opera-house transformation see Lord Mount-Edgcumbe, *Musical Reminiscences*, 66; he calls it 'one of the prettiest, and by far the most genteel and comfortable theatres I ever saw'. It must apparently have been shortly before the transformation that the ingenious and active Abbé Vogler, being in England on one of his highly successful recital tours, reconstructed the organ (see Grove, and also Fétis, s.v. 'Vogler, Georg Joseph'). The main principles of his alteration were: (*a*) the suppression of all mutation stops; (*b*) the rearrangement of the pipes in chromatic scale order, instead of the equal

It may be of interest to read a contemporary account of the destruction of the famous place of entertainment. The following comes from *The Gentleman's Magazine* of January 1792, the fire occurring on the 14th of that month:

'This morning, between one and two o'clock, the painters' room, in one of the new buildings which had been added to the Pantheon, to enlarge it sufficiently for the performance of Operas, was discovered to be on fire. Before any engines were brought to the spot, the fire had got to such a height, that all attempts to save the building were in vain. The flames, owing to the scenery, oil, paint, and other combustible matter in the house were tremendous, and so quick in progress, that not a single article could be saved. It was even with difficulty, that the family of Mr. Kempe, the clerk of the house, which occupied the apartments adjoining the painters' room, got out of the house before the total destruction of his furniture was completed. The fire kept burning with great fury for about ten hours, by which time, the roof and part of the walls having fallen-in, it was so much subdued, that all fears for the safety of the surrounding houses were quieted.

'We are happy in stating, that no lives were lost, nor any person hurt during the whole time, though the hurry and confusion, as may naturally be expected on such an occasion was very great. It was a fortunate circumstance, that the engines, after they did arrive, had a plentiful supply of water, otherwise it would have been impossible to have prevented the flames from spreading devastation through that populous neighbourhood.

'The house, it seems, was insured to the full value, or nearly to its amount, so that the loss will fall upon the Insurance-offices.

'The performers, next to the Insurance-offices, will be the greatest sufferers: for they have put themselves, as usual, to great expences in preparing for the season; many of them were obliged to do this on credit, but their salaries ending with the existence of the house, and before any of them had their benefit nights, they have now no means of extricating themselves from their difficulties.'

Here is an anecdote of the conflagration from the *Reminiscences* of the then famous singer Michael Kelly (published 1826):

'On the 14th of January, 1792, the Pantheon theatre was burned. Mr. Sheridan was with me on that day; I went with him into Oxford Street, to view the conflagration. While Mr. Sheridan was observing how very high the flames were, he said, "Is it possible to extinguish the flames?" An Irish fireman who was close to us, and who heard him make the observation, said, "For the love of Heaven, Mr. Sheridan, don't make yourself uneasy, Sir; by the Powers, it will soon be down; sure enough, they won't have another drop of water in five minutes". Pat said this in the natural warmth of heart, for he imagined that the burning of the Pantheon theatre must have been gratifying to Mr. Sheridan, as the proprietor of Drury Lane.'

division of long and short pipes between the two sides, as was, and is, usual—as to this point see Hopkins and Rimbault, *The Organ*, 3rd edition, 1877, part ii, p. 290; (*c*) the addition of pedals (one of the earliest British organs to possess them); (*d*) the enclosure of the whole instrument in a swell box. For the last two points see Burney, in Rees's *Cyclopaedia*, s.v. 'Vogler'.

There is a most graphic description of the fire in the *Reminiscences of Henry Angelo* (1828), i. 95:

'It is a remarkable fact, that Mr. Wyatt [the architect of the building], who was travelling to town from the west, in a post-chaise with the ingenious Dixon, his clerk, saw the glare of this memorable fire illuminating the sky, whilst crossing Salisbury Plain, and observed, "That vast light is in the direction of London; surely, Dixon, the whole city is on fire", little dreaming that this awful spectacle was blazing away so fatally for himself.'[1]

The Pantheon was rebuilt in 1795, but on a different plan, and with its glories diminished. Masquerades and a few concerts took place, but apparently did not enjoy Burney's approval, for if we read his *Cyclopaedia* article it is clear that for him the Pantheon went out of existence in the fire of 1792. Perhaps we get a hint of the reason for his feeling on the matter in a letter he wrote in old age to his friend Lady Crewe, in which he speaks of the various discouragements of his life, of which, says he, one was, 'The Pantheon being burnt down in wch. I had purchased a share wch. cost me £700, and the loss of 100 Guineas a year as foreign secretary to engage singers from Italy and Germany'.[2]

Choral Music

At Covent Garden there was, in Lent, 'Oratorio'—sometimes true oratorio (as in the case of the first British performance of Haydn's *Creation*, in 1800; see II. 117), but often a mere miscellaneous programme, in which not all the items were even of a strictly religious character.

The Academy of Antient Music had suffered by the death of Dr. Pepusch in 1752 and by the period now under consideration was in decline. Its last conductor was Dr. Samuel Arnold, who was in office from 1789 to 1792, when it went out of existence, having enjoyed a

[1] The crow-flight distance of Salisbury Plain from London is about 80 miles; during the European war of 1939–45 fires were reported to be visible up to 125 miles.

[2] In 1834, after about twenty years of disuse, the building was reconstructed as a bazaar, stalls being let to various tradespeople (for a description see *Punch*, July 1842, p. 24). And so in the London newspapers we find advertisements like this in the *Daily Telegraph* of 12 Dec. 1866:

> Pantheon Bazaar, Oxford-street,—Open as usual, from ten to six o'clock daily. An extensive assortment of toys, fancy and useful articles suitable for Christmas presents.

In 1867 the building was acquired by Messrs. W. and A. Gilbey, the wine merchants. Up to 1937 the original Wyatt front, with projecting portico, remained as a prominent feature in Oxford Street. In that year an entirely new building rose on the site, erected by Messrs. Marks & Spencer. The façade, with its portico, has, by the efforts of the Society for the Protection of Ancient Buildings, been preserved for re-erection on another site.

To avoid confusion, note that London had another building also, from its shape, called 'Pantheon'—a more 'popular' place of amusement, in Spa Fields, North London. This latter was the building that was taken over by Lady Huntingdon for a chapel; she had a house there, and there she died.

There were also Pantheons, imitative of that in Oxford Street, elsewhere in the world. Mrs. Fay, in her *Original Letters from India* (Calcutta, 1817) mentions one at Madras—'where the assemblies are held'.

period of some usefulness of eighty-two years. From 1784 its place of meeting had been the Freemasons' Hall, Great Queen Street. Its subscribers were largely of the wealthy city merchant class. Towards the end the annual subscription was five guineas, and there were eight concerts in the season, at which vocal soloists of the front rank were engaged. The choir and orchestra, according to the *Public Advertiser* in 1789, then comprised about sixty-five performers.[1]

Often to-day confused with the Academy of Antient Music is its younger rival, the CONCERT OF ANTIENT MUSIC (Why did not its sponsors present it at the font with a more distinctive name?). It was founded in 1776 at the suggestion of Burney's friend the Earl of Sandwich (see I. 193–4, 195 n., II. 68 n.):

'The Concert of Ancient Music, originally suggested by the Earl of Sandwich in 1776, in favour of such solid and valuable productions of old masters as an intemperate rage for novelty had too soon laid aside as superannuated, was supported with spirit and dignity by the concurrent zeal and activity of other noblemen and gentlemen of the first rank, who united with his lordship in the undertaking till 1785, when it was honoured with the presence of their Majesties, whose constant attendance ever since has given to this institution an elevation and splendor, which perhaps no establishment of this kind ever enjoyed before. Here the productions of venerable old masters, particularly those of Purcell and Handel, are performed by a select and powerful band, with such correctness and energy, as the authors themselves never had the happiness to hear.'[2]

'Ancient' times were interpreted as being those of at least twenty years back, no music composed at a lesser interval from the date of a concert being admitted to its programme. As the *Harmonicon* of 1831 (p. 28) intelligently remarks of this regulation: 'It was, in fact, proclaiming to every musical aspirant that he might toil over his midnight lamp for years; he might rival Purcell in genius, Handel in sublimity, and Arne in grace, but he must not look forward to any one of his compositions being performed at the most fashionable and most influential concerts in London, till, nine chances to one, the composer himself was dead.'

Fanny Burney, when resident in the Court at Windsor, says that she got 'a very gracious message from the King', asking her if she would like him to put her name down 'among the subscribers to the Tottenham

[1] See *Reminiscences of Michael Kelly* (1826), i. 326: 'There was at this time a subscription concert, held at Freemasons' Hall, called the Academy of Ancient Music, under the direction of Dr. Arnold; I was engaged also at that concert for the season. The subscribers were chiefly bankers and merchants from the city; I think I hardly ever saw a greater assemblage of beautiful women.'

[2] *Hist.* iv. 683 (Mercer, ii. 1022). The founder of the Institution, the Earl of Sandwich, was an amateur kettledrummer. In Rees's *Cyclopaedia*, under 'Solo', Burney says that solos were then (early nineteenth century) 'wholly laid aside' (in favour of full orchestral pieces), and implies that this was due to a fashion set at the Ancient Concerts, 'where a composition was never thought complete by the late earl of Sandwich, without a kettle-drum, nor with, unless he beat it himself'.

Street Oratorio' [an informal name for this organization],—a 'condescension' which she 'accepted very willingly'. Later the King dropped into her room to inquire 'with whom I should go and some other questions, all very gracious and condescending' (she arranged to go with her father's friend Mrs. Ord—see II. 90).[1]

For some time the performances were given in the Society's own room in Tottenham Street, known as 'The New Room'. Then (1794) they were removed to the concert room (again called 'The New Room') attached to the King's Theatre in the Haymarket (see II. 164), and in 1804 to the Hanover Square Rooms (at that time, apparently, called 'The Festino Rooms'). Joah Bates (see II. 62–3) was the conductor until 1793 and Greatorex until 1831. There were twelve meetings every year, and the subscription was at first twelve guineas (later eight guineas).

This concert body was very aristocratic—'your social position had to be as carefully vouched for as for a ball at Almack's'[2] (see I. 39 n.).

From 1785 the attendance and active interest of George III led to the organization being spoken of as 'The King's Concert' (or 'The King's Concerts'). The King's private band and the boys of the Chapel Royal choir (in their uniforms) formed part of the body of performers. The Royal Family sat in a special box, and etiquette required that applause and demands for encores should strictly follow the lead that came therefrom. In effect, then, this organization ranked almost as a part of the musical activities of the Court.

Women had only lately been admitted to sing in choirs and qualified women were scarce in London; hence fine sopranos were imported from Lancashire and maintained in London for the season. There were, as above mentioned, choirboy sopranos also (from the Abbey, St. Paul's, and the Chapel Royal). The altos were all men. The abilities of one of the Lancashire girls so impressed the Directors that they determined to educate her and to do the thing legally they formally apprenticed her—to the Duke of Cambridge (the only time in British history, surely, that a son of the reigning monarch has taken an apprentice!). The account of the sums paid to the various teachers (general and musical), &c., is extant: it includes sixty guineas to Kirkman (successor to Burney's boyhood friend; see I. 35) for a grand piano. This girl, Deborah Travis,[3] after three years appeared as a principal singer at the concerts, and hereafter took a good place on the oratorio platform. In effect the Directors of the Concerts, in the absence of any musical

[1] *Diary and Letters*, iii. 216.

[2] James E. Matthew, paper on 'The Antient Concerts' in *Musical Association Proceedings*, 1906–7. Mr. Matthew possessed an almost complete set of programmes of the concerts, with account books and other documents. His paper is most interesting. For other sources of information on these concerts see Pohl, *Mozart und Haydn in London* (1867), ii. 11, and E. Beresford Chancellor, *London's Old Latin Quarter* (1930), 108.

[3] She is to be found in books of reference as Deborah Knyvett, for she married the well-known singer of that surname.

educational institution in the country, gave a promising young musician a scholarship of nearly £300 a year—and a very good thing to do! However, this 'apprenticeship' occurred at a later period than that we are now considering—the year before Burney's death in fact.

The Antient Concert lasted for seventy-two years—till 1848. There was a secession from it in 1792 which led to the inauguration of another body, THE VOCAL CONCERTS, which held its meetings in Willis's Rooms and apparently provided performances of glees, vocal solos (by very eminent artists), &c., as also chamber music. Ten concerts were given each season. This organization ceased in 1794, and was then revived in 1801 on an orchestral-choral basis, and with very varied and interesting programmes, and no limitation of ancientry. In 1811 a rival to this scheme was set up, supported by three of the King's sons (the Dukes of Kent, Sussex, and Cambridge), known (from the names of the two vocalists who promoted it) as MESSRS. KNYVETT AND VAUGHAN'S VOCAL SUBSCRIPTION CONCERTS. After two years these two organizations amalgamated.

COVENT GARDEN ORATORIO. The Lenten seasons that had been begun by Handel were continued after his death in 1755 by his amanuensis and secretary, J. C. Smith, and the famous blind organist, Stanley; after Smith's retirement in 1774 by Stanley and Thomas Linley; and after Stanley's death in 1786 by Linley and Dr. Samuel Arnold. After 1795 there was a series directed by J. Ashley and then by his son, but its programmes took on more and more the character of a miscellaneous musical entertainment.

We now come to the various convivial-choral bodies whose activities were, towards the end of the century, a feature of musical life in London (and in the provinces similar bodies existed).

The MADRIGAL SOCIETY (see I. 22) continued its activities, as, indeed, it still does to-day. Its headquarters shifted every few years from tavern to tavern.

THE NOBLEMEN AND GENTLEMEN'S CATCH CLUB (also still alive) was founded in 1761, Burney's friend the Earl of Sandwich, who had a finger in every musical pie, being again one of the founders. The membership was limited to twenty-one, all members of the aristocracy, plus a modicum of 'Privileged Members', who were professional musicians condescendingly admitted for their choral utility. At the period now under consideration it was at the height of its activity. In the 1780's five of George III's sons were members and two more joined later—making seven out of nine, and including the future George IV, the future William IV, and the future King of Hanover.

The Club met weekly, and dined, after which every member proposed a toast, the toasts alternating with songs, catches, and glees.

Amongst the rules (codified in 1767) were the following:

'If any person who takes a part in any piece of music during the first round is found deficient in his part, and actually sings out of time or tune or stops before the piece is finished, he is to drink a glass of wine of any sort at that time upon the table, at the requisition of any Member, and by order of the President. . . .

'No coffee, tea, or other such heterogeneous beverage is to be brought upon, or drank near the table where the Club is seated upon any account; but if a Member either for himself or any other submits to call for such unnatural mixtures, they must be carried to a distant table, and the parties concern'd must take them at that place, with a due sense of the Society's indulgence.

'All coffee, tea, etc., must be paid for by the Member or Members who call for them, and must not be charg'd in the Society's account upon any pretence whatsoever.'[1]

The Club offered prizes for the compositions of catches, canons, and glees, and Burney's close friend J. W. Callcott, who had taken lessons from Haydn when he was in England, used to send in quite extraordinary quantities of pieces in the hope of winning a prize or two, which he sometimes did. Indeed, during the five years 1789–94, out of 23 prizes given this composer carried off 13. In 1785, out of 114 competing compositions, 60 were by Callcott, and the next year, out of 167, his numbered 98; thereupon the committee made a rule limiting the number of pieces to be submitted by each candidate to three, and Callcott, apparently discouraged or offended, did not compete. However, the following year he bobbed up again—with the full quota of three pieces in each of the four classes, with which outdistancing all rivals he carried off the whole of the four prizes. Haydn, when in England, wrote several catches for the Club.

In the last volume of Burney's *History* he says of this Club:

'The spirit and liberality with which this establishment has been . . . supported has not only much improved the manner of performing the catches, canons, and glees of old masters, but been productive of innumerable new compositions of that kind which are still of a more ingenious and elegant texture.'[2]

The Glee Club came into existence more or less informally in 1783 and was definitely established under this name in 1787, at the Newcastle Coffee House, thence moving its headquarters from time to time to various well-known taverns. Some of the finest glees in existence were composed for this Club, e.g. Webbe's *Glorious Apollo*. At the meetings (on alternate Saturday evenings) first the officials and then the members,

[1] Viscount Gladstone, *The Story of the Noblemen and Gentlemen's Catch Club* (privately printed, and copy kindly supplied to the present author, 1930). *The Evening Standard* of 31 Oct. 1938 gave the then membership as limited to twenty and the annual subscription (once £25) as £5. The President was at that date Lieut.-Colonel Edmund Royds, and the members included the Earl of Buckinghamshire, Lord Hollenden, Lord Davies, Sir Archibald Weigall, Sir Hugh O'Neill, Bt., Sir John Barran, Bt., Colonel the Hon. Stuart Pleydell-Bouverie, and Judge Hargreaves.

[2] *Hist.* iv. 683 (Mercer, ii. 1022).

in order of seniority, each chose a glee to be sung. This Club, unlike the one just mentioned, had a middle-class membership, consisting in part of leading professional musicians (as full members, not condescendingly 'privileged'), such as Burney's friends Drs. Arnold, Dupuis, and Callcott. The Club lasted until 1857.

There was another GLEE CLUB (called simply that) founded in 1793. It had fortnightly meetings at the Garrick's Head Coffee House, Bow Street, the meetings terminating with supper. Apparently it did not last very long.[1]

There seems to have been still another, called the AD LIBITUM SOCIETY, for there is an anonymous publication of 1794 entitled *Glees as sung by Messrs. Incledon, Dignum, Bellamy and Suett, composed for, and at their request dedicated to the Gentlemen of the Ad Libitum Society*. There were certainly many of these convivial singing societies for the various social strata of masculine society, but traces of them are to-day mostly lost.

The period of Burney's professional life was roughly the period of the growth and flowering of the English glee (a purely national product). It was a male-voice type and, as will have been realized, it was a good deal cultivated in a convivial way: it will be understood that all the members of the above clubs were singing members, but it would appear that they were eating and drinking members also.

It is curious that Burney, in his *History*, has nothing to say about the Glee as a distinctive type. Where he uses the word (only once or twice) it is always applied in the older general and indefinite way, except for the mention in the reference to the Catch Club above quoted. However, we have to remember that the last volume of the *History* appeared in 1789, when the genuinely musical importance of the new type (as distinct from its utility as a gathering point for convivial musical males) was, perhaps, not so freely recognized as it became a little later. The Glee Club, it will be noted, had been in existence only five or six years when Burney's volume was published, and hence only four or five when he wrote its final chapters; however, the Catch Club had for more than twenty years offered an annual reward for a 'Serious Glee' and another for a 'Cheerful Glee'.

It would have been interesting and valuable if in Burney's closing pages he had given a careful conspectus of music in Britain as he saw it at the moment of closing his great task. This would necessarily have brought in the leading Glee composers. As it is, only two or three of the names we to-day associate with Glee compositions are mentioned, and then it is always in connexion with theatrical compositions or something of that sort.

THE NEW MUSICAL FUND ('new' in contradistinction from the older organization, the Society of Musicians, later the Royal Society of Musicians) was a musical-charitable society with influential supporters.

[1] W. T. Parke, *Musical Memoirs* (1830), i. 175.

It was founded in 1786. It gave orchestral and choral concerts on a large scale (200–400 performers) in the King's Theatre, the Pantheon, &c. In 1795 Haydn conducted (at the piano) a new symphony.

THE CHORAL FUND was founded in 1791 by Dr. Arnold. It opened with a performance of *Messiah* in a chapel in Fetter Lane. As its name suggests, it, also, had a charitable purpose—to help distressed choral singers (sometimes instrumentalists also) and their widows and orphans.

THE FESTIVAL OF THE SONS OF THE CLERGY (the annual field-day of the mid-seventeenth century charitable society, the Corporation of the Sons of the Clergy), consisted of a choral programme in St. Paul's Cathedral (formerly Purcell, now almost entirely Handel, whose overture to *Esther* opened it from about 1720 to 1843).

Other musical societies (probably all choral) mentioned in *The Musical Directory* for 1794 are the Long Acre Society; the Titchfield Chapel Society, Marylebone; the Handelian Society, Wych Street; the Surrey Chapel Society, Southwark (these last two combining later with the Choral Fund), and the Cecilian Society. It will be noted that the Anacreontic Society, already discussed under the head of 'Concert Organizations', might have also been discussed under the present head of 'Choral Music'.

LVIII. VIRTUES AND VAGARIES OF A SEPTUAGENARIAN ENCYCLOPAEDIST

(1801–1805; Burney aged 75–79)

BURNEY's activity of mind and body was such that, as it seems, it took people about him a very long time to realize that he was growing old. He continued his teaching until he was seventy-eight and for three years before this he was combining with it a very heavy new literary task—nothing less than the writing, single-handed, of a whole big *Encyclopaedia of Music*. For his contribution of the musical articles in Rees's *Cyclopaedia* amounts to nothing less than that. His friend Rousseau's similar articles for the French *Encyclopédie*, thirty years earlier, had been afterwards extracted by their writer and separately published as a *Dictionnaire de Musique* and if Burney's own contributions to this great English encyclopaedia, in which he has quite obviously taken Rousseau as his model, had been similarly treated we should not only have possessed a valuable compendium of musical knowledge and thought as it existed at the opening of the nineteenth century, but also a demonstration of the vigorous vitality of its writer at an age when the Biblical three-score-and-ten was well in the past.

What editor of any many-volumed encyclopaedia to-day, looking round for a specialist writer to whom he could confide the survey of a whole big section of learning (a survey that must necessarily take some years to achieve), would pick, out of the several writers available, a man of seventy-five? The editor who showed this bold confidence in Burney's health, strength, and mental vigour was Abraham Rees, D.D., a much respected London Presbyterian minister and a man of solid learning (see pl. 37, II. 154). He had already won recognition as an encyclopaedist by his new edition of Chambers's *Cyclopaedia*, which he brought out from 1779 to 1786 in over 400 sixpenny parts (making four great folio volumes plus a volume of plates) and with over 4,000 new articles—being elected an F.R.S. in recognition of this contribution to the tools of study.

The first reference we see to Burney's new undertaking is in a letter of 1801 to some person unknown, printed by his daughter in the *Memoirs*:

'I have entered now into concerns that leave me not a minute, or a thought, to bestow on other matters. Besides professional avocations, I have deeply engaged in a work that can admit of no delay; and which occupies every instant that I can steal from business, friends, or sleep. A new edition, on a very enlarged plan, of the Cyclopaedia of Chambers, is now printing in two double volumes 4to, for which I have agreed to furnish the musical articles, on a very large scale, including whatever is connected with the subject; not only definitions of the musical technica, but reflexions, discussions, criticism, history, and biography. The first volume is printed, and does not finish the letter A. And in *nine months' hard labour*, I have not brought forth two letters. I am more and more frightened every day at the undertaking, so long after the usual allowance of three score years and ten have expired. And the shortest calculation for the termination of this work is still ten years.'[1]

Burney's description of the work as 'a new edition . . . of the Cyclopaedia of Chambers'[2] is inexact: it was a totally new work that was projected, and the words 'two double volumes 4to' must involve some copying slip of Fanny's. Clearly a work whose first volume 'did not finish the letter A' was not going to progress in a second volume to the end of the letter 'Z'. The word 'two' seems to have been intruded here, or else has been substituted for 'twenty-two', or 'thirty-two', or even 'forty-two', or more likely still, the phrase should read 'two double volumes quarto *per annum*'. For the work was issued in parts, each two parts constituting a volume (which is evidently what Burney means by 'double volumes'), and when publication was completed, twenty years later, it consisted of seventy-eight parts, or thirty-nine volumes, plus six volumes of plates, i.e. forty-five volumes in all, the present writer's set occupying over seven feet of his shelving—space that is not grudged since the work, though much of it is dull, still has its vitality in parts and can often be referred to for useful information as to the state of knowledge and opinion at the beginning of the last century.

The price of the immense work was necessarily high. A virulent little footnote in De Quincey's essay on Dr. Samuel Parr tells us what it was. De Quincey has been attacking the Duke of Sussex (sixth son of George III) for placing 'the bust of a hack dissenting book-maker, rather than that of Aristotle or Lord Bacon, as the presiding genius of his fine library at Kensington Palace', and then footnotes 'book-maker' as follows:

'I trust that in so describing Dr. Rees I do him no wrong. The doctor was understood to be the editor of an immense encyclopaedia, originally charged to the public at £80,—latterly, I believe, at about 80 shillings. Southey, who was an admirable judge of such compilations, had received a copy as a present from the very liberal proprietors in its early or 80-pound stage; and he privately showed me such transformations and specious creations worked by paste and scissors as are elsewhere unexampled.'

The year after Burney wrote that gloomy letter of 1801 he wrote

[1] *Mem.* iii. 302.

[2] The Chambers's *Cyclopaedia* here mentioned took its name from its first Editor, Ephraim Chambers. It first appeared in 1728, and Rees's edition of it in 1779–86 was the seventh and last. The musical articles in this work were, says Burney, largely provided by Alex. Malcolm (or else cribbed from that writer's *Treatise of Music*, Edinburgh, 1721). It is not to be confused with the well-known Chambers's *Cyclopaedia* of to-day, which first appeared in 1860–8 and took its name from its publishers, the public-spirited William and Robert Chambers of Edinburgh. It was the first of these two Chambers's *Cyclopaedias* that formed the inspiration and basis of the celebrated French *Encyclopédie* of d'Alembert and Diderot (1751–72), which may be said to have revolutionized the philosophical thought of Europe.

another in a tone of equal discouragement: 'This enormous Cyclopedia fills up all my thoughts. I have been long an A.B.C.derian, and now am become so for life.' And a little later he says that he has given up 'town business' and is neglecting correspondence:

> 'I had a mind to see what I could really do in twelve months, by driving the quill at every possible moment that I could steal from business or repose, by day and by night, in bed and up; and, with all this stir and toil, I have found it impracticable to finish three letters of the alphabet.'[1]

However, by dropping his teaching ('town business') he was free to give almost his whole time to the work. Fanny says that in a letter to her, at about the time he wrote the one just quoted, 'He mentions that, to fulfil his engagement, he generally rises at five or six o'clock every morning—in his seventy-sixth year!'

The old man did not, however, expend on this task the ten years he had anticipated, but perhaps half that length of time. On 7 May 1805 he wrote to a friend of the family (Mrs. Waddington, formerly Miss Port, niece of Mrs. Delany) that his work for Dr. Rees was almost finished and that he was no longer a slavish A.B.C.derian.[2] There was still some revision to do and there were proofs to read, but the actual writing was done and he felt a happy sense of freedom.

It is stated in various books of reference that Burney received £1,000 for his work. The statement, so far as the present writer is aware, first appears in a good five-column 'Memoir of Charles Burney, Mus.Doc., F.R.S.' in *The Harmonicon* for 1832 (p. 215). This says 'His remuneration for the assistance was £1,000, and as most of the matter was extracted without alteration from his *History of Music*, the price was perhaps not inadequate to the service rendered.' The article by Dr. Rimbault in Grove's *Dictionary* (all four editions) tells the world that 'as most of the matter was extracted without alteration from his *History* the price was large'. (Rimbault should be the last man to mention this fact, if true. Presumably he himself was paid for the article in which he makes the criticism and it is nearly all cribbed from the *Harmonicon* article above mentioned, generally without even change of wording.)

The *Dictionary of National Biography* says that Burney wrote 'the musical biographies for Rees "Encyclopaedia", for which work he received the large sum of £1,000'.

Burney's will (see II. 271) confirms the sum received, but all these statements, with their emphasis on the amount, are unfair. It is true that the 'biographies', so far as they concern musicians treated at any length in the *History*, are largely (not, by any means, entirely) extracted from that work, as are some of the articles on Ancient Greek music and the like, but Burney wrote for Rees far more than the biographies and articles on the music of the Ancients. The articles of a strictly scientific

[1] *Mem.* iii. 331.

[2] The letter can be seen in 'George Paston's' *Side Lights on the Georgian Period*, 1902.

or very mathematical type were, apparently, written by a specialist in science, spoken of in the Preface as 'Farey senior',[1] but there are very numerous articles other than biographical (some of them very long ones) that are plainly to be recognized as Burney's. To grudge the poor old man his thousand pounds for all the work he did before others had risen or after they had gone to bed, and this continued through a long term of years, is very mean, and the writers in *The Harmonicon* and Grove are hereby condemned for the spreading of such a false impression as to Burney's willingness to *earn* any money he ever received for his literary labour.

Burney had a willing helper in his work in his admiring friend J. W. Callcott (see pl. 37, II. 154). There are in the British Museum a number of copies of letters written by Callcott to Burney in 1802–3[2] showing that he was not only putting at Burney's service material he had for years, by a wide reading of ancient and modern musical literature, been collecting for a *Musical Dictionary* of his own (which was, as things turned out, never to appear), but that he also undertook research into certain historical points concerning late-eighteenth-century London musical activities on which Burney required more definite information than he possessed.

The publication of the *Cyclopaedia* dragged on from January 1802 until August 1820, so Burney never saw it completed. The impression one gets is that he finished his contributions about 1809 or 1810 (Rees then keeping the later ones in cold storage and taking them out as required).[3] The fifteen plates of engravings (some of them beautiful) which embellish the musical articles bear all sorts of engraving dates between

[1] Evidently John Farey (1766–1826), chiefly known as a geologist, but also a writer on the velocity of sound and other general scientific subjects (see *D.N.B.*). Do you ask why Burney did not do the whole job himself, instead of accepting a colleague? Well, here is one of Farey's articles, one of the shortest, for many of them run to pages and pages of this kind of popular chit-chat:

> 'HALF-TONE, hemitone, or chromatic toniæum of Aristoxenus and Holden, half the tone major, $= 2\sqrt{2} \div 3 = 52{\cdot}003932\,\Sigma + f + 4m$, or $52\,\Sigma + f + 4\frac{1}{2}m$; whose common logarithm is ·9744237,3877, and its Euler's log. = ·084962, such being its decimal relation to the octave 1. It is = 4·740705 major commas.'

And that is only one of three articles on different sorts of 'Half-tone', to say nothing of four on different sorts of 'Half-note' (whatever the distinction may be!).

What Burney thought of that sort of thing we find from his article on Pepusch, who, he says, attached himself to a certain mathematician and a certain classical scholar and then, having absorbed their lore: 'He bewildered himself and some of his scholars with the Greek genera, scales, diagrams, geometrical, arithmetical, and harmonical proportions, surd quantities, apotomes, lemmas, and every thing concerning ancient harmonics, that was dark, unintelligible, and foreign to common and useful practice.'

[2] Add. MS. 27667, fol. 596–696. The present writer possesses many of the letters of Burney to which these letters of Callcott's are replies, or which reply to them.

[3] There is an allusion in one article, 'Instrument', to something that happened in the beginning of this month, April 1811, but it has probably been added in proof. Fanny (*Mem.* iii. 414) says the work was finished 'about 1805', but her dates are always untrustworthy and two letters dated 1807, in the possession of the present writer, show that in that year there was still a lot of work to be done.

1803 and 1818, so presumably, though now to be found bound up together in one of the volumes of illustrations, they originally appeared in the various parts and attached to the articles on the subjects with which they are concerned. One of them reproduces a graceful sketch by Burney's nephew, Edward—*The Pandean Minstrels in Performance at Vaux-Hall.*

As to the reproduction of matter from the *History*, the biographical articles do, as already admitted, where they treat of musicians who flourished prior to the publication of the relevant volume of that work, simply quote (sometimes literally). In such cases Burney often puts a reference at the end (e.g. 'Burney Hist. Music, Vol. III'), sometimes also adding a reference to his rival (e.g. 'Hawkins Music, Vol. IV'). Sometimes he much expands the *History*'s articles; for instance Blavet, who has merely three lines in the *History*, has in the *Encyclopaedia* nearly half a column (see also II. 196).

Often, however, in discussing some subject, he saves his space by stating that a particular aspect of it 'has been fully detailed in the Gen. Hist. of Music'—which is hardly fair, since he surely could not take it for granted that all his readers possessed those four specialist volumes, published long years before.

Quite naturally Burney often relieves himself of trouble by 'lifting' extended passages out of his friend Rousseau's *Dictionary of Music* (or Rousseau's articles in the French *Encyclopédie*, which is the same thing). Such passages usually, however, give credit where credit is due, being ushered in with some such phrase as, 'The reasoning of the citizen of Geneva on this principle is very specious and ingenious . . .' There is indeed quite a lot of that 'citizen of Geneva' scattered here and there. Sometimes Burney lifts a whole article, justifying himself to his honest soul by adding Rousseau's name at the end.

One rather comical way of Burney's of referring to his own *History* is found under 'Arkadelt'—'Why du Verdier and others have called Arkadelt a Frenchman Dr. Burney doth not know.'

Other writers freely quoted by Burney are Framery and Ginguené,[1] who both wrote musical articles for the *Encyclopédie méthodique* (1791), and poor, guillotined Laborde, author of the *Essai sur la musique ancienne et moderne* (1780). It is curious that Burney, who had such a low opinion of French music, set such a high value on French writings on music. It may almost be said that he does not quote German or Italian writers—always French.

And, very curiously, he gives an enormous quantity of matter under actual French headings, and thus in alphabetical positions where it will rarely be found by those looking for it. To mention only a very few cases at random, he has entries headed, 'Bon', 'Bruit', 'Dix-neuvième',

[1] The poor old chap spells this name in various other ways—'Guinguené', 'Gingiuné', &c. He has a fair number of other names loosely spelt.

'Dix-septième', 'Echelle', 'Fausse', 'Feinte', 'Filer un son', 'Fragmens', 'Frappe', 'Fredonner', 'Jouer', 'Oreille', 'Renversement' (i.e. 'inversion' of chords), 'Réponse' (i.e. 'answer' in fugue), 'Septième', 'Tons de l'église', 'Travailler', 'Valeur des notes'. In most cases these entries are 'lifted' from Rousseau and apparently it has not occurred to Burney, when translating the matter, to translate the heading also, and then to place the article in its English alphabetical position.

Another oddity is that there exists not only a long and full article, 'Organ', but also a short entry, 'Orgues', this latter serving only as an opportunity to recount one or two facts concerning the early history of the instrument in France.

It cannot be said that Burney shows much sense of the nature of a book of reference—in which, surely, every entry should be confined to answering the question that can be expected to have sent the reader to it. Here is an example of his discursiveness:

'Accelerando, in *Music*, is an Italian term for accelerating the time in the middle of a piece of music, as *ralentando* is for retarding it. This last is a fashionable effect lately introduced in the performance of music, and much abused by the excess and too frequent use of it. The gradual change of measure, when practised in the midst of a regular movement, seldom produces any other effect on common hearers than that of breaking time. Perhaps in a very pathetic and expressive passage, even in an allegro, when very delicately done from real feeling, the effect may be approved; but the imitators of the licences and retimements [a good word but not to be found in his friend Johnson's Dictionary] of great masters disgrace the compositions which they mean to embellish, and disgust their hearers. Daring imitators of the bold modulation of Haydn, and of the rapid running up and down the keys in half notes, as Mozart did in his juvenile days, have deformed melody, and corrupted harmony. These great masters knew when to stop; but their apes think they never can season their productions too highly; and, it is to be feared, that the lovers of simplicity will never be indulged again with plain food, even by those who have no means of gratifying them with luxuries.'

As will be noticed, a line or two here suffices to define 'Accelerando', and then Burney goes on to discuss two or three other subjects (and, shall we say, to express his prejudices thereon)—Rallentando and its abuse, excessive Modulation in composition, excessive Chromaticism, and the general decline of taste owing to the crude imitativeness of the 'modernist' composers of the day—all that under 'Accelerando'!

This is a persistent fault in Burney, and often he muddles the mind of the reader thereby. Thus under 'Accent', after briefly discussing the emphasis on the first and third beats in four-time and on the first *and third* in three-time (surely a little disputable), he goes on, to the length of a column, intermixing with such discussion the quite different subject of 'accent' in the sense of 'the peculiar tone or tune by which nice observers discover the residence of the speaker' (the 'cantilena by which an Englishman discovers a native of Scotland', &c.). Then follows an account of what, 'in a conversation with Metastasio', the writer had heard as to the musical nature of the Italian language, and totally irrelevant quotations from Eximeno, Dionysius Halicarnassus, Dryden, Rousseau, and Holder. And, to end, we have reference to what to-day we call 'phrasing' on the violin and violoncello, the flute, and the hautboy. In fact we are given a confusing display of heterogeneous learning rather than a plain answer to the question, *What is Accent in music?* That is typical of Burney throughout his work on the *Cyclopaedia*. If one did not know the man one would almost suppose that, like a 'penny-a-liner', he was trying to fill as much space as possible.

Here is another amusing example of Burney's discursive style—the entry 'Facteur' (which entry, of course, properly belongs merely to a dictionary of the French language):

'FACTEUR, Fr. in *Mechanics*, a maker; as in music, a flute or fiddle-maker, an organ-builder. How great a demand there was for flutes in Athens, may be conceived from a circumstance mentioned by Plutarch in his life of Isocrates. This orator, says he, was the son of Theodorus, a flute-maker, who acquired wealth sufficient by his employment not only to educate his children in a liberal manner, but also to bear one of the heaviest public burdens to which an Athenian citizen was liable, that of furnishing a choir or chorus for his tribe, or ward, at festivals and religious ceremonies. Each tribe furnished their distinct chorus; which consisted of a band of vocal and instrumental performers, and dancers, who were to be hired, maintained, and dressed during the whole time of the festival: an expence considerable in itself, but much increased by emulation among the richer citizens, and the disgrace consequent to an inferior exhibition. The fluctuations of trade and public favour have rendered the business of boring flutes far less profitable at present than it was in the time of Theodorus. But then we have had a harpsichord-maker in our own country (old Kirkman) who died worth £100,000 and who was as able to maintain a choir as Theodorus, or any dean and chapter of a cathedral.'

If anyone wishes to realize the distance Burney wandered in the course of some of his articles they should look at their opening and closing words. For instance, from this beginning:

'HORNPIPE, the name of an instrument and of a tune. The hornpipe air, so frequently danced . . .',

we arrive at this ending:

'We had very good church music in our cathedrals from the time of Tallis and Bird, to the arrival of Handel, in 1710, but being set to English words, it never reached the continent.'

It is pretty common with Burney, this dear, unpractical old gentleman, when he has an idea he wished to make public, to bury it where the public is least likely to come across it. As one out of very many instances, he wants to express his agreement with d'Alembert's sound opinion that 'the calculation of ratios is of no use in practical music'—in other words, that acoustics is Science and composition is Art (which is one for Farey!). Instead of neatly introducing this under either 'Acoustics' or 'Composition', as he might well have done, he gives it a place to itself where no musical inquirer will ever look for it, under 'Calculation'.

Similarly, a long, practical article on 'Singing' is found under the head 'Cantare, Ital. to sing' (there is another, shorter one under 'Chanter' and still another under 'Singing', and one has to find all three to cover the ground). And at the end of this 'Cantare' article, having given twenty-two rules for singers, and stated that they are by Aprile (*evirato* contralto, 1738–1814), Burney goes on to apologize for the fact that 'to him we did not allow an article when we were at work upon the letter A, not knowing whether he was singing Alleluiahs in this world or the next' (though how that affects the matter is not easy to realize), and adds, 'we shall endeavour here to make him and our musical readers some amends for the omission'. Whereupon in letter 'C' of the *Cyclopaedia*, sandwiched between 'Cantare' and 'Cantarilla', we find a fair-sized article on 'Aprile, Giuseppe'. Surely rather comical! Who wanting an article on either Singing or Aprile is likely to look under 'Cantare'? Similarly Burney ends the article 'Filer un Son' by a reference to the style of singing of the great soprano Agujari and then says: 'We have just now recollected that Agujari was forgotten in the alphabetical order where she ought to have had a niche, for which we beg pardon of her manes, and shall try to deserve it, by doing her justice here.' Whereupon, misplaced in this volume 'Exu to Foo', there follows a full-sized article on 'Agujari'.

And so, too, in writing of 'Gizziello, Gioachino', Burney has occasion to mention Anibali, remembers he had omitted him in the A volume, and at once inserts him here under 'G'![1]

Perhaps one of the most extraordinary entry headings in the *Cyclopaedia* is one in the 'R' volume—'Robes to Minstrels'. Of all things! ('In good time', as Mrs. Thrale would say: see I. 355.) Imagine anyone taking it into his head to see what a work of reference had to say on 'Robes to Minstrels'! When the article is looked into it turns out to consist of nearly a page of quite interesting records of the way in which, in the fourteenth century, were rewarded minstrels in regular attendance at a court or visiting there—matter that really belongs to a specialist antiquarian or historical treatise, and decidedly not to a general work of reference.

And there is actually an article 'Red Notes in Music'!

[1] The touch about not knowing whether Aprile 'was singing Alleluiahs in this world or the next' has its counterpart in the article on the tenor, 'Davide, Giacomo', which ends: 'We have heard nothing of him lately; and he has probably ere now retired from the stage, if not from this world' (which latter retirement, as a matter of fact, did not occur until forty years later).

One suspects that such unlikely entries as these represent matter that Burney found he had by him and that he realized that he had not used at the proper time when compiling his articles for earlier volumes. Obviously the articles just mentioned should have formed part of the general articles on 'Minstrels' and 'Notation' respectively.

An instance of totally unfindable matter is that of a certain discussion of Plato's views on music which is buried under the tombstone, 'Period of Perfection in Greek Music', whence perhaps, to this day, no inquirer has ever dug it out.

Then how many readers, we may ask, ever turned to a work of reference for an article on 'Simplicity in Music'? This should have made a part of the article 'Composition'.

Who would turn up a work of reference for a study of 'Unity of Melody'? Obviously this should form part of the general article 'Melody'.

There is a long article 'Modes of the Ancient Greek Music'. But if we want to know anything about the so-called 'Church Modes' (based on the ancient Greek modes), which underlay all European composition up to the seventeenth century, we have to know the French term, 'Tons de l'Eglise', for it is under this head that Burney discusses them. And when he does so (it must be admitted in a somewhat ignorant manner, exhibiting the general lack of understanding of the subject which a couple of centuries of composers' disuse of the modes had brought about), he refers to a setting out of them on a plate which, on turning to the volumes of plates, we find does not exist.

There is an entry 'Testo, Ital. literally "text"', which is an article existing solely in order to allow Burney an opportunity of explaining his views about false accentuation in the song settings of his time.

It is really astonishing what an amount of solid information and careful reasoning is hidden where it never can have been found when wanted.

Of one demand that the user of any work of reference has a right to make Burney has no conception—the demand that it shall, so to speak, dig over more or less the whole surface of each subject, the depth to which the digging is done naturally varying according to the nature of the subject and the general scope of the book. In many articles we find Burney digging hard in one particular spot or another, just as happens to come into his septuagenarian (or possibly by now, octogenarian) head, and leaving other parts of the field quite untouched. Thus under 'Cathedral Service' there is a pretty full treatment of plainsong, the responses, &c., with three pages of reproduction of Marbeck's 'Booke of Common Praier Noted', but never a single word about the long line of English cathedral composers who had by Burney's time provided the Church with such an enormous and admirable repertory of choral settings of the canticles and of anthems, never a mention of the Anglican

Chant, of the offices of Precentor, Lay Vicar, Organist, &c. This is purely a plainsong article.

Under 'Clarinet', though there is discussion of some recent improvements, Burney never in any way defines or describes the instrument. An inquirer turning to this article would realize that it is a wooden wind instrument, but would get no further precise information. It might resemble a flute, oboe, or bassoon for all Burney tells him.

There are abundant examples of ambiguous or puzzling expressions, as when, after defining 'Cadence', Burney tells us 'Regularly it is to be made on the final or dominant, though sometimes also on the mediant or middle chord of a note'. The most plausible guess here is that Burney is thinking of the treble part, and is referring to one particular cadence (the 'Perfect Cadence' or 'Full Close'), and that for 'middle chord of a note' we are to read 'middle note of the chord'. However, this is merely a guess, and the present reader may be able to achieve a better one.

Occasionally Burney is himself puzzled, having to describe things on mere hearsay. For instance, after an article 'Gongong' ('an instrument used by the Hottentots'), he says: 'We hope our readers will understand this description, by which we frankly own ourselves not to be much enlightened.' And then ends—by the mild expression of his opinion that 'we have little reason to lament our ignorance of the construction and use of the gongong'.

Here is an example of Burney's questionable statements. It occurs under 'Design in Music':

> 'In all Haydn's best productions, where his invention seems inexhaustible, the hearer is never allowed to forget the text; which, amidst all the variety and contrast of pathos, grace, spirit, and playfulness of the principal melody, is heard by means of double counterpoint, in one part or other throughout the composition.'

Some of Burney's mis-statements are inexplicable except on the view that he did not trouble to think before writing. Thus he defines 'Fuga' as 'a movement in which *the leading part or first treble is pursued by the second, the second treble by the tenor and tenor by the base*' (which is true of merely a proportion of fugues), and gives as a 'certain and unexceptionable rule' that in the Answer, as compared with the Subject, '*if one part rises a fifth the other will only rise a fourth*' (which might more properly read 'if one part rises a fifth from the tonic the other will rise only a fourth', but would, even then, neglect cases where one part falls a fourth from the tonic and the other should fall a fifth). We have surely a right to expect more care from a man of Burney's standing!

And, by the way, if in order to cover the subject of Fugue we glance about the 'Fu' pages, we find out that he has arbitrarily distributed his information under three headings, 'Fuga', 'Fughe', and 'Fugue', alphabetically separated by others of the *Cyclopaedia*'s 'Fu' articles.

There is a considerable element of carelessness in the way the cross-references of this book have been drafted and checked. For instance, if we wish to know something of the famous London opera institution of Burney's earlier days, the so-called 'Royal Academy of Music', we turn to that head, which refers us back to 'Opera'—an article of a purely general nature with no mention whatever of the said Royal Academy. Or if we want to know the meaning of 'Rosalia', and look under that head, we are referred elsewhere—'See "Repetitions"'; but from 'Repetitions' we are merely rebounded to 'Rosalia'! Let us not, however, tamely abandon our search! If we only set to work to read right through the 'R' volumes we shall in time come across a very full, interesting, and even amusing treatment of the subject of 'Rosalia'—occupying more than half the space of the article on 'Richter, Francis-Xavier'—a composer who, as it happens, was addicted to this particular device.[1]

Talking of biographical articles, a curious feature of one or two of these is that they are duplicated—as though Burney had somehow written two articles on the same subject and unwittingly sent both to the editor, who had, so as to waste nothing, tacked one at the end of the other. So under 'Brossard', for instance, we get two treatments. And having read a rather solemn discussion of the indebtedness of Rousseau and Grassineau, in their musical dictionaries, to the earlier one of Brossard, we start again and read another solemn discussion of the indebtedness of Rousseau and Grassineau, in their musical dictionaries, to that of Brossard.

A good example of duplication is the explanation of notation—or rather this is for the most part triplication, for much of it occurs under 'Characters used in Music', under 'Note', and also as a couple of self-explanatory pages in one of the volumes of plates. The familiar table showing that two minims equal one semibreve, two crotchets one minim, &c., is thus supplied in three separate places.

Other articles that are duplicated are some of those on subjects admitting of a scientific or mathematical treatment. It seems as though Burney and his scientific colleague, Farey, both wrote on some of these

[1] Of course the learned Editor is much to blame. One can guess that the Rev. Dr. Rees did not himself read, in copy or proof, every article he sent to the press, and one is forced to that view not only by the peculiarities of the musical department but by others also. How ever did such an entry as this come about?:

> 'ASPE, a valley of Berne, in Swisserland, between the Pyrenées and the town of Oleron. The river of Oleron passes through the valley, and is called the Gave of Aspe.'

Suggested explanation: for 'Berne' read 'Béarne', which has been transformed in proof and then had the elucidation 'in Swisserland' added by some sleepy sub-editor, so making nonsense of the whole thing. (And for 'Oleron' read 'Oloron'—a different place altogether.)

Here is the opening of an article which suggests that the editorial department of the *Cyclopaedia* lacked a sense of humour:

> 'LEGS, in *Rural Economy*, are the extremities that, for the support of animals . . .'

That department lacked also a sense of proportion: eighty columns on 'Shipbuilding' and sixty on 'Sheep' are much too ample allowances for a general work of reference, and if the Editor had been up to his job he would never have allowed our dear old Burney over eighteen columns on his old friend Metastasio (far more than is given to any composer).

subjects and the editor just sent both articles to the printer without attempting to merge the treatments. Thus under 'Horn' there is a general treatment which necessarily brings in the system of crooks and then a highly mathematical treatment, showing (to four or six decimal points) the vibration ratios of the various notes of the harmonic scale, &c., and bringing in an explanation of the crooks, exactly as though they had not before been mentioned.

There is an oddity under 'Corno da Caccia'. Under this rubric we are referred to 'French Horn' (an entry that does not exist!), and then, as though we had not been directed to apply elsewhere, we are, after all, supplied with an article on the spot. Incidentally, we are also referred to 'Russian Music', an article on which does exist, but which includes no mention at all of any sort of horn! This is the sort of accident which occurs, one supposes, through writing articles to an alphabetical scheme; one commits oneself, by a cross-reference, to a treatment under a later head and when the time comes to write under that head, perhaps some years later, forgets one's commitments. It is impossible to write a good reference book alphabetically. The various subjects should be written by category and then distributed alphabetically.

Burney is really rather amusingly free with his intimate particulars, especially of persons he has known. Thus of the very celebrated hautboy player, Fischer (Gainsborough's son-in-law), he says: 'He had not a grain of sense but what he breathed through his reed; he never spoke more than three words at a time, and those were negatives or affirmatives. But peace to his ashes!'

And there is plain speaking about a one-time friend, the great violinist Giardini (Burney quotes nearly a column of it as having been written by a close associate of the man and as having 'lately come to our hands accidentally'):

'His disposition is so truly diabolical, that, preferring the evil principle of the Manicheans to the good of the Christians, if it is a matter of indifference to his interest, whether he shall serve or injure an individual, he would always chuse the latter.'

(Despite the use of the present tense in the above, the diabolical Giardini was dead—died in 1796 in Moscow, apparently unknown to Burney.) So too, 'Jackson, William' possessed 'genius, judgement, taste', but 'these qualities were strongly alloyed by a mixture of selfishness, arrogance, and an insatiable rage for superiority'. (His judgement and taste did not, apparently, extend to his dietary—'He latterly dined on milk-porridge and drank water. The experiment proved fatal.')

Here, too, is a bit of plain speaking. Under 'Howard, Samuel' we have been told that 'he took the lead in managing the affairs of the musical fund' (i.e. the Royal Society of Musicians):

'He was a dull, vulgar, and unpleasant man; and by over-rating his own importance, and reigning paramount over his equals, he rendered the monthly meetings disagreeable, and cooled the zeal of many well-wishers to the society.'

Then there is 'Immyns, John', remembered to-day as the founder of the still-existent Madrigal Society. He never got high in the profession:

'Yet he was always in cheerful spirits; and the honour of having established the Madrigal Society, and being its chairman at different alehouses in the city, presiding over dilettanti tradesmen, mechanics, and psalm singers, contributed as much, perhaps, to his pride and felicity, as the being president of the Royal Society, or speaker of the house of commons could have done. But alas! the tyrant Death dragged him from all his sublunary felicity in 1764.'

And here is a line that reads oddly. It refers to 'Hunt, Mrs. Arabella'. 'Whether this siren was a professional singer or a lady, does not appear.' (However the cricketing world, it is understood, to this day, maintains a similar distinction, 'players' and 'gentlemen'.)

Then there is the sad case of 'Quilici, Gaetano', an opera bass. Burney thinks he is 'still living in London, we fear in penury and obscurity', and supporting 'himself, a bed-ridden wife and an idiot boy, by teaching to sing, and has made some admirable scholars'. (We almost get the impression that a benevolent purpose prompts this very personal information.)

Under 'Vento, Matteo' (the Neapolitan composer, d. London 1776) we find a case of a musician who died 'very rich, as there was every reason of industry, parsimony and avarice, to imagine; but by some strange disposition of his property and affairs, none of his effects could be found at his death; and his widow and her mother were left wholly destitute of support, but from charity and the lowest menial labour'.

Here is a moral and domestic touch, rather unexpected in a work of reference. Under 'Blavet' we read of the 'respectable virtues' of this celebrated performer on the German flute:

'He married at eighteen, and lived upwards of fifty years with his wife in uninterrupted harmony and affection. We are always glad when to great professional abilities, such a character can be joined.'

The notice of 'de Amicis, Anna' terminates equally pleasingly with this satisfactory testimonial of character: 'Her private conduct seems to have been equally correct with her public, as no irregularities have ever arrived at our knowledge to sully her professional fame and amiable character.'

Another little intimate touch is this (the ending of the article on 'Domenico, Anibali'):

'We found a music book of one of Anibali's scholars at a stall in Middle-row, with graces to all the airs of Siroe, in his own hand-writing, which, for the time, were good.'

How characteristic of Burney to introduce the irrelevance of *where he bought* the book. (He alludes to the middle-row of the Strand, now destroyed—all but two churches surviving as islands: *Siroe* is Handel's opera of that name.)

Who invented the 'Musical Switch', which we to-day suffer under as a modern touch? Burney, under 'Charke, Richard', says that this gentleman was supposed to be the first who produced that species of buffoonery called a 'Medley Overture', wholly made up of shreds and patches of well-known vulgar tunes (he suggests, however, that Pepusch's overture to *The Beggar's Opera* has a claim to priority). This Charke was a queer character. He wrote a 'slang hornpipe, which used to be a favourite among the tars', and he was 'a facetious fellow, gifted for a turn for b.g. humour'. (What on earth is that? One suspects the worst!) As for Mrs. Charke (to which the *D.N.B.* gives an entertaining page or two), Burney cannot tell us all he would, as her memoirs, 'softened by being her own biographer, could never be read by persons of her own sex not wholly-abandoned'.

This entry ends:

'Though this couple was allowed to possess talents of various kinds, there was nothing in which they manifested more ingenuity than in plaguing each other.'

What tales Burney does sometimes tell! Here is one about 'Thevenard, Gabriel Vincent', of Paris, one of Lulli's singers:

'He was more than sixty years old, when, seeing a beautiful female slipper in a shoemaker's shop, he fell violently in love, on sight, unseen, with the person for whom it was made; and having discovered the lady, married her, after obtaining the consent of an uncle on whom she was dependent, with the assistance of many bottles of wine which they cracked together with the utmost cordiality, and which Thevenard meliorated with the charms of his voice.'

Can we believe the statement in the last lines of the following entry:

'CHANT *sur le livre, French,* is discant, or singing extempore in the plain song in the cathedral service of the Romish Church; which is done by three or four singers on the Gregorian notes, in the mass book on the desk in the middle of the choir, so that, except the *canto fermo* in the missal, which is generally sung by the tenor, the singers have nothing to guide them. However, there are choral singers, so versed in counterpoint, that they even lead off and pursue subjects of fugue and canon on this foundation, without confusion, or violating the rules of harmony.'

Is Rousseau here to be believed? For Burney has quietly lifted the whole passage as it stands, as his early acquaintance, Handel, used sometimes to lift movements of Stradella or Kerll. Only he has added, as a touch of his own, the reference to 'canon'. (No, no! Something colourably resembling a free fugue perhaps just barely possible—but *canon*!)

Burney did not merely write the definitely musical articles of the *Cyclopaedia*. In many articles on more general subjects there is included a slice of musical matter, in which it is easy to detect his hand. Such are, for instance, the articles 'Italy', 'Languages' (with a discussion of the relative value of French and Italian 'for vocal purposes'), 'Leopold II, Emperor of Germany' (with a short account of the music of his court and his own compositions), 'Liége' (the college belonging to it at Rome, to which the young Grétry journeyed), 'Liturgy', 'Luther', 'Mason, William', 'Parody', 'Russia', and 'Saxony'. It is odd that whilst Louis XIII and XIV of France are treated in general under 'Lewis', descriptions of the music of their courts appear under 'Louis', where the musical side of the subject and nothing else is treated. (It appears as though Burney, noticing the omission in the general 'Lewis' articles, had taken this ingenious way of remedying it a little later down the alphabet.)

A very rum article indeed is that on 'Queen'. It begins with a column of general information as to the status of a queen, of a queen consort, of a queen dowager, and this is followed by a mass of musical stuff that Burney has evidently been tolerantly allowed to shove in—a few inches about Queen Caroline's musical proclivities, a column about ecclesiastical music in the reign of Queen Mary, and nearly four columns about the musical activities of Queen Elizabeth and the musicians about her court. These various queens have all been treated in a general biographical and historical way in their proper positions earlier in the book, but Burney, realizing that the musical side of the subject has been there omitted, finds this way of supplying the omissions. And so long as a subject is somewhere in the book he never seems to worry as to whether anyone interested will ever get it *out* again.

Did Burney write the following passage in the article 'Seville'? And if so, does his authority incline the reader to believe in the cathedral organ bellows mentioned, which were so 'ample' that the player could have filled them himself, and then, if Bach had only been known in Spain, have played two or three of his fugues without refilling:

> 'The construction of the organ is peculiar; it contains 5300 pipes, with 110 stops, being, as it is said, 50 more than those of the famous one at Haerlem, yet, so ample are the bellows, that when stretched they supply the full organ fifteen minutes. The mode of filling them with air is singular; for instead of working with his hands, a man walks backwards and forwards along an inclined plane of about six feet by three and a half. These communicate with five other pair united by a bar; and the latter are so contrived, that when they are in danger of being overstrained, a valve is lifted up, and gives them relief. Passing ten times along the inclined plane fills all these vessels.'

Another entry in which Burney intervenes is that on the painter-poet-musician Salvator Rosa. When in Rome in 1770 he had bought from Rosa's granddaughter a music book that had belonged to Rosa, and so he tacks on at the end of some other writer's quite short biography of the great man a page of critical description of everything in this book—item by item, whether by Rosa himself or by some other composer.

There is in the *Cyclopaedia* an article, 'Westminster Abbey'. It is pure Burney, being entirely occupied with the 1784 Commemoration of Handel—not a word about the architecture or history of the Abbey. Nothing but the Commemoration! (Shocking editing, Dr. Rees!)

One of the most curious Burneyan additions is to be found at the end of the article '*Umbrella*, a well-known shade or guard from the sun or rain . . . not long introduced but now become very common'. Burney, who had evidently been experimenting, adds at the end of this article a long paragraph beginning, 'An umbrella, held in a proper position over the head, may serve to collect the force of a distant sound by reflecting, in the manner of a hearing trumpet', and goes on to discuss the Whispering Gallery at St. Paul's, and 'Mr. Charles's paradoxical exhibition of the invisible girl'—as to which latter he disappoints us by revealing that it was all a deception. But who would think of looking under 'Umbrella' for a discussion of acoustical phenomena? And what musical writer but Burney would have seized such an opportunity to hold forth?

A long, learned, and useful article of which Burney wrote a part was 'Liturgy'. At the end of this article occur brief references to the musical practices of the Calvinists, including the Scottish Presbyterians and their objection to the 'box of whistles', on the Methodists and their love of 'light, airy and familiar music' and admission of 'ballad and barrel organ tunes, out of the street, adapted to their hymns', and on the Quakers, who 'have no liturgy', but 'wait till the spirit moves them to speak, and never sing', but only 'sigh and groan'.

Now apparently the Presbyterians and Methodists had no wish to deny what was said about them or treated it with quiet contempt; it was the pacifist Quakers who pounced on the editor; for in a later volume, under the heading 'Service, Choral' (another long, learned, and useful article), we find the following:

> 'The Quakers object to singing as a part of public worship, and accordingly it is never practised in their meetings. To this respectable body we here make an apology for a jeu d'esprit of our learned coadjutor, Dr. B., who compiled part of the article LITURGY, which escaped him, notwithstanding his well-known liberality and candour, and which was undoubtedly unseasonably introduced, in an account of their public worship. Religious scruples, though in some respects unfounded and unwarrantable, when seriously avowed, are not fit subjects of ridicule.'

So poor Burney, who had never in his writings shown the slightest sympathy with any branch of Nonconformity but at last found himself writing under the editorship of an eminent Nonconformist divine, stood publicly rebuked! (We shall see in a moment another of Burney's references to Quaker sighs and groans.)

Was Burney a pedant? Some have said that he was, but the present writer flatly denies it. For example, he had a great admiration for the mathematician George Lewis Scott, F.R.S., F.S.A., whose articles on 'Temperament' and such subjects in Chambers's *Cyclopaedia* he highly commends, but he smiled at Scott's mathematical preoccupations when engaged in music-making:

'Mr. Scott was a performer on the harpsichord, and very fond of music; but always calculating, during his own performance and that of others, as to the legality of modulation. And we well remember his being much disturbed at the unrelative succession of chords, in the opening of Pergolesi's "Stabat Mater", at the second bar, where that most pleasing author surprises the ear, as well as the eye and intellect, in modulating from F minor to E♭ major.'

Then Burney had a very proper contempt for music that was merely 'learned'—canon for canon's sake, or fugue for fugue's sake. So of John Travers (d. 1758) he says:

'His passion for fugues resembled that of an inveterate punster, who never hears a phrase or sentence uttered in conversation, without considering what quibble or pun it will furnish: so Travers seems never to have seen or heard any series of sounds, without trying to form them into a fugue, and meditating when and where the answer might be brought in.'

Now a word or two as to Burney's literary style. Sometimes it is shockingly slipshod, but when he is at his best he really writes neatly, picturesquely, and, in every way, effectively. Space shall be found for one complete entry in the *Cyclopaedia* to illustrate his style when in good form:

'JONES, a Welshman who was blind, and the best performer on the harp of his time. The old duchess of Marlborough would have retained him in her service, with a pension, as an inmate; but he could not endure confinement, and was engaged by Evans, the landlord of a well-accustomed home-brewed ale-house, at the Hercules' Pillars, opposite Clifford's Inn passage in Fleet-street, where he performed in a great room up stairs during the winter season. He played extempore voluntaries, the fugues in the sonatas and concertos of Corelli, and most of his solos, with many of Handel's opera songs, with uncommon neatness, which were thought great feats, at a time when scarcely any thing but Welsh tunes with variations was ever attempted on that instrument in the hands of other harpers. He also played on the violin, and accurately imitated on that instrument, to the great delight of the home-brewed ale-drinkers, the sobs, sighs, and groans of a Quaker's sermon.'

That is the vivid and picturesque Burney. But in the more dignified style our friend is at times equally successful. His words are well chosen and well placed, and there is a swinging rhythm in his prose which his friend Johnson himself would have approved. Take this, as a chance example (from the article 'Italy', the musical portion of which is clearly by him):

'If the great musicians of antiquity, whose names are so familiar to our ears, had not likewise been poets, time and oblivion would long since have swept them away. But these having been luckily writers themselves, took a little care of their own fame; which their brethren of after-ages gladly supported for the honour of the *corps*.

'But since writing and music have become separate professions the celebrity of the poor musician dies with the vibration of his strings; or if, in condescension, he be remembered by a poet or historian, it is usually but to blazon his infirmities, and throw contempt upon his talents. The voice of acclamation, and thunder of applause, pass away like vapours; and those hands which were most active in testifying temporary approbation, suffer the name of those who charmed away their care and sorrows in the glowing hour of innocent delight, to remain unrecorded.'

Johnson and Burney, in their many conversations at Streatham, must sometimes have discussed the effective writing of English. Indeed we have a hint of this in a letter from Twining to his brother which touches on a detail of good writing. Twining urges the avoidance of 'a form of reference that I abominate, i.e., the latter, the former'. As he rightly remarks, it is 'abominable' for two reasons: (*a*) one is always 'forced to look back', and (*b*) 'There is an appearance always of aiming at antithesis'—' "*As long as you have the use of your tongue and your pen*," said Dr. Johnson to Dr. Burney, "*never, sir, be reduced to that shift*." '

Here, to close, is another well-worded paragraph (from the article on 'Trial, Jean Claude', who at the age of fifteen (so Burney assures us) was appointed director of the concert and opera at Montpellier, and later held a similar position in Paris:

'Permit us here to define the office of director of the academy of music, or serious opera. The management of the opera is a painful and embarrassing administration. It is necessary for the director of this complicated machine to attend to all the springs, to dissipate all impediments to their action, flatter the taste and sometimes the caprice of the inconstant public, unite to a point of concord very rarely attainable, a crowd of various and often rival talents, excite emulation without awakening jealousy, distribute rewards with justice and delicacy, censure and punish with address, limit the unbounded demands of some by flattery, check the independence of others by apparent concessions, and try to establish in the interior government of this republic as much harmony as reigns in the orchestra. It is manifest that nothing but the most subtile, artful, and pliant character can hope to accomplish such Herculean labours.'

LIX. DEATH OF AN OLD FRIEND—THE INVENTIVE MERLIN

(*d. 1804, aged 69; Burney aged 78*)

IN 1804 the Burneys lost an old friend, one who had been a frequent visitor in the St. Martin's Street days and who, from the amusement his visit always provided, deserves a special word in any chronicle of the Burney family—the harpsichord maker and general inventor, Merlin, 'the very ingenious mechanic' as Fanny calls him.

'He is a great favourite at our house. He is very diverting also in conversation. There is a singular simplicity in his manners. . . . He speaks his opinion upon all subjects and about all persons with the most undisguised freedom. He does not, though a foreigner, want *words*; but he *arranges* and *pronounces* them very comically. He is humbly grateful for all civilities that are shown him; but is warmly and honestly resentful for the least slight.'[1]

It was, apparently, about the time the above was written (1775) that the Burneys acquired an instrument of Merlin's make, and we find its qualities displayed to all the family's friends, such entries as the following occurring in Fanny's diary:

'We went into the library and Hetty was prevailed upon to play a Lesson of Bach of Berlin upon our Merlin harpsichord.'

And a few days later:

'Mr. Bruce, who is so very fond of music, had appointed that day to accompany Mrs. Strange hither to hear Mr. Burney play upon our Merlin harpsichord.'[2]

Bach of Berlin is, supposedly, Burney's friend C. P. Emanuel Bach, formerly attached to the Court there, though he might be the elder brother, Wilhelm Friedemann, if we are willing to suppose that Fanny had heard that he had settled there the previous year; Bruce is the great explorer; Mrs. Strange the wife of the engraver; by 'Mr. Burney' is always meant Dr. Burney's nephew and Hetty's husband, Charles Rousseau Burney.

Some special qualities of Merlin's instruments are mentioned in Burney's article 'Harpsichord' in Rees's *Cyclopaedia*:

'Merlin, we believe, was the first who changed the octave stop to a third unison, about the year 1770, which rendered the instrument equally powerful and less subject to go out of tune; the octave stop being so much affected by the least change in the temperature of the air, that it almost instantly discovered when there was a change in the wind.'

The article goes on to say that Merlin introduced also 'great improve-

[1] *Early Diary*, ii. 58. For a portrait, &c., of Merlin see pl. 41, II. 206.

[2] Ibid. 10, 24.

ments in the mechanism' of 'large piano-fortes'. He was one of the first to make these in the 'grand' shape, and he took out a patent for a combined harpsichord and pianoforte.[1] This latter novelty was patented in 1774, the year previous to that of the above diary entries, and it is quite likely that they refer to an example of it, for the inventor could find few more effective means of making his new type of instrument known in the right quarters than that of getting a specimen into such a centre of musical activity as the house in St. Martin's Street. The fact that people were invited to the Burneys specially to hear their new instrument supports this suggestion. This may possibly have been the instrument thus described in one of Merlin's catalogues:

'A superb Patent *Double-bass Piano-Forte Harpsichord* with twenty different Stops, and less complicated than a common double-keyed Harpsichord with a Swell, although it is not so liable to be out of Order or Tune. Price from 90 to 100 Guineas.'[2]

A year or two later Merlin was commissioned by Burney to make for him a pianoforte of a special compass. It is mentioned in Burney's Will as 'my large Piano Forte, with additional keys at the top and bottom . . . made by Merlin, with a Compass of six Octaves . . . constructed expressly at my desire for duets à Quatre Mains'. The Will also states that this instrument of enlarged compass was 'the first that was ever constructed', and the year of construction is given as 1777. That is the year of publication of the first music ever to be printed for two performers at one keyboard—Burney's own *Four Sonatas or Duets for Two Performers on One Pianoforte or Harpsichord*, and the construction and publication were connected. Not that in these 'Sonatas or Duets' themselves the full compass of Burney's own instrument is employed (which would have debarred them from any sale), but that his mind was, at this moment, employed on the general problems of duet playing and composition.[3]

[1] Rosamond E. M. Harding, *The Pianoforte* (1933), 48, 70.

[2] The following occurs in a *Morning Post* report of a performance of *The Beggar's Opera* at Covent Garden (issue of 30 Sept. 1776): 'At the performance of *The Beggar's Opera*, at Covent Garden Theatre. . . . The orchestra [was disappointing.] Mr. Fisher . . . in avoiding one extreme, has run into another equally unjustifiable, in accompanying the airs only with a first and second fiddle, and Merlin's new forte piano.—By this super delicate pianissimo, the melody and harmony of the matchless airs in this celebrated opera were filtered down to nothing, but the obligato flourishings of the first fiddle, and the chord of the new invented harpsichord . . . [were] more absurd, if possible, than the old style of overpowering the voice with the full force of a large band.'

[3] Burney's lead as to an extended compass was slowly followed. Thirteen years later (1790) Broadwood put on the market what is usually spoken of as the first pianoforte of five and a half octaves, and four years after that (1794) he at last produced one, like Burney's, of six octaves. Six octaves remained the limit for a long time; Liszt in Paris in 1824 was using an Erard of this compass. (The works of Schumann and Chopin require only six and a quarter octaves; the present-day instruments have only seven and a quarter but some have been made with eight.) As regards Burney's priority in the publication of four-hand music for one keyboard, note that one or two pieces of such music were written in the late sixteenth century, though these never attained the dignity of print (see *Oxford Companion to Music*, s.v.

It is curious that this specially constructed instrument referred to in the Will as a 'Piano Forte' appears in one of Burney's articles in Rees's *Cyclopaedia* ('Ravalement') as a harpsichord:

'In the year 1777, when Dr. Burney first composed and published duets "à quatre mains," or for two performers on one instrument, the ladies, at that time wearing hoops, which kept them at too great a distance from each other, [he] had a harpsichord made by Merlin, expressly for duets, with six octaves; extending from the octave below double C in the base, to the octave above C in alt. in the treble. And as duets à quatre mains have been composed by all the great masters in Europe since that time, instruments with additional keys are now become general. At first it was only in the treble that the compass was extended, except in the instrument above-mentioned by Merlin; but at present notes are added in the base to complete the six octaves: and, indeed, the additional notes in the base are better worth having for particular effects, than those in the treble; which often, from the shortness of the strings and feeble vibration, more resemble the tone of wood than wire; whereas the tone of those in the base of large piano fortes, by the best makers is so rich and full that each sound below double F resembles that of an organ-pipe in slow notes, more than the transient tone of a string.'

A harp on some new system was another novelty of Merlin's introduction. We hear of Edward Jones, the Welsh harper (later the author of a famous book on the Welsh bards), playing at one of the St. Martin's Street musical evenings on 'a very sweet instrument with new pedals, constructed by Merlin'.[1] This may be the instrument listed in a catalogue of 'Merlin's Mechanical Exhibition' as 'Merlin's Vocal Harp, played with keys', which—

'displays a celestial body of sound, resembles the human voice, gives the effect of Fiddles and Bases, and is most admirably calculated for the Expressivo'.

Then in *The Public Advertiser* of 30 March 1778 is an advertisement of a concert, 'Mrs. Barthélemon's Benefit', at which 'Mr. Barthélemon will play a solo on the Ipolito, an instrument of five strings, invented by him, and made by Mr. Merlin'.

Merlin was, however, many things besides instrument maker. He was a remarkable man of high ingenuity very variously applied.

The story of his earlier life, so far as the present writer has been able to discover it, is as follows. He was born in 1735 at Huy, between Namur and Liége.[2] He must have shown early inventive powers, for the French Academy of Sciences encouraged him to settle in Paris. He there

'Pianoforte', 21). Three years after Burney's *Four Sonatas or Duets* had appeared, Theodore Smith published nine such sonatas in Berlin. Smith was an Englishman and a Londoner and it is likely that he had become acquainted with Burney's Sonatas.

[1] *Mem.* ii. 14.

[2] Sophie v. La Roche, in her diary of a visit to London in 1786, calls him 'Merlin von Lüttich' (i.e. of 'Liége'). See the translation of this diary, *Sophie in London* (1933).

seems to have met the Count de Fuentes, who, on coming to London in 1760 as Spanish Ambassador, brought him over in his suite.[1]

A few years later he was serving as manager of Cox's Museum, in Spring Gardens.[2] We read in Fanny's *Evelina* of a party being made up to visit Cox's Museum—'very astonishing and very superb', says the heroine, 'yet it afforded me but little pleasure, for it is a mere show, though a wonderful one'; however, it was pronounced by another lady of the party to be 'the grandest, prettiest sight in England'.[3]

The Museum was apparently an exhibition of all kinds of automata—'a pine-apple which, suddenly opening, discovered a nest of birds, which immediately began to sing', and the like.

'This entertainment concluded with a concert of mechanical music: I cannot explain how it was produced, but the effect was pleasing. Madame Duval was in ecstasies; and the Captain flung himself into so many ridiculous distortions, by way of mimicking her, that he engaged the attention of all the company; and, in the midst of the performance of the Coronation Anthem, while Madame Duval was affecting to beat time, and uttering many expressions of delight, he called suddenly for salts, which a lady, apprehending some distress, politely handed to him, and which, instantly applying to the nostrils of poor Madame Duval, she involuntarily snuffed up such a quantity, that the pain and surprise made her scream aloud.'[4]

Later Merlin established a similar exhibition of his own, in Prince's Street, Hanover Square; it was known as 'Merlin's Cave', the proprietor, in this way, adroitly setting up an attractive association between himself and his namesake the great magician of Arthurian legend.[5]

In the Bodleian Library at Oxford are preserved two catalogues of this place of entertainment, belonging to different periods but having the same wording on the title-page:[6] *Morning Amusement. Merlin's Mechanical Exhibition. Catalogue of the Different Pieces of Mechanism exhibited at his Great Room, No. 11, Prince's Street, Hanover Square, which is open every Day (Sundays excepted) from eleven 'till Three o'Clock. Admittance 2s. 6d. N.B. Such Persons as visit the Exhibition will have the Liberty of using not only the Hygaeian Chair, but also the Escarpolette.* This Chair, in which (it is

[1] Rimbault (ed. Clinch), *Soho and its Associations* (1895), 28.

[2] Austin Dobson; footnote in *Diary and Letters of Madame D'Arblay*, i. 458.

[3] John Wesley's opinion coincided with that of Fanny's heroine, not with that of the 'other lady'. See his *Journal*: '3 March 1773. I was invited to see Mr. Cox's celebrated museum. I cannot say my expectation was disappointed; for I expected nothing, and I found nothing but a heap of pretty, glittering trifles, prepared at an immense expense. For what end? To please the fancy of fine ladies and pretty gentlemen.'

[4] *Evelina*, ch. xix.

[5] Perhaps, too, there was an idea of reviving a name previously known to London pleasure seekers. The following is from E. Beresford Chancellor's *The Pleasure Haunts of London* (1925), 383. The place referred to was near Sadler's Wells. '*Merlin's Cave*, near the New River Head (Merlin's Place perpetuates its name), was a Sunday resort for many years from 1735, when it is said to have been first constructed. It was obviously an imitation of the cave made for Queen Caroline in the gardens at Richmond with which the thresher-poet, Stephen Duck, is associated, but possessed a skittle-ground which was probably its chief source of attraction.'

[6] They are respectively '2704, f.4' and 'Jessel 56' (item 72).

reassuring to be told) 'the Nobility and Gentry may swing themselves with perfect safety', was a wonderful remedy for 'Pulmonary Consumption and other Disorders', and the 'Escarpolette' was something of the same kind and with similar valuable properties. Amongst the exhibits of Merlin's establishment, as in the earlier one of Cox, was 'an automatic organ, imitating the performance of a full band'.[1]

But Merlin, as we have already seen, not only exhibited novelties; he also sold them. Horace Walpole, in 1791, writes to Miss Mary Berry as follows:

'An odd adventure has happened. The Primate of Poland has been here, the King's brother. He bought some scientific toys at Merlin's, paid fifteen guineas for them in the shop, and was to pay as much more. Merlin pretends he knew him only for a foreigner who was going away in two days, and literally had his holiness arrested and carried to a sponging-house; for which the Chancellor has struck the attorney off the list.'[2]

Amongst Merlin's ingenious inventions was (1770) a machine for notating music, which he sent to Prince Galitzin, in St. Petersburg. Fétis says that 'the difficulty of translating the signs caused this machine to be dropped'.[3] Another was 'a Table, which may be formed into desks for 8 performers, with brass furniture for Candle light: by a winch it can be elevated to any height, for writing or playing standing, with drawers and various contrivances for secret deposits'. Burney himself possessed such a 'curious Merlin Table', and it figures, in the above description, in his Will (II. 271).

Another invention was a 'pedal tea table' (which was contrived to cause a succession of cups automatically to pass before the pouring hostess), and still another, as it appears, the roller-skate:

'One of his ingenious novelties was *a pair of skaites* contrived to run on small metallic wheels. Supplied with a pair of these and a violin he mixed in the motley group of one of the celebrated Mrs. Corneily's masquerades at Carlisle-house, Soho-square; when, not having provided the means of retarding his velocity, or commanding its direction, he impelled himself against a mirror of more than five hundred pounds' value, dashed it to atoms, broke his instrument to pieces, and wounded himself severely.'[4]

A safer, if slower, means of progression introduced by this never-resting inventor was the 'Merlin Chair', which is still sold under that name—an invalid chair propelled by the occupant, the wheels on each side of him having attached to them other wheels of slightly smaller diameter (so as not to touch the ground), which smaller wheels are turned by the

[1] Sir John Graham Dalyell, *Musical Memoirs of Scotland* (1849), 147.

[2] *Letters of Horace Walpole* (Toynbee's edition), xiv. 410.

[3] Fétis, *Biographie Universelle des Musiciens* (1870), s.v. 'Merlin'. The authority quoted by Fétis is a notice of the machine in the *Correspondant musical de Spire* (1792), 398.

[4] Thomas Busby, *Concert Room and Orchestra Anecdotes* (1835), ii. 137. *The Examiner* of 24 Aug. 1823 announces the invention of the roller-skate at that date. Probably Merlin never put his article on the market, so that it became forgotten and had to be reinvented. (The name 'roller-skate' seems to be American and to date from the early 1870's.)

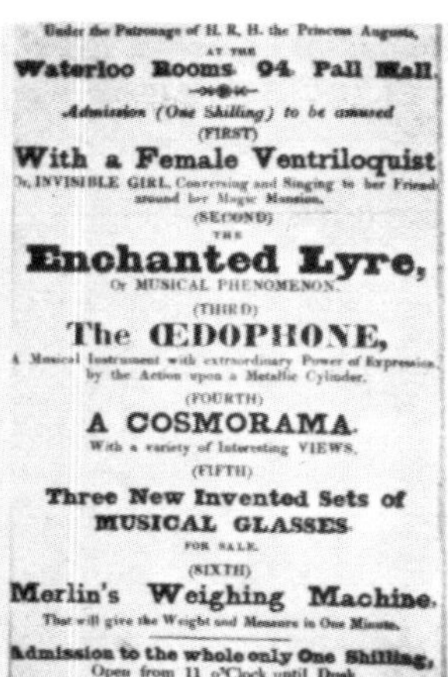

Under the Patronage of H. R. H. the Princess Augusta,
AT THE
Waterloo Rooms, 94, Pall Mall.
Admission (One Shilling) to be amused
(FIRST)
With a Female Ventriloquist
Or, INVISIBLE GIRL, Conversing and Singing to her Friends around her Magic Mansion.
(SECOND)
THE
Enchanted Lyre,
Or MUSICAL PHENOMENON.
(THIRD)
The ŒDOPHONE,
A Musical Instrument with extraordinary Power of Expression, by the Action upon a Metallic Cylinder.
(FOURTH)
A COSMORAMA.
With a variety of Interesting VIEWS.
(FIFTH)
Three New Invented Sets of MUSICAL GLASSES
FOR SALE.
(SIXTH)
Merlin's Weighing Machine.
That will give the Weight and Measure in One Minute.
Admission to the whole only One Shilling,
Open from 11 o'Clock until Dusk.

MERLIN, HIS CARRIAGE, AND AN EXHIBITION

e dial in front of the carriage registered the distance traversed. The Exhibition comprised both musical and non-musical inventions.

M E R L I N'S
NECROMANCIC CAVE,
PRINCES STREET, HANOVER SQUARE.

THE AUTHOR, having for many Years paſt made Mechanics his Study, has reached a Species of Perfection hitherto unknown in is or any other Country, in inventing a great Variety of Machines, not ore curious than uſeful. Among other ingenious Pieces of Mechaniſm, e humbly ſubmits the following Outlines of a Deſign equally novel as e preſumes it will appear aſtoniſhing.

P L A N.

I. On Entrance, the Company will be accommodated in a CIRCU-AR SALOON, moſt judiciouſly adapted to its Uſes, and ornamented ith uncommon Taſte. In the Centre of the SALOON will be the ECROMANCIC CAVE, on which the Automaton Figure of MBROSIUS MERLIN will be ſeated; holding in his Right-hand a Leaden ceptre, or conjuring Rod, a Symbol of his abſolute Power, by which he ill apparently animate all inanimated Things, ſuch as Chairs, Paintings, nd Magical Looking-glaſſes; all which will obey his Commands; he ill likewiſe tell the Fortunes of the Ladies. Two AUTOMATON FIGURES ill then walk in a Gallery in the Saloon, and play on ancient Inſtruments f Muſic, by Means of a wonderful Exertion of Mechaniſm, preſenting Re-freſhments to the Ladies only.

II. Under the Entrance to the Cave will be a dark ſubterraneous Cavern n Feet deep, wherein the Author will make Uſe of his ſuppoſed Necro-mancic Power, in Imitation of the celebrated AMBROSIUS MERLIN, alled the NECROMANCER. A Variety of Phantoms, red and white ragons, Rattle-ſnakes, all Sorts of Reptiles, creeping Animals and noc-urnal Birds, will be ſeen and heard making the moſt horrid mournful Shrieks and Noiſe, ſo as to ſtrike the Beholders with the utmoſt Aſto-niſhment; the Goddeſs of Darkneſs will alſo appear in a ſable Habit, wearing Bat's Wings. By an extraordinary Diſplay of Mechanical Inge-nuity, the Prince of Darkneſs and Chief of the Devils, will be diſcovered in a deep, extenſive and tremendous Cavern, which will alſo contain all the Furies and infernal Harpies.

III. After having explored this dark Receſs, the Company will be deſired to walk into a Circus, richly adorned and ornamented with the Temple of Apollo, where a Concert will be performed, entirely the Effect of an amazing Effort of Mechanical Invention, and ſo well directed as nearly to equal, both in Vocal and Inſtrumental Muſic, FIVE or SIX HUN-DRED PERFORMERS, in a Selection of the moſt approved Works of the moſt celebrated Maſters that have appeared throughout Europe.

P R O P O S A L S.

I. That the Sum of *Five Thouſand and Forty Pounds* be raiſed for the Purpoſes of this Undertaking, by Means of *Four Hundred Shares* at Twelve Guineas each Share.

II. That the firſt Two Hundred Subſcribers be furniſhed each with a Ticket marked A; and the other Two Hundred, with a Ticket marked B.

III. That Two Evenings be ſet apart every Week for the Entertainment of the Subſcribers; one for the Proprietors or Holders of the Ticket A, and the other for that of B; which will give free Admiſſion for Two Years from the Commencement of the Exhibition.

IV. That the Tickets be transferable.

V. That Sir HERBERT MACKWORTH, Bart. DORSET, JOHNSON, and Co. Bankers, No. 68, Bond Street, be appointed to receive the Subſcriptions.

For NON-SUBSCRIBERS.——VI. That there will be *a Morning* and an *Evening Exhibition* Four Days in the Week, (of which proper Notice will be given in due Time;) the former, at Half-a-Guinea each Perſon; and latter, in conſequence of the Illuminations, &c. &c. at *One Gu*

DESCRIPTION OF 'THE NECROMANCIC CAVE'

e small type of this reproduction is well worth perusal (with a magnifying-glass if necessary) as it gives ood idea of the variety of accomplishment of Merlin's clever automata. It will be noted that this eighteenth-century magician connects his powers with those of his legendary Celtic namesake. (For an account of this 'Merlin the Second' *see* ii. 202–9.)

invalid himself. The 'Morpheus Chair' (or 'Morfus Chair' as Charlotte Burney alternatively and tentatively spells one of its names), was (and is) 'made to fall back and form a Bed for the Repose of the Infirm'. It cost forty guineas.

Apparently it was this chair that figured in 1780 in a certain masquerade already mentioned (see II. 41; was this regarded as an opportunity for advertising the novelty?). Dr. Burney's daughter, Charlotte, says:

'Merlin was there as a Sick Man in his Morpheus Chair as he calls it. He was a very good mask Edward says, but the newsmongers are not so good natured to him, for *they* say that there was a sick man in his Chair who made everybody sick of him!'[1]

For those who were not infirm but venturesome the Exhibition provided a more exciting form of progression, the 'Ærial Cavalcade' on which 'Ladies and Gentlemen may ride perfectly safe, over the heads of the rest of the Company'—presumably keeping out of the way *en route* of 'An Artificial Bat which flies in the Cupola'. Back on *terra firma* they could enjoy the sight of 'the Bust of a Turk who will chew and swallow an artificial Stone as often as any of the Company chooses to put one in his Mouth'. Or they could apply themselves to the 'Gambling Machine' which would 'play the game of Odd or Even' with them 'for four hours by once winding up'.

An attractive trait of this inventor was his generous willingness to share the benefits of his ingenuity. One of the catalogues just mentioned has a preface addressed 'To ALL ARTISTS OF GENIUS', inviting 'ingenious Mechanics' to visit the Exhibition at the usual admission price of half a crown, and 'take drawings and dimensions, and if they make them Mr. Merlin will recommend them to the Nobility and Gentry'.

Having helped the suffering by one of the inventions just described this kindly man had the thought, apparently, of doing something to help the aged, for Mrs. Thrale writes to Fanny, in 1781:

'Merlin has been here to tune the fortepiano. He told Mrs. Davenant and me that he had thought of inventing a particular mill to grind old ladies young, as he was so prodigiously fond of their company.'[2]

With the Thrales, Merlin, it appears, was on friendly visiting terms—not merely making professional calls, and Fanny gives a descriptive account of one of his visits in which (as seems to have been usual with

[1] *Early Diary*, ii. 289.

[2] *Diary and Letters*, i. 458. There is a startling reflection on the capacity of early nineteenth-century pianoforte tuners in Burney's article 'Acute', in Rees's *Cyclopaedia*. As often, Burney after defining a quality goes on unthinkingly to discuss its opposite. Here, beginning by a definition of the word as the equivalent of 'sharp, shrill or high', he goes on to tell us that the 'grave additional tones in our large pianofortes become the more difficult to tune as they descend', and actually states that—'The octave below double C can, with the utmost difficulty, be made to satisfy a nice ear by the most experienced tuner.' No wonder that Merlin preferred to be the tuner of his own instruments when they were to be played by musicians like his friend Burney!

those who knew Merlin) the company tried to pull his leg. They loved to see Merlin appear—'that ridiculous Merlin, who contrived to divert Mrs. Thrale and me with his inconceivable absurdities', Fanny calls him on one occasion. 'Merlin supped here and was very diverting; I think you must introduce him in your next work', writes Susan to Fanny from St. Martin's Street, on another occasion.[1]

It was partly Merlin's command of English that so much pleased his friends. Here is an extract from a letter of young Charlotte Burney:

'Merlin has taken to visiting us again, to my delight. If ever I am at all my own mistress, I'll certainly always have my doors open to Merlin. He said that *Sir Crostopher Wichcurt's* daughter had *affront* him. But that he knows a Turk who is very civil, and not at all *Barbarative*.'[2]

Merlin seems to have been a friend of the very musical Gainsborough who, when he painted the well-known portrait of his son-in-law, the celebrated oboeist Fischer, took care to put Merlin's name pretty boldly on the pianoforte against which Fischer is leaning. More than that, he painted a portrait of Merlin himself, and one of which its subject highly approved. It will be remembered that amongst the family gallery of Reynolds's portraits commissioned by Mr. Thrale was one of Burney, and Fanny tells this Streatham dinner-table anecdote of Merlin's comments on it:

'Oh! for that picture of Dr. Burney, Sir Joshua Reynolds has not taken pains, *that is*, to please me! I do not like it. Mr. Gainsborough has done one much better of me, which is very agreeable indeed. I wish it had been at the Exhibition, for it would have done him a great deal of credit indeed.'[3]

The 'that is' was evidently a recognized Merlinian expression. We meet with it elsewhere, as in a letter from Fanny to Mrs. Thrale:

'Merlin was here last night, & to know in what I had offended him I went down Stairs: & I find the mischief was all done by Mr. Seward, who told him we all laughed at him here—but he had the wit to say he did not thank him for such a *disagreeable sort of compliment*, though he does not *think it worth while that is to take notice of it to him*. So we parted very good friends.'[4]

Fanny, in *Cecilia*, though she does not, as her sister had suggested she should do, use Merlin as a model for a comic character, does, like Gainsborough, manage to work in a touch of advertisement for him, since her heroine, being in danger of boredom, 'amused herself with walking and reading' and 'commissioned Mr. Monckton to send her a Piano Forte of Merlin's'.

[1] *Diary and Letters*, i. 503, ii. 18; *Early Diary*, ii. 242.

[2] Ibid. 300. Merlin meant the daughter of *Sir Christopher Whitchott*.

[3] *Diary and Letters*, i. 505. The following year, 1782, it was 'at the Exhibition', i.e. of the Royal Academy, but I cannot now trace its whereabouts, nor can any authority to whom I have referred the problem. See, however, a little information in W. T. Whitley, *Thomas Gainsborough* (1915).

[4] W. Wright Roberts, *Burney in the Light of the New Thrale Correspondence in the John Rylands Library* (1932), 13.

They all made fun of Merlin but they all liked him—and it appears that they pushed his wares.

Leaving now the subject of Merlin it may here be recorded that shortly after his death (some time in 1805) Burney had the pleasure of seeing in Chelsea Hospital the King, Queen, 'and all the Royal Family in England, I believe, except the Prince and Princess of Wales':

'They went over every ward, the Governor's apartments, and all the offices; with the chapel, refectory, and even the kitchen. I was graciously summoned when they entered the chapel, and most graciously, indeed, received. The first thing the King said on my appearance, was, holding up both his hands as if astonished, "Ten years younger than when I saw you last, Dr. Burney!" The first words of the Queen were, "How does Madame d'Arblay do?" And after my answer, and humble thanks, she added in a low voice, "I am extremely obliged to you, Dr. Burney, for the hymn you sent me." "What? what?" cried the King. Her Majesty answered: "The Russian air, Sir." "Ay, ay; it's a very fine thing; but they performed it too slow. It wanted more spirit in the execution. They commonly perform too slow, and make things of that sort languid that should be animated." . . .

'Their Majesties then both condescended to make some inquiries after my family, though by name only after my daughter d'Arblay. I heard from her very seldom, I answered; I was afraid of writing to her; and I saw she was afraid of writing to me. Buonaparte, I said, was so outrageous against this country, that I doubted not but that a sheet of blank paper that should pass between us, would be turned into a conspiracy! My grand-daughter, Fanny Phillips, I mentioned, now lived with me: for she had often and most condescendingly been noticed by the Royal Family, during the time that my daughter d'Arblay had had the honour of belonging to the Queen's establishment. The Queen said she had heard of my young companion from Lady Aylesbury. When I left their Majesties, I went in search of my grand-daughter, and brought her under my arm into the governor's great room.

'The Queen no sooner perceived, than she graciously addressed her: while the King held up his hands at her growth since he had seen her, at the Palace, in her childhood. All the Princesses remembered, and spoke to her with the most pleasing kindness.

'"And what are you doing now, Dr. Burney?" said the King.

'"I am writing for the new Cyclopaedia, Sir."

'"I am glad the subject of music," he answered, "should be in such good hands." . . .

'The King then resumed again his old favourite topic of amusement, my daughter d'Arblay's concealed composition of Evelina; inquiring again and again into the various particulars of its contrivance and its discovery. I could not have been honoured with so much of his Majesty's notice, but that, being at home in Chelsea College, I was naturally permitted to follow in his suite the whole morning; and all I have written passed at different intervals, between matters of higher import.'[1]

[1] *Mem.* iii. 360–1. Is there any significance in the fact that it was in the year following this visit of the King and Queen to Chelsea Hospital that Burney received his pension (see II. 254)?

LX. THE OCTOGENARIAN BURNEY BECOMES A CONVERT TO BACH

(1807–1814; aged 81–88)

BURNEY's opinion of Bach at the time he wrote his *History* has been summarized in an earlier chapter (see I. 312). Before we set righteously to work to assess the culpability of Burney and the musicians of his day in their failure to realize the greatness of Bach we must in justice consider what was the extent of their opportunities. What published music of Bach was available at the date of Bach's death? Here is the list:

1. CHORAL MUSIC. One early Cantata (vocal parts only), and a few chorales in Schemelli's hymn book.
2. ORGAN MUSIC. 27 Choral Preludes and what we to-day call the 'St. Anne's' Fugue.
3. HARPSICHORD MUSIC. 7 Partitas, the Italian Concerto, the Goldberg Variations, and the *Musical Offering* to Frederick the Great.

Soon after Bach's death his sons added to this the *Art of Fugue*, which, however, sold very few copies and did not become much known.

Burney's second volume of his *History*, in which he treated Bach so scantily and scurvily (as we now think), appeared in 1782, thirty-two years after the composer's death. What of Bach's music had been published in those thirty-two years? So far as the present writer knows, nothing except 200 of the four-part chorals harmonized by him, which were collected by his son Emanuel and published in 1765–9.

Where Bach's compositions were known at all, then, they were confined to the above-listed tiny handful of printed material, with a few other things, that, in Germany at any rate, circulated in manuscript—more particularly, we may suppose, some of the organ works.

And as for those organ works it must be remembered that they were all totally unplayable on English organs, of which during Burney's lifetime only rare specimens possessed a pedal board—and then almost certainly not of a range that would allow of the performance of Bach's pedal parts.

About 1800 a strange new interest in Bach began suddenly to grow and to spread, and it looks as though almost the first signs of it appeared in England, where there was made public a suggestion for the issue of the *Well-tempered Clavier*. Burney's friend, the German-born Organist of the German Chapel of St. James's Palace, Augustus Frederic Christopher Kollman, published in 1796 and dedicated to Burney himself *An Essay on Musical Harmony, according to the Nature of the Science and the Principles of the Greatest Musical Authors* (2nd and 3rd editions in 1799 and 1812), including in it examples from the *Well-tempered Clavier*; and three years later, in 1799, he published *An Essay on Practical Musical Composition* in which he included a prelude and fugue from the '48' and one of the Organ Trios. In this latter work he announced his intention of producing an 'analysed' edition of the '48'. At the time he made the announcement the *Well-tempered* had not been published in any country, and Kollman's intention to become a pioneer was at once favourably noticed in the Leipzig journal, the *Allgemeine Musikalische Zeitung* (October 1799):

> 'England is not unacquainted with the state of music in Germany. Even those higher departments of German art in which we ourselves begin to be strangers are so well known there that an English organist can have the courage of publishing Sebastian Bach's "Well Tempered Clavier, with Explanations", when but a few years ago an attempt of printing that work was made in vain at two different places in that great composer's own country.'

The appearance of foreign editions, however, took the wind out of Kollman's sales. Writing twelve years later in a journal he had started, the *Quarterly Musical Register* (January 1812—one of the only two numbers of this journal that ever appeared), he took credit for stimulating a competition he had felt himself unable to face. As his announcement had, he said, led to the publication of two German editions and a Swiss one and to their importation into England, he had dropped the idea. These editions were those of Simrock, of Bonn; Hoffmeister and Kühnel, of Leipzig; and Nägeli, of Zürich. They had all appeared in or about 1801.

Kollman being, as already mentioned, a friend of Burney's (one whose musicianship he much respected—see Fanny's *Memoirs* of her father, iii. 393), and his book being dedicated to Burney, the old man must surely have followed with some interest this intended bold enterprise and its final abandonment. It does not appear that he possessed himself of a copy of one of the editions of the *Well-tempered Clavier* that were now on the market: he already, however, possessed a manuscript copy of the first book of this work that had been given to him by the composer's son, Carl Philipp Emanuel Bach, and with that, we may suppose, he was satisfied. He called it a 'very curious and beautiful copy', but, as we shall see, it possessed a rather better title to the first adjective than to the second.

It may be here remarked that Burney had clearly never got into the spirit of the more sprightly of the forty-eight fugues, or he would not have tended, as he did, to look on the fugue style as essentially a grave ecclesiastical type of musical expression. In Rees's *Cyclopaedia*, under 'Eximeno', in criticizing that Spanish theorist for his condemnation of fugues, he says:

> 'Let fugues be banished from the theatres and private concerts, if he pleases, and let them remain in the church as a distinct species of composition, where they were first generated, and where they can never become vulgar or

obsolete. The style being naturally grave, requires musical learning, and will, by the solemnity of the words and place of performance, continue to be reverenced and respected. It is allowed that variety is more wanted in music than in any other art and by totally excommunicating canons and fugues from the church, the art will lose one capital source of variety, as well as ingenuity; and intelligent hearers will be deprived of a solemn style of music, to be heard no where else.'

The present author possesses a long letter of Burney to the poet-precentor Mason, written in 1782, in which he develops this same idea: 'I sometimes wish the art of the Fugue to be cultivated *only* for the use of the Church where . . . it might preclude the levity of secular melodies.' And so on!

There was in London at that time a most promising young violinist, pianist, and composer of mixed Italian, German, and British descent, called George Frederic Pinto. His promise all came to nothing, for he died in 1806 at the age of twenty. Before he died he had somehow got hold of some of Bach's music—most probably the *Well-tempered Clavier*, but perhaps also the Six Sonatas for Violin and Keyboard, for Nägeli, of Zürich, gave these latter to the world. And Pinto, an enthusiastic convert, began preaching the Gospel according to St. Bach, and preached it vigorously to Samuel Wesley. Then Karl Friedrich Horn, a Saxon musician, Music Master in Ordinary to Queen Charlotte, gave Wesley a copy of the *Well-tempered Clavier*, and he became an immediate convert and himself an ardent preacher.[1]

Now the talented brothers Charles and Samuel Wesley were friends of Burney. Fanny tells us:

'The two Wesleys, Charles and Samuel, those born rather than bred musicians, sought, and were welcomed by the Doctor, whenever his leisure agreed with his estimation of their talents. With Samuel he was often in musical correspondence.'[2]

Most likely Burney had followed the careers of these two sons of Charles Wesley, the hymn writer, since the time when, as child prodigies, they first began to be known in London musical circles. Almost certainly he would sometimes be present at those wonderful fortnightly subscription concerts at their father's house in Chesterfield Street, Marylebone, which began in 1779, when the brothers, aged respectively twenty-two and thirteen, gathered around them such a distinguished company —musicians like Lord Mornington, Dr. Worgan, and Dr. Arnold, and a miscellaneous group of well-known people, such as the great Corsican

[1] The fact of young Pinto's connexion with the matter is recorded by Wesley himself in his manuscript autobiography in the British Museum. See Jas. T. Lightwood, *Samuel Wesley* (1937), 119. Horn's gift of the *Well-tempered Clavier* to Wesley is recorded in *The Musical World*, 13 Oct. 1874; Samuel Wesley's daughter Eliza copied this information from that journal (Brit. Mus. Add. MS. 35027), so apparently she more or less endorsed the statement.

[2] *Mem.* iii. 134. For a portrait of Samuel Wesley see pl. 42, II. 218.

patriot and refugee General Paoli, General Oglethorpe, the Archbishop of Canterbury, and the Bishop of London (on one or two occasions, anyhow), the Dean of Windsor, and (several times, as entries in his diaries show), the concert-givers' uncle John, who appeared in full canonicals, but was not always quite at ease on these occasions. ('I spent an agreeable hour at a concert of my nephews. But I was a little out of my element among lords and ladies. I love plain music and plain company best.')[1]

In 1807 Samuel Wesley, now in his early forties, began to tackle Burney, now in his early eighties, about his Bach opinions. Apparently he could quickly boast of some success, for in July 1808 he is found writing to Burney in a way that shows that he knew he could count on his sympathetic interest in his Bach propaganda. Wesley had been visiting Cambridge and says that 'this Journey has advanced Sebastian Bach's cause not a little, for I made a point of playing him (even at their glee parties, upon the Piano Forte) whenever an Evening Meeting took place . . . it surprized one to witness how they drank in every note'.[2] A letter of Wesley to his friend Benjamin Jacob (organist of Surrey Chapel) is extant, dated 17 September 1808, which refers to the slighting references to Bach in Burney's *History*. Wesley had, it appeared, recently converted Jacob to Faith in Bach and this was the year in which Jacob and Wesley began their remarkable series of Bach instrumental programmes at Surrey Chapel. The opening of this long letter runs as follows:

'I am grieved to witness in my valuable Friend Doctor Burney's Critique (for he is a man whom I equally respect and love), so slight an acquaintance with the great and matchless Genius whom he professes to analyze: and I have however much satisfaction in being able to assure you, *from my own personal experience*, that his present judgment of our Demi-God is of a very different Nature from that at the Time he imprudently, incautiously, and we may add, *ignorantly* pronounced so rash and false a verdict (although a false Verdict is a contradiction in Terms), as that which I this Day read for the first Time upon "the greatest Master of Harmony in any Age or Country".

'It is now I think nearly a twelvemonth since I wrote to the Doctor respecting my profound admiration (and Adoration if you like it as well) of Sebastian: I stated to him that I had made a Study of his Preludes and Fugues, adding that his compositions had opened to me an entirely new musical World, which was to me at least as surprising as (when a child) I was thunderstruck by the opening of the Dettingen Te Deum, at the Bristol Cathedral with about an hundred Performers (a great Band in those Days). I went into something like a general Description of what I conceived to be his characteristic Beauties, and particularly specified *Air* as one of the chief and

[1] Wesley's *Journal*, 25 Jan. 1781. It is rather curious that we have no record of any meeting between John and Charles Wesley and Burney. They must have known one another—especially as they had friends in common, e.g. Johnson was a friend of John and Garrick of Charles (see Boswell; and, for Garrick, Wesley's *Journal*, 28 Dec. 1789).

[2] Letter quoted in Colbeck Radford & Co.'s catalogue (*The Ingatherer*), No. 11, Oct. 1930.

most striking. I have by me the Doctor's reply to my letter, although I cannot at the present moment advert to it, but I fully remember his observing in nearly the following Words:—"In order to be consistent with myself with regard to the great Sebastian Bach, before I presently coincide with you, I must refer to what I have written at various Times and in various Places of my History, Travels, &c., in which I had occasion to mention him; but I shall feel exceedingly gratified in hearing his elaborate and erudite Compositions performed by you (for I never yet HEARD any one of them), and can tell you that I have a very curious and beautiful Copy of *his Fugues*, which was presented to me many years since by his son Emanuel, and which I shall have much pleasure in shewing you."

'When I waited on my venerable Friend he had been kind enough to previously lay upon his Music Desk, the MS. in question (together with several other beautiful and superb Works of our immortal Master); but when I came to examine this said rare Present, how much was I surprised to find it so full of *scriptural* Faults, that it was not without some Difficulty I could manage to do justice to one of the Fugues which I had been formerly the most familiar with; and although I did not *boggle*, yet I played with extreme Discomfort. My Friend, however, was extremely delighted, and the very first Part of his Critique expressed his Wonder *how such abstruse harmony* and such perfect and enchanting melody could have been so marvellously united!

'What a convincing Proof this is, that his *former* criticism upon our matchless Author was an hasty and improvident Step!

'I conceive that the Fact stands thus: When Burney was in Germany, the universal Plaudits and Panegyricks upon the Father of *universal Harmony* were so interesting that it would have been impossible for him to have avoided giving such a Man a Place in his Account of Musical Authors in his General History. Nevertheless it appears very evidently from the erroneous Sentence he has pronounced therein upon the Comparative Merit of him and Handel, that he never could have taken due Pains to make himself Master of the Subject, otherwise his late candid acknowledgement would not have been made, and is proof sufficient that he only wanted *experience* of the *Truth* to make him ready and willing to own it.

'I must tell you another Piece of News;—namely that this imperfect and incorrect volume, this *valuable* and inestimable Gift of Sebastian's dutiful Son, happens to contain only the 24 *first* Preludes and Fugues; all written in the Soprano Clef (to make them more easily understood, I suppose), and the Preludes so miserably mangled and mutilated that had I not met them in such a collection as that of the learned and highly illuminated Doctor Burney, I verily believe that I should have exclaimed, "An Enemy hath done this". I should have at once concluded that such a manuscript could have been made only by him who was determined to disgrace instead of promote the cause of correct Harmony.

'Ever since I had the privilege of so great a triumph (for I can call it nought else) over the Doctor's Prejudice, he has evinced the most cordial veneration for our Sacred Musician, and when I told him that I was in Possession of 24 *more* such precious Relicks, he was all aghast in finding that there could be any Productions of such a Nature which he had not seen: this again is another proof of his having hastily judged, and also how remiss the Germans must have been not to have made him better acquainted with the Works of their transcendant Countryman.'[1]

Six months later (2 March 1809) another letter refers to Burney. Somebody had apparently been lending Wesley some more of the Bach music (perhaps that old copy of the Partitas published during Bach's lifetime, or, it may be, some of the Suites or the Inventions in manuscript). In this letter there is another attack upon Burney's old friend Emanuel Bach:

'By the way I have had the Loan of many *exercises* [i.e. Suites, Partitas, &c.] of his for the Harpsichord, which are every Whit as stupendous as the Preludes and Fugues, and demonstrate him (what every fresh scrap of his I meet with does) the very quintessence of all Musical Excellence.

'It's droll enough, that amongst these is inserted a beautiful Air which is published along with a sett of Emanuel Bach's Lessons [Sonatas], and which I saw at Bath: I am very much inclined to think that this Son, like many others, made but little scruple of robbing his Father; and that he was not concerned for his Honour seems plain enough by the vile and most diabolical Copy that he gave Dr. Burney as a Present, and from which the latter was wise enough to judge of and damn his Works (as he thought), but the Phoenix must always revive.'

And five months after this (September 1809) there is another letter. Wesley seems now to have got hold of a copy of the Six Sonatas for Violin and Keyboard, published by Nägeli, of Zürich, nine years earlier:

'I have just received a letter from Dr. Burney, an extracted Portion of which will not be uninteresting to you—"I believe Mr. Salomon is now out of Town; but when I saw him last, he said you were in Possession of some Sonatas of his [Bach's] *divine Manufacture*, with a very fine Violin Part to them which he wished me to hear. I have no Violin in Order; but when I return home [Burney was then staying with the Duke of Portland, at Bulstrode] and you are both at Leisure, I wish you would prevail on him to fix a Day, and to send one of his own Violins any time before 2 o'clock; while you are charming me with two Parts, I shall act in a Triple Capacity and play the parts of Pit, Box, and Gallery in rapturously applauding the Composition and Performance."

'You see one is never too old to learn, and here is an instance that it is never too late to mend!

'What more could the Dr. have said, even had he originally been the like Enthusiast with ourselves in the Cause of Truth.

'His *Repentance* (tho' he does not profess it yet in Words) seems so evident from the *zealous* Expressions he uses, that I really think we must cordially forgive the past, for we can hardly expect him, when tottering over the Grave, and having attained (whether justly or otherwise) a Reputation for Musical Criticism, publickly to revoke what he advanced at so distant a Period of Time, and when perhaps he thinks that his Strictures are forgotten, or at

[1] The originals of the Bach letters of Wesley to Jacob are now in the British Museum. They were published in 1875 (reprint 1878) by Wesley's daughter, Eliza Wesley.

least overbalanced by his present Acknowledgement of the real State of the Fact.'

Apparently the sonatas were in due course performed by Jacob as pianist and Wesley as violinist, for the following letter (undated) from Wesley to Jacob exists:

'Dear Friend,—I am in the utmost Distress, and there is no one on Earth but yourself who can help me out of it. Dr. Burney is starke staring mad to hear Sebastian's Sonatas, and I have told him all how and about your adroit management of his Music in general. He was immediately resolved on hearing you on the Clavicembalum [properly 'Harpsichord' but what Burney used now was a pianoforte] and me on the Fiddle at them. He has appointed *Monday next* at 12 o'clock for our coming to him, as this is the only time he has left before a second Excursion into the Country. You see it is an extreme Case. I had appointed three private Pupils for Monday, but shall put them all off to Tuesday. Would to Heaven that you may be able to do the like: the Triumph of Burney over his own Ignorance and Prejudice is such a glorious event that surely we ought to make *some* sacrifice to enjoy it.

'I mentioned young Kollman as quite capable of playing the Sonatas, but you will see by the enclosed (just received) that he prefers you. Pray comply in this arduous Enterprise. Remember our Cause, "Good will towards Men" is at the Bottom of it, and when Sebastian flourishes here, there will be at least more musical "Peace on Earth".

'You see we are utterly ruined unless you come forward To-morrow.—Think of what we shall have to announce to the Public; that Dr. Burney (who has heard almost all the Music of other Folks) should be listening with Delight at almost 90 years old [83½, or so, really] to an Author whom he so unknowingly and rashly had condemned.

'Only imagine what an Effect this must have in confounding and putting to Silence such pigmy puerile Puppies as Williams and Smith and a Farrago of other such musical Odds and Ends.'

(Williams was probably George Ebenezer Williams, then Deputy Organist, and later Organist, of Westminster Abbey: 'Smith' may have been John Stafford Smith, Organist of the Chapel Royal; he had helped Hawkins with his History; see I. 296.)

In this year of 1809, at Wesley's 'Musical Morning Party' at the Hanover Square Rooms, Bach's motet, *Jesu, meine Freude* (now known to British singers as 'Jesu, Priceless Treasure'), was first heard in our country.

In 1810 Wesley and Horn began to issue their edition of the *Well-tempered Clavier*; it appeared in four sections at nine shillings each, and was complete in 1813. It was apparently not the first British edition of the work, as Wesley wrote to Dr. Crotch, in 1808: 'Let me advise you, as a friend, to burn your London copy, without delay or ceremony: it is a libel upon the great author it affects to announce.'[1]

[1] James T. Lightwood, *Samuel Wesley*, 128. However, this 'London copy' *might* be a manuscript copy made in London.

Vincent Novello had now, it seems, joined the little band of Bachites, and in a letter from Burney to Wesley on 27 June 1810 we find an allusion to this. We note that the eighty-four-year-old Burney had become a good deal of an invalid (cf. II. 257), but what a zest he still had for the making of new friendships!

Chel. Coll. June 27th 1810.

My dear Friend

Since we last met I have been but 3 days *see*able; not so much from age and infirmities as from other complaints with wch. I have been persecuted. However, this delightful warm weather has hit my several cases so well as to enable me to quit my bedroom, and to breathe the more pure air of my Library, wch. being in a Northern aspect I dare not enter during winter, or wintery weather in Summer. But now ours is so much a Summer Island, I shall be very happy in the honour of receiving you and your illustrious Portuguese friend[1] in any room of my étage *in alt*; but not till the ensuing week: as I have two or three engagements hanging over me wch. prevent my offering you and M. Novelli [*sic*] any specific time till after next Sunday the 30th inst. Your comprehensive encomia on the Talents as well as intellects and mental cultivation of M. N. render me extremely impatient to enjoy both. And if, at noon, any day in the ensuing week shall be more convenient to either of you than another, I beg you will let me know your choice and I shall be ready to shake a hand with you, not only con tutta la stima, but con amore

C. B.

My daughter Sarah is not at home, or I am sure she w^d. have returned your complim^ts. wth. thanks.[2]

And about three weeks later there is a letter to Wesley and Novello jointly. They had evidently got hold of the Goldberg Variations, published by Bach himself about seventy years before. These Variations were composed for a double-manual harpsichord; Burney must, in earlier days, have possessed such an instrument, but harpsichords had now been almost entirely superseded by pianofortes (Burney tells in Rees's *Cyclopaedia*—'The harsh scratching of the quills of a harpsichord can no longer be borne'), and so Wesley and Novello had turned the variations into a duet for two pianos, and planned to give the eager old gentleman a treat. The trouble was to arrange for the use of the two instruments. To this the following two letters of Burney allude:

'Now my French packet is off my mind I have time to think of your last plan of rehearsing the quips and quiddities of the great S. B. to the best advantage, concerning which I must have seemed very cold (in spite of the heat of the weather) by the enumeration of difficulties that, at first, occurred to me for want of room sufficient for 2 large instruments of sufficient force and magnitude; and time in one day to do justice to, and enjoy the effects of such learned and ingenious arcana. But, allowing the old adage, which you have already quoted, that second thoughts are best—instead of sending you and Signor Novello to a P. F. maker's to find 2 instruments of equal magnitude—

[1] Novello was Organist of the Portuguese Chapel in South Street, Grosvenor Square.

[2] Brit. Mus. Add. MS. 11730, fol. 33.

wisely tuned together—upon examining my little parlour or keeping room (in health and warm weather) I find that, when unbelittered, there would be sufficient space for 2 such first rate Giants to be alongside of each other, and that when I thought of sending you and your friend to a P. F. shop for trial of your 30 very comical pieces (as the most learned, ingenious and original productions of Haydn, Mozart and Beethoven[1] are often said to be, by ignorant and vulgar hearers) I never once thought of my sweet and precious self, to whom your performance would be as inaudible as the music of the spheres —for I never intend going into the open air again.

'But now, though I have caught a fresh cold, and have 2 decayed teeth in my upper jaw, that give me a very acute twinge whenever I inhale fresh air, I beg, during the warm weather, your performance may be within my obtuse *earshot*, that I may acquaint the *Larvae* I shall meet with (post obit.) how the wonderful wonders produced by the pen of the great S. B. have been played, as a game at *all fours* by the zealous and indefatigable Messrs. Wesley and Novello.

'Therefore send your instrument, name your day, or days, and your hours, before the end of the present month, and I hope nothing sinister will occasion a new procrastination of our promised pleasure.

C. B.

'Suppose we decimate the 30 variations, and divide them into 3 decads, performing 10 once, or twice, if we like or dislike them much, each day? which will allow us time to breathe, digest and judge.'[2]

The eagerness and humour of this old man, who never expects to leave the house again, are surely refreshing! And note how he, who had grown up in the Handelian period and had known and admired Handel, had continued to develop, and in old age was defending Beethoven 'nearly all' of whose works he possessed (at the date when he made his Will—given in a later chapter).

Chel. Coll. July 19 $\frac{1}{2}$ past 2
Thursday [1810]

With best Comp. a. Virtuosisi$^{mo.}$ Sigr. Vincenzo Novello.

I shall now begin my final note, in the dual number, with

My dear Friend*s*.

If you c$^{d.}$ send your Lumber-dy Instrum$^{t.}$ sooner than 10 to-morrow morn$^{g.}$ I sh$^{d.}$ be right glad; that it may be tuned in unison with mine: for if its pitch sh$^{d.}$ be altered the 2 Giants will not remain in perfect friend$^{p.}$ an hour. While the weather continues warm, I had rather wait on ye at 11, than 12 or 1—I am now entirely for the performance of the 30 Wariations *de suite*: as you two virtuous gemmen, doubtless, are so *parfet* in all these pretty *chunes*, that you'll go on as swimming from beginning to end, as if wind and tide were both strongly in your favour. I think the forte, i.e. fortés, may begin

[1] In 1803 Burney wrote in his diary, as Fanny tells us (*Mem.* iii. 334): 'Beethoven's compositions for the piano-forte were first brought to England by Miss Tate, a most accomplished *dilletante* singer and player. I soon afterwards heard some of his instrumental works, which are such as incline me to rank him amongst the first musical authors of the present century.'

(It may be of interest to add here that Beethoven possessed a copy of Burney's *History*, as the inventory taken at his death shows.)

[2] Lightwood, op. cit. 131.

HORACE WALPOLE
By Dance
Burney visited Walpole at Strawberry Hill (*see* i. 371 n.).

SAMUEL WESLEY
By John Jackson
He converted Burney to Bach enthusiasm (*see* ii. 210–23).

My dear & Revd Grandson

I congratulate you & my worthy Gran-
daughter on the happy event of wch you have kindly
informed me. I must confess that I had my fears:
having often heard nursury Gossips say that the
agonising throes of a first birth are more painful
and liable to accident than all others. There is no
part of your narrative wch I cd possibly wish otherwise
than my not being honrd wth a Male Great Grand Child.
A mother has always more domestic comfort from a daughter
than a Son: boys, when at school: come home mere ruffians. &,
if at College, they are so totally weaned from childish amusemts
that nothing but public places and Town bustle can afford them
any delight. So we may suppose that "whatever is, is right." And
his we beg all relations around you to accept of the best compliments &
and regards, of your affectionate Grandsire

C. B.

Chel. Coll. May 2d
1812.

'BOYS AT SCHOOL COME HOME MERE RUFFIANS',
says Burney, in congratulating his grandson, Rev. Charles Parr Burney, on the birth of a daughter.

to storm the works of Engineer Bach, before 12. And if we have any time to spare, after being played over, we can *talk* them over—or (what w$^{d.}$ be shtill petter auch coot) if little i were to say *bis* there might, may-hap, be time for a Da Capo. So *fin Dimani*, at least, God bless ye!

C. B.[1]

To Sam$^{l.}$ Wesley Esq$^{r.}$
11, Adam's Row,
Hamstead Road.'

And now Pinto having converted Samuel Wesley, and Samuel Wesley having converted Burney, the last-named wishes to add another link to the chain—he proposes an attempt at the conversion of the great Roman Catholic lawyer (co-editor of *Coke upon Littleton*), philologist, historical, biographical, and ecclesiastical author, Charles Butler—whose musical proclivities are, by the way, unmentioned in the long notice of him in the *Dictionary of National Biography*. The following letter of Butler to his co-religionist, Vincent Novello, is to be found in the British Museum.[2]

Dear Sir

I have a note from Doctor Burney expressing a wish that You and I would, as he calls it,—'mount his lofty apartment next Sunday about 12 at Noon, and let him hear from You a thorough Bach of the Great Sebastian's Golden Grain.'

I hope the party will be agreeable to You—May I request the favour of a line from you by the return of the Post.—I am so serious about the Gregorian Note that I have sent to Paris for a Work respecting it.

Most sincerely your's
Ch: Butler
Lin: Inn 7 Oct. 1812

During the following year (1813) the Bach meetings that had begun four years earlier are still proceeding, for we find Burney administering a sharp reproof to Wesley for not keeping his engagements:

'Though the weather grows daily more cold to my bodily feelings my mind is not sufficiently cool to forget the vexation [of] your breach of an engagement made upon your own day and hour, without seeming to think it of importance enough to require an excuse. I am sorry to recollect that you have formerly more than once, for frivolous reasons, let me expect you in vain—having, on the way hither met w$^{th.}$ some person or thing that caught your attention and made you relinquish or drive from remembrance your engagement. I cannot, at least immediately, bring myself, cordially to name any future time for such a meeting as you seem to wish. I have been long so much detached from the active world and weaned from musical delights

[1] These two letters of Burney are in the British Museum—Add. MS. 11730, fols. 33 and 35. The latter has been dated by E. van der Straeten (in *Musical Times*, June 1926) as 1806, but Mr. P. E. T. Edwards of the British Museum points out to me that the watermark on the paper is 1809 (not as the authority mentioned read it) and that in 1810, but not in 1806, 19 July fell on a Thursday.

[2] Add. MS. 11729, fol. 36.

that I now no more wish to renew them than a child who has been several years deprived of the breast—unless coax'd by the civilities of such a performer as yourself.'[1]

Burney, aged eighty-seven, was now within eight months of his death. Whether any more Bach meetings took place we do not know. But the good work was accomplished, and the learned historian of music who had thirty years before told the world that 'Sebastian Bach disdained facility so much that his genius never stooped to the easy and graceful', that his music suffered from 'unmeaning art and contrivance', died, we may almost say, with the praises of Bach on his lips.

And when, over twenty-two years later, Wesley himself approached his own end, we find him exulting in the memory of his missionary success:

'The late learned and ingenious Writer on musical Subjects, Dr. Charles Burney, with whom I had the Honour to be intimate, had but a slight knowledge of the inimitable Merits of Sebastian Bach, until I had the Pleasure of making him become better acquainted with his Music.

'He shewed me a very incorrect Copy of the first twenty four Preludes and Fugues, which he informed me were presented to him by his son Emanuel, and seemed quite surprized when I assured him that there was a second Sett of twenty four more upon the same Plan and of quite equal Excellence. I brought to him my own Copy of the whole forty eight, and played over the greater Number of them, with which he was inexpressibly delighted. He had formerly mentioned this great Man not in Terms of that high Praise which he afterwards did. When he had heard me perform the Pieces to which he had been a Stranger, from a correct Copy, and given with Exactness and Precision he made ample Amends for the Defects in his former Criticism.'[2]

In closing this chapter the author wishes to pose a little technical problem to which he himself can offer no satisfactory solution. Many previous authors of books and articles have discussed Samuel Wesley's enthusiastic study of Bach and his efforts to induce other musicians to study him but nobody ever raises questions like this: HOW COULD WESLEY PLAY THE FORTY-EIGHT PRELUDES AND FUGUES OF THE 'WELL-TEMPERED CLAVIER' ON THE ORGANS AND PIANOS OF THE DAY, SINCE THESE WERE NOT 'WELL-TEMPERED'?

Before expanding this question by a little explanation of its nature a word may be said on the allusion above to the playing of the *Well-tempered Clavier* on the organ. When Wesley, in organ programmes, included a Bach fugue it was usually one of the *Well-tempered* '48'. The real organ fugues, as already stated, were quite unplayable on almost all English organs, from lack of a pedal-board. On one occasion we hear of the very considerable feat of playing on the organ the whole of the '48' at one sitting, for Wesley writes to his friend the great violinist,

[1] Brit. Mus. Add. MS. 35027, fol. 12b.

[2] Samuel Wesley's autograph Reminiscences. Brit. Mus. Add. MS. 27593, fols. 141, 151.

Bridgetower, inviting him to meet him and 'a few friends' next day at Davis's organ works, off Tottenham Court Road, when he will play on 'an excellent instrument for a church at Surinam in the West Indies', the '*whole of the Preludes and Fugues*'.[1]

Now, as we understand, the English organs and pianos of those days were tuned on 'mean-tone temperament', equal temperament not coming in, so far as pianos are concerned, until near the middle of the nineteenth century (Broadwood's first began to use it in 1846), and, so far as organs are concerned, rather later.[2]

It is not possible to tune any keyed instrument *perfectly* for more than one key; if you tune it correctly for key C, the moment you play in another key some of the notes will be out of tune. On the mean-tone system not a single key was perfect, but, by a compromise, a certain number of keys were made near enough perfect for the ear to tolerate them, the rest being left outside the pale. There were '*six* practicable major scales (C, G, D, A, F, and B flat), in place of the one perfect scale; and *three* practicable minor scales instead of one (A, D and G)'.[3]

Naturally, then, composers could not use, as they do to-day, just *any* key for their compositions (nor could they modulate quite freely in any composition). Burney's own *Preludes, Fugues and Interludes for the Organ, alphabetically arranged in all the keys that are most perfectly in tune upon that Instrument* include pieces in the following keys:

MAJOR, C, D, A, B flat

MINOR, A, C.

One of these keys (C minor) does not come into the above list of the practicable. Presumably Burney could tolerate it: there is nothing absolute about the list; it is all a matter of what the ear can bear, and individual ears differ; many keys, however, would be so much out of tune as to distress almost any hearer. As keys that 'had not, in fact, any

[1] Lightwood, *Samuel Wesley*, 137. Bridgetower was, on his father's side, an African negro. It was for him that Beethoven composed the 'Kreutzer Sonata' and with him he played it.

[2] The organ of St. George's Hall, Liverpool, built in 1855, to the specification of Samuel Wesley's son, Dr. Samuel Sebastian Wesley, was, by his directions, not 'well-tempered'. The organs of Norwich Cathedral and St. George's Chapel, Windsor, were not 'well-tempered' until 1877 and 1880, respectively (see Grove's *Dictionary of Music* and *The Oxford Companion to Music*, s.v. 'Temperament' for facts such as these; the latter makes an attempt at a popular general discussion of the difficult subject of temperament). According to Orlando A. Mansfield, in *The Musical Quarterly* of April 1935, there was one London organ tuned in equal temperament in Wesley's day—that very organ at Surrey Chapel on which he and his friend Jacob gave their performances. I do not know the source of this statement, which surprises me, and the accuracy of which I doubt. Burney, in Rees's *Cyclopaedia* (article, 'Organ', written some time shortly before 1805), says, 'On the organ an equal temperament has certainly never been used'. George Hogarth in an article in *The Musical World* in 1836 says that at that date the organ in England was 'tuned according to a system of temperament differing from that which prevails on the Continent, and the effect of which is that the harmony is intolerably impure in all keys which require more than three sharps or three flats'. It may then surely be taken that Burney and Samuel Wesley never heard an equally-tempered organ.

[3] Edward J. Hopkins and Edward F. Rimbault, *The Organ* (3rd edn., 1877), 162.

practicable existence on keyed instruments as then tuned', Hopkins and Rimbault mention—MAJOR, E, B, F sharp, C sharp, E flat, A flat; MINOR, E, B, F sharp, F. Of some of these the same authorities say that they 'could not fail to produce an effect very offensive to sensitive ears and a little investigation would reveal that the main cause of the untunefulness arose from the fact that each of the five short keys [i.e. 'black notes', as we call them] was tuned *either* as the *sharp* to the long key to the *left*, or as the *flat* to the long key to the *right*, but in no case so as to serve in the two capacities'.

That brings us again to Bach and his 'well-tempered' (meaning equal-tempered) system. Bach tuned his clavier not (*a*) perfect in one key and hence imperfect in all the others ('Just Intonation'), and (*b*) not nearly perfect in a few keys and grossly imperfect in the rest ('Mean-tone' System); but (*c*) imperfect in all keys, the out-of-tuneness being shared out with an attempt at mathematical exactitude amongst the twelve notes of the octave, making it so small everywhere that the accustomed ear could tolerate it ('Equal Temperament'). Bach then could (and did) write music in all keys, major and minor, and the two books of this *Well-tempered Clavier*, each book containing a prelude and fugue in each of the twelve major and twelve minor keys, was a demonstration of the advantage of this fair-compromise method.

To correct a popular misconception it may be interpolated that the system was not of Bach's introduction, but it was largely his practical object lesson of its advantages that reconciled purists to its adoption and so paved the way to a freedom of modulation that the evolution of musical form was shortly to reveal as indispensable to further advance.

We now come back to that intriguing question—How could Pinto, Wesley, Jacobs, Horn, and Burney, and the rest of the growing tribe of Bachites, tolerate such a work as the *Well-tempered Clavier* when played on the Unwell-tempered Claviers of their country at that period? Very few living persons have ever heard a 'mean-tone' tuned organ, but, by all that the acousticians tell us, music in the extreme keys played upon such an organ must have been excruciating. And, as Burney's piano was presumably 'mean-tone' tuned, did he not suffer when Wesley played him the famous '48'? And if not, why not?

The present writer has had the curiosity to go through the whole series of such of Burney's compositions as he himself possesses and can, therefore, easily examine. They amount to just on one hundred separate pieces or movements, and their range of keys exceeds that given by the authorities quoted (particularly as to minor keys). It comprises the following:

MAJOR, C, G, D, A, E, F, B flat, E flat.
MINOR, C, G, D, A, E, B, F, B flat.

(The more extreme keys are rarer than the less extreme.)

It would seem that this whole question of keys in use before the introduction of Equal Temperament needs study. Handel (to take one instance) sometimes used certain keys that we should not expect to find him using. Nevertheless it remains true that there were keys that no composer would have thought of using before the days of Equal Temperament. Burney, it will be noted, leaves eight unused—four major and four minor—and certainly it would seem that these eight, on a mean-toned instrument, would produce a very bad effect. Yet they must have been used in playing through the '48'—unless Wesley transposed certain of Bach's preludes and fugues, and we hear nothing of that.

It looks as though, in asking the simple question, 'How did Wesley play Bach's "48" on Burney's piano?' one is challenging the acousticians and scientific musical historians to a little fresh consideration of a subject on which they have so far pronounced rather too dogmatically, and without sufficiently checking their statements by an examination of the actual musical repertory of the eighteenth century.

And there, modestly admitting that 'a fool can ask questions that a wise man cannot answer', the present author quietly leaves the matter.

LXI. FANNY'S TEN YEARS' ABSENCE IN FRANCE AND HER RETURN

(*1802–1812: Fanny aged 50–60, her Father 76–86*)

FANNY and her emigrant General, it will be remembered, married on the last day of July 1793. Just two months later, Fanny, who for that period had been 'the happiest of all human beings', suddenly suffered 'such a blow of sorrow' as 'reversed the whole scene', for her husband felt it to be his duty to offer his services to the British Government in the defence of Toulon. Burney sympathized with his daughter on the prospect of the departure of her husband on so dangerous an errand, though, as he remarked, 'To military men who, like M. d'Arblay, have been but just united to the object of their choice and begun to domesticate, it is no uncommon thing for their tranquillity to be disturbed by "the trumpet's loud clangour" '.

Fanny was to present the offer in person to the King at Windsor, whilst d'Arblay himself hurried to present it to Pitt. Just what happened is not known, except that the offer was not at once accepted—and of course Toulon did not long hold out, so that the offer soon lapsed.[1] D'Arblay therefore continued his quiet domestic and horticultural pursuits.

In 1798 an old friend from France, Lajard (Minister of War in the last period of the reign of the unhappy Louis XVI), spent a week with the d'Arblays in their little 'Camilla Cottage', and in November 1800, being back in Paris, he wrote sending a message from a cousin of d'Arblay's to the effect that 'some of his small property is yet unsold, to about the amount of £1000, and can still be secured from sequestration if he will immediately go over and claim it, or, if that is impossible, if he will send his *procuration* to his uncle from some country *not at war with France*'.

It was therefore decided that d'Arblay should run over to Holland and send his procuration from there. He did this, and in about a month, to Fanny's joy, was back again. Then came the preliminary articles for the Peace of Amiens (October 1801), and France and Britain being now friends again he was able to go over to see his long-lost relatives and his old friends, and to do his business in person.[2] He seems to have had some hope of obtaining the half-pay to which, as a retired officer under the old régime, he was entitled—a benefit much to be desired, since, as he wrote to his wife, 'Il est impossible de nous dissimuler que depuis plusieurs années nous n'avons vécu, malgré toute notre économie, que par le moyen de ressources qui sont ou épuisées ou bien prêtes à l'être'.

[1] *Diary and Letters*, v. 221–31.

[2] Ibid. v. 466 et seq. The account of the adventures of the voyage there given is well worth reading.

Then, too, he had some faint hope of an appointment as one of the new Trade Commissioners representing the French Government in England.

This latter project came to nothing. As for the half-pay—Napoleon himself looked into his claim. He

'inquired minutely into the merits of the case, and into the military character of the claimant; and, having patiently heard the first account, and eagerly interrogated upon the second, he paused a few minutes, and then said: "Let him serve in the army, if only for one year. Let him go to St. Domingo, and join Le Cler; and, at the end of the year, he shall be allowed to retire, with rank and promotion".'

The prospect of military service in a distant part of the world was one that had never entered into d'Arblay's calculation, 'yet, to a military spirit, jealous of his honour and passionately fond of his profession, it was a proposition impossible to be declined'. He argued that to undertake this duty was not 'to combat for Buonaparte, nor to fight against his original allegiance; it was to bear arms in the current cause of his country in resisting the insurgents of St. Domingo, against whom he might equally have been employed by the Monarch in whose service he had risked, and through whose misfortunes he had lost his all'.

He therefore accepted the offer and came back to England to settle his private affairs and take leave of his wife and little son. He 'sunk a considerable sum to be expeditiously accoutered', and then hurried back to Paris. The day before leaving London, however, he wrote a personal letter to Napoleon (a bold and manly letter, but one of which the consequences would have been foreseen by a less simple-minded warrior than he); in this, as a precaution, he clearly repeated the stipulation he had made that in thus rejoining the French army he was not to be considered as bound in any way or at any time to fight against the country of his wife.[1] This letter he handed to the French Minister in London for urgent dispatch and then set off on his journey.

Napoleon, without 'demonstrating any suspicious resentment', quietly annulled the reappointment of d'Arblay to his position in the army. To Lafayette, who as a friend of d'Arblay sought an audience on the subject, he exclaimed, 'Il m'a écrit un diable de lettre!'—remarking, however, that he must remember that it came from the husband of the authoress of *Cecilia*, 'and then abruptly broke up the conference'.[2]

And now d'Arblay was trapped. He had obtained his passport in London only on the harsh condition that he stayed away for a whole

[1] Fanny gives the letter (*Mem.* iii. 313). It was written without her knowledge (doubtless as the result of a sudden impulse) after he had left her at Bookham.

[2] Lafayette's own account of his interview with Napoleon on behalf of d'Arblay will be found in *Diary and Letters*, v. 488.

twelvemonth, and so could not return.[1] So he wrote to Fanny asking her to bring little Alex and join him in Paris.

Burney, who had so lately lost both his wife and his daughter Susan, was quite broken down by the prospect of this further separation; he had a premonition that it would be more extended than was contemplated.

And so it was! The Peace of Amiens was, of course, shortlived; the very next year Britain and France were again at war and d'Arblay and his wife and child were in Paris with no prospect of returning.[2]

On arrival in Paris Fanny had been very pleased at the civilities shown her by d'Arblay's old friends and his relatives—'the kind, I might say *distinguished* reception I have been favoured with'.[3] The city was *en fête* and she was taken to the opera, to assemblies, to military parades, and to the ante-room of a *levée* of the First Consul, where she had the gratification of seeing the great man at close quarters, as afterwards of watching him review his troops.

She spent a fortnight at Joigny, about ninety miles south-east of Paris, where, she records:

> 'M. d'Arblay is related, though very distantly, to a quarter of the town, and the other three-quarters are his friends or acquaintance; and all of them came, first, to see me; next, were all to be waited upon in return; next, came to thank me for my visit; next, to know how the air of Joigny agreed with me; next, to make a little further acquaintance; and, finally, to make a visit of congé. And yet all were so civil, so pleasant, and so pleased with my Monsieur's return that, could I have lived three lives, so as to have had some respite, I could not have found fault; for it was scarcely ever with the individual intruder, but with the continuance or repetition of interruption.'

Here she had a good deal of acquaintance with Louis Bonaparte—then Colonel of a regiment there quartered, afterwards King of Holland, who 'was very kind to my little Alex, whom he never saw without embracing, and he treated M. d'Arblay with a marked distinction very gratifying to me'.

D'Arblay's many friends continued active in his behalf, and the First Consul at last, apparently, signed a document giving him a retiring allowance. It was only small (1,500 francs a year—about £60), but it was something. As for the family property it was unfortunately found to be impossible to recover any of that without incurring expenses that would outweigh all advantage.[4]

[1] This is clear from a letter he wrote to his wife (*Diary and Letters*, v. 486). But in the *Memoirs* of her father her octogenarian muddlement led her to give another reason (iii. 318).

[2] All these matters are recorded in ibid. 310 et seq. and *Diary and Letters*, v. 482 et seq. Fanny's long letter to her father recounting the incidents of travel is one of her best bits of descriptive writing, and shows that when she was not deliberately attempting 'literature' (as she did in her later novels and occasionally in her later diary and her letters) her hand had not lost its cunning.

[3] Ibid. vi. 3.

[4] Ibid. 40–1.

A small apartment at Passy was taken 'but not a quarter furnished', and there the three of them settled down, d'Arblay obtaining a small position in a government department which enabled the family to live —in a very simple manner, but still to live.

For a time some letters got through to Dr. Burney and some came through from him, the latter of the old vivid 'newsy' sort, relating how he and Dr. Charles Burney junior (Glasgow and Aberdeen had now both of them conferred on the younger Charles the LL.D. degree) had dined at Lord Melbourne's with the Prince of Wales, who had 'quoted Homer in Greek to my son, as readily as if the beauties of Dryden or Pope had been under consideration', and had talked to Burney himself on music with equal facility—that kind of thing, with, of course, all sorts of welcome details of family happenings.

But some letters were lost, and there were long periods when none could be conveyed, and one period when Burney was 'in prudence imploring all your living old correspondents and my friends not to venture a letter to you, even by a private hand, lest it should accidentally miscarry, and, being observed, should injure M. d'Arblay in the eyes of zealous Frenchmen'.

Thus from the autumn of 1808 to the spring of 1810[1] there seem to have been no letters in either direction. Then Lafayette quietly contrived to use a returning prisoner-of-war as a means of Fanny's sending a letter to her father, and at last the 'terrible arrears of knowledge' of family affairs were paid off in a long answering letter which Burney by some means managed to get carried to her.

Whenever, by rare luck, any letter from Chelsea reached Passy its receipt made a gala evening for the d'Arblay trio. Thus did, on one occasion, Fanny write to her father about one lately come to hand:

'Seated round our wood fire by one, by two, by three, we gave to it a whole evening, stopping upon every phrase, commenting upon every paragraph, and I, the reader, indulging them and myself by expounding and dilating upon every allusion, quotation, and family story or saying. It was therefore a long and delicious banquet; and we have agreed to lock it up, and take it out again once in every three months for another family reading, till another arrives.'[2]

It was in 1810 that Fanny wrote to her father telling him that he had had the honour of being elected a corresponding member of the Institute of France—'Classe des Beaux Arts'.[3] For though France and Britain were indeed at war yet there were men of eminence (including Suard, Perpetual Secretary of the 'Classe de la Langue et de la Littérature Française' of the Institute, to whom Burney years before had presented himself with an introduction from Garrick) who did not forget him, nor

[1] See ibid. 48, and *Mem.* iii. 384, which contradict one another slightly as to date.

[2] *Diary and Letters*, vi. 55.

[3] In *Mem.* iii. 391, she says that the election itself had taken place as far back as 1806.

mean the old man to be neglected. The diploma was delivered to Fanny, together with a medal, 'a mark of distinction reserved for peculiar honour to peculiar select personages', but all these she had to put by until the means could be found to convey them safely to her father.

Meantime the education of young Alex d'Arblay was being carried on, apparently by means of a private tutor. Fanny, later in 1810, reports of him:

'Alex is thin and pale, but strong and without complaint. He is terribly singular, and more what they here call *sauvage* than any creature I ever beheld. He is untameably wild, and averse to all the forms of society. Where he can have got such a rebel humour we conceive not; but it costs him more to make a bow than to resolve six difficult problems of algebra, or to repeat twelve pages from Euripides; and as to making a civil speech, he would sooner renounce the world.'[1]

D'Arblay was often overworked and grew thin, and he had for a time the anxiety of seeing his wife dangerously ill, with the menace of a cancer—from which menace she was relieved by an operation performed by Napoleon's famous surgeon, Baron de Larrey.

'Whenever Bonaparte left Paris there was always an immediate abatement of severity in the police', and so, when in 1812 he was in Russia, one of Fanny's influential friends took advantage of the opportunity to get her and her son a pass to go to some part of America—a pass that could be illicitly used for landing in England, the police, who well knew the real intention, winking at the intended evasion.

D'Arblay made inquiries and found that an American boat was about to sail from Dunkirk, and that it would take a certain number of passengers with American passports and permits, who would be privately dropped at some English port at which it would touch before it proceeded across the Atlantic. He arranged that his wife and son should travel by this boat.

But, arrived at Dunkirk, through the mismanagement and misconduct of the captain of the vessel the whole party was held up for 'the most painfully wearisome six weeks'. Fanny came into real peril with the police through having been seen to give money to some Spanish prisoners and the present reader should be encouraged to read her own very spirited account of the incident, which would occupy too much space here.[2]

The passage from Dunkirk to Deal, owing to a calm, took two days and a night, and when the ship anchored off this latter port, Fanny, who lay helplessly sick in the cabin, was startled in the morning by Alex running down to her and crying 'in a tone of rapture', '*Maman, we are taken by the British! We are all captured by British officers!*' It turned out

[1] *Diary and Letters*, vi. 54.
[2] Ibid. 69 et seq.

that the American captain had innocently put into a port of a hostile country, since war had been declared by the American Congress in June and news of it had just reached Britain. Fanny and her son, as British subjects, were, of course, allowed to go free, and after being entertained by Lady Foley, wife of the governor of the port, and staying there three or four days so as to give the old gentleman at Chelsea warning of their approach (for there had been no means of letting him know that they were on their way or even that they intended to come, and they did not dare unannounced to burst in on him in his weak state of health), they set out for London.

What they did not know was that a false report that they were coming had prepared their family. A 'French-headed, fluttering bustler', in London (the words are Sarah Harriet's in an indignant letter to her brother Charles)[1] had sent them a message leading them to suppose that she had some special intelligence, whereas, as inquiry revealed:

> 'Her reason for believing that Mde. d'Arblay was *en route* to Chelsea was simply this: a vessel from Dunkirk was said by the newspapers to have arrived at an English port, and she thought that my sister *might* have come over in it! . . . My father's disappointment is now proportioned to his preceding delight. *Whip the Woman!*'

However, the false news was, happily, soon followed by the true, and the delight returned.

Poor Burney! For ten years he had not seen his daughter, and now that he heard she was coming he had told all the rest of his family to keep away until the first meeting was over and:

> 'He had the precaution, kindly, almost comically, to give orders to his immediate attendants, Rebecca and George, to move all the chairs and tables close to the wall; and to see that nothing whatsoever should remain between the door and his sofa, which stood at the farther end of a large room, that could interfere with her rapid approach.'[2]

How did Fanny find her father? When she left him he was seventy-six, when she returned he was eighty-six—and those ten years had, of course, left their mark on him:

> 'She had left him, cheerful and cheering; communicating knowledge, imparting ideas; the delight of every house that he entered.
>
> 'She had left him, with his elegantly formed person still unbroken by his years; his face still susceptible of manifesting the varying associations of his vivid character; his motions alert; his voice clear and pleasing; his spirits, when called forth by social enjoyment, gay, animating, and inspiring animation.
>
> 'She found him—alas! how altered! in looks, strength, complexion, voice, and spirits.

[1] In the present writer's possession.
[2] *Mem.* iii. 401.

'But that which was most affecting was the change in his carriage and person: his revered head was not merely by age and weakness bowed down; it was completely bent, and hung helplessly upon his breast; his voice, though still distinct, sunk almost to a whisper: his feeble frame reclined upon a sofa; his air and look forlorn; and his whole appearance manifesting a species of self-desertion.'[1]

[1] *Mem.* iii. 402.

LXII. BURNEY'S FAMILY IN 1814

(*Burney aged 88*)

ESTHER, Burney's eldest child, was in 1814 a woman of about 65; she had now been married forty-four years, and had, apparently, had ten children.[1] Of these seven appear to have been alive in 1814—two having died in infancy and the adventurous Charles Crisp (see Ch. LI) in later boyhood.

Esther and her husband lived long in Great Titchfield Street and there they sometimes gave parties of the old St. Martin's Street type. Their own duet playing was famous, and the great vocal performers of the day, such as Pacchierotti, came and sang to their guests as they did to Dr. Burney's.

When Fanny was in the Queen's service she used to take advantage of the Royal Drawing Room visits to London to receive Esther in her own apartment at St. James's Palace, or to borrow her father's carriage and pay a visit to Great Titchfield Street. (The Burneys were what is called 'a very united family' and from childhood to old age any of them who could get together did so.)

We hear of some severe illnesses on the part of both Esther and her husband and also of some of the children, and as we have seen there were family trials such as the tragic death of Esther's father-in-law and the disappearance of her eldest son.

In 1814 a number of Esther's children were in or approaching their forties. Anne, or Anna Maria (or 'Marianne'), had in 1803 married a French refugee named Bourdois, a friend of her uncle d'Arblay, and had gone with him to France. But she had three years later been left a widow. She stayed in France for a little time, settling up her affairs and getting some comfort from the society of her Aunt Fanny. She then managed to get home, joining with another lady in taking a coach and evading Napoleon's prohibition of travel to England by driving first into Germany and thence through Holland. She then settled at Batheaston near Bath, 'and took her sister Sophia to reside with her'.[2] Here from 1811 to 1814 she and her sister associated a good deal with Prince Lucien Bonaparte and his family, who were then prisoners-of-war (see II. 42 n.). Apparently she did not marry again; at all events in 1821 she is still spoken of as 'Mrs. Bourdois'.

[1] The names of six are to be found in *Early Diary* and there are four more mentioned in Blakeway. The ten names are (1) Anne Maria ('Marianne'), (2) Charles Crisp, (3) Frances, (4) Sophia Elizabeth, (5) Richard Allen, (6) Cecilia, (7) Harriet (died young), (8) Henry (died young), (9) Charlotte Esther, (10) Amelia Maria. The present writer (without embarking on more investigation than he is prepared to undertake) cannot quite guarantee all the names in this list or the order in which they should be placed.

[2] *Family Memoranda* (some dates there given being, however, palpably wrong).

In 1814 Burney's eldest son, JAMES (see pl. 20, I. 288), was sixty-four years old.

After the action off Cuddalore, in 1783 (see II. 26) he returned home in bad health and despite all his efforts (see II. 106) never held another command. It seems amazing that the Admiralty should waste the nearly quarter of a century of varied experience of an officer still young (when he returned only thirty-three; he had, as we remember, gone to sea at the age of ten). But so it was; after 1783, so far as we know, James Burney never set foot on deck again.

In 1785 he had married Sally Payne (see II. 25), with whom he seems to have been very happy. He bought a small property at Mickleham, near his sister Susan,[1] but in 1791 he inherited a good house in the best part of London, and probably, also, a considerable sum of money (see I. 71).

A true Burney, James could not be idle. When he visited Susan at Mickleham in 1787 she wrote of a walk she took with him:

> 'James talked to me all the way of his studies. He is studying very hard, and all kinds of things at once—Law—Physic—Politics—and History—besides French and Latin. He has set himself a task for a year I think, to read a certain number of pages a day, I believe he said a hundred on an average. It keeps him in full employment which is always a good thing—but I think he is attempting too much at a time.'[2]

It is worth recording that in addition to all these varied studies Captain James was something of a musician. We hear of his brother-in-law Molesworth Phillips and him practising the fiddle together.[3]

In 1790 James edited for his friend Bligh, just returned from his thrilling adventure, his *Narrative of the Mutiny on Board H.M.S. Bounty*, and in 1792 his *A Voyage to the South Sea in H.M.S. Bounty.*

In 1797 he published his two pamphlets, *A Plan of Defence against Invasion* (second edition a few months later) and *Measures Recommended for the Support of Public Credit.* In 1803 there came out the first volume of his *magnum opus*, *A Chronological History of Discoveries in the South Sea or Pacific Ocean*, and during the following fourteen years there were issued at intervals its four further great quarto volumes. It remains to-day the standard work on its subject. In 1803 we find Southey, entrusted with a review of one of the volumes, grumbling that it was not very easy to write to the length required to earn his three-guineas fee, for 'it is always more difficult to dilate praise than censure'.[4] (A quite incompetent journalist! He ought to have been able to 'dilate' anything.)

The passion for writing seems to have been ingrained in the family constitution. Here is a Burney whose general education (as distinct

[1] Manwaring, *My Friend the Admiral*, 188.

[2] Letter in the possession of Countess Ferrers, quoted in Manwaring, op. cit., 186, from which book many of the particulars of James Burney are here taken.

[3] Letter in Armagh Library.

[4] Quoted in *Early Diary*, ii. 14n.

from his purely technical education) ceased at the age of ten, and yet he is competent to write for publication and pours out his compositions! And, be it said, the work is well done. James Burney was no mere hack writer.

Some time about the opening of the century James struck up a warm friendship with John Rickman, the statistician, census expert, and Secretary to the Speaker of the House of Commons, then a young man of about thirty. Rickman was a friend of Southey and of Lamb, and at his house, in 1803, Lamb and James met. Lamb's account of the meeting is a pleasant one:

> 'I supped last night with Rickman, and met a merry *natural* captain, who pleases himself vastly with once having made a pun at Otaheite in the O. language.
>
> 'At first the natives could not make out what he meant, but all at once they discovered the pun and danced round him in transports of joy.'[1]

Southey speaks on one occasion of escaping from the learned and serious Dr. Charles Burney, junior, whom he met at a dinner party, to his brother James, the bluff sailorman. Charles, he says:

> 'after a long silence, broke out into a discourse upon the properties of the conjunction *Quam*. Except his *quamical* knowledge, which is as profound as you will imagine, he knows nothing but bibliography, or the science of title-pages, impresses, and dates. It was a relief to leave him, and find his brother, the Captain, at Rickman's smoking after supper, and letting out puffs at one corner of his mouth and puns at the other.'[2]

In 1803 Charles and Mary Lamb and the James Burneys made holiday together in the Isle of Wight and Burney and Lamb wrote a joint letter to Rickman. The following, which comes from Lamb's part of the letter, gives us some news of James as a parent, the children referred to being Martin (then about fifteen) and Sally (then about ten):

> 'Capt. Burney does nothing but teach his children bad habits. He surfeits them with cherries and black currants till they can eat no supper, and then claps down the fruit expended to the common stock, and deducts what the surfeit saves from his part. There's a little girl he's brought with him that has cost I don't know what in codlings. No ordinary orchard would be a jointure for her. To add to our difficulties Martin has brought down a Terence, which he renders out loud into canine Latin at Breakfast and other meals till the eyes of the infatuated parent let slip water for joy and the ears of everybody beside shed their wax for being tired. More I could add but it is unsafe.'[3]

[1] Here the present writer has (he thinks logically) brought into one a passage from a letter from Lamb to Manning and another from Mrs. Shelley to Leigh Hunt, in which she quotes Lamb. See Manwaring, *My Friend the Admiral*, 216.

[2] Southey, *Life and Correspondence* (1850), ii. 292.

[3] Ainger's edition of the *Letters of Charles Lamb*, i. 253–5.

For some years the Lambs used to hold a Wednesday evening reception ('Like other great men I have a public day—cribbage and pipes'), and there were, too, frequent whist parties at the Burneys; and these meetings provided the material for one of Lamb's most delightful essays, *Mrs. Battle's Opinions on Whist*, Mrs. Battle being Mrs. James Burney. It is really too well known to quote, but a few lines from the opening may possibly justify themselves as tending to send readers once again to their copy of Lamb and so to enable them to capture the spirit of the gatherings at James Burney's house:

'"A clear fire, a clean hearth, and the rigour of the game." This was the celebrated *wish* of old Sarah Battle (now with God), who, next to her devotions, loved a good game at whist. She was none of your lukewarm gamesters, your half-and-half players, who have no objection to take a hand, if you want one to make up a rubber; who affirm that they have no pleasure in winning; that they like to win one game and lose another; that they can while away an hour very agreeably at a card-table, but are indifferent whether they play or no; and will desire an adversary who has slipped a wrong card to take it up and play another. These insufferable triflers are the curse of a table. One of these flies will spoil a whole pot. Of such it may be said that they do not play at cards, but only play at playing at them.

'Sarah Battle was none of that breed. She detested them, as I do, from her heart and soul, and would not, save upon a striking emergency, willingly seat herself at the same table with them. She loved a thorough-paced partner, a determined enemy. She took, and gave, no concessions. She hated favours. She never made a revoke, nor ever passed it over in her adversary without exacting the utmost forfeiture. She fought a good fight: cut and thrust. She held not her good sword (her cards) "like a dancer". She sat bolt upright; and neither showed you her cards, nor desired to see yours. All people have their blind side—their superstitions; and I have heard her declare, under the rose, that hearts was her favourite suit.

'I never in my life—and I knew Sarah Battle many of the best years of it—saw her take out her snuff-box when it was her turn to play; or snuff a candle in the middle of a game; or ring for a servant until it was fairly over. She never introduced, or connived at, miscellaneous conversation during its process. As she emphatically observed, cards were cards; and if ever I saw unmingled distaste in her fine last-century countenance, it was at the airs of a young gentleman of a literary turn, who had been with difficulty persuaded to take a hand; and who, in his excess of candour, declared that he thought there was no harm in unbending the mind now and then, after serious studies, in recreations of that kind! She could not bear to have her noble occupation, to which she wound up her faculties, considered in that light. It was her business, her duty, the thing she came into the world to do,—and she did it. She unbent her mind afterwards over a book.'

The James Burneys (the Captain himself, his wife, and his son Martin) were always great whist players, and the present writer, who is no such thing, nevertheless cherishes his copy of *An Essay by way of Lecture on the Game of Whist, by James Burney Esq.* (1821; there were other editions), which seems to his non-expert mind to be a work of admirable conciseness and clear expression.

The injustice of James Burney's treatment by the Admiralty rankled in his mind. In the promotion of Captains to Flag rank in 1804 he was passed over. His retired pay, as Captain, was only ten shillings a day. In 1806 he petitioned the King in Council, but without avail. So far as one can see he was very badly treated.[1] It was not until 1821 that he received the promotion due to him and he was then able to enjoy it for only four months.

In 1809 James had the honour of election as a Fellow of the Royal Society, but for, some reason did not complete the formalities until six years later.

In 1814 James's son, Martin, was twenty-six years old and his daughter Sally about twenty-one. Sally inherited the family musical gifts. She 'learnt Thorough Bass and played classic music in a professional manner'.[2]

Of Martin a good many whimsical particulars can be learnt from the letters of the various literary friends of the family. Southey in 1804 calls him 'the queerest fish out of water', but 'a sharp lad'.[3] He was educated under his uncle, Dr. Charles, junior, at his Greenwich Academy and then articled to a literary solicitor friend of the family, Sharon Turner, author of the *History of the Anglo-Saxons* and many other solid historical works (more literature than law seems to have come out of this articling).

Martin was constantly with the Lambs, and his name often crops up in connexion with them and their circle, generally with some allusion to his oddity and helplessness, but coupled with the thought of his lovableness and purity of mind—as in the closing couplet of Lamb's sonnet addressed to him:

> In all my threadings of this worldly maze
> (And I have watch'd thee almost from a child),
> Free from self-seeking, envy, low design,
> I have not found a whiter soul than thine.

Of Burney's second daughter, FRANCES, her husband, and her son we have read in the last chapter.

By 1814 Burney's second son, CHARLES, now fifty-seven, had accumulated money and honours.

In 1786 he had opened a school of his own at Hammersmith.[4] Here, apparently, the boys had no easy time. Charles had been serving as

[1] The circumstances, with documents, are set forth in Manwaring, *My Friend the Admiral*, 229 et seq., and appear conclusive.

[2] Ann Rickman, quoted in Constance Hill, *Good Company at Westminster*.

[3] Southey, *Life and Correspondence*, ii. 292.

[4] Fairlawn House, according to Henry Angelo, who taught fencing there, see *Angelo's Pic Nic* (1834), 45. Angelo says that 'the Doctor, after Parr, was considered, with George Glass [should be 'Glasse'] the two best Grecians'. (There was no English syntax taught at Eton when Angelo was a boy there.)

assistant to William Rose, who leaned towards the modern, milder methods of controlling youth. We remember Johnson's remark to Rose on this very subject, 'What the boys gain at one end they lose at the other': that, apparently, was Charles Burney's idea, and when he set up for himself he applied it: 'We have heard from an officer of the Guards, who not unfrequently smarted under his castigations, that, like the learned Busby, he was a grand assertor of the ancient discipline.'[1]

In 1789 he published his *Appendix in Lexicon Graecum a Scapula constructum* and in 1791 his *Remarks on the Greek Verses of Milton* (as an appendix to Thomas Warton's edition of Milton's poems).

By 1792 his reputation for scholarship had risen high and both his own University of Aberdeen and that of Glasgow conferred on him their LL.D.

In 1793 he removed his school (already a very flourishing institution) to Greenwich.[2]

In 1801 he was elected Professor of Ancient Literature at the Royal Academy, succeeding his father's friend, Bennett Langton, who had succeeded Johnson (what all these professors did is a mystery to the present writer; most of them never gave any lectures). In the same year he was elected a Fellow of the Society of Antiquaries and in the following year Fellow of the Royal Society.

In 1807 there appeared his *Richardi Bentleii et doctorum virorum epistolae*, and the next year the University of Cambridge, from which thirty years earlier he had fled as a discovered thief, conferred on him its honorary M.A.—which must have been a satisfaction both to him and to his father (he had been readmitted to the books of Caius College in 1807).

In 1809 he published his *Tentamen de Metris Æschyli*, in 1810 his *Abridgement of 'Dr. Pearson on the Creed'*, and in 1812 his *Philemonis Lexicon Technologicum.* In this last year the Archbishop of Canterbury, at whose request he had undertaken some textual research described by Fanny as 'collating a newly found Greek Testament',[3] by virtue of the ancient powers vested in his office (powers to-day strangely, and surely not very properly, still claimed and used), made him a D.D.

He was now, says Fanny (and she is not far out according to reports from other quarters), as to Greek scholarship, 'generally held, after Porson and Parr, to be the third scholar in the kingdom'.

The following year, 1813, he retired from his school,[4] which was henceforth carried on by his son Charles Parr Burney. Before this he had taken orders (deacon, 1807; priest, 1808), becoming at once an eminent pluralist—Rector of Little Hinton, Wilts., 1811; Vicar of

[1] An article of 17 April 1818 preserved in the Public Library of King's Lynn, but not bearing the name of the journal from which it is extracted.

[2] For a picture of the school and a portrait of its proprietor see pl. opposite.

[3] *Mem.* iii. 410.

[4] One of his pupils, by the way, was the painter, art-critic, forger, and poisoner, Thomas Griffith Wainewright.

CHARLES BURNEY JUNIOR

Famous Greek scholar (*see* ii. 235–9), successful schoolmaster and (in later life) divine.

Engraving by William Sharp after the portrait of Sir Thomas Lawrence, R.A.

THE SCHOOL AT GREENWICH

By means of which this 'Grand Assertor of the Ancient Discipline' earned the fortune which enabled him to amass those huge collections of books, newspapers, playbills, and other literary material which are now amongst the irreplaceable treasures of the British Museum.

Herne Hill, 1811–15; Vicar of St. Paul's, Deptford, 1811–17; Rector of Cliffe-at-Hoo, 1815–17.[1]

Charles's library was famous. Not only was his collection of the classics enormous but it was arranged systematically so as to admit of easy comparison of all (or nearly all) the existing editions of the various authors; there were also some valuable manuscripts, including the Townley Homer, which alone was on his death officially valued at £1,000. Charles's library of the classics was, indeed, more complete than that of the British Museum.

'That munificent disposition, in consequence of which he expended a large portion of his hard-earned gains on the acquisition of a library, seemed to shed a lustre around his head, while it communicated a certain portion of it to his family, relations and friends. Since the days of the Medicis, no private person had before his time been seen to employ agents both at home and abroad, to purchase whatever was rare, valuable and learned. Few men, with such limited means, have achieved so much in this way; no obstacles prevented, no sum, however large, obstructed, no difficulties, however formidable, deterred him in his pursuit. By devoting nearly the whole of his fortune to this particular propensity, he was enabled to achieve great things; and some of the richest of our nobility were startled at a competition, in which a private gentleman, with but very scanty resources, fairly outbid the proprietors of large hereditary estates.'[2]

The library had a lighter side—one strongly contrasting. For it included a most comprehensive collection of playbills and other material for a history of the English stage from the time of Queen Elizabeth, arranged in some hundreds of volumes. The amazing industry of this pedagogue, divine, and classical scholar as a collector of English theatrical material is seen by a glance at the catalogue of the British Museum, where the fruits of his diligent pursuit of his hobby are now garnered:

Notebooks on the History of the Stage in England, 1538–1807. 46 vols.
Notebooks on British Actors, 1560–1816. 7 vols.
Theatrical Register, 1660–1801. 84 vols.
Theatrical Register, Playbills of Drury Lane, Covent Garden, Haymarket, etc. 59 vols.
Notes on the History of the Theatre in Goodman's Fields, 2 vols.
Collection of Playbills, etc., dealing with Private Theatrical Performances, 1750–1808 (This, however, is also attributed to S. S. Banks).
Playbills of Brighton, 1804–8.

And besides these we find:

Collection of Newspapers, 700 vols.

Altogether, then, the present-day student of British theatrical history has at his disposition 900 volumes of invaluable material collected by

[1] J. A. Venn, *Alumni Cantabrigienses,* Pt. II, vol. i.
[2] Article preserved at King's Lynn Public Library, already alluded to.

Charles Burney, junior, and how any man whose mind was occupied with the oversight of an important educational establishment and with classical and theological study could, in his off-moments, get together that bulk of material treating of matters so totally different from those that necessarily chiefly engaged his attention must remain a mystery. However, the school was profitable, there was no shortage of money, and perhaps he employed agents in the pursuit of this hobby as of the other. Probably, too, every second-hand bookseller and auctioneer in London knew of his interests and called his attention to anything relevant to these that happened to come their way.

An amusing personal peculiarity of Dr. Charles Burney, junior, is revealed to us in the following, which shows us the imperious pedagogue, accustomed to be obeyed:

'Among his peculiarities, at home, were two of a very innocent kind; the first was the possession of the best wine, of the best vintage; the next a dread of a fresh current of air. Shut the door! was the first salutation uttered by him to anyone, who entered his apartment, and but few of his associates neglected this rule. This custom it seems, did not abandon him even on the most critical and trying occasions; for it is said, that having been robbed while returning home one evening in his own carriage, along the Greenwich road, by a couple of footpads, who were more eager in obtaining his money, than contributing to his accommodation, he called them back in a peremptory tone, and while they were wondering what he wanted with them, he exclaimed in his usual manner, and with his own peculiar emphasis: "Shut the door!" A voice, accustomed to command, produced the desired effect, and he was instantly obeyed.'[1]

According to the *Biographie Universelle* (Paris, 1835), Charles's relinquishment of his school was due to a scandal. It says that he would have made his fortune in his school, 'si quelques traits qui décèlent de l'indélicatesse, pour ne rien dire de plus, ne l'eussent mis dans la nécessité de se retirer en la cédant à son fils vers 1813'.

[1] Article at Lynn already quoted. In some other publications this incident is related as occurring to Charles Burney, senior—to whom, however, the 'peremptory tone' was not nearly so habitual. That gives us a hint of Charles as a disciplinarian. And so does this, from the introduction to his abridgement for schools of *Pearson on the Creed*:

'Let me trespass a little further on the patience of the Reader; in order to recommend this Abridgement, with affectionate respect, to my Brethren, who are employed in the laudable, but anxious, duty of instructing the RISING GENERATION; to which service, between twenty and thirty years of my life have been constantly devoted. During the latter part of this period the difficulties, the toils, and the solicitude of a Schoolmaster's occupation have been gradually and greatly increased: not nearly so much, let me add, by the *evil days*, on which *we have fallen*; as by those extraordinary and destructive indulgences, with which children are now gratified, during the seasons at which they are under the roof of their Parents.'

The following entry in the catalogue of a second-hand bookseller a few years ago testifies to the firmness of Charles's disciplinary principles:

'BURNEY (Dr. Charles). A.L.S., in verse, 3 pp., 4to., to Wm. Parsons, of the *Florence Miscellany*, etc., dated from York House, Jany. 22. 1795. [But why from York House?]

'The letter is in reply to one by Parsons on the subject of the birching of small boys, and others, of which Burney is strongly in favour. The letter-poem is of 62 lines and on the reverse of the last sheet Parsons has drafted part of his reply in the same medium.'

There is very unlikely to be any truth in this story. Firstly he *had* (in a modest way) 'made his fortune', which was probably why he retired; and, secondly, his immediate admission to orders and the preferments that so quickly followed (Prebendary of Lincoln; Chaplain to the King) seem quite to preclude any theory of disgrace.

Burney's fourth daughter, CHARLOTTE (his youngest child by his first wife), has been a good deal neglected in these pages. As a girl she was gay, frivolous, and perhaps a little flirtatious, so that Fanny, from the superior height of seven years' seniority, had some little regret for the impression her manner was likely to make upon strangers.[1] Like Fanny she had a descriptive pen. (See examples of her writing at I. 368, 379; II. 41, 207, 208.)

When she was twenty-seven she found a husband in an odd way. A family account says:

'Clement Francis had been secretary to Warren Hastings in India, and while there he read, and was so charmed with "Evelina", that he was seized with a desire to make the authoress his wife, and, with that intent, came home from India and obtained an introduction to Dr. Burney and his family; but the result was that he married the younger sister—Charlotte.'[2]

The marriage took place on 11 February 1786—the year in which Hastings returned from India, so that we may suppose that Francis had travelled home with him.

To have been secretary to Hastings would, in itself, constitute a favourable introduction to the Burney family, who admired the great man and when the famous trial began two years after this were amongst his most vehement supporters.

Francis, though when in India he had been engaged in secretarial duties, was by profession a medical man and on the list of the officers of the East India Company he figures as such. After his marriage he practised at Aylsham, in Norfolk.

Fanny, in her Court days, passed 'an agreeable evening' with Charlotte and her husband at Beaumont Lodge, Hastings's house at Windsor. And during the Westminster Hall trial the Queen, on one occasion, gave Fanny tickets for herself and Charlotte and Francis, and on another occasion tickets for herself and Charlotte and their youngest sister Sarah.[3] In Fanny's distress at the effects the life at Court were having on her health she consulted Francis, describing all her symptoms, and he at once wrote to Burney telling him that he must at any cost get his daughter away. The Queen, on more than one occasion, tried to 'pump' Fanny as to what Francis had said, but the ever dutiful Fanny felt that she had to parry the Queen's questions until her father should have written to her giving his views, based on Francis's report.[4]

[1] *Early Diary*, ii. 272.
[2] Ibid. 272–3.
[3] *Diary and Letters*, iii. 19; iv. 351.
[4] Ibid. 437 et seq.

The year after Fanny's escape from Windsor (i.e. in 1792) she was staying with her sister and brother-in-law at Aylsham (they had wanted her to live with them entirely)[1] when Francis had an apoplectic fit and died. Apparently he left his wife and three children (Clement, Marianne, and Charlotte) well provided for, but a few years later his brother, to whom a part of his capital had been lent, became bankrupt and disappeared, so probably a considerable loss was thus sustained.[2]

In 1798, after about six years of widowhood, Charlotte married again, her husband being again a man of Indian experience—Captain Ralph Broome of the Bengal Army. He, too, was a supporter of Warren Hastings and as the trial had proceeded he had published in the *World* a series of rhyming letters on it—*Letters of Simpkin the Second, Poetic Recorder of all the Proceedings upon the Trial of Warren Hastings, Esq. in Westminster Hall.*[3] By him she had a son who died young. Captain Broome was said by Fanny to 'have by no means the wit and humour and hilarity his *Simpkins letters* prepare for', but, as she added, 'the pen and the tongue are often unequally gifted', and she admitted that he had a reputation for being 'deeply skilled in languages, and general erudition' and was 'full of information on most subjects that can be mentioned'.

RICHARD THOMAS, Burney's youngest son (by his second wife), was now dead. 'He had gone to India, become Head Master of the Military Upper Orphan School at Kidderpore, Calcutta, and died at Rangoon on 8 March 1808, aged thirty-nine.'[4] The family always spoke of him as 'Bengal Dick', so distinguishing him from his uncle Richard and two cousins Richard. He left 'a large and prosperous family'. There may just possibly have been some minor scandal or family unhappiness connected with his going abroad, for we find Susan writing on one occasion that his life there is 'always a subject from which I feel inclined to shrink'.[5] Such an expression could be explained by the mere sadness of being parted from a favourite brother, but it may be significant that there is so little about Richard to be gleaned from such family diaries and letters as have been allowed to remain in existence. However, 'Bengal Dick's' life in India seems to have been one of the greatest piety. His funeral sermon, preached on 15 May 1808, was published (with voluminous footnotes) in London no less than thirty years after (1838).

[1] *Diary and Letters*, iv. 224.

[2] Letter from Susan Burney to her sister Fanny, in the Armagh Library, reproduced in Brimley Johnson, 225.

[3] Anstey's *New Bath Guide* (1766) had been written in the name of 'Simpkin', and 'Simpkin the Second' adopted the same style of writing. Broome's work is reviewed at much length and with high praise and extensive quotations in *The Monthly Review*, Jan. 1791.

[4] Extract from the Records of the College of Arms, communicated to Canon F. d'Arblay Burney in 1895, and by him communicated to the present author. Richard Thomas Burney's will was proved on 4 May 1808. A portrait of him will be found on pl. 44, II. 244.

[5] Letter from Susan Burney to her sister Fanny, in the Armagh Library, reproduced in Brimley Johnson, 168–9.

It tells us that 'The Bible was his constant companion; he never went forth of the doors but, like the staff in his hand, it accompanied his steps', and 'On the Sabbath he would not allow any token of levity to appear, such as thoughtless whistling, or any sort of play, however innocent in itself', and 'On Wednesdays he distributed charity to the blind, lame, and aged, around his neighbourhood, who were incapable of obtaining a subsistence for themselves; these he distinguished from common sturdy beggars to whom he would give nothing', and 'Even when he entered his salary in his cash-book, he would add a note thanking God for his mercies to so unworthy a creature'. His last utterance was a stanza of one of Watts's hymns.

The Burney Prize at Cambridge was founded by Richard Thomas's eldest son, Richard (d. 1845); he interpolated into a military career in the service of the East India Company a furlough long enough to enable him to take a degree at that University, and there is a memorial to him in the chapel of Christ's College.

In the *Proceedings of the Royal Asiatic Society* (Anniversary Meeting, 16 May 1846) is a 'Tribute to the Memory of Lieut. Col. Henry Burney'. This was another son of Richard Burney's. Many of his papers appear in the *Proceedings* just mentioned. He also wrote a book on *The Political Relations between British India and Ava* (Calcutta). Several volumes of reports of his have in recent years been published by the Government of Ava, in the history of whose State he figures importantly.

In 1814 Sarah Harriet, Burney's youngest child, was forty-four years of age. She was unmarried, and was all her life to remain so. She was a good French and Italian scholar. Like most of her brothers and sisters she must be writing, and so in 1796 she had published (anonymously) her first novel, *Clarentine*; in 1808 her second, *Geraldine Fauconberg*; and in 1812 her third, *Traits of Nature*. Her father admired her books:

> 'There is, I think, considerable merit in her novel, Geraldine, particularly in the conversations; and I think the scene at the emigrant cottage really touching. At least it drew tears from me, when I was not so prone to shed them as I am at present.'[1]

He had the satisfaction of seeing these novels 'well received and favoured in the best society',[2] but it is not the present writer's experience that they can be read to-day without sturdy determination.

Presumably, after her mother's death, she directed the household, though, as already quoted (II. 150), her father stated that she 'had no experience in household affairs'.[3] Let us hope, for his comfort, that she quickly gained it!

[1] *Mem.* iii. 225. [2] Ibid. 410. [3] Ibid.

LXIII. BURNEY'S BROTHER-IN-LAW, ARTHUR YOUNG

(*From 1784 to 1814; Young aged 43–73, Burney 58–88*)

A BRIEF sketch of the doings of Burney's famous brother-in-law, Arthur Young, up to the year 1783, has already been given (II. 43). In 1785 Young's mother died and the family estate of Bradfield, near Bury St. Edmunds, became his. Here he was much visited by students of agriculture from all over Europe.

In 1788 he was a leader in opposing the Wool Bill, published pamphlets against it, and was examined at the Bars of both Houses. It passed, however, and its Norwich supporters burnt Young in effigy. In that same year and the next he made his second and third journeys to France, the second on his own mare and the third, which was extended to the northern parts of Italy, in a post-chaise so as to be able to bring back samples of soils, wools, &c. Burney wrote to him in Italy in October 1789, giving him various commissions to inquire about new musical books and old friends there:

'Pray go to the church of Sant' Antonio [Padua] on a festival; there Tartini used to lead and Guadagni sing. If Padre Valetti is living, the Maestro di Capella, pray present my compliments to him and enquire after the sequel of his Treatise. I have as yet only seen the first part. I likewise beg to be remembered to Signor Marsili, the Professor of Botany, and Padre Columbo, the Professor of Mathematics: the first was some time in England and speaks our language; the second was the great friend of Tartini, and left in possession of all his manuscript papers. Enquire what is become of them, and try to get intelligence of the disposal of Padre Martini's papers, books, and sequel of his "History of Musick" at Bologna. Enquire likewise, when you meet with intelligent musical people, what are the defects of the newest and best of the great Italian theatres. No plan is, I believe, as yet adopted for rebuilding ours. [The King's Theatre, burnt to the ground four months earlier—June 1789.] Le Texier has a model made with many conveniences and more magnificence than our former theatre could boast, but whether it will be adopted, or whether it is to be wished that a Frenchman should ever have the management of an Italian opera, I know not. However partial he or his countrymen may seem to German and Italian musick, I know by long observation that they are totally ignorant of, and enemies to *good singing*, without which what are the two or three acts of an opera but intermezzi or act tunes to the ballets? I perceive, however, that, amidst all the horrors of Paris, they suffer Italian operas to be performed in Italian and by Italians, which were never allowed before except at Versailles; but these are only burlettas; serious operas so performed might have some effect on the national taste in singing. But les Dames des Halles, their excellencies *Mesdames les Poissardes*, furnish them with "other fish to fry" at present; so I shall say no more of France, but that I pity most sincerely every honest man who has the misfortune to be resident in that distracted kingdom.

'God bless you, my dear Sir, and give you health and spirits to enjoy your rational and useful enquiries.

CHARLES BURNEY.'[1]

On this journey Young saw the opening flare-up of the Revolution—at its very centres, Paris and Versailles.

In 1791 he was in correspondence with both Washington and Lafayette. Washington asked him to 'procure some implements for his husbandry', which he not only did, but also gave him a plan for a barn, which was duly erected and of which Young then gave a picture in his *Annals of Agriculture*.[2] In the same year George III made him a present of a Spanish merino ram, of which he published a picture in his *Annals*.

In 1792 his *Travels in France and Italy during the years 1787, 1788, and 1789* were published, and, of course, they have been much republished since and are still on sale in various languages. To-day, well as Young's name is known in Britain, it is, apparently, still better known in France. The French have always remained grateful to Young for his gift to them of 'de précieux renseignements sur la vie journalière des Français à la veille de la Révolution'—to quote a popular book of reference.[3] The French Government of the Convention period (1792–5) printed 20,000 copies of a French translation of the *Travels* and distributed them gratuitously in every commune—to the advantage of French agriculture.[4] Later Napoleon, on Elba, procured them and read them 'with much approbation'.

In that same year of 1792 Young made a proposal for the protection of Britain against the French by means of a volunteer organization of Horse Militia. It was at once taken up by the nation but was not carried out in the way Young himself proposed. He was for 'arming *the property* of the kingdom', and the Government extended the scheme so that men of *no property* were soon carrying arms—to the grave danger of the Constitution, as the now anti-Jacobinical Young thought. He soon found his health being drunk after the King's at gatherings of the various new corps, as the originator of a scheme he did not altogether approve. This scheme, by the way, in a few years, brought poor Burney into trouble, for we find him, in 1797, writing from Chelsea to Young:

'The ballot has fallen upon me to furnish a man and a horse to the

[1] Arthur Young, *Autobiography*, 183.

[2] Op. cit., 189.

[3] *Larousse Universel*, 2 vols., 1923.

[4] Garat, *Mémoires sur la Révolution* (1794). In 1938 it was announced that it had been decided to celebrate the coming 150th anniversary of the publication of the *Travels in France* by the erection of a monument 'on the exact spot where Young first set foot on French soil after disembarking from one of the small cross-Channel boats which operated between Dover and Calais in those days.' *The Times*, 11 May 1938. That paper honoured Young by making the announcement the subject of a leading article.

Provisional Cavalry, which has occasioned me much trouble and vexation. The expense, had it been double, I would have paid with alacrity, for the defence of everything dear to honest men, during such a war and with such enemies; but the business of recruiting, clothing, accoutring, &c., is so new to men of peace, that they know not how to go to work. Three substitutes that I had engaged have disappointed me, and the horse I have purchased I am not sure will pass muster. Had Government levied a tax of five or ten guineas upon each horse that was kept for pleasure, either in or out of harness, and done the business of raising a certain number of cavalry themselves, it would have been better done, and ladies and superannuated gentlemen (like my worship) would have escaped infinite plague and vexation.'[1]

Then Young, having the chance of buying for next to nothing an estate of 4,400 acres near Pateley Bridge in Yorkshire (mostly moorland which he thought he could bring under cultivation), seized it, but just then had offered to him by Pitt the Secretaryship of the newly-founded Board of Agriculture, so sold his new territory and settled in London. Here, on the strength of his many and various writings, he immediately became a Society favourite ('I find by an old memorandum book that I dined out from twenty-five to thirty days in the month, and had, in that time, forty invitations from the people of the highest rank and consequence').[2]

He still kept his family estate at Bradfield, and in his house there, in 1797, died his beloved fourteen-year-old daughter, 'Bobbin'.

From that moment Young was a broken man. The stern, practical rule of his brother-in-law, Burney, not to let bereavement spoil his life (see II. 53), was not his: 'I have torn my heart to pieces with looking at my dear child's hair! Melancholy remains, but how precious when their owner is no more! I am to see her no more in this world. Gone for ever!' He buried the child under his pew in the village church, 'fixing the coffin so that when I kneel I will be between her head and her dear heart. This I did as a means of preserving the grief I feel, and hope to feel while the breath is in my body. It turns all my views to an hereafter.'

Pathetically, the poor fellow started entertaining poor children in Bobbin's memory. So his memorandum book records, in 1798:

'*March.*—A dinner for fifteen poor children, 11*s.* 10*d.*
Another dinner for thirty-seven children, 16*s.* 6*d.*
Another dinner for forty-seven children, £1. 6*s.* 6*d.*
April.—This month seven dinners to about forty-eight children each time.
May.—Four dinners to about forty-eight children each time.'[3]

A devout seriousness now seized the mind of Young and it soon (at times, at any rate) approached the quality of melancholia or religious

[1] Young, *Autobiography*, 301. A little later we find Burney feeling gratified at having some connexion with the 'Chelsea Armed Association'—presumably the Chelsea branch of the 'Provisional Cavalry' (see letter on II. 295).

[2] Op. cit., 223.

[3] Op. cit., 319.

PLATE 44. *MORE FAMILY PORTRAITS*

SUSANNA ELIZABETH BURNEY
By her cousin Edward F. Burney
Burney's 3rd daughter (*c.* 1754–1800). She married her brother's comrade in the Cook explorations, Molesworth Phillips. The story of her life will be found at ii. 29 and 142–8.

'BENGAL DICK'
Burney's youngest son, Richard Thomas (1768–1811). For his story *see* i. 319 et seq. and ii. 30 and 240. (Miniature by George Chinnery, probably executed during this painter's long sojourn in the East.)

ARTHUR YOUNG
griculturalist and copious author. His wife as a sister of Burney's second wife and he was uch associated with the Burney family life (*see* 136–7 and ii. 43 and 242 et seq.). Miniature by an unknown artist.

'BOBBIN' YOUNG
Her loss in 1797 was the ruin of Young's reasonable outlook on life, driving him into a distressing state of religious melancholia of which a brief account will be found at ii. 244–5. Miniature by Plymer.

mania. He gave up society and spent his time reading sermons. Wilberforce's *Practical View of Christianity* helped him, and he struck up an acquaintance with the author. (Years later this acquaintance was, as we shall see, to bring on him a great misfortune—the culminating one of his troubled life.)[1]

In the early years of the nineteenth century Young was still pouring out book after book and the magnitude of his output may be imagined when it is mentioned that, in the year these lines are written (1939), the Bodleian Library, despite the amplitude of its collections, published a list of thirty-four works of Young still 'wanting'.[2]

The French Directory, in 1801, ordered the translation and publication, at the public expense, of all Young's works, in eighteen big volumes. In the same year Catharine the Great sent the author a gold snuff-box, with ermine cloaks for his wife and a daughter. Three years later came another Russian gold snuff-box, studded with diamonds—this time from the Governor of Moscow, and inscribed 'From a Pupil to his Master'. All over Europe Young had become famous. He was elected an honorary member of innumerable foreign scientific societies and 'breakfasting at Bradfield on one occasion the Duke of Bedford found him surrounded by pupils from Russia, France, America, Naples, Poland, Sicily, and Portugal'.[3]

But though Young was still incessantly at work for the improvement of agriculture his real interest in his efforts was now tempered. In 1800 he wrote:

> 'What is the tendency of all these improvements except to add to the wealth and prosperity of a country that is already under a most heavy responsibility to the Almighty for innumerable temporal blessings, repaid with the black ingratitude of irreligion and a general contempt of everything serious or sacred. . . . Our fields are made to smile with cultivation for the profits of men thankless to Heaven. Can such a country continue to be thus blessed? I fear and dread some terrible reverse, and have the only hope that the prayers of religious men, Methodists as they are called, may be heard, and avert the misfortunes we deserve. It damps all vanity of public good attending such attempts as mine to think of the use that is made of great wealth.'[4]

Troubled by the thought that general 'affliction and poverty' might more conduce to the real welfare of the nation than the prosperity he had long been trying to increase, Young nevertheless went on working. One mitigation of his anxiety was the undoubted fact that he was helping to lift the very poor out of their hopeless position. At home, however,

[1] *The Practical View* greatly impressed another of Burney's circle, for it is on record that Burke spent a great part of the last two days of his life in reading this book, and one of his last messages was to Wilberforce to thank him for writing it. This is recorded by Burney's friend, Mrs. Crewe, who was with Burke a good deal when he was on his death-bed (see R. Coupland, *Wilberforce*, 1923, 244).

[2] *Bodleian Library Record*, June, 1939.

[3] *D.N.B.*

[4] Young, *Autobiography*, 333.

he had little consolation: 'Mrs. Y. in great health, and when that is the case in too much irritation. God forgive her! . . . quarrels and irritation never subsiding. My daughter and daughter-in-law reading cart loads of novels.'[1] (At a later date this relative of Burney, the father of novelists, exclaims 'Oh! the number of miserables that novels have sent to perdition'.)

It is a relief a year or two later to find a pleasanter matrimonial record: 'I have never lived so well with Mrs. Young as for five weeks past.'

Every day he was up 'at 4 a.m. and sometimes at 3 a.m.'. He then, when at Bradfield, walked up to his neck in the garden pond (in winter breaking the ice to do so, and on one occasion, as an experiment, rolling naked in the snow after his bath), and returned to the house for his devotions. Here is a characteristic diary entry of April 1801:

'12th, *Sunday*.—The ground white with snow, and the wind cutting. I am up every morn at 4 a.m., and walk to the garden pond; habits will do anything. I do not mind it at all, and sometimes stand in the wind till dry; it is, however, sharp work.'[2]

He was vexing his spirit, as people do, by finding in the political events of the moment a fulfilment of the prophecies of the Book of Daniel and the Book of The Revelation, and was also, more practically, regularly visiting the poor of the neighbourhood, relieving their wants and instructing them:

'As there was no church this morning I had eleven poor women from the village to talk to upon their neglect of church. I read many passages on public worship and prayer out of Dodd's Commentary on the Bible, and explained, preached, and reasoned with them. One made a defence, and was inclined to prate. I took it cooly, and presently brought her to better reason. I doubt they liked a sixpence apiece better than my sermon, yet three of them cried.'

Every Sunday he heard 'sixteen or eighteen children read the Scripture and say their catechism' and he paid 'for the schooling of all that would learn'.[3]

Once fond of music, and greatly enjoying what he heard at Burney's, he now began to think time ill spent on it. So, visiting the Earl of Bristol, Bishop of Derry, at his family seat of Ickworth, Suffolk, he says:

'On Monday I breakfasted, dined and slept at Lord Bristol's; Lady B. and her sister, Miss Upton, sung Italian airs till twelve o'clock at night. They were many years ago a horrible temptation, now a frivolous waste of time, but ever a bad tendency on the heart. . . . All this visiting is very bad for my soul.'[4]

[1] Young, *Autobiography*, 339, 389, 421.
[2] Op. cit., 356.
[3] Op. cit., 360, 433.
[4] Op. cit., 401. Here is an example of that yielding to the 'horrible temptation', those

With time-wasters, indeed, he had no sympathy. Reading Dr. Johnson's *Prayers and Meditation* he reflects (not altogether justly), 'His sloth seems to have been dreadful. What a contrast to the life of John Wesley!'

At last, in 1811, to add to all his miseries (real and invented, unavoidable and self-imposed), this gifted, diligent worker for the good of his country and of the whole world went blind from cataract. There was a chance of saving his sight by the operation of couching, but unfortunately, Wilberforce visited him and broke to him in such a touching way the news of the death of their friend the Duke of Grafton, that he burst into tears, and so made recovery of his sight for ever impossible.[1]

It was a sad thing to see him preaching to the villagers on Sunday evenings in his house, Bradfield Hall, for sometimes in his movements he would gradually turn round until his back was to the congregation, and then Burney's granddaughter, Marianne Francis, who at this time tended him, would place her hands on his shoulders and gently turn him back again. This loving assistant (Charlotte Burney's elder daughter, a girl in the early twenties) was apparently a very remarkable polyglot and read every day in 'Greek, Latin, Hebrew, Arabic, German, Spanish, French, Dutch, &c., &c.'.

'She sleeps over the servants' hall, with a packthread tied round her wrist, and placed through the keyhole, which he pulls at four or five times, till he awakens her, when she gets up and accompanies him in a two hours' walk on the turnpike road to some cottage or other, and they take milk at some farmhouse; and she distributes tracts (religious ones), and questions the people about their principles, and reads to them and catechises them. They return at half-past six, as that is the hour Mr. St. Croix gets up (his secretary) who finds it quite enough to read and write two hours and a half before breakfast.'[2]

And with this manner of life, at the age of seventy-seven, six years after Burney's own death, ended the useful, busy, troubled existence of his dear friend and brother-in-law, Arthur Young.

'many years ago'. On setting out to France in 1789 he wrote in his diary on 2 June: 'To London. At night, Il Generosité [*sic*] *d'Alessandro*, by Tarchi, in which Signor Marchesi exerted all his powers and sung a duet that made me for some moments forget all the sheep and pigs of Bradfield!' (*Travels in France*). And here is another, from an earlier date (1768): 'This year I made many visits to my friend, Dr. Burney, in Poland Street, to whom my wife's sister was married, and whose daughter Hester (by a former marriage) entertained, or rather, fascinated me, by her performance on the harpsichord and singing of Italian airs. I was never tired of listening to the "Ah, quelli occhi ladroncelli," and "Alla larga," of Piccini, and [he is recording this years later, in his Autobiography] it is marvellous to me now to recollect that I was thus riveted to her side for six hours together.'

[1] Op. cit., 454 n.

[2] Letter from Young's daughter Mary to her brother in Russia, quoted by the Editor of Young's Autobiography.

LXIV. FANNY'S LAST NOVEL

(1814; Fanny aged 62, her Father aged 88)

FANNY brought with her from Paris the manuscript of her fourth novel, *The Wanderer, or Female Difficulties*—so far as it had gone, that is to say nearly three volumes of the ultimate five. Held up at Dunkirk she had sent back to Paris for her manuscript in order to occupy herself by working on it.[1] It was dangerous at that time to attempt to carry any papers with one out of France, but her husband used his influence with the Secretary of the Minister of Police and obtained special permission. When she had got the manuscript she found she was in too great a state of anxiety to do any effective work, and the having this long English document in her possession increased her trouble with the police; indeed, she says that it would certainly have been destroyed but for the intervention of an English merchant settled in Dunkirk and much respected in that town.

Her arrival in England occurred in the middle of August 1812, and in March 1814 the book appeared. Apparently she had already been negotiating from Paris for its publication six months before she left for England, since we find Byron, in December 1811, writing to a friend that a publisher, Cawthorne, had told him, 'with a most important face', that he was 'in treaty for a novel of Madame D'Arblay's for which 1000 guineas are asked'—which looks as though Fanny had begun counting her chickens before they were hatched. Byron modestly adds, 'He wants me to read the MS. (if he obtains it), which I shall do with pleasure; but I should be very cautious in venturing an opinion on her whose *Cecilia* Dr. Johnson superintended [an error, of course]', and, still more modestly, 'If he lends it to me I shall put it into the hands of Rogers and Moore, who are truly men of taste'.[2]

Presumably, as not Cawthorne but the many-partnered firm of Longman, Hurst, Rees, Orme, and Brown published the book, Byron was not called upon to pronounce as to its qualities. If he had been what would he have said? *The Wanderer* is Fanny's last work of fiction, and we will examine it a little in detail to see what had been her development since she published *Evelina* thirty-six years before.

The novel begins, very topically, with a party of English people in a boat, escaping from France at the time of 'the dire reign of the terrific Robespierre'. Amongst them is a young woman whose 'Female Difficulties' on arrival in England form the theme of the plot. Her painful efforts to earn a living are constantly frustrated by the passively

[1] This and the following information comes from *Diary and Letters*, vi. 69 et seq.

[2] Moore, *Life of Lord Byron* (1844), 147, quoted by Dobson in his edition of *Diary and Letters*, vi. 70. It seems very strange that with communications so difficult any business between an author in Paris and a publisher in London should be possible.

unsympathetic or actively malicious conduct of a variety of 'Society' people amongst whom she is thrown.

It is curious how this obsession of Fanny's persists through all her fiction from beginning to end. The age *was* one of extreme 'difficulty' for lone 'females'; and any female without friends, such as the heroine of this novel, was indeed, almost as helpless as an abandoned babe. In the present book Fanny emphasizes that idea by frequently bringing up in capitals the word, 'FEMALE', or the word 'DIFFICULTIES' or the pair of words, 'FEMALE DIFFICULTIES'.

Fanny was a good deal of what about a century later was called a 'Feminist'. She seems to have had thoughts of the 'Rights of Women', and to have resented the current notions of woman's mental inferiority. She slyly introduces a male character who, after declaring (i. 201) that, 'as to ladies, though they are certainly very pleasing, they are but indifferent judges in the political line', calmly adds that he 'speaks without offence, inferiority of understanding being no defect in a female'. And she gives us, too, a female character who (i. 164) 'was of opinion that every woman ought to live with a needle and thread in her hand'.[1] And as a manifesto against this attitude we have brought before us one heroic woman character who actually claims that marriage proposals may as fittingly come from women as men.

Fanny's picture of an empty-minded and almost entirely heartless upper class is Hogarthian; it is hard to realize that such people ever existed as Fanny's tyrannical and capricious ladies of wealth and position, her curious old maids always going about asking people intimate questions about their private affairs, and her almost inevitable bad baronet living merely to seduce innocent young girls of the lower classes and then to abandon them.

What we should have expected Fanny (politically such a Tory) to denounce as 'democratic' or 'levelling' ideas seem sometimes to have her keen sympathy. There is a wealthy lady who had at first taken the heroine to belong to her own exalted class ('a young lady of family and fashion') and then, as she thinks, discovers her to be 'a mere nothing'; a coarse-grained individual who is present turns on her as follows:

'"Faith, Madam, as to her being a mere nothing, I don't know that any of us are much better than nothing, when we sift ourselves to our origin. What are you yourself, Ma'am, for one?"

'"O, Sir? I'm descended from a gentleman's family, I assure you! I don't know what you mean by such a question!"

'"Why then you are descended from somebody who was rich without either trouble or merit; for that's all that your gentleman is, as far as belongs to birth. The man amongst your grand-dads who first got the money, is the only one worth praising; and he, who was he? Why some one who baked sugar or brewed beer better than his neighbours; or who slashed and hewed

[1] The Bluestocking Movement (if we may use that expression) was, of course, a protest against this very notion (see Ch. XLVII).

his fellow-creatures with greater fury than they could slash and hew him in return; or who culled the daintiest herbs for the cure of gluttony; or filled his coffers with the best address, in emptying those of the knaves and fools who had been set together by the ears. Such, Ma'am, are the origins of your English gentlemen."'

All the dramatis personae are strongly differentiated in the way that persisted from the 'Characters' of the seventeenth century to the novels of Dickens, that is to say there are throughout the book few or no 'ordinary people', such as we meet by thousands in real life, every person Fanny describes being a type. And, as usual with Fanny (and here again she anticipates Dickens), the vulgar people and the social oddities are the best drawn. After pages of the most stilted expressions from the 'educated' and well-to-do, and these thrown into long formal paragraphs, we at last emerge into the sunlight with pages (alas, too few!) of delightfully vivid conversation amongst shopkeepers or the peasantry and do so with the relief of a traveller who has been wading painfully through bogs and suddenly finds his feet touching hard ground. There is, in particular, a naïve rustic who appears and reappears episodically to whom every reader must give a recurring welcome: at his final appearance he is engaged in carrying out a country merry-making that for life and spirit may almost be ranked with that of *The Winter's Tale.*[1]

The plot of *The Wanderer* is wonderfully rich in incident. Some new turn in the fortunes of the heroine occurs in every chapter, until the reader is almost dizzied by her recurring peripetia. The whole plot is really in the highest degree absurd, the poor girl's manifold troubles on English ground arising from her penniless condition due to her having carelessly thrown her purse into the English Channel as she crossed it (a refugee who does not take better care of her money is 'asking for trouble'—and this one actually loses a second purse in her fifth volume and so reaps a small crop of fresh troubles!) Then, as in so many eighteenth-century novels, the group of individuals picked out of the whole population of the country to carry forward the plot are constantly meeting and re-meeting in all sorts of places in a manner providential for the plans of the authoress but utterly incredible—even in this human life of ours, so strangely full of coincidences. And, still more astonishing, pretty nearly all the *good* people we find in Fanny's pages, after all these strange and unexpected meetings and re-meetings, discover themselves finally, to their great astonishment, to be family relations, thus triumphantly bringing about a thoroughly happy ending.

The fact seems to be that Fanny was a fool at tragedy or serious narra-

[1] This merry-making is at the farm of a Sussex peasant who 'would not believe a word about all those battles and guilotines and the like of Mounseer Robert Speer in foreign parts' until he met the heroine of the tale, who had herself been in France. We get a hint as to where Fanny got her knowledge of country talk and country ways of thought when we find that Kitty Cooke, at Chesington, had been just as incredulous until she met d'Arblay (cf. *Wanderer*, iii. 202 and *Diary and Letters*, v. 200).

tive and a genius at comedy and never realized either the limitations that should have restrained her or the powers she should have developed. Her melodramatics and her heroics are painful, but as soon as she condescends to be comical she becomes a delightful companion. So in *The Wanderer* she tells a crazy tale that soon becomes in the highest degree fatiguing, and just here and there brightens its boredom with real fun. Nine-tenths of her characters, though she does not know it, are tiresomely mad, and the other one-tenth have to bear all the responsibility of maintaining the interest of the reader.

But what a cynic quiet little Fanny must all her life have been. Delighting, as she and her father and all the Burneys did, in 'the best society' (kings and queens; lords and ladies; statesmen and dignitaries of the church), they evidently realized that behind the more intellectual section of that society (their own, better section) there lay a mass of social pretence and heartlessness that merited the severest reproof—and if this book of Fanny's was read (but Leslie Stephen in the *Dictionary of National Biography* avers that it was 'never read by anybody') it may perhaps have done some good.

Over a century later, in the 1930's, there was a protracted correspondence in *The Times* about the thoughtlessness of well-to-do people who let their tradespeople wait for their money, never stopping to think that this 'time-lag' in payment must then be passed on to those who supply the tradespeople, and by them passed on again, so creating wide-spreading eddies of financial embarrassment and becoming a serious impediment to commerce. Fanny was something of a pioneer in calling attention to that evil, amongst others, and deserves credit for a kind heart and some courage.

Well, whether or not people read the book they bought it and perhaps that was the main thing. It was sold at what its authoress herself calls 'the rapacious price' of two guineas and in the end, apparently, she pocketed £3,000.[1]

The reviewers dropped on it heavily—especially Croker and Hazlitt. As the latter said (and Macaulay later said the same thing), the faults of the book seemed to come 'not from a decay of power but from a perversion of it'.[2] Her diary and her letters, to the very end, show that she could when she wanted write forceful, vivid English, yet sometimes, led astray by a desire for high dignity and grandeur, she degenerated into ridiculous pomposity and magniloquence. A very simple example,

[1] What became of all the many copies sold? Why should it now be so rare that the present writer, 120 years after the book's publication, had to pay five guineas for a copy? (And by the way, as supporting the statement of Leslie Stephen, the copy in question *did* bear evidence of never having been read until it came into the present owner's possession.)

[2] *Diary and Letters*, vi. 102 n.; Austin Dobson, *Fanny Burney*, &c. Hazlitt's account of it in the *Edinburgh Review* (Feb. 1815) was made by him an occasion for discussing all Fanny's fiction, and he did this in such a way that her brother James wrote him a letter definitely breaking off the acquaintance between them (G. E. Manwaring, *My Friend the Admiral*, 249).

here chosen for its brevity, occurs at i. 150. Fanny wishes to express the thought 'Easier said than done' but stretches it out into 'But the idea of this project had a facility of which its execution did not partake'. A longer example occurs at iii. 40, where she wants to express the idea that the public professional concert platform has its dangers for a young woman and that hence the person speaking means to remain a mere amateur; this becomes, under her florid pen:

> 'Much as I am enchanted with the art, I am not going to profess it! On the contrary, I think it so replete with dangers and improprieties, however happily they may sometimes be combatted by fortitude and integrity, that, when a young female, not forced by peculiar circumstances, or impelled by resistless genius, exhibits herself a willing candidate for public applause;—she must have, I own, other notions, or other nerves than mine!'

But these are mild. The stronger examples, of which there are hundreds, would take too much space for quotation here.

Long before *The Wanderer* appeared Boswell, in selecting passages from various prominent English writers to demonstrate the influence of Johnson's style, had (with satisfaction) included one from Fanny's *Cecilia*. To-day it reads as very mannered and stilted, for though Fanny, as Fanny, still arouses admiration, as a female Johnson she merely invites derision.

Whatever the defects of *The Wanderer* it was translated into French, for the Duchesse d'Angoulême pleased Fanny's husband by her statement that she was reading it in that language.[1] Apparently all Fanny's novels achieved the honour of translation into other languages, but on the bibliography of Fanny Burney the present writer can claim no special authority and by those better qualified than he the subject appears to have been neglected.

The Wanderer is Fanny's last novel—which is a good thing!

[1] *Diary and Letters*, vi. 134.

LXV. THE LONG LIFE ENDS

(12 April 1814; aged 88)

As the reader will have noticed, Burney all his life overworked and underslept in a most imprudent way. Of course, he had to pay the penalty and the wonder is that it was not a heavier one.

At times he suffered a good deal from rheumatism. As far back as 1775, when he was still under fifty, we find him complaining of this and telling Crisp that at the moment of writing 'not one straight finger have I on my right hand'—a statement confirmed by the character of the handwriting itself. This painful condition lasted some time—'Never, surely, was an attack more obstinate', says Fanny.[1] At this time he visited Buxton, Clay in Norfolk (for sea bathing), and also Bristol Hotwells.

Considering the date, it came as a momentary surprise to the present writer to find in a letter in his possession, written to Burney whilst he was suffering from this very obstinate and prolonged attack, by his country doctor friend Bewley, the suggestion, 'As you seem to have exhausted the common *Materia medica*, electricity sometimes presents itself to me as perhaps worthy of a trial', followed by a little discussion of the type of case in which it has been found of service. He adds that he had written on this subject in *The Monthly Review* in 1767. However, on reflection it was realized that the suggestion of electrical treatment, at this date, is not so remarkable. Electricity was 'in the air' during the 1760's and Bewley was only one of several who recommended its remedial use. See, for instance, the references to electricity in the index of the Standard Edition of John Wesley's *Journal*: Wesley used it as early as 1757, and in 1760 published a pamphlet on the subject.

In 1792 Fanny speaks of her father as ill and depressed (an unusual thing with him at this period). She told the King, who inquired about him, 'that all he had done of late to soothe his retirement and pain had been making canons to solemn words, and with such difficulties of composition as in better health and spirits would have rather proved oppressive and perplexing than a relief to his feelings'.[2] In 1793 he had feverish attacks of a nervous type. These were followed by an acute attack of his old malady, rheumatism, for which he took a course of Bath waters.[3] (Burke was then at Bath and Burney records with pleasure that he dined with him eight times.)

According to a French work of reference (*Biographie Universelle*; Paris, 1835; vol. lix), in 1793 several journals announced Burney's death and

[1] *Early Diary*, ii. 34, 45.
[2] *Diary and Letters*, v. 75.
[3] *D.N.B.*

'the most flattering expressions of regret broke out everywhere'. It may have been so.

In 1794 he was able to report to Fanny that he was in better health.[1]

In 1795 he was keeping his room with some other illness and for three months could not venture out of doors, and as soon as he was released became engaged in a turmoil ('engagements, scholars, printers, proofs, revises, etc., etc.') greater than even he could remember; but he had been born with a tough constitution, and, says he, 'the best part of the story is that I have been gathering strength and spirits through all this bustle faster than I did by nursing and enquiries after my own health'.

Throughout 1802–3 he was plagued by an unremitting cough. He got rid of it in the first of these years during a visit to Hampshire, but on return, walking up Richmond Hill with Hetty, 'What shd. I meet, *full butt*, on the way, but that curse of every Xtian. country within my beat, a N.E. wind wch. brought back, in its pestilential train my Cough, in a worse humour than when we parted, and now, being on the wrong side the port to expect any relief from a mild and balmy sky, I have every reason to fear that we shall have a Dog and Cat winter together.' In the second year his ever devoted friend, Mrs. Crewe (see pl. 37, II. 154), took him to Cheltenham, but he could get only four hours' sleep every night, so to drive off 'the foul fiend hypochondria' he spent the rest of each night in 'lexicographic labours' (making fair copies of his articles for the earlier letters of the alphabet of Rees's *Cyclopaedia*); naturally, then, he brought his malady back 'in nearly the same state as I took it out'.[2]

In 1804 he had a bad attack of influenza, and henceforth, he says, 'dreaded cold and night air as much as they are dreaded by a trembling Italian greyhound'.[3] Perhaps it was on account of this illness, as also because his eyes and ears were becoming less sharp, that he now dropped teaching—getting rid of his carriage. Next year he spent a good deal of time in his bedroom. He found his memory now somewhat failing.

In 1806, about the time that Burney finished his trying labours as Cyclopaedist, he was cheered by the award of a Government pension of £200 a year.[4] For the initial steps in securing him this solace, he had to thank his friend Lady Crewe (her husband had this year been raised to the peerage), whom, sixty years earlier, when she was Baby Greville, he had held at the font down in Wiltshire; who, ever since she came to years of discretion, had shown her deep affection for him; and who in his old age abounded in kindnesses, caring for him almost like a daughter. She, it seems, had put the suggestion to another warm friend of Burney's, Windham (see pl. 37, II. 154).

[1] *Diary and Letters*, v. 238.

[2] Bodleian MS. Add. C 89, fol. 4, and MS. Malone 38, fol. 131.

[3] *Mem.* iii. 369.

[4] Later, apparently, increased to the somewhat odd sum of £248. See note on his Will, II. 272.

Amongst the Windham Papers in the British Museum is the draft of a letter Windham sent on his behalf to some person in authority. From its opening words it must have been written about 1802, but it was not until 1806 that it took effect. It does not minimize Burney's financial distresses which, to judge from his Will (see II. 264), can surely not have been as serious as here laid down.

'He is about 76 years of age, well and hearty during *some* Months in the year but often laid up in the winter by the most severe Rheumatism!—he is acknowledged to be at the head of his profession, and has been noticed by *all* the *Royal* Family in the *most flattering manner* and several of the first Ministers in various administrations have declared to me and to *many other Persons* that they had it truly at heart to serve so honest and ingenious a Man, but here he is, *obliged* still to teach little Misses their Gammut *for bread*!—all he possesses in the world besides the money he had earned, is an Appart. in Chelsea College which saves him House rent,—Mr. Burke appointed him Organist of that place and the salary of it just pays for the Chaplain's Rooms, and while he had a large family to Lodge, he found this a very great Convenience, and the Air still suits his Constitution, but the distance of Chelsea from London makes it *necessary* for him to pay for a Carriage and Horses and the expence of these, with the *Income tax* &tc, &tc, have now almost weighed him *quite* down!—he never *complains* but his *Confidential Friends* know but *too well* what his situation is, and wd. to Heaven there cd. be some relief!—£200 a year wd. make him quite *rich*, at least it wd. allow him to get some sleep which he cannot do at this time! he told me yesterday evng. that he got up every Morg. at five o'clock lately to finish a musical work [his work on Rees's *Cyclopaedia*: see II. 186] on which he hopes to get a little money for this year, and in all the *heat* of yesterday he was forced to go to five places to teach scholars ! ! !'

This rather strikes one as 'telling the tale'. It is likely that in a missing portion of this document Windham developed his case on the sounder grounds of the definite services Burney had rendered. The old man had, in his time, certainly advanced the cause of musical scholarship by the publication of his two books of travel, his enormous *History*, his book on Handel and the Handel Commemoration, and his *Life and Letters of Metastasio*; moreover, his articles for the *Cyclopaedia*, though not yet before the public, were known to be in preparation. As a music teacher he had had through his hands hundreds of the young females of the aristocracy, some of whom presumably had now become supporters of musical institutions and activities. He had been interested in all worthy operatic enterprises and one of the first promoters and warmest adherents of the Antient (or 'King's') Concert. Apart from music, he was one of the few remaining links with the circle of Johnson (who had enjoyed a similar pension), and, as such, an object of veneration to the lovers of literature. He was the father of a family that had distinguished itself in exploration, classical learning, and the art of the novelist. He was, too, a known patriot and—a good Tory!

His eightieth year was about to close when the happy news reached him in his chamber, to which he had long been confined, and his long letter of thanks to Lady Crewe, dated 18 April 1806, concluded:

'The warmth of the weather to day, and of your friendly heart, have enabled me to think of quitting my bedchamber in order to travel across the cold library into the parlour, where I shall now be most happy in the honour of a call from you any day you will have the goodness to name, Dearest Madam.

Your most devoted
Obliged and Affectionate Servant
The Octogenarian
Chas. Burney
born Apr. 7th O.S. 1726.'[1]

In this same year of 1806 he spent some time at the Bristol Hotwells (i.e. Clifton)—to 'do my cough good and enable me to bear the ensuing winter more heroically than I have done what preceded it'. He and his young companion, his granddaughter, Fanny Phillips, re-read, as they travelled, the now twenty-eight years old *Evelina*, the scene of which is partly laid in the city to which they were bound, and they then tried to get *Cecilia* from the library, but were disappointed as it was always out—a pretty good testimony to the popularity of a novel published a quarter of a century earlier.[2] This jaunt seemed to do him good, but three days after return to Chelsea, on Michaelmas Day, he reports:

'I had an alarming seizure in my left hand, which neither heat, friction, nor medicines could subdue. It felt perfectly asleep; in a state of immoveable torpor. My medical friends would not tell me what this obstinate numbness was; but I discovered by their prescriptions, and advice as to regimen, that it was neither more nor less than a paralytic affection; and, near Christmas, it was pronounced to be a Bath case.

'On Christmas eve, I set out for that City, extremely weak and dispirited: the roads terrible, and almost incessant torrents of rain all the way. I was five days on the journey; I took Fanny Phillips with me, and we had excellent apartments on the South Parade, which is always warm when any sun shines. I put myself under the care of Dr. Parry, who, having resided, and practised physic at Bath more than forty years, must, *caeteris paribus*, know the virtues and vices of Bath waters better than the most renowned physicians in London. To give them fair play, I remained three months in this City; and I found my hand much more alive, and my general health very considerably amended. But I caught so violent a fresh cold in my journey home, that it was called what the French style a *Fluxion de poitrine*, and I was immediately confined to my bed at Chelsea, and unable to eat, sleep, or speak. Strict starvation was then ordered; but softened off into fish and asparagus as soon as possible, by our wise and good Æsculapius, Sir Walter Farquhar: and

[1] Letter of Burney to Lady Crewe in Windham Papers, vol. lxxv. British Museum Add. MS. 37916, fol. 16. It is given in full at II. 306 of the present work.

[2] *Mem.* iii. 369.

now I am allowed poultry and game, under certain restrictions, and find myself tolerably well again.'

It sounds as though Burney had had a 'stroke'. Fortunately that was the first and last. 'The Sword of Damocles', as he mournfully declared, 'seemed eternally waving over his head', but it never fell. We see from the date of his Will (12 Jan. 1807) that he made it at Bath during this visit.[1]

In his latest years Burney took to sparing himself more than he had done ('Till dinner he lies in bed with a little establishment of desks and books to read and write'), but when he was eighty-two he outwalked his daughter Charlotte in Kensington Gardens.

The year 1810 seems to have been an oasis-year in Burney's long-stretching desert of ill health. That was a year when, as we have seen, he was able to get into touch again with his exiled Fanny, and he wrote to her in June:

'With regard to my own health, I shall say nothing of past sufferings of various kinds since my last ample family letter; except that "Here I am", in spite of the old gentleman and his scythe. And the few people I am able to see, ere the warm weather, tell me I look better, speak better, and walk better than I did "ever so long ago". God knows how handsome I shall be by-and-by:—but you will allow it behoves the fair ladies who make me a visit now and then, to take care of themselves! That's all.

'People wonder, secluded as I am for ever from the world and its joys, how I can *cut a joke and be silly*: but when I have no serious sufferings, a book, or a pen, makes me forget all the world, and even myself; the best of all oblivions.'

His eyes, for which he had feared, came to be in a good state again, for when Fanny was back with him in 1812, her son records, 'Mama went to Chelsea this morning, and there found Grandpapa stout and well, and reading to her a small print without spectacles in a dark room.'[2] As for some years his letters had alluded to his extreme difficulty in reading and writing, and as reading and writing made up a large part of his daily occupation this recovery must have been a very welcome miracle.

[1] Ibid. 381–3. The attack of paralysis is also described in letters to Malone of Nov. 1806 (Bodleian, Malone MS. 38, fols. 133 and 135). Sir Walter Farquhar's prescription was Mustard Seed twice a day and pedestrian exercise, and as winter was now coming on Burney says, 'When I cannot go out I shall walk a mile or two by a pedometer in my own apartments.'

Dr. Parry, of Bath, was a friend of Charles Burney junior, who wrote a letter recommending his father to his care (now the property of Dr. G. B. Harrison, of King's College, London; communicated to me by Dr. L. F. Powell, of Oxford).

Burney's Bath cure was certainly not assisted by the news of a mishap that occurred to a part of the manuscript of his work which he had sent to the publishers, Longman & Co.: 'The sad calamity of their mislaying the Letter C. of the Cyclopaedia; but I trust it will be found, as there is no doubt it was left at the house.' (Letter of Fanny Phillips to her uncle, Charles Burney, Junior, 4 Feb. 1807, in the possession of the present writer; from this letter it is apparent that Burney had not only his niece with him at Bath, but also his daughter, Charlotte—Mrs. Broome. See also Burney's letter to his son Charles, on II. 311.)

[2] W. Wright Roberts, *Charles and Fanny Burney in the Light of the New Thrale Correspondence in the John Rylands Library*, 18–19.

At last the time arrived when Burney felt that to mount the staircase to his room in Chelsea Hospital had become too much for him and he resolved to go out no more:

'The height of his apartments, which were but just beneath the attic of the tall and noble Chelsea College, had been an evil when he grew into years, from the fatigue of mounting and descending; but from the time of his dejected resolve to go forth no more, that height became a blessing, from the greater purity of the air that he inhaled, and the wider prospect that, from some of his windows, he surveyed.

'To his bed-chamber, however, which he chiefly inhabited, this good did not extend: its principal window faced the burying-ground in which the remains of the second Mrs. Burney were interred; and that melancholy sight was the first that every morning met his eyes. And, however his strength of mind might ward off its depressing effect, while still he went abroad, and mingled with the world; from the time that it became his sole prospect, that no change of scene created a change of ideas must inevitably, however silently, have given a gloom to his mind, from that of his [own] position.'[1]

We approach now the fall of the curtain. He remarked to Fanny, one day: 'I have gone through so rough a winter, and such severity of bodily pain; and I have held up against such intensity of cold, that I think now, I can stand anything!'

For three or four days after this, Fanny, who with her son was lodging in Chenies Street, Tottenham Court Road, was kept away from her father by business, and then she sent her son to see how he was getting on and to tell him that she was coming to see him later in the day. Alexander returned at once with a disquieting report, and Fanny rushed off to Chelsea.

'I found the beloved invalid seated, in his customary manner, on his sofa. My sister Sarah was with him, and his two faithful and favourite attendants, George and Rebecca. In the same customary manner, also, a small table before him was covered with books. But he was not reading. His revered head, as usual, hung upon his breast—and I, as usual, knelt before him, to catch a view of his face, while I inquired after his health.

'But alas!—no longer as usual was my reception! He made no sort of answer; his look was fixed, his posture immoveable, and not a muscle of his face gave any indication that I was either heard or perceived!

'Struck with awe, I had not courage to press for his notice, and hurried into the next room not to startle him with my alarm.

'But when I was informed that he had changed his so fearfully fixed posture I hastened back, reviving to the happy hope that again I might experience the balm of his benediction.

'He was now standing, and unusually upright, and, apparently, with unusual muscular firmness. I was advancing to embrace him, but his air spoke a rooted concentration of solemn ideas that repelled intrusion.

'Whether or not he recognized or distinguished me I know not! I had no

[1] *Mem.* iii. 411.

command of voice to attempt any inquiry, and would not risk betraying my emotion at this great change since my last and happier admittance to his presence.

'His eyes were intently bent on a window that faced the College burial-ground, where reposed the ashes of my mother-in-law [stepmother], and where, he had more than once said, would repose his own.

'He bestowed at least five or six minutes on this absorbed and melancholy contemplation of the upper regions of that sacred spot that so soon were to enclose for ever his mortal clay.

'No one presumed to interrupt his reverie.

'He next opened his arms wide, extending them with a waving motion that seemed indicative of an internally pronounced farewell! to all he looked at; and shortly afterwards he uttered to himself, distinctly though in a low but deeply-impressive voice, "All this will soon pass away as a dream!"'[1]

His attendants seized the opportunity of his attitude with arms extended to draw off his dressing-gown, and put him to bed.

Next morning, 11 April 1814, there was glorious news. Napoleon had abdicated! That evening, as Fanny watched by the bedside, she says, 'The brilliance of mounting rockets and distant fire-works caught my eyes, to perceive, from the window, the whole apparent sky illuminated to commemorate our splendid success.'

All night she continued to sit beside her father, and when morning dawned waited for an opportunity to call his attention to the happy events which had just occurred:

'But when I entered into the marvellous details of the Wellington victories, by which the immortal contest had been brought to its crisis; and told him that Buonaparte was dethroned, was in captivity, and was a personal prisoner on board an English man-of-war, a raised motion of his under lip displayed incredulity; and he turned away his head with an air that shewed him persuaded that I was the simple and sanguine dupe of some delusive exaggeration. I did not dare risk the excitement of convincing him of his mistake!'

Burney's children gathered round him and his son Charles administered such spiritual consolation and preparation as a dying man's condition permitted. In the afternoon Burney became tranquil and as evening advanced fell quietly asleep.

'An awful stillness thence pervaded the apartment, and so soft became his breathing, that I dropped my head by the side of his pillow, to be sure that he breathed at all! There, anxiously, I remained, and such was my position when his faithful man-servant, George, after watchfully looking at him from the foot of his bed, suddenly burst into an audible sob, crying out, "My master!—my dear master!"

'I started and rose, making agitated signs for forbearance, lest the precious rest, from which I still hoped he might awake recruited, should prematurely be broken.

'The poor young man hid his face, and all again was still.

[1] Ibid. 425.

'For a moment, however, only; an alarm from his outcry had been raised, and the servants, full of sorrow, hurried into the chamber, which none of the family that could assemble ever quitted, and a general lamentation broke forth.

'Yet could I not believe that all had ceased thus suddenly, without a movement—without even a sigh! and, conjuring that no one would speak or interfere, I solemnly and steadily persisted in passing a full hour, or more, in listening to catch again a breath I could so reluctantly lose: but all of life—of earthly life, was gone for ever!'

A week later Burney's remains were placed beside those of his wife in the spot which he had so often regarded from his window. James and Charles 'walked as chief mourners' and the leading pall-bearers were their father's friends, the Hon. Frederick North (the future Earl of Guilford, son of George III's Prime Minister, Lord North, and famous both as a very efficient Governor of Ceylon and as an outstanding Greek scholar and Philhellene), and the great impresario, Salomon (who had been instrumental in bringing Burney's beloved Haydn to England, and who had the year before been active in promoting our still-enduring Philharmonic Society).

The others, according to *The Gentleman's Magazine*, were 'Sir G. Beaumont, Dr. Moseley, Mr. Townsend and Mr. Rogers, the poet'. I take 'Sir G. Beaumont' to be Sir George Howland Beaumont, Bt., the painter and patron of painters (1753–1827), one of the Reynolds circle which Burney had frequented—the Beaumont who is famous for his dictum that 'a good picture, like a good fiddle, should be brown' and 'there ought to be a brown tree in every landscape'. 'Dr. Moseley' was undoubtedly Benjamin Moseley, M.D. (1742–1819), physician to Chelsea Hospital, and the celebrated surgeon, 'a large number of whose patients died of tetanus'. 'Mr. Townsend' was probably a younger son of General Lord Townshend, Burney's old friend of his Lynn days and for a short period Governor of Chelsea Hospital (see I. 71). Rogers, the banker-poet, remained to the end a friend of Fanny Burney.

Thus were the worlds of letters, science, painting, and music very appropriately represented in this last scene.

LXVI. BURNEY'S WILL AND HIS MEMORIAL

THE Will Burney left behind him is an interesting and even touching document. It has been copied for the present book at Somerset House,[1] and seems to be worth reproduction *in extenso*. It was made at Bath in January 1807 during the visit mentioned on II. 256 and was subsequently altered here and there as one or two changes in the family affairs made necessary.[2] The care the old man took, not only to deal justly with his children and other relatives, but also to make clear to them the principles upon which he acted, will be observed. He was eighty when he made the Will, and in a very weak state of health, and did not, perhaps, express himself very coherently or systematically. The original document is one solid mass of writing, without a full stop or a comma from beginning to end (in this latter respect conforming to the strange legal convention which is still observed by English solicitors). In reproducing it, punctuation, paragraphing, and head-lines have been freely introduced, as conducing to easier reading, and some footnotes have been added.

Bath. South Parade, 5
Jany. 12th, 1807.

The Longevity in which it has pleased God to allow me my feeble state, and the rapid encrease of my infirmities, render it necessary to settle my affairs, for which gloomy task I have had little leisure or inclination to set about since the death of my dear wife, Elizabeth, in 1796, though the births and deaths in my own Family, the events and vicissitudes in my own life since that period, render a new arrangement absolutely necessary. Be it therefore understood by my Family and executors that I, Charles Burney, Doctor in Music and Fellow of the Royal Society, do make and publish this to be my last Will and Testament, bearing date, at Bath, January 12th, 1807, written with my own hand and sealed with my own seal, by which, annulling all former Wills, I bequeath—

A. DISPOSITION OF HIS MONEY

(1) To Children by First Wife.

To my eldest daughter, Esther Burney, the sum of one thousand Pounds, five per cent. Navy.

To my second daughter, Frances d'Arblay, do.

[1] Reference indication, '202 Bridport'—Bridport being the name of the Registrar of the Prerogative Court of Canterbury at the time the Will was proved.

[2] As to those corrections—It was the Wills Act, 1837 (7 Will. IV and 1 Vict. c. 26), that imposed the formalities still in force for the making of valid Wills. Before that, considerable latitude of execution, attestation, and alteration was allowed in Doctors' Commons. Preceding Burney's Will is an Affidavit by his son, Charles (18 April 1814), concerning the alterations in it.

To my Grand daughter, FRANCES PHILLIPS, daughter of the deceased and much beloved Susan Phillips, the third daughter by my first marriage, one thousand one hundred pounds. Having been bereaved of my dear daughter, Susan Phillips, Jany. 6th, 1800, who died at Park Gate,[1] and who so much wished to be an inmate with me when she could be spared by her family, I have in a manner adopted my Grand daughter aforesaid as heiress to my affection and designs in her mother's favor, and this as a Portion, her Father's affairs by his second marriage, and their previous deplorable state, having rendered it impossible for him to make that provision for the children of his first wife to which they were entitled.[2] I wish I could do more for this dear Grand daughter but treating her as my own Child was all I could fairly do without injuring my daughters Esther and Frances, her Aunts.

I bequeath to my fourth daughter by my first marriage, CHARLOTTE BROOME, Two hundred Pounds. This was my intention at the decease of the worthy Mr. Clement Francis,[3] as it was always my wish to proportion my female family bequests to the wants of my Children, and Charlotte, being left in possession of a certain and ample dowry for herself and considerable improving fortune to her Children during their minority, she was in no want of parental assistance, and her second marriage has not altered my Opinion.

To my eldest son, CAPTAIN JAMES BURNEY of the Royal Navy, I leave Two hundred Pounds and the same Sum to my second Son the REVEREND CHARLES BURNEY, of Greenwich, F.R.S. and LL.D.

(2) TO CHILDREN BY SECOND WIFE.

To my Son RICHARD, of Kiddapore, I bequeathed Two hundred Pounds, and to his sister, SARAH, One thousand Pounds and one hundred Pounds more for a wedding Garment if ever she marries. The Legacy to my Son Richard was intended to be paid immediately after my decease, but he died at Rangoon 1808. The Sum would have been more considerable was he not, at the death of his Mother, Heir to the house in Lynn Regis, called the Rookery, left to him by his Grand mother, the late Mrs. Elizabeth Allen of that place, and to my daughter Sarah; this was all settled entirely to the satisfaction of all parties at the death of Mrs. Allen of the Rookery and on the decease of my second Wife, Elizabeth, by her brother Mr. Maxey Allen, Executor to his Mother.

[1] See II. 147.

[2] This granddaughter, Fanny Phillips, within the next year or so became Mrs. C. Raper (letter of Burney to Malone; Bodleian, Malone MS. 38, fol. 143). Her father, Major Phillips, as we have seen (II. 142–8), though a hero in the South Seas, was not, when at home, a man of much judgement, prudence, or even principle (at all events during one phase of his career), and it is likely that the Irish estate he inherited involved him in more loss than gain.

[3] See II. 240.

(3) To his Sister.

To my dear Sister, Rebecca Burney,[1] of Richmond in Surry, I leave the rent of my house in York Street, Covent Garden, now let to Mr. John Hanon for Twenty seven Pounds a year nett, he paying Ground Rent, Taxes, and Repairs, and if my Niece, Letitia Brooke,[2] survive her Aunt, whom she has long nursed with great care and affection, I wish the said Rent may be continued to her during her life till the lease is expired, and afterwards the same annuity to be paid to her by my daughters, Esther, Frances, Sarah, and Grand daughter, Fanny Phillips.

(4) To Grandchildren.

To all my Grand Children severally I bequeath One hundred Pounds each namely—

5 daughters and one son of my eldest daughter, Esther:	6
of my eldest son, James:	2
of my second daughter, Frances:	1
of my third daughter, Susan:	3
of my second son, Doctor Charles:	1
of my son Richard, offspring of my second Marriage:	8
	21

(5) To Children of his Brother Richard.

To the above bequests, confined entirely to my children and Grand children, I wish to leave a testimony of my affection to one Nephew, the modest and ingenious Mr. Edward Burney, and to three Nieces, namely the worthy Mrs. Hawkins,[3] widow of the late Revd. [blank] Hawkins, Elizabeth Burney,[4] Spinster, and Mrs. Sandford,[5] Wife of [blank] Sandford Esquire, of Worcester, to each of whom I bequeath one hundred Pounds.

(6) To Servants.

It is hoped that the Residue of my Stock in the five per cent. Navy, after the above bequests are paid, will cover the few debts I may leave unpaid and my Funeral Expences, together with thirty Guineas to each of my female Servants, namely Rebecca More, my Cook, who has served me with probity and diligence eleven [altered to '13'] years. [The following passage in the original is here marked to be deleted—'and Lucy Band, who has taken care of my books, paid my bills, acted as Woman to Fanny Phillips, my Grand daughter, and attended me during my last illness with care and tenderness'.] To my boy, George, but lately come to me, Six Guineas and a year's wages.[6]

[1] She died before the Will came into effect. See II. 34.
[2] Not traced.
[3] Ann, Hannah, or Nancy Burney. See II. 42.
[4] Elizabeth Warren Burney. See II. 42.
[5] Rebecca Burney. See II. 42.
[6] For Rebecca, the cook, and George, the boy, see II. 258, 259.

(7) Sum of Money Available.

Though at present I have only £7,800 in the Funds, yet if I live to return to Chelsea I shall leave in my Banker's hands, in arrears of Salaries, Pension, and Jany. dividend at the Bank, more than sufficient to complete the Sum in the Funds mentioned above.

B. DISPOSITION OF HIS OTHER EFFECTS, ETC.

(1) The Miscellaneous Books.

(with certain exceptions)

I shall now proceed to specify my other effects and the manner in which, and to whom, I wish to distribute them—

The miscellaneous books in various languages (particular books hereafter excepted) in my Library, Parlour, Bed-Room, Lockers, Back room, and passage presses, it is my wish that they should be disposed of, entire or by auction, for the profit of my two Eldest Daughters, as they shall themselves amicably settle, the produce of which all to be divided equally between them.

(2) Residuary Legatees.

Item: It is my wish that my two Eldest Daughters by my dear first Wife be my residuary Legatees and have an equal share in such of my property as, when my debts, Funeral Expences, and legacies are paid, shall remain.

(3) Appointment of Executors.

I have long denied myself many comforts and enjoyments to avoid breaking into my savings, and constantly lived on the interest of my money in the Funds, by my Scholars, and (after I ceased teaching) by my Pen, in order to leave some solid memorial of my affection for my Children, Grand Children, and other relations, endeavouring to dispose of my Property so equitably and conscientiously (to the best of my judgement) that my Children shall have no cause to complain of my partiality or prejudice, and I have such an Opinion of their rectitude and affection for each other that it seems to me unnecessary to appoint Executors. However, as I am informed that such an appointment is necessary lest difficulties and litigation should arise, I hereby appoint as my Executors and Trustees my two eldest Sons, Captain James, of the Royal Navy, and Doctor Charles, of Greenwich, more to assist their Sisters with their advice how best to act and make the most of the Property I have bequeathed them than to be a check upon their inclinations.

(4) Books on Music.

With respect to my books in various languages on the Art and Science of Music, chiefly set apart in the closet of my Library, with others on the same subject that will be found among the Miscellaneous books (particularly on the shelves of D in the Parlour), I began to make a Catalogue 'raisonné' pointing out each author's intention, or at least his promises in the title page and degree of success in the execution, and had advanced through the Greek, Latin, Italian, and part of the French Tracts and Treatises previous to my engagement to write for the new Cyclopaedia, for which I have made use of some of the Articles.

It is my wish that all the books, tracts, and treatises on the particular Faculty of Music (many of which are very scarce) should be separated from those on all other subjects and disposed of together to some liberal collector or public library for the advantage of my two eldest daughters, ESTHER AND FRANCES. But on this subject I shall leave instructions to my son Charles, who will, I doubt not, with alacrity endeavour to fulfill my intentions for the advantage of his sisters, who in such a transaction will be unable to act for themselves.

(5) CERTAIN SPECIAL BOOKS.

I bequeath to my SON CHARLES, Walther's Lexicon Diplomaticum Fol°, a book of wch. I have never seen another copy, together with all such Classics and splendid editions of learned and scientific books of which he is not already in possession as are in the glazed book-case standing in the parlour of my Apartments at Chelsea, chiefly given to me by my late worthy and dear friend, John Hayes Esquire, but the models and coins contained in the drawers of the said Case I bequeath to my GRANDSON CHARLES,[1] now a Student at Oxford, with the Book Case itself. But such books in the above mentioned Book Case as my Son Charles, his father, may already possess I bequeath to my daughter, FRANCES D'ARBLAY, and my Grandson, ALEXANDER D'ARBLAY.

(6) BEQUESTS TO TWO OLD FRIENDS.

To my dear and honoured Friend through life, LADY CREWE, I bequeath my Nephew Edward's Copy of Sir Joshua Reynolds's Sleeping Child, over the Parlour fire place, of which her Ladyship has often expressed admiration. Of the books lent to Lady Crewe for her villa at Hampstead I beg her Ladyship to accept any that she particularly wishes to retain except Malone's Shakespeare, of which, though an excellent edition in other respects, she thinks the type too small. I therefore bequeath that set of books to my daughter Sarah, and any other of the duplicates lent to Lady Crewe which she does not wish to retain.

To LADY BRUCE, with whose constant regard and partiality I have been honoured ever since her days of adolescence, I bequeath the most beautiful book that the Parma press can boast, in point of typography and embellishments from antique gems, of which only 25 Copies were

[1] Charles Parr Burney; see II. 276.

printed before the plates were destroyed. This rare and most elegant work was presented to me by my Friend, Pachierotti [?]. Its title is [blank].

(7) Various Portraits and Prints.

To my daughter Mrs. d'Arblay I bequeath the original Portrait of my Friend, and the friend of my Family in all its branches, Samuel Crisp Esq. of Chesington in Surry, painted by my Nephew, Edward Burney. His excellent Copy of Mr. Lawrence's excellent Portrait of Mr. Lock of Norbury Park,[1] whom I and my whole Family have ever revered, which is placed over the door of my Parlour, is the property of my Grand daughter Phillips,[2] having been painted for her Father, Col. Phillips, by my nephew.

The 42 prints, framed and glazed, most of them presents from my friend Sir Robert Strange,[3] which for want of room in my apartments have been lodged in an upper room of Chelsea College, I bequeath to my most worthy and meritorious Nephew, Mr. Edwd. Burney, to be sold or kept by him as he shall chuse.

(8) His own Compositions.

A great number of Manuscript Fugues and pieces for the Organ, many of them composed so late as the Sumr. of 1791, to amuse me during confinement by indisposition, will be found among my papers. These I bequeath to the care of my worthy Nephew and Son in law, Mr. Charles R. Burney of John Street. Perhaps he may find 10 or 12 among the most modern not unworthy to be printed as a second Book to my organ Pieces already published in a pocket form for young organists.[4]

To my Grandson, The Reverend Richard Burney, of Kimpton Sherbourne, Dorset, eldest Son of Charles R. Burney, it was my intention during his youth to bequeath my large Fol° MS. book of Voluntaries, some of which were composed more than 50 years ago, but there are Fugues and other pieces more modern in the book and the whole might perhaps have served as a Study for Organ playing in the old grave and voluntary style, or at least as a memento of his old Grand father. But this Grandson has long out-grown such old-fashioned Studies and can play extempore and compose for himself and others more modern and better music. My Nephew, his father, may therefore do with the book what he pleases. If put among the books on sale it may perhaps find a purchaser.

[1] See II. 129.
[2] Frances Phillips. See II. 262.
[3] See I. 134.
[4] See I. 60. (They never were printed.)

(9) His Collection of Printed and Manuscript Music.

My Collection of Music, printed and manuscript, I wish to be sold by auction. It was most of it good in its day, though now some of it is out of fashion, but there are many curious scarce and excellent compositions for voices such as the [blank] works of Carissimi, Stradella, Colonna, Steffani, Clari, Motetti di Bassani, Leo, Alessandro Scarlatti, Durante, Jomelli, Perez, Galuppi, and Sacchini, and, for instruments, the entire works of Tartini, printed and MS. of [illegible—? Domenico] Scarlatti, Sebastian and Emanuel Bach, Schobert, nearly all the works of Haydn, Mozart, and Beethoven.

To these may be added a Legacy of the late Lady Mary Duncan,[1] of the Operas, in Score MS., composed by Perez for the Court of Lisbon in the years 1752, 3 and 4, in 31 Vols. 4to., superbly bound in Red Morocco, lettered and Gilt. These Operas were performed by the greatest Singers of the Italian School in Europe previous to the Earthquake in 1755. The sale of this Music I should suppose would be very productive, as much of it is only to be found in my Collection, but among my most curious MSS. will be found 20 works by the most renowned Old Masters, from Palestrina to Marcello's Salmi in 8 vol. ffol^{o}., original Venice Edition. These are invaluable not only from their scarcity but excellence.

(10) A Remembrance for General d'Arblay.

To my worthy Son in Law, Alexander d'Arblay Esq., I bequeath my new and General Biographical Dictionary in 12 Vol^{s}. 8vo.

(11) The History of Music.

The remaining copies in sheets of the 4 Vols. in 4to. of my general Hist^{y}. of Music, of which the frontispieces and ornamental plates, many impressions, will be found in a drawer of my bedroom, and the plates themselves in the bureau of the parlour glass book case marked E, and I think if the Pewter Plates of Music, which have been so injured by the Robinson's[2] Warehouse Men and miserably reprinted by an ignorant

[1] See II. 80.

[2] Presumably G. Robinson, of Paternoster Row, one of the booksellers who figures on the title-page of the *History*. In a letter to Malone a little later (23 June 1807—or possibly 1808) Burney says:

'I have been extremely occupied for some days past abt. the removal of the remaining letter-press copies of my Histy. wch. have lain in a hopeless state in a lumber-room ever since the Bankruptcy of the Robinsons—no impressions of plates to be found for another copy, as I believe I have told you more than once—the music plates seemed all spoiled by being put by in so dirty and damaged a state—and were so worn out and ill used that new good impressions from them cd. never be more obtained. But we have lately been told of a method to dissolve the obdurate Iron in the black notes of the Music Plates (wch. are of Pewter and stampt, not engraved) by a Lexyvium of Soap Lee or Lye and Fern Ashes. My Nephew has had 2 or 3 boild in this liquor and impressions taken from [them] as distinct and perfect as in the first Edition of my Histy. so that I am meditating a new edition of all the

person unused to the work, were to be restamped the expence would soon be made good by the Sale of the Work at six Guineas a Set, at least as far as the remaining Copies of the 2d. vol. go, and in time would enable the Proprietor of the work to reprint the 2d. Vol. intire which has long wanted a 2d. Edit. This work I leave to my Son DR. CHARLES, who, being a man of Letters accustomed to the press and bibliopolieto [?], will know best not only how to preserve the credit of the work, which has cost me so much money in procuring materials and more than 30 years labour in digesting them, but how to turn it to some advantage to himself.

(12) WORKS OF HANDEL, PIRANESI, AND LEONARDO DA VINCI.

Arnold's edition of Handel's works on large Paper to be disposed of for the profit of my two Nephews, MR. CHAS. R. BURNEY and MR. EDWD. BURNEY, his Brother.

To my ingenious, worthy, and too modest Nephew, EDWARD BURNEY I likewise bequeath my Piranesi views of Rome[1] and the ffol°. edit. of Leonardo da Vinci's Art of Painting.

(13) FRENCH BOOKS—INNOCENT AND DANGEROUS.

To my daughter, SARAH, and my Grand daughter, FRANCES PHILLIPS, I bequeath the French books in the Glass Book Case of my Parlour marked E, except the works of Voltaire many of which are unfit for the perusal of Females, and Bolingbrokes Philosophical works,[2] if they have any respect for the Christian religion. The book case itself I bequeath to my said GRAND DAUGHTER PHILLIPS and one of the glazed book cases in my bed room to my daughter SARAH.

(14) PIANOFORTES.

My large Piano Forte with additional keys at the top and bottom, originally made by Merlin, with a Compass of six Octaves, the first that was ever constructed, expressly at my desire, for duets à Quatre Mains, in 1777,[3] I bequeath to my ['Grand' deleted] daughter ['Phillips' deleted] ESTHER, to keep or to sell, and to my daughter SARAH I bequeath my small Piano Forte made by Broadwood, with additional keys in the Treble, an excellent instrument for a small room, chosen out

Plates, Copper by Bartolozzi and Cipriani, as well as Pewter.' (British Museum, Malone MS. 38, fol. 161.)

There is an earlier allusion to the trouble with the Robinson firm in a letter of November 1804 to a Mrs. Blore, of Ashford, Bakewell, Derbyshire. In this Burney complains, 'I have not a single complete set of my Hist. Mus., the labour of 30 years, and near £7000 expense in printing, fit for use or sale.'

[1] The gift of Piranesi himself. See I. 175, and pl. 13, I. 174.

[2] Cf. the conversation on Bolingbroke, between Burney and Johnson, on I. 94. Apparently Burney possessed some of the works which had originally appeared in French or some of the French translations of those which had originally appeared in English.

[3] See II. 203.

of a great number: this will probably be more convenient to Sarah as, while a Spinster, it is to be feared that she will not be rich enough to afford an Apartment sufficiently spacious to contain so unwieldy an instrument as that by Broadwood in the Merlin Case and, moreover, Sarah is no lesson player.[1]

(15) A Special Heirloom.

My Silver Standish, a present from the late Earl of Macartney for providing his Excellency a Military Band, an organ, books, and other matters in his embassy to China, in which I had such pleasure that I refused all remuneration from his Lordship and the India Company, on whom he would have drawn for such a Sum as he supposed professionally I deserved, but, proud of his Lordship's long acquaintance and confidential Attachment, I positively refused all pecuniary reward. When taking my leave I found in my Carriage this honorable testimony of his regard, which he has kindly expressed in an elegant Latin Inscription on the Standish itself—Carolo Burney, Mus. Doctor hocce minusculum amicitiae pignori dono dedit Georgius Dominus Vice Comes Macartney, 1792. This flattering expression of friendship from such an eminent and accomplished nobleman I bequeath to my Son Charles and his descendants, to be preserved in the Family.[2]

(17) A Portrait of Handel.

My half length Picture of Handel, painted by Wolfgang at Hanover in the year 1710, where he stopt at the Elector's Court (afterwards Geo. the first, King of England) on his way from Italy to London, this portrait I intended to present to the Concert of Ancient Music, if the noble directors would have done me the honour to accept of it as a mark of respect for that Establishment and for the great master whose unrivalled excellence has so justly endeared him to the Nation, as it is the best picture of him and must have a strong resemblance in his 24th year when it was painted. Mrs. Delany, who saw him the first year of his arrival, to whom this portrait was shewn, said no resemblance on canvas could be stronger,[3] and Sir Joshua Reynolds, when he saw it, said that he was sure it was like, as it was not a made up face.[4]

[1] 'Lesson' was the seventeenth- and eighteenth-century term for a Suite of Pieces. What Burney probably means is that Sarah did not play what some of her kind to-day would call 'classical music', but merely strummed a little to amuse herself.

[2] It *is* so preserved, being now in the possession of the Misses Burney, descendants in the direct line from Dr. Burney, and daughters of the fifth Charles Burney in succession. It is described as 'a charming silver inkstand with two bottles and a container for sand'. A water-colour, by Wilde, of the Library of Charles Burney junior, shows Reynolds's portrait of his father on the wall and this standish on the table.

[3] Mrs. Delany was an early friend of Handel. See II. 18.

[4] Apparently Burney, in this clause, merely puts on record an offer which had been refused. Why it was refused we cannot tell, but the suggestion of the clause seems to be that of defence against unkind reflections that had been made as to the value of the picture as a

(18) Remembrances for his Physician.

To Sir Walter Farquhar a Print on large Paper of my head, and a Ring I wish may be presented at my decease, as a small testimony of my regard and sense of his liberal and voluntary kindness to me and my late wife Elizabeth in several long and severe fits of sickness. I am now transcribing my Will at Chelsea where dear Sir Walter again most kindly attends me.

(19) References to Malone and Mrs. Ord.

Mr. Malone, the worthy and zealous Treasurer and Historiographer of the Club established by Sir Jos. Reynolds, Dr. Johnson, Mr. Burke, etc., of which I had the honour of being unanimously elected in 17– [blank], having determined to procure, for a book, prints of such deceased members as could be obtained, I presented to him (Mr. Malone) at his request a print of my head on large paper for his collection, engraved by Bartolozzi from an original painting of the late most worthy, admirable, and ever to be lamented member, Sir Jos. Reynolds. I intended to have presented a Ring and my print on large paper to my dear and firm friend Mrs. Ord,[1] of Queen Anne Street West, whom I have always respected, loved, and revered. But alas she died in May 1808.[2]

portrait. As no legatee is mentioned it is to be presumed that the picture was to be sold and the sum realized to merge in the general estate.

Mr. Wm. C. Smith, of the British Museum, the eminent Handel authority, tells me that amongst his notes is one to the effect that in 1789 there was offered for sale in London, '*A very fine original Half-length Portrait of that much esteemed and celebrated Musician, George Frederick Handel, Esq. Painted by Wolfgang, is in fine preservation and admirably adapted to decorate an elegant Concert, Music, or Ball-room.*'

We may plausibly assume that this is the portrait in question, and that it came into Burney's possession at the date mentioned. However, there were, during the Handel period, several painters and engravers named 'Wolfgang' or 'Wolffgang'. There is (or was lately) a Wolffgang miniature of Handel 'on parchment, in pencil and sepia' in the Peters Music Library at Leipzig. Information about this and a reproduction are given in the *Jahrbuch der Musikbibliothek Peters*, 1896, and there is also a reproduction in Fritz Volbach's life of Handel. Two engravings of it are said to have been published. It appears, however, to be a much later portrait than Burney's, as it bears on the back the information, in old writing, '*Georg Frideric Hendel, G. A. Wolffgang, Pinx, London 1737.*' There is also a miniature of Handel by Wolffgang in Windsor Castle.

What may or may not be Burney's Handel portrait is included in the catalogue of the sale of the Snoxell Collection, by Puttick & Simpson, in 1879—'*Portrait of George Friderick Handel by Wolfgang, with the Engraving*'. A manuscript note in the British Museum copy of the catalogue says 'Sold to Mr. W. Clark, £15. 10.' The name of Clark as the purchaser of this portrait is given in Grove's *Dictionary*. Where is it now? And if engravings of it existed, where are they? (There are two 'Wolffgang' engraved portraits of Handel in the British Museum.)

[1] See II. 90.

[2] Here again, as in several other clauses, Burney goes out of his way to explain what he would have done if the beneficiary in mind (here Mrs. Ord) had not predeceased him, or what he has already done which renders it unnecessary for him to do it again (here for Mr. Malone). This Will, it will be gathered, is not a mere legal document, but also a record of feelings and intentions.

(20) Some Family Portraits.

A miniature of my first wife, Esther, admirably painted by Spencer just before our Marriage,[1] I bequeath to my eldest daughter, Esther, and a Picture in Miniature, painted by Miss Reed, of my 2d Wife, Elizabeth, to my daughter Sarah, to whom it naturally belongs. A miniature of myself painted by Humphreys, if it can be found, I bequeath to my 2d daughter, Mrs. d'Arblay, together with my Nephew's excellent Copies of Sir Jos. Reynolds portrait of Doctor Johnson and of himself, as these were her first literary patrons.[2]

(21) Some Particular Objects.

If I live to return to Chelsea there are many particulars of my profession, hitherto unnoticed, to specify, such as my two Gongs and oriental instruments in Chests sent from Canton by Mr. Matthew Raper and two of inferior quality brought by Lord Macartney when he returned from his Chinese embassy. [Also] A very curious and delicately painted procession of the Great Mogul through a triumphal Arch, on an Elephant, with his Wives, Concubines, and great Officers of State: the heads of the females are very beautiful and highly finished, as if each were intended to be set in a Ring. This was painted at Delhi and a present from Mrs. Pleydel. It hangs over the fire place in my Bed room.[3]

A curious Merlin Table, which may be formed into desks for 8 performers, with brass furniture for Candle light. By a winch it can be elevated to any height, for writing or playing standing, with drawers and various contrivances for secret deposits. Merlin valued it at 11 Guineas 20 years ago; one could not now be made like it for twice that sum. This is to be sold for the profit of my three daughters, Esther, Frances, and Sarah.

(23) Bequest to a God-daughter.

To the eldest Child of Sarah Walter,[4] my God daughter, I bequeath Twenty Pounds.

(24) A Note on Income.

In recollecting my Property at present it appears, and will be found by my Executors, that, notwithstanding the thousand Pounds which was due before the Income Tax was imposed for my Articles written for the new Cyclopaedia, the present of 100 Guineas with which I was honoured by the noble directors of the Concert of Ancient Music,[5]

[1] See I. 45.

[2] See I. 353. The portraits were copies of those Reynolds painted for the Thrales' house at Streatham (see I. 325).

[3] See I. 137–8.

[4] I have not traced Sarah Walter; possibly an old servant.

[5] The present from the Ancient Music directors was, presumably, for some service rendered

Lady Mary Duncan's bequest of £600,[1] and my Pension of £200 a year,[2] neither my income nor my possessions have been increased for, besides my relinquishing Scholars since I became a Cyclopaedist, and resigning Oxford Chapel[3] to Mr. Burney, the defection of my Income, I fear, by the great expence of my Bristol and Bath journeys,[4] the stoppage of the £50 per annum by Mr. Lewis[5] and of £80 a year by Col. Phillips,[6] amounting to £130 nett. and the Reviewing for Griffiths,[7] must, at a moderate computation, diminish my income at least £400 per annum.

(25) CANCELLATION OF PREVIOUS WILLS.

I have cancelled, but not destroyed, the records of my instructions as to the disposal of my property at different periods of my life according to births, deaths, and other events in my Family, and changes in my circumstances, to manifest to my heirs and Executors that I always thought of my Children, Grandchildren, and other relations, with equity and kindness.

CHARLES BURNEY, Chelsea College.

Signed, Sealed, and delivered in the presence of us, who are Witnesses to the signing of each Page, on 25th April 1807—W. North, Chelsea Hospital; J. R. Reid, Chelsea Hospital.

Proved at London, 30th April, 1814, before the Worshipful Sherrard Beaumont Burnaby, Doctor of Laws and Surr., by the Oath of The Rev[d] Charles Burney, Doctor in Divinity, the Son, one of the Exors. to whom Admōn was granted, having been first sworn duly to administer Power to James Burney Esquire the other son.

The passage which follows concerns a small portion of Burney's estate which had been overlooked in the papers leading to the original grant. The two original executors (Charles and James) being both by now deceased, their sister Charlotte receives what would to-day be called a grant of *De Bonis Non.*

On the 17th day of May, 1823, Admōn. of Goods, Chattels, and Credits of Charles Burney, Doctor in Music, late of Chelsea College in

—probably help in engaging foreign artists. Cf. II. 177, where it will be seen that the directors of the Pantheon employed Burney in this way.

[1] See II. 80. Lady Mary Duncan left Burney also 'her great and curious collection of music, printed and manuscript' (Mem. iii. 345). See also Clause 9 *ante*.

[2] This Will, as we have seen, was drafted in 1807, and the pension was then £200 a year. But it must later have been increased, for the Report of the Commissioners of Military Enquiry in 1812 gives Burney's income from government sources as £248 pension, plus £50 salary at Chelsea Hospital (see II. 55), plus £2 for 'opening the organ' (see II. 55 n.), plus £30 as a member of the King's Band (see II. 322), altogether, then, £330.

[3] See I. 259.

[4] See II. 256.

[5] Mr. Lewis has not been traced.

[6] Probably interest on a mortgage. See II. 144.

[7] For many years Burney was a contributor to Griffith's *Monthly Review*. See II. 93–4.

the County of Midx. dec[d], left unad[d]. by the Revd. Charles Burney, Dr. in Divinity, the son and one of the Exors. named in the said Dec[d]'s Will, was granted to Charlotte Ann Broome, Widow, heretofore Francis, Widow, theretofore Burney, of Richmond in the County of Surry, limited so far only as concerns all the right Title and Interest of him, the said Dec[d], in and to a certain half yrs. dividend on the Sum of five thousand five hundred Pounds Stock three per Cent. Consolidated Bank Annuities, amounting to the sum of Eighty two Pounds and ten Shillings, and all benefit and advantage to be had, rec[d] and taken therefrom, but no further or otherwise or in any other manner what[r] having been first sworn duly to adm[r]. The said Charles Burney died Intestate, and James Burney Esqre., the son also, and other Exor., died without proving the said Will.

THE DISPOSAL OF BURNEY'S LIBRARY.

1. The non-musical portion of Burney's library was sold by auction on 9 June 1814 and the eight following weekdays. In the British Museum is *A Catalogue of the Miscellaneous Library of the late Charles Burney*: it has manuscript notes of prices and purchasers, and shows the total amount realized to be £1,414. 18*s*. 6*d*.

2. The sale of the music was advertised in *The Times* on 13 July:

> 'The late Dr. BURNEY'S MUSICAL LIBRARY.—To be SOLD by AUCTION, by Mr. White, in the last week of this month (July), pursuant to his will, the valuable and very fine COLLECTION of MUSIC, printed and MS., of the late Charles Burney, Mus.D., F.R.S., and Correspondent to the Institute of France; in which are many scarce, curious, and excellent compositions for voices, such as the inedited works of Carissimi, Stradella, Colonna, Steffani, Clari, Bassini, Leo, Scarlatti, Durante, Jommelli, Perez, Galuppi, and Sacchini, Palestrina, Salvator Rosa, &c.; and for instruments, the entire works of Tartini, Scarlatti, Sebastian, and Emmanuel Bach, Schobert, nearly all the works of Haydn, Mozart, and Beethoven; with many rare articles not to be found in any other collection. Catalogues are preparing, and due notice will be given of the day of sale, viewing, &c.'

This sale lasted nine days. The catalogue announces it as to open on 8 August—not during the last week of July as the above newspaper advertisement had stated. Two copies of the catalogue are in the British Museum: there are included one thousand and eighty items. One of these copies is Sir George Smart's copy in which he has inserted particulars of a few purchasers and prices. The other is fully priced and there is a note to the effect that the amount on each page is copied from Mr. White's (the auctioneer's) own copy. Dr. Rimbault's copy, also fully priced, is in the Library of Congress, Washington. The total realized was £686. 0*s*. 6*d*.

3. At the foot of the catalogue of the above-mentioned sale is an intimation to the effect that:

'The books, tracts, and treatises on the particular faculty of music in all languages will be sold by auction at a future period unless previously disposed of by private sale.'

Apparently there was some idea that the British Museum should buy the collection, for Add. MS. 18191, fol. 20, in the Museum, is a letter dated 22 July from Burney's son Charles, then in the Isle of Wight, to the auctioneer, 'Mr. White, Storey's Gate, Westminster', saying, 'If a Person should come to you commissioned by Mr. Baber of the British Museum, to value the Books on the subject of Musick, on the part of the Trustees of that Institution, pray let him see them—as often as may be needful.'

A month later an advertisement in the *London Gazetteer* of 24 August announces that 'this day' was to be sold by White, at his rooms in Storey's Gate, the collection of books and also the portrait of Handel and the 'original and very curious Indian pictures from the Collection of Governor Holwell'. What happened to the portrait of Handel and the very curious Indian pictures I do not know. Possibly they were duly disposed of as intended. Apparently, however, the auction of the books on music did not take place. Perhaps representations on the part of the British Museum were the motive for a postponement pending further negotiations, for this collection was purchased *en bloc* by the Museum during 1815, the sum paid being £253.[1]

Thus the total for the whole of the Library (non-musical books, music, and books on music) was £2,353. 19*s*.

Grove's *Dictionary of Music* (s.v. 'Libraries') has in all its four editions to date stated that Burney's musical library was 'bequeathed by its owner to the Museum and transferred to Bloomsbury on his death in 1814'. The Will shows that there was no such bequest and the above statement, it is believed, at last gives the full facts.

Burney's family naturally desired that some permanent public memorial of him should exist. Details of the arrangements for the erection in Westminster Abbey of the tablet still to be seen there are found in two letters of Charles to his sister Fanny.[2] The fee to the Dean and Chapter was to have been £35, but was raised to £60, the expense being shared by Esther, Charles, and Fanny, to the last-named being confided the drafting of the epitaph:

'Our dear Hetty has entrusted me with twenty pounds as her *third portion* of the fees of that *Cormorant*, Westminster Abbey! My share of 20 pounds is also ready, and if you will write to Hoares, they will pay the same sum of twenty pounds, and I will then march off to Mr. Gell's, the agent of the

[1] Information kindly disinterred by Mr. C. B. Oldman of the Museum.

[2] Sold about 1933 by Messrs. Colbeck Radford & Co., Ltd., of Bruton Street, London, and by them very kindly communicated to the present writer. The *Music List 32* of Mr. Leonard Hyman, Reading (1946), gives considerable extracts from correspondence in the Burney family concerning the wording, &c., of the tablet.

Cormorant, pay the stuff and there will be an end of that part of the business. The Monument will [be] ready in three weeks. So Lady fair! down with your Epitaph, before that time; as it must for form's sake be exhibited to the Dean of the Cormorant's next [? Chapter meeting].'

The monument is a tablet in the North Choir Aisle, and there is a little unintended significance in the fact that it is immediately below that of Blow (see I. 310–11).

SACRED TO THE MEMORY OF

CHARLES BURNEY MUS.D. F.R.S.

WHO, FULL OF YEARS, AND FULL OF VIRTUES,
THE PRIDE OF HIS FAMILY, AND THE DELIGHT OF SOCIETY,
THE UNRIVALLED CHIEF, AND SCIENTIFICK

HISTORIAN,

OF HIS TUNEFUL ART!
BELOVED, REVERED, REGRETTED,
BREATHED, IN CHELSEA COLLEGE, HIS LAST SIGH!
LEAVING TO POSTERITY A FAME UNBLEMISHED,
BUILT ON THE NOBLE BASIS OF INTELLECTUAL ATTAINMENTS.
HIGH PRINCIPLES AND PURE BENEVOLENCE,
GOODNESS WITH GAIETY, TALENTS WITH TASTE,
WERE OF HIS GIFTED MIND THE BLENDED ATTRIBUTES;
WHILE THE GENIAL HILARITY OF HIS AIRY SPIRITS
ANIMATED, OR SOFTENED, HIS EVERY EARTHLY TOIL;
AND A CONSCIENCE WITHOUT REPROACH
PREPARED,
IN THE WHOLE TENOUR OF HIS MORTAL LIFE,
THROUGH THE MEDIATION OF OUR LORD JESUS CHRIST,
HIS SOUL FOR HEAVEN.—AMEN.
BORN APRIL 7. O.S. 1726. DIED APRIL 12. 1814.

In strong contrast with this is the simplicity of the inscription on the stone above the grave of Burney and his wife in the little cemetery at Chelsea College.

In Memory of

ELIZABETH BURNEY

Died 20th October 1796
Aged 68

Also CHARLES BURNEY 1814

LXVII. BURNEY'S FAMILY AFTER HIS DEATH

Less than four years after Burney's death he was followed by his second son and namesake, Charles, who died of apoplexy at Deptford 28 December 1817, aged only sixty. Six months earlier he had become a Prebendary of Lincoln. He was also a Chaplain to the King.

His famous classical library and his huge collections of playbills and materials for a history of the stage and of newspapers were, by a special Resolution of Parliament, bought for the British Museum (see II. 237), the large sum of £13,500 being paid for them.[1]

The British Museum's elaborate and beautifully reproduced folio volume of 1840, *Catalogus Librorum Manuscriptorum Bibliothecae Burneianae*, testifies to the extent, variety, and value to scholars of one part of the possessions Charles had accumulated.

Besides his library, Charles left behind him his one child, the Rev. Charles Parr Burney (1785–1864. See II. 236), who became Archdeacon of St. Albans and then of Colchester.[2]

A tablet to the memory of the second Charles Burney (as one to that of the first) is to be seen in Westminster Abbey. It is surmounted by a bust by Nollekens (see opposite).

The present author possesses a number of very affectionate letters that passed in both directions between Charles and his son Charles Parr when the latter was at Oxford; those from the father abound in sage advice on practical academic matters.

Charles has descendants to-day. Of three of them I am told that they are the daughters of the fifth Charles Burney in succession. The five are (1) Charles Burney, the musician; (2) Charles Burney, the classical scholar; (3) Charles Parr Burney, Archdeacon of St. Albans and then Colchester; (4) Charles Burney, Archdeacon of Kingston-on-Thames; and (5) Charles Burney, Master of the Supreme Court.

Charles's elder brother, James, to his great satisfaction promoted Rear-Admiral in 1821, died at his house in London only four months

[1] Hansard (xxxviii, passages beginning in cols. 328 and 501, 24 April and 4 May 1818) shows that there took place a spirited debate between some of the classical scholars of the House and some of the economically minded. It was explained to the latter that the duplicates of the collection could be thriftily resold for about £3,000, and that the remaining £10,500 would be made up by withholding the Museum's 'usual allowance' until the remaining sum had been wiped out. A long and convincing speech by the eloquent and able Sir James Mackintosh (Burke's old opponent of the French Revolution days) closed the debate. Particulars of the material acquired will be found in the *Report from the Committee on Petition of Trustees of the British Museum, relating to the collection of the late Dr. Burney. Ordered, by the House of Commons, to be printed 17 April 1818*.

[2] Archdeacon Charles Parr Burney was an amateur artist. There are etchings by him in the Print Room of the British Museum. One of his great-grandchildren writes to me: 'He was a very good amateur artist and belonged to a club, with Turner and other contemporary artists, where they exchanged drawings and in consequence we have some beautiful water colours by Turner and others.'

The tablet to Charles Burney, Junior, is surmounted by a bust by Nollekens. It is well that a high reputation for scholarship has been recorded for all time in sonorous Latin, as it appears otherwise to have faded from the public memory.

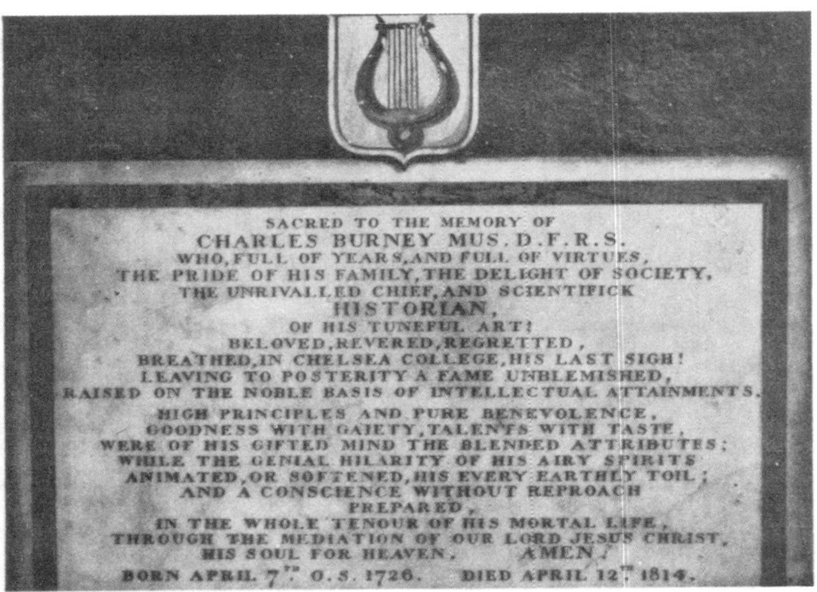
SACRED TO THE MEMORY OF
CHARLES BURNEY MUS. D. F. R. S.
WHO, FULL OF YEARS, AND FULL OF VIRTUES,
THE PRIDE OF HIS FAMILY, THE DELIGHT OF SOCIETY,
THE UNRIVALLED CHIEF, AND SCIENTIFICK
HISTORIAN,
OF HIS TUNEFUL ART!
BELOVED, REVERED, REGRETTED,
BREATHED, IN CHELSEA COLLEGE, HIS LAST SIGH!
LEAVING TO POSTERITY A FAME UNBLEMISHED,
RAISED ON THE NOBLE BASIS OF INTELLECTUAL ATTAINMENTS,
HIGH PRINCIPLES AND PURE BENEVOLENCE,
GOODNESS WITH GAIETY, TALENTS WITH TASTE,
WERE OF HIS GIFTED MIND THE BLENDED ATTRIBUTES;
WHILE THE GENIAL HILARITY OF HIS AIRY SPIRITS
ANIMATED, OR SOFTENED, HIS EVERY EARTHLY TOIL;
AND A CONSCIENCE WITHOUT REPROACH
PREPARED,
IN THE WHOLE TENOUR OF HIS MORTAL LIFE,
THROUGH THE MEDIATION OF OUR LORD JESUS CHRIST,
HIS SOUL FOR HEAVEN. AMEN!
BORN APRIL 7TH O. S. 1726. DIED APRIL 12TH 1814.

For this tablet to Charles Burney, Senior, *see* ii. 274–5.

later (17 November), aged seventy-one. *The Gentleman's Magazine* paid him a worthy tribute which included this passage:

'As an officer Admiral Burney was particularly remarkable for his great and enlightened humanity to those under his command: at a period, too, when severity in discipline was generally considered a proof of zeal, of spirit, and of ability, and when the wiser and more generous opinions and practice of the present day were considered heterodox and pernicious. This humanity was characteristic of him.'

In 1817 he had completed publication of his enormous work, *A Chronological History of the Voyages and Discoveries in the South Sea or Pacific Ocean* (5 vols. quarto), begun fourteen years earlier (see II. 232), and two years after this there appeared his *Chronological History of the North Eastern Voyages of Discovery and of the Early Eastern Navigation of the Russians* (1 vol. octavo). And there were various papers and pamphlets, and, in the year of his death, the little book on whist (see II. 234). As already suggested, in view of the fact that his schooling had ceased at the age of ten the clarity and rhythm of his writing are worth remark.[1]

A host of literary friends deplored the death of James—Lamb, Hood, Southey, Wordsworth, Coleridge, Crabb Robinson, and others. Lamb's essay entitled *The Wedding* humorously describes the marriage of James's daughter Sally in April 1821:

'The union itself had long been settled, but its celebration had been hitherto deferred, to an almost unreasonable state of suspense in the lovers, by some invincible prejudices which the bride's father unhappily had upon the subject of the too early marriages of females. He had been lecturing any time these five years—for to that length the courtship has been protracted—upon the propriety of putting off the solemnity till the lady should have completed her five-and-twentieth year. We all began to be afraid that a suit, which as yet had abated none of its ardours, might at last be lingered on till passion had time to cool and love go out in the experiment. But a little wheedling on the part of his wife, who was by no means a party to these over-strained notions, joined to some serious expostulations on that of his friends, who, from the growing infirmities of the old gentleman, could not promise ourselves many years' enjoyment of his company, and were anxious to bring matters to a conclusion during his lifetime, at length prevailed; and on Monday last the daughter of my old friend, Admiral —, having attained the *womanly* age of nineteen [actually twenty-eight!], was conducted to the church by her pleasant cousin J—, who told some few years older.'

As James Burney is here spoken of as 'Admiral' and he held this rank for only a few months, it will be gathered that Sally's marriage was one of the last events of his life. She married her cousin, John Payne, who had succeeded his and her grandfather and his father in the bookshop

[1] In the Scottish Admiralty township of Rosyth there is a 'Burney Place' which we may suppose to be so named with the intention to do honour to James Burney. There is also a 'Burney Road' which recently came into existence as a part of the Admiralty's temporary housing scheme.

'in the Mews Gate'.[1] This Wedding took place in St. Margaret's, Westminster, and the officiating clergyman was another cousin of the bride, Rev. Charles Parr Burney, son of Dr. Charles Burney, junior. Both Charles and Mary Lamb were present. Some details of Lamb's essay are purposely falsified (e.g. the name of the clergyman), but his humorous description of the wedding breakfast (three hours long, with 'stores of cold fowls, tongues, hams, botargoes, dried fruits, wines, cordials, &c.') is probably pretty close to the facts, as also his account of the bride's parents' house, where the breakfast was held:

> 'I have been at my old friend's various times since. I do not know a visiting place where every guest is so perfectly at his ease; nowhere, where harmony is so strangely the result of confusion. Every body is at cross purposes, yet the effect is so much better than uniformity. Contradictory orders; servants pulling one way; master and mistress driving some other, yet both diverse; visitors huddled up in corners; chairs unsymmetrized; candles disposed by chance; meals at odd hours, tea and supper at once, or the latter preceding the former; the host and the guest conferring, yet each upon a different topic, each understanding himself, neither trying to understand nor hear the other; draughts and politics, chess and political economy, cards and conversation on nautical matters, going on at once,[2] without the hope, or indeed the wish, of distinguishing them, make it altogether the most perfect *concordia discors* you shall meet with.'

Another daughter, Catherine, had died young.

Here is one of Lamb's allusions to the odd, lovable Martin Burney, James's only son (who was constitutionally impecunious):

> 'There is a class of street readers whom I can never contemplate without affection,—the poor gentry, who, not having wherewithal to buy or hire a book, filch a little learning at the open stalls; the owner, with his hard eye, casting envious looks at them all the while, and thinking when they will have done. Venturing tenderly, page after page, expecting every moment when he shall interpose his interdict, and yet unable to deny themselves the gratification, they "snatch a fearful joy". Martin B—, in this way, by daily fragments, got through two volumes of "Clarissa", when the stall-keeper damped his laudable ambition, by asking him (it was in his younger days) whether he meant to purchase the work. M— declares, that under no circumstances in his life did he ever peruse a book with half the satisfaction which he took in those uneasy snatches.'[3]

Lamb's *Prose Works* of 1818 were dedicated to Martin Burney.

James's wife, Sarah, died at Penshurst, Kent, in 1832.

The sweet-tempered Esther ('Hetty'), the only one of Burney's children who was markedly musical and who attained what we may call professional skill as a performer, was, apparently, at or about the

[1] See G. E. Manwaring, *My Friend the Admiral*, 264.

[2] This surely did not have the sanction of 'Mrs. Battle'. See II. 234.

[3] Essay, 'Detached Thoughts on Books and Reading'.

time of her father's death, living at Turnham Green. Thence, years later (1817), she and her husband removed to the neighbourhood of Bath, where, after about another two years (1819), her husband, now aged seventy-two, died. Esther survived him by about thirteen years, dying at Bath in 1832, aged about eighty-three. Six or seven of her ten children had predeceased her.

Burney's grandchild, Sophia Elizabeth Burney, daughter of Esther and Charles Rousseau Burney, inherited the family propensity for authorship. At Sothebys in 1930, there were put up for sale the following great works by her (still in manuscript, however):

Novels, Plays and Poems, written for the Instruction of People of all Ages (70 pp.; written at the age of thirteen).

The Juvenile Magazine (6 parts, consisting of short stories, charades, etc.; 1792).

Stories for her sister Cecilia, then aged five (illustrated with 9 water colour drawings by her uncle Edward Burney).

FANNY outlived her father by nearly twenty-six years. In the month of her father's death (April 1814) she was presented, in London, to Louis XVIII; he greeted and parted from her as 'Madame La Comtesse' —a title which she could claim but never used. Soon after this her husband, now an officer in the new King's bodyguard, arrived from Paris, to which he later in that year took her back, their son, Alexander, being left to pursue his studies at Cambridge.

When, in March 1815, Napoleon escaped from Elba, Fanny, on her part, managed to escape from Paris to Brussels, and her long account of her experiences there, in her diary, is supposed to have been drawn on by Thackeray in the relevant chapters of *Vanity Fair*.

Just one Brussels incident shall be recorded here because it has a slight musical interest and concerns a composition of Burney's old master, Arne:

'Our last entertainment here was a concert in the public and fine room appropriated for music or dancing. The celebrated Madame Catalini had a benefit, at which the Queen of the Netherlands was present, not, however, in state, though not incognita; and the king of warriors Marshal Lord Wellington, surrounded by his staff and all the officers and first persons here, whether Belgians, Prussians, Hanoverians, or English. I looked at Lord Wellington watchfully, and was charmed with every turn of his countenance, with his noble and singular physiognomy, and his eagle eye. He was gay even to sportiveness all the evening, conversing with the officers around him. He never was seated, not even for a moment, though I saw seats vacated to offer him frequently. He seemed enthusiastically charmed with Catalini, ardently applauding whatsoever she sung, except the "Rule, Britannia"; and there, with sagacious reserve, he listened in utter silence. Who ordered it I know not, but he felt it was injudicious in every country but our own to give out a chorus of "Rule, Britannia! Britannia, rule the Waves!"

'And when an encore began to be vociferated from his officers he instantly crushed it by a commanding air of disapprobation, and thus offered me an opportunity of seeing how magnificently he could quit his convivial familiarity for imperious dominion when occasion might call for the transformation.'[1]

In July, Fanny's husband, whose important conference with the Duke of Wellington is mentioned in Fanny's account, whilst on recruiting service for the Allies amongst the deserters from Napoleon's army, was injured by a kick from a horse. Fanny heard alarming rumours of his accident and set out to find him at Trèves. D'Arblay, in poor health, then retired from the French service with the rank of Lieutenant-General and, three years later (May 1818), died at Bath.

Fanny for some years lived in Bolton Street, Piccadilly. In 1832 she published her *Memoirs* of her father, which aroused wide interest (the present author possesses a copy of an edition published in Philadelphia the year following the appearance of the original). Southey warmly praised the *Memoirs* saying that 'Except Boswell's there is no other work in our language which carries us into such high society, and makes us fancy that we are acquainted with the people to whom we are introduced', but Croker, in a tremendous article in *The Quarterly Review* (April 1833), brutally told the octogenarian that her style could not have been 'more feeble, anile, incoherent, or *sentant plus l'apoplexie*'—a criticism which expresses some truth but no delicacy.

A complaint which he might legitimately have made, but which evidently does not occur to him, is that whilst Fanny occupies a large amount of space with accounts of her own writings she does not even mention the long tale of literary productions, some of them of real importance, by her brothers James and Charles and her half-sister Sarah Harriet: this is really a rather shocking example of senile vanity. He condemns her long adjectival phrases and, to make them look more ridiculous than they already are, supplies them with hyphens. Thus we are led to chuckle over *the yet-very-handsome-though-no-longer-in-her-bloom Mrs. Stephen Allen* and (the longest adjectival phrase in the language, claims Croker) *the sudden-at-the-moment-though-from-lingering-illness-often-previously-expected death.* And, as already mentioned (I. 359), he goes thoroughly into the grounds (very insufficient ones) for his allegation that Fanny had deceived the public as to her age at the time she wrote *Evelina.*

In 1837 Fanny lost her son, Alexander Charles Louis, who had gone through Cambridge with credit, becoming tenth Wrangler and a Fellow of his college (Christ's). The year before his death he had been appointed Minister of Ely Chapel, Holborn (then a Protestant and Anglican place of worship, now Roman Catholic). As a boy he was a great chess enthusiast and it may be added here that his enthusiasm was maintained and that his poem on the famous match between

[1] *Diary and Letters*, vi. 207.

Alexander O'Donnell and the Frenchman, Labourdonnais, is not entirely forgotten by chess enthusiasts of to-day.[1]

Fanny died on 6 January 1840, in Lower Grosvenor Street, Bond Street, and was buried beside her husband and son in the churchyard at Wolcot, Bath, the officiating clergyman being the Rev. Charles Burney, great-grandson of her father (son of the Rev. Charles Parr Burney who was son of her brother Charles; see II. 276). *The Times* account of the funeral (18 Jan.) reads:

'The funeral of the late Madame d'Arblay took place at Bath on Wednesday last. It was strictly private, in accordance with her own last directions and was attended only by some female relatives and her nephews, Mr. Martin Burney, Lieutenant-Colonel H. Burney, East India Company's service, late resident at Ava, who is appointed her executor; the Rev. Charles Burney, and Mr. Richard Barrett, who is appointed her heir.'[2]

Two years after Fanny's death (1842) her niece, Mrs. Barrett (Charlotte, daughter of Fanny's sister, Charlotte, by her first husband, Francis), began publication of the *Diary and Letters*—completing publication four years later. The vicious Croker again made a savage attack in *The Quarterly Review* (June 1842), again developing his *Evelina* allegation, and was then himself attacked by Macaulay in *The Edinburgh Review*, in the essay which is still reprinted and read and has, no doubt, had much to do with the permanent establishment of Fanny's fame as an authoress.[3]

The *Diary and Letters*, representing Fanny's earlier and more vivacious literary style and supplying a compendious account of literary and social activities and personalities during her long life, largely superseded the *Memoirs* in public favour. It remains one of the most celebrated books of its kind in the English language. Fanny's younger sister and fellow novelist, Sarah Harriet Burney, wrote thus to her friend Crabb Robinson, shortly after its publication:

'You want to know what I think of the "Diary". I will tell you fairly and impartially.—After wading with pain and sorrow through the tautology and vanity of the first volume I began to be amused by the second, and every

[1] See P. W. Sergeant, *A Century of British Chess* (1934).

[2] *The Times* of 13 Jan. had reported: 'The will of the late Madame d'Arblay (formerly Miss Burney) was read before her family on the Friday previous to the remains leaving London for Bath, where they will be buried on Wednesday next. The personal estate amounts to about 15,000*l*. Three per Cent. Stock, out of which she has bequeathed to Mr. Burney, the barrister, her eldest nephew, an annuity of 100*l*. a year for life, and legacies of various sums of money to other nephews and nieces, leaving Mr. Barrett, her sister's grandson, her residuary legatee.'

[3] Whatever justification there might have been for Croker's attack on the *Memoirs* there was little or none for the equally vicious attack on the *Diary and Letters*: 'We are conscientiously obliged to pronounce these volumes to be, considering their bulk and pretentions, nearly the most worthless we have ever waded through, and we do not remember in all our experience to have laid down an unfinished work with less desire for the continuation. That it may not mend as it proceeds we cannot—where there is such room for improvement—venture to pronounce; and there is this much to be said for it, that it can hardly grow worse.'

succeeding volume has, to my thinking, encreased in power to interest and entertain. That there is still considerable vanity I cannot deny. In her life she bottled it all up, and generally spoke with the most refined modesty, and seemed ready to drop if ever her work was alluded to. But what was kept back and scarcely suspected in society, wanting a safety valve, found its way to her private journal. Thence, had Mrs. Barrett been judicious, she would have trundled it out by half quires and even whole quires at a time.'[1]

The more youthful portion of Fanny's record was, rather strangely, omitted by the first editor and did not see the light until 1889, when it was separately published under the admirable editorship of Mrs. Annie Raine Ellis.

Rogers, in his *Table Talk*, relates a pathetic circumstance concerning Fanny's last years: he says that he once asked her if she remembered those lines of Mrs. Barbauld (her old friend of the Bluestocking period) entitled *Life*, the last stanza of which runs:

> 'Life! We've been long together
> Through pleasant and through cloudy weather.
> 'Tis hard to part when friends are dear;
> Perhaps 't will cost a sigh, a tear;
> Then steal away, give little warning,
> Choose thine own time.
> Say not *Good Night*, but in some brighter clime
> Bid me *Good Morning*.'

'*Remember them!*' she replied, '*I repeat them to myself every night before I go to sleep.*'

The memory of Fanny is kept before Londoners by a street name. D'Arblay Street runs at right angles to that Poland Street in which she spent some of the years of childhood: in this street is to be found a 'D'Arblay Dairy'.

Burney's youngest child, SARAH HARRIET (see above), died at Cheltenham in 1844, unmarried and aged seventy-four. In addition to the works of fiction already mentioned as coming from her pen (see II. 241) she had in 1815 published her *Tales of Fancy*, in 1819 her *Romance of Private Life*, and in 1820 her *Country Neighbours* (which last prompted the sonnet of Charles Lamb mentioned on II. 139). She spent some years in Florence, and in 1829 Crabb Robinson met her in Rome (see his *Diary and Reminiscences*). Burney once said of her that she had 'native spirits of the highest order and distinguished ability'. These qualities hardly appear in her fiction but perhaps contributed to her personal popularity in the society around her, which popularity seems to have been considerable.

When the death occurred of CHARLOTTE ANN, Mrs. Ralph Broome (Burney's youngest child by his first wife), is unknown to the present

[1] Letter reproduced by Edith A. Morley, in an article on Sarah Harriet Burney in *Modern Philology*, xxxix. 2, Nov. 1941.

writer. Like two of her sisters she was a novelist. Her *Trials* appeared in 1824, and there were one or two smaller works.

Her son Clement (by her first husband, Francis) died in 1829. Her daughter Charlotte (also by her first husband), who at sixteen had married a Mr. Barrett, became well known as the first editor of her aunt Fanny's *Diary and Letters* (1842–6). There was a daughter Marianne (also a Francis), and a son (a Broome) who died young.

Burney's son by his second wife, RICHARD THOMAS ('Bengal Dick'), had, of course, predeceased him by several years (see II. 240).

Of the later life of Burney's three STEPCHILDREN the present writer has little knowledge. Stephen Allen's career has been mentioned on II. 31. Maria died in 1821. Bessy, whose runaway match made her Mrs. Meeke, simply fades out of history.

Of Burney's nephews and nieces, children of his favourite brother Richard, several survived him. Charles Rousseau Burney, the harpsichordist (Esther's husband), has already been mentioned. Elizabeth Warren Burney died, unmarried, in 1832. Rebecca, who married the surgeon, Sandford, died in 1835. Anne (or Hannah, or Nancy), who married the Rev. John Hawkins, vicar of Halstead, Essex, died in 1819.

There is just one of Burney's nephews of whom something should be recorded before this account closes—EDWARD FRANCIS (or 'Francesco', or 'Francisco') BURNEY, son of Burney's brother Richard. Some allusions to his artistic abilities have already been made (II. 40–2). Of his work a large amount remains in the form of illustrations to books and ladies' annuals, frontispieces, vignettes on title-pages, and the like.

Edward's uncle Charles sometimes employed his skill, as in the plates of his book on the Handel Commemoration of 1784 (see II. 65), one or two plates in the *History of Music*, and a plate of a party of 'Pandean Minstrels' at Vauxhall, illustrating one of his articles in Rees's *Cyclopaedia*. And Edward's cousin James employed him in the illustration of his *Discoveries in the Pacific*. Apparently nobody has ever attempted to compile a list of this once popular illustrator's work. Amongst books said to contain such work are an edition of Glover's *Leonidas: a Poem* and *The Cabinet of the Arts* (1799); and the 1893 edition of Sainte-Beuve's *Portraits Littéraires* reproduces some of his work. But there must be extant dozens of books illustrated by him.

The famous Mrs. Montagu (see II. 83–5), in her wonderful house in Portman Square, had a room hung with 'elegant paintings by our ingenious Edward' (Fanny, in *Diary and Letters*, v. 68).

Beside the works in the National Portrait Gallery and Victoria and Albert Museum there are drawings of Worcestershire Churches in the Prattinton Collection now in the possession of the Society of Antiquaries. The British Museum has some pencil drawings (including a portrait of Garrick), water-colours, and prints 'after' Burney, the last including a strange apocalyptic *Hieroglyphical Print of the Church of God in the Fivefold*

State, including the Holy Jerusalem, together with a Scriptural Exhibition of the . . . Artists, Mechanicks and Manufacturers engaged in their respective Pursuits (said to have been executed to the order of Providence Chapel, Titchfield Street, and Monkwell Chapel in the City; the date is 1791). This is a very strange production, containing perhaps 300–400 minute figures of divine and human beings (and some animals variously engaged). It should be 'accompanied by another Print containing the Ground Plan of the Heavenly City, together with a Key to the Whole', and certainly requires such aids if it is to mean anything to the ordinary beholder.

Edward had, however, quite another side to him than the graceful designer, the skilful portraitist, and the artist-mystic. He possessed a sort of Hogarthian humour, which expressed itself in caricatures crowded with figures, every figure highly individualized and typical of some human eccentricity. This feature of his work seems to have been forgotten until in 1931 the Victoria and Albert Museum acquired his *Musicians of the Old School, The Waltz* (see pl. 27, II. 41), and *An Elegant Establishment,* satirically representing, respectively, a music party, a dancing party, and a young ladies' seminary of deportment. Then, at last, the press got hold of him, several journals reproducing pictures of his—including the august *Times,* which also gave him a column of letter-press, and so started a correspondence which brought to light a useful fact or two.

But Edward Burney had been immortalized before all this—quietly but surely. He is the 'E. B.' of Lamb's essay, *Valentine's Day.* The present collection of Burneyana could not be considered complete if this tribute to a worthy member of the Burney tribe did not in it receive some attention: the relevant part of this essay is, therefore, here reproduced.

'All Valentines are not foolish; and I shall not easily forget thine, my kind friend (if I may have leave to call you so), E—— B——. E. B. lived opposite a young maiden whom he had often seen, unseen, from his parlour window in C— Street.[1] She was all joyousness and innocence, and just of an age to enjoy receiving a Valentine, and just of a temper to bear the disappointment of missing one with good-humour. E—— B—— is an artist of no common powers; in the fancy parts of designing, perhaps inferior to none; his name is known at the bottom of many a well-executed vignette in the way of his profession, but no further; for E—— B—— is modest and the world meets nobody half-way. E—— B—— meditated how he could repay this young maiden for many a favour which she had done him unknown; for when a kindly face greets us, though but passing by, and never knows us again, nor we it, we should feel it as an obligation: and E. B. did. This good artist set himself to work to please the damsel. It was just before Valentine's Day three years since. He wrought, unseen and unsuspected, a wondrous work. We need not say it was on the finest gilt paper, with borders; full, not

[1] Clipstone Street, Fitzroy Square. Here Edward Burney was, apparently, residing up to 1832 (*Mem.* ii. 382).

of common hearts and heartless allegory, but all the prettiest stories of love from Ovid, and older poets than Ovid (for E—— B—— is a scholar). There was Pyramus and Thisbe, and be sure Dido was not forgotten, nor Hero and Leander, and swans more than sang in Cayster, with mottoes and fanciful devices, such as beseemed,—a work, in short, of magic. Iris dipt the woof. This on Valentine's Eve he commended to the all-swallowing indiscriminate orifice—(O ignoble trust!)—of the common post; but the humble medium did its duty; and from his watchful stand, the next morning, he saw the cheerful messenger knock, and by and by the previous charge delivered. He saw, unseen, the happy girl unfold the Valentine, dance about, clap her hands, as one after one the pretty emblems unfolded themselves. She danced about, not with light love, or foolish expectations, for she had no lover; or, if she had, none she knew that could have created those bright images which delighted her. It was more like some fairy present; a God-send, as our familiarly pious ancestors termed a benefit received where the benefactor was unknown. It would do her no harm. It would do her good for ever after. It is good to love the unknown. I only give this as a specimen of E—— B—— and his modest way of doing a concealed kindness.'

It is worth recording that Edward Burney, like so many of his clan, was something of a musician (a violinist, apparently). When he was staying once with his cousin Susan and her husband at Norbury we find her writing, 'We do not apply to Edward for music commonly till after supper—and then he is grown very good. He has an excellent ear, and memory, and taste, and has given me, I believe, a dozen sweet bits of Pleyell's, at least.'

Edward Burney exhibited regularly at the Royal Academy from 1780 to 1793, and then stopped. He died (unmarried) in Wimpole Street, in 1848, at the age of eighty-eight.

There are many of Charles Burney's descendants amongst us to-day, some of them before the public in various useful capacities and others not publicly prominent. But the present chronicle, having given some information concerning the lives and activities of the Burney family during a period of two centuries and a half (and, indeed, nearly three centuries and a half if every casual allusion be counted), must here be brought to an end.

SOME BURNEY LETTERS

[To Miss Dorothy Young, of King's Lynn, October 1761.][1]

I had not thought it possible that anything could urge me to write in the present deplorable disposition of my mind; but my dear Miss Young's letter haunts me! Neither did I think it possible for any thing to add to my affliction, borne down and broken-hearted as I am. But the current of your woes and sympathetic sorrows meeting mine, has overpowered all bounds which religion, philosophy, reason, or even despair, may have been likely to set to my grief. Oh Miss Young! you knew her worth—you were one of the few people capable of seeing and feeling it. Good God! that she should be snatched from me at a time when I thought her health re-establishing, and fixing for a long old age! when our plans began to succeed, and we flattered ourselves with enjoying each other's society ere long, in a peaceable and quiet retirement from the bustling frivolousness of a capital, to which our niggard stars had compelled us to fly for the prospect of establishing our children.

Amongst the numberless losses I sustain, there are none that unman me so much as the total deprivation of domestic comfort and converse—that converse from which I tore myself with such difficulty in a morning, and to which I flew back with such celerity at night! She was the source of all I could ever project or perform that was praise-worthy—all that I could do that was laudable had an eye to her approbation. There was a rectitude in her mind and judgment, that rendered her approbation so animating, so rational, so satisfactory! I have lost the spur, the stimulus to all exertions, all warrantable pursuits, except those of another world. From an ambitious, active, enterprizing Being, I am become a torpid drone, a listless, desponding wretch!—I know you will bear with my weakness, nay, in part, participate in it; but this is a kind of dotage unfit for common eyes, or even for common friends, to be entrusted with.

You kindly, and truly, my dear Miss Young, styled her one of the greatest ornaments of society; but, apart from the ornamental, in which she shone in a superior degree, think, oh think, of her high merit as a daughter, mother, wife, sister, friend! I always, from the first moment I saw her to the last, had an ardent passion for her person, to which time had added true friendship and rational regard. Perhaps it is honouring myself too much to say, few people were more suited to each other; but, at least, I always endeavoured to render myself more worthy of her than nature, perhaps, had formed me. But she could mould me to what she pleased! A distant hint—a remote wish from her was enough to inspire me with courage for any undertaking. But all is lost

[1] *Mem.* i. 140. For Miss Young see the present work, I. 75; for the death of Mrs. Burney see I. 103. Burney's age at the date of this letter was thirty-five.

and gone in losing her—the whole world is a desert to me! nor does its whole circumference afford the least hope of succour—not a single ray of that fortitude She so fully possessed!

You, who knew her, respected and admired her understanding while she was living. Judge, then, with what awe and veneration I must be struck to hear her counsel when dying!—to see her meet that tremendous spectre, death, with that calmness, resignation, and true religious fortitude, that no Stoic philosopher, nor scarcely Christian, could surpass; for it was all in privacy and simplicity. Socrates and Seneca called their friends around them to give them that courage that perhaps solitude might have robbed them of, and to spread abroad their fame to posterity; but she, dear pattern of humility! had no such vain view; no parade, no grimace! When she was aware that all was over—when she had herself pronounced the dread sentence, that she felt she should not outlive the coming night, she composedly gave herself up to religion, and begged that she might not be interrupted in her prayers and meditations.

Afterwards she called me to her, and then tranquilly talked about our family and affairs, in a manner quite oracular.

Sometime later she desired to see Hetty, who, till that day, had spent the miserable week almost constantly at her bed-side, or at the foot of the bed. Fanny, Susan, and Charley, had been sent, some days before, to the kind care of Mrs. Sheeles in Queen Square, to be out of the way; and little Charlotte was taken to the house of her nurse.

To poor Hetty she then discoursed in so kind, so feeling, so tender a manner, that I am sure her words will never be forgotten. And, this over, she talked of her own death—her funeral—her place of burial,—with as much composure as if talking of a journey to Lynn! Think of this, my dear Miss Young, and see the impossibility of supporting such a loss—such an adieu, with calmness! I hovered over her till she sighed, not groaned, her last—placidly sighed it—just after midnight.

Her disorder was an inflammation of the stomach, with which she was seized on the 19th. of September, after being on that day, and for some days previously, remarkably in health and spirits. She suffered the most excruciating torments for eight days, with a patience, a resignation, nearly quite silent. Her malady baffled all medical skill from the beginning. I called in Dr. Hunter.

On the 28th., the last day! she suffered, I suppose, less, perhaps nothing, as mortification must have taken place, which must have afforded that sort of ease, that those who have escaped such previous agony shudder to think of! On that ever memorable, that dreadful day, she talked more than she had done throughout her whole illness. She forgot nothing, nor threw one word away! always hoping we should meet and know each other hereafter!—She told poor Hetty how sweet it would be if she could see her constantly from whence she was going, and begged she would invariably suppose that that would be the case. What a lesson to leave to a daughter!—She exhorted her to remember how much her example might influence the poor younger ones; and bid her write little letters, and fancies, to her in the other world, to say how they all went on; adding, that she felt as if she should surely know something of them.

Afterwards, feeling probably her end fast approaching, she serenely said, with one hand on the head of Hetty, and the other grasped in mine: 'Now this is dying pleasantly! in the arms of one's friends!' I burst into an unrestrained agony of grief, when, with a superiority of wisdom, resignation, and true religion,—though awaiting, consciously from instant to instant awaiting the shaft of death,—she mildly uttered, in a faint, faint voice, but penetratingly tender, 'Oh Charles!—'

I checked myself instantaneously, over-awed and stilled as by a voice from one above. I felt she meant to beg me not to agitate her last moments.—I entreated her forgiveness, and told her it was but human nature. 'And so it is!' said she, gently; and presently added. 'Nay, it is worse for the living than the dying,—though a moment sets us even! life is but a paltry business—yet

'Who to dumb forgetfulness a prey
This pleasing, anxious being e'er resign'd,
Left the warm precincts of the cheerful day,
Nor cast one longing, lingering look behind?'

She had still muscular strength left to softly press both our hands as she pronounced these affecting lines.

Other fine passages, also, both from holy writ, and from what is most religious in our best poets, she from time to time recited, with fervent prayers; in which most devoutly we joined.

These, my dear Miss Young, are the outlines of her sublime and edifying exit—What a situation was mine! but for my poor helpless children, how gladly, how most gladly should I have wished to accompany her hence on the very instant, to that other world to which she so divinely passed!—for what in this remains for me?

BURNEY, IN ITALY, REPORTS PROGRESS TO HIS FRIEND GARRICK[1]

Naples, Oct. 17th, 1770.

Thus far into the bowels of the land have we marched on without impediment, except such as every traveller must encounter who has to deal with Italian innkeepers, Camerieri, Veturini, Postiglioni, &c.

[1] From *The Private Correspondence of David Garrick* (1831). A number of names there wrongly transcribed have been corrected and paragraphing has been introduced. Burney's age at the date of this letter was forty-four.

&c.; but for the honour of Italy, as well as for my own honour, I must say that my reception and treatment among the men of learning and genius throughout my journey have been to the last degree flattering. After the accounts I had heard and read of this country, I expected to meet with a people shy of strangers and difficult of access; but *au contraire*, in every great town where I have stopped, I have not only met with politeness and civility, but even with kindness and friendship. I am almost ashamed to tell you how many men of eminence, both in the literary and musical world, have interested themselves in my enterprise; but as you, who rank so high among the former class in our own country, have kindly manifested your good wishes in an effectual manner by your hearty recommendations to your friends at Paris, I shall continue to tell you, without fear of incurring the character of a puffer, what reason I have to be satisfied with the success of my journey.

When I left England, I had two objects in view; the one was to get from the libraries to the *viva voce* conversation of the learned, what information I could relative to the music of the ancients; and the other was to judge with my own eyes of the *present state* of modern music in the places through which I should pass, from the performance and conversation of the first musicians in Italy. I shall here only mention the most remarkable of both sorts. As my general history must be a work of time, I intend publishing, as soon as I get home, in a pamphlet, or small volume, an account of the present state of music in France and Italy, in which I shall describe, according to my judgment and feelings, the merits of the several compositions and performers I have heard in travelling through those countries.

At Turin I often saw and conversed with the famous Padre Beccaria; and the two Bezozzis not only performed to me for two hours, but were friendly all the time I was there. I found some things I wanted, too, in the King's Library.

At Milan, Padre Boscovich, Padre Frision, Signor Oltrocchi, Ambrosian librarian, D. Triulzi, the Abate Bonitti, Padre Sacchi, Conte Po, &c.; and on the side of practical music, the famous San Martini, Lampugnani, il Padre Maestro Florione, of the Duomo, &c.

At Brescia I stopped but two days, and only one at Verona and Vicenza; but at Padua I was six or eight days, and there I found your friend Dr. Marsili, Cav. Valeinicis, Padre Colombo, Padre Vallotti, Maestro di Capella at *Santo*, one of the greatest composers for the church now alive; and on the other side of practice, Signor Guglietti, poor Tartini's scholar and successor at St. Anthony's Church, from whom I got the *last drop of his pen*, or, in other words, the last solo he composed.[1]

At Venice, I had high entertainment for all sorts of learning and

[1] The printed *Tour* alludes not to 'Signor Guglietti' in this connexion, but 'Signor Tromba'.

theory. I conversed with Dr. Reghellini, the Abate Martini, the librarian of St. Marc's, il Conte Tassis; and for modern music with the famous Galuppi, Latilla, and Sacchini.

At Bologna I almost lived in the house of the celebrated theorist and historian, Padre Martini, whose library of books relative to music amounts to 16,000 or 17,000 volumes;[1] he was very communicative, and we compared *notes*, and have already opened a correspondence. I had great civilities from Farinelli, with whom I spent two whole days. I visited here the famous Dottoressa Laura Bassi, upon the merits of a recommendation from her friend Padre Beccaria.

At Florence, il Prefetto Fossi, Dr. Guadagni, Signor Bandini, the Grand Duke's librarian, il Canonico Dominico Cavaluc, and Dr. Perelli, were all open and friendly. I was almost every night at an *accademia*. The first-rate practical musicians I found here, were Mansoli, Nardini, Campioni, Dottel Figlio, &c.

By the time I got to Rome my Italian acquaintance and letters were much accumulated; I stayed there near a month. Several friends and first-rate artists are on the hunt for me, and are making original drawings of musical instruments from bassi rilievi, and ancient sculpture of the first class. As to the music of the Pope's Chapel, I shall be enabled to speak of it from the best authority my own eyes and ears can afford. Signor Santarelli, the Pope's Maestro di Capella, who has loaded me with civility and friendly offices, is now getting made out for me copies of the best compositions that are in constant use in the Pope's Chapel. I have found out the music of the first *opera* and first *oratorio* that were set to music. The Duke of Dorset had a very good concert every night, and took a great deal of pains to get curious and clever performers together, often on my account. I was presented to Cardinal Alissandro Albani, the principal librarian at the Vatican, who gave me permission to go into it, and to have whatever would be of use to my work copied. I spent most of my mornings in this library, and the Abate Elie, one of the Custodi, was very obliging and serviceable to me in my researches after *Canto Fermo*, *Contrapunto*, Provencal songs, &c., and I have been pretty fortunate. The Cardinal Albani is likewise prefetto of the Pope's Chapel, and gave me leave to ransack the archives there.

But though this is sport and special fun to me, I forget by the time this arrives both your hands and your head will be too full to admit flutes and fiddles. However, this I am sure of, that you have a heart which glows with friendship, and will excuse my breaking in upon you at an unseasonable time, when it is to pay an old debt from hence of several years standing. I remember you sent me an excellent letter from Naples, which was never answered, and this is more an acknowledgement of the debt than a payment of it. But d—n your speeches, you

[1] It seems incredible that at that date so many books on music could have existed. Has the figure been wrongly transcribed?

will say; and so I have done, first begging my best respects to Mrs. Garrick.

I shall stay here till after the 4th November, St. Charles's Day, which you know is that on which the serious opera begins, when the great theatre is doubly illuminated. I would not take 100*l*. not to be here then; indeed, it will cost me more, but Jomelli is here, and is the composer; De Amicis and Apribeau, the principals. The Gabriele is still in banishment in Palermo. I was with Piccini all the morning; there is a pretty comic opera of his now in run, as to music, but the libretto is terrible stuff. I have been here but three days. Mr. Hamilton is at his villeggiatura. I dine with our little Consul to-morrow, and with Mr. Hamilton in the country on Sunday. Vesuvius begins to throw up fire finely, and an eruption is hourly expected.

Adieu, my dear Sir. Believe me yours most affectionately,

CHARLES BURNEY.

BURNEY DESCRIBES A DINNER PARTY AT SIR JOSHUA REYNOLDS'S[1]

[early 1791].

To Mr. Burney at his Academy, near Hammersmith, Middlesex.

I dined after the Abbey performance with Sr. Jos. by appointment and he had 14 or 15 people to meet me—tho' I only asked for a family dinner with himself and Miss Palmer. There were Lds. Inchiquin & Eliot—Malone and his 2 Sisters, Bozzy and his 2 daughters—Devaynes—Mrs. Siddon's brother and, after dinner, Dr. Beatie, who inquired very kindly after you—he is in affliction for the loss of a Son,[2] & I think you shd. find him out, & call on him as soon as you can. The Eumelian Club[3] was mentioned—Davaynes sd. you were not there—though the compy. amounted to 34—Bozzy was very drole abt. the number of Drs. all paying court to Davaynes—Mr. D. you look very well today—I am happy to see you, quoth another. Mr. D. your health says a 3d. and Mr. D. shall I have the pleasure to help you? cries a 4th &c. Oh, but now I think of it, Bozzy sd. he was to be with you at Hammersmith on Sunday—& he hoped with me at Chelsea, on Monday—meaning in the hall, being the founder's day—I have had an invitation from Sr. Geo. Howard, our Governor, & shall go, though I want the Eveng. terribly for Haydn's *Passione Stromentale*—and for one of the *Concerts*

[1] Unpublished letter from Burney to his son Charles; original in the possession of the present writer. Burney's age at the date of the letter was sixty-five.

The dinner described evidently followed one of the Handel Commemoration performances of 1791.

Devaynes was Apothecary to the King.

[2] His younger son, who died 19 Nov. 1790, and whose life he wrote. His elder son died six years later and this quite broke him up.

[3] Founded 1788; met at the Blenheim Tavern, Bond Street. Burney and his friends Reynolds, Windham, and Boswell were members.

ambulans, at Ld. Cadogan's, where the Pac. & Giornovichi perform[1]—God bless you—as you cannot dine from home, perhaps you will try to call here before dinner—Love to Rosette,[2] & believe me yrs

very affectionately
CHAS. BURNEY.

THE SEPTUAGENARIAN BURNEY TELLS HOW HE READ HIS ASTRONOMICAL POEM TO AN APPRECIATIVE AUDIENCE[3]

[To Fanny] 24th. April, 1798, Chelsea College.

Mrs. Crewe has frequent singing parties with young people of *ton*, to bring out Miss Crewe. All the world that I know are there. Last week I was at Mrs. Ord's, to meet my old sweethearts, Mrs. Garrick, Betty Carter, Hannah More, and my new sweetheart, Mrs. Goodenough, the Speaker's sister, etc. To-morrow at Lord and Lady Inchiquin's: Friday again at Mrs. Crewe's, with evening music at Lady Northwick's, *ci-devant* Lady Rushont's; Saturday to dine with Lady Jones, relict of Sir William.—And so we go on.

Well, but in the midst of all this hurly burly, and business besides, I have terminated the twelfth book of my Poem, and transcribed it fair for your hearing or perusal. Mrs. and Miss Crewe, and Miss Hayman, who is now privy purse to the Princess of Wales, have been attending Walker's astronomical lectures,[4] and wanted much to hear some of my *Schtoff*; so, also, Windham and Canning. An evening was fixed upon for a meeting. Windham, after dinner, was to read us his balloon journal; Canning a manuscript poem; and I a book of my astronomy.[5] The lot fell on me to begin. When I had finished book the first, 'Tocca Lei', quoth I to Mr. Windham. 'No, no, not yet; another book first!' Well, when that was read, 'Tocca Lei', I cried to Mr. Canning. 'No, no', all called out, 'let us go on! another book!' Well, there was no help; so hoarse as I now was, I began a third book. Mrs. Crewe, however, soon offered to relieve me; and Miss Hayman to relieve Mrs. Crewe; and then supper was announced; and thus I was taken in! and

[1] 'Pac.' is Pacchierotti, who was then in London and performed at the Commemoration. Giornovichi was the famous violinist.

The *Passione Stromentale* was the original (instrumental) version of Haydn's *Seven Last Words*, of which several performances were given in London during the composer's stay there in 1790–1.

[2] Mrs. Charles Burney, junior, had been, it will be recalled, a Miss Rose.

[3] *Mem.* iii. 256. Burney's age at the date of this letter was seventy-two.

[4] Adam Walker (1731?–1821) was a Yorkshire schoolmaster who became a considerable inventor, mathematician, and astronomer, and gave every season a series of popular and fashionable astronomical lectures at his house in George Street, Hanover Square.

[5] Windham's 'Balloon Journal' was evidently an account of his ascent thirteen years before (5 May 1785). He took notes, a sort of log, scribbled in pencil on cardboard (British Museum Add. MSS. 37925): selections can be seen in R. Wyndham Ketton-Cramer's *The Early Life and Diaries of William Windham* (1930). Canning's manuscript poem may have been one of those published in *The Anti-Jacobean* in the following year and two succeeding years.

the rest with the balloon and the manuscript poem, are to be read, *comf.* at Mrs. Crewe's villa at Hampstead, as soon as finished.

BURNEY IS PROUD TO HAVE HELPED THE VOLUNTEERS[1]

Chelsea, College,
15th June, 1799.

To Matthew Yateman, Esq.,
Commandant of the Chelsea Armed Association.

Sir,

I cannot resist the desire with which the testimony of your approbation, and that of the special committee of the Chelsea Armed Association has impressed me, of returning thanks for the thanks with which you have honoured me for a small service, in the performance of which I had infinite pleasure. And, loving my country, and its established government as I do, I shall, to the last hour of my life, regard the loyalty, zeal, and truly patriotic spirit of your very respectable corps, manifested on the King's birth-day, as the most honourable to his Majesty and to his subjects, which any country has ever shewn.

'We know that the Roman legions were *paid*, as well as the individuals of every other army, ancient or modern; and that the title of soldier is derived from *solidus*, a piece of money; but a body of eight or nine thousand men, voluntarily mounted, exercised and clothed at their own expense, is an instance of such real patriotism as does not, perhaps, occur in the history of the world. I feel, therefore, proud of my country, and the noble efforts it is making to avert the misery and horrors with which Gallic principles and plunder have desolated the rest of Europe, and shook the globe.

I have the honour to be,
Sir, etc.,
CHARLES BURNEY.

BURNEY ATTENDS ONE OF THE WINDSOR CASTLE NIGHTLY CONCERTS[2]

Chelsea, Tuesday, three o'clock
[23 July 1799]

[To Fanny]

Not a moment could I get to write till now; and I am afraid of forgetting some part of my history, but I ought not, for the events of this visit are very memorable.

[1] *Mem.* iii. 266–7. Burney's age at the date of this letter was seventy-three. In 1799 the Chelsea Armed Association (to which Burney had contributed a man and a horse; see II. 243) mustered at Chelsea College. Burney composed a march for the occasion, drew up the Order of the Procession, and played the organ in the Chapel at the Consecration of the Colours. That explains this letter.

[2] *Diary and Letters*, v. 440. Some quotations from this letter, from Burney to his daughter Fanny, have already been given at II. 156. For the Griesbachs, who are mentioned, see the note on that page. It will be noted that the nightly concerts at court were divided into three

When the King and Queen, arm in arm, were approaching the place where the Herschel family and I had planted ourselves, one of the Misses Parry heard the Queen say to His Majesty, 'There's Dr. Burney', when they instantly came to me, so smiling and gracious that I longed to throw myself at their feet. 'How do you, Dr. Burney?' said the King. 'Why you are grown fat and young.' 'Yes, indeed', said the Queen; 'I was very glad to hear from Madame d'Arblay how well you looked.' 'Why, you used to be as thin as Dr. Lind', says the King. Lind was then in sight—a mere lath;[1] but these few words were accompanied with such very gracious smiles, and seemingly affectionate good-humour—the whole Royal Family, except the Prince of Wales, standing by—in the midst of a crowd of the first people in the kingdom for rank and office—that I was afterwards looked at as a sight. After this the King and Queen hardly ever passed by me without a smile and a nod. The weather was charming; the Park as full as the Terrace, the King having given permission to the farmers, tradesmen, and even livery servants, to be there during the time of his walking.

Now I must tell you that Herschel proposed to me to go with him to the King's concert at night, he having permission to go when he chooses, his five nephews (Griesbachs) making a principal part of the band. 'And', says he, 'I know you will be welcome.' But I should not have presumed to believe this if His Majesty had not formerly taken me into his concert-room himself from your apartments. This circumstance, and the gracious notice with which I had just been honoured, emboldened me.

A fine music-room in the castle, next the Terrace, is now fitted up for His Majesty's evening concerts and an organ erected. Part of the first act had been performed previous to our arrival. There were none but the performers in the room, except the Duchesses of Kent and Cumberland, with two or three general officers backwards. The King seldom goes into the music-room [? until] after the first act; and the second and part of the third were over before we saw anything of him, though we heard His Majesty, the Queen, and Princesses talking in the next room. At length he came directly up to me and Herschel, and the first question his Majesty asked me was—'How does Astronomy go on?' I, pretending to suppose he knew nothing of my poem, said, 'Dr. Herschel will better inform your Majesty than I can.' 'Ay, ay', says the King, 'but you are going to tell us something with your pen'; and moved his

parts, which, as was usual at that period, were spoken of as 'Acts'. The oratorio of *Joseph* mentioned was doubtless that of Handel. It may be of interest to some readers to compare the account of this nightly concert at the British Court with that of a similar concert, at a somewhat earlier period, at the Court of Prussia (see I. 233).

Burney's age at the date of this letter was seventy-three.

[1] There were two eighteenth-century Drs. Lind, both of them named James and both of some eminence. The 'lath' was the one who lived 1736–1812. He was Physician to the Royal Household, and a fellow astronomer and fellow F.R.S. of Burney's.

hand in a writing manner. 'What—what—progress have you made?' 'Sir, it is all finished, and all but the last of twelve books have been read to my friend Dr. Herschel.' The King, then looking at Herschel, as who would say, 'How is it?' 'It is a very capital work, Sir,' says H. 'I wonder how you find time?' said the King. 'I make time, Sir.' 'How, how?' 'I take it out of my sleep, Sir'. When the considerate good King, 'But you'll hurt your health. How long,' he adds, 'have you been at it?' 'Two or three years, at odd and stolen moments, Sir'. 'Well', said the King (as he had said to you before) 'whatever you write, I am sure will be entertaining,' I bowed most humbly, as ashamed of not deserving so flattering a speech. 'I don't say it to flatter you', says the King; 'if I did not think it, I would not say it.'

After this he talked of his concert, and the arrangements of the pieces performed that evening from the oratorio of *Joseph*. His majesty always makes the list himself, and had made a very judicious change in the order of pieces, which I told His Majesty, as there were no words in question which, as a drama, might require the original arrangement. He gave me his opinion very openly upon every musical subject started, and talked with me full half an hour. He began a conversation with General Harcourt and two other general officers which lasted a full hour, and we durst not stir till it was over, past eleven.

All this Windsor and Slough visit has turned out delightfully. I have not room to say anything more, only God bless you all!

C. B.

BURNEY TELLS OF GAY DOINGS AT DOVER[1]

Dover, 9th. Sept. 1799.

Why you Fanny!—I did not intend to write you my adventures, but to keep them for *vive voix* on coming to Camilla Cottage; but the nasty east wind is arrived, to the great inconvenience of our expedition, and of my lungs—all which circumstances put it out of my power to visit Camilla Cottage at present, as I wished, and had settled in my own mind to do. But let me see—where did I leave off? I believe I have told you of my arrival here, where, at first, I found Mr. Crewe, as you might observe by the frank. But two days after he went to Hythe, where he is now quartered with the Cheshire Militia corps, of which he is Colonel.

You may be sure that I hastened to visit the harbour and town, which I had not seen for near thirty years. . . . Did I tell you Mr. Ryder, our Chelsea joint paymaster, is here, and that we all dined on Wednesday with him and his sposa, Lady Susan? a most sweet creature, handsome, accomplished, and perfectly well-bred, with condescending good-humour; and who sings and plays well, and in true taste. Thursday,

[1] *Mem.* iii. 272. Two days after he had thus written to his daughter Burney wrote a similarly descriptive letter to his brother-in-law Arthur Young (see *Autobiography of Arthur Young*, p. 326). Burney's age at the date of this letter was seventy-three.

bad weather; but Canning came to *Longchon* to brighten it: and at night I read astronomy to Mrs. Crewe, and her fair, intelligent daughter.

On Friday I visited with them Lady Grey, wife of the Commander in Chief, at the Barham Down Camp. I like Lady Grey extremely, notwithstanding she is the mother of the vehement parliamentary democrat, Mr. Grey, who is as pleasing, they pretend, as he is violent, which makes him doubly dangerous. She is, indeed, a charming woman, and by everybody honoured and admired; and as she is aunt to our ardent friend *Spotty*, the Dean of Winchester's daughter, I was sure to be much flattered and *fêted* by all her family.[1]

Sir Charles's mother, old Mrs. Grey, now eighty-five, is a great and scientific reader and studier; and is even yet in correspondence with Sir Charles Blagden; who communicates to her all the new philosophical discoveries made throughout Europe.[2] What a distinguished race! The democrat himself,—but for his democracy, strikingly at their head! Mrs. Grey took to me mightily, and would hardly let me speak to anybody else. Saturday we visited Mr. and Lady Mary Churchill, our close neighbours here, and old acquaintances of mine of fifty years' standing or more.

Next day, after church, I went with Miss Crewe and Canning—I serving for chaperon—to visit the Shakespeare Cliff, which is a mile and more beyond the town: and a most fatiguing clamber to it I found. We took different roads, as our eye pointed out the easiest paths; and in so doing, on my being all at once missed, Canning and Miss Crewe were so frightened 'you can't think' as Miss Larolles[3] would say. They concluded I had tumbled headlong down the Cliff. It has furnished a story to everyone we have seen ever since; and that arch clever rogue, Canning, makes ample use of it, at Walmer Castle, and elsewhere. 'Is there any news?' if he be asked, his ready answer is, 'only Dr. Burney is lost again.'

This day, 5th September, pray mind! I went to Walmer Castle with Mrs. and Miss Crewe to dine with Lady Jane Dundas—another charming creature, and one of my new flirtations; and Mr. Pitt dined at home. And Mr. Dundas, Mr. Ryder, Lady Susan, Miss Scott, the sister of the Marchioness of Titchfield, and Canning, were of the party; with the Hon. Colonel Hope, Lady Jane's brother. What do you think of that, Ma'am?

Mr. Pitt!—I liked this cabinet dinner prodigiously. Mr. Pitt was all politeness and pleasantry. He has won Mrs. Crewe's, and even Miss Crewe's heart, by his attentions and good-humour. My translation of

[1] Sir Charles Grey (later 1st Earl Grey) then commanded the Southern District, residing at Barham Court, near Canterbury. His son (later 2nd Earl) was the active Whig politician and, as such, obnoxious to the Tory Burney.

[2] Sir Charles Blagden, M.D., F.R.S. (1748–1820), was the great friend of Cavendish, the chemist, and of Sir Joseph Banks, the naturalist. He was Secretary of the Royal Society and contributed to its Transactions many papers on both physical and medical subjects.

[3] A character in *Cecilia*.

the hymn, 'Long live the Emperor Francis!' was very well sung in duo by Lady Susan Ryder and Miss Crewe; I joining in the chorus.[1] Lady Jane Dundas is a good musician, and has very good taste. I not only played this hymn of Haydn's setting, but Suwarrow's March to the great minister: and though Mr. Pitt neither knows nor cares one farthing for flutes and fiddles, he was very attentive; and before, and at dinner, his civility to me was as obliging as if I had half a dozen boroughs at my devotion; offering to me, though a great way off him, of every dish and wine; and entering heartily into Canning's merry stories of my having been lost; and Mrs. Crewe's relation of my dolorous three sea voyages instead of one, when I came back from Germany;[2] all with very civil pleasantry.

Monday the 2d. Dine with Sir Charles Grey, and twenty or thirty officers from the camp, for whom he keeps a table, and is allowed ten guineas a day towards that expense alone. Sir Charles placed me on Lady Grey's right hand, and took the liberty of placing himself on mine! What do you say to that, Ma'am? You cannot imagine how cordially and openly he talked to me on all sort of things that occurred. I only wish he had kept his eldest hopes in better order. However, he is a charming man; very animated, and, for his time of life, very handsome. To Miss Grey, a very sweet girl of ten or eleven, I gave a copy of the hymn and of the march; and made her try them with me; much to the satisfaction of Sir Charles and his lady. Next day, Lady Grey and her young people came to breakfast with Mrs. Crewe; and Lord Palmerston and his eldest son, Mr. Temple, came in the evening. Lord Palmerston is a great favourite of Mrs. Crewe; she would have his character stand for the leading one in the periodical works at which she wants you to preside.[3] Wednesday, we visited the castle at Dover, its Roman towers, and remains, etc.

Thursday, we go to the camp at Barham Down, and see Mr. Pitt at Sir Charles Grey's. The Duke of Portland and Lady Mary Bentinck arrive at *our* house, where they take up their abode. Friday, go with his Grace and the ladies to the parade, where a *feu de joie*, by two or three thousand militia and regulars, took place for excellent Dutch news. After which, all but the Duke went to the Camp to visit Mr. John Crewe, just appointed Lieutenant-Commandant of the 9th. Regiment, and going abroad. The Duke went on horseback to Walmer Castle, and lent me his chaise and four to follow the three ladies, who occupied Mrs. Crewe's demi-landau. And I dined very comfortably and sociably with the good and gay Sir Charles and his charming Partner, and their engaging young folks. 'Tis a delightful family; all spirit and agreeability. There were likewise a few select officers. I came home alone in the Duke's carriage and four,—in which Canning reports I was again lost!

[1] For Burney's arrangement and translation of this hymn see Bibliography, II. 350.

[2] See I. 240.

[3] See II. 151.

Saturday we go encore to Walmer Castle; Lady Mary Bentinck, Mrs. and Miss Crewe, in Mr. Crewe's chaise and four; and Mrs. Churchill and I in the Duke's. His Grace on horseback. The Duke of York was at the Castle; and all were preparing for the third embarkation for Holland, which did not take place till Sunday, the eighth; when we were all called up at five in the morning. The three ladies set out at six for Deal, which is just by Walmer Castle: but the Duke, who took me in his chaise, did not set off till between seven and eight: and we arrived just before the first boat of transports was launched. After seeing five or six launches, in a very high and contrary wind, we gazers all repaired to lunch at Walmer Castle. Mr. Pitt and Mr. Dundas all hurry, but all attention to his Royal Highness the Duke of York; and to the business of the day. But just as we were going to depart, Mr. Pitt pressed us to stay and take a scrambling dinner, that we might see the Duke of York himself launched. This offer was gladly accepted.

It was truly a scrambling dinner; his Royal Highness, with his aides-de-camp, Lord Chatham, two or three general officers, the Duke of Portland, Mr. Dundas and Lady Jane, and Mrs. Crewe, filled the first table. Lady Mary Bentinck, with her youngest brother, Lord Charles, going also as aide-de-camp to his Royal Highness; Messrs. Ryder and Lady Susan, Miss Scott, Canning, etc., and I, filled the second. Canning is delightful in social parties; full of wit and humour. The cannon on the castle battlements of Walmer and of Deal, and those of all the ships, to the number of at least one hundred and fifty, were fired when his Royal Highness embarked. He looked composed, princely, and noble. It was a very solemn and serious operation to all but the military, who went off in high spirits and glee; though there was a violent east wind against them, which must oblige them to roll about all night, if not all the following day. I pity the sea-sickness of the fresh water sailors more than their fighting.

And so here's my Journal for you up to this day, 9th. September, 1799. And take note, Lady Jane Dundas, Lady Susan Ryder, and Lady Grey, I regard as my *bonnes fortunes* in this expedition. All three have pressingly invited me to their houses in town, and begged that our acquaintance may not drop here. And I don't intend to be cruel!—But *for 'll* this, I hope to get away in a week; for I dread letting the autumn creep on at a distance from my own chimney corner.

BURNEY CONTINUES HIS ACCOUNT OF HIS GAY DOINGS AT DOVER[1]

[To Fanny] 15th. September, 1799.

The Duke and Lady Mary left us two days after my last, but a dinner was fixed for Messrs. Pitt, Dundas, Ryder, and Canning, with *us* at

[1] *Mem.* iii. 278. Burney's age at the date of this letter was seventy-three.

Dover. Now I must give you a little episode. Canning told me that Mr. Pitt had gotten a telescope, constructed under the superintendence of Herschel, which cost one hundred guineas; but that they could make no use of it, as no one of the party had knowledge enough that way to put it together; and, knowing of my astronomical poem, Canning took it for granted that I could help them. The first day I went to Walmer Castle, I saw the instrument, and Canning put a paper in my hand of instructions; or rather, a book, for it consisted of twelve or fourteen pages; but before I had read six lines, company poured in, and I re-placed it in the drawer whence Canning had taken it; and, to say the truth, without much reluctance; for I doubted my competence. I therefore was very cautious not to start the subject! but when I got to Dover, I wrote upon it to Herschel, and received his answer just in time to meet the Dover visit of Mr. Pitt. It was very friendly and satisfactory, as is everything that comes from Herschel; I shewed it to Mr. Pitt, who read it with great attention, and, I doubt not, intelligence.

After discussing all the particulars concerning the telescope, Herschel says: 'When I learn that you are returned to Chelsea, I shall write again on the subject of memorandums that I made when I had the pleasure of hearing your beautiful poetical work'. This I did not let Mr. Pitt see; but withdrew the letter from him after Herschel had done speaking of the telescope, lest it should seem that I more wished Mr. Pitt should see Herschel's civilities to me, than his telescopical instructions. But Mrs. Crewe, in the course of the evening borrowed the letter from me, and shewed it to Lady Jane Dundas; who read it all, and asked what the poetical work meant. Miss Crewe smilingly explained.

The dinner was very cheerful, you may imagine, for these Messieurs had brought with them the important news of the taking of Seringapatam; truly gratifying to Mr. Pitt; but doubly so to Mr. Dundas, who plans and directs all India affairs.

No one can be more cheerful, attentive, and polite to ladies than Mr. Pitt; which astonishes all those who, without seeing him, have taken for granted that he is *no woman's man*, but a surly churl, from the accounts of his sarcastic enemies.

The Major of Mr. Crewe being ill, Mr. Crewe himself could not dine at home, being obliged to remain at Hythe with his regiment; and, after the ladies left the dining room, it having been perceived that none drank port but Mr. Pitt and I; the rest all taking claret, which made the passing and repassing the bottle rather awkward; I was voted into the chair at the head of the table, *to put the bottle about*! and that between the first ministers, Pitt and Dundas! what '*only think*', and '*no notions*', would Miss Larolles[1] have exclaimed! I, so notorious for always stopping the bottle.

When we went to the ladies, music and cheerfulness finished the

[1] See note on II. 298.

evening. The hymn and the march were not forgotten. In talking over Pizarro, Mr. Pitt related, very pleasantly, an amusing anecdote of a total breach of memory in some Mrs. Lloyd, a lady, or nominal housekeeper of Kensington Palace: 'being in company', he said, 'with Mr. Sheridan, without recollecting him, while Pizarro was the topic of discussion, she said to him, "And so this fine Pizarro is printed?" "Yes, so I hear", said Sherry. "And did you ever in your life read such stuff?" cried she. "Why I believe it's bad enough!" quoth Sherry; "but at least, Madam, you must allow it's very loyal." "Ah!" cried she, shaking her head, "loyal? You don't know its author so well as I do!"'

In speaking, afterwards, of the great number of young men who were just embarked for Holland, Miss Crewe, half jocosely, but no doubt half seriously, said it would ruin all the balls! for where could the poor females find partners? 'O', said Mr. Pitt, with a pretended air of condolence, 'you'll have partners plenty—both Houses of Parliament!'

'Besides', said Canning, 'you'll have the whole Bench of Bishops!'

To be sure nobody laughed! Mr. Pitt, by the way, is a great and loud laugher at the jokes of others; but this was so half his own, that he only made *la petite bouche*.

Two days after all this, Mrs. and Miss Crewe brought me on in my way as far as Canterbury.

Now what say you? Is this not a *belle histoire*?

BURNEY HAS WRITTEN A PATRIOTIC SONG[1]

[To Fanny] [November 1799.]

Pray take note, that I have made a song on the five naval British heroes of the present war, to an easy popular tune, which any one with a good ear may sing by memory, after twice hearing. To this I was provoked by Lady Spencer's complaining to me, that though several pretty poems, and a few good songs had been produced by our late victories, yet there were no good new tunes. I have gotten Lady Harrington to send a copy of this naval ditty, both words and music, to the Queen at Windsor: and I have sent another copy to Lady Spencer herself who has bestowed on me the following flattering answer:

'Dear Sir,

I should have returned you my best thanks for your excellent song, and popular air, as soon as I received them; but I have been severely ill: . . . however, I am now somewhat recovered, and able to thank you; which I do most sincerely. I wish you would get it sung at Covent Garden theatre: that is always the progress of these kind of songs; they begin on the stage, and come thence into the street; and this last is the highest honour such music can look to. I declare that whoever composed "Rule Britannia", is next to Handel in my list of composers. That your song may have the same honour,

[1] *Mem.* iii. 269. Burney's age at the date of this letter was seventy-three.

and have it long, my dear Sir, I most heartily hope. I am sure your talents and your excellent intentions, deserve such fame.

I am, dear Sir, etc.
Lav. Spencer.'

Mrs. Crewe, and two or three more, to whom I have communicated this patriotic hullaballoo, join in the opinion of Lady Spencer, that it should be sung at the theatres. That, however, should it be thought worth while, must be negociated by some one else—not by me.

Lord and Lady Spencer are charming people: *he*, now first Lord of the Admiralty, is everything one could wish a man, in his high station, to be; active, accessible, and well-bred. In private life, a lover of literature and talents; manly at once, and elegant in his pursuits; and a model for husbands, for fathers, and for masters. *She* has a natural cheerfulness and sport about her, joined to considerable acquirement; designs and paints well; is a good musician; and has a keenness in reading characters which I have but lately found out; with great eagerness for knowledge of whatever is the subject of conversation.[1]

7th. Nov. Well, Lady Harrington has received the most gracious of requests relative to my ballad; and it is written by Her Royal Highness the Princess Elizabeth:

'Mamma has just commanded me to beg you to return Dr. Burney her thanks for the song he has sent her, which she has already sung; and she thinks it has so much merit, that she wishes Dr. Burney would give her leave to send it to Covent Garden theatre, to be performed there; for she thinks the tune so pretty and simple, that it will become popular.'

BURNEY PUTS A MAN UP FOR THE CLUB[2]

[1800]

Fanny Phillips and I have dined thrice lately with your excellent neighbours, the Lockes, who rise in my esteem and affection at every visit. I have been long thinking of putting up Mr. William Locke at our club, but would not venture without his permission. After our last dinner, therefore, I drew him aside, and fairly asked him whether he would give me leave to try for his election at a club, established under Dr. Johnson, Sir Joshua Reynolds, and Mr. Burke? and he said, after

[1] Lord Spencer was First Lord of the Admiralty for the six years beginning at the end of 1794, i.e. for one of the most glorious periods in British naval history, and has been spoken of as 'the organizer of victory'. He also reorganized the family library, the famous Althorp Collection, which formed the nucleus of the present John Rylands Library at Manchester. He was one of Burney's fellow-members of the Club. His wife, Lavinia, daughter of the Earl of Lucan, was famous for her beauty, intelligence, and conversational gifts, and as such one of the most admired hostesses of London. As a child she knew Johnson and in later life she was the friend of Gibbon, of Nelson and Collingwood, and of prominent men and women in all the major activities of national life.

[2] *Mem.* iii. 298. Burney's age at the writing of this letter was seventy-three. Fanny Phillips was his granddaughter (daughter of Susan; see II. 262). For William Locke see II. 129. For Lord Macartney see II. 115. For Mr. Langton see I. 333.

some modest scruples of being unworthy, that nothing would flatter him more. Yesterday, therefore, I began to canvass Malone, at his own house, and Lord Macartney, *a sotto voce* in the club room before dinner. Malone was readily *de mon avis*; but Lord Macartney, following up the known plan of Dr. Johnson, to select the first man in every profession, for the more exact information of the rest upon those points of which they were ignorant, argued that we ought to have a great painter to supply, as well as he could, the loss of Sir Joshua Reynolds.

And you will have one, my Lord, I cried. The painters all honour themselves in being of that mind with respect to Mr. William Locke. He only happens, by chance, to be heir to a considerable estate; he would else have been a painter by profession, as well as by talent and excellence. In Mr. William Locke we shall have every gratification we can wish for in a new member; he is a scholar, a traveller, a gentleman; and, when he can be prevailed with to talk, the best informed and most pleasing converser with whom men of cultivated minds can wish to associate.

This gave me Lord Macartney as well as Malone; and, after dinner, on that very day, Lord Macartney himself, seconded by Mr. Langton, put up your dear friend's 'eldest hopes'. I was applied to for giving the Christian name, and an assurance that the election was desired by the proposed new member. An entry then was made in the books, and the election will come on at the next club.

BURNEY GETS HIS MAN IN

[To Fanny] [10 January 1800]

I went to the club to-day with fear and trembling, lest I should have involved Mr. William Locke in any disappointment. Langton, though he had willingly seconded Lord Macartney's motion, could not be there: it was a great day at the House, where they were debating the Adultery Bill, which lost us Windham, Canning, Bishop Douglas, Lords Spencer, Ossory, Palmerston, and Mr. Frere, of all whose suffrages I was sure. There were only nine members present; and I saw, on entering the room, with fear and dismay, the person suspected as a general black-baller. I'll try to recollect the nine members: Lord Macartney, Sir Robert Chambers, Malone, Sir Charles Bunbury, Marsden, Dr. Fordyce, Mr. Thomas Grenville, Dr. Vincent, and your humble servant. Canning, whose turn it was to be President, being away, Lord Macartney and two or three more, invited me to take the chair; but I modestly declined the honour! Well, we all seemed in perfect good-humour, and I hobbed a nob; and got two or three more to hob a nob, with the Knight of the Negro Ball; and, after dinner, when the box went round, Sir Charles Bunbury acted as Vice President, and opened it, and—would you think it?—all was as white as milk!—and Mr. William Locke, jun. was declared duly elected.

Sir Charles wrote the usual letter of inauguration, and I one of congratulation; and I sent my own man with both to Manchester Square. And so that fright, at least, is happily over.

If Mr. and Mrs. Locke are with you, pray lay my best respects at their feet; and my love at the hearts of your two Alexanders.[1] And so good night. It is past twelve, and time for all but owls and bats to be at roost.

C. B.

BURNEY IS PRESENTED WITH A PERPETUAL ADMISSION TO THE KING'S CONCERT, AND RETURNS THANKS[2]

Berkeley Square
May 27th. [1804]

Lord Dartmouth is happy to have it in charge from his brother-Directors of the Ancient Concerts, to present the enclosed General Ticket to Dr. Burney; and to beg his acceptance of it as a token of their sense of his merits in the cause of music; and especially that part of it which is more immediately the object of their attention: as well as of the respect in which they all hold his person and character.

Chelsea College
27th May, 1804.

To the Right Honourable the Earl of Dartmouth, Lord Chamberlain of His Majesty's Household, and one of the Directors of the Concerts of Ancient Music.

Dr. Burney presents his most humble respects to the Earl of Dartmouth, and to the rest of the Right Honourable and Honourable Directors of the Concerts of Ancient Music; and feels himself flattered beyond his powers of expression, with the liberal testimony of the esteem and approbation with which he has been honoured by the illustrious Patrons of an Establishment at the formation of which he had the honour to be present; and for its prosperity constantly zealous.

So uncommon and unexpected a token of approbation of his exertions in the cultivation and cause of an art which he has long laboured, and still labours to improve, as well as to record its progress, and the talents of its Professors, from the time of Orpheus to that of Handel; will gild his latter days, and generate a flattering hope that his diligence and perseverance have been regarded in a more favourable light than, in his vainest moments, he had ever dared to hope or imagine.

[1] The 'two Alexanders' were Fanny's husband and son.

[2] *Mem.* iii. 338. Burney's age at the date of this letter was seventy-eight.

BURNEY AND HIS SON SPEND A HAPPY EVENING WITH THE PRINCE OF WALES[1]

[To Fanny] July 12, 1805.

Your brother, Dr. Charles, and I, have had the honour last Tuesday of dining with the Prince of Wales at Lord Melbourne's, at the particular desire of H.R.H. He is so good-humoured and gracious to those against whom he has no party prejudice, that it is impossible not to be flattered by his politeness and condescension. I was astonished to find him, amidst constant dissipation, possessed of so much learning, wit, knowledge of books in general, discrimination of character, as well as original humour. He quoted Homer in Greek to my son as readily as if the beauties of Dryden or Pope had been under consideration. And as to music, he is an excellent critic; has an enlarged taste—admiring whatever is good in its kind of whatever age or country the composers or performers may be; without, however, being insensible to the superior genius and learning necessary to some kinds of music more than others.

The conversation was general and lively, in which several of the company, consisting of eighteen or twenty, took a share, till towards the heel of the evening, or rather the *toe* of the morning; for we did not rise from table until one o'clock, when Lady Melbourne being returned from the opera with her daughters, coffee was ordered; during which H.R.H. took me aside and talked exclusively about music near half-an-hour, and as long with your brother concerning Greek literature. He is a most excellent mimic of well-known characters: had we been in the dark any one would have sworn that Dr. Parr[2] and Kemble were in the room. Besides being possessed of a great fund of original humour, and *good humour*, he may with truth be said to have as much wit as Charles II, with much more learning—for his merry majesty could spell no better than the *bourgeois gentil-homme*.

THE OCTOGENARIAN BURNEY, ON BEING GRANTED A PENSION, RECALLS SOME OF THE LOSSES AND DISAPPOINTMENTS OF HIS LIFE[3]

Chel. Coll., 18th Apr. 1806.

My ever and very dear Lady Crewe.

I had been so long hopeless as to Place or Pensions, after being so many years honoured with the Countenance of the Great and even the friendship of several persons in power, that not a ray of hope had glanced through my mind for many years, till you lately assured me with such confidence, that Mr. Windham had kindly and readily

[1] *Diary and Letters*, vi. 44. Burney's age at the date of this letter was seventy-nine.

[2] Dr. Parr the great classical scholar, a friend of Charles Burney, junior, who named his son after him—Charles Parr Burney (see II. 276).

[3] *Windham Papers*, vol. lxxv. British Museum; Add. MS. 37916, fol. 16. Burney's age at the date of this letter was eighty.

undertaken my cause at your request. This revived all the hopes of youth and inexperience from Patronage: as Mr. Windham, though a Statesman, is not a loose and insincere distributor of moonshine; but like Johnson 'promises others only what he promises himself.'

Were I to give a list of my losses and Disappointments in the course of my long and laborious life, my friends wd. not wonder at my scepticism in the smiles of fortune.

In 1764, I lost a friend by a sudden death (Mr. Honeywood the banker) who gave me £100 a year for dining with him at Hampstead of a Sunday; by whose sudden death I was supposed by his partner and connections, to have lost much more than the £100 a year.

In 1767, I lost my 2d. wife's Dower of £5000, by the bankruptcy of Mr. Gomm the great Russian Timber Merchant to whom the whole had been lent, previous to our marriage, by the advice of Dr. King, Chaplain to our Factory at Petersburg.

I lost the reversion of the place of Master of the King's Band of £300 a year twice. 1st by Ld. Hertford the Chamberlain, 4 of whose daughters were my scholars, and who had promised me the place in case of a vacancy; but asking the K. on the death of Dr. Boyce, whether his Majesty wished him to appoint any particular person, without mentioning my name, Stanley was appointed. 2dly. by Lord Salisbury appointing Parsons the instant he heard of Stanley's death, for fear I shd. be named to the musical profession to be Stanley's successor as a thing of course.

When the Duke of Rutland was Ld. Lieut. of Ireland, Mr. Secretary Ord had procured me a promise of the place of composer and Master of the King's band in Ireland of £200 a year in case of a vacancy during the D. of Rutland's regency: a vacancy *did* happen, when the Prince of Wales knowing nothing of my claim asked the place of the Duchess of Rutland for Crosdill, young enough to be my grandson.

The Pantheon being burnt down in wch. I had purchased a share wch. cost me £700, and the loss of 100 Guineas a year as foreign secretary to engage singers from Italy and Germany.

Two Mortgages in Wales of £1,000, and one in Ireland of £2,000, and I fear gone beyond recovery. I have recd. no interest from either for many years.

Booksellers breaking who had recd. subscriptions for my Histy. of Music; and lately others in whose hands I had placed all the remaining copies of the 4 vols. 4to.—and many *Et ceteras* might be added to the unfortunate events of my life.

But though I have not teazed the Great for favour, they have honoured me with Notice and civilities, wch., though not so solid as place and pension, have flattered and gratified my heart, and made life pass more smoothly and honourably than mere filthy lucre cd. have done. And at last when something of a more solid kind *is* arrived, wch. for some time I have felt myself in danger of wanting, its coming through the medium of persons, whom I have always respected, loved, and honoured, swells its value from 200, to at least 2,000, and so for the present, I shall dilate no more on the subject.

But will your Ladyship (I have kept it off a great while) have the goodness to instruct me how to demean myself (having had no practice that way) on this important occasion? Would it not be right for me to wait upon Lord Grenville, to leave a card at least, and on our Right Honble. and *most* Honourable Advocate Mr. Windham, with a card of grateful thanks to the benignant Mrs. Windham for her benevolent Annunciation of the glad tidings?

The warmth of the weather to day, and of your friendly heart, have enabled me to think of quitting my bed-chamber in order to travel across the cold library into the parlour, where I shall now be most happy in the honour of a call from you any day you will have the goodness to name to,

Dearest Madam, your most devoted
Obliged and Affectionate Servant
The Octogenarian
Chas. Burney
born Apr. 7th O.S. 1726.[1]

BURNEY AND HIS GRAND-DAUGHTER VISIT THE BRISTOL HOTWELLS, RE-READING 'EVELINA' ON THE ROAD THERE[2]

[To Fanny—in France] [May 1806]

I have so much to say that I hardly know where to begin.

At the close of this last summer, I took it into my head that the air, water, rocks, woods, fine prospects, and delightful rides on the Downs, at Bristol Hotwells, and in their vicinity, would do my cough good, and enable me to bear the ensuing winter more heroically than I have done what have preceded it; for since the Influenza of 1804, I have dreaded cold, and night air, as much as they are dreaded by a trembling Italian greyhound. Do you remember Frisk, the pretty little slim dog we had, as successor to Mr. Garrick's favourite pet, Phill?[3] who always pestered Garrick to let him lick his hands and his fingers,—till Garrick, though provoked, could not, in the comic playfulness of his character, help caressing him again, even while exclaiming, when the animal fawned upon him: 'What dost follow me for, eh—Slobberchaps? Tenderness without ideas!' Well, as chill am I now as that poor puppy, Frisk,—though not quite as tender, nor yet, I trust, as void of ideas.

[1] His point in adding this date of birth is that he was writing on his eightieth birthday, for 7th Apr., Old Style = 18th Apr., New Style.

[2] *Mem.* iii. 369. Burney's age at the date of this letter was eighty.

[3] Garrick's Phill had been left in the care of the Burneys when Garrick and his wife went to France and Italy in 1763 (ibid. i. 168).

Well, to the Hotwells at Bristol I went; and took with me Fanny Phillips.[1] And we both took Evelina, as many of its best scenes are at the Wells and at Bath. However we devoured it so eagerly on the journey, that we had only half a volume left when we arrived at No. 7, on Vincent's Parade; where we were sumptuously lodged; and Fanny Phillip's maid went to market; and our landlady dressed our dinners; and, as I had my carriage, and horses, and servant, we did very well: except that we were too late in the season, for we had not above three balmy days in our whole month's residence.

I liked little Evelina full as well as ever; and I have always thought it the best—that is, the most near to perfection of your excellent penmanships. There are none of those heart-rending scenes which tear one to pieces in the last volumes of Cecilia and Camilla. They always make me melancholy for a week. But, for all that, Fanny Phillips and I proposed going through the whole while at Bristol, for our social reading. However, it was not possible; for we could never procure the first volume of Cecilia from any of the Libraries. It was always, as the Italians say of the English when they vainly try for admission, '*Sempre* not at home'.

I made an excursion to the city of Wells for one day and night, to see its admirable cathedral. The Bishop, Dr. Beadon, is an old musical acquaintance of mine, of thirty years' standing. He wished me to have remained a week with him. And I should have liked it very well,—'ma—ma!—ma!'—as the Italians say, I have no weeks to spare!

BURNEY IS CHEERED BY FINDING AN OLD LETTER FROM ROUSSEAU[2]

12th. October [1806]

My dear Fanny,

Do you remember a letter of thanks which I received from Rousseau for a present of music which I sent him, with a printed copy of The Cunning Man, that I had Englishized from his *Devin du Village*?[3] I thought myself the most fortunate of beings, in 1770, to have obtained an hour's conversation with him; for he was then more difficult of access than ever, especially to the English, being out of humour with the whole nation, from resentment of Horace Walpole's forged letter from the King of Prussia;[4] and he had determined, he said, never to read or write again! Guy, the famous bookseller, was the only person he then admitted; and it was through the sagacious good offices of this truly eminent book-man, urged by my friends, Count d'Holbach, Diderot, etc., that the interview I so ardently aspired at was procured for me.

[1] See II. 262.

[2] *Mem.* iii. 371. Burney's age at the date of his writing this letter was eighty.

[3] For an extract from this letter see I. 116.

[4] The mock letter which Walpole wrote at Paris in 1765, which purported to come from Frederick the Great and to offer Rousseau an asylum in his dominion. It greatly pleased Rousseau's enemies and helped to embitter his quarrel with Hume. See I. 111–13.

Well, this letter from the great Jean Jacques, which I had not seen these twenty years, I have lately found in a cover from Lord Harcourt, to whom I lent it, when his lordship was preparing a list of all Rousseau's works, for the benefit of his widow; which, however, he left to find another editor, when Madame Rousseau relinquished her celebrated name, to become the wife of some ordinary man. Lord Harcourt then returned my letter, and, upon a recent review of it, I was quite struck with the politeness and condescension with which Jean Jacques had accepted my little offering, at a time when he refused all assistance, nay, all courtesy, from the first persons both of England and France. I am now writing in bed, and have not the original to quote; but, as far as I can remember, he concludes his letter with the following flattering lines:

'The works, Sir, which you have presented me, will often call to my remembrance the pleasure I had in seeing and hearing you; and will augment my regret at not being able sometimes to renew that pleasure. I entreat you, Sir, to accept my humble salutations.

JEAN JACQUES ROUSSEAU.'[1]

I give you this in English, not daring, by memory, to quote J. J. Rousseau. It was directed to M. Burney, in London; and, I believe, under cover to Lord Harcourt, who always was his open protector.

But is it not extraordinary, my dear Fanny, that the most flattering letters I have received should be from Dr. Johnson and J. J. Rousseau? I can account for it in no other way than from my always treating them with openness and frankness, yet with that regard and reverence which their great literary powers inspired. Much as I loved and respected the good and great Dr. Johnson, I saw his prejudices and severity of character. Nor was I blind to Rousseau's eccentricities, principles, and paradoxes in all things but music; in which his taste and views, particularly in dramatic music, were admirable; and supported with more reason, and refinement, than by any writer on the subject, in any language which I am able to read. But as I had no means to correct the prejudices of the one, nor the principles of the other of these extraordinary persons, was I to shun and detest the whole man because of his peccant parts? Ancient and modern poets and sages, philosophers and moralists, subscribe to the axiom, *humanum est errare*, and yet, every individual, whatever his virtues, science, or talents, is treated, if his frailties are discovered, as if the characteristic of human nature were perfection, and the least diminution from it were unnatural and unpardonable!

God bless you, my dear Fanny. Write soon, and long, I entreat.

[1] Rousseau's letter, in the original French, can be seen in Théophile Dufour's *Correspondance Générale de Jean-Jacques Rousseau* (1924–34) xx. 111.

BURNEY HAS A FRIGHT ABOUT THE LOSS OF HIS ENCYCLOPAEDIA ARTICLES[1]

To
Dr. Charles Burney,
Greenwich,
Kent.

Bath, 5, South Parade
Wedy. Morng. 4th Feb. 1807.

My dear Charles,

I want very much to know how your cold and Rheumatism do, & how you got home. Hearing that you did not leave the York Hostel till 12 o'clock, & had a 70 miles journey to Oxford, on not a good day, & a dark night, I feared it wd. require too great an exertion & be accomplished at a very late hour. Pray let me know how you are, & how you found Carlach [?], and our dear Rosette, when you arrived at your *Dulce Domo.* I consign this letter to the care of Clement Francis, and one to Lady Burke, giving him a power of franking them, equal to a *Membre du Parliament.*

I think my general health is more improved by the pump and air of Bath, than my paralysed Thumb.

But, the 31st of last month, I recd. a letter from Longman, Hurst & Co. wch. was a thunderbolt to me, & has made me sick at heart ever since. I believe I told you, that 8 or 10 days after I had recd. the last instalms. of an agreement, I exerted all my strength when very feeble & out of spirits, in revising for the last time all the remaining articles in letter C,[2] and arranging the references to all the plates that were finished; and this without waiting till these articles were called for—& sent them in a new blue bag, tied, sealed, and directed to Messrs. Longman, Hurst and Co. with wch. parcel I sent my boy into the City on purpose—he delivered the parcel to some young people in the front shop, & did not stay for an answer. I told him, as he had other places to go to, that it was unnecessary. And now I receive with horror & despair the following short Requisition from the partners in Pater Noster Row.

'Dear Sir

Dr. Rees is aground for want of more articles from you; and as we are now printing the Cyclopaedia with great expedition he will thank you to favour him with the remainder of the Letter C.

We are Dear Sir your most humble servants

Longman & Co.'

London, Jany. 29 1807

[1] Unpublished original in the possession of the present author. Burney's age at the date of this letter was eighty.

[2] In view of the fact that Burney began his work on the Rees's *Cyclopaedia* in 1801 he must by 1807 have passed well beyond letter C. He had probably in his first draft travelled very much deeper down the alphabet than this and then, as the printer called for more copy, revised and dispatched his articles. The *Cyclopaedia* was in the first instance published in parts, the issue of these being spread over some years.

Is Longman the Bookseller got into Parliamt.? because, though the preceding letter was not franked, & cost me 8d., in a postcript he says: 'If you have occasion to write to us, you will please to inclose your letter in a cover addressed to

George Longman Esqr. M.P.'

What is all this? and what *can* I do? if I were to live 20 years longer, I cd. never think of re-writing these articles, amounting to 50 or 60, some of them of considerable length. All I can imagine possible is, that the parcel was recd. but thrown aside & put in some improper place and forgotten. The back rooms are in such litters & so crowded with books, papers, proofs, & copies of works printed & to be printed by the firm, that it is likely that my parcel was never conveyed thither—and this accounts for Rees, Straker, Ditton, and all the pater-noster partners applying to me for books, copy, & proofs corrected, without the least allusion to my illness, and Bath Journey—in my parcel I had inclosed a note to Longman & Co. to tell them of my paralytic seizure, and being ordered to Bath by all my Medical advisers—but if this note was never seen, it will acct. for the seeming ill breeding & total want of feeling or common humanity of those who applied to me. This is all I can suggest possible to be the case. If you shd. chance to pass by Longman's House pray step in & inquire whether all possible inquiry and search have been made for my parcel, & the result. And pray beg Mr. Payne[1] to advertise my Histy. now the Town is full & peoples' ready [? money] not all gone.

Near 11 o'clock. Here comes a message from Mrs. Broome to say that Clement is not very well today,[2] & the apothecary thinks he had better not set out today.

BURNEY'S LOST ARTICLES ARE FOUND: CATALANI'S SINGING AND SOME OTHER MATTERS[3]

Bath, 4th Mar. 1807

Dear Charles,

Your long silence made me uneasy for you, and myself. I feared the complaint with which you left Bath had been increased by the hurry and fatigue of your journey—and accidentally hearing that you had written more than once to Ld. Crewe without a word to me as concerning my terrors and vexation concerning the loss of the articles I had sent to Longman and Co. did not contribute to my ease on that

[1] Payne the bookseller and publisher, father of James Burney's wife; he published Hawkins's *History* and Burney's Handel volume and his poem of welcome to Haydn. Evidently Burney had now commissioned him to sell what remained of the volumes of his *History*.

[2] Mrs. Broome was Burney's daughter Charlotte. Clement was one of her children by her first husband, Clement Francis. Mother and son were staying at Bath at the same time as Burney and his granddaughter Fanny Phillips.

[3] Unpublished original in the possession of the present author. Burney at the date of this letter was nearly eighty-one.

Chapter. It was a full week ere I recd. any answer to my complaints addressed to the Pater-Noster Row folks concerning the lost articles. Mr. Strahan did not write a syllable to me on the subject, he only franked the following laconic letter—

'Dear Sir

I write to inform you that the Copy wch. was missing, and wch. was supposed to have been lost, is now found.

I am Sir
Your most obedient servant
Andrew Spottiswood'

New Street
Feby. 2nd.

Not a syllable of apology for the trouble and vexation into wch. I had been plunged, or for the constant requisitions wth. wch. I was teased at setting out & on the road to Bath when I was going in an alarming state of health. Nothing can be more rude & unfeeling than the whole gang, Mr. Strahan among the rest, of whom I used to think better than of the Editor & publishers. I had before I recd. your counsel determined never to part with a line of Copy, without a *receipt* from the person to whom it is delivered.

I shall be obliged to J. Robinson if he will get the dividend for me, & deliver it to you.

I have had an excellent acct. of the Catalani's[1] Talent from my friend Mr. Chinery, a superior Judge of Italian singing, & from Lords Cardigan & Ailesbury of the Concert given to the Queen & princess by the Duke of York, & though I have not heard her, nor perhaps never shall, I can *talk Catalani* with any of the Critics that may either praise or censure her performance. I have had a visit and long conversation with the ingenious & worthy Rauzzini on the subject not only of her Talents but Rapacity—she had the conscience to demand of him for singing at his benefit concert at Bath, 500 Guins. or to procure 700 subscribers at a Guinea a Ticket—that being declined—30s. for a ticket—the prices are low at Bath, & so is the Compy. compared to old times—she having liberty to sing where she pleases, boasts of being engaged at 60 different Concerts—at 200 pds. or Guins. a Night—Harry Greville's select concerts & Masquerade are included in these Concerts.

I fear you have not begged Mr. Payne to advertise my Histy. wch. was one of my petitions when I last wrote to you.[2] These poor books sleep on the peaceable shelves in the back shop—& I am perpetually asked where my Histy. may be had.

I am sorry that sickness has got among your boys. Mrs. Broome & the girls give but a bad acct. of the health of Clement.

[1] Catalani (born 1780) first appeared in London in December 1806, two or three months before the date of this letter.

[2] See II. 312.

Remember me kindly to Rosette, wth. compts. to Mrs. Bicknell. I hope to be able to leave this terrible expensive place the last week in the present Month. Almost all my most agreeable frds. & Visitors are *off*, & none to supply their places except Lady Lowther & 2 of her daughters who call themselves my Grandchildren, I having been Ly. Lowther's Master before her Marriage, when Ly. Augusta Fane. Mrs. Gratton, the charming Mrs. Gratton, wife of the *energetic* Champion for Catholic Emancipation, & 2 of her daughters are at present parade Neighbours, most pleasant & agreeable for myself & Fanny.

Adieu—the post hour is come—so God bless you—

C. B.

BURNEY REQUESTS THE ATTENDANCE OF THE PIANO TUNER[1]

Chel. Coll. June 29th. 1812.

Dr. Burney sends his best compliments to Mr. Broadwood, and shall be much obliged to him if he will have the goodness to let one of his ingenious Foremen regulate the Hammers and touch of his 6 Octave Piano Forte, of wch. each Octave is so ill voiced as to seem of a different register. It is only during the height of summer that Dr. B. has inclination to quit his bed room or strength to put down a key. He hopes his very worthy old Friend Mr. B. Junr. is well, & if able and willing to go out shd. be very glad to see him whenever he will favour him wth. his company. Has Mr. B. seen & heard the little Miss Paton from Edinburgh?[2]

To Mr. Broadwood,
Great Pulteny Street
Golden Square.

[1] Unpublished original in the possession of the present author. Burney's age at the date of this letter was eighty-six.

[2] 'Little Miss Paton' had appeared in Edinburgh two years before, at the age of eight, as singer, reciter, and violinist. She later became a very celebrated operatic soprano. In 1826 she took part in the first performance of *Oberon* and its composer, Weber, wrote home to his wife about her in great enthusiasm. She was singing up to about 1845 and died in 1864.

APPENDICES

EXTRACTS FROM PARISH REGISTERS CONCERNING THE BURNEY FAMILY

(chronologically arranged)

Date	*Church*	*Entry*	*Relationship to Charles*
1678; June 13	Hanwood, near Shrewsbury	'Jacobus, filius Jacobi Mac Burny et Mariae, born May 23, baptised'	Father
1704–5; Jan. 22	St. Julian, Shrewsbury	'James, son of James Macburny, a stranger, and Rebekah, his wife, baptised'	Half-brother
1706; Apr. 25	St. Chad, Shrewsbury	'Mary, daughter of James Mackburney, a Surveior, and [*blank*], Mr. Simit's, Dogg Lane, baptised'	Half-sister
1706; Apr. 28	St. Chad, Shrewsbury	'Mary, daughter of James Mackburney, sirvaor, Dogg Lane, buried'	The same half-sister
1707; Sept. 17	St. Chad, Shrewsbury	'Thomas, son of James Mackburney and Rebecka, Dogg Lane, baptised'	Half-brother
1708–9; Feb. 14	St. Chad, Shrewsbury	'William, son of James and Rebecca Mackburney, baptised'	Half-brother
1712; Apr. 20	St. Chad, Shrewsbury	'Mary, daughter of James and Rebecka Mackburney, baptised'	Half-sister
1714; June 10	St. Mary, Shrewsbury	'Askeboleham [should be Ashburnham], son of James Mack-Burney, at Cotton Hill, and Rebecca, baptised'	Half-brother
1716; Sept. 27	St. Chad, Shrewsbury	'William, son of Mr. Mach Burney, buried'	Half-brother (for birth see above under 1708–9)
1721–2; Mar. 18	St. Chad, Shrewsbury	'Anne, daughter of Ja: Burney, buried'	Half-sister (not mentioned above)
1721; May 6	Abbey Church, Shrewsbury	'Married by lic. James Mackburney and Anne Cooper, both of St. Chad's p'sh'	Father and Mother
1723; July 21	St. Chad, Shrewsbury	'Richard, son of James Berney, baptised'	Brother
1724–5; Mar. 15	St. Chad, Shrewsbury	'Rebecca, daughter of Mac: Burney, baptised'	Sister
1726; May 5	St. Mary, Shrewsbury	'Charles and Susannah, son and daughter of James Mackburny and Anne, baptised'	Self and twin sister

Date	*Church*	*Entry*	*Relationship to Charles*
1732; Apr. 29	St. Alkmund—(information in Newling MS. no. 325, f. 59, in Shrewsbury Public Library)	'James Burney married to Anne Wood'	Half-brother
1733; Apr. 9	St. Mary, Shrewsbury	'Letitia, Daughter of Mr. James Mackburney and Anne, baptised'	Niece (i.e. daughter of half-brother)[1]
1734; Sept. 19	St. Alkmund—(information as under 1732, above)	'Letitia, daughter of James and Anne Macburney, buried'	Niece (see above)[1]
1750; July 5	St. Dionis's Backchurch, London	'*James*, son of Charles Burney and Esther Burney, Organist of this parish, born 13 June, Baptised'	Son
1751; June 16	,,	'*Charles Burney*, Son of Charles and Esther Burney (Organist of this par:); born 3 June. Baptised'	Son
1752; July 7	St. Nicholas, King's Lynn	'*Frances* (born 13 June). Baptised'	Daughter
New Style begins; 11 days lost, Sept. 2nd being immediately followed by Sept. 14th.			
1752; Oct. 12	St. Nicholas, King's Lynn	'*Charles*. Buried' (apparently the child whose baptism is recorded 16 June 1751)	Son
1754; Jan. 5	,,	'*Charles*. Buried' (no record of birth or baptism apparently)	Son
1755; Jan. 31	St. Margaret, King's Lynn	'*Susanna Elizabeth*. Baptized' (no record of birth, apparently)	Daughter
1758; Jan. 2	,,	'*Charles*. Baptized. Born 4 Dec. 1757'	Son
1760; May 10	,,	'*Henry Edward*. Buried' (no record of birth, apparently)	Son
1767; Oct. 2	St. James, Westminster (= St. James, Piccadilly)	'Charles Burney, of this parish, to Elizabeth Allen, of Lynn Regis, Norfolk, by Licences of the Archbishop of Canterbury'	Self and second wife
1789; June 19	St. Mary, Shrewsbury	'Mr. James Burney (organist) buried'	Half-brother (birth under 1704–5 above)

[1] As the names of Charles's half-brother and his wife are the same as those of his father and mother there is here no absolute certainty, but only a strong probability that the former and not the latter are in question. In other words this *might* be a younger sister of Charles. However, information in the *Family Memoranda*, &c., tells against this suggestion.

SOME ORGANS BURNEY PLAYED

James Burney's Organ at St. Chad's, Shrewsbury

(Played by Charles Burney, as his pupil and assistant)

THE builder was Thomas Schwarbrook, of Warwick, and the date 1716. Like other organs of the period this one was strong in mutation and mixture stops—especially on the Great Organ, which, out of thirteen stops, appears to have included only two flue stops of the normal 8-foot pitch and two of 4-foot.

Other features characteristic of the period are: (*a*) the lack of any pedal-board (here Britain lagged about 300 years behind Germany); (*b*) the extension of two of the manuals downwards half an octave beyond the present lowest note—so compensating a little for the lack of pedals; (*c*) the use of 'short octaves' at the bottom of the keyboard—for an explanation of this term see the article 'Short Octaves' in the *Oxford Companion to Music*; (*d*) the economy of running certain stops down merely to middle C, so saving the cost of the larger pipes (of the twenty-six stops on the organ no fewer than eleven are thus curtailed).

Less common features of the instrument are the following: (*a*) the combination of Choir and Swell on one manual (the swell box device, in the crude form of a shutter rising and falling, had been introduced only four years before this organ was built, the first organ to possess it being that built by Jordan, at St. Magnus the Martyr, London Bridge, in 1712: in this detail Britain was in front of Germany, for when Burney came to travel in that latter country sixty years later he came across only one organ supplied with a swell box); (*b*) the Flageolet stop, possibly the first instance of this; (*c*) the Drum-pedal, which admitted wind to the lowest two notes of the Great Organ, so producing a drum or thunder effect.

GREAT ORGAN. 13 stops.

Compass: GG (short 8ves) to D in alt.

1. Open Diapason.
2. Stopped Diapason.
3. Principal.
4. Octave, to middle C.
5. Twelfth.
6. Fifteenth.
7. Tierce (17).
8. Lesser Tierce (19).
9. Cornet, treble.
10. Sesquialtera, bass.
11. Fourniture.
12. Trumpet.
13. Clarion.

CHOIR ORGAN. 6 stops.

Compass: same as Great Organ.

14. Open Diapason, to middle C.
15. Stopped Diapason.
16. Principal.
17. Flute, to middle C.
18. Fifteenth.
19. Trumpet, to middle C.

Nos. 14 and 19 were enclosed as a Swell, and the box was opened by a pedal.

ECHO. 7 stops.

Compass: Middle C to D in alt. = 27 notes

20. Open Diapason.
21. Stopped Diapason.
22. Principal.
23. Flageolet.
24. Twelfth.
25. Fifteenth.
26. Trumpet.

Drum-pedal, sounding G and F♯

Burney's Organ at St. Dionis's Backchurch, London

The builder was Renatus Harris, junior,[1] and the date 1723–4. Some of the remarks just made on the Shrewsbury organ apply to this equally. The following appears in the first and second editions of Grove's *Dictionary of Music*:

'This admirable organ, made by one of the fourth generation of Harrises, who died young, was remarkable for the number and excellence of its reed-stops, as well as for the general goodness of its Flue-work. This organ had several stops by "communication", either wholly or partially, and from different notes. The introduction of the GG♯ was an unusual feature. It appears to have been the earliest organ to contain a "French Horn" stop. "Tenor D" was a peculiar note for it to be terminated upon; but it nevertheless remained the standard note for special stops for many years. The Swell had no separate Principal. Where this was the case, the Principal was included in the Cornet.'

GREAT ORGAN. 12 stops, plus one borrowed.

Compass: GG (with GG sharp) to D in alt.

	Pipes
1. Open Diapason	56
2. Stopped Diapason	56
3. Principal	56
4. Twelfth	56
5. Fifteenth	56
6. Tierce	56
7. Larigot	56
8. Sesquialtera, 4 ranks	224
9. Cornet, to middle C, 5 ranks	135
10. Trumpet	56
11. French Horn, to tenor D	37
12. Clarion	56
13. Cremona, from Choir Organ by communication	00
	900

CHOIR ORGAN. 8 stops, plus one borrowed.

Compass: same as Great Organ.

14. Open Diapason to middle C, by communication below	27
15. Stopped Diapason to Gamut G, by communication below	44
16. Principal	56
17. Flute	56
18. Fifteenth	56
19. Cremona	56
20. Bassoon	56
21. Vox Humana	56
22. Clarion, from Great Organ by communication	00
	407

[1] See, however, footnote on I. 48.

SWELL ORGAN. 7 stops.

Compass: Fiddle G to D in alt.

23. Open Diapason	32	27. Clarion	32
24. Stopped Diapason	32	28. Cremona	32
25. Cornet, 4 ranks	128	29. Vox Humana	32
26. Trumpet	32		320
		Total	1627

It will be noted that the manual compass (Great and Choir) extended downwards half an octave beyond that of to-day.

Burney's Organ at St. Margaret's, King's Lynn

This was built in 1754 by John Snetzler, to Burney's specification or a specification approved by him. The following remarks appear in Hopkin & Rimbault's *The Organ* (1855 and later editions):

'The Lynn organ is the first that contained a Dulciana, of which it had two, one in the Choir and one in the Swell. It also had a Bourdon in the Great Organ, to CC, of metal throughout, except the lowest two notes, which were of wood. The three manuals were complete, and a Bass to the Swell was obtained from three of the Choir Organ Stops, by three additional sliders and as many separate drawstops.'

GREAT ORGAN. 12 stops.

Compass: GG to E in alt.

	Pipes		*Pipes*
1. Bourdon, to CC	53	7. Tierce	57
2. Open Diapason	57	8. Sesquialtera, 4 ranks	228
3. Stopped Diapason	57	9. Furniture, 3 ranks	171
4. Principal	57	10. Cornet, to middle C, 5 ranks	145
5. Twelfth	57	11. Trumpet	57
6. Fifteenth	57	12. Clarion	57
			1053

CHOIR ORGAN. 7 stops.

Compass: GG to E in alt.

13. Dulciana, of metal throughout	57	16. Flute	57
14. Stopped Diapason	57	17. Fifteenth	57
15. Principal	57	18. Bassoon up to Fiddle G	36
		19. Vox Humana	57
			378

SWELL. 8 stops, plus 3 borrowed bass stops.

Compass: Tenor F to E in alt.

20. Open Diapason	36	26. Trumpet		36
21. Stopped Diapason	36	27. Hautboy		36
22. Dulciana	36	a. Stopped Bass from Choir		
23. German Flute, to Middle C	29	b. Dulciana Bass	do.	
24. Cornet, 4 ranks	144	c. Flute Bass	do.	389
25. French Horn	36		Total	1820

This organ had no pedals until 1852, when they were added by Holdich. It will be noted that the manual compass (Great and Choir) extended downward half an octave beyond that of to-day.

'BISHOP'S FACULTY TO SELL THE OLD ORGAN AND ERECT A NEW ONE IN ST. MARGARET'S CHURCH IN KING'S LYNN, NORFOLK

Dated the Eighth Day of December 1753

THOMAS by Divine permission Bishop of Norwich.

To our beloved in Christ James Fysh and Edmund Elsden churchwardens of the Parish and Parish Church of St. Margaret in King's Lynn in the County of Norfolk and our Diocese of Norwich, Greeting. Whereas it has been represented unto us by a petition under your hands that the Mayor Aldermen and Common Council of the Borough of King's Lynn, aforesaid, have presented the said parish, to be set up in the Church of St. Margaret aforesaid (lately rebuilt) a new Organ. That the Parishioners, pursuant to Public Notice given, met together, at which meeting you the said Petitioners were directed to apply for our License or Faculty for the taking down and selling the Old Organ now erected in the said Church. Whereof you the said Petitioners have accordingly desired our Licence and Faculty to take down and sell the said Old Organ, and to erect the new one at the west end of the said Church. Now know ye that we the said Bishop being fully satisfied of the truth and reasonableness of your said petition, Have therefore thought fit to give and grant and by these presents Do (as far as by Law we may) Give and grant unto you our license and faculty to take down and sell the said old Organ and to erect the new one at the west end of the said church.

Hereby strictly enjoining you to render an account to us or our Vicar General when lawfully required of what money shall arise by the sale of the said Old Organ and how the same shall have been applied and expended.

Given under the Seal of Office of our Vicar General in Spirituals (which in this case we use) this 8th day of December in the year of our Lord one Thousand seven hundred and fifty three.

Original deposited in the Church Chest. } HEN. FIELD. Dep. Regr.'

BURNEY'S ATTEMPTS TO SECURE ROYAL APPOINTMENTS

1765. First Attempt (*Failure to be appointed a Musician to the King*)

Fanny (*Mem.* i. 185) speaks of her father, in 1765, making efforts to be appointed 'Master of the King's Band', as 'the highest professional honour to be obtained', and narrates at length the circumstances of his attempt and of his disappointment. But there can have been no vacancy in 1765, for Boyce had been appointed in 1755 and remained in office until his death in 1779. It is true that about 1765 Boyce became too deaf to continue his church appointments, but he did not relinquish his royal office, which was really that of composer (the Band had also a 'Conductor', 'C. Weidemann, £100'), and *The Musical Times* of July 1901 contains a list of all his royal New Year Odes and Birthday Odes, without missing a year, from his appointment to his death. It will be seen in a moment that on Boyce's death, fourteen years after the date Fanny mentions as that of her father's application, Burney did seek to succeed him and was foiled. All the details Fanny gives undoubtedly attach to the year 1779.

Then why does she mention the year 1765? Probably because she remembered that when she was a child of thirteen there was disappointment in the family over her father's failure to obtain a royal position, and what is related immediately below suggests that the position was merely that of an 'Extra Musician' (which he obtained two years later), or that of 'Musician in Ordinary' (which he obtained nine years later). Fanny has then, writing in old age, naturally enough confused two of her father's several attempts to obtain places about the Court.

1767. Second Attempt (*Success in appointment as 'Extra Musician' in the King's Band*)

The Royal Kalendar shows that 'C. Burney' was appointed to the King's Band in this year, as an 'Extra Musician'. His name henceforth remains in the list until his death. The first appearance of his name is at the bottom of the list, and it then moves gradually upwards, apparently by seniority, until at his death he is fifth from the top.

At the time of his appointment as 'Extra Musician', in 1767, he was not a Doctor of Music. Even when he became such the list in the Kalendar shows no cognizance of the fact—until 1811, when he figures as 'Charles Burney, D.M.' (The fact is, however, earlier recognized in the official Appointment Book—see below.)

1774. Third Attempt (*Appointment as 'Musician in Ordinary' to the King*)

In this year Burney received promotion, for in the Public Record Office is the following document (Records of the Lord Chamberlain's Department: Appointment Books; Series I, 1754 to 1775, vol. 58, fol. 418):

'Whereas Dr. Charles Burney is by my Warrant Sworn and admitted into the Place and Quality of Musician in Ordinary to His Majesty, in the room of James Dell Deceased. To Commence on the 20th of May 1774. Given under my Hand, the 10th of June 1774. Hertford.

'These are to Certify that I have Sworn and admitted Doctor Charles Burney, into the Place and Quality of Musician in Ordinary to His Majesty, in the Room of James Dell, Deceased; In witness whereof I have hereunto Set my Hand and Seal the 13th of June 1774.

Edwd. Sneyd
Gentn. Usher, Daily Waiter.'

As this appointment and the previous one are never mentioned by Fanny (nor, it is thought, by any writer previous to the present) one feels at first a little sceptical as to whether the documents cited refer to *our* Burney. Can the 'Charles Burney' mentioned be not himself but his nephew, the harpsichordist, Charles Rousseau Burney? The use in the above of the prefix 'Doctor' (twice) answers this question. We never hear of Burney's nephew attaining academical rank, and at a later date, as will be seen, there is mention in certain Government reports of Burney himself as occupying the position in question.

The salaries of the rank and file members of the band are mentioned in the *Court and City Register* as '£24–40'. As all we know about Burney shows him to have been a man very busily engaged professionally about London it is clear that he could not, for this small remuneration, be constantly running down to Windsor to perform his duties. Probably, however, this was never required. The Band (i.e. the *full* Band of about thirty members) would play only at St. James's Palace. The *Court and City Register* says that Levee Days were weekly on Wednesday and Friday, with Monday, also, when Parliament was in session. For these levees the Court came up from Windsor (indeed, to judge by Fanny's *Diary* when she was, later, Lady-in-Waiting at the Court, the King and Queen spent a good deal of their time on the road). It is not by any means to be taken for granted that the Band was present even on all Levee Days, and probably Burney's duties (if his post was not a complete sinecure, as it may have been) were quite light: New Year's Days and King's Birthdays were the great occasions, a specially composed 'Ode' by the 'King's Master' being performed whenever one of these came round.[1]

The Report of the Select Committee on Finance in 1798 shows that at that date Burney was receiving a salary of £40 a year, whilst that of the Commission of Military Inquiry, in 1812, shows that his salary was then only £30. He held the post to the end of his life, for his name

[1] Since the above was in type an article by Mr. Adam Carse, embodying the results of his recent research into the royal music, has confirmed the suggestion that Burney's post might be 'a complete sinecure'. It appears that the Lord Chamberlain appointed as nominal (yet salaried) members of the band 'his friends, or their butlers, valets, or other servants', many of whom 'could not play upon any instrument' (*Music and Letters*, July 1946).

appears in the list up to 1814. As latterly he was in feeble health, the post must either have always been, or have now become, a sinecure—or the duties have been done by deputy. Possibly the reduction of salary from £40 to £30 is explained by the appointment of a deputy.

It will be noted from the signature on the above document that the Lord Chamberlain was Lord Hertford, lately Ambassador in Paris—and we remember that Burney, when he took his children to that city, had somewhat frequented the Embassy there, becoming very friendly with Hume, its Secretary. Hertford returned to England about the same time as Burney did, served for a very short period as Lord Lieutenant of Ireland and became Lord Chamberlain in 1766. Burney had doubtless kept in touch with him since, and it is just possible that this facilitated his appointment as 'Extra Musician' and his promotion to 'Musician in Ordinary'. On the other hand, it is equally possible that the promotion was automatic on the death of a colleague in the Band.

1779. FOURTH ATTEMPT (*Failure to succeed Boyce as Master of the King's Band*)

Some information as to this comes from a letter of Burney, in old age, to Lady Crewe (given on II. 306–8), in which Burney, recounting some of the disappointments of his life, says: 'I lost the reversion of the place of Master of the King's Band, of £300 a year twice, 1st by Ld. Hertford, the Chamberlain, 4 of whose daughters were my scholars, and who had promised me the place in case of a vacancy, but asking the K. on the death of Dr. Boyce, whether his Majesty wished to appoint any particular person, without mentioning my name, Stanley was appointed.'

Fanny, who, as we have seen, wrongly dated the incident as occurring in 1765, gives a slightly different account, also implicating Lord Hertford who, it will be remembered, had an official connexion with Burney's appointment to minor positions previously. It appears, according to her, that the Lord Chamberlain, Burney's acquaintance, Lord Hertford, had promised that Burney should have the position when a vacancy should occur, that Burney, immediately he heard that a vacancy *was* occurring, recalled the promise, and that he received the 'confounding intelligence' that 'the place was disposed of already'.[1]

Somebody 'had a pull' with one higher than the Lord Chamberlain—with the King's brother, the Duke of York. To learn this was an additional blow to Burney, for, when playing at private concerts in the great houses of London, he had often had pleasant relations with the Duke, and so he felt entitled to look for his support. However, the Duke had been 'got at' by somebody possessing early intelligence, and had put in his word at the right moment, the vacancy had been immediately filled, and despite the warm efforts of Hume, who tried to get hold of Lord Hertford (his former chief at the Paris Embassy; see above),

[1] *Mem.* i. 185; see also *Letters of David Hume*, ed. Greig, 2 vols., 1932.

and, failing him, did get hold of the Countess (who 'had an esteem for' Burney and said the matter 'gave her great uneasiness'), nothing could now be done. Life *is* like that!

The one satisfaction Burney felt was that of having had the warmest and most energetic action taken on his behalf by Hume, 'a man who was then almost universally held to be at the head of British literature'.

The discrepancy between Fanny's account of the incident in her *Memoirs* of her father, and Burney's in the letter above mentioned, may possibly be accounted for as follows:

Lord Hertford's explanation at the time, exculpating himself, was as Fanny relates it, and this remained in her mind (possibly, indeed, being the only explanation she ever heard).

Burney himself would at the time accept this as accurate, but at some later date (possibly many years later, and perhaps during Fanny's long absence in France, when for a long period no communications passed between her and her father or family) he may have heard the truth from one of his Court friends in reminiscent mood.

The probability is that this second tale is correct. Hertford most likely forgot his promise to Burney until reminded of it too late, so giving the Duke of York his chance. He then slightly twisted the facts in order to clear himself of blame. After all, he was a diplomat by profession!

1782. Fifth Attempt (*Failure to succeed Kelway as 'Organist in the Queen's Band of Musick'*)

The only information as to this attempt seems to be that in a letter from Mrs. Thrale to some person unknown, which letter was included some years ago in catalogue No. 980 of Messrs. Tregaskis, the eminent London experts in old books and autographs. The firm most generously supplied me with a copy and I here give this in full:

Dear Sir—

You will think me mad about Musick and Musicians, when I intreat your Friendship to assist me in serving Dr. Burney: but he wishes to succeed Kelway as Queen's Master, & well do you know that no Man breathing can produce such Claims for the Honour. If a consummate Knowledge of the Theory of his Art, if Perfection in the practice of it; if the Knowledge of a Scholar, the elegance of a Gentleman, and the Conduct of an amiable inoffensive Man, can be urged as Claims—my dear Doctor Burney will not fail of Success—but all this will not shew him the way to Court Preferment; and what I torment you now for, is to *put us in the Road.*

Do but tell me *who,* & *how* & *where*; and we will not rest till something can be done: the Duke of Montagu I am told should be applied to—how shall I get at the Duke of Montagu?

Mrs. Crewe will I hope be a Canvasser in his Favour, Mrs. Boscawen I know is deeply engaged in the Business. Pray forgive me. I am always interrupting *your* Business or your Pleasure, but it is never in behalf of unworthy Objects; & nothing can more effectually prove my Zeal to serve them, than the Risque I am perpetually running of displeasing You, for whom I have so perfect an Esteem & to whom I owe such Obligations. Let me this *once* hope for Excuse & Assistance, & I was going to protest!—but I thought better of it; & am rather inclined to hope that such will be very soon your Situation, as may encourage a variety of Teizers: & among them Your already infinitely Obliged

& Grateful Servant

Streatham H. L. Thrale.

June 14: 1782.

It will be seen that Mrs. Thrale speaks of the desired appointment as that of 'Queen's Master' in succession to Kelway (who had just died), and since Grove's *Dictionary* and the *Dictionary of National Biography* both tell us that Kelway was Queen Charlotte's harpsichord teacher from her arrival in the country in 1761, it is, at first sight, natural to take it for granted that the position Burney sought was also that of teacher. But those works of reference are wrong. The Queen's harpsichord teacher was never Kelway. John Christian Bach had been appointed to that position in 1762. The title-page of his Six Sonatas, Op. 11 (1764), describes him as 'Maître de Musique de S.M. la Reine d'Angleterre'. Mrs. Papendiek (i. 64) tells us that he was in constant attendance at the Court and, as the royal children one by one grew old enough, taught them as well as their mother. He continued in the position until his death on 1 January 1782, and then, before he was even in his grave, J. S. Schröter was appointed in his stead—see the *Public Advertiser*, 5 January 1782.

When Mrs. Thrale wrote this letter, six months after that last date, there was, then, no vacancy for 'Queen's Master', in the sense of *teacher of the harpsichord*. Schröter already held that position.

Kelway's appointment has been misdescribed in Grove and *D.N.B.* He was not, as Grove puts it, the Queen's 'instructor on the harpsichord', but '*Organist*' (with the implication also of harpsichordist) in '*the Queen's Band of Musick*'. This Band (see *Court and City Register*, 2nd edition, 1775, p. 71) consisted of 4 Violins, 1 Tenor, 1 'Cello, 1 Double Bass, 2 Oboes, and 'Mr. Kelway, Organist'.

As we have just seen, Burney already held a position in the King's Band, and he evidently wished to become a pluralist—about which wish there was nothing at all abnormal, since the lists of the two bands show that several musicians were members of both.

Apparently, however, this attempt of Burney's failed, for we hear no more of the matter.

1783 or 1784. Sixth Attempt (*Failure to obtain the post of 'Composer of the State Music in Ireland'*)

Our information here comes from Burney's letter to Lady Crewe already mentioned—'When the Duke of Rutland was Ld. Lieut. of

Ireland, Mr. Secretary Ord had procured me a promise of the place of composer and Master of the King's band in Ireland of £200 a year in case of a vacancy during the D. of Rutland's regency: a vacancy did happen, when the Prince of Wales knowing nothing of my claim, asked the place of the Duchess of Rutland for Crosdill, young enough to be my *grandson*.'

There are certain minor difficulties here. For example, Crosdill obtained the appointment in 1783 (according to Grove's *Dictionary*), whereas it was in 1784 that the Duke of Rutland became Viceroy of Ireland. Also Crosdill, born in 1751 was *not* young enough to be the grandson of Burney (born 1726). However, these are probably merely details of mis-statement. No doubt the facts are substantially as Burney above gives them.

But would he have gone to Ireland? It would probably have been unnecessary. There seems to be no evidence that Crosdill ever did so. Just as Boyce's duties at the English Court seem to have been merely those of the composition of *pièces d'occasion*, so probably would Burney's at the Irish Court. He would, so to speak, have done his duties by post.

However, Dublin was at that period a great social and musical centre and it is just possible that, like his early acquaintances, Arne and Handel, and the many instrumentalists and singers of the day, he would have been glad occasionally to spend a little time in the Irish capital, which until the Union of 1801, with the consequent disappearance of its residential importance as the seat of a Parliament, was one of the musical cities of Europe.

1786. SEVENTH ATTEMPT (*Failure to succeed Stanley as 'Master of the King's Band'*)

In the letter to Lady Crewe just quoted Burney refers to this as follows: 'I lost the reversion of the place of Master of the King's band . . . 2dly by Lord Salisbury appointing Parsons the instant he heard of Stanley's death, for fear I shd. be named to the musical profession to be Stanley's successor as a thing of course.' Fanny's fuller version of the occurrence has been given on II. 23–4.

It will be seen that Burney on at least seven occasions endeavoured to secure royal appointments, failing in all but two of them. In the investigations concerning five of these occasions I had the assistance of the late Professor Charles Sanford Terry, author of (amongst many other works on English, Scottish, and musical history) what must ever remain the standard work on John Christian Bach. On account of this last-named musician's Court appointment Professor Terry had accumulated a good deal of information on such matters, which he was good enough to place entirely at my disposition. The conclusions reached above, so far as they concern the five occasions mentioned, had his assent. Of another occasion (the Irish position) I have learnt only since his death, by the discovery in the British Museum of the letter from Burney to Lady Crewe.

Although Burney was not a very successful applicant for Court position for himself he had the satisfaction of seeing one offered to his daughter. And, in addition to the appointment as Musician in Ordinary to the King, he was to receive a minor government appointment as Organist of Chelsea Hospital and also, in old age, to be gratified with the grant of a royal pension. So he did not do so badly! But, in any case, he never seems to have adopted, in any serious way, the pose of a disappointed man, and the letter to Lady Crewe is the only complaint on his part which has come to the present writer's notice.

THE STRANGE CEREMONIES OF REFFLEY SPRING, NEAR LYNN, AND ARNE'S MUSIC FOR THEM

IN the list of Arne's 'opera and other stage pieces' in Grove's *Dictionary* is found '*Reffley Spring 1772*' (a work not referred to in Cummings's book on Arne).

I do not know where the date 1772 comes from, but it is possibly correct, as the work was published by 'C. & S. Thompson, No. 75 S. Paul's Church Yard', and according to Kidson's *British Music Publishers* this firm, under this style, was publishing from 1764 to 1776–8.

Reffley Spring is not, properly, an 'opera' or a 'stage piece'. Its title-page styles it *A Cantata composed for the Dedication of the Water to the Deities of Love and Social Enjoyment, the Music by Dr. Arne.* This refers to ceremonies still maintained at the chalybeate spring in the parish of Gaywood, about two miles from Lynn. The waters of the spring were celebrated for the brewing of punch, which liquor, made according to a secret recipe, is still, it is said, consumed annually beside it.

The spring 'rises, amongst overhanging trees, in a large basin with a fine central obelisk, backed by an octagonal temple, and with convenient seats surrounding a bright verdant lawn. It belongs to Sir William ffolkes, Bart.,[1] and by the first baronet, member for Lynn, was appropriated as a place of resort for the people of the town.' (Lecture by Rev. E. J. Alvis, Vicar of East Winch, in St. James's Hall, Lynn, 23 Nov. 1900.)

The octagonal building is small; it bears the inscription, 'REFFLEY TEMPLE—ERECTED BY A FRIENDLY SOCIETY, A.D. 1789. WHOEVER DEFACES IT WILL BE PROSECUTED. ENLARGED A.D. 1851.' A raised flat stone in the Temple enclosure is lettered: 'THIS STONE TABLE WAS PRESENTED TO THE MEMBERS OF REFFLEY BY A FRIEND, JUNE 22ND 1778.' There is also a very large tree-stump, apparently serving as an

[1] Now to Sir Francis ffolkes.

additional table. In front of the Temple are two sphinxes: behind it is a small kitchen.

On the visit of the present writer to this spot he apparently overlooked a Latin inscription at the base of a column. Of this the Hon. Secretary informs him that it conveys the information that the spring was dedicated to 'Bacchus and Venus, the gods of this place' on the 24 June 1756, when 'the column rose more beautiful than before from its ruin'. The original date of the dedication of the spring to its quasi-religious purposes is unknown: local tradition associates it with anti-government gatherings in the time of the Commonwealth. The earliest remaining document of the Society is a 'Bett Book', dated 1789, which records some very odd wagering amongst the members.

Arne's Cantata consists of recitatives, airs, and choruses, all very convivial and very amorous, designed to accompany the elaborate ceremonial which is thus set out as the music proceeds:

'The Company being ranged near the Spring, the High Priest, standing in the centre (Crown'd with a wreath of Ivy, Myrtle, and Roses), begins the Recitative.

1. Here all advance to, and encircle the Spring.
2. From a charger, brim full of excellent Punch (a Liquor for which this Chalybeate Water is Celebrated) a Goblet is filled, and handed to the High Priest).
3. Here a quantity of Loaf Sugar is thrown into the bason, which the Water flows into.
4. Whilst the Symphony is playing, the High Priest gives the most Beautiful Toast in the Universe, Venus, which goes round, and the Air is sung.
5. From the Charger a copious Bowl is filled, and delivered to the High Priest, as before.
6. Here a Bottle of Brandy is poured into the bason.
7. Again, while the Symphony is playing, the High Priest gives the Toast most pleasing to those "Who, impotent of thought, puff away Care". Bacchus goes round.
8. A Lemon is squeezed into the Bason.
9. Here the Bowl is again replenished, and given to the High Priest.
10. Venus and Bacchus, the Deities of Reffley United, constitute the Toast that goes round, previous to the Song.'

It will be realized that, if the cantata was actually, as appears, performed on the spot, a considerable body of musicians must have been in attendance, and it is curious that written or printed record has not been found and that no Lynn tradition seems to exist as to a performance or performances of the work. Some revival of the music and ritual would offer an opportunity for local pageantry. Why not?—say at five years' intervals. It is not every place that can boast the possession of a musical work of local intention by a composer of Arne's standing and ability. It is gloomily reported that present musical efforts of the 'Sons of Reffley' (always thirty in number) at their annual celebration do not rise above *Cock Robin.* They play bowls, drink punch out of some beautiful old china, eat a lavish lunch and smoke churchwarden pipes (lit at an ancient lantern), sing their simple song—and that, it is disappointingly reported, is all they do.

The purposes of mentioning this cantata of Arne's in the present book are mainly two: (*a*) the work has been generally overlooked by writers on Arne and it seems desirable that its existence in print should be recalled to notice; (*b*) it has been suggested in Lynn (e.g. in the lecture by the Rev. E. J. Alvis above quoted) that the friendship between Burney and Arne led the one to induce the other to pay a visit to him at Lynn and that this was the result of the visit. This may be, but it must be observed that Burney left Lynn at least four or five years (or even, according to Grove's date of the Cantata, twelve years) before the *publication* of the music and that no mention of the work appears in Fanny Burney's *Memoirs* of her father, or in Burney's treatment of Arne in his *History of Music.* Further, as Burney himself had already successfully composed for the London theatres, one would suppose that he himself would be called on to compose any convivial music required for local use.

BURNEY AND THE DUKE OF YORK

THE following occurs in the article on Burney in an old work (undated), *The Lives of Eminent and Illustrious Englishmen from Alfred the Great to the Latest Times*:

> 'Dr. Johnson, in one of his letters to Mrs. Thrale, states that his friend Burney had given fifty-seven lessons in one week. The Duke of York was so captivated by some of the most wild and difficult lessons of Scarlatti, which he had heard his little daughter play, that he desired him to put parts to them in the way of concertos. These were frequently performed to His Royal Highness and his friends by Pinto, at the head of a select band.'

I do not know the source of this anecdote and think that the value Fanny Burney set upon royal contacts and approval would have ensured the recording of such an incident in her *Memoirs* of her father.

The same consideration seems to dispose of the statement concerning Burney's return from Lynn, in the *Nouvelle Biographie Universelle* (1853), to the effect that he was 'rappelé dans la capitale par un de ses protecteurs, le duc de York'. The Duke of York referred to is clearly Edward Augustus, 1739–67, brother of George III. This statement that the Duke of York recalled Burney from Norfolk goes back at least as far as Gerber's *Historisch-Biographisches Lexicon der Tonkünstler* (Leipzig, 1790).

BURNEY BICENTENARY COMMEMORATION

THE following is taken from the London *Daily Telegraph of* 12 April 1926:

'On April the twelfth, 1814, Dr. Charles Burney died at Chelsea College, "full of years, and rich in all that should accompany old age." He was born on April 12, 1726, and, yesterday, to mark the bicentenary of that event, the Londoners' Circle held a commemoration at the Royal Hospital, Chelsea (by kind permission of the governors). At half-past two, members assembled at the main entrance to the hospital, and then proceeded to visit the organist's quarters in the hospital, which were formerly occupied by the Burney family. In 1783, after his appointment at Chelsea College, Dr. Burney moved from his house in St. Martin's-street, Leicester-square (formerly Newton's residence) and took up residence in a suite of rooms provided for him in the college, where he passed the last twenty-five years of his life.

'After visiting the organist's quarters, the circle assembled in the chapel to hear Professor Joseph C. Bridge (who was chairman for the afternoon) deliver a short lecture on "Burney the Musician." During the few minutes at his disposal Professor Bridge briefly outlined the chief events of Burney's life at Shrewsbury, Chester, King's Lynn, and later London. Later Mr. Percival J. Ashton (founder of the Londoners' Circle) delivered a short tribute to "Burney the Londoner," during which he referred to Fanny Burney's descriptions of the musical evenings at her father's house.

'During the afternoon Mrs. Hawes (who, incidentally, has been organist at the Chelsea Hospital for exactly the same period as that of Burney's holding the appointment), played a few examples of her predecessor's organ music, including a Fugue in F minor, a "Cornet" (which was a type of composition written for echo effects), and an Introduction. The recital was admirably carried out. The Chelsea Hospital Choir also sang a "Nativity Hymn," which made appeal through the freshness of the vocal line. Finally, from the London Studio, a Sonata for two performers on piano and harpsichord was broadcast. This was one of a set written by Burney, which, if they were not the first examples of this kind of duet, were certainly among the earliest.

'This most happy commemoration was fittingly ended by a pilgrimage to Dr. Burney's grave in the Hospital Cemetery; there a wreath was placed by Miss Mabel Burney as a tribute from the Londoners' Circle to her great-great-grandfather. It should be mentioned that a further bond of association was supplied by the broadcasting of Chester Cathedral bells during the afternoon. Thus it was that Johnson's words were still found apt and fitting by those who came to honour a great Englishman: "Dr. Burney is a man for everybody to love."'

(It will be noted that there are a good many inexactitudes in the dates and allusions in this account.)

A similar commemoration was held in St. Margaret's Church, King's Lynn, the church being crowded. The organist, Mr. A. Heath, used only such stops as formed part of the organ when it was built during Burney's organistship.

BIBLIOGRAPHY

BURNEY'S PUBLISHED BOOKS

1769 (aged 43)

An Essay towards a History of the Principal Comets that have appeared since the year 1742, including a Particular Detail of the Return of the Famous Comet of 1682 in 1759, according to the Calculation and Prediction of Dr. Halley. Compiled from the Observations of the Most Eminent Astronomers of this Century with Remarks and Reflections upon the Present Comet. To which is prefixed, by way of Introduction, a Letter upon Comets addressed to a Lady by the late M. de Maupertuis, written in the year 1742. London. Printed for T. Becket and P. A. de Hondt, in the Strand. (Anonymous.) **See I. 146.**

Copies in the British Museum and the Library of Congress (Rare Books Room). The contents are: a dedicatory letter 'To the Right Honourable the Countess of Pembroke', a summary account of the life of Maupertuis, and then his letter upon Comets (which we know to have been translated by Burney's first wife, who came of a French family), the Essay itself, and a Postscript ('London, October 25, 1769'). The whole consists of 93 pages.

1771 (aged 45)

(*a*) *The Present State of Music in France and Italy, or the Journal of a Tour through those Countries, undertaken to collect Materials for a General History of Music.* London. Printed for T. Becket & Co. in the Strand (8vo). **See I. 190–2.**

(*b*) The same. 'The Second Edition corrected.' Printed for T. Becket & Co., Strand; J. Robson, New Bond Street; and G. Robinson, Paternoster Row. 1773.

This edition has, facing the title-page, and dated 'London, April 20, 1773', some 'Proposals for Printing by Subscription a General History of Music', etc.

In the Library of the Royal College of Music there is a copy of this book with manuscript remarks by Charles Wesley, junr.

The incidents of travel which Burney omitted from his book as published he nevertheless preserved, copying them twice, once in a set of note-books now in the British Museum (Add. MS. 35122) and once in another set in the possession of the present author. These two sets have been roughly collated for the sake of the present work; they are found to be substantially the same but occasionally vary slightly in the wording; each of them also contains a little matter not found in the other one and the British Museum copy repeats a little matter to be found in the published volume which the copy in the possession of the writer does not. (Complete collation has not been undertaken, as it could hardly be achieved without copying out the whole of the two sets in some system of parallel columns and corresponding pages—an immense and probably not very profitable task.)

(*c*) *Carl Burney's der Musik Doctors Tagebuch einer musikalischen Reise durch Frankreich und Italien welche er unternommen hat um zu einer allgemeinen Geschichte der Musik Materialen zu sammeln. Aus dem Englischen übersetzt von C. D. Ebeling, Aufsehern der Handlungsakademie zu Hamburg.* Hamburg, 1772. Bey Bode (8vo). **See I. 204.**

(*d*) *De l'état présent de la musique en France et en Italie, dans les Pays Bas. . . .* Translation by Charles Brack. Genoa, 3 vols., 1809–10.

Nearly forty years after the original! There is a copy in the British Museum. Fétis calls it 'une traduction fort médiocre'.

(*e*) *Viaggio Musicale in Italia, 1770. Translation by Virginio Attenasio.* Naples, 1921 (8vo).

This is not a direct translation; it is a translation of Brack's French version of 1809–10 (see above). There are sixteen illustrations, including some reproductions of contemporary prints depicting the Italian conservatorios of the eighteenth century.

1771 (aged 45)

(*a*) *Lettera del defonto Signor Giuseppe Tartini alla Signora Maddalena Lombardini inserviente ad una importante Lezione per i Suonatori di Violino.* With English title also: *A Letter from the late Signor Tartini to Signora Maddalena Lombardini (now Signora Sirmen) published as an important lesson to performers on the Violin. Translated by Dr. Burney.* London, R. Bremner. Small folio; 7 pp. Italian and 8 pp. English. **See I. 166.**

(*b*) Second Edition of the above. 1779.

(*c*) Third Edition of the above, as *An Important Lesson to Performers on the Violin.* Wm. Reeves, London, 1879.

(Still on sale in the nineteen-forties.) The Italian and English are on facing pages. This letter has been reprinted many times as a part of larger works, e.g. G. Dubourg's *The Violin* (1836 and later editions to 1878).

1773 (aged 47)

(*a*) *The Present State of Music in Germany, the Netherlands, and the United Provinces, or the Journal of a Tour through those Countries, undertaken to collect Materials for a General History of Music.* London. Printed for T. Becket & Co., Strand; J. Robson, New Bond Street; and G. Robinson, Paternoster Row. 2 vols. (8vo). **See I. 243–4.**

Opposite the title is an announcement of the coming *History*.

(*b*) The same. 'The Second Edition Corrected.' 1775 (8vo).

(*c*) *Carl Burney's der Musik Doctors Tagebuch seiner Musikalischen Reisen. Zweyter Band. Durch Flandern, die Niederlande und am Rhein bis Wien. Aus dem Englischen übersetzt.* Hamburg, 1773. Bey Bode (8vo).

No translator's name, but see I. 244–8 of the present work. The explanation of this being called the second volume is that it forms a part of the travel series in German that began with the volume listed on II. 331 under '1771 (*c*)'.

(*d*) *Carl Burney's der Musik Doctors Tagebuch seiner Musikalischen Reisen. Dritter Band. Durch Böhmen, Sachsen, Brandenburg, Hamburg, und Holland. Aus dem Englischen übersetzt. Mit einigen Zusätzen und Anmerkungen zum zweyten und dritten Bande.* Hamburg, 1773. Bey Bode (8vo).

No translator's name, but see I. 244–8 of the present work.

(*e*) *Ryk Gestoffeerd Geschiedverhaal van der Eigenlicken Staat de hedendaagsche Toonkunst of sir Karel Burneys Dagboek van Zyne onlangs gedaane Reizen door Frankryk en Deutschland, etc.* 1786. ('Highly detailed Account of the

Real State of Music To-day, by means of Mr. Charles Burney's Diary of his Recent Journey through France and Germany, etc.')

Fétis (copying, apparently, Gerber's *Neues . . . Lexikon* of 1812) says that this Dutch translation is excellent, and has interesting notes. Eitner words the title rather differently, so there may have been two editions. The translator was J. W. Lustig, Organist at Groningen, whom Burney mentions in his *German Tour*, ii. 280.

(*f*) *Dr. Burney's Continental Travels*. London, 1927.

This is a volume of selections from the two printed *Tours* and from the British Museum MS. mentioned on II. 331 under '1771 (*b*)', with also the addition of connective matter. Its compiler is Cedric Howard Glover.

1774 (aged 48)

A Plan for a Music School, alias *A Plan for the Formation of a Musical Academy*, alias *A Plan for an English Conservatorio*, &c. **See I. 263.**

These various titles are given in various books of reference, &c. It seems impossible to trace a copy. No library in which search has been made possesses one; this includes the British Museum, the Bodleian, the Rylands Library, the Library of Congress, and the Library of the Foundling Hospital. The present writer's conviction is that no such work ever existed in print—that a mere written scheme was presented to the Governors of the Hospital. The variety of titles quoted supports this suggestion; they are probably rather descriptions than actual titles. Dr. Rimbault, who wrote the article on Burney in Grove's *Dictionary of Music*, uses in it the first of these titles, but uses the second in a letter to *Notes & Queries*, Series I, vol. i, 135 (29 Dec. 1849): he adds the indication '8vo. n.d.,' as though he knew the work, and concludes, 'As your *Notes & Queries* will become a standard book of reference, strict accuracy on all points is the grand desideratum.' In the Grove article, which was written many years later, he gives the date '1774'. Fétis gives the date as 1767, which would obviously be too early.

Apparently the impression that Burney had actually published his 'Plan' was current in his own lifetime, for the present writer possesses a detached article from some magazine, title untraced, volume of 1798–9, which includes it (as *Plan for a Public Music School*) in the list of his works. It is possible that this article, which is a rather slipshod production, is the fount and origin of the often-repeated statement that the 'Plan' was a published work.

1776–89 (aged 50–63)

(*a*) *A General History of Music from the Earliest Ages to the Present Period. To which is prefixed a Dissertation on the Music of the Ancients.* 4 vols. (4to) as follows in the first edition: i, 1776; ii, 1782; iii and iv, 1789. Vol. i is 'Printed for the Author, and sold by T. Becket, Strand; J. Robson, New Bond Street; and G. Robinson, Paternoster Row'; in vols. ii, iii, and iv the mention of Becket drops out, and in vols. iii and iv 'Payne & Son, at the Meuse Gate' is added. **See I. 289–315.**

Some perplexity arises from the existence of diversities in copies of the different volumes.

VOLUME I exists in editions dated 1776 and 1789.

The 1776 edition has two slightly varying forms.

Variant 1 has the original frontispiece, a Cipriani design of Apollo playing the lyre to the Nine Muses, engraved by Bartolozzi.

Variant 2 has, instead, the frontispiece that originally appeared in 1789 in vol. iii or vol. iv (varying in different sets of copies), i.e. Reynolds's portrait of Burney, engraved by Bartolozzi; it bears the date 1784. (The List of Plates, at the end of the book, however, still describes the frontispiece as 'Apollo and the Nine Muses'.)

It seems clear then that when Burney, in 1789, completed his great work by publishing vols. iii and iv there were some copies of the original 1776 edition of vol. ii remaining in sheets, and that these were utilized to make up complete sets, the frontispieces in the various volumes of those sets being readjusted so as to bring the portrait into the opening volume of the work.

The Variant 1 copies have a List of Subscribers, the Variant 2 copies have not, it having now, of course, in thirteen years, become out of date. There are also other slight differences: for instance, in some copies the bulk of the plates are collected at the end of the volume instead of being dispersed.

Having in 1789 used up the remaining copies of the 1776 edition of vol. i, Burney then had this volume reprinted, with the new date and the description 'Second Edition'. The imprint now becomes 'Payne and Son, at the Mews Gate; Robson and Clark, Bond Street; and G. G. and J. Robinson, Paternoster Row'. The portrait, of course, again appears as frontispiece, but (strangely) its entry in the List of Plates is even now unchanged, still giving it as 'Apollo and the Nine Muses'. The title-page is altered by the omission of the lines about the 'Dissertation', thus assimilating the wording to that of the other volumes. The pagination also is different, the type having been entirely reset. The Preface has alterations. And there are other innovations.

In the 1776 copies (both variants) certain page numbers occur twice, first with an asterisk and then without. This seems to be due to Burney's having inserted at this point a considerable quantity of new information supplied to him late in the day by his friend the Abyssinian explorer, Bruce.

The above account by no means exhausts the bibliographical details that could be listed, but copies vary so much (in some respects, perhaps merely by the vagaries of binders) that the drafting of a complete statement would call for extensive travels from library to library—and probably result in no important conclusion.[1] Some information additional to the above will be found in Allen T. Hazen's *Samuel Johnson's Prefaces and Dedications* (1937). Hazen states, by the way, that Burney's chapter on Hebrew Music in volume I exists also as a separate pamphlet, but does not, apparently, know the date. I have never seen a copy of this.

Volume II exists in two editions, though the words 'Second Edition' are not used. Both are dated 1782.

Edition 1 was actually published in 1782. It uses the long *ʃ*, as do the other volumes of the work. It has no index.

Edition 2 is also dated 1782 but was actually issued over a quarter of a century later, since the paper bears the water-mark '1809'. It is carelessly printed (Hazen, *Johnson's Prefaces and Dedications*). Mr. Frank Mercer, in his 1935 edition of the *History*, mentions a copy of this edition with an index.

The existence of this second and misdated edition is a puzzle. Burney's Will, made in 1807, mentions that the second volume of his work has 'long wanted a second edition' (see II. 268) and presumably this was produced two or more years later to meet the demand: but why was it misdated and why was it carelessly printed?

VOLUMES III AND IV (both 1789) had only the one edition. Copies differ in the plate used as frontispiece, but this may be due simply to the bookbinders: the Reynolds's portrait of Burney is to be found in vol. iii in some sets, in vol. iv in others, and, as already mentioned, pushed forward to vol. i in still others.

THE PLATES. Some passing remarks on these have been made above. A certain number of them are small and delicate engravings by Bartolozzi of elegant classical designs by Cipriani or by the author's nephew, Edward Burney. These had had a previous use. The author in his 'List and Description of the Plates to Vol. I' says:

[1] There are attempts to clear up the confusion in *Notes & Queries* as follows: x. x. 9, 57; x. xii. 494.

'As each of these plates had fulfilled its destination of serving as a concert ticket for one performance only, it seemed a hardship upon the admirable artists who designed and engraved them, as well as upon the public, that such productions should be buried in oblivion. This idea, and the want of sufficient time to have others executed, suggested to me a desire of ornamenting my History with them, and a wish to publish and preserve them in a work to which they seem naturally to belong.' For the very artistically designed and produced concert tickets of the late eighteenth century see pl. 40, II. 169.

In the Print Room of the British Museum are preserved drawings intended for the *History* (some by Burney's nephew Edward); many were never engraved; some of them bear notes in Burney's hand. There are also proofs of engravings that did appear in the book.

The Public Advertiser, 19 January 1775

January 1, 1775.

HISTORY OF MUSIC

A long and severe Indisposition having wholly put it out of the Power of Dr. Burney, to publish the First Volume of his General History of Music at the Time mentioned in the Proposals, he is under the Necessity of intreating his Subscribers to indulge him with a few Months longer, in order to enable him to render it less unworthy of the Patronage with which it has been honoured. He can with the utmost Truth assure his Subscribers, that when he fixed upon the End of 1774, for Publication, he promised them no more than he promised himself; however more than half the First Volume is already printed; and the whole will be pursued with all the Diligence and Expedition which his Health will permit.

Subscriptions will continue to be received by the Author, at his House in St. Martin's street, Leicester Fields; by Messrs. Becket, Strand; Robinson, Paternoster Row; and Robson, Bond Street; till the First Volume is published.

The Public Advertiser, 22 February 1776.

This Day is published.

In One Large Volume Quarto, Price 1£ 11s 6d in Boards.

Dedicated to Her Majesty.

A GENERAL HISTORY OF MUSIC, from the earliest Ages to the present Period; embellished with ornamental Plates engraved by Bartolozzi, from Designs of Cipriani, and with Representations of ancient Instruments, engraved by other eminent Artists. To which is prefixed a Dissertation on the Music of the Ancients.

By Charles Burney, Mus.D. F.R.S.

Volume The First.

Printed for T. Becket, Strand; J. Robson, New Bond Street; and by G. Robinson, Pater Noster Row.

*** The Subscription Books are delivered by the Author only, at his House in St. Martin's Street, Leicester Fields.

The Public Advertiser, 17 May 1780.

HISTORY OF MUSIC

This Day is published Volume the First.

[Then follows an announcement of the first volume, much as above.]

The Second Volume of this Work, a great Part of which is already printed, will be published in the course of next Winter; and those who have purchased the First Volume at the advanced Price of One Guinea and a Half, will be admitted as Subscribers to the Second Volume, upon sending in their

Names to the Author, and taking out Receipts; upon the original Conditions of One Guinea.

Subscribers to the first Volume are likewise intreated to send for their Receipts for the Second, that the Author may be enabled to ascertain the Number of Copies necessary to be set apart for their use.

The Morning Herald and Daily Advertiser, 22 May 1782

On Wednesday the 29th inst. will be published, A General History of Music, By Charles Burney, Mus.D. F.R.S. Vol. II Printed for the Authors in St. Martin's Street, Leicester-square . . .

Where may be had the First Volume; and where Subscribers, at One Guinea, will be received for the Second, till the time of publication; after which, the price to Non subscribers will be raised to a Guinea and a half.

(*b*) The same. Edited by Frank Mercer. 2 vols. 1935.

(*c*) Pamphlet reprint of the chapter on Hebrew Music from vol. i.

See reference on II. 334.

(*d*) *Dr. Karl Burney's Abhandlung über die Musik der Alten.* Translation of the 'Dissertation' in the first volume of the *History*, by J. J. E. Eschenburg. Leipzig, 1781, 4to.

An allusion will be found in a MS. essay by J. W. Callcott in the British Museum, Add. MS. 27646. The book itself is in the Museum.

(*e*) *Versuch über Musik Kritik.* Translation of the introduction to the third volume of the *History*, by J. J. E. Eschenburg. In the *Berliner Musik-Wochenblatt*, 1792, pp. 73–5 and 81–8.

(*f*) *Sketch of the Life of Handel.* In Logier's *Theoretical and Practical Study for the Pianoforte*, No. 3. (n.d.)

This number consists of a piano arrangement of Handel's *Occasional Oratorio*, and the Sketch is a mere extract from Burney's *History*.

1779 (aged 53)

Account of the Infant Musician Crotch. London. J. Nichols. 26 pp. (4to).

A reprint from the *Philosophical Transactions of the Royal Society*. See List of Contributions to Periodicals, same year (II. 337).

1784 (aged 58)

Cantata written in German for Mademoiselle Paradis, by her blind friend, M. Pfeffel, of Colmar, and set to music by her music-master, M. Leopold Kozeluch, of Vienna, 11th November, 1784. Imitated by Dr. Burney.

The 'Mademoiselle Paradis' here mentioned was a blind vocalist and player on harpsichord and organ who came to London to relieve 'the state of her finances'. The Cantata was for her own singing and it narrates her own experiences. Burney 'translated or rather imitated' it, took measures for having it brought to the notice of the Queen (who 'humanely cheered and revived the blind minstrel with essential tokens of royal liberality'), and 'printed and dispersed' copies of the words at his own expense. The words are reproduced in full in Fanny's *Memoirs* of her father (iii. 25), from which come the above quotations. The German original is to be found in *Poetische Versuche von Gottlieb Conrad Pfeffel* (Vienna, 1792); Burney's 'imitation' is very free.

1785 (aged 59)

(*a*) *An account of the Musical Performances in Westminster Abbey and the Pantheon in Commemoration of Handel.* Payne; also Robinson, 1785, 4to. 'Printed for the Benefit of the Musical Fund.' **See II. 64–75.**

(*b*) The same. Dublin edition, in the same year, 1785.

There is a copy in the British Museum. (Pirated Dublin editions of successful London books were very usual at this period.)

(*c*) The same. Duff and Hodgson, London, 1834.

There are copies in the British Museum, the Bodleian Library, and the Library of Congress. It is an incomplete reprint (a mere forty pages) and includes 'A Notice of the forthcoming Royal Musical Festival of 1834', so that it is really of the nature of a prospectus of the 1834 Westminster Abbey Festival.

(*d*) Partial reproduction of the same in George Farquhar Graham's *An Account of the First Edinburgh Musical Festival held between the 30th October and 5th November 1815.* Blackwood, Edinburgh, 1816. (It includes Burney's discussion of *Messiah* and other works.)

(*e*) *Dr. Karl Burneys Nachricht von Georg Friedrich Händels Lebensumständen und der zu ihm zu London im Mai und Juni 1784 angestellten Gedächtnissfeyer.* Translated by J. J. Eschenburg. Berlin and Stettin, 1785. **See I. 314 n.**

There is a copy in the British Museum and another in the Library of Congress.

1791 (aged 65)

Verses on the Arrival in England of the Great Musician Haydn. A shilling quarto pamphlet of 14 pp. with the imprint of Payne and three other booksellers. (Not, as sometimes reported, first published in *The Monthly Review*, January 1791, but reviewed in that journal, June 1791.) **See II. 111.**

1796 (aged 70)

Memoirs of the Life and Writings of the Abate Metastasio in which are incorporated Translations of his Principal Letters. 3 vols. 'London: Printed for G. G. and J. Robinson, Paternoster Row', 1796, 8vo. **See II. 149.**

BURNEY'S CONTRIBUTIONS TO PERIODICALS, TO WORKS NOT ENTIRELY HIS OWN, ETC.

1773, &c.

The *Annual Register* has much matter by Burney, but it is all extracted from his existing works—1773, vol. xvi, forty-one pages of extracts from the *German Tour*; 1779, vol. xxii, the Crotch paper (see below and also list of Burney's books, 1779), apparently intact; 1784–5, vol. xxvii, four pages from the Handel book. And in 1789, vol xxxi, are reproduced the three translations of hymns by Dionysius, from the *History*, and also ten pages of prose from it.

1779 (aged 53)

Account of the Infant Musician Crotch. In vol. lxix, part 1, of the *Philosophical Transactions of the Royal Society*, 1779.

It appeared in the same year in the *Annual Register* (see above) and had also a separate existence (see list of Burney's books, 1779). As a separate publication it is included in the list of works on music at the end of the last volume of Burney's *History* (*Paper on Crotch, the Infant Musician*, 1779). There is a copy in the British Museum and another in the Library of the Liceo Musicale G. B. Martini at Bologna—doubtless sent by Burney to his friend Martini; it may have become scarce, as the present writer, in addition to a printed copy, possesses a hand-written copy made in 1836, which belonged to some member of the Callcott family.

Apparently this was Burney's only contribution to the *Philosophical Transactions*.

Ten years after the publication of this *Account* Burney came under rebuke from a correspondent in *The Gentleman's Magazine* (13 June 1789; reproduction in Nichols, *Illustrations of the Literary History of the Eighteenth Century*, vii. 608). One R. N. (believed to be Archdeacon Nares) complains that Burney, who 'was the first to bring his [Crotch's] superior genius to public notice' (by the above-mentioned publication when Crotch was four years old), had neglected the present-day Crotch, now 'a complete master of the science'.

1782 (aged 56)

Poem in the *Morning Herald*, 12 March 1782. **See II. 92.**

1785 to **1802** (aged 59 to about 75)

Contributions to *The Monthly Review*. **See II. 93–4.**

The file of this *Review* in the Bodleian Library, Oxford, is that of the editor, Griffiths, and each article has attached to it some indication of its authorship. Burney's articles are marked, 'Dr. B', Dr. By.', or 'Dr. Bu—y.' The articles ran from November 1785 to June 1802 (Fanny in the *Memoirs* gives two dates of beginning, both too late—1789 and 1791).

There is a list of Burney's articles during the first part of the period in B. C. Nangle's *Index to the Monthly Review, 1749–1789* (1934); note, however, that one or two of the articles of Charles Burney, junior, have been included not only in his own list but also in that of his father. The present writer sees reason to doubt whether one or two others are by Burney, e.g. one (1788, 1st vol. 177) where there is something rather slashing about the poet, Mason, who was a much respected friend of Burney.

1789 (aged 63)

Striking Views of Lamia, the Celebrated Athenian Flute Player.

Not a separate publication, as has been implied, but merely an article in *The Massachusetts Magazine*, vol. i, 284 (1789, not 1786 as reported by Fétis and copied from him by others). It is of merely 400 words or so. The present writer has seen it at the New York Public Library. His recollection is that it reproduces the information given by Burney in the *History of Music* and in his article on Lamia in Rees's *Cyclopaedia*.

1799 (aged 73)

Notes contributed to Malone's edition of Boswell's *Johnson*.

They are all signed 'B'.

1802 to *c.* **1820**

Articles in Rees's *Cyclopaedia* (45 vols., appearing serially, some of them after Burney's death). **See II. 184–201.**

1804 (aged 78)

Ode: To the People of Great Britain on the Threatened Invasion. In the *Annual Register*, 1804, vol. xlvi, 901. Also in *The Monthly Visitor*, July 1804, vol. vii, 299.

A very stirring piece of work beginning,

Arm, Britons, arm! Your Country's Cause
Your Monarch, Constitution, Laws,
Religion, wives and infant train
Now call to arms!—nor let their call be vain.

There is some question whether these verses are by Charles Burney the Mus.D. or his son, Charles Burney the D.D. The father was all his life an habitual writer of English verse, whereas the son is not known to have been such. The *Annual Register* and *The Monthly Visitor* vaguely attribute the verses to 'Dr. Charles Burney', which might be either. If the father was the author he entrusted the son to see through the press a separately printed edition of which the British Museum possesses two copies, for one of these, which appears to be a proof, has been corrected in the son's handwriting, and the printer is one whose address (Deptford) is near his (Greenwich).

1820

Introduction to *The Late C. F. Abel's Adagios, in Score, and J. B. Cramer's Specimens in the Fugue Style.* London; printed for the Royal Harmonic Institution.

This is a mere posthumous reprint of part of Burney's treatment of Abel in the *History.*

BURNEY'S UNPUBLISHED LITERARY WORK

(See also under 'Manuscript Sources')

1756 (aged 30)

Dizionario portativo Italiano ed Inglese. Compilato da Carlo Burney per l'uso proprio di se stesso. MDCCLVI. **See I. 73.**

In the possession of the present author.

1782 (aged 56)

Memoirs. Begun in 1782; then dropped; resumed 1807.

Destroyed after his death by his daughter Fanny (see her remarks in her own *Memoirs* of her father).

1787 (aged 60)

Poem on the Queen's Birthday. **See II. 101.**

Written for Fanny to present to the Queen (see *Diary and Letters,* iii. 162). It is presumably now either stored in the royal archives or lost.

Undated.

Verses on the Marriage of Miss Susan Burney; Verses on his daughter Esta's [*sic*] *recovery from a dangerous illness; Song; Epitaph on Samuel Crisp Esq.* (see II. 47); *To my daughter Charlotte, on her Marriage with Clement Francis Esq., Feb. 11th 1786; Verses to Miss Francis.*

The above manuscripts were included in the catalogue of C. A. Stonehill jr., Museum Street, London, in 1934. Their present whereabouts is unknown to the present author.

BURNEY'S COMPOSITIONS, ARRANGEMENTS, ETC.

1748 (aged 22)

Six Sonatas for two Violins, with a Bass for the Violoncello or Harpsichord. Most humbly dedicated to the Rt. Honble. the Earl of Holderness. Opera Prima. London. Printed for the Author by Wm. Smith in Middle Row, Holborn, and sold at Mr. Richd. Burney's in Hatton Garden. **See I. 43.**

This is, of course, in parts, not score. The only copies known to the present author are in the University Library, Cambridge, and in his own possession. This is evidently the set which Fanny in her *Memoirs* of her father describes as 'printed in 1747 and dedicated to the Earl of Holderness'. As will be remarked from the advertisements below, the first edition was quickly exhausted and a reprint or second edition issued.

The General Advertiser, 13 February 1748.

NEW MUSICK.

In May next, will be publish'd by subscription, Six Sonatas or Trios for two Violins and a Bass, which will be carefully figur'd for the Organ or Harpsichord. Compos'd by Charles Burney, Opera Prima. The Price to Subscribers will be a Guinea for the Large, and half a Guinea for the Small Paper, the whole to be paid at the Time of Subscribing.

Subscriptions are taken in, and Receipts delivered at Mr. Walsh's, in Catherine-street in the Strand; at Mrs. Walmsley's, in Piccadilly; at Mr. Johnson's in Cheapside; at Mr. Simpson's, in Swithin's Alley; at Mr. Smith's in Middle Row, Holborn; and Mr. Richard Burney at his House in Hatton-Garden near Holborn.[1]

The General Advertiser, 27 May 1748.

NEW MUSICK.

Mr. Burney gives notice to his Subscribers, that on Monday next the 30th inst. will be ready to deliver according to the printed Proposals, at Mr. Richard Burney's, 12 Doors on the Right Hand Side of Hatton-Garden, near Holborn, His Six Sonatas for two Violins, and a Bass, for a Violoncello or Harpsichord. Op. Prima.

The General Advertiser, 24 July 1749.

MUSICK.

Just publish'd A Second Edition, of Six Sonatas for Two Violins and a Violoncello, figur'd for the Organ or Harpsichord. Compos'd by Charles Burney.

Which may be had at Mr. Oswald's in St. Martin's Church-yard; Mrs. Hare's opposite the Mansion-House; and at Mr. Burney's in Hatton Garden, near Holborn, Price Half a Guinea.

1750 (aged 24)

Robin Hood. A New entertainment as it is perform'd at the Theatre Royal in Drury-Lane. The Musick compos'd by the Society of the Temple of Apollo. **See I. 53.**

This was apparently not published as a whole, but the following are in the British Museum (the Cambridge University Library has the 'Linnet' and 'Woodbine' songs):

(*a*) The Libretto (from which is taken the above title), 'London, printed and sold at the Theatre, and by M. Cooper in Pater-noster-row. Price Six Pence.'

In *The General Advertiser* of 15 December 1750, it was advertised as published.

[1] Richard Burney was Charles Burney's brother, the dancing master; see II. 32–3.

(The first performance had taken place two days earlier.) The Bodleian Library has the libretto (anonymous but catalogued as by 'Moses Mendez, M.A.'), dated 1751.

(*b*) *I'll sing you a song that shall suit you all round* (a single sheet), 1751. This song also appeared in *The Universal Magazine*, vol. xix, 271, 1756.

(*c*) *As blyth as the Linnet sings in the Green Wood* (a single sheet), 1751. It also appeared in *The London Magazine*, 1755, p. 444.

(*d*) *To an Arbor of Woodbine* (a single sheet), 1751; another edition in 1755 (?). It also appeared in *The Universal Magazine*, vol. xv, 323, 1754; and in *The New Universal Magazine*, March 1755 and again March 1756.

1750 (aged 24)

(*a*) *The Comic Tunes in Queen Mab as they are perform'd at Drury Lane, set for the Violin, German Flute or Hoboy; with a Thorough Bass for the Harpsichord. Publish'd by authority. London; printed for J. Oswald and sold at his Musick Shop in St. Martin's Lane.* **See I. 54–7.**

There was a later edition 'sold by W. Randall and Straight and Skillern'; and it ascribed the composition of the music to the first publisher, Oswald. Randall's name appears on various publications from 1771 to 1783; for a little time before this the imprint was 'Randall and Abell'.

There is a copy of the Comic Tunes of *Queen Mab* in the British Museum.

(*b*) *The Songs of Queen Mab as they are performed at the Theatre Royal in Drury Lane, Composed by the Society of the Temple of Apollo; Sung by Mr. Vernon. Printed for J. Oswald in St. Martin's Church Yard and published by permission of the Society.*

This is mentioned by the late Wm. Barclay Squire, of the British Museum, in *The Musical Antiquary*, April 1910. There is a copy in the British Museum.

Joseph Vernon was born in 1738, so that he was but a boy of twelve or thirteen when, at the end of 1750, *Queen Mab* was first performed. Later he became a well-known tenor vocalist. In the early days of *Queen Mab* he sang the fairy's songs (see Burney's recollections of this on I. 55 of the present work. Probably the 'Mr.' is to be interpreted as 'Master' rather than 'Mister'—cf. Swift, 'Maids, misses, and little masters').

(*c*) *The Overture in all its Parts to that celebrated Entertainment call'd Queen Mabb.*

There are sets of these parts in the British Museum and the Bodleian Library. They consist of 1st and 2nd Violin, Viola, Violoncello, Oboe, Bassoon, and Harpsichord (this last merely a bass line figured). The 1st Violin part has the title-page, which describes the work as 'composed by the late James Oswald Esq., Chamber Composer to His Majesty'. (This dates the copies as after 1769, when Oswald died, and thus twenty years or so after the first performance of the work.) The publisher was 'Henry Thorowgood, Musical Instrument Maker, No. 6 North Piazza, Royal Exchange—where may be had the above Overture for the Harpsichord, price 0. 0. 6'.

It would seem that Oswald himself never claimed to have composed the music to *Queen Mab*, and that the attribution of the music to him was conjectural and arose after his death. In view of Fanny Burney's quite definite statement as to the work being her father's, it would seem that we need not take this later attribution seriously.

(*d*) *The Overture to Queen Mabb. Printed for H. Thorowgood.*

This is a keyboard arrangement. There is a copy in the British Museum, dated in the catalogue '1753?'

c. **1750** (aged about 24)

Six Songs composed for the Temple of Apollo. To which is added, A favourite Cantata set to musick by Mr. Chas. Burney. Opera II, Lib. I. London, printed for and sold by J. Oswald at his Musick shop in St. Martin's Church-yard in the Strand.

The cantata is Gay's *The Despairing Shepherd.* It is scored for two violins and a bass. At the end there are four songs arranged for two German flutes.

The only copy of this publication known to the present author is in the National Library of Scotland, Edinburgh; catalogue number 'Inglis 200 (7)'.

1750 (aged 24)

We've fought, we have conquer'd. **See I. 24.**

The copy in the British Museum has no title-page or title, but in handwriting at the top of the page appear the words 'Air in the Mask of Alfrid [sic], set by C. B. 1750'. In engraved copperplate writing are the words 'Sung by Mr. Beard'. The music is set for 2 violins, viola, bass, 2 oboes, side drum, and voice.

1750 (aged 24)

Lovely Harriote. A Crambo Song, the words by Mr. Smart. Set to music by Charles Burny [*sic*]. *Printed by J. Oswald. By authority G. R.*

Copy in the British Museum.

'Crambo Song' seems to have reference to the game in which one selects a word to which another finds a rhyme. In the song *Lovely Harriote* the point evidently was to find numerous (and humorous) rhymes for 'Harriote', e.g. (first verse)

Great Phoebus in his vast career,
Who forms the self-succeeding year,
Thron'd in his amber *Chariot*,
Sees not an object half so bright,
Nor gives such Joy, such Life, such Light,
As dear delicious HARRIOTE.

Other words rhyming with 'Harriote' are (seven verses in all) 'Marriotte', 'Barry Hot', 'carry ought', 'Iscariote', 'war riot'.

Apparently 'Crambo Songs' had a long run of popularity. Fanny Burney (*Diary and Letters*, iv. 262), nearly half a century later, refers to Dr. Willis, who had just succeeded in curing the King of his insanity (1789), being rewarded by celebration in such a song:

'Dr. Willis this morning lent me a crambo song, on his own name, which he had received by the penny post. I shall copy and show it you. It is sportive enough and loyal.'

For Burney's relations with Smart see I. 42, 135.

1751 (aged 25)

Six Cornet Pieces, with an Introduction for the Diapasons, and a Fugue. Proper for young Organists and Practitioners on the Harpsichord. Printed for J. Walsh, in Catherine Street in the Strand. **See I. 60, 61.**

Copies in the British Museum; in the University Library, Cambridge; in the Library of Congress; and in the possession of Mr. Alfred Moffat and of the present author. The publication is advertised in *The London Evening Post*, 2 to 5 November 1751, and *The General Advertiser*, 7 November 1751.

1754 (aged nearly 28)

Six Sonatas or Duets for Two Violins or German Flutes. Printed for J. Oswald. **See I. 343 n.**

No copy in the British Museum.

The General Advertiser, 12 March 1754.

NEW MUSICK.

This Day is published,

Six Sonatas or Duets for two Violins or German Flutes. Composed by Mr. Burney. Price 3s. Printed for J. Oswald, in St. Martin's Church-yard.

The same announcement appears in *The Public Advertiser* three months later (20 June) with the same indication 'This day is published'. (See also following item.)

1755 (aged 29)

Six Sonatas for Two German Flutes.

The present writer knows of these only from the announcement below and from mention in Grove, in Brown and Stratton, and in *The Harmonicon*, 1832, p. 217. They may just possibly be the same as the 'Six Sonatas for Two Violins or German Flutes' mentioned above, the intimation 'This day is published' carrying with it, at this period, no definite significance beyond that of the publication being actually on sale.

The Public Advertiser, 12 May 1755.

NEW MUSICK.

This Day is published, Price 3s.

Six Sonatas for two German Flutes composed by Mr. Charles Burney.
Printed for J. Oswald in St. Martin's Church-yard.

1757 (aged 31)

The Man to my Mind (Song).

Copy in the British Museum; it bears no publisher's name; the above date has been written on it.

Also in *The Universal Magazine*, May 1757, with the title, *Since Wedlock's in vogue, the Man to my Mind.*

1759 (aged nearly 33).

Six Sonatas for Two Violins and a Bass, addressed to the Hon. and Rev. Mr. Home. Opera 4ta. Printed for John Johnson, opposite Bow Church in Cheapside. **See I. 63.**

Copies in the British Museum and the Henry Watson Music Library, Manchester; also in the possession of the present writer (Parts only; no score would be published).

The Public Advertiser, 23 March 1759.

NEW MUSICK.

This Day is published,

Six Sonatas for two Violins and a Bass, addressed to the Hon. and Rev. Mr. Home. By Charles Burney, organist, at Lynn, Opera Quarta.

The 'Pastorale' from the sixth Sonata, arranged, is included in Alfred Moffat's *English Classical Album* (for Violin and Piano; Augener's edition 7523).

Ode on St. Cecilia's Day, adapted to the Ancient British Musick. **See I. 95–7.**

Apparently unpublished and no copy remaining.

c. **1760** (aged about 34)

Six Concertos in Seven Parts for Four Violins, a Tenor, a Violoncello, and Thorough Bass for the Organ and [i.e. 'or'] *Harpsichord Op. 5.*

Copies in the Henry Watson Music Library, Manchester, and the Library of Congress (Parts only; no score would, of course, be published).

The Public Advertiser, 29 September 1761.

New Music.

This Day is published, Price 5s. A Collection of the best old English and Scotch Songs, with Symphonies and Accompanyments. By James Oswald. Chamber Composer to His Majesty. Printed for James Oswald and sold at his Music-Shop on the Pavement in St. Martin's Church-yard.

Where may be had, Six Concertos in seven Parts, by Mr. Charles Burney, Price 10s. 6d.

Undated

Six Concertos for Violin, etc., in Eight Parts.

Mentioned in Grove and Fétis; not in Eitner. No copy traced by the present writer. It is possible that Fétis and Grove take their information as to the existence of the work from the obituary in *The Gentleman's Magazine*, 1814, and that an error has there been made by the substitution of 'eight' for 'seven' (see above), the organ and harpsichord both being counted instead of being recognized as alternatives.

1760? (aged 34?)

Constancy (Song).

A single sheet publication. Copy in the British Museum.

1761 (aged 35)

Six Sonatas or Lessons for the Harpsichord. **See I. 101.**

No copy known to the present writer. (But see below—1766.)

The Public Advertiser, 27 April 1761.

New Music for the Harpsichord,

This Day is published, Price Half a Guinea, Six Sonatas or Lessons for the Harpsichord, composed by Charles Burney. Printed for the Author and sold at his House in Poland-street, Golden Square.

(Advt. many times repeated. There had been an advance announcement on 19 March.)

1763 (aged 37)

Songs for Garrick's Drury Lane production of '*A Midsummer Night's Dream*', *23 November.*

There had been a good many adaptations of this play, all with much musical development, but this (also an adaptation) was the only production under the original title between 1662 (see Pepys) and 1816. It was a fiasco, having merely one performance in its full five-act form and then, three days later, being reduced to a two-act after-piece under the title, *A Fairy Tale*, in which latter form it continued to be performed from time to time to 1777.

In the five-act version there were 33 songs, of which 14 were by Burney; in the two-act version there were 12 songs, of which 4 were by him. In the 1777 version (Haymarket) only one song of Burney's was retained (or possibly two). The music is lost and the above facts as to it are taken exclusively from 'A Table of the Songs with the Names of the several Composers' appended to a copy of the libretto in the King's Library of the British Museum (642. e. 19, 4). Fanny Burney, in the *Memoirs*, does not mention her father's connexion with this production, to which attention was first called in an article by Alfred Loewenberg in *Theatre Notebook*, April 1946, from which article has been taken the above information.

1765 (aged 39)

Sonata for Two Violins and a Bass.

Mentioned in Brown and Stratton's *British Musical Biography*; otherwise unknown to the present writer (Brown was a professional librarian and may have met with such a work).

1766 (aged 40)

Six Sonatas for the Harpsichord. Printed for the Author and Sold by R. Bremner opposite Somerset House in the Strand.

British Museum Catalogue gives the date as 1766 (Bremner opened his London house in 1762). But if this date is correct, is this a reprint of the 1761 set with a slightly different title? There is a copy in the Library of Congress, and the present writer possesses one. Mr. C. B. Oldman, of the British Museum, writes: 'I am sure that this is identical with the work entered above under 1761. I have observed innumerable instances of discrepancy between the titles given in the newspaper advertisements and the titles on the music itself.'

One or two movements in this set have long passages of repeated notes, of such a character that they may have formed the basis for a criticism of Burney as harpsichord composer which is found in *A B C Dario Musico* (1780), an alphabetically arranged, sometimes satirical (and even libellous) account of composers in England, in which Charles and Charles Rousseau Burney receive the following entries:

B. RN. Y. Doctor

Has written a learned and elegant history of Music. We can't say much in his praise as a composer, his lessons having nothing remarkable in them, but the frequent repetition of one note, which *trick* we think rather ill-adapted to the harpsichord. He first wrote lessons for two performers on one instrument, which are very inferior to some since published by Mr. Bach [J. C. Bach; see I. 122].

B. RN. Y. Nephew to the Doctor. A performer on the harpsichord of most capital and original execution, particularly neat in the performance of the *trick* above alluded to, and which nothing but the ability of Mr. B.rn.y could excuse. We are surprised that this gentleman has never published any lessons, as they would certainly prove very acceptable from such a great master of his instrument, and from such only.

It may be noted that Gerber's *Lexicon der Tonkünstler* (Leipzig 1790) mentions as known in Germany 'VI Klaviersolos'.

1766 (aged 40)

(*a*) *The Cunning-Man, a Musical Entertainment. In Two Acts. As it is performed at the Theatre Royal in Drury Lane. Taken from the Devin du Village of Mr. J. J. Rousseau and Adapted to his Original Music by C. Burney. Price 5 sh. London. Printed and Sold by R. Bremner, Opposite Somerset House in the Strand. Of whom may be had this Opera printed seperately* [sic], *for the German Flute and Guitar.* **See I. 107–17.**

The voice parts are given, with keyboard accompaniment. Copies in the British Museum (catalogued under 'Rousseau', press mark D. 281, 1), in the University Library, Cambridge, and in the possession of the present writer; copies with same year, but the imprint 'T. Becket and P. A. de Hondt' in the Library of Congress (catalogued as '2nd edition') and Library of the University of Chicago.

(*b*) *The Comic Tunes in the Devin du Village or Cunning Man. For the Harpsichord, Violin, German Flute, or Hoboy.* Also published by Bremner.

Copy in the British Museum.

(*c, d*) *Arrangement of Tunes of the Opera for the German Flute. Arrangement of Tunes of the Opera for the Guitar.*

The writer's sole knowledge of the existence of these publications comes from the advertisement on the title-page of the first of the *Cunning Man* publications above mentioned.

(*e*) *The Favorite Air from the Devin du Village, with Variations.*

The present writer possesses no information about this beyond what is given in the advertisement of the 'Second Rondo', below (s.v. 'Between 1803 and 1809').

Libretto. There appear to have been at least six editions of this:

1766, two editions, London, Burney's name appearing on the second.
1767, Dublin.
1784, in the Supplement to *Bell's British Theatre* (vol. ii).
1786, in *A Collection of the Most Esteemed Farces* (vol. ii), Edinburgh.
1792, in another edition of the 1786 *Collection*.

The following note appears in the first and second editions:

'Upon rehearsing the Music, it has been thought necessary to retrench the Second Act for fear of satiety; for though the Airs and Dances, after the reconciliation of Colin and Phoebe, are by no means inferior to the rest in point of composition, yet as no other business remains to be done after that circumstance, the Editor, with some reluctance, submitted to the omission of such airs etc. as are printed with inverted commas, which, however, are all published with the music, by Mr. Bremner in the Strand.'

The second edition has also the following:

'The Translator cannot send this edition to the press, without making his acknowledgements to the Managers of Drury Lane Theatre, for their great care in getting up this little piece; to the Performers, for their excellent representation of it; and to the Public for their favourable acceptance of his feeble endeavours to contribute his mite toward their innocent amusements.'

1769 (aged 43)

ANTHEM. *I will love Thee, O Lord, my Strength* (From Psalm XVIII).

See I. 142–5.

Written as the Exercise for the doctorate in music at Oxford, there performed on the occasion of the taking of the degree and on later occasions, as also at Hamburg under Carl Philipp Emanuel Bach (for particulars of these performances see Chapter XIII). The work is of considerable length. It has never been published, but since its performance has always been available for examination in the Bodleian Library.

The work is orchestrated for Strings, Oboes, Bassoons, and Horns. The layout of the work will be seen from the printed programme, of which, also, a copy is preserved in the Bodleian Library, and of which a reproduction is given on pl. 12, I. 144 in the present work. (The writer possesses a complete photostat.)

1769 (aged 43)

ANTHEM. *Thanks be to God.* **See I. 145.**

This is in eight real parts, unaccompanied. It was prepared as an additional exercise for the Oxford doctorate but not required. It is printed in full in the original edition of Burney's *History of Music* (iii. 351), but is not included in the modern reprint of the work.

1769 (aged 43)

Nine tunes in *A Collection of Psalm and Hymn Tunes*, being the 'Lock Hospital Collection', ed. Rev. Martin Madan (new edn. in 1792).

Perhaps *c.* **1770** (aged perhaps 44)

Two Sonatas for the Harpsichord or Forte Piano with Accompanyments for a Violin and Violoncello. London (3 part-books).

Copy in the Royal Music Library in the British Museum. In the Berlin Library, according to Eitner (see a 'Second Number' below).

1771 (aged 45)

La Musica che si Canta Annualmente nelle Funzioni della Settimana Santa nella Cappella Pontificia. Composta dal Palestrina, Allegri, e Bai. Raccolta e Pubblicata da Carlo Burney Mus.D. Londra Stampata per [blank] *nella Strand.*

See I. 196.

The Public Advertiser, 29 January 1772.

SACRED MUSIC.

This Day is published, Price 10s. 6d,

The Compositions which are annually sung in the Pope's Chapel during Passion Week, including the famous Miserere of Allegri. Collected and published by Dr. Charles Burney. To which is prefixed an Historical Preface by the Editor, and an Inside View of the Pontificial Chapel, engraved from Invara, of Rome.

Printed and sold by R. Bremner, opposite Somerset House, in the Strand.

The title as above given is taken from a copy in the possession of the present writer. This copy does not tally with the description supplied in the advertisement, since there is no Preface (and clearly never has been one): and there are no illustrations; moreover the place for the publisher's name is left vacant. This copy may, then, be an incomplete reprint. A copy recently in the market bore the words 'stampata per Roberto Bremner' and the date 1771. It had a four-page preface by Burney. The copy in the Library of Congress has Bremner's name where the above blank occurs.

There was a later reissue by 'Preston e figli, Londra', of which the British Museum catalogue's suggested date is 1790.

Books of reference are sometimes at fault as to the date of first publication of this collection. Fétis is badly out at '1784'.

1772 (aged 46)

A Second Number of Two Sonatas for the Harpsichord and [i.e. 'or'] *Forte Piano, with Accompanyments for a Violin and Violoncello.*

The Public Advertiser, 21 March 1772.

NEW MUSICK.

This Day is published, Price 5s.

A Second Number of two Sonatas for the Harpsichord, or Piano Forte, with accompanyments for a Violin and Violoncello. Composed by Dr. Burney.

Printed and sold by R. Bremner, opposite Somerset House in the Strand. Of whom may be had, just published, the Music annually sung in the

Pope's Chapel during Passion Week, including the famous Miserere of Allegri.

No copy in the British Museum. Copy in the possession of the present author. The pagination of the keyboard part runs from 18 to 33 and that of the string parts from 6 to 12: it would appear, therefore, that it is continuous with that of the 'First Number', which is apparently the item previously listed under 'Perhaps *c.* 1770'. Gerber's *Lexicon der Tonkünstler* (Leipzig, 1790) mentions as known in Germany the *IV Klaviersonaten mit einer Violin und Violonzell* of Burney. This would appear to be a combination of the Two Sonatas of *c.* 1770 and the 'Second Number' of 1772.

The distinction of method should be understood between Burney's (or any other composer's) 'Sonatas for Two Violins and a Bass' (and similar combinations) and 'Sonatas for the Harpsichord, with Accompaniments for a Violin and Violoncello'.

(*a*) Those for 'Two Violins and a Bass', &c., include a figured-bass from which both the violoncellist and harpsichordist (if both present) would play, the latter extemporizing his part from the harmonies indicated by the figuring.

(*b*) Those for 'Harpsichord or Forte Piano', with 'Accompaniments' for the stringed instruments, possess a keyboard part written out in full, in all but a few passages, and of prime importance. (The 'few passages' just mentioned are those where the violin momentarily becomes the leading performer and here the keyboard player is supplied with a figuring indicating the chords out of which he is to evolve an accompaniment.)

1777 (aged 51)

Four Sonatas or Duets for two Performers upon one Piano Forte or Harpsichord.

See II. 203.

This appears to be (as the composer claims in his long and interesting preface) the first music for two players *at one keyboard* ever to reach print, though a little such music had been composed as far back as the Elizabethan period. Copies are in the British Museum; the University Library, Cambridge; the Library of Congress; and the possession of the present author. The publication is an oblong folio with the two parts printed one above the other and the indications 'Cembalo 1 mo' and 'Cembalo 2 do'. Eitner speaks of the set as being in two books, but seems to be wrong.

An article in the American journal, *The Musician*, April 1930, says, 'In 1777 the music publisher [*sic*] Burney is generally supposed to have been the first to publish a set of four sonatas transcribed by one Wulf of Weimar, and known as the Burney-Wulf duet publications': of that statement the present writer can make nothing; but 'Wulf of Weimar' is clearly Ernst Wilhelm Wolf (1735–92), known as 'der Weimarer', according to Eitner.

The Public Advertiser, 24 January 1777.

New Music.

Speedily will be published, Price 10s. 6d.

Four Sonatas or Duets for two Performers upon one Forte Piano or Harpsichord.

Composed by Charles Burney, Mus.D. Printed for the Author, and sold by R. Bremner, in the Strand; and at all the Music Shops.

1778 (aged 52)

A Second Set of Four Duets, for Two Performers upon one Forte Piano or Harpsichord.

A copy is in the British Museum, whose catalogue gives the date as 1778: other copies are in the University Library, Cambridge, and in the Library of Congress.

The Public Advertiser, 17 April 1778.

NEW MUSIC.

Speedily will be published

A Second Set of four Duets, for two Performers upon one Forte Piano or Harpsichord. Composed by C. Burney.

Printed for the Author; and sold by R. Bremner, in the Strand; and at all the Music Shops.

(At the date when the present book was being completed it was stated that a modern edition of one of these duets, by Alec Rowley, was about to be published by Messrs. Schott.)

c. **1780** (aged about 54)

Sonate à Trois Mains for Harpsichord.

The present writer's only knowledge of this unusual composition comes from the final paragraph of the following advertisement, and from one of Bremner's catalogues (1782) in the possession of Mr. Alfred Moffat.

The Public Advertiser, 27 January 1781.

NEW MUSIC.

This Day are published. Price 7s. 6d.

The favourite Songs in the Opera Rinaldo, composed by Signor Sacchini.

Printed and sold by R. Bremner, opposite Somerset House, in the Strand.

Of whom may be had, several new Publications, among which is a Harpsichord Sonate à trois mains, by Dr. Burney. Price 2s. 6d.

1782? (aged 56?)

'Dr. Burney's Trios for Violin and Bass.'

This is an entry in Bremner's catalogue of March 1782. The item is most likely one of those earlier recorded, the catalogue including many compositions dating back twenty years or more. (Information communicated by Mr. Alfred Moffat, who possesses a copy of the catalogue.)

1787 (aged 61)

Preludes, Fugues and Interludes for the Organ. Alphabetically arranged in all the keys that are most perfectly in tune upon that Instrument and printed in a Pocket size for the convenience of Young Organists: for whose use this book is particularly calculated and Published. Book I. London. Printed for the Author and sold at the Music Shops. **See I. 60, 61.**

The above date is established by an advertisement in *The General Advertiser* of 27 May. Copy in the British Museum. The present writer also possesses a copy (it bears the autograph of that keen music-lover, the late Lord Balfour).

No 'Book II' can be traced, and probably none was published.

1789 (aged 63)

Hymn Tunes, *Dartmouth* and *Fordwich* in *Psalmodia Evangelica, a Collection of Psalm and Hymn-tunes in three parts, for Public Worship.* Edited by Thomas Williams. London, S. A. and P. Thompson.

See pl. 7, I. 60.

In addition to these two tunes there appears anonymously in this publication the tune *Truro*, which has long been found in many British and (especially) American collections of hymn tunes with Burney's name attached. There seems to exist no evidence at all for this attribution; the very carefully compiled and reliable Historical Edition of *Hymns Ancient and Modern* (1909) does not mention Burney's name in connexion with the tune and the late J. T. Lightwood, author of *Hymn Tunes and their Story* (1905), a very thorough researcher, states that he could find no reason for associating this popular tune with Burney. The earliest attribution of this kind that has come to the author's notice is in Dobson and Gauntlett's *Tunes, New and Old* (1864), where, curiously, whilst Burney's name is attached to the tune itself, the index gives it to Gauntlett.

c. **1789** (aged about 63)

Catch, *Peter White can ne'er go right*, in Thompson's *Apollonian Harmony*, vol. iii, p. 21.

It is also to be found in *Boosey's Family Glee Book* (2nd Selection).

c. **1790** (aged about 64)

XII Canzonetti a due voci in Canone. Poesia dell' Abate Metastasio. Presso Longman and Broderip, Londra.

Copies in the University Library, Cambridge, in the British Museum, and in the Bodleian Library, Oxford.

1791 (aged 65)

Hymn Tune, *Millbank.*

This first appears, apparently, in Dr. Rippon's *Selection of Psalms and Hymn Tunes from the Best Authors*, where it is credited to Burney.

1794 (aged 68)

Two Sunday Hymns written by W. Mason and set by Dr. Burney.

Copy in the Harvard College Library. Four pages; words only. Whether the music was published is unknown to the present writer.

1799 (aged 73)

Hymn for the Emperor, translated by Dr. Burney, composed by Doctor Haydn. London: Printed by J. Dale. (For publisher see below.) **See II. 117.**

In the *Memoirs*, iii. 274, a letter from Burney to Fanny (reproduced on II. 297–300 of the present work) speaks of his playing this to Pitt at Dover, in September 1799, and giving a copy of it to Miss Grey, daughter of Sir Charles Grey.

The following is an extract from Dr. Otto Erich Deutsch's exhaustive article 'Haydn's Hymn and Burney's Translation' in *The Music Review*, August 1943:

'Shortly after the first publication of the Emperor's Hymn, Haydn, it would seem, in about 1798, sent one or more copies to London, and Charles Burney . . . was inspired to translate the hymn, with alterations, into English. The original hymn, written for a single voice with accompaniment, consists of three four-bar phrases, the first and third of which are repeated. In Burney's version, set for two sopranos, bass and pianoforte, each stanza of which contains eight lines instead of six as in the original, all three phrases are repeated. (In both versions the last two lines are repeated as a refrain.) This version was published in 1799 by Broderip and Wilkinson in London under the title *Hymn for the Emperor / Translated by Dr. Burney / Composed by Doctor Haydn.* Copies are to be found in the British Museum, the University Library, Cambridge, and the Paul Hirsch Library. There exist two later editions published in about 1805 (British Museum).

'In the summer of 1799 Burney sent a copy to Haydn with the following letter [first published in *The Harmonicon* V, 63, 1827]:

"*Al Celeberrimo Signore Giuseppe Haydn, in Vienna.*
"My dear and much-honoured Friend,

. . . The Divine Hymn, written for your imperial master, in imitation of our loyal song, 'God save great George our King', and set so admirably to music by yourself, I have translated and adapted to your melody, which is simple, grave, supplicating and pleasing. *La cadenza particolarmente mi pare nuova e squisitissima.* I have given our friend, Mr. Barthlemon, a copy of my English translation to transmit to you, with my affectionate and best respects. It was from seeing, in your letter to him, how well you wrote English, that I ventured to address you in my own language, for which my translation of your hymn will perhaps serve as an exercise; in comparing my version with the original, you will perceive that it is rather a paraphrase than a close translation; but the liberties I have taken were in consequence of the supposed treachery of some of his Imperial Majesty's generals and subjects, during the unfortunate campaign of Italy, of 1797, which the English all thought was the consequence, not of Buonaparte's heroism, but of Austrian and Italian treachery. . .

Your enthusiastic admirer and affectionate Servant,
Charles Burney."'

c. **1799** (aged about 73)

Suwarrow's March.

This evidently commemorated the exploits of the Russian Marshal Suvarov, who in 1799 subdued Poland and defeated the French Revolutionary armies in Italy. Burney played it to Pitt on the occasion mentioned above. No copy is known to the present writer.

1799 (aged 73)

Song on the Naval Victories (alias 'Song on the Five Naval Heroes').

See II. 302.

Deliberately set in a popular 'ballad' or 'hallaballoo' style (see *Memoirs*, iii. 268). It was sung in private by the Queen, and in Covent Garden Theatre before the King and Queen, the Queen having sent it there with a request. It must surely have been published but no copy has come to the notice of the present writer.

c. **1800** (aged about 74)

Bella Donna. A Favorite Ariette as sung by Mrs. Ashe at the Ladies' Concerts, Composed by C. B. Printed and sold by Rt. Birchall, No. 133, New Bond Street.

The Bodleian Library catalogue attributes this to Burney. Mrs. Ashe (*née* Comer) was the wife of Andrew Ashe (*c.* 1758–1838), one of London's chief flautists and a composer for his instrument.[1]

Probably *c.* **1801** (probably aged about 75)

A Favorite Rondo (for pianoforte).

Not in the British Museum, and no copy traced by the present writer, whose information of the existence of the piece comes from the advertisement on the 'Second Rondo', below.

[1] Next to the above, in the Bodleian volume, is another song, *Il Pegno*; a Favorite Arietta composed and Inscribed to Dr. Burney, by F. B., Author of *L'Inganno*. It also is published by Birchall. I have not traced 'F. B.'—possibly Frances Burney the Second, daughter of Hester and Charles Rousseau Burney.

1803 (aged 77)

Courtenay's Four Patriotic Songs, addressed to the British Sailors, Soldiers and Volunteers. London. Printed by Broderip and Wilkinson, No. 13 Haymarket.

There are copies in the British Museum, the Bodleian Library, Oxford, and the University Library, Cambridge.

The songs are four in number: 1, *John Bull's Call to the Sailors* ('Ye guardians of Britain, ye sons of the waves'). 2, *To Arms! A Call to the Volunteers* ('Ye Volunteers renown'd in Song'). 3, *The Devoted and Victorious British Soldier* ('To battle let Despots condemn the poor Slave'). 4, *Britannia's Triumph, written during the late War* ('Let France her vain Republic boast').

The words of the songs above are not in a collection of 'Verses addressed to His Royal Highness the Prince Regent' by John Courtenay, but are very similar in style and evidently by the same person—John Courtenay, the politician (1714–1816).[1]

Between **1803** and **1809** (aged 77–83)

A Second Rondo in which is Introduced the favorite Air of The Old Highland Laddie with Variations. Printed by Lavenu and Mitchell, 29 New Bond Street, where may be had by the same author A Favorite Rondo; 2/-; The favourite Air from the Devin du Village with Variations, 1/-.

The dates above given are those when Mitchell was in partnership with Lavenu. No copy in the British Museum; the present writer possesses one.

(The air of *The Old Highland Laddie* tune is not that of *The Blue Bells of Scotland.*)

Undated

Nativity Hymn.

Manuscript in the British Museum (Add. 36871, fol. 206). It is a setting of Charles Wesley's *Hark the Herald Angels sing* (or, as Wesley wrote it, *Hark how all the welkin rings*). Whether it was ever published is doubtful. A 'Nativity Hymn' (probably this) was sung at the Burney Bicentenary Celebration at Chelsea in 1926 (see II. 330).

1832

A Canzonetta to Humorous Words by Metastasio. Reproduced in *The Harmonicon* of the year mentioned.

Undated

Round, *Jack and Jill.*

This is found in *The Rounds, Catches, and Canons of England*, by J. Powell Metcalfe and Edward F. Rimbault, published (n.d.) by Cramer, Wood, & Co., where Burney's name is attached to it.

1897

Alla Trinità; melody from the 15th Century harmonized by Chas. Burney (S.A.T.B.) G. Schirmer, New York: also a version with English words, 1903.

The basis of the ascription is that Burney in his *History* (ii. 328; Mercer, i. 631), after giving the melody, in plainsong notation, as he had copied it from a volume of

[1] Next in the album in the Bodleian Library is *Lady Avondale's Song. The words taken from 'The Refusal', by Mrs. West. Composed and respectfully inscribed to Mrs. Holyroyd by Miss Cecilia Burney. London. Chappell & Co., 124 New Bond Street.* This shows us a granddaughter of Burney as a composer—Esther Burney's youngest child (1789–1821). The *Family Memoranda* states that she had a talent for music and 'began composing elegant little songs in her 13th year', whilst 'those which she produced in later life were masterly compositions'.

Laudi Spirituale in the Magliabecchi Library at Florence, has followed it with an (imperfect) attempt at a reproduction in modern notation, to which he has added a bass.

WORKS OF JAMES BURNEY

1797. *A Plan of Defence against Invasion.* **See II. 232.**

Pamphlet; 2 edns., in the same year.

1797. *Measures Recommended for the Support of Public Credit.* **See II. 232.**

Pamphlet; no copy now known to exist.

1803–17. *A Chronological History of the Voyages and Discoveries in the South Sea or Pacific Ocean.* 5 vols. **See II. 232.**

Observations on the Progress of Bodies Floating in a Stream.

New Method proposed for Measuring a Ship's Rate of Sailing.

The last two were papers read before the Royal Society but not included in its *Philosophical Transactions.* They are mentioned here for completeness, but apparently they were never printed.

1818. *A Memoir on the Geography of the N.E. Part of Asia and on the Question whether Asia and America are Contiguous, or are Separated by the Sea.*

Paper read to the Royal Society in Dec. 1817 and printed in the Society's *Philosophical Transactions* the following year.

1819. *A Chronological History of North-Eastern Voyages of Discovery and Early Eastern Navigations of the Russians.* **See II. 277.**

1819. *A Commentary on the Systems that have been advanced for Explaining the Planetary Motions.*

A 60-page pamphlet dedicated to Sir Joseph Banks.

1820. *A Memoir of the Voyage of D'Entrecasteaux in Search of the Pérouse.*

Pamphlet. La Pérouse was a French explorer who disappeared in the Pacific in 1788.

1821. *An Essay by Way of Lecture on the Game of Whist.* **See II. 234.**

There was a 2nd edn., in 1823, as *A Treatise on the Game of Whist;* the posthumous 4th edn., in 1848, was called *A Concise Treatise on the Game of Whist.*

WORKS OF FANNY BURNEY (LATER D'ARBLAY), PUBLISHED AND UNPUBLISHED

(Chronologically arranged according to dates of first editions, when published)

1778. *Evelina, or a Young Lady's Entrance into the World.* 3 vols.; 2nd, 3rd, and 4th edns. 1779. Other edns. in 1783, 1784 (London and Dublin), 1788 (English edn. published in Dresden), 1791, 1793, 1794, 1808, 1810, 1815, 1821, 1822, 1829, 1881, 1903, 1904, and 1930 (probably this list is incomplete). **See I. 349–60.**

French translations, 1779, 1780, 1784 (transl. Griffet de Labaume) and 1797.

German translation, 1779.

The 1st edn. is not rare and did not fetch high prices until 1912 when a specially fine copy sold for £49. Since then prices have soared, varying within absurdly wide limits according to condition. *The Times Literary Supplement* of 18 Jan. 1936 remarked that three copies had recently been sold within a few months at prices ranging from £10 to £4,000.

1779. *The Witlings.* **See I. 360–1.**

Comedy written for Sheridan, but, at Dr. Burney's desire, not acted. Never printed.

1782. *Cecilia, or the Memoirs of an Heiress.* 5 vols. Other edns. in 1783, 1784 (Dublin), 1791, 1796, 1809, 1812 (Birmingham), 1819, 1820, 1882, 1893, and 1904 (probably this list is incomplete). **See II. 26–9.**

Prices for the 1st edn. have recently ranged from £1. 10*s.* to £15 or more, according to condition.

The *Königlicher Grossbritannischer Historischer Genealogischer Calendar* for 1789 (Lauenburg; 16mo) includes what Fanny Burney describes (*Diary and Letters*, iv. 233) as 'an abridgement of *Cecilia*': every month's instalment opens with an illustrative copperplate by Daniel Chodowiecki, 'the Berlin Hogarth'.

There were probably many translations, beginning with the French one published at Neuchâtel in 1783, which may be the same as the translation by Rieu in that year.

In May 1930 there was sold at Sothebys, for £195, draft of a page advertisement of *Cecilia*, in Fanny Burney's autograph, the property of Lieut.-Col. A. E. C. Burney.

1793. *Brief Reflections relative to the Emigrant French Clergy. . .* **See II. 136–7.**

There was only one edn. Copies sell at from £2. 10*s.* to £10. 10*s.*

1794. *Edwy and Elgiva* (or *Edwin and Elvina*). **See I. 361.**

Tragedy produced at Drury Lane and withdrawn after one performance. Never printed.

1796. *Camilla, or a Picture of Youth.* 5 vols. **See II. 134, 138–41.**

Copies of the 1st edn. have recently sold at prices from £1. 10*s.* to £7. 7*s.* A Dublin edn. same year. Later edns. in 1840, &c. There was at least one French translation, by Desprez and Deschamps (1798), and a German one (also 1798).

1799. *Love and Fashion.* **See I. 361.**

Comedy put into rehearsal at Drury Lane, but withdrawn without performance, at Burney's desire. Never printed.

1800. Poem, *In Memory of Susan Elizabeth Phillips.*

MS. in catalogue of C. A. Stonehill, jr., London, in 1934; there are other poems apparently by Fanny in the same catalogue, as well as many by other members of the family, their relatives by marriage, and their friends.

1814. *The Wanderer, or Female Difficulties.* 5 vols. **See II. 248–52.**

Apparently some copies are dated 1815, copies of both dates being sold to-day as 1st edns. and at prices ranging from £2 to £36.

There was a French translation by Breton and Lemierre d'Argy, in the very year of the publication of the original. Its title is *La Femme errante, ou les embarras d'une femme.*

1832. *Memoirs of Doctor Burney, arranged from his own Manuscripts, from Family Papers, and from Personal Recollections.* Published by Moxon. **See II. 280.**

Copies sell at prices from £2. 10*s.* to £5.

There was an abridged edn. in one volume in Philadelphia in the year following the appearance in the original (copy in the possession of the present author).

At the opening of the English edition appears the following 'Advertisement' of a projected fourth volume that was never published:

'It was the intention of the Biographer of Dr. Burney, to have printed the Doctor's Correspondence, in a fourth volume, at the same time with the Memoir; but upon examining the collection, there appears such a dearth of the Doctor's own Letters, of which he very rarely kept copies, that it seems to be expedient to postpone their publication, till it can be rendered more complete; to which end, the Biographer ventures earnestly to entreat, that all who possess any original letters of Doctor Burney, whether addressed to themselves, or retained by inheritance, will have the goodness—where there seems no objection to their meeting the public eye—to forward them to Mr. Moxon, who will carefully transmit them to the Biographer, by whom they will afterwards be restored to their owners, with the most grateful acknowledgements.'

1842–6. *The Diary and Letters of Madame d'Arblay.* 7 vols. Edited by her niece, Mrs. Charlotte Francis Barrett (daughter of her sister Charlotte).

Vols. 1 and 2 exist in two issues, differing in pagination.

See II. 281.

Later editions are as follows:

1854, Reprint of the above, but in 4 vols.

1876, Reprint of the above, also in 4 vols. ('revised').

Two impressions of this, differing slightly.

1890–4, 3 vols., edited (and somewhat abridged) by W. C. Ward.

1892, 4 vols.

Reprint of the first impression of the 1876 edn.

1904–5, 6 vols. edited by Austin Dobson.

This is now the standard edition and is the one to which reference is made throughout the present work; it is, strangely, out of print. It includes, as an appendix, a list of all editions to its own date of publication. There is room for a new and more scholarly edition with a better index.

1912. The Johnsonian passages alone, edited by C. B. Tinker, as *Doctor Johnson and Fanny Burney.*

1931, a 1-vol. selection by Muriel Masefield (Cambridge University Press).

1940, a 2-vol. selection by Lewis Gibbs (Everyman Edn.).

The *Diary and Letters* have long been a favourite subject of the hobby of the 'Grangerizer' or 'extra illustrator'. The present writer possesses a handsome set of the Austin Dobson edition enriched in this way by some enthusiast unknown, but the finest set in existence is undoubtedly that of the late Mr. Leverton Harris, of Camilla Lacey (Fanny's old residence), now in the National Portrait Gallery; in this the original has been extended to twenty folio volumes.

In May 1930 there was sold at Sothebys, for £400, 'a portion extending to 53 pages quarto of the autograph of Fanny Burney's *Diary*, written in the year 1786 and dealing with the duties as Second Keeper of the Queen's Robes'. About 11 pages of the manuscript are lightly scored out and have not been published. The purchaser was Mr. Gabriel Wells.

The general body of the manuscript of the *Diary* was in the possession of Mr. Leverton Harris (above mentioned). It was consumed in the disastrous fire at Camilla Lacey in 1919 (cf. I. 350 n.).

1889. *The Early Diary of Frances Burney, 1768–1778, with a Selection from her Correspondence and from the Journals of her Sisters Susan and Charlotte Burney.* Edited by Mrs. Annie Raine Ellis. 2 vols.; revised edn. 1907; cheap edn. 1913. (Still on sale in Bohn's Standard Library.)

1890. *Fanny Burney and her Friends.* A selection from her Diary and other writings, compiled by L. B. Seeley.

WRONGLY ATTRIBUTED. *Elizabeth or the Exiles of Siberia*, 'from the French of Mad. Cottin'. 1807.

Also 1809 and 1810; it is in the reprint of 1810 that this is described on the title page as translated by 'Miss Burney'. The present writer is of the opinion that if any Miss Burney of the family in which he is interested were really the translator it would more probably be Fanny's half-sister, Sarah Harriet, but second-hand booksellers of to-day assume that Fanny is intended, which is improbable as she would at that date have been called 'Madame d'Arblay'.

WRONGLY ATTRIBUTED. *Tragic Dramas.*

See under 'Frances Burney II (daughter of Hester and Charles Rousseau Burney)'.

Fanny's husband, General Alexandre d'Arblay, was also an author—at least to the extent of producing a pamphlet in defence of a colleague and friend. In 1792 Antoine Rivarol published at Liége a pamphlet *De la Vie Politique, de la Fuite et de la Capture de M. Lafayette*, whereupon d'Arblay promptly replied with another *Sur le pamphlet de M. de Rivarol contre M. de Lafayette* (copies in the British Museum and the Bodleian Library). It is signed at the end: 'Alexandre d'Arblay, ci-devant adjutant général de l'armée aux ordres de M. de Lafayette'.

WORKS OF CHARLES BURNEY, JUNIOR

c. 1783–6. Articles in *The Monthly Review*, especially an attack on Huntingford's *Monostrophica.*

c. 1783–1800. He became Editor of *The London Magazine* on the recommendation of Dr. Parr (*D.N.B.*) and presumably himself contributed articles.

Article on Porson's *Hecuba* and Wakefield's *Diatribe.*

Part of this was translated into Latin by Gaisford and inserted in a note appended to a reprint of Markland's *Supplices of Euripides* (see *D.N.B.*).

1789. *Appendix in Lexicon Graecum a Scapula constructum.*

1791. *Remarks on the Greek Verses of Milton.*

Also appended to Warton's edn. of Milton's early poetry. (For a discussion of these 'Remarks' see *The Monthly Review*, January 1793.)

1807. *Richardi Bentleii et doctorum virorum epistolae.*

Printed for presentation only (reprinted by Friedmann, 1825).

1809. *Tentamen de Metris Æschyli.*

1810. *Abridgement of 'Dr. Pearson on the Creed'.*

1812. *Philemonis Lexicon Technologicum.*

For some remarks on *Verses on the Threatened Invasion*, attributed by the British Museum Catalogue to this writer, see II. 338–9. For reference to another poem, see II. 238 n.

WORKS OF CHARLOTTE ANN BURNEY

(MRS. FRANCIS AND THEN MRS. BROOME)

1824. *Trials.*

WORKS OF SARAH HARRIET BURNEY

1796. *Clarentine.*

Published anonymously; another edn. 1816.

1808. *Geraldine Fauconberg.*

Another edn. in 1813. There was a French translation, by 'Mme. Saint-H***', in 1811.

1812. *Traits of Nature.*

First and second edns. same year; third in 1813. There was a French translation by Defauconpret, in 1819; its title was *Le Jeune Cleveland, ou Traits de Nature.*

1815. *Tales of Fancy.*

Some copies are apparently dated 1816.

1820. *Country Neighbours.*

1839. *The Romance of Private Life.*

For the translation of Madame Cottin's *Elizabeth or the Exiles of Siberia* see a note under 'Fanny Burney'.

WORKS OF ALEXANDER D'ARBLAY, JUNIOR

(Fanny's only child)

1830–6. A number of Sermons, or 'Discourses'. (See British Museum Catalogue.)

1831. *Chant guerrier des Polonais, ou Sckrynecki devant Varsovie: Poème lyrique, avec traduction en Anglais par l'Auteur.* London.

c. 1833. *Urania, or the Spirit of Poetry, an Ode.* Privately printed.

n.d. *Poem on the famous match between the British and French chess champions O'Donnell and Labourdonnais.* **See II. 280–1.**

WORKS OF CHARLES PARR BURNEY

(Son of Charles Burney, junior)

1809. *The Love of our Country; a Prize Essay recited in the Theatre at Oxford.* Oxford. Also in *Oxford English Prize Essays*, 1836, vol. ii.

WORKS OF MRS. CHARLOTTE FRANCIS BARRETT

(*née* Francis: Charlotte's daughter)

1855. *Handbook to the Marbles, Casts and Antiquities in the Fitzwilliam Museum.* Cambridge.

1859. *Charades, Enigmas, and Riddles.* Published anonymously, as 'Collected by a Cantab'.

See also under Fanny Burney, *Diary and Letters.*

WORKS OF FRANCES BURNEY II

(Daughter of Hester and Charles Rousseau Burney)

1818. *Tragic Dramas chiefly intended for Representation in Private Families, to which is added 'Aristodemus', a Tragedy from the Italian of Vincenzo Monti.*

In the *Cambridge Bibliography of English Literature* (1941), and in some library catalogues, this work by one of Burney's granddaughters has, by oversight, been attributed to his daughter, Frances Burney I, i.e. to Fanny, the aunt of the actual author. Some reference to the work will be found in Brimley Johnson, *Fanny Burney and the Burneys*, 367.

WRITINGS ON THE BURNEYS

(OR INCLUDING REFERENCES TO THEM)

ABC Dario Musico. Bath, 1780. Has short notes on prominent British musicians of the time, including Burney.

ANON. 'Charles Burney.' In *The Organist and Choirmaster*, xxi, 550, 1913–14.

AUSTEN, JANE. *Northanger Abbey.* 1818. Has reference at the end to Fanny Burney's *Camilla.*

—— *Pride and Prejudice.* 1813. Named from a phrase in Fanny Burney's *Cecilia.*

BLACKBURN, VERNON. 'A Journalist on Tour—Charles Burney.' In *The Fringe of an Art*, 1898.

—— 'A Forgotten Enthusiast.' In *Musical Record and Review*, July 1903.

BROWN, REV. DAVID (Senior Chaplain at the Presidency of Fort William, Bengal). *A Sermon preached at the Mission Church, Calcutta, Sunday evening, May 15th, 1808, on the occasion of the Death of Mr. Richard Thomas Burney, late Head Master of the Military Upper Orphan School at Kidderpore, near Calcutta, Bengal, who died at Rangoon, Pegul, March 8th, 1808.* London, 1838, i.e. thirty years after the event!

BUTTNER, CARL. *Die Sprache in Fanny Burney's 'Evelina'.* Giessen, 1924.

CLYNE, ANTONY. 'Viewing the Accomplishments of Dr. Burney.' In *Musical America*, xliii, 27 March 1926.

'COLLIER, JOEL'. *Musical Travels in England.* 4 edns., 1774–5–6, 1818. (See I. 272–5.)

CROKER, JOHN WILSON. Attack on Fanny Burney in *Quarterly Review*, June 1842.

DANZ, K. *Frances Burneys Evelina und das Aufkommen der Frauenromane.* In the German periodical *Anglia*, xxxvi, 1924.

DEAN, CAPTAIN C. G. T. 'Dr. Burney's Connection with the Royal Hospital, Chelsea.' In *Transactions of the London and Middlesex Archaeological Society*, New Series, viii, pt. 3, 1944.

DELACHAUX, E. 'Fanny Burney, intermédiaire manquée entre l'Angleterre et la France.' In the *Revue de Littérature comparée*, Sept. 1935.

DEUTSCH, OTTO ERICH. 'Haydn's Hymn and Burney's Translation.' In *The Music Review*, Aug. 1943.

DICKINSON, CLARENCE. *A Music Lover's Tour of Europe with Dr. Burney.* 1930. This is a booklet programme of a series of four Historical Lecture Recitals given in the chapel of the Union Theological Seminary, New York. It comprises seventy items (solo vocal, choral, and instrumental) ingeniously arranged in geographical succession according to Burney's two itineraries, being compositions that he heard at the places mentioned, or by composers whom he met at those places.

DOBSON, AUSTIN. *Fanny Burney*, 1903. The best general treatment.

EDWARDS, F. G. 'Dr. Charles Burney.' A Biographical Sketch in *The Musical Times*, xlv, Oct. 1904.

FORSHALL, J. *The Burney Manuscripts in the British Museum*, i.e. the collection of Charles Burney, junior. It forms Part 2 of the Catalogue of Manuscripts.

GALLOWAY, TOD BUCHANAN. 'The Genial Dr. Burney.' In *The Etude* (U.S.A.), liii, Oct. 1935.

GERBER, ERNST LUDWIG, *Historisch-Biographisches Lexicon der Tonkünstler*. 2 vols., Breitkopf, Leipzig, 1790–2.

—— *Neues historisch-biographisches Lexicon der Tonkünstler*. 4 vols., A. Kühnel, Leipzig, 1812–14.

It is of interest to observe that Burney in 1790 received the recognition of a long article in a continental biographical dictionary of musicians.

The information given, though pretty adequate in the general impression it leaves, is faulty in detail. It gives his birthplace as 'Worchester' (possibly confusing him with his nephew Charles Rousseau Burney, born at Worcester), and his birth date as 1727 instead of 1726. It speaks of him as the pupil of his father (no doubt confusing his father, James Burney, with his brother, James Burney). Instead of sending him to King's Lynn in 1751 it, oddly, sends him to the neighbouring town of Swaffham. The attaining of the Oxford doctorate is spoken of as occurring after the Italian journey. And so on!

Readers of the *Lexicon* are referred by it to *Cramer's Magazin*, vol. ii, for further information, and this journal is the source of the incorrect statements.

GONSALVES, AUGUSTO LOPES. 'Une Viagem Musical à Italia no seculo XVIII.' In *Revista Brasileira da Música*, i, March 1934.

GOUDGE, ELIZABETH. Three plays (one being *Fanny Burney*, in eight scenes). 1939.

HALL, WILLIAM T. *Madame d'Arblay's Place in the Development of the English Novel*. Indiana University Studies, 1916.

HAZEN, ALLEN T. *Samuel Johnson's Prefaces and Dedications*. 1937. Has bibliographical information concerning the *History of Music* and the *Commemoration of Handel*.

HAZLITT, WILLIAM. Review of Fanny Burney's *Camilla* in *The Edinburgh Review*, Feb. 1815. Reproduced, with some changes, in Hazlitt's *English Comic Writers*, 1819.

HEGAR, E. *Anfänge der neueren Musikgeschichtsschreibung um 1776 bei Gerbert, Burney und Hawkins*. Strassburg, 1930. This book is to be found in the British Museum and the Library of Congress.

HILL, CONSTANCE. *The House in St. Martin's Street, being Chronicles of the Burney Family*. 1907.

—— *Fanny Burney at the Court of Queen Charlotte*. 1912.

—— *Juniper Hall*. 1904. On the French refugees and the Burneys' relations with them.

HOLMES, EDWARD. *A Ramble amongst the Musicians of Germany*. Three edns.,

1828, 1835, 1838. Has a chapter on 'The Voyage made by Dr. Burney in search of the Origin of Counterpoint'.

Horae Burneienses. Greenwich. Printed by Harriet Richardson, 1829 (150 pages). This is a collection of poems, essays, &c., by pupils of the school which C. P. Burney had taken over from his father in 1813. The preface alludes with disdain to the publication a few months earlier of a similar collection that was not entirely genuine.

ISAACS, LEWIS M. 'A Friend of Dr. Johnson.' In *The Musical Quarterly* (U.S.A.), i. 583, 1915.

JOHNSON, R. BRIMLEY. *Fanny Burney and the Burneys*. Family documents from the 'Worcester Journal' of the Burneys, selected and edited. 1926.

KERSHAW, S. W. 'Fanny Burney and Surrey.' In *Memorials of Old Surrey*, ed. Cox, 1911.

KIDSON, FRANK. 'James Oswald, Dr. Burney, and the Temple of Apollo'. In *The Musical Antiquary*, Oct. 1910. See remarks on I. 55–7 of the present book.

LAMB, CHARLES. Essay, *Detached Thoughts on Books and Reading*. (Refers to Martin Burney.)

—— *Letters*. Ed. E. V. Lucas. Has references to James Burney, &c.

LIGHTWOOD, JAMES T. ('L'). 'Dr. Charles Burney, Organist, Historian, and Gossip.' In *The Choir*, x, Jan.–Apr. 1919.

LLOYD, CHRISTOPHER. *Fanny Burney*. 1936.

LOCKWOOD, ELIZABETH M. 'At Dr. Burney's.' In *Music and Letters*, xi, Jan. 1930.

—— 'A Musical Pilgrimage in Vanishing London.' In *Musical Opinion*, xlix, Mar. 1926.

MACAULAY, THOS. BABINGTON. Review of *The Diary and Letters of Madame D'Arblay*. In *The Edinburgh Review*, Jan. 1843. To be found in all reprints of Macaulay's *Essays*.

MANWARING, G. E. *My Friend the Admiral*. 1938. The authoritative book on James Burney.

MASEFIELD, MURIEL. *The Story of Fanny Burney; an Introduction to the Diary and Letters of Mme d'Arblay*. 1927.

MOORE, FRANKFORT. *The Keeper of the Robes*. On Fanny Burney's Court life; a 'popular' treatment.

MOORE, THOMAS. *Letters and Journals of Lord Byron*. 2 vols., 1830. Has references to Fanny Burney as novelist.

MORLEY, EDITH J. *Fanny Burney*. English Association Pamphlet, 1925.

—— 'Sarah Harriet Burney, 1770–1844.' In *Modern Philology*, xxxix, 2 Nov. 1941. Includes sketch of her life and reproduces a number of her letters to Crabb Robinson.

New South Wales Historical Records. Vol. i, part 1, has letters that passed between James Burney and Captain Cook.

NICHOLS, R. H. and WRAY, F. A. *The History of the Foundling Hospital*. 1935. Contains an account of Burney's scheme for a School of Music there.

OBERMAN, A. A. *An Investigation into the Character of Fanny Burney*. Amsterdam, 1933. A University Thesis (in English).

PAPENDIEK, MRS. *Court and Private Life in the Time of Queen Charlotte, being the*

Journals of Mrs. Papendiek, Assistant Keeper of the Wardrobe and Reader to her Majesty. 2 vols. 1887. 'Journals' is a misnomer, as the contents of the volumes are reminiscences begun forty years after the events they narrate. They include statements concerning Fanny Burney's Court position. For a criticism of this very slipshod work see *Early Diary*, ii. 333.

PARKER, JOHN R. *A Musical Biography, or Sketches of the Lives and Writings of Eminent Musical Characters.* Boston, Mass., 1825. It includes a life of Burney—and speaks of this life as still in being!

'PASTON, GEORGE' (Mrs. E. M. Symonds). 'A Burney Friendship.' In *The Monthly Review*, viii, 1902. Also in *Side Lights on the Georgian Period*, 1902. Has some letters of Burney and of Fanny Burney to Miss Port (later Mrs. Waddington), niece of Mrs. Delany.

Probationary Odes by the Various Candidates for the Office of Poet Laureat to His Majesty. In the Room of William Whitehead Esq., Deceased (1785 and many other editions, with changes in titles and in text). Includes a skit on Burney (see II. 72 of the present work).

Public Characters in 1798–9. Has a four-page sketch of Burney's career to that date, and a tiny portrait.

PULVER, JEFFREY. 'Burney in Berlin.' In *The Monthly Musical Record*, lix, June 1929.

REICHARDT, JOHANN FRIEDRICH. *Vertraute Briefe eines aufmerksamen Reisenden die Musik betreffend.* 2 vols., 1774–6 (includes a vigorous attack on Burney's German Tour).

Report from the Committee on Petition of Trustees of the British Museum, relating to the collection of the late Dr. Burney. Ordered by the House of Commons to be printed, 17 April 1818. This refers to the collection of Charles Burney, junior—the D.D., not the Mus.D. It was reproduced in *The Gentleman's Magazine*, 1818, Pt. I, pp. 419–21; also in *The Gentleman's Magazine Library*, in the volume entitled *Literary Curiosities.* It includes a comparative table of the Greek literature in the British Museum and in Burney's library, divided into twenty-four classes and showing the latter to possess from two to three times as many volumes in almost every class.

RICCI, CORRADO. *Burney, Casanova e Farinelli in Bologna.* 1890. A pamphlet of 44 pp. Ricordi, Milan. Illustrations in text from drawings by A. Sezanne.

ROBERTS, W. WRIGHT. *Charles and Fanny Burney in the Light of the New Thrale Correspondence in the John Rylands Library.* Pamphlet. 1932. Also in *Bulletin* of the Library, xvi, No. 1; Jan. 1932.

—— *The Trial of Midas the Second or Congress of Musicians.* Burney's satirical poem on Hawkins's *History* described, with extracts. In *Bulletin* of John Rylands Library, Manchester, 1933; reprint in *Music and Letters*, Oct. 1933; separately published 1933.

ROLT, M. S. (Ed.). *A Great Niece's Journal, being Extracts from the Journals of Fanny Anne Burney (Mrs. Wood), 1830–42.* 1926.

SEELEY, L. B. *Fanny Burney and her Friends*, 1895. Largely extracts from her writings.

SHUCKBURGH, S. 'Fanny Burney's "Edwy and Elgiva".' Article in *Macmillans' Magazine*, Feb. 1890 (see also *The Times Literary Supplement*, 22 Nov. 1934).

SOTHEBY. Sale Catalogue of Fanny Burney's (Mme D'Arblay's) Library, by Sothebys, 12 Jan. 1883. There is a copy in the Printed Books Department of the British Museum, with MS. notes as to prices obtained. This sale is a continuation of a larger sale.

SYMONDS, MRS. E. M. *See* 'Paston, George'.

TINKER, CHAUNCY B. *Dr. Johnson and Fanny Burney, being the Johnsonian passages from the works of Mme. d'Arblay.* 1912.

TOURTELLOT, A. B. *Be Loved no More; the Life and Environment of Fanny Burney.* 1938. Condemned in *The Times Literary Supplement* in March 1938 as an example of 'the tawdry colours of the less satisfactory type of transatlantic prose' and defended in the same journal by its author on 2 April as 'an informal narrative' not 'an academic thesis'.

VILLENOISY, F. DE. *Le Journal de Voyage en France et en Italie d'un Musicien Anglais* [i.e. Burney]. Pamphlet of 21 pp. (8vo). 'Extrait de la *Correspondance Historique et Archéologique,* année 1916, tiré à 50 exemplaires.'

WAUCHOPE, A. J. 'The D'Arblays in July, 1815.' In the *Cornhill Magazine,* cliv, 1936.

WOOD, MRS. *See* Rolt.

(For particulars of the sale catalogues of Burney's library see II. 273–4.)

WORKS THROWING LIGHT ON THE CONDITIONS OF BURNEY'S PROVINCIAL LIFE

SHREWSBURY

AUDEN, H. M. *Notes on Condover.* Shrewsbury, 1932.

AUDEN, J. E. *Shrewsbury School Registers, 1734–1908.* 2nd edn., Oswestry, 1909.

FISHER, G. W. *Annals of Shrewsbury School.* 1899.

LLOYD, T. B. *Notes on St. Mary's Church, Shrewsbury.* 1900.

—— *Shrewsbury Neighbourhood.*

OWEN, HUGH. *Some Account of the Ancient and Present State of Shrewsbury.* 1808.

—— and BLAKEWAY, J. B. *History of Shrewsbury.* 2 vols., 1825.

Parish Registers of Hanwood. Shropshire Parish Register Society.

CHESTER

BRIDGE, JOSEPH C. 'The Organists of Chester Cathedral.' In *Journal of the Architectural, Archaeological, and Historical Society for the County and City of Chester and North Wales,* xix, part 2, 1913.

Memorials of the Dutton Family. London and Chester, 1901.

KING'S LYNN

ALVES, REV. E. J. *Lecture on the History of King's Lynn.* King's Lynn, 1900.

—— *A Record of Music in King's Lynn.* 1900.

BELOE, EDWARD MILLIGEN. *Our Borough; our Churches.* 1899.

BESANT, WALTER. *The Lady of Lynn.* Novel. 1901.

BLOMEFIELD, FRANCIS. *Topographical History of Norfolk.* 1806.

BULWER-LYTTON, E. G. E. L. *Eugene Aram.* Novel, 1832.

HILLEN, HENRY J. *History of King's Lynn,* 2 vols.

HOOD, THOMAS. *The Dream of Eugene Aram, the Murderer.* Poem. 1829. Hood's Preface, with its allusions to James Burney, can be seen in a separate edition of 1831, with Wm. Harvey's illustrations.

Norfolk Tour. 1829.

RICHARDS, WILLIAM. *History of Lynn.* 2 vols. 1812.

ROCHEFOUCAULD, FRANÇOIS DE LA. *Mélanges sur l'Angleterre.* Transl. S. C. Roberts and ed. J. Marchand as *A Frenchman in England, 1784* (1933). This has descriptions of both town and country life in Burney's day, gives a good description of some of Burney's haunts in Norfolk, and alludes a good deal to the author's friend (and Burney's brother-in-law), Arthur Young.

WALE, HENRY JOHN. *Grandfather's Pocket Book.* 1883.

WATSON, ERIC R. *Eugene Aram; his Life and Trial.* 1913.

YOUNG, DOROTHY ('D. Y.'). *Translations from the French.* Lynn, 1770.

WORKS THROWING LIGHT ON THE CONDITIONS OF BURNEY'S LONDON LIFE

ANGELO, HENRY. *Reminiscences.* 2 vols. 1830. (Reprint in 1904.)

—— *Angelo's Pic-Nic.* 1834.

Annals of The Club, 1764–1914. Printed for the [Literary] Club, 1914.

ANON. *See* Ring, John and *Queen's Concert Rooms.*

BESANT, SIR WALTER. *London in the Eighteenth Century.* 1902. A volume of his great *Survey of London.*

BROWNLOW, JOHN. *Memoranda or Chronicles of the Foundling Hospital.* 1847.

BUSBY, THOS. *Concert-Room and Orchestra Anecdotes.* 3 vols. 1825.

CARDWELL, REV. JOHN H. *Men and Women of Soho.* 1903.

CASANOVA DI SEINGALT, G. J. *Memoirs.* 12 vols., Leipzig, 1826–38; 8 vols., Paris 1885; &c. Has some particulars of Mrs. Cornelys and her establishment.

(CASTLE CONCERTS.) *The Laws of the Musical Society at the Castle Tavern in Pater-Noster Row. Printed in the year MDCCLI.* There were other editions in 1759 (almost exactly the same) and 1764 (somewhat altered). These later editions speak of the place of meeting as 'Haberdashers' Hall'. Cf. I. 23 n. There are copies of all these in the Bodleian Library.

CHANCELLOR, E. BERESFORD. *London's Old Latin Quarter* (The Tottenham Court Road district). 1930. *The Pleasure Haunts of London.* 1925. *The Eighteenth Century in London.* 1933.

DEAN, C. G. T. See II. 358.

DE CASTRO, J. P. *The Gordon Riots.* 1926.

DUFF, SIR M. E. GRANT. *The Club, 1764–1905.* A history of the Literary Club, of which Burney was a member. Privately published, 1905.

FAULKENER, THOMAS. *Historical and Topographical Description of Chelsea.* 1810 edition (not the later one).

GEORGE, M. DOROTHY. *London Life in the Eighteenth Century.* 1925.

GLADSTONE, VISCOUNT. *The Story of the Noblemen and Gentlemen's Catch Club.* Privately printed, 1930.

HARLEIAN SOCIETY PUBLICATIONS; Registers, vol. iii, 1878, being *The Register Booke of Saynte Denis Backchurch Parishe* (*City of London*).

HARRISON, BERTHA. 'Hickford's Rooms.' In *The Musical Times*, Sept. and Oct. 1906.

HENNESSY, REV. GEORGE. *Novum Repertorium Ecclesiasticum Parochiale Londiniense*, 1898.

HILL, CONSTANCE. *Good Company in old Westminster and the Temple.* 1925.

HODGSON, REV. ROBERT. *Life of Bishop Beilby Porteus.* 1811.

HUNT, J. H. LEIGH. *The Town.* 1844.

JACKSON, WILLIAM (of Exeter). *The Present State of Music in London.* 1791.

KELLY, MICHAEL. *Reminiscences.* 2 vols. 1826.

KENT, WILLIAM. *Encyclopaedia of London.* 1937.

KIDSON, FRANK. 'Nurseries of English Song' (the 'Gardens'). In *The Musical Times*, Aug. and Sept. 1922.

Laws of the Musical Society at the Castle Tavern in Pater-Noster Row. See Castle Concerts, above.

LEWIS, WILMARTH SHELDON. *Three Tours through London, 1748–1776–1797.* 1941.

LOCKMAN, JOHN. *Sketch of the Spring Gardens, Vauxhall.* 1762.

LONDON COUNTY COUNCIL. *Survey of London* (20 vols. published to date). The volume devoted to Trafalgar Square and neighbourhood has pictures of two of the mantelpieces in Burney's St. Martin's Street house and also one of the exterior of the house and adjoining chapel.

LYONS, SIR HENRY. *The Royal Society, 1660–1940.* 1944.

MACKINLAY, T. *Mrs. Cornelys' Entertainments at Carlisle House.* 1840(?).

MATTHEW, JAS. E. 'The Antient Concerts.' In *Musical Association Proceedings*, 1906–7.

'Memoirs of the Metropolitan Concerts.' In *The Harmonicon*, 1831.

MILLER, EDWARD. *Letters on behalf of Professors of Music residing in the Country.* 1784. This is a plea that the benefits of the Handel Commemoration should not be restricted to musicians living in London.

MOUNT-EDGCUMBE, LORD (2nd Earl). *Musical Reminiscences.* 2 vols. 1825, and three later edns., to 1834.

NANGLE, B. C. *The Monthly Review (1749–89).* 1934. It lists the contents and gives the names of the contributors from the editor's marked copy.

NICHOLS, R. H. and WRAY, F. A. *History of the Foundling Hospital.* 1935.

OLIPHANT, THOMAS. *A Brief Account of the Madrigal Society.* 1835.

OULTON, WALLEY CHAMBERLAIN. *History of the Theatres of London from 1771 to 1795.* 2 vols. 1796.

PARKE, WM. THOS. *Musical Memoirs.* 1830.

PARRY, JOHN. *A Sketch of the Rise and Progress of Her Majesty's Concerts of Ancient Music.* 1847.

PENNANT, THOMAS. *A Journey from Chester to London.* 1782.

—— *London.* 1790.

—— *Additions and Corrections to 'London'.* 1791.

—— *Literary Life.* 1793.

Queen's Concert Rooms, Hanover Square, Notes Historical and Miscellaneous concerning the. 1862.

Registers of St. Dionis Church, London (Harleian Society, 1878).

Report of the Select Committee on Finance, 1798.

Report of the Commissioners for Military Enquiry, 1812.

RIMBAULT, EDWARD F. (ed. Clinch). *Soho and its Associations.* 1895.
RING, JOHN. *The Commemoration of Handel: a Poem.* 2 edns., 1786 and 1819—the first anonymous.
ROCHE, SOPHIE V. LA. *Sophie in London* (transln. of her diary of 1786). 1933.
SOUTHGATE, T. L. 'Music of the London Gardens.' In *Musical Association Proceedings*, 1911–12.
TIMBS, JOHN. *Clubs and Club Life in London.* 1872.
TURBEVILLE, A. S. (ed.). *Johnson's England.* 1933.
VICTOR, BENJAMIN. *Original Letters, Dramatic Pieces, and Poems.* 1766.
WALFORD, EDWARD. *Old and New London.* 1872–8.
WEBB, SIDNEY and MRS. SIDNEY. *English Local Government.* 8 vols., 1906–29.
WESLEY, JOHN. *Journal* (1739–91). Definitive edition in 8 vols., ed. Nehemiah Curnock, 1909–16.
WHEATLEY, H. B. *Hogarth's London; Pictures of the Manners of the Eighteenth Century.* 1909.
WINNETT, REV. A. R. *History of St. Dionis Backchurch.* 1935.
WOOD, SIR HENRY TRUEMAN. *A History of the Royal Society of Arts.* 1913.
WROTH, WARWICK. *The London Pleasure Gardens of the Eighteenth Century.* 1896.

SOME WORKS OF INTEREST IN CONNEXION WITH BURNEY'S CONTINENTAL TRAVELS

BERNARDI, G. G. 'La Musica a Venezia nell' Età di Goldoni.' In *L'Ateneo Veneto*, xxxi, Fasc. 3, 1908. Also separately published.
BRENET, MICHEL. *Les Concerts en France sous l'Ancien Régime.* Paris, 1900.
BROSSES (PRÉSIDENT) CHARLES DE. *Lettres d'Italie.* Posthumously published 1799 (Modern edn. 1927). This work has much information on music and musicians.
BRUFORD, W. H. *Germany in the Eighteenth Century: the Social Background of the Literary Revival.* 1935.
CURZON, HENRI DE. *La Musique (XVIIIe Siècle): Textes choisis et commentés.* 1914.
DORAN, DR. JOHN. *'Mann' and Manners at the Court of Florence, 1740–86.* 2 vols., 1876.
LA LANDE, J. J. L. DE. *Voyage en Italie.* 9 vols., 1769; 2nd edn. 1786.
LAMBERT, R. S. (ed.) *Grand Tour, a Journey in the Tracks of the Age of Aristocracy.* 1935.
LEE, VERNON. *Studies of the Eighteenth Century in Italy.* 2 edns., 1881 and 1907.
MAXWELL, CONSTANTIA. *The English Traveller in France, 1698–1815.* 1932.
MONNIER, PHILIPPE. *Venice in the Eighteenth Century.* 1910.
ROLLAND, ROMAIN. *Voyage Musical au Pays du Passé.* Paris, 1920.
SMOLLETT, TOBIAS. *Travels through France and Italy.* 1766 and later editions to present day.
STRIFFLING, LOUIS. *Esquisse d'une Histoire du Goût Musical en France au XVIIIe Siècle.* Paris, 1912.
WIEL, TADDEO. 'I Teatri Musicali Veneziani del Settecento.' In *Archivio Veneto*, 1891–7. Separately published, Venice, 1897.

See also, in *Select List of Writings on or by the People Burney met and knew*,

Armstrong, Baretti, Diderot, Ebeling, Frederick the Great, Hamilton, Martini, Metastasio, Mozart, Quantz, Rousseau, and Young. And see *Writings on the Burneys* (several entries).

SELECT LIST OF WRITINGS ON OR BY THE PEOPLE BURNEY AND THE BURNEYS MET AND KNEW

Intended to give an idea of the literary circles in which he and they moved, and including many books referred to in the preparation of the present work.

JOHN ARMSTRONG, M.D. (1709–79). 'The poetical *Æsculapius*', as Fanny called him. Early medical adviser and warm friend of Burney and his family.

JOHN ARMSTRONG. *A Short Ramble through France and Italy* (written under the *nom de plume* of 'Launcelot Temple Esq.'). 1771.

—— *The Art of Preserving Health.* 1774.

SAMUEL JOHNSON, Essay on Armstrong in *The Lives of the Poets.* 1781.

I. A. WILLIAMS. *Seven Eighteenth-Century Bibliographies.* 1924. Has an Essay on Armstrong, and a Bibliography of his works.

For a more complete list of Armstong's own numerous poetical, medical, and other works, see *The Cambridge Bibliography of English Literature.*

THOMAS AUGUSTINE ARNE, D.Mus. (1710–78). Composer, orchestral director, violinist, and occasional singer and actor, to whom the young Burney was apprenticed and in whose house he for some time lived.

WM. HAYMAN CUMMINGS. *Dr. Arne and 'Rule, Britannia'.* 1912.

HUBERT LANGLEY. *Doctor Arne.* 1938.

C. P. EMANUEL BACH (1714–88). Second son of J. S. Bach and friend of Burney in Hamburg.

C. P. E. BACH. *Versuch über die wahre Art das Klavier zu spielen.* 2 parts, 1753–62, and other editions to 1920 or later.

HEINRICH MIESNER. *Philipp Emanuel Bach in Hamburg.* Leipzig, 1929.

For general biographies, &c., see the list in Grove's *Dictionary.*

JOHN CHRISTIAN BACH (1735–82). Youngest son of J. S. Bach and in touch with Burney in London.

CHARLES SANFORD TERRY. *John Christian Bach.* 1929.

For other works see list in Grove's *Dictionary.*

MRS. BARBAULD (*née* Aikin; 1743–1825). Learned lady and voluminous authoress. Known to the Burneys.

ANNE LAETITIA BARBAULD (with her brother Dr. Aikin). *Evenings at Home* (for children). 12 vols., 1792–8.

—— *Poems.* 1773 (3 edns.), and other edns. to 1792.

—— *Works.* 2 vols., 1825 (with Memoir by her sister).

G. A. ELLIS. *A Memoir, Letters, and a Selection from the Writings of Anne Laetitia Barbauld.* 2 vols., 1874.

A. L. LE BRETON. *A Memoir of Mrs. Barbauld.* 1874.

J. MURCH. *Mrs. Barbauld and her Contemporaries.* 1877.

For a fuller list of writings by and on Mrs. Barbauld see *The Cambridge Bibliography of English Literature.*

GIUSEPPE BARETTI (1719–89). Teacher of languages, member of the Streatham circle, and Burney's adviser in the planning of his Italian Tour.

GIUSEPPE BARETTI. *A Dissertation on the Italian Poetry.* 1753.

—— *An Introduction to the Italian Language.* 1755.

—— *An Italian Library.* 1757.

—— *A Dictionary of the Italian and English Languages.* 1760.

—— *An Account of the Manners of Italy.* 1768.

—— *A Journey from London to Genoa.* 4 vols., 1770.

—— *Easy Phraseology for the Use of Young Ladies who intend to learn the Colloquial Part of the Italian Language.* 1773.

—— *The Carmen Seculare of Horace.* Translation with 7-page Introduction [1779]. 16 Aug. 1941.

LACY COLLISON-MORLEY. *Giuseppe Baretti and his Friends.* 1909.

DAINES BARRINGTON (1727–1800). K. C. (and later Judge), naturalist, musical dilettante, and versatile miscellaneous writer. An habitué of the Burney home.

DAINES BARRINGTON. *Observations on the More Ancient Statutes.* 1766 and later edns.

—— *The Anglo-Saxon Version from the Historian Orosius, by Alfred the Great.* 1773.

—— *Gorcheston Beirdd Cymru.* 1773.

—— *Miscellanies.* 1781. (Includes his papers on the young musicians, Mozart, Charles and Samuel Wesley, and Crotch.)

—— *Progress of Gardening.* 1782.

—— *Observations on the Practice of Archery in England.* 1785.

GILBERT WHITE. *Natural History of Selborne.* 1789, &c. (About half consists of letters to Barrington.)

JAMES BARRY (1741–1806). Painter and writer on painting; fiery opponent of Burney's friend Reynolds but admirer of Burney himself, whom he introduced into one of his murals at the Society of Arts.

JAMES BARRY. *Real and Imaginary Obstructions to the Acquisition of the Arts in England.* 1775.

—— *A Letter to the Dilettanti Society respecting the Improvement of Public Taste.* 1798.

—— 'Remarks on the Present State of the Art of Painting.' In Pilkington's *The Gentleman's Dictionary of Painters*, 1798.

—— *Lectures on Painting delivered at the Royal Academy.* 1809.

—— *Works.* 2 vols., 1809.

—— *An Account of the Pictures in the Great Room of the Society of Arts, Manufactures and Commerce at the Adelphi.* 1783; other edns., with slightly altered titles in 1803 and 1833.

SIR TRUEMAN WOOD. *A Note on the Pictures in the Great Room of the Society of Arts.*

BENJAMIN R. HAYDON. *Autobiography and Memoirs.* Ed. Tom Taylor. 1853. Several edns. in recent times.

JAMES BEATTIE (1735–1803). Professor of Moral Philosophy and poet; member, like Burney, of the Streatham circle.

JAMES BEATTIE. *Essays on Poetry and Music as they affect the Mind, etc.* London,

1775; Dublin, same year; Edinburgh, 1776; London, 1779. French translation, 1797.

JAMES BEATTIE. *A Letter to the Rev. H. Blair on the Improvement of Psalmody in Scotland.* 1778.

M. FORBES. *Beattie and his Friends.* 1904.

RALPH S. WALKER (Editor). *James Beattie's London Diary, 1773.* Aberdeen University Press, 1946.

For a complete list of Beattie's poetical and prose works see *The Cambridge Bibliography of English Literature.*

WILLIAM BECKFORD (d. 1799). Historian. Hospitable to Burney in Rome, an habitué of Burney's home in London, and visited by Burney and his friends in the Fleet Prison. (This William Beckford must not be confused with his namesake and younger contemporary, of Fonthill and the author of *Vathek.*)

WILLIAM BECKFORD. *A Descriptive Account of Jamaica.* 2 vols., 1790.

BLUESTOCKING LADIES. (*See also* Mrs. Boscawen, Mrs. Carter, Mrs. Chapone, Mrs. Delany, Mrs. Montagu, Hannah More, Mrs. Thrale, &c.)

SAMUEL HOOLE. *Aurelia, or the Contest.* 1783. An heroic-comical poem in four cantos, which towards its close gives a few lines each to various members of the Bluestocking group, including, notably, Fanny Burney.

A. K. ELWOOD. *Memoirs of the Literary Ladies of England from the Commencement of the Last Century.* 2 vols., 1843.

E. R. WHEELER. *Famous Blue-Stockings.* 1910. Includes Mrs. Montagu, Mrs. Delany, Mrs. Thrale, Mrs. Vesey, Mrs. Chapone, Fanny Burney, Elizabeth Carter, and Hannah More.

R. BRIMLEY JOHNSON. *Bluestocking Letters.* 1926. A selection from the letters of Mrs. Boscawen, Elizabeth Carter, Mrs. Chapone, Mrs. Montagu, and Mrs. Vesey.

MRS. BOSCAWEN (d. 1805). Wife of the celebrated naval commander, one of the Bluestocking ladies and a close friend of the Burneys.

C. ASPINALL-OGLANDER. *Admiral's Wife.* 1941.

—— *Admiral's Widow.* 1943.

ROGER BOSCOVICH (1711–87). Jesuit, physicist, and astronomer. Friend of Burney in Milan.

ROGER BOSCOVICH. *Philosophiae naturalis theoria reducta ad unicam legem virium in natura existentium* (his chief work). 1759.

H. V. GILL, *Roger Boscovich, Forerunner of Modern Physical Theories.* Dublin, 1942.

JAMES BOSWELL (1740–95). Advocate, traveller in Corsica, *Fidus Achates* and biographer of Johnson, and friend of Burney and of Fanny Burney.

JAMES BOSWELL. *A Journal of a Tour in the Hebrides with Samuel Johnson, LL.D.* 1785, and other edns.

—— *The Life of Samuel Johnson, LL.D.* 2 vols., 1791, and innumerable later edns. to the third of which Burney contributed notes.

—— *Private Papers of James Boswell from Malahide Castle. In the Collection of Lt.-Col. Ralph Heyward Isham.* Prepared for the Press by Geoffrey Scott. 18 vols., privately printed, 1928. (Index to this by Fredk. A. Pottle and others, independently published, 1937.)

F. A. Pottle. *The Literary Career of Boswell.* 1929.

C. E. Vulliamy. *James Boswell.* 1932.

J. L. Smith-Dampier. *Who's Who in Boswell.* 1936.

For the long list of works of and about Boswell see *The Cambridge Bibliography of English Literature.*

JAMES BRUCE (1730–94). African explorer and member of the intimate circle of the Burneys in their London home.

James Bruce. *Travels to Discover the Source of the Nile.* 5 vols., 1790. Other edns. 1805, 1813, and (abridged) 1830.

EDMUND BURKE (1729–97). Statesman, orator, and author, admirer of Fanny Burney's novels and warm friend of Burney, who was indebted to him for his appointment as organist of Chelsea College.

Edmund Burke (ed. Lawrence and King). *Works of the Right Honourable Edmund Burke.* 8 vols., 1792–1827. Many similar collected edns. since.

—— *Correspondence.* Ed. Earl Fitzwilliam and Sir R. Bourke. 4 vols., 1844.

—— *Correspondence of Edmund Burke and William Windham.* Ed. Gilson. 1910. (Both close friends of Burney.)

—— *Extracts from Mr. Burke's Table Talk at Crewe Hall* (the seat of Burney's friends, Lord and Lady Crewe). 1862.

John Morley (Viscount Morley). *Burke.* 1879.

For the long list of separate works by Burke, and of works of others upon him, see *The Cambridge Bibliography of English Literature*; for the many translations into French see Lanson, *Manuel Bibliographique,* 1921.

CHARLES BUTLER (1750–1832). Lawyer, author, lover of music, defender of the Roman Catholic faith, and friend of Burney in his last years.

Charles Butler. *Reminiscences.* 2 vols., 1822.

JOHN WALL CALLCOTT, Mus.D. (1766–1821). Organist, composer of innumerable glees, pupil of Haydn, and friend of Burney and his willing helper in the literary labours of his latest years.

John Wall Callcott, *Musical Grammar.* 1806.

—— *Glees, Catches and Canons.* Ed. Horsley—with a Memoir. 1824.

ELIZABETH CARTER (1717–1806). Learned lady, friend of Richardson, of Johnson, and of Burney and his daughter Fanny (*see also under* Blue-stocking Ladies).

Elizabeth Carter. *Poems on Several Occasions.* 1738 and several later edns.

—— *An examination of Mr. Pope's Essay on Man, translated from the French of M. Crousaz.* 1739.

—— *Sir Isaac Newton's Philosophy explain'd for the Use of Ladies, translated from the Italian of Sig. Algarotti.* 2 vols., 1739.

—— *All the Works of Epictetus which are now Extant.* 1758, and four later edns. to 1910.

—— *A Series of Letters between Mrs. Carter and Miss Talbot to which are added letters from Mrs. Carter to Mrs. Vesey.* 4 vols., 1809.

—— *Letters from Mrs. Elizabeth Carter to Mrs. Montagu.* 3 vols., 1817.

—— Essays 44 and 100 in Johnson's *The Rambler.*

MONTAGUE PENNINGTON. *Memoirs of the Life of Mrs. Elizabeth Carter.* 1808.

A. C. C. GAUSSEN. *A Woman of Wit and Wisdom; a Memoir of Elizabeth Carter.* 1906.

AUSTIN DOBSON. 'The learned Mrs. Carter.' (In *Later Essays*, 1921.)

HESTER CHAPONE (1727–1801). Learned lady, moral writer, and friend of Burney and of his daughter, Fanny (*see also under* Bluestocking Ladies).

HESTER CHAPONE. *Letters on the improvement of the Mind, addressed to a young Lady.* 2 vols., 1773 (3 edns.), and later edns. to 1806 ('with the life of the author').

—— *The Works of Mrs. Chapone.* 2 vols., Dublin, 1786; 4 vols., 1807.

—— *The Posthumous Works of Mrs. Chapone, containing her Correspondence with Mr. Richardson, a Series of Letters to Mrs. Elizabeth Carter, and some Fugitive Pieces never before published; together with an account of her Life and Character, drawn up by her own Family.* 2 vols., 1807–8.

JOHN COLE. *Memoirs of Mrs. Chapone; newly Developed, from Various Authentic Sources.* 1839.

For one or two other works see *The Cambridge Bibliography of English Literature.*

THEOPHILUS CIBBER (1703–58). Actor, playwright, and author, and husband of Arne's sister, the famous contralto. In the Cibbers' house, the young Burney, in his early period in London, found himself amid a constellation of wits, poets, actors, and men of letters.

THEOPHILUS CIBBER. *The Lives and Characters of the Most Eminent Actors and Actresses.* 1753.

—— *The Lives of the Poets of Great Britain and Ireland.* 5 vols., 1753.

—— *An Epistle to David Garrick, Esq.* 1755.

—— *Two Dissertations on Theatrical Subjects.* 1756.

For other works of Cibber, including his plays, see *The Cambridge Bibliography of English Literature.*

CHARLES CLAGGET (1740–*c.* 1795). Ingenious improver of musical instruments, whom Burney tried to help in the difficulties into which his ill-requited ingenuity brought him.

CHARLES CLAGGET. *Musical Phænomena; an Organ made without Pipes, Strings, Bells or Glasses, the Only Instrument in the World that will never require to be Retuned; A Cromatic Trumpet, capable of producing Just Intervals and Regular Melodies in all Keys, without undergoing any change whatever; A French Horn, answering the above description of the Trumpet.* 1793.

—— *A Discourse on Musick to be delivered at Clagget's Attic Consort.* October 31, 1793.

—— *Improvements on the Violin and other Instruments played on Fingerboards* (Patent Specification No. 1140, date 1776).

—— *Certain new Methods of Constructing and Tuning Musical Instruments which will be Perfect in their kind and much Easier to be performed on than any hitherto discovered* (Patent Specification No. 1664, date 1788).

JAMES COOK (1728–79). The celebrated circumnavigator, who visited Burney in his London home and one of whose officers on two of his voyages was Burney's son James.

JAMES COOK. *An Account of a Voyage round the World.* First printed in Hawkesworth's *Voyages*, 1773. (*See under* Hawkesworth.)

—— *A Voyage to the South Pole and round the World.* 2 vols., 1777.

—— *A Voyage to the Pacific Ocean.* 3 vols., 1784.

MAURICE THIERY. *The Life and Voyages of Captain Cook.* 1929.

SIR J. CARRUTHERS. *Captain James Cook One-hundred-and-fifty Years After.* 1930.

ANDERS SPARRMAN. *A Voyage round the World with Captain James Cook in H.M.S. Resolution.* 1945 (Sparrman, a Swede, was the botanist of the expedition).

For further literature on Cook see *The Cambridge Bibliography of English Literature.* There were French translations of Cook's Voyages from 1774 onwards (see Lanson, *Manuel Bibliographique*, 1921).

MRS. (later Lady) CREWE (*c.* 1750–1818). Daughter of Burney's early patron, Fulke Greville. Society leader and one of Burney's most devoted and helpful friends in his old age.

MRS. CREWE. *The Muses and Graces on a Visit to Grosvenor Square, being a Collection of the Original Songs sung by the Masquers at Mrs. Crewe's Elegant Ball.* 1775.

SAMUEL CRISP (d. 1783). Lover of music, disappointed playwright, the reputed first importer of a pianoforte into Britain, and devoted friend and thoughtful counsellor of Burney and all his children.

SAMUEL CRISP. *Virginia: a Tragedy.* 1754. (See II. 187–9.)

—— *Burford Papers, being Letters of Samuel Crisp to his Sister at Burford.* Ed. W. H. Hutton. 1905.

WILLIAM CROTCH (1775–1847). Child musical prodigy, to whose amazing talent Burney was the earliest to call attention and who became in later life a well-known organist and composer and Professor of Music in the University of Oxford.

WILLIAM CROTCH. *Elements of Composition.* 1812, and later edns.

—— *Substance of Several Courses of Lectures on Music.* 1831.

—— *Specimens of Various Styles of Music.* 3 vols., n.d.

CHARLES BURNEY. *Account of the Infant Musician, Crotch.* See list of Burney's literary works.

DAINES BARRINGTON. *Little Crotch.* See I. 136.

For a more complete list of Crotch's books and list of his compositions see Grove's *Dictionary of Music* and Brown and Stratton's *British Musical Biography.*

RICHARD CUMBERLAND (1732–1811). Dramatist, novelist, and miscellaneous writer, and member of the literary circles frequented by Burney.

RICHARD CUMBERLAND. Memoirs. 2 parts, 1806–7.

For the very long list of his works see *The Cambridge Bibliography of English Literature.*

MARY DELANY (1700–88). Friend of Handel, of Swift, and of Queen Charlotte, and in old age of Fanny Burney, whom she introduced to the royal circle (*see also under* Bluestocking Ladies).

LADY LLANOVER. *Autobiography and Correspondence of Mrs. Delany.* 6 vols., 1861–2.

R. Brimley Johnson. *Mrs. Delany, at Court and among the Wits.* 1925.

C. E. Vulliamy. *Aspasia; the Life and Letters of Mary Granville, Mrs. Delany.* 1935.

'George Paston.' [E. M. Symonds.] *Mrs. Delany, a Memoir.* 1900.

Austin Dobson. 'Dear Mrs. Delany'. (In *Side-walk Studies*, 1902.)

DENIS DIDEROT (1713–84). French philosopher and man of letters, projector and editor (with d'Alembert) of the famous *Encylopédie* (35 vols., 1751–80), lover of music; friend of Burney in Paris and thereafter one of his correspondents.

Denis Diderot. *Le Neveu de Rameau* (German transln. by Goethe, 1805; French transln. from this German transln. by de Saur, 1821; French text, from an actual copy, by Brière, 1823. For other edns. see Lanson, *Manuel Bibliographique*).

—— *Principes de l'acoustique.* 1748.

J. G. Prud'homme. 'Diderot et la Musique'. In the volume *Place au Théâtre*, Paris, 1933; also in *Monthly Journal of the International Musical Society*, March and April 1914.

John Morley (Lord Morley). *Diderot and the Encyclopedists.* 2 vols., 1891.

For particulars of Diderot's general production and of biographical and critical works upon him, see Lanson, *Manuel Bibliographique*, 1921.

CHRISTOPH DANIEL EBELING (*c.* 1741–1817). Supervisor of the Commercial Academy of Hamburg, keen music-lover, and translator of Handel's *Messiah* and of Burney's *Tour in France and Italy.*

Grohmann. *In Memoriam Christ. Dan. Ebelingi.* Hamburg, 1818.

Petersen. *Geschichte der Hamburgischen Stadtbibliothek.* 1838.

FREDERICK THE GREAT (1712–40–86). King of Prussia, flute player and flute composer, whose performance Burney heard in the palace of Potsdam.

Frederick the Great. *Briefwechsel . . . mit dem Grafen Algarotti* (the Italian writer on music). 1847.

Thos. Carlyle. *The History of Frederick II of Prussia, called Frederick the Great.* 6 vols., 1858–65, and subsequent edns.

K. F. Müller. *Friedrich der Grosse als Kenner und Dilettant.* 1847.

W. Kothe. *Friedrich der Grosse als Musiker.* 1869.

G. Thouret. *Friedrichs des Grossen Verhältniss zur Musik.* 1895.

—— *Friedrich der Grosse als Musikfreund und Musiker.* 1899.

George Müller. *Friedrich der Grosse; seine Flöten und sein Flötenspiel.* 1932.

Philipp Spitta. *Zur Ausgabe der Kompositionen Friedrichs des Grossen.* 1890.

Henry de Catt. *Frederick the Great: Memories of his Reader*, transl. F. S. Flint, 1916.

A selection of this monarch's flute compositions, ed. Spitta, was published by Breitkopf and Härtel in 1899. Dance music by him is in G. Thouret's *Musik am preussischen Hofe*, vol. xx, 1906.

DAVID GARRICK (1717–79). Famous actor-manager and playwright; one of Burney's associates from almost his first arrival in London, and a warm friend of all his family.

The Private Correspondence of David Garrick, Ed. Boaden. 2 vols., 1831–2.

THOS. DAVIES. *Memoirs of the Life of David Garrick.* 2 vols., 1780, and later editions.

ARTHUR MURPHY. *Life of David Garrick.* 2 vols., 1801 (London and Dublin edns.).

PERCY FITZGERALD. *Life of David Garrick.* 1868; revised edn. 1899.

J. KNIGHT. *David Garrick.* 1894.

MRS. C. PARSONS. *David Garrick and his Circle.* 1906.

For the very long list of Garrick's plays and adaptions, poems, pamphlets, &c., and of books on him, see *The Cambridge Bibliography of English Literature.*

EDWARD GIBBON (1737–94). Militia officer, Member of Parliament, historian; and acquaintance of Burney and his daughter Fanny.

EDWARD GIBBON. *The Decline and Fall of the Roman Empire.* 1776–88, and many later edns. to the present time.

—— *The Autobiography of Edward Gibbon.* Ed. Lord Sheffield. 1796; many later edns. to the present time.

For full list of works by Gibbon and a very extensive one of works on him see *The Cambridge Bibliography of English Literature.*

THOMAS GRAY (1716–71). The poet, who was also a keen lover of music.

H. E. KREHBIEL. 'Gray's Musical Collection.' (In that author's *Music and Manners in the Classical Period*, New York, 1898.)

For the general bibliography of Gray see *The Cambridge Bibliography of English Literature.*

FLORA GREVILLE (*née* Macartney; d. 1789). Wife of Fulke Greville, friend of Burney and of his first wife, and mother of his warm admirer and supporter in later life, Mrs. (afterwards Lady) Crewe.

FLORA MACARTNEY. *Ode to Indifference* (reprinted in Campbell's *Specimens of the British Poets*, 1819).

'COUNTESS OF C.' *The Fairy's Answer to Mrs. Greville's Prayer for Indifference.* (In Vicesimus Knox's *Elegant Extracts*, 1789.)

FULKE GREVILLE (dates unknown). Man of wealth and fashion; Burney's early patron and friend; for a period British minister at a German court.

FULKE GREVILLE. *Maxims, Characters and Reflexions—Critical, Satirical and Moral.* 1756; 2nd edn. 1757.

—— *Letter to James Boswell, Esq., with some remarks on Johnson's Dictionary,* &c. Publ. anonymously, 1792.

Some particulars of Greville and his wife will be found in *Notes & Queries*, III. iv. 5, 97, and IV. iii. 459, the last-mentioned including a list of references to him in the literature of his period.

SIR WILLIAM HAMILTON (1730–1803). British Ambassador at Naples, Burney's host and helper there, as also his guest in London.

SIR WILLIAM HAMILTON. *Observations on Mount Vesuvius.* 1772.

LADY HAMILTON (d. 1782). The first wife of the above and a notable harpsichordist.

G. JEAN-AUBRY, 'A Forgotten Musician, Lady Hamilton'. In *The Chesterian*, XVI, No. 121, May–June, 1935.

GEORGE FRIDERIC HANDEL (1685–1759), in whose band the young Burney often played, and of whom he was one of the earliest biographers.

REV. JOHN MAINWARING. *Memoirs of the Life of the Late George Frederick Handel, to which is added a Catalogue of his Works and Observations thereon.* 1760 (the year after Handel's death, this being the first biography of him—in book form, at all events).

VICTOR SCHOELCHER. *The Life of Handel.* 1857.

W. S. ROCKSTRO. *Life of George Frederick Handel.* 1883.

CHARLES BURNEY. *An Account of the Musical Performance in Westminster Abbey in Commemoration of Handel.* 1785. See II. 62–76.

For other books on Handel see Grove's *Dictionary of Music* and the present writer's *List of Books on Music in the English Language*, &c.

JAMES HARRIS (1709–80). Statesman, philosopher, keen lover of music; in Salisbury organizer of musical performances and in London habitué of the musical parties in Burney's house.

JAMES HARRIS. *Three Treatises. The First concerning Art. The Second concerning Music, Painting and Poetry. The Third concerning Happiness.* Edns. in 1744, 1765, 1772, 1783, and 1792.

—— *Hermes, or a Philosophical Inquiry concerning Universal Grammar.* 1751, and other edns. to 1794. Also a French transln., 1796.

AUSTIN DOBSON. 'Hermes Harris.' In *Later Essays.*

For other books by this author see *The Cambridge Bibliography of English Literature.*

JOHN HAWKESWORTH (*c.* 1715–73). Editor and miscellaneous writer, for whom Burney obtained the commission to compile for the Admiralty the volumes of Southern Voyages—disappointment as to the reception of which led to its compiler's death.

JOHN HAWKESWORTH. *The Adventurer.* 140 numbers, 1752–97.

——*An Account of the Voyages undertaken in the Southern Hemisphere.* 3 vols., 1773. French and Dutch translations, 1774.

For a list of Hawkesworth's plays, and other works see *The Cambridge Bibliography of English Literature.*

SIR JOHN HAWKINS (1719–89). London solicitor and magistrate, for a time a member of the Literary Club and Burney's rival as an historian of music.

SIR JOHN HAWKINS. *Observations on the State of the Highways.* 1763.

—— *A Charge to the Grand Jury of Middlesex.* 1770 (another in 1780).

—— *An Account of the Institution and Progress of the Academy of Ancient Music.* (Anonymous.) 1770.

—— *Principles and Power of Harmony.* 1771.

—— *A General History of the Science and Practice of Music.* 5 vols., 1776; reprints in 2 vols. (plus a vol. of portraits), 1853 and 1875.

—— *A Dissertation on the Armorial Ensigns of the County of Middlesex.* 1780.

—— *The Works of Samuel Johnson.* 15 vols., 1787–9. (The first vol. is his Life of Johnson.)

For a somewhat more complete list of the varied books of Hawkins, and a list of some writings on him, see *The Cambridge Bibliography of English Literature.* For the satire on him in *Probationary Odes* (first 9 edns., 1785–91), see I. 302 n. of the present work.

FRANZ JOSEPH HAYDN (1732–1809), whose compositions and whose personality won Burney's highest admiration and whose visits to London brought about a warm friendship between the two.

CHARLES BURNEY. *Verses on the Arrival in England of the Great Musician Haydn.* Pamphlet. 1791. (See II. 111.)

HENRY E. KREHBIEL. 'Haydn's London Diary.' (Essay, with extracts from the Diary, in *Music and Manners in the Classical Period*, New York, 1898.)

J. E. ENGL. *Joseph Haydns handschriftliches Tagebuch aus der Zeit seines zweiten Aufenthaltes in London, 1794 und 1795.* 2 vols., Leipzig, 1875–1909.

C. F. Pohl. *Mozart und Haydn in London.* 1867.

—— and H. BOTSTIBER. *Joseph Haydn.* 2 vols., Leipzig, 1875–1927.

GEORG AUGUST GRIESINGER. 'Biographische Notizen über Joseph Haydn.' (In the *Allgemeine Muzikzeitung*, July–Sept., 1809; and in book form, Vienna, 1810.)

ALBERT CHRISTOPH DIES. *Biographische Nachrichten über Joseph Haydn.* Vienna, 1810.

ROSEMARY S. M. HUGHES. 'Haydn at Oxford.' In *Music and Letters*, vol. xx. 3, July 1939.

——'Dr. Burney's Championship of Haydn.' In *The Musical Quarterly*, vol. xxvii, 1, Jan. 1941.

For other books on Haydn see Grove's *Dictionary of Music*, the present writer's *List of Books on Music in the English Language*, &c.

SIR WILLIAM HERSCHEL (1738–1822). Oboist, organist, band-master, and organizer of concerts; then Astronomer Royal and the discoverer of Uranus, and Burney's warm friend and willing helper in the writing of his poetical History of Astronomy.

SIR WILLIAM HERSCHEL. *Scientific Papers.* (Collected by the Royal Astronomical Society.) 2 vols., 1912.

M. C. HERSCHEL. *Memoir and Correspondence of Caroline Herschel.* 1876.

A. M. CLERKE. *The Herschels and Modern Astronomy.* 1895.

CONSTANCE A. LUBBOCK. *The Herschel Chronicle; the Life Story of William Herschel and his sister Caroline Herschel.* 1933.

EDWARD MILLER. *History and Antiquities of Doncaster.* 1804. Long footnote on p. 162 with personal recollections of Herschel's early musical career in this country.

'The Musician Astronomer.' (In *Monthly Journal of the International Musikgesellschaft.* Oct. 1907: in English.)

ROBERT SOUTHEY. *The Doctor.* 7 vols., 1834–47, and later edns.

JOHN ZEPHANIAH HOLWELL (1711–98). Survivor and historian of the Indian Mutiny, Governor of Bengal, and friend of Burney.

JOHN ZEPHANIAH HOLWELL. *A Genuine Narrative of the Deplorable Deaths of the English Gentlemen and others who were suffocated in the Black Hole.* 1758, and later reprints to 1899.

—— *India Tracts.* 1758.

—— *Interesting Historical Events relative to the Province of Bengal and the Empire of Indostan.* 1765–7. French transl. 1768.

DAVID HUME (1711–76). Diplomat, philosopher, and historian, and Burney's friend and helper both in France and in England.

David Hume. *Letters.* Ed. J. Y. T. Greig. 1932. These include the letter trying to secure for Burney a royal appointment (see II. 323 of present work), but have no other reference to him.

—— *The Life of David Hume Esq. written by himself.* Hume died in 1776 and from the following year this was included in most edns. of his *History of England,* &c., and of his *Essays.* It appeared in French in 1777.

—— *A Concise and Genuine Account of the Dispute between Mr. Hume and Mr. Rousseau.* 1766.

J. Y. T. Greig. *Life of David Hume.* 1931.

Ernest Mossner. *The Forgotten Hume.* 1943.

E. B. Greene (?). *A Defence of Mr. Rousseau against the Aspersions of Mr. Hume, Mons. Voltaire, and their Associates.* 1766.

Anon. *Justification de J. J. Rousseau dans la contestation avec M. Hume.* 1766.

H. Fuseli. *Remarks on the Writings and Conduct of J. J. Rousseau.* 1766.

Mme de la Tour de Franqueville. *Précis pour M. Rousseau en réponse à l'exposé succinct de M. Hume.* 1767.

Bergerat (?). *Plaidoyer pour et contre J. J. Rousseau et le Docteur D. Hume.* 1767.

It will be observed that the above pamphlets on the Hume–Rousseau controversy all appeared about the time of the correspondence for and against Rousseau's *Le Devin du Village* as arranged by Burney (see I. 111–16).

J. H. Burton. *Life and Correspondence of David Hume.* 2 vols., 1846.

T. H. Huxley. *Hume.* 1879.

J. Churton Collins. *Voltaire, Montesquieu, and Rousseau in England.* 1908.

For a long list of Hume's historical and philosophical works, and another of books on Hume, see *The Cambridge Bibliography of English Literature;* also Lanson, *Manuel Bibliographique,* 1921.

SAMUEL JOHNSON (1709–84). Lexicographer, miscellaneous author, conversationalist, close friend of Burney, the acknowledged king of the social-literary circle of which Burney was an active member, and devoted friend of all the Burney family.

Samuel Johnson. *Irene; a Tragedy.* 1749.

—— *The Rambler.* 280 numbers, 1750–2. Many reprints in volume form.

—— *The Idler.* 104 numbers, 1758–60. Many reprints in volume form.

—— *The Prince of Abissinia* (= *Rasselas*). 1759, and many later edns.

—— *A Dictionary of the English Language.* 2 vols., 1755, and many reprints.

—— *The Plays of William Shakespeare, to which are added Notes.* 8 vols., 1765.

—— *A Journey to the Western Isles of Scotland.* 1775; 3 edns. in that year and many later.

—— *Lives of the Poets.* 1779–81, and later editions.

—— *Letters.* Ed. G. Birkbeck Hill. 2 vols., 1892.

—— *Poems.* Ed. D. Nichol Smith and E. L. McAdam. 1941.

James Boswell. *Life of Samuel Johnson.* 1791. The later edns. by Malone, Croker, &c., have been consulted by the present author for the additional information on Burney which they include. The best edn., that of Dr. George Birkbeck Hill, in 6 vols., 1886, with elaborate annotations, has been found extremely useful; it has appeared, as revised by Dr. L. F. Powell, from 1934 onwards.

George Birkbeck Hill. *Johnsonian Miscellanies.* 2 vols., 1897.

Sir John Hawkins. *Collected Edition of Johnson's Works.* 11 vols., 1787.

—— *Life of Johnson.* 1787. (2 edns. in that year.)

Arthur Murphy. *Essay on the Life and Genius of Samuel Johnson, LL.D.;* 1792. Reprinted in G. Birkbeck Hill's *Johnsonian Miscellanies.*

Mrs. Piozzi (formerly Mrs. Thrale). *Anecdotes of the Late Samuel Johnson, LL.D., during the Last Twenty Years of his Life.* 1786; current edn. 1932. (Also reprinted in G. Birkbeck Hill's *Johnsonian Miscellanies,* 1897.)

—— *Letters to and from the late Samuel Johnson, LL.D.* 2 vols., 1788.

Miss Reynolds. *Recollections of Dr. Johnson.* In Croker's edn. of Boswell. Also in G. Birkbeck Hill's *Johnsonian Miscellanies.* 1897.

A. M. Broadley. *Dr. Johnson and Mrs. Thrale.* 1910.

The R. B. Adam Library relating to Dr. Samuel Johnson and his Era. 3 vols., 1929–30.

C. B. Tinker. *Doctor Johnson and Fanny Burney.* 1912. (The Johnsonian passages from Fanny's Diary.)

For a full list of the enormous contributions to literature by and about Johnson see *The Cambridge Bibliography of English Literature.*

AUGUST FRIEDRICH CHRISTOPH KOLLMAN (*c.* 1756–1829). Organist of the royal German Chapel, one of the earliest Bach students in England and admirer and friend of Burney.

August Friedrich Kollman. *Essay on Practical Harmony.* 1796.

—— *Essay on Practical Musical Composition.* 1799.

—— *Practical Guide to Thorough Bass.* 1801.

For other books by this author see Grove's *Dictionary of Music*; also a good article in *The Musical Times,* Oct. 1907, which gives extracts from Kollman's periodical *The Quarterly Musical Register* (only two issues, Jan. and April 1812).

LOCK (or Locke) FAMILY. Wealthy and cultivated family of Norbury, Surrey, and dear friends of Burney's daughters Susanna and Fanny and of the other Burneys.

Duchess of Sermonetta. *The Locks of Norbury.* 1940.

ANDREW LUMISDEN or LUMSDEN (1720–81). Brother of Burney's friend, Lady Strange. Active Jacobite and Secretary to the Young Pretender and as such long an exile from England; one of Burney's advisers on his Italian tour.

Andrew Lumisden. *Remarks on the Antiquities of Rome and its Environs.* 1797.

E. Denniston. *Sir R. Strange and A. Lumsden.* 1855.

FANNY MACARTNEY. *See* Flora Greville.

GEORGE MACARTNEY (1737–1806). First Earl Macartney, diplomatist; friend of Burney, who helped him in the preparations for his Embassy to China.

George (Earl) Macartney. *An Account of an Embassy to Russia.* 1768.

—— *A Political Account of Ireland in 1773.* (In Sir J. Barrow's *Memoir of Macartney,* 1807.)

Samuel Holmes. *Journal during Lord Macartney's Embassy to China.* 2 vols., 1798.

SIR J. BARROW. *Memoir of Lord Macartney.* 1807. A French translation of Macartney's travels appeared in 1810.

JOHN BAPTIST MALCHAIR (1731–1812). Violinist and water-colour artist. Burney's leader in the performance of his D.Mus. Exercise at Oxford.

PAUL OPPÉ. 'John Baptist Malchair of Oxford.' In *The Burlington Magazine*, Aug. 1943.

JOHN H. MEE. *The Oldest Music Room in Europe.* 1911.

J. GRIEG. *The Farington Diary*, vol. i. 1922.

EDMOND MALONE (1741–1812). Literary critic and Shakespearian scholar, fellow member with Burney of the Literary Club, and his friend and frequent correspondent.

His work was mainly editorial and critical. For his editions of the works of Shakespeare, Goldsmith, and Sir Joshua Reynolds, of Boswell's *Johnson*, &c., his voluminous critical writings, and biographical notices on him, see *The Cambridge Bibliography of English Literature.*

GIOVANNI BATTISTA MARTINI, known as 'Padre Martini' (1706–84). Musical theorist and historian, friend of Burney, who spent much time with him in Padua and long maintained with him a correspondence.

GIOVANNI BATTISTA MARTINI. *Storia della Musica.* 3 vols., 1757–70–81.

—— *Esemplare ossia saggio . . . di contrappunto*, 2 vols. and vol. of examples. 1774–5.

—— *Onomasticum seu Synopsis musicarum graecarum atque obscuriorum vocum earum interpretatione ex operibus J. B. Doni.* 1763.

—— *Dissertatio de uso progressionis geometricae in musica.* 1766.

—— *Compendio della teoria de' numeri per uso del musico.* 1769.

—— *Regola agli organisti per accompagnare il canto fermo.* c. 1756.

—— *Serie cronologica de' principi dell' Accademia dei Filarmonici.* 1777.

(In addition to the above there are a number of occasional writings by Martini—controversial pamphlets, &c.)

PIETRO DELLA VALLE. *Memorie storiche del Padre Giovanni Battista Martini.* 1785.

G. B. MORESCHI. *Grazione in lode del Padre Martini.* 1786.

FEDERICO PARISINI. *Della vita e delle opere del Padre Martini.* 1887.

—— *Lettere di Padre Martini.*

LEONIDA BUSI. *Il Padre Giovanni Battista Martini.* 1891.

G. GANDOLFI. *Elogio di Giovanni Battista Martini.* 1913.

WILLIAM MASON (1724–97). Poet and musician, Precentor of the Cathedral of York, and friend and correspondent of Burney.

WILLIAM MASON. *Ode performed in the Senate House at Cambridge.* 1749. (Also published with Boyce's music to it.)

—— *A Copious Collection of those Portions of the Psalms of David, Bible, and Liturgy, which have been set to Music, and sung as Anthems in the Cathedral and Collegiate Churches of England. Arranged in Chronological Order, according to the Times in which the several Musical Composers lived. And published for the Use of the Church of York, under the Direction of William Mason, M.A., Precentor of that Cathedral. By whom is prefixed, a Critical and Historical Essay on Cathedral Music.* York 1782; another edition, 1834.

WILLIAM MASON. *Essays, Historical and Critical, on English Church Music.* York, 1795.

J. W. DRAPER. *William Mason: a Study in 18th Century Culture.* New York, 1924.

EDWARD MILLER, Mus.D. *History of Doncaster.* 1804. (Discusses Mason adversely from personal recollections, in a long footnote on p. 161.)

For a full list of Mason's poetical and prose publications and of literature on him see *The Cambridge Bibliography of English Literature.* For others of his works on Church music see Grove's *Dictionary of Music.* An Anthem by him, *Lord of all Power and Might* (of which Miller says only the melody is his), was in use comparatively recently and is possibly still to be heard.

MOSES MENDEZ (d. 1758). Poet and dramatist, and one of Burney's early librettists.

MOSES MENDEZ. *The Chaplet, a Musical Entertainment at the Theatre Royal in Drury Lane.* 1749 (separately and with Boyce's music); very many later edns.

—— *Robin Hood, a New Musical Entertainment.* 1750. (Set by Burney; see I. 53.)

—— *The Shepherd's Lottery; a Musical Entertainment at the Theatre Royal in Drury Lane.* 1751 (separately and with Boyce's music).

—— *A Collection of the Most Esteemed Pieces of Poetry that have appeared for several years, with variety of Originals.* 1767.

PIETRO ANTONIO DOMENICO BONAVENTURA METASTASIO (*né* Trapassi; 1698–1782). Poet and Europe's most famous and productive opera librettist; friend, in Vienna, of his warm admirer Burney.

CHARLES BURNEY. *Memoirs of the Life and Writings of the Abate Metastasio.* 3 vols., 1796.

LUIGI ROSSI. *Metastasio.* 1921.

It is impossible to give here the long list of Metastasio's dramatic works, and of writings upon him. Grove's *Dictionary of Music* gives these fairly fully and Riemann's *Musiklexikon* (Einstein's edition of 1929) still more so. *The Cambridge Bibliography of English Literature* supplies much information as to the many English editions and translations of Metastasio, but it should be noted that it has inadvertently conferred on him duality by dividing his productions according to two sets of Christian names.

ELIZABETH MONTAGU (1720–1800). Woman of learning, sagacious conversationalist (and as such praised by Johnson), a leader in the Bluestocking circle frequented by Burney and his daughter Fanny, and one of their most respected friends (*see also under* Bluestocking Ladies).

ELIZABETH MONTAGU. *An Essay on the Writings and Genius of Shakespeare . . . with some Remarks upon the Misrepresentation of Mons. de Voltaire.* 1769 and 3 further edns., to 1777.

—— *The Letters of Mrs. Elizabeth Montagu, with some of the Letters of her Correspondents.* Edited by Matthew Montagu. 4 vols., 1809–13.

EMILY J. CLIMENSON. *Elizabeth Montagu, the Queen of the Blue-Stockings. Her Correspondence from 1720 to 1761.* 2 vols., 1906.

JOHN DORAN. *A Lady of the Last Century (Mrs. Elizabeth Montagu): illustrated in her Unpublished Letters. With a Chapter on Blue Stockings.* 1873.

REGINALD BLUNT. *Mrs. Montagu, Queen of the Blues, from Material left by her great-niece Emily J. Climenson.* 2 vols., 1923.

R. HUCHON. *Mrs. Montagu and her Friends.* 1907.

HANNAH MORE (1745–1833). Playwright, novelist, writer in the interests of the manners of the poor and of the great, and a leading member of the Bluestocking circle frequented by Burney and by his daughter Fanny (*see also under* Bluestocking Ladies).

HANNAH MORE. *Collected Works.* 8 vols., 1801; and other edns.

—— *The Bas Bleus; or Conversation.* 2nd edn. in 1787.

—— *Thoughts on the Importance of the Manners of the Great to General Society.* 1788. (French translns. 1790.)

WILLIAM ROBERTS, *Memoirs of the Life and Correspondence of Mrs. Hannah More.* 2 vols., 1834; 4 vols., 1838.

R. BRIMLEY JOHNSON (ed.). *Letters of Hannah More.* 1925.

HENRY THOMPSON. *Life of Hannah More, with Notices of her Sisters.* 1838.

A. M. B. MEAKIN. *Hannah More.* 1911.

For a much more complete list of works by and on Hannah More see *The Cambridge Bibliography of English Literature.* And for the *Cheap Repository Tracts* see a long article by Augustus de Morgan in *Notes & Queries,* III. vi. 241.

WOLFGANG AMADEUS MOZART (1756–91), the great composer, who in youth was well known to Burney.

O. JAHN. *Wolfgang Amadeus Mozart.* 4 vols., 1856–9 and later edns. to 1905–7. Engl. transln. by Miss P. D. Townsend, 3 vols., 1882. New German edn. thoroughly revised, by H. Abert, 2 vols., 1919–21 and 1923–4.

T. DE WYZEWA and G. DE SAINT-FOIX. *W. A. Mozart.* 2 vols., 1912; also 2 further vols. by the latter author alone, 1936 and 1939; another in preparation.

EMILY ANDERSON. *The Letters of Mozart and his Family.* 3 vols., 1938. (Excellent English transln.)

For more information as to the extensive Mozart literature see Grove's *Dictionary of Music,* and the present writer's *List of Books about Music in the English Language,* &c.

ARTHUR MURPHY (1727–1805). Actor and industrious and successful playwright, and miscellaneous author, biographer of Burney's friend Garrick, and friend of Burney and Fanny Burney.

ARTHUR MURPHY. *Works.* 7 vols., 1786.

JESSE FOOT. *The Life of Arthur Murphy Esq.* 1811.

For a list of Murphy's plays and other writings see *The Cambridge Bibliography of English Literature.* Some of his plays appeared in French in Mme de Vasse's *Théâtre Anglais.* 1784.

JOSEPH NOLLEKENS (1737–1823). Able sculptor and sordid miser; known to Burney and the executant of busts of him and of his son Charles.

J. T. SMITH. *Nollekens and his Times.* Original edn. 1828; modern edn. by W. Whitten, 1920; abridged edn. in 'The World's Classics', 1929.

JOHN CHRISTOPHER PEPUSCH (1667–1752). Theatrical musical director, musical compiler, and arranger of *The Beggar's Opera*, learned theorist and deep student of the ancient Greek music; friend and counsellor of the young Burney.

JOHN CHRISTOPHER PEPUSCH. *A Treatise of Harmony, containing the chief Rules for Composing in Two, Three and Four Parts.* Anonymous unauthorized edn., 1730; authorized enlarged edn. 1731.

—— 'The Ancient Genera.' In the *Philosophical Transactions of the Royal Society*. 1746.

THOMAS PERCY (1729–1811). Bishop of Dromore, Ireland; fellow-member with Burney of the Literary Club.

THOMAS PERCY. *Reliques of Ancient English Poetry.* 3 vols., 1765 and many edns. to the present day.

—— *Northern Antiquities.* 2 vols., 1770.

For the pretty long list of works by and on Percy see *The Cambridge Bibliography of English Literature.*

JOHANN JOACHIM QUANTZ (1697–1773). Flautist, composer, author of a still famous book on flute playing, and musical director to Frederick the Great, at whose Court Burney became acquainted with him.

JOHANN JOACHIM QUANTZ. *Versuch einer Anweisung die Flöte . . . zu spielen.* 1752. Dedicated to Frederick the Great. Several edns. in German, French, Dutch, &c.

ALBERT QUANTZ. *Leben und Werken von J. J. Quantz.* 1877.

RUDOLF SCHÄFKE. *Quantz als Æsthetiker.* 1924.

ABRAHAM REES (1743–1825). Nonconformist divine and encyclopaedist, in which latter capacity Burney served him as musical contributor.

ABRAHAM REES. *The Advantages of Knowledge recommended to the Supporters of a New Academical Institution among Protestant Dissenters.* 1788.

—— *Sermons.*

—— *Cyclopaedia.* (See II. 184–201.)

SIR JOSHUA REYNOLDS (1723–92). Famous painter, first President of the Royal Academy of Arts, co-founder with Johnson of the Literary Club, and warm friend of Burney, whose portrait he painted.

SIR JOSHUA REYNOLDS. *A Discourse delivered at the Opening of the Royal Academy, 1769, by the President.* Similar opening discourses and discourses to students were delivered and published, up to 1791—the year before Reynolds's death. There have been several (partial) collected edns., as also some translns. into French, Italian, and German. A number of cheap edns. are now on sale.

—— *The Works of Sir Joshua Reynolds.* Ed. Malone. 2 vols., 1797, with new edns. and revisions, added memoirs, &c., up to 1845.

—— *Letters.* Ed. F. W. Hilles. 1929.

J. NORTHCOTE. *Memoirs of Sir Joshua Reynolds.* 1813; supplement in 1815; new edn. 1818.

C. R. LESLIE and T. TAYLOR. *The Life and Times of Sir Joshua Reynolds.* 1865.

J. STEEGMAN. *Sir Joshua Reynolds.* 1933.

Fuller particulars of Sir Joshua Reynolds's own writings can be found in

F. W. Hilles's *The Literary Career of Sir Joshua Reynolds*, 1936, and of books about him in *The Cambridge Bibliography of English Literature.*

JEAN-JACQUES ROUSSEAU (1712–78). Philosopher, political and social theorist, writer on music and composer, whose *Le Devin du Village* Burney translated and arranged for London performance, whom he visited in Paris, and who addressed to him some famous observations on Gluck.

JEAN-JACQUES ROUSSEAU. *Dissertation sur la musique moderne.* 1743.

—— *Discours sur la question proposée par l'Académie de Dijon.* 1750.

—— *Lettre à M. l'Abbé Raynal au sujet d'un nouveau mode de musique inventée par M. Blainville.* 1751 (not 1754 as usually stated).

—— *Lettre à M. Grimm au sujet des remarques ajoutées à sa lettre sur Omphale.* 1752.

—— *Lettre sur la musique française.* 1753.

—— *Lettre d'un symphoniste de l'Académie royale de musique à ses camarades de l'orchestre.* 1754.

—— *Le Devin du Village.* First performed 1753; score published 1754; with six new airs, 1779. (Transl. arranged and published by Burney, 1766; see I. 107–17. There was also an anonymous transln., *The Village Conjuror*, in 1767.)

—— *Lettre à D'Alembert contre les spectacles.* 1758. (Transl. as *A Letter on the Effects of Theatrical Entertainments on Mankind.* 1759.)

—— *Du Contrat Social.* 1762. (Transl. as *The Social Contract.* 1763.)

—— *Émile, ou de l'Éducation.* 1762. (Transl. as *Emilius, or an Essay on Education.* 1763.)

—— *Dictionnaire de Musique.* 1767. (Poor English transln. by Wm. Waring, 1770.)

—— *Pygmalion.* One-act spoken piece with musical interpolations. First produced 1770.

—— *Daphné et Chloé.* Unfinished opera published posthumously. 1780.

—— *Consolations des misères de ma vie.* Collection of songs, &c., published posthumously. 1781.

—— *Confessions.* 1782. English transln. 1783. Many edns. since.

—— *Lettre à M. Burney sur la Musique, avec des fragments d'observations sur l'Alceste de M. le chevalier Gluck.* Posthumous (see I. 183–4).

—— *Extrait d'une réponse du Petit Faiseur à son Prête-Nom, sur un morceau de l'Orphée de M. le chevalier Gluck.* Posthumous.

—— *Correspondance Générale*, ed. Dufour and Plan. 1924–34.

LE CHEVALIER DE MOUHY. *Justification de la musique française.* 1754.

ANON. *Lettre d'un académicien de Bordeaux sur le fond de la musique française, à propos de la Lettre de M. Rousseau.* 1754.

ANON. *Réponse critique d'un académicien de Rouen à l'académicien de Bordeaux sur le plus profond de la musique.* 1754.

A. POUGIN. *Jean-Jacques Rousseau, Musicien.* Paris, 1901.

A. JANSEN. *Jean-Jacques Rousseau als Musiker.* Berlin, 1884.

J. TIERSOT. *Jean-Jacques Rousseau.* Paris, 2nd edn., 1920.

AMALIE ARNHEIM. 'Le Devin du Village von Jean-Jacques Rousseau und die Parodie des amours de Bastien et Bastienne.' In *Sammelbände der Internationalen Musikgesellschaft*, iv. 4, July–September 1903.

LORD MORLEY. *Rousseau.* 1873.

The above does not comprise a complete list of Rousseau's own works, general or musical. For that, as also for the enormous literature on Rousseau, see Lanson's *Manuel Bibliographique*, 1921. And see under 'Hume' above.

WILLIAM SAVAGE (*c.* 1720–89). Gentleman of the Chapel Royal and Master of the Choristers at St. Paul's Cathedral.

H. G. FARMER. Article in *Music and Letters*, July 1936.

RICHARD BRINSLEY SHERIDAN (1751–1816). Dramatist, theatre proprietor, Member of Parliament, and renowned political orator; admirer of Fanny Burney as novelist.

THOMAS MOORE. *Memoirs of the Life of the Right Honourable Richard Brinsley Sheridan.* 2 vols., 1825.

WILLIAM FRASER RAE. *Sheridan: a Biography.* 2 vols., 1896.

MARGARET OLIPHANT. *Sheridan.* 1883.

For the long list of Sheridan's Plays, Poems, Political Speeches and Pamphlets, &c., and of books on him see *The Cambridge Bibliography of English Literature.*

CHRISTOPHER ('KIT') SMART (1722–71). Poet; friend of Burney, who helped him in his poverty and during his incarceration in a madhouse.

CHRISTOPHER SMART. *A Song to David.* 1763.

—— *Psalms of David.* 1765.

K. A. MCKENZIE. *Christopher Smart, sa Vie et ses Œuvres.* 1925.

LAWRENCE BINYON, *The Case of Christopher Smart.* English Assocn. Lecture, 1934.

For a complete list of Smart's poetical works, his libretti for oratorios, &c., see *The Cambridge Bibliography of English Literature.*

GEORGE STEEVENS (1736–1800). Shakespeare commentator, friend of Burney's friend Johnson and of Burney himself, and fellow member of Burney in the Literary Club.

His work was mainly editorial. For a list of his editions of Shakespeare, Hogarth, &c., and other writings by and upon him see *The Cambridge Bibliography of English Literature.*

BENJAMIN C. STILLINGFLEET (1702–71). Botanist, amateur violoncellist, and habitué of the Bluestocking circle.

BENJAMIN C. STILLINGFLEET. *Principles and Power of Harmony.* 1771. (Founded on Tartini's *Trattato di Musica*, 1754.)

—— *Miscellaneous Tracts in Natural History.*

—— *A Poem on Earthquakes.*

ARCHDEACON WILLIAM COXE. *Literary Life and Select Works of Benjamin Stillingfleet.* 2 vols., 1811.

BONNELL THORNTON (1724–68). Writer and wit, whose humorous St. Cecilia Ode Burney set to music.

BONNELL THORNTON, *An Ode on St. Cecilia's Day, adapted to the Ancient British Musick.* Published anonymously in 1749, and again, with the author's name, in 1763; also in the *Annual Register*, 1863 (pp. 243–6); in Mendez's *Collection of the Most Esteemed Pieces of Poetry that have appeared for Several Years*, 1767; and in W. H. Husk's *An Account of the Musical Celebrations of St. Cecilia's Day*, 1857.

For other works of this author see *The Cambridge Bibliography of English Literature*.

HESTER LYNCH THRALE, later PIOZZI (1741–1821). Friend and hostess of Johnson, and of a wide circle of men and women of literature and the arts, including, notably, Burney and his daughter Fanny. (*See also under* Johnson *and under* Bluestocking Ladies.)

HESTER LYNCH THRALE (PIOZZI). *Anecdotes of the late Samuel Johnson, LL.D., during the last Twenty Years of his Life.* 1786, 5 edns.; other edns. in 1822–56–84–87. Ed. S. C. Roberts, 1925, 1932. Included, with notes, in G. Birkbeck Hill's *Johnsonian Miscellanies*, I, 1897.

—— *Letters to and from the late Samuel Johnson, LL.D.* 2 vols., 1788 (London and Dublin edns.).

—— *Observations and Reflections made in the Course of a Journey through France, Italy and Germany.* 2 vols., 1789 (London and Dublin edns.); German transln., 1790.

—— *British Synonomy.* 2 vols., 1794 (London and Dublin edns.).

—— *Three Warnings to John Bull before he dies* (pamphlet). 1798.

—— *Retrospection; or a Review of the Most Striking and Important Events . . . which the last Eighteen Hundred Years have presented to the View of Mankind.* 2 vols., 1801.

—— *The French Journals of Mrs. Thrale and Doctor Johnson.* Ed. Moses Tyson and Henry Guppy, 1932.

—— *Three Dialogues by Hester Lynch Thrale, from the hitherto unpublished original manuscript now in the possession of the John Rylands Library.* Ed. M. Zamick (Bulletin of the Library, Jan. 1932).

—— *Thraliana, the Diary of Mrs. Hester Lynch Thrale (later Mrs. Piozzi), 1776–1809.* Ed. K. C. Balderston. 2 vols., 1942.

ABRAHAM HAYWARD. *Autobiography, Letters, and Literary Remains of Mrs. Piozzi.* 1861; two edns. in that year, the latter having much new matter (see also 'Lobban' below).

J. H. LOBBAN. *Dr. Johnson's Mrs. Thrale* (Hayward's work, as above, selected and edited). 1910.

C. E. VULLIAMY. *Mrs. Thrale of Streatham.*

L. B. SISLEY. *Mrs. Thrale, afterwards Mrs. Piozzi.* 1891.

R. BRIMLEY JOHNSON (ed.). *Letters of Mrs. Thrale.*

JAS. L. CLIFFORD. *Hester Lynch Piozzi (Mrs. Thrale).* 1941.

P. MERRITT. *Piozzi Marginalia.* 1925.

CHAS. HUGHES. *Mrs. Piozzi's 'Thraliana'* (with some extracts). 1913.

There were attacks on Mrs. Piozzi by Baretti in *The European Magazine* in 1788 (xxx, 313, 393, and xl, 89).

For further writings on or by this lady see *The Cambridge Bibliography of English Literature* and the excellent work by Clifford mentioned above.

THOMAS TWINING (1735–1804). Country clergyman, classical scholar, musical enthusiast, and Burney's close friend and constant correspondent.

THOMAS TWINING. *Aristotle's Treatise on Poetry, translated, with Notes and Two Dissertations on Poetical and Musical Imitation.* 2 vols., 1789, 1812: a reprint appeared in Cassell's National Library in 1894. The musical theories are discussed in *The Harmonicon*, 1830, p. 511; also in Ernest Newman's *Gluck and the Opera*, 1895.

—— *Recreations and Studies of a Country Clergyman of the Eighteenth Century*. 1882.

—— *Selections from Papers of the Twining Family*. 1887.

RICHARD TWISS (1747–1821). Traveller and author; acquainted with the Burneys as a member of the Streatham circle.

RICHARD TWISS. *Travels through Portugal and Spain*. 1775.

—— *A Tour in Ireland*. 1775.

—— *A Trip to Paris*. 1793.

HORACE WALPOLE (1717–97). Son of the great Prime Minister, and himself a Member of Parliament, famous as a collector of objects of beauty and historical interest, proprietor of a private printing press, author of the famous 'Gothic story' mentioned below and proprietor of the 'little Gothic castle', Strawberry Hill, where he was visited by his admired friends Burney and Fanny Burney.

HORACE WALPOLE. *Anecdotes of Painting in England*. 2 vols., 1763, and later edns. to the present day.

—— *The Castle of Otranto*. 1765 and later edns. to the present day. French translns. in 1767 and 1797.

—— *The Works of Horatio Walpole, Earl of Orford*. Ed. Mary Berry and others. 9 vols., 1798–1825.

—— *Letters*. Ed. Mrs. Paget Toynbee. 16 vols., 1903–5, with 3 vols. supplements ed. Paget Toynbee, 1918–25. The Yale Edn. ed. W. S. Lewis, begun 1937, will be still more inclusive and may amount to as many as 50 vols.

See also the very extensive list of works of and on Horace Walpole in *The Cambridge Bibliography of English Literature*.

REV. DR. JOSEPH WARTON (1722–1800, Headmaster of Winchester College).

JOSEPH WARTON. *Ranelagh House, a Satire in Prose*. 1747. This is reproduced in the work of Wooll mentioned below.

REV. JOHN WOOLL. *Biographical Memoirs of Joseph Warton; to which are added a Selection from his Works and Literary Correspondence*. Vol. i (all published), 1806. This includes a letter of Burney to Warton on the musical treatises of Gafori (1451–1522).

For a full list of Warton's poetical and prose works, works edited by him, and works of others discussing him, see *The Cambridge Bibliography of English Literature*.

JOHN WEAVER (1673–1760). Celebrated dancing master, in which capacity he had the boy Burney as a pupil.

JOHN WEAVER. *Orchesography, or the Art of Dancing by Character and Demonstrative Figures*. 1706; 2nd edn. *c*. 1716. (It is a transln. of Feuillet's *Chorégraphie*.)

—— *A Small Treatise of Time and Cadence in Dancing, reduc'd to an Easy and Exact Method*. 1706.

—— *An Essay towards a History of Dancing*. 1712.

—— *Anatomical and Mechanical Lectures upon Dancing*. 1721.

JOHN WEAVER. *The History of the Mimes and Pantomimes.* 1728.

For a reference to Weaver's contribution to *The Spectator* see I. 8.

SAMUEL WESLEY (1766–1837). Organist, composer of music of solid worth, and pioneer enthusiast for the music of Bach, into the enjoyment of which he successfully initiated the aged Burney.

SAMUEL WESLEY. *Letters to Mr. Jacobs relating to the Introduction into this country of the Works of Bach.* Edited by Eliza Wesley. Two edns., 1875 and 1878.

JAMES T. LIGHTWOOD. *Samuel Wesley, Musician.* 1937.

Valuable articles on Wesley as a Bach pioneer have appeared in *The Musical Times* as follows: 1902, 799; 1908, 236; 1920, 170; 1926, 515 and 544.

WILLIAM WINDHAM (1750–1810). Statesman; from his childhood acquainted with Burney, and one of Burney's steady friends, who exerted influence with the government to secure him a pension.

WILLIAM WINDHAM. *Diary of the Right Hon. William Windham.* Ed. Mrs. Henry Baring. 1866.

—— *The Windham Papers.* With Introduction by the Earl of Rosebery. 1913.

R. W. KETTON-CREMER. *The Early Life and Diaries of William Windham.* 1930.

Correspondence of Edmund Burke and William Windham. Ed. Gilson. 1910.

ARTHUR YOUNG (1741–1820). Active in agricultural research and frequent traveller in pursuit of information; Burney's brother-in-law and close friend.

ARTHUR YOUNG. *On the War in North America.* 1758.

—— *A Farmer's Letters to the People of England.* 2 vols., 1768. French transln. 1770.

—— *A Six Weeks' Tour through the Southern Counties of England and Wales.* 1768 and later edns. There were several Tours through other parts of England and Ireland published in subsequent years. French translns. appeared.

—— *Political Arithmetic.* 1774. French transln. 1775.

—— *Travels . . . undertaken with a view of ascertaining the Cultivation, Wealth, Resources, and Natural Prosperity of the Kingdom of France.* 2 vols., 1792–4 and later edns. French transln. 1793–4.

—— *Autobiography.* Ed. M. Bentham Edwards. 1898.

The above is a mere selection of Young's very numerous works. Larger lists may be seen in *The Cambridge Bibliography of English Literature, D.N.B.*, &c.

DOROTHY YOUNG (dates unknown). Learned lady of Lynn, and devoted friend of the Burneys during their residence in that town.

DOROTHY YOUNG. *Translations from the French, by D.Y.*

BOOKS FOR CONSULTATION—GENERAL AND VARIOUS

Catalogue of Five Hundred Celebrated Authors of Great Britain now living. 1788.

Court and City Register. (There is a copy in the British Museum.)

CRADOCK, JOSEPH. *Literary and Miscellaneous Memoirs.* 2 vols., 1826.

CUMMINGS, WILLIAM HAYMAN. *God save the King*. 1902.

DAVEY, HENRY. *History of English Music*. 1895 and later edn.

DISRAELI, ISAAC. *Curiosities of Literature*. 2 Series, 1791–3 and 1823.

DITTERSDORF, KARL DITTERS VON. *Autobiography*. Transl. A. D. Coleridge. 1896.

DOBSON, AUSTIN. Many volumes of Essays, largely on eighteenth-century subjects. Now republished in 'The World's Classics'.

DORAN, DR. JOHN. *'Their Majesties' Servants' or Annals of the English Stage from Thomas Betterton to Edmund Kean*. 1865.

GEORGE, M. DOROTHY. *England in Johnson's Day*. 1928.

—— *Catalogue of Political and Personal Satires*. The 2 vols. by this author cover the period in question. British Museum, 1935–8.

—— *English Social Life in the Eighteenth Century*. 1923.

GREVILLE, ROBERT FULKE. *The Diaries of Robert Fulke Greville*. Edited by F. McK. Bladon. 1931. This is not the Fulke Greville of Burney's early life but the one who appears as 'Colonel Wellbred' in Fanny Burney's diary, and his diaries amplify her description of life at Court.

HAMPDEN, JOHN. *An Eighteenth-Century Journal*. 1940.

HARDING, ROSAMOND E. M. *The Pianoforte*. 1933.

HAWKINS, LAETITIA M. *Anecdotes, Biographical Sketches and Memoirs*. 1822.

—— *Memoirs, Anecdotes, Facts and Opinions*. 2 vols., 1824.

HIPKINS, EDWARD J., and RIMBAULT, EDWARD F. *The Organ*. 3 edns., 1855–70–77.

JOHNSTONE, JOHN. *Memoirs of Dr. Samuel Parr*. Vol. i of *Collected Works*. 1828.

LAMB, CHARLES. *Essays of Elia*. 2 series, 1823 and 1833.

—— *Letters*. Edited by E. V. Lucas. 2 vols., 1905, 2nd edn. 1912. Complete edn., 3 vols., 1935.

LAWRENCE, W. J. *Old Theatre Days and Ways*. 1935.

LOEWENBERG, ALFRED. *Annals of Opera, 1597–1940*. 1943.

LYSONS, D.; AMOTT, J.; WILLIAMS, C. LEE; CHANCE, H. G. *Origin and Progress of the Meeting of the Three Choirs*. These authors were concerned with the successive cumulative edns. dated respectively 1812, 1864, and 1894.

MOORE, THOS. *Life of Lord Byron*. 1830.

MORITZ, K. P. *Reisen eines Deutschen in England im Jahre 1782–1783*. There have, from 1795, been several edns. of an English translation (as *Travels in England*), and it is still in print. The book gives a good idea of the England of the middle of Burney's lifetime.

NICOLL, ALLARDYCE. *A History of Late Eighteenth-Century Drama, 1750–1800*. 1927.

—— *The English Theatre*. 1936.

NICHOLS, JOHN. *Literary Anecdotes of the Eighteenth Century*. 9 vols., 1812–15.

—— *Illustrations of the Literary History of the Eighteenth Century*. 8 vols., 1817–58.

Oxford History of Music. Ed. Hadow &c., 8 vols.

'PASTON, GEORGE' (Mrs. E. M. Symonds). *Social Caricature in the Eighteenth Century*. 1905.

—— *Sidelights on the Georgian Period*. 1902.

POOLE, MRS. REGINALD LANE. *Catalogue of Portraits in the Possession of the University, Colleges, and County of Oxford*. 3 vols., 1912–25.

QUENNELL, MARJORIE and C. H. B. *A History of Everyday Things in England*, III.

ROGERS, SAMUEL. *Table Talk.* 1856.

SCHOLES, PERCY A. *The Puritans and Music in England and New England.* 1934.

—— *God save the King: its History and its Romance.* 1942. (Larger work awaiting publication.)

SOUTHEY, ROBERT. *The Doctor.* 1837–47.

—— *Life and Correspondence.* 1850.

STEPHEN, LESLIE. *English Thought in the Eighteenth Century.* 2 vols., 1876.

TURBERVILLE, A. S. *English Men and Manners in the Eighteenth Century.* 1929.

—— (ed.) *Johnson's England.* 2 vols., 1933.

VICTOR, BENJAMIN. *Original Letters, Dramatic Pieces and Poems.* 1766.

WALKER, EMERY, and FLETCHER, C. R. L. *Historical Portraits.* 4 vols., 1909–19.

WESLEY, JOHN. *Journal.* 21 pts., 1739–91; 4 vols., 1827; definitive issue ed. N. Curnock, 8 vols., 1909–16.

JOURNALS—CONTEMPORARY AND MODERN

(See exact references in text)

British Journal, 1724.

European Magazine, vols. xiii and xiv, 1788 (for Baretti's attacks on Mrs. Piozzi), 1798, &c.

General Advertiser for the period.

Gentleman's Magazine for the period.

Harmonicon, 1823–33.

Ipswich Journal, 1754.

London Evening Post, 1754, 1789.

London Gazetteer, 24 Aug. 1814.

Monthly Review for the period.

Morning Herald and Daily Advertiser for the period.

Musical News, 3 May 1919.

Norwich Mercury, 1753, 1757, 1759, 1768.

Notes & Queries, passim.

Oxford Journal, June 1769 (for the performance of Burney's Mus.D. exercise).

Public Advertiser, 1760, 1765.

Yorkshire Herald, 1928.

BOOKS OF REFERENCE

ABDY-WILLIAMS, C. F. *A Historical Account of Degrees in Music at Oxford and Cambridge.* 1893.

ADLER, GUIDO. *Handbuch der Musikgeschichte*, 1928.

Allgemeine Deutsche Biographie. 33 vols., 1875, &c.

Alumni Oxoniensis, 1715–1886. Ed. John Foster.

Annual Register for the period covered by the present book.

BAKER, D. E. *Companion to the Playhouse.* 1764. Edited and brought up to date, as *Biographica Dramatica*, by Isaac Reed in 1782 and by Stephen Jones in 1812–13.

BATESON, F. W. (ed.). *The Cambridge Bibliography of English Literature.* 4 vols., 1940.

BROWN, JAS. D., and STRATTON, STEPHEN S. *British Musical Biography.* Birmingham, 1897.

Cambridge History of English Literature. 15 vols., 1907–16.

Catalogue of Opera Librettos printed before 1800. Library of Congress, Washington, D.C. 1914.

CHAMBERS, EPHRAIM. *Cyclopaedia or an Universal Dictionary of Arts and Sciences.* 7th edn. in 4 vols. and vol. of plates, ed. Rev. Abraham Rees, 1779–86. (Original edition, in 2 vols., 1728; other editions in 1738, 1739, 1741, &c.) This work gives attention to music but includes no biographical articles.

Dictionary of Musicians. 2 vols., 1822–7.

Dictionary of National Biography. 1882 onwards.

EITNER, ROBERT. *Biographisch-bibliographisches Quellen-Lexikon der Musiker.* 10 vols., 1900–4.

FÉTIS, F. J. *Biographie Universelle des Musiciens et Bibliographie Générale de la Musique.* 8 vols. 2 edns. 1835–44 and 1860–5. Supplement by A. Pougin, 2 vols., 1878–81.

GENEST, JOHN. *Some Account of the English Stage from the Restoration in 1660 to 1830.* 10 vols., 1832.

Grove's Dictionary of Music and Musicians. Four edns., all of them used in the preparation of this book. 4 to 6 vols., 1878–89, 1904–10, 1927, 1940.

KIDSON, FRANK. *British Music Publishers, Printers and Engravers . . . from Queen Elizabeth's Reign to George the Fourth's.* 1900.

LANSON, G. *Manuel Bibliographique.* 1913; 2nd edn. 1921.

MENDEL, HERMANN. *Musikalisches Conversations Lexikon.*
The 2nd edn. in 12 vols., 1879–83, is the one that has been used in the preparation of this book.

MICHAUD, L. G. *Biographie Universelle.* 83 vols., 1811–53.

REDGRAVE, SAMUEL. *Dictionary of Artists of the English School.* 1874.

REES, ABRAHAM. The *Cyclopaedia or Universal Dictionary of Arts, Science, and Literature.* 39 vols., *c.* 1805–19.

RIEMANN, K. W. J. H. *Musik-Lexikon.*
The 11th edn. in 2 vols., by Alfred Einstein, 1929, is the one that has been used in the preparation of this book.

SCHOLES, PERCY A. *The Oxford Companion to Music.* 7th ed. 1947.

TIEGHEM, PAUL VAN. *Répertoire Chronologique des Littératures Modernes.* 1935.

VENN, J. A. *Biographical History of Gonville and Caius College, Cambridge.* 3 vols., 1897–1901.

—— *Alumni Cantabrigienses.* 4 vols., 1922–7.

MANUSCRIPT SOURCES

(See precise references in text)

1. IN THE BRITISH MUSEUM.

Letters to and from Burney and members of his family; also to Garrick, J. W. Callcott, Vincent Novello, Samuel Wesley, &c. (Add. MSS. 11730, 35027, 35126, 37916).

Twining Papers. Correspondence of the Rev. Thos. Twining with Dr. Burney and others (Add. MS. 39929–30–32–36).

Three exercise books in Burney's writing containing travel material omitted from his Italian Tour as printed. (Three similar books, also in his handwriting, are in the present author's possession; the two copies differ somewhat in details.) See I. 190–1.

Burney's *Specimens of Dr. Blow's Beastialities* (Add. MS. 11557).

Harpsichord Solos, &c., by Handel, Arne, and others, copied by Burney at Chester in 1744 (Add. MS. 39957).

Chansons, Madrigals, &c., from Burney's Collections (Add. MS. 34071).

Drawings intended for the *History* but never used, &c. (See II. 335.)

Eleven Volumes of Extracts from Various Musical Writers and Composers with Remarks and Criticisms by Burney (Add. MS. 17581–91).

Catalogue of all the Books, Tracts, and Treatises, of all the Original Authors . . . in Greek, Latin, German, French, Italian, Spanish, and English, on the particular Faculty of Music . . . of the late Charles Burney, Mus.D., F.R.S. (Add. MS. 18191).

Letters from Latrobe to Vincent Novello (Add. MS. 11730).

Letters of Garrick to Sir William Young (Add. MS. 37916).

Letters from Arthur Young to Fanny Burney (d'Arblay), 1792 (Add. MS. 35127).

James Burney's *Journal to the Pacific*, 1776–80 (Add. MS. 8955).

Notebooks on British Actors, 1560–1816, of Charles Burney Junr. 7 vols. (Add. MS. 939 b.1).

Notebooks on the History of the Stage in England, 1538–1807, of Charles Burney Junr., 46 vols. (Add. MS. 938 e-f).

Collections of Playbills, &c. of Charles Burney Junr. (1750–1808) (Add. MS. 939, 1. 9).

History of Theatres in Goodman's Fields, by Charles Burney Junr. 2 vols. (Add. MS. 939, 6. 2).

Theatrical Register (1660–1801), by Charles Burney Junr. 8 vols. (Add. MS. 938 a-d).

Theatrical Register: Playbills of Drury Lane, Covent Garden, Haymarket, &c. (1768–1817). Collected by Charles Burney Junr. 59 vols. (Add. MS. 937 b-e).

Collection of Notebooks on Garrick, by Charles Burney Junr. 48 vols. (Add. MS. 939 d-e).

Miscellaneous Newspaper Cuttings. Collected by Charles Burney Junr. (Add. MS. 936 g).

Playbills of Ipswich, Lynn, &c., 1773–1801. Collected by Charles Burney Junr. (Add. MS. 937 f).

Formal Letters of the Boys of the School of Charles Burney Junr. (Add. MS. 39303).

Notebooks with Dormitory List of the School of Charles Burney Junr. (Add. MS. 39303).

Horae Burneienses (Add. MS. 11601 d). Cf. reference on II. 360 to a printed work of the same name.

Windham Papers.

William Cole, Collections for an Athenae Cantabrigiensis Alphabetically Arranged (Add. MS. 5864).

Samuel Wesley, Reminiscences (Add. MS. 27593).

J. W. Callcott, Account of the Graduates' Meeting, a Society of Musical Professors, established in London, Nov. 24, 1790 (Add. MS. 27693).
J. W. Callcott's Miscellaneous Papers.

2. In The Records Office.

Journal of the Voyage of the 'Adventurer' (Adm. 51/4523).

3. At Somerset House.

Burney's Will (202 Bridport).

4. In The Bodleian Library, Oxford.

Burney's Mus.D. Exercise, with printed programme of its official performance.
MS. Malone 38, fol. 129 (16 letters of Burney to Malone, 1802–10).
MS. Montague; MSS. Add.; MS. Eng. Misc. (7 letters by Burney to various people).
MS. Blakeway 5 (concerning Shrewsbury, and including a pedigree of the Burney family).

5. In The John Rylands Library, Manchester.

A few Letters of Burney (Eng. MS. 5466, &c.).
Burney's satirical poem on Hawkins's History.

6. At King's Lynn.

Minutes of the Corporation.
Parish Records of St. Margaret's.

7. In The Norwich Public Library.

Mann Manuscripts (Collection of the late A. H. Mann, D.Mus., concerning Norfolk music and musicians, and including a volume of 'King's Lynn Musical Events').

8. In The Shrewsbury Public Library.

St. Mary's Parish-book (Wm. Phillips MS., 231).

9. In The Public Library, Armagh, Northern Ireland.

Copies of seventy-nine letters from Mrs. Molesworth Phillips (Susan Burney) to her sister Fanny (1787–99).

10. In The Liceo Musicale G. B. Martini, Bologna.

Letters from Burney to Martini (photostats of these are in the possession of the present author).

11. In The Possession of the Present Author.

Many letters from and to Burney and various members of his family.
Album of Correspondence between Callcott and Burney.
Three exercise books in Burney's writing, containing travel material omitted from his Italian Tour as printed (See I. 190–1).
Bound volume of 98 typescript pages and index of 10 pages, *Memoranda of the Burney Family*, 1603–1845, being evidently the document referred to by the late R. Brimley Johnson, in his *Fanny Burney and the Burneys* (1926),

as 'Journal of the Worcester Burneys in the possession of Mr. Leverton Harris'. (See I. 1 n.)

Burney's manuscript Italian-English Dictionary (referred to on I. 73).

Miscellaneous family documents of smaller or greater importance.

The descriptive catalogues of various dealers in old manuscripts, and of various dates, have often been useful in the preparation of the present book, such catalogues often including manuscripts no longer to be traced, of which the extracts they supply are informative. These are mentioned by name in footnotes as reference is made to them in the text.

INDEX

By MARION FINCH, M.A.

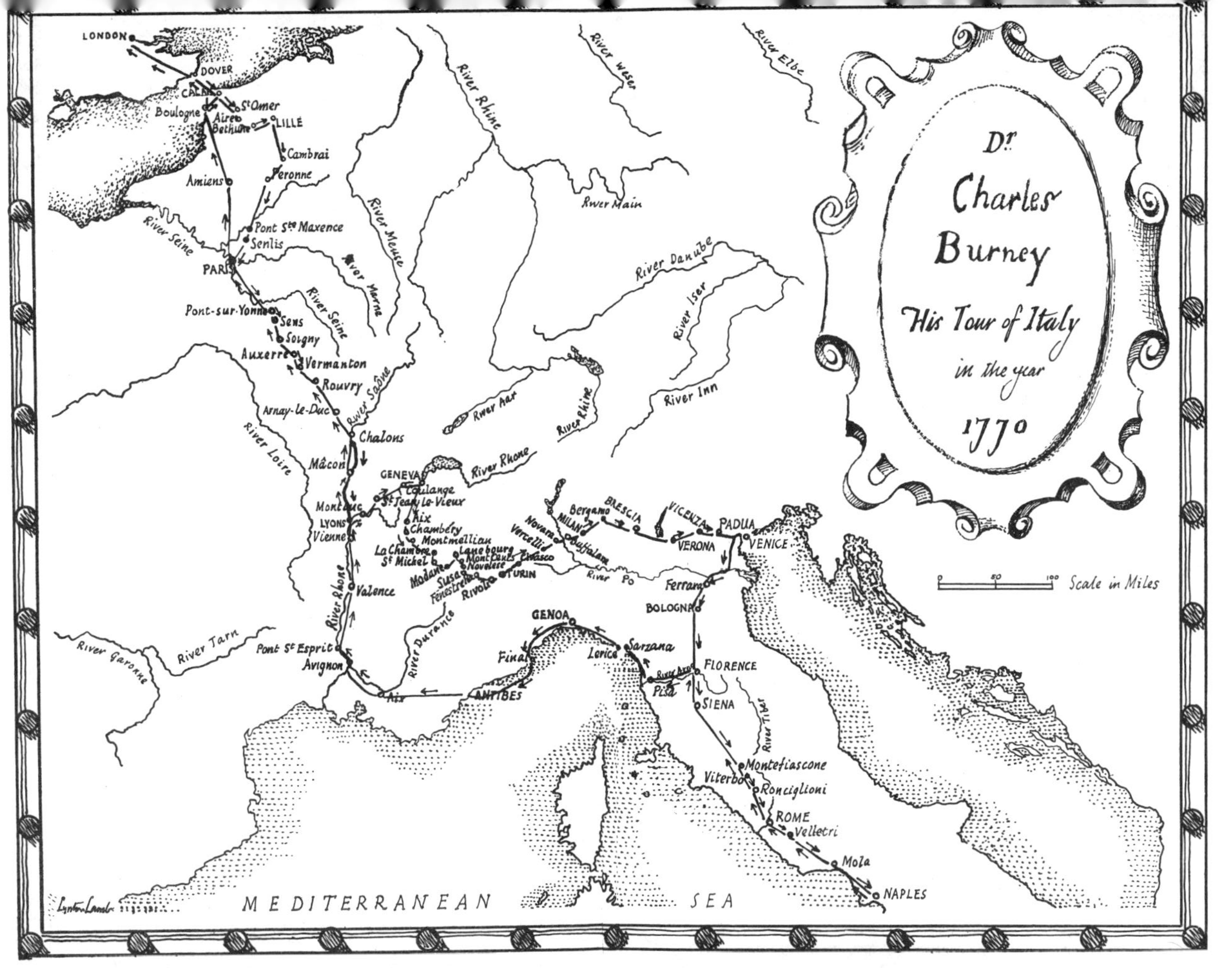
Dr. Charles Burney
His Tour of Italy
in the year
1770
Scale in Miles
0
50
100
LONDON
DOVER
St Omer
Boulogne
Aire
Bethune
LILLE
Cambrai
Peronne
Amiens
Pont Ste Maxence
Senlis
PARIS
Pont-sur-Yonne
Sens
Soigny
Auxerre
Vermanton
Rouvry
Arnay-le-Duc
Chalons
Mâcon
GENEVA
St Jean le Vieux
Aix
Chambery
Montmellian
La Chambre
St Michel
Modane
Susa
Rivoli
TURIN
LYONS
Vienne
Valence
Pont St Esprit
Avignon
Aix
ANTIBES
Final
GENOA
Lerici
Sarzana
Pisa
FLORENCE
SIENA
BOLOGNA
Ferrara
Novara
Vercelli
MILAN
Bergamo
BRESCIA
VICENZA
VERONA
PADUA
VENICE
Montefiascone
Viterbo
Ronciglioni
ROME
Velletri
Mola
NAPLES
River Seine
River Marne
River Meuse
River Rhine
River Weser
River Elbe
River Main
River Danube
River Iser
River Inn
River Aar
River Rhone
River Saône
River Loire
River Tarn
River Garonne
River Durance
River Po
River Arno
River Tiber
MEDITERRANEAN SEA

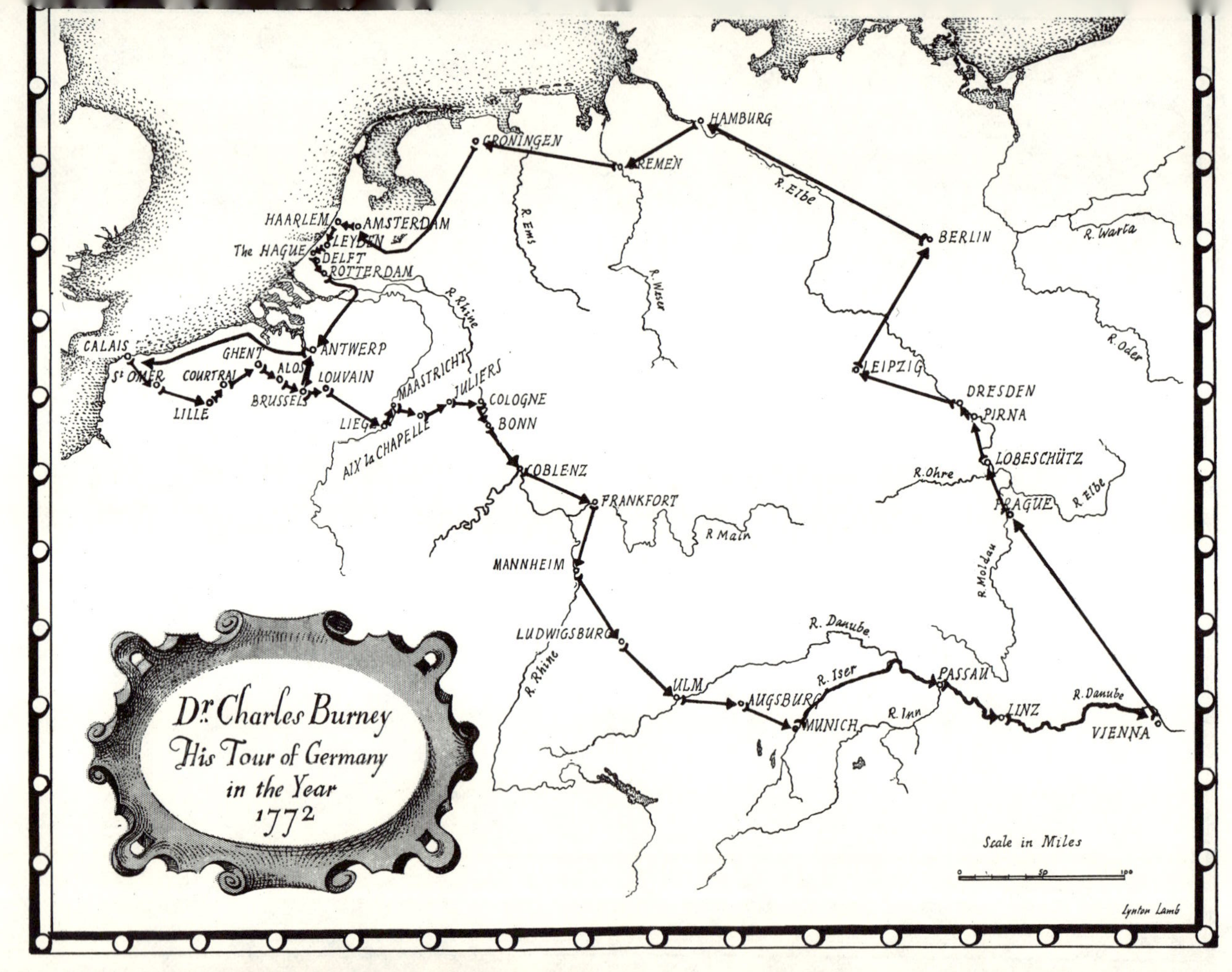
Dr. Charles Burney
His Tour of Germany
in the Year
1772
CALAIS
St OMER
LILLE
COURTRAI
GHENT
ALOST
BRUSSELS
LOUVAIN
ANTWERP
ROTTERDAM
DELFT
The HAGUE
LEYDEN
HAARLEM
AMSTERDAM
GRONINGEN
BREMEN
HAMBURG
BERLIN
LEIPZIG
DRESDEN
PIRNA
LOBESCHÜTZ
PRAGUE
VIENNA
LINZ
PASSAU
MUNICH
AUGSBURG
ULM
LUDWIGSBURG
MANNHEIM
FRANKFORT
COBLENZ
BONN
COLOGNE
JULIERS
AIX la CHAPELLE
MAASTRICHT
LIEGE
R. Rhine
R. Ems
R. Weser
R. Elbe
R. Warta
R. Oder
R. Ohre
R. Moldau
R. Main
R. Danube
R. Iser
R. Inn
Scale in Miles
0
50
100
Lynton Lamb

LIBRARY OF DAVIDSON COLLEGE